CAR
One hundre

TOONS

years of cinema animation

by
Giannalberto Bendazzi

John Libbey

LONDON • PARIS • ROME

British Library Cataloguing in Publication Data

Bendazzi, Giannalberto
  CARTOONS: One Hundred Years of Cinema Animation
  I Title
  791.433

ISBN: 0 86196 445 4 (paperback)
ISBN: 0 86196 446 2 (hardback)

CARTOONS is co-published with Indiana University Press, 601 North Morton Street, Bloomington, Indiana 47404 (USA) and is available in North America and Canada through this publisher.

This book is dedicated to the loving memory of Robert and Shirley Edmonds and to the smile of Ilaria, three years old.

Translated by Anna Taraboletti-Segre

Published by

John Libbey & Company Ltd, 13 Smiths Yard, Summerley Street, London SW18 4HR, England.
Telephone: +44 (0)81-947 2777: Fax +44 (0)81-947 2664
John Libbey Eurotext Ltd, 127 rue de la République, 92120 Montrouge, France.
John Libbey - C.I.C. s.r.l., via Lazzaro Spallanzani 11, 00161 Rome, Italy

Printed in Hong Kong by Dah Hua Printing Press Co Ltd.

Contents

**VII
Indexes:
Names and Titles**

List of Figures

Black and white figures

Colour figures

Foreword

A little over one hundred years separate the first animated shows (Pantomimes lumineuses, Paris, 1892) from the date of publishing this book. In the meantime, animation has become an imposing trade, a job for hundreds of thousands of people, a ubiquitous art. Its development underwent cycles and changes, often influenced by major historical events. Such an event is the recent fall of the Soviet system, which re-drew the world map, politically as well as economically. For animation a whole marketplace disappeared, studios were shut, jobs, careers, schools, styles ended. In addition to these dramatic changes, another revolution came, centered on the media. The markets were 'globalized' in a very short time, and the trend is currently developing. As a result of cable and satellite television, the programmes were exported, as beforehand, but private producers – as well as those nations with existing power to do so - were able to conceive, produce and distribute on an international scale. The IDATE report, commissioned by Media 95's CARTOON programme in 1992, showed that from 1989 to 1992 animated programmes in the Western European televisions had had a growth of 15 per cent a year: an unforeseen challenge, after many years of stagnation.

The history of animation is thus entering a completely new stage, and it will be years before it will be possible to describe its real shape and analyse its events. This means that the first century of animation's life is a completed era, which we can and should analyse like all things belonging to the past, even though many of its men and women are alive and active at the time of writing. Besides, studies on animation are rather young. The first serious historical works go back no more than twenty years. They have had to face a large number of misunderstandings which still endure among many filmgoers, critics, historians of live action cinema. Yet it must be reiterated here that animation cinema is not necessarily for children, is not always comic, and has only a faint relationship with printed comic strips (with the exception of the first twenty years of this century in the United States of America). Unfortunately, the historical and critical literature on animation is comparatively one of the most scanty in the field of cinema The following chapters aim to demonstrate that, on the contrary, animation deserves to be studied and that this rich, eclectic field includes some of the most valuable works of our time.

Why is there such a chasm between the richness of creative minds on one side and the lack of a receptive audience on the other? It may rightly be argued that animation would be more popular if the mechanisms of film distribution were different. Equipped with a most concise instrument, animators release primarily short films, while the theatrical market favours feature films over all other forms. Thus, animation makes rare appearances in movie theatres, except in its most commercial and therefore aesthetically-lesser forms (animated feature films are rarely major artistic achievements). True, there is television, however this irreparably distorts the formal values of works made for the big screen. The television market, moreover, does not provide the

economic conditions necessary to encourage a careful creative process. Animated television series are most appropriately discussed within a framework of the history and theory of television, and are, therefore, almost entirely excluded from this work.

Under these circumstances, it is quite understandable that animation has taken a course parallel to, but not the same as, that of mainstream cinema and has a history of its own. The fashionable currents and trends of live action cinema (which are also its most visible and imposing aspects) have little influence on animators who have chosen to develop instead, their own trends and movements.

The last step in this process of isolation is the cultural ghetto into which the men and women who work in the field have segregated themselves, and which has acquired world-wide proportions, especially over the last thirty years. From within, animators attend specialized festivals to show their works, view those of their peers and discuss topics which are familiar to a few, while outsiders remain uninformed.

The critic is therefore forced to make much use of footnotes, explanatory paragraphs and outlines of methodology.

Some of the most active followers of animation cinema believed in its aesthetic autonomy and proclaimed it 'an art in its own right' (with the ironic result that someone nicknamed it 'Seventh art-bis', after the cinema).

Linguistically, technically, stylistically, animation as an expressive form is indeed autonomous, and there is no need of examples to prove it. For a long time, filming technique was considered the discriminating element on the basis that in live action cinema, actions are filmed exactly as they take place, at twenty-four frames per second, whereas in animation the action is constantly reinvented: objects or drawings are filmed frame by frame and, in between frames, they are moved or changed by the animator.[1] The earlier introduction to the ASIFA[2] statute stated that live action cinema was produced by mechanical analysis, through pictures of events similar to the ones which appeared on the screen; whereas animation cinema created events through different instruments which differed from actual reproduction. In an animation film, events took place for the first time on the screen. Later on, the development of new techniques (especially electronics) as well as the rise of philosophical issues (from the standpoints of aesthetics and language, the characteristics of production work do not count) suggested a 'negative' definition, so that the 1980 statute of ASIFA defined animation as everything which is not a simple representation of live action shot at 24 frames per second.

With this explanation, the author does not intend to solve an aesthetic conundrum or exhaust all themes in the theory of animation cinema, which have been treated in specialized texts listed in the bibliography section of this book.

More modestly, the intent is to warn against self-complicating problems as well as to point out how unfair it is to isolate a phenomenon (in this case, animation) from the context in which it belongs (in this case, visual communication or visual art). A precise separation between animation and other media is not easily identifiable. In its most realistic version, animation expands to 'live action cinema'; in its own abstract forms animation expands into kinetic art. In pursuing this research, I have not pre-established any kind of paradigm but have rather worked pragmatically.

In this light, some classic questions arise: whether

---

1   In fact, there were one, two or more frames, as required by different creative needs. The procedure gave rise to the expressions 'single frame' or 'frame by frame'.

2   ASIFA is the acronym of the French name of the International Association of Animation Film Artists.

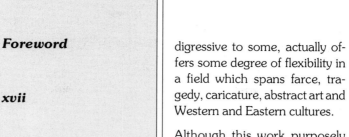

Foreword

xvii

animation is or is not cinema and whether it can be considered plastic art in motion. The system of 'dynamic' visual communication is not separated from static visual communications such as drawing or sculpture. Interchanges and analogies between these related forms are more than legitimate. The world of animation, in particular, has held an ongoing dialogue with contemporary schools of painting and graphics.

This work covers little more than one century of animation. It begins in 1888 because in that year Emile Reynaud released (although to an audience of only friends and relatives) the *théâtre optique* and dramatically improved the quality of animated drawings which, for the first time, recounted stories and thoughts. The first films of animated drawings were born that year.

This study focuses on works and consequently, artists, and stresses a documentary, critical approach rather than an analysis of economic, industrial or political events. It is not a 'history of animation cinema' (it does not involve a study of facts and intentions) but attempts to fill the void of knowledge on the topic and to give an interpretive introduction to little known filmmakers.[1]

Pages filled with names, titles and dates may be boring to the reader, but are necessary because the often fragmentary, uncertain sources require classification, and information had to be definitively written so as to become available to other scholars. In short, it was imperative to do some 'preventive archaeology' (pardon the oxymoron) and trace a map which could be later used for monographic studies. As for the critical approach, filmmakers have been studied within their own single, specific cultures and inspirations, creative projects and ideas; they have not been compared to any pre-determined aesthetic credo to which they might or might not answer. This approach, which may appear incoherent or digressive to some, actually offers some degree of flexibility in a field which spans farce, tragedy, caricature, abstract art and Western and Eastern cultures.

Although this work purposely abstains from historic or philosophic interpretations, it cannot avoid some general observation on the past century. This fascinating period has witnessed the birth and development – albeit with pauses, contradictions and dead-ends – of a new language which has been opened to the creativity of individuals and groups of artists. Animation in the strict sense of the term, as the invention or orchestration of forms allowed by the development of optical machines at the turn of the 20th century, has offered no less artistic opportunity than have colour, line and volume. Animators have been able to develop forms in the dimension of time, as opposed to the two-dimensions of painting or three-dimensions of sculpture. This opportunity, which at times has been misunderstood, is at the root of an evolution which, after one century, has not yet seen its full potential.

Much of the information presented in this book has been made possible by the cooperation and courtesy of the filmmakers themselves. I wish to thank them all without doing them the injustice of naming them on a page which does not mention their artistic work. Similar thanks should be given to the relatives of deceased filmmakers.

I am grateful to the Canadian critic Robi Roncarelli, a computer animation expert who not only provided me with information, but actually wrote the chapter on this topic. My thanks to the Swiss historian Bruno Edera, a tireless, meticulous researcher who furnished me with copies of his published and unpublished works; and similarly to my American colleague John Canemaker. I thank my British colleague Ken Clark for having very kindly revised my paragraphs on British animation. The following people (listed in alphabeti-

---

1   To give a complete listing of each artist's complete filmography was not the main purpose of this study. The works cited here are merely representative.

cal order) gave me information and first-hand documents:

István Antal, Budapest; Jordi Artigas, Barcelona; Sergej Asenin, Moscow; Mike Barrier, Washington, DC; Alfio Bastiancich, Turin; Louise Beaudet, Montreal; Maria Benesová, Prague; Jehangir S. Bhownagary, Paris; Fulvio Capezzuoli, Milan; Joan Cohen, Los Angeles; Nico Crama, The Hague; Harvey Deneroff, Los Angeles; Robert and Shirley Edmonds, Chicago; Robi Engler, Lausanne; Simón Feldman, Buenos Aires; June Foray, Los Angeles; Lisbeth Gabrielsson, Stockholm; Luis Gasca, San Sebastian; Rolf Giesen, Berlin; Marcin Gizycki, Warsaw; Mattias Gordon, Västerås; Vasco Granja, Lisbon; Lalla Grimes, New York; León Herman, Buenos Aires; Robert Jung, Munich; Torsten Jungstedt, Stockholm; Mark Kausler, Los Angeles; Jan Klava, Sydney; Jerzy Kotowski, Lodz; Joachim and Detelina Kreck, Wiesbaden; Jirí Kubícêk, Prague; Manfred Lichtenstein, Berlin; Rubens Francisco Lucchetti, São Paulo; Raymond Maillet, Paris; Massimo Maisetti, Milan; Marie Catherine Marchetti, Paris; György Matolcsy, Budapest; Anne Melblom, Milan; Inni-Karine Melbye, Copenhagen; William Moritz, Los Angeles; Antoinette Moses, Cambridge; Ranko Munitic, Zagreb; Takashi Namiki, Tokyo; Giuliana Nicodemi, New York; Huguette Parent, Montreal; Angie Pike, Los Angeles; Fazo Premilovac, Zagreb; Karen Rosenberg, Brookline; Michel Roudevitch, Paris; Charles Samu, New York; Georges Sifianos, Paris; David R. Smith, Burbank; Charles Solomon, Santa Monica; Véronique Steeno, Genk; Gunnar Strom, Volda; Hélène Tanguay, Montreal; Juan Gabriel Tharrats, Madrid; Naoki Togawa, Tokyo; Rinaldo Traini, Rome; Christine Tréguier, Chatillon; Ervin Voiculescu, Bucharest; Anatolij Volkov, Moscow; Pat Webb, London; Ytzhak Yoresh,

CARTOONS
Bendazzi

xviii

Jerusalem; Fiorello Zangrando, Venice. Thank you also to Markku Salmi for his very detailed reference checking.

More information was very kindly given to me by: Rodolfo Alegria, Managua; Roberto Chiti, Genoa; Daniel Marranghello, San José de Costa Rica; Norma Martinez, Havana; Nelson Garcia Miranda, Lima; Felix Nakamura, Caracas; Timothy R. White, Singapore; Ken O'Connell, Eugene; Alessandra Biagini, Beijing; Yan Ding Xian, Shanghai; Robin Allan, Stockport; María Manzanera, Murcia.

I have been provided with documents by the following institutions: Art Institute of Chicago; ASIFA; Associazione Italia-URSS; British Film Institute; Cinémathèque Québécoise; Cinémathèque de Toulouse; Danske Filmmuseum; Embrafilme; Film Polski; Filmbulgaria; Goethe Institut; Hungarofilm; ICAIC; Danish Cultural Institute; Joop Geesink Dollywood; Kinostudioja Shqiperia e Re; Len Lye Foundation; Library of Congress, Motion Picture Division; Museum of Modern Art; National Film Board of Canada; Stiftung Deutsche Kinemathek; Suomen Elokuvasäätiö; UCLA, Theater Arts Library; USIS.

Last but not least, my sincere thanks to family and friends who helped and advised me, at different times and in different ways, and made my task a little easier, to Anna Taraboletti-Segre who has translated this work into English, and to Ellis Edmonds who helped her.

I wish to express my gratitude to my editor, Manuel Alvarado, who made the best out of the text I submitted him, and to my publisher, John Libbey, who had faith in this book. Last, but not least, I thank my wife, Graziella, for having been at my side in this endeavour.

Giannalberto Bendazzi
Milan, 1994

Preface

In Praise of Animated Film

Serge Diaghilev to Jean Cocteau, while riding a gig in the Bois de Boulogne: "Stupefy me!"
Louis Pasteur to Odilon Redon, during the opening of the artist's exhibition: "Your monsters are alive!"

The task Giannalberto Bendazzi took upon himself with this book was to reconstruct the events of animation cinema throughout the years, and to describe the linguistic aspects which group the visual arts into families. I will limit myself to simply adding a few notes.

Among all the animal species, man is undoubtedly the only one which challenges his faculties in order to extend his limits. (Have we ever seen a deer training by repeatedly jumping over the same barrier so as to outdo himself?) Yes, man's nature is that of a challenger. Every new exploit gives him a new challenge.

Classical antiquity was aware of this, organizing the Olympic games; and further, challenging future generations by inventing the actions of fictitious heroes in the form of metaphors disguised as myths.

Our century has seen an identification with the image of Icarus, not to mention Prometheus, who moulded human features in mud and then blew life into them. Now, from the graffiti of Altamira to the canvasses by Balla, painters endeavour to create *living* forms. They have never attained actual movement, but only the idea of movement. In the 15th century, through the discovery of perspective, Italian painters added the illusion of a third dimension – of depth – to the two-dimensional image. But it wasn't until the end of the 19th century that we were able to see the two-dimensional image (already put in perspective) gain a fourth dimension: with a *fictitious, but evident* movement. And this happened long before man learned to fly.

It happened in 1892, in Paris, three years before the introduction of cinema. This Prometheus was Emile Reynaud, and nobody seemed to understand the meaning of that invention; as H. G. Wells once said, 'When a thing is strange enough and great enough, nobody seems to notice'.

After Emile Reynaud, there have been men able to create living images, and this does not surprise anybody. What are the reasons?

Animation film falls victim to an error in classification – or rather, to two errors. One consists in mistaking animation for animated drawings (as one might mistake an airplane for a kite); another, in considering it simply as a sort of 'cinema', while it could just as well be *painting, drawing, engraving* or even, *sculpture* in movement (do we ever consider an oil portrait as a sort of photo?)

This confusion between *animation* and 'cinema' dates from the first film projection by the Lumière Brothers, in Paris, in 1895. Now, Emile Reynaud had already been showing his Théâtre Optique at the Grévin museum since 1892. All images by Reynaud had been drawn by hand. It is certain that the invention of 'cinema' had been patented by Reynaud who did not have enough money to sue the Lumière brothers and win.

Anyhow, it is legitimate to consider cinema as a particular kind of animation, a sort of cheap, industrial substitute; which was destined to replace the creative work of an artist, such as Emile Reynaud, with photography of human models 'in movement'.

It should be remembered that photography itself was still too new for its non-artistic aspects to be evident: at that time and even much later, photographers loved to dress as 'artists', with Rembrandt-style hats and Lavallière ties, like painters. Nadar felt a closeness to Manet.

In reality, it is possible to take pictures artistically, exactly as it is possible to paint canvasses with craftsmanship. However, there is still a major difference between the work of a photographer such as Nadar, who chose his model and many other elements, but who did not filter 'indifferent' details with an awareness of the meaning and the form of *all* the details he used; and Manet, whose work precisely does not have anything to do with 'nature', but with the idea that he – Manet – had of nature. The great naïveté of the public should also be remembered; when it saw photographs for the first time, one can imagine the enthusiastic and indiscriminate shouts, in front of all the mechanically reproduced *details*: 'here is the ring on mum's finger, and here the wart on dad's nose, and here the fly on the dish'. How can one be surprised at such an incomprehension for works of art, since such naïve observations are uttered still today? Thus, the presentation of *L'arrivée du train à La Ciotat* in the first cinema was amazing: a *real train*! (Real, because photography is 'real'). Thus, a still unsolved problem emerged: What is reality? What do we mean by 'objective reality'? In another place I will deal with the absence of any relationship of the flat image of a monocular photographic view with the binocular understanding of the world which is typically human. The only possible relationship between these two views is filtered through the words 'there is even the fly … ' (a relationship which is false and sad because of its stupidity, since the fly is present only by chance. In art there is no place for the superfluous, and in a photograph almost everything is superfluous). Thus did the Lumière brothers' cinema overshadow Emile Reynaud's Animation; the industrial product won over the genius's work easily because it proved to be more marketable. The proliferation of photographic 'cinema' was such that Emile Cohl's drawings could be shown only in public theatres equipped with 'cinematographic' projectors; this element contributed to their classification as 'cinema' because, as much as they were bizarre vaudeville performances, they still were 'cinema'. Thus one of the two errors in classifying Animation was made.

Once Emile Cohl's animated drawing was considered as a particular kind of 'cinema', Reynaud's work found a way to survive. Several talented artists drew many animated drawings and always used movie theatres for the projection of their drawings, printed (exposed) on standard film stock, at a standard speed of 24 frames per second. In a word, the big brother of cinema accepted its role as a junior. But the 'art-animators' did not have the personality of Reynaud, who was an inventor even before being an artist. When some artists, mainly Europeans, came up with the idea of establishing a non-industrialized animation cinema with an awareness of its mission as a new art-form, it was treated as cartoons, industrialized caricatures, produced on an assembly-line in order to survive the competitive prices of photographic cinema. Gradually however, animated film looked for new techniques which were suited to the creation of individual works; the works of these artists became renowned, and in recent years the public has become aware of the existence of a newborn plastic art in movement called 'animation'.

Now, any registered patent is usually accompanied by a list of claims (exactly like the claims accompanying the application for exclusive rights over a gold mine). The higher the number of the 'claims' in a patent, the more important is the invention. But the high number of the possible applications of animation is precisely what makes its classification so difficult. How shall the new vein of animation be adapted to the old forms such as Cinema, Art Galleries, Television or Museums?

Film directors do not see any relationship between animation and the full-length feature films whose audiences go to see the stars advertised by billboards and by the press. Television programmers do not find, in animated fantasies, the advantages of direct and immediate reproduction of real events, such as coronations, revolutions, robberies and so on (this is the basic goal of television, isn't it?). Art dealers (serious people, if ever there were any) look for 'the signature' and inquire about the 'original work'.[1] No, art collectors and dealers do not buy or sell 'fantasies'. They need *goods* to be measured and, sometimes, even weighed!

As for Museum Directors, they compare animation to toys ' ... and after all, museums lack projectors, because whenever electricity is present, there is the danger of fire ... '.

The absence of animated films in the Automata collections, such as in the Museum of Arts and Industries in Paris, is more difficult to explain. Do we have to hope that videotapes will give Animation the communication tool it needs?

What are, then, the 'claims' of animation?

Before starting the praise of animation, let's point out the changes in values acting on performances as a whole, which have occurred in our society in the last 50–150 years. If it was easy to amaze the public with thread-controlled marionettes, wise elephants, musical tobacco boxes or with Vaucanson's mechanical duck which ate, digested and eliminated food, it was because the public loved to be amazed.

It is probable that today's public is no less naïve than in the old times, but it loves to look 'knowledgeable'. In praising animation, therefore, I will have to be careful to avoid old expressions such as 'miracle', or 'magic'.

I will praise animation, a pure work of the spirit

Animation, which has found numerous production techniques, presents itself as a 'frame by frame' method of creation of movement, no matter which technique has been used. Using the word 'creation' clearly involves some exaggeration, since man cannot create anything: stones, plants, animals. Rather, this word describes a manipulation, or an arrangement of existing things. This is the case, for example, in the photographic-film, when the director chooses a certain actor, a certain framing, a certain mimicry, a certain lighting, and so on. One can believe that, in such a repertoire, there is only a limited range of choice, which only faintly represents the director's creative will.

Once these components have been chosen and arranged, more or less well, they move on to the final result exactly as they were before, without

---

1   For movie animators, the movement which happens on the screen *for the first time* is the one which makes the original work: contrary to the 'photo-film', which is satisfied with a photomechanical analysis of the real events that the synthesis of the screen recreates as *déjà vu*.

the director becoming aware of them through analysis. The making of a live action film is thus easy, quick and abundant ... What else can this century wish, being so obsessed by notions of quantity and speed? These are the producers' obsessions; are the public's similar? Nothing is less certain. The steady decrease of attendance at the movies is well-known and normally explained by competition from television. Is such an explanation sufficient? What should we think of the flood of violent or pornographic films? It seems that, in motion pictures, any means is justified to attract the public. If we remember that the wave of pornography had been preceded by two decades of uninteresting technical inventions, such as the large screen, the several 'ramas', the circular screens and so on, we have the right to suppose that the motion picture industry has realized that it has exhausted the interest in novelties which had been its own characteristic, and no longer knows what to invent in order to attract a bored, saturated and indifferent public.

In considering the popular movies, it can be noted that, other than by violence or pornography, the public is interested by unusual subjects (such as undersea filming or erupting volcanoes). It is already evident that the day is near when machine guns and nudity will be boring. In short, the repertoire of photographic cinema is limited and close to exhaustion. After all, closing doors, cars coming and going, musketeers' and cowboys' costumes, Belmondo's uppercuts as well as men's and women's anatomies offer very few variations.

Contrary to live action cinema, Animation draws the elements of its future works from a raw material made *exclusively of human ideas*, those ideas that different animators have about things, living beings and their forms, movements and meanings. They represent these ideas through images they make with their own hands. In the causal concatenation of their images – a concatenation they conceive themselves – nothing

can be left to chance. For this reason, creation requires an exceedingly long time which is out of proportion to live action cinema. But the repertoire of human ideas is inexhaustible.

For animators of my generation this slowness has been a very serious handicap. The barbaric need for immediate economic revenue took animated films away from distribution circuits. But times are changing, and the increase of free time will relegate to the past the inattentive rush of the last fifty years spent in old vestiges of wild superproduction. Thus, the same economy which had pushed companies to adapt to a get-fast mode of action, will soon force managers to change their minds and to understand that economic gain has always been alien to really important activities, such as discoveries and inventions. And what is the art work which is not an invention as well? Isn't such work a copy, or plagiarism? The fifty years spent alternating engraved illustrations with film animation have taught me the values of Gutenberg's culture (a stable culture) as well as the values of modern culture (a mobile one). The second will never be able to substitute for the first, and vice versa. Being complementary, these two cultures will remain incomparable as well as irreplaceable, because they represent two opposite processes of the spirit.

To the artist, animation is a totally new discipline. It is, first and foremost, ethic: the painter's intention to greedily keep in his files even the smallest sketches, with the hope of selling them in the future, is foreign to the animator. A 12-minute film is formed by about 16,000 frames. Have the masters done as many drawings in their entire lives? Therefore, the animator does not have time for a Bohemian life.

When I make an illustration, I look for the most valuable exposures, avoiding difficult angles and unrewarding fore-shortening. While animating a film, I cannot omit any of the aspects which the logic of movement forces me to go through. I must study many elements which are not necessary to painting: I must know optics, physiological optics, psychology, neuropsychology of visual perception (sorry, but this is its name), sensitometry as well as music (and I am forgetting others).

In animating composite pendulums in order to trace abstract figures, I took up again the study of basic physics. Moreover, I learned that man has three ways of perceiving objects in movement. Examples of these modes of observation are: an aeroplane propeller, perceived as a translucent and shiny, 'totalized' disc; the moon, the movement of which cannot be seen (but which can be 'totalized' with a long photographic exposure); and finally, the universally known way of seeing, which perceives both the form of the object and its movement (and which photography can 'totalize' as well). These methods of spectatorship are according to their speed in relation to something I am not capable of explaining and which I had to call 'speed of observation'. *Totalization* has taught me the relativism of the notions of speed and form. I can affirm that animation teaches how to know better the way man sees and thinks. It allowed me to enter the true fourth dimension, introducing me to an unknown universe, which I used to create new effects.

In the same way that painting develops an awareness of colours, values and forms, animation develops an awareness of movements and time spans.

I spend beautiful moments in my tiny garden, observing the effects of thousands of small, blurred suns, the images of which are filtered through the foliage of my lime tree. This celebration, caused by the slightest breeze, is a choreography which you cannot perceive, because you do not make animation.

Yet, young people are no longer satisfied by seeing animated films: they want to make some. They are right. Let the new generation reform the economy of future society in such a way as to honour 'the well-done work', in the words of Peguy's mother. This is the challenge!

Alexandre Alexeïeff
Paris, 1973

I

The first four decades (1888–1929)

Chapter 1

Origins

The beginning

The 19th century was the century of science. In physics, and particularly in optics, the scholars, academicians and simple practitioners who determined the course of techno-logical progress in that era found time to study the persistence of images on the retina. In 1824, Peter Mark Roget, who was then examiner of physiology at the University of London, published *Persistence of Vision with Regard to Moving Objects*.[1] As Roget explained, images were retained by the retina of the human eye for fractions of a second before being replaced by the succeeding ones. If the succession was sufficiently rapid, the viewer had the impression of movement even when looking at still pictures. This phenomenon led to further exploration over the next fifty years.

One year later, in 1825, a famous English physician, John A. Paris, created the prototype of optical toys, the thaumatrope: a disc with a complementary image on each side, and strings attached at each end of its horizontal axis. When the disc is spun on the strings, the two complementary images appear to merge. In 1832, the Belgian scientist Joseph Plateau invented the prototype of optical toys, the phenakistiscope.[2] This was a device made of a pivot and a cardboard disc, along the edge of which successive images of an object in motion had been drawn. By focusing on one drawing while viewing the rotating disk through a slit, one had the illusion that the drawing moved. Improvements and analogous research soon added to Plateau's invention. New devices with Greek sounding names (praxinoscope, kinematoscope, fantascope) brought together the laws of physics and the principles found in the old 'magic lantern' in the attempt to transform a simple curiosity into an instrument of entertainment. The interest in moving images, rooted in the ancient human need to reproduce existence as faithfully as possible, was finding its first technological realizations. Toward the end of the century, Edison in America and the Lumières in Europe would give birth to what is known today as cinema, but even earlier, the French inventor, Emile Reynaud, made pioneering discoveries.

Emile Reynaud

Emile Reynaud was born in Montreuil-Sous-Bois on 8 December, 1844. As a young boy, he apprenticed in a precision-mechanics shop and worked for Salomon, the French photographer who imported Hafenstaegl's art of retouching from Bavaria to France. This knowledge of optics and mechanics enriched Reynaud's artistic skills, which he had learned from his mother who had been a student of the painter Redouté (the 'Raphael of the Flowers'. 1759–1840).

In 1872, Reynaud came upon an issue of *La Nature* magazine which illustrated the latest findings on the optical reproduction of movement. Combining experience and ingenuity, he built a device of his own, the praxinoscope. It consisted of a cylindrical box attached to a pivot. A coloured strip of paper on the inside face of the cylinder showed the consecutive stages of a movement. When the cylinder rotated, these stages were reflected in rapid succession on a mirrored prism mounted on the pivot, and the viewer who looked at the prism would see the drawn image move freely. Reynaud patented the praxinoscope in 1877, and the following year he received honourable

mention at the Paris World Exposition. He later opened a small workshop and began manufacturing the instrument in large quantities, selling it throughout Europe as a children's toy.

Unwilling to return to anonymity, Reynaud modified the praxinoscope hoping to transform this family amusement into an entertainment device for large audiences. After several metamorphoses (all of them patented), in 1888, the praxinoscope became what the inventor had wished. In October, Reynaud invited some friends to an experimental projection in his home and showed one film, *Un bon bock* (A Good Beer), his very first work of the kind. Pleased with the response, in December he applied for a patent at the Prefecture of Seine.

Fig. 1. Emile Reynaud's 'Théâtre optique'. The images of the reel are projected (B–C) on to the screen (E) by a mirror (M). Another projector (D) throws the background's fixed image on to the screen (France, 1892–1900).

1 This is the same Peter Mark Roget who, in 1852, published the first edition of the *Thesaurus of English Words and Phrases Arranged so as to Facilitate the Expression of Ideas and Assist in Literary Composition.*

2 Plateau always called his device a 'phenatisticope', without the central 's'.

The patent, numbered 194482, was granted on 14 January 1889. Although the new device was a modification of the praxinoscope, Reynaud gave it a new name, *théâtre optique* (optical theatre). By means of a projector and more mirrors, the images which the viewer of the praxinoscope had once seen directly on the prism were now brought to a screen. Images were no longer arranged on a short, self-terminating strip placed within the cylinder, but were painted on a long ribbon, a true film with a canvas support that unwound from one spool and rewound on another. Finally, an auxiliary 'magic lantern' projected a fixed background on the same screen where the action film was taking place.

This rather complex and fragile instrument had one fundamental defect: it had to be turned manually by a skilled operator. The projection included stops and rewinds at pre-established times, acoustical effects, and so on. In other words, the operator had to be a cinematic puppeteer – animated cinema and animated theatre were walking hand in hand. Reynaud planned to sell his device to entrepreneurs at home and abroad. He hoped to establish a profitable business supplying new films for his clients who would want a variety of programmes. This proved to be an illusion. Excessive costs, the fragility of the instrument and the difficult operations it involved dissuaded any potential buyers.

Reynaud himself had to be the projectionist if he wanted his *théâtre optique* to be shown. On 11 October 1892, four years after his first experimental performance, he signed a contract with the Grévin Museum, the well-known wax museum which also offered variety programmes. The contract required daily performances, which Reynaud had to run in person, and an entirely new repertory every year. A clause prohibited the sale or rental of similar instruments and films in France and abroad. Reynaud was also tied hand and foot, having to spend all his free time creating new films. He complied, however, and showed his first *pantomimes lumineuses* (Lit pantomimes) on 28 October 1892. The billboards read *Le clown et ses chiens* (The Clown and His Dogs), *Pauvre Pierrot* (Poor Pierrot), and *Un bon bock*.

As the years went by, Reynaud made some improvements on his device (by pushing a lever he was able to simulate the sound of Pierrot's thrashings). He also painted new films. There was always an audience for the *pantomimes lumineuses*; for when they ended screenings in 1900, it was estimated that over half a million people had seen them. In 1895, however, after the Lumières' historical projection only a few hundred yards from the Grévin Museum, the audience began to wane. Reynaud tried new techniques to speed up the manual work. He saved some time by using photographic instruments while drawing, but did not want to make films 'Lumière style'. Whenever he used photographs, he reworked them by hand, till they were transformed into drawings. Because of his craftsman way of working, he was left behind the times, which were becoming ever more fast-paced. The Grévin Museum offered the *théâtre optique* until 1 March 1900, when English marionettes and a Gypsy orchestra replaced the *pantomimes lumineuses*.

At fifty-six, Reynaud did not want to retire and kept experimenting with new machinery, such as the stereoscopic viewer. But cinema was opening its door to the industrialists, not to the craftsmen who could not compete. With the sale of his inventions alone, Reynaud was no longer able to support himself: the praxinoscope was a toy without a future, and the *théâtre optique* had not been improved from its inception ten years earlier. In a moment of vexation, a depressed Reynaud smashed the three *théâtres optiques* he owned. Then, day after day, he threw the long and painstakingly painted films into the Seine. His last years were marred by poverty and solitude. He died on 9 January 1917.

'The device is designed to create the illusion of movement, no longer limited to the repetition of the same poses each time the instrument is turned, as happens with all of the current devices; on the contrary, its indefinite length and variety produce true animated scenes with unlimited length.' In this awkward prose (from the report accompanying the patent application for the *théâtre optique*) Reynaud summarized the meaning of his work. He was aware of his unique contribution which expanded the time dimension and theoretically opened unlimited possibilities to images in rapid succession. From that time on, images would no longer be repeated at each turn of the crank, but would flow, telling a story, forming a narrative movement. Before, the available devices were visual music boxes which displayed a few images over and over again. After Reynaud's invention, the core of the performance was no longer the simple 'wonder' originated by a drawing (or a picture) which moved, but 'entertainment' itself.

Two films by Reynaud remain: *Pauvre Pierrot* and *Autour d'une cabine* (Around a Bathing Hut), true little comedies performed by drawn actors in the spirit of the times. The exquisitely delicate *Autour d'une cabine* displays an amiable turn-of-the-century taste, a narrative enriched by details (a flight of seagulls, a group of comic bathers) and a feeling for colour. While the drawing itself is nothing more than an example of good graphics, the movement is impressive even to the present-day viewer. Indeed, animation is not the art of drawing that moves, but the art of movement which is drawn, as Norman McLaren remarked fifty years later. Reynaud's drawing becomes beautiful when it moves, because the inventor of animation sensed that drawings had to be functional to their dynamics.

Reynaud did not want to use photography for his pantomimes, despite the advantages that this might have brought him. A one-time photographer, he did not like the exact reproduction of physical reality. On the contrary, he was a graphic artist in the tradition of Salomon, who had brought the art of retouching to virtuoso levels, working by hand on the negatives and obtaining images that had little to do with the original, but were graphic and pictorial creations. When Reynaud agreed to use photographic equipment in the last years of the century, he did so in order to lighten his workload as a draftsman. He called upon two comics, Footit and Chocolat, and filmed their routines. He asked the actor Galipaux to perform the piece which had made him famous, *Le premier cigare* (The First Cigar), in front of the camera. Then he chose the photo-

Fig. 2. Autour d'une cabine *by Emile Reynaud (France, 1895).*

graphs one by one, and re-touched them. What counted was human intervention; craftsmanship, to Reynaud, was the mother of art.

Frame by frame

The age of the movie camera and the projector began in 1895, after several decades of experimentation with all kinds of photographic and optical techniques and equipment. The practical outcome of those studies was followed by a sudden easing up of research as the Lumière brothers' instrument, and the somewhat similar one developed by Edison in America, satisfied immediate technical and industrial needs. A few people still pursued research, aiming for colour, three-dimensionality and sound, but remained outside the mainstream. The truly significant advancement was the invention of the little camera capable of taking (manually) from sixteen to twenty photographs per second. Because of this camera, which would generate economic empires and significant sociological phenomena, for the first time in history people were able to visualize a believable kinetic portrait of their world and themselves.

The time was ripe for the rediscovery of animated cinema. By the turn of the century a slew of advancements laid the groundwork. The first step was to redevelop the principle of animation by successive frames through which one could direct movement. The American Alfred Clark was probably the first to find out that the crank of a camera could be stopped and then started again, thus allowing the images in front of the lens to be changed uninterruptedly during projection. While working for Edison on *The Execution of Mary, Queen of Scots*, in August 1895, Clark substituted a puppet for the actress who was

going to be beheaded. The first artist to make objects move was perhaps Georges Méliès, who animated the letters of the alphabet for advertising films in 1898. James Stuart Blackton was probably the first to obtain a speeded-up caricature by modifying drawings during a pause of the crank (*The Enchanted Drawing*, 1900). Still, could this be called animation, or was it rather a stop-motion technique? And what if the operator only slowed the crank, instead of stopping it, and speeded-up the entire scene, drawing and artist included, during projection?

Luckily, it is not as necessary to unravel this tangled controversy, as to point out that the frame-by-frame (or single frame) technique was one of the first special effects needed by any good technician.[1] This 'trick', as well as the procedures of slow motion and reverse or double exposure, did not require any special creativity on the part of the person who manually controlled the movement of the film. If animation comes into play not when its techniques were first applied, but when they became a foundation for creativity, then the first animated film could very well be *Matches: An Appeal*, by the Briton Arthur Melbourne Cooper. Made in 1899 with animated matches, *Matches: An Appeal* was a public address inviting British citizens to donate matches to the soldiers fighting in the Boer war. For those who subscribe to the teachings of archaeologist C.W Ceram, (in history, a process does not 'begin' at its inception but when it gives rise to a new productive stage),[2] the history of animation begins with the films made by the Frenchman Emile Cohl in 1908.

In any case, the contribution to cinema by the 'paleoanimators' should not be undervalued. This group includes the American Edwin S.

---

1   As late as in 1927, the German filmmaker and animator Guido Seeber listed the frame by frame techniques as only one of the many special effects ('tricks') a cameraman should handle, and complained that the current German language called by autonomasia 'Trickfilm', just animation (Guido Seeber *Der Trickfilm in seinen grundsätzlichen Möglichkeiten* (Verlag der Lichtbildbühne, Berlin, 1927).

2   C.W. Ceram, *Archaeology of the Cinema* (London: Thames and Hudson, 1965).

Porter (director of the first western, *The Great Train Robbery*, a live action film of 1903), whose best animated work is a famous sequence of *The 'Teddy' Bears* (1907), featuring fluidly animated bear puppets; the Spaniard Segundo de Cho-

món, who will be discussed later; the Briton Walter P. Booth, author of *The Hand of the Artist* (1906); and James Stuart Blackton.

Fig. 3. Humorous Phases of Funny Faces *by James Stuart Blackton (USA, 1906).*

James Stuart Blackton

Born in Sheffield (Great Britain) in 1875, Blackton moved to the United States at the age of ten. As a teenager, he showed an interest in journalism. In 1896, while interviewing Thomas Alva Edison, Blackton confessed to an aptitude for drawing, and was asked by Edison to draw his portrait while a camera filmed the scene. The episode started Blackton's cinematographic career as cameraman, director and producer.

Blackton had direct experience with 'chalk talks' (or 'lightning sketches' in British English), vaudeville acts during which an artist drew quick caricatures of viewers, or modified a drawing while doing his monologue. (Many English and American animated proto-films were no more than lightning sketches which had been transposed to the screen). After *Enchanted Drawing*, Blackton persisted in this formula. His most famous production, *Humorous Phases of Funny Faces* (1906), featured comic portraits of a man rolling his eyes and puffing smoke, a long-nosed character and a dog jumping through a ring. Here, the drawings displayed an exceptional autonomy while the artist-designer's presence was merely suggested by the appearance of his hand on the screen.

In 1907, Blackton released *The Haunted Hotel*, a live action film in which the frame-by-frame technique enlivened the supernatural effects of the haunted hotel. Although the film was no better than others, it was extraordinarily successful. It was amply imitated, and it spurred a search for the trick behind that uncanny movement that many were seeing for the first time. It also triggered many people's interest in cinema, among them, Emile Cohl's. In 1909, Blackton quit animation. He died in Los Angeles in 1941.

For their animated works, Blackton and his contemporaries used the frame by frame technique as a way to 'stupefy' by creating 'magical' effects. After Blackton's contribution, only one more step was needed before film animation became

such in the full sense of the word. That step would be taken by Emile Cohl in Paris.

Emile Cohl

Emile Cohl was born Emile Courtet on 4 January 1857 in Paris. He was proud of his surname, as Parisian as the Seine. His family, he wrote, had lived for centuries in the neighbourhood where the Bourse is situated, and his most distant ancestor was mentioned in the civil annals of 1292. Courtet worked as an apprentice to a jeweler and an assistant to a magician. He discovered his artistic talent while serving in the military when he sketched portraits of the entire regiment, including his colonel. Having returned to civilian life, he studied with artist André Gill. Just as he was about to become famous, he changed his name to the Alsatian-sounding Cohl, thinking that a pinch of the exotic might be helpful.

Cohl was like a chameleon of many colours. He worked as a caricaturist for several magazines, such as *Les hommes d'aujourd'hui*, to which he supplied caricatures of Verlaine and Toulouse-Lautrec. (In 1894, that same magazine confirmed Cohl's vast notoriety by dedicating to him a cover caricature signed by Uzès.) In the 1880s, Cohl turned successfully to photography. His light comedies were performed in the theatres of the boulevards and, last but not least of his numerous hobbies, he was interested in puzzles and magic tricks.

Cohl did not approach cinema until 1907, when he entered Gaumont's offices, with other purposes than looking for employment. He had noted that Gaumont had plagiarized one of his vignettes, and was now demanding a compensation. Not only did Gaumont make no objections to offering excuses, but he also invited Cohl to

join his 'brains trust' in the department of film tricks. Cohl accepted. At this point history and legend overlap. According to the latter, at the same time that Cohl entered the world of cinema, Blackton's *The Haunted Hotel* arrived on the French screens. Filmmakers racked their brains to understand how it was done. The legend goes that the only one to solve the problem, discovering the basic laws of what was to become his own art form, was Emile Cohl.

Indeed, the American film caused much commotion. As for Cohl, he did come to understand the technical process, and after a few months of work he completed the first animated French film, *Fantasmagorie*. Moving ahead of Blackton's works, Cohl improved the quality. Worried about verisimilitude, Blackton was always careful to introduce or justify the presence of a cartooned world next to a real world. On the contrary, the Frenchman jumped into the graphic universe, animating the adventures of autonomous characters. The four-minute-long *Fantasmagorie* was first shown at the Théâtre du Gymnase on 17

Fig. 4. Le cauchemar du fantoche *by Emile Cohl (France, 1908)*.

August 1908. The public welcomed this new type of show, and the producers entrusted Cohl with the creation of more new films.

Before the year 1908 ended, Cohl had made five and perhaps more films – an exceptional number considering the time-consuming workmanship and the rudimentary techniques and equipment used. Production continued frantically until 1923. By then, Cohl remembered having made over three hundred shorts, but he forgot many, the actual number being much larger, adding animated films to special effects comedies, live-action shorts and so on. By the end of 1909, he had made more than forty films. In 1910, he left Leon Gaumont and signed a contract with Pathé. In 1912, after joining the Eclair company, he was transferred to the American branch office in Fort Lee, where he animated Snookums, a comic character by McManus in a series that should be considered among the most outstanding of the early animated cartoons era.

In the United States, Cohl found an already well-trained team since animated drawings had been fashionable for some time. The possibility that some American colleagues stole some secrets from him was regularly suggested but without tangible evidence; in any case it is certain that studying and copying other people's techniques was common. A passage from a letter he wrote from Fort Lee shows his high-spirits and admiration for the teamwork and for the producers' generous compensation to the artists. His mood changed in the following years when he saw that the rationalization of labour and the economic-managerial machine enabled the Americans to produce films for the European market, in such a way as to defeat competition by individual filmmakers.

In March 1914, three months before the outbreak of World War I, Cohl returned to Paris. During the war he worked on a series similar to the ones he had produced in the United States, this time featuring characters by the cartoonist Benjamin Rabier. The series was entitled *Flambeau* . He also made war propaganda films. The inspiration of his earlier years weakened, as he limited his productions to series. Even the most famous *Pieds nickelés* (Lacking Agreement), with drawings by Forton, no longer had the stamp of Cohl's personality. The postwar period definitively signaled the waning of Cohl's genius. He concerned himself primarily with scientific and advertising films for other studios before his death on 20 January 1938 at the age of eighty-one.

The most interesting period of Emile Cohl's cinematographic career was certainly the first, which ended in 1910. During the Gaumont stage, the draftsman and director brimmed with fantasy. In an age when cinema was swamped by conceited theatrical costumes, he gave lessons in stylization and before-the-fact surrealism. His characters create and destroy themselves, undergo limitless metamorphoses, are run through by umbrellas without losing a drop of blood and fall victim to monsters with humanoid faces and eyeballs on the tips of their tails. Nor did Cohl content himself strictly with drawing. He animated puppets and

Fig. 5. Les joyeux microbes by Emile Cohl (France, 1909).

objects (a famous film of his featured animated matches), studied new tricks and hand-painted colours on film, as in *L'éventail animé* (The Animated Fan).

Such a fertile imagination commands interest even today, when other films of the same period may appear tiresome. This is due primarily to Cohl's crisp, albeit elementary, graphics. Those critics who emphasize the graphic element in film animation consider Cohl's visual, two-dimensional fantasy as the first and highest example of this art. His films are tied to humour and comedy. For example, the episodes featuring Fantoche are little comedies of intrigue, based on the contrast between characters, the intervention of competitors (such as a policeman), and misunderstandings. Cohl's drawings emphasize lines over volume, and his comedies favour plot over psychology, but his films display one exceptional element: the dazzling trick which spurts without explanation or logical connection like a rabbit from a magician's top-hat. This joyousness reverberates in the drawings, which are naïve, despite Cohl's fine craftsmanship. Cohl's stylization depended on his need to reduce the number of lines to be animated, but perhaps never as in this occasion had an artist known how to make a virtue of necessity.

The years directly following 1910 marked a slow decline, although Cohl still released a few good works. His last spectacular film was *Fantoche cherche un logement* (The Puppet Looks for Lodging, 1921). For this film, the sixty-four year old artist resuscitated a character which had been dear to him in the happier times of *Drame chez les fantoches* (Drama Amongst the Puppets) or *Le cauchemar du fantoche* (The Nightmare of the Puppet). In Fantoche's company, Cohl marked his retirement from the world of animated drawing.

Georges Méliès

Georges Méliès (born in Paris on 8 December

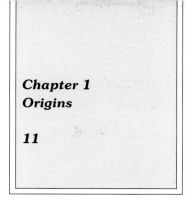

1861) was an illusionist who bought the Robert Houdin theatre and became an artist-impresario of magic and variety shows. As a prospective client of the Lumières, he was invited to the historical projection of 28 December 1895. That event had a dramatic impact on him: he turned to directing and producing and was a leader in his field for the next ten years. In a world of documentary filmmakers, Méliès was the first to view cinema as the realm of the imagination. He was also a pioneer in studying the effects obtainable with the camera, anticipating breakthroughs which have transformed into today's cinematic language.

Screening Méliès's films today is like viewing an animated film … without animation. The story unravels against unnaturally painted backgrounds; the actors themselves seem purely figurative elements, covered by masks, costumes or camouflages. In addition to this, the movie camera is stationary (Méliès filmed according to the principle that the movie camera should be like a gentleman in his armchair); therefore all the action occurs as if in an animated puppet theatre. This is where Méliès's cinema contains the seeds of its own negation; for, if there is a stylistic clash in his films, it lies in the contrast between the two-dimensional scenery and the clumsy movement of the three-dimensional actors. Still, Méliès paved the way for a similarly rooted cinema in which this contradiction would be overcome by improved technology. Characters and scenery (drawn or modelled) were to be stylistically homogeneous and movement would no longer be left to the actors, but would be created by the directors. Méliès' work is perhaps one of the most convincing pieces of evidence that there is no actual borderline between live action and animated cinema.

The first abstract cinema

The years from the end of the 19th century to

post-World War I were decisive for the history of film as well as the history of art culture. Cinema affirmed itself both as art and industry in Europe and in the United States. At the beginning of the century, the major companies of the newborn film industry, such as Pathé and Gaumont, Itala and Ambrosio, Edison and Biograph, competed in the field with investment and income worthy of a great traditional industry. Permanent movie theatres replaced the projections in circus big tops and country fairs, and, in the United States, store fronts. First Méliès, then the Brighton school and finally Edwin S. Porter laid the foundation for a cinematographic style that Griffith would later bring to its greatest heights. (*The Birth of a Nation* was made in 1915). Cinema was a new phenomenon, and the filmmakers a new breed: only rarely did artists from other disciplines, intellectuals or philosophers embrace and praise this new medium. Without a history of its own, masters to emulate or models to follow, cinema displayed all the problems of a newborn language, needing gifted technicians and amateurs as well as artists skilled in the use of the camera.

Such circumstances were ignored by universities and art schools, which considered cinema as a poor copy of theatre and a place the artistically gifted should avoid. With very few exceptions, a similar attitude greeted the avant-garde movements which were subverting the formal and ideological order of the traditional arts. Fauvism and Cubism scandalized through their daring innovations. A few years later, Futurism proclaimed itself not only an artistic movement, but an ideological and political current as well. Dada and Surrealism followed this pattern. Facing ostracism by the bourgeois intelligentsia, cinema and avant-garde movements led a somewhat parallel life and each caused a division in the humanist culture of the century.

Contacts between the two were sporadic. While Futurists, Dadaists and Surrealists loved filmed shows, there was no corresponding interest from film producers toward the fine arts, and even less toward the avant-garde. With a few exceptions, cinema was the industry of the masses.

The avant-garde, restrained by technical and economic obstacles, produced only a few marginally successful films. These include: *Vita futurista* (Futuristic Life) by Ginna; the Dada films by Man Ray, Fernand Léger, and Clair-Picabia; and *Un chien andalou* (An Andalusian Dog) and *L'âge d'or* (The Golden Age) by Buñuel-Dalí. Why were these artists interested in film? Because cinema offered movement. The search for movement, which had constantly marked the history of art, had become pressing after Impressionism, when paintings strove ever more to capture life itself, leaving static representations to photography. Seurat succeeded in painting the vibrations of air; while the Futurists, who believed in 'dynamism' as an ideological and aesthetic principle, forgot the figure and painted the action. Balla painted the scurrying of a bassethound in *Dog on a Leash* (1912), and hands moving rapidly on the instrument in *The Violinist's Hands* (1912). Bragaglia actuated 'photodynamics', synthesizing the development of a gesture in a single image; in the same years, Marcel Duchamp created the *Nude Descending a Staircase*, and the list of examples continues.

These artistic currents were all based on a 'plastic' concept of movement: the new mode of painting and taking photographs tried to express optical effects or psychological concepts of action. From there to film, the step was short. Capable of moving, or in Futurist terminology, of rendering mobile any object, animation was the medium closest to the purposes of designers, sculptors and painters. The history of animation is marked by contact with painters, as well as the equally fertile attention of animators to the innovative currents in graphics and plastic arts (Picasso himself was on the brink of entrusting some of his drawings to animator Giulio Gianini).[1] In the 1950s, the birth of 'kinetic' art supplied the missing link in the evolutionary chain that tied the traditional plastic arts to animation. Europe, a cultural centre for the first forty years of this century, was also host to experiments, debate and a large number of talented animators. In America, experimental and art films began in the late 1930s.

Arnaldo Ginna

'Since 1907 I understood the kinetic-pictorial potential of cinema,' Arnaldo Ginna recalled. 'In 1908–09, a movie camera which could film one frame at a time did not exist. I thought of painting directly on the film.'[2] Writer, Futurist theoretician, painter of what was probably the first abstract painting in the history of Western art (*Neurasthenia*, 1908) and director of the only official Futuristic film, *Vita futurista* (Futuristic Life, 1916, filmed in Florence with the participation of the movement's major exponents), Ginna created a radically new technique for film animation – a technique which Len Lye and Norman McLaren would skilfully develop 25 years later.

Ginna, whose real name was Arnaldo Ginanni Corradini, was born in Ravenna, Italy, on 7 May 1890. With his brother Bruno (Ravenna, 9 June 1892 – Varese, 20 November 1976), who used the pen-name of Bruno Corra, he developed an original theory of the arts. According to the two brothers, a mutual relationship exists among the arts: a *musical motif* is formed by sounds changing within a time sequence; and likewise, in painting a *chromatic motif* can be obtained by cinematographic techniques which offer colours changing within a time sequence. Just as the musical chord is a fixed sound in space like that emitted by an organ when one presses a key, the

'chromatic chord', in Ginna's terms, defines what would later be called an 'abstract painting'. Ginna wrote:

'Pointillism was the starting point for the studies on the chromatic chord, the chromatic symphony and so on, because the different dots or segments of painting paralleled the succession of different musical notes. This allowed us to approach certain areas of colour in the paintings of Segantini. For example: a particular colour area in a field by Segantini was a chromatic chord taken precisely from the nature of those mountain meadows.'[3]

Ginna painted four works directly on film: *A Chord of Colour* from Segantini, *Study of the Effects of Four Colours* and *Song of Spring*, from Mendelssohn, and *Flowers* from Mallarmé. While the first film was the development of a colour chord, the second studied the effects among complementary colours (red-green, blue-yellow) and the last two were chromatic renderings of music and poetry.

'I have not seen frames of the experiments done in 1910 for many years. Perhaps someone has them? Are they lost? Or destroyed? You will understand, it was so many years ago, with so many events and moves from one city to another! Besides, no one gave them much importance. Those experiments, especially the sequence regarding Segantini's work, were made in order to produce chromatic music, chromatic motifs and symphonies. Even small black and white animations were made. The very earliest consisted of a little book whose many pages, when flipped quickly, yielded the impression of movement. These were then transcribed by hand on to the celluloid film, but without pigment sensitive to

1   Curiously, the Spanish master had another bout with animation: animated experiments featuring his drawings appear in *Le mystere Picasso* (1956), a documentary by Henri-Georges Clouzot.

2   Quotation from *Cinema e letteratura del Futurismo* by Mario Verdone (Edizioni di Banco e Nero, Rome, 1968).

3   Letter received from Arnaldo Ginna, 1 March 1972.

silver nitrate. This film was sent to us by our optician Magini, in Ravenna. That's all: very distant recollections, almost a dream. I noticed later that these little books with animated drawings were being sold to entertain small children.'[1]

Ginna continued his unpublicized artistic activity, but he never ventured into cinema again. He died in Rome on 24 September 1982.

Léopold Survage

Around 1914, the Cubist painter Léopold Survage, of Scandinavian, Russian and French descent, responded to the Futurists. He wanted to make a film based on the rhythm of colours, filming image-by-image according to traditional principles. 'Coloured rhythm is not at all an illustration or interpretation of a musical work. It is an autonomous art form, even if it is based on the same psychological data as music,' Survage wrote on the pages of Apollinaire's magazine, *Soirées de Paris*. Survage's long but ideologically weak manifesto, however, explored the same field as Ginna and arrived at somewhat similar conclusions. The war put an end to Survage's cinematographic ambitions, and the film never came to be. As a result, only a few preparatory paintings remain.

1   Letter received from Arnaldo Ginna, 18 February 1972.

Chapter 2

Animation in the United States of America

A ndré Martin wrote: 'From 1913 on, American film animation can be compared to a boiling pot. All the movements are simultaneous, and the influences are countless. Directors and animators jump like fleas from one studio to another, from New York to Hollywood. Producers can participate in various studio productions simultaneously, and films of the same series can be circulated through several distributors.'[1] As if the matter was not muddled enough, the historian searching for reliable information on this period must also deal with poorly preserved copies and titles in which names of directors and artists were often omitted. Moreover, since animation attracted little public interest, only a few pieces of news or interviews related to this subject have been preserved. Taking into account that the world of animation did not have widespread origins, American production was an impressive phenomenon and its main lines can be safely outlined.

Winsor McCay

A clever cartoonist (his comic strip *Little Nemo in Slumberland*, published from 15 October 1905 in the *New York Herald*, is still one of the best in the field), Winsor Zenis McCay can be considered the first 'classical' artist of American animation. McCay was born on 26 September 1871, near Spring Lake, Michigan.[2] Like many of his colleagues and contemporaries, he was a self-taught artist, who started by drawing billboards and vaudeville stage settings and newspaper comic strips. After fifteen years in Cincinnati, he was invited to New York by James Gordon Bennett, a legendary figure in American journalism, publisher of the *New York Herald* and the *New York Evening Telegram*. There, McCay made a name for himself. Admired and respected by his colleagues, he was an amiable artist who managed to combine high quality work with mass success, topped with a keen intuition for public relations.

In June 1906, McCay returned to vaudeville, this time performing on the stage. His act was a typical 'chalk talk', in which he drew caricatures of spectators and performed *The Seven Ages of Man* (he sketched two faces and aged them by progressive modification). For eleven years he toured with his successful show, never neglecting his comic strips and illustrations.

It was for his vaudeville act that McCay prepared his first animated movie. The excuse was a bet with some of his fellow cartoonists who challenged him to film the thousands of drawings he tirelessly created. With the few techniques known at the time, and possibly at the suggestion of James Stuart Blackton, McCay filmed *Little Nemo* (1910). Beginning on 12 April 1911, McCay incorporated *Little Nemo* into his vaudeville act. The film was also shown simultaneously in movie theatres. Blackton's production company, Vitagraph, distributed the movie with an introductory 'frame' by Blackton, describing the bet and showing the artist at work. In January 1912, McCay created *The Story of a Mosquito* (or *How a Mosquito Operates*). This time, however, he requested that the movie not be distributed while he was exhibiting it in the theatre. *Little Nemo* is truly a 'first movie'; without plot or background, it is little more than a sequence of images, materializing and then vanishing as if to prove their ability to exist on screen. This experimentalism is overcome in *The Story of a Mosquito*, the funny,

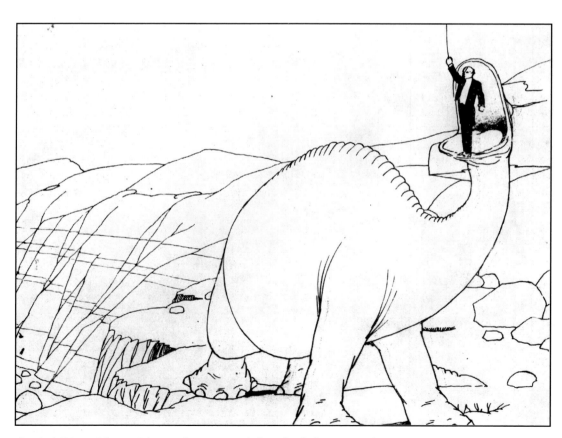

Fig. 6. Gertie the Dinosaur *by Winsor McCay (USA, 1914).*

1   André Martin *Arbre généalogique des origines et de l'âge d'or du dessin animé Americain* (Montreal Cinémathèque Québécoise, 1967).

2   According to John Canemaker, McCay's biographer, the date should rather be 1867, and the place was Canada (personal communication to the author)

ironic tale of a huge mosquito, wearing a top hat, which is insatiably hungry for the blood of a drunkard. The gluttonous bug ends up exploding.

The first part of McCay's production is characterized by extraordinarily sharp drawings and animation. The rich, elegant art-nouveau style of his comic strips is simplified but not impoverished. Movements are slow, fluid, perfectly suited to such personal graphics, with a display of elegance which is nearly unmatched in the history of animation. Since McCay produced his own movies, he could afford expensive workmanship, using thousands of drawings on paper and a careful control over the fluidity of animation (he used an old mutoscope roll to flip through the drawings before filming them).

On 8 February 1914, at the Palace Theater in Chicago, McCay showed his masterpiece, *Gertie the Dinosaur*. The film features the unlikely act of an animal tamer and his dinosaur. The large animal peeks from behind some rocks, eats an apple, drinks a lake, plays with a mammoth and dances at McCay's command. Sometimes she is reluctant and when scolded, she cries. The animation and drawings are not only admirable, but also surprising for the personality they give to this puppy-like brontosaurus. Certainly the animal's performance, well-endowed with timing and mimicry, reduced McCay's stage role to that of a straight-man. A unique chronicler, Emile Cohl, in a letter from the United States wrote: 'The main actor, or perhaps the sole actor, was a prehistoric animal ... . McCay stood very elegantly in front of the screen, armed with a whip. He would give a short speech and then, turning toward the screen like an animal trainer, he would call the animal. (Gertie) would come out of the rocks, and at this point, an exhibition of the highest quality would begin ... '.

McCay ended his theatrical career when the newspaper for which he worked claimed the exclusive rights to his performances of *Gertie the*

Dinosaur. Because he wished to avoid any battle, McCay first limited his performances to New York and eventually quit. He re-edited *Gertie* by adding a prologue and a few live action scenes and by the end of 1914, he delivered it to William Fox for distribution in the movie circuits.

Four years were to pass before another movie by McCay could be seen on the screen. This time it was a totally different film lasting over 20 minutes. Entitled *The Sinking of the Lusitania* (July 1918), it was based on a sad episode of wartime history, the sinking of the British ship *Lusitania* by a German submarine in May 1915. Of the 1,198 passengers who died, 124 were US citizens. American public opinion was indignant, and the accident played a determining role in favour of American participation in the war. An outraged McCay created a dramatic, extremely detailed, gripping movie which maintained the rhythm and style of contemporary documentaries or newsreels. Basically, it was a filmic version of the very popular illustrated reenactments of accidents, which appeared in American and European newspapers of the time. McCay's characteristic floral style emerged even in the ethical and dramatic undertones of the movie, as can be seen in the beautifully drawn head of the child surfacing in the waves.

Among McCay's remaining movies and fragments, the most relevant are the three *Dreams of a Rarebit Fiend*, filmed by McCay and his son Robert, around 1921. The first, *The Pet*, tells the story of a dog which grows to a monstrous size and wanders around the city. The second, *Bug Vaudeville* features non anthropomorphic insects performing sleights of hand, dances and bicycle acts. In the third movie, *The Flying House*, a middle-aged husband and wife equip their house with wings and an engine and fly away through the universe. *Bug Vaudeville* is a serene and elegantly animated film with much originality; undoubtably, it is the best of the three. Yet, these movies are far from McCay's initial efforts.

Having abandoned the technique of drawing on paper, he used the cel process, with sometimes unfortunate results; his inspiration and his rhythmic sense, similarly, seemed less assured.

In the following years until his death on 26 July 1934, McCay limited his production to drawings and illustrations. Even so, he always considered himself an animator, declaring in an interview that he was most proud of his movies. In the 1920s, during a famous dinner for New York's animators, McCay did not mince words when recalling his colleagues to their responsibilities. 'Animation should be an art, that is how I conceived it,' he said. 'But as I see what you fellows have done with it is make it into a trade … not an art, but a trade … bad luck.'

Birth of the industry

After 1910, other pioneers of animation emerged everywhere, but with little organization. New York City became a major centre of animation, housing the most thriving studios that offered the best opportunities and the most

efficient systems of production.

The link between the two very American forms of comic strips and animated cartoons was clear from the start. Many animators were either creators of comic strips or started in that field. Many characters, also, moved to the screen directly from the printed page, and for the most part they communicated through the balloons typical of comic strips.

The early movies were also inspired by vaudeville, a secondary but still significant influence. The commonly used formula of the drawing which is sketched by an artist and then becomes alive, for instance, derives from the acts of vaudeville artists and magicians. In the following years, popular shows still influenced animated movies, although vaudeville was soon replaced by live action cinema.

Raoul Barré

Raoul Barré, a French Canadian painter and cartoonist (born in Montreal on 29 January 1874) moved to New York in 1903, after a few trips to Europe. From 1912 to 1913, he collaborated

Fig. 7. Animated Grouch Chasers *by Raoul Barré (USA, 1915).*

with William C. Nolan to produce and direct animated advertising films. The following year, they set up their own studio for entertainment films. Shortly thereafter they were joined by some future talents: Gregory La Cava, Frank Moser, Dick Huemer and Pat Sullivan.

Barré introduced the use of standard perforations in the drawing paper – thus avoiding jerkiness from one image to the following one – and the slash system. The slash system consisted of drawing the set only once, leaving a blank space for the characters' movements and inserting sheets of paper cut to shape in the blank space. The character was drawn in progressive phases of movement on those paper cuttings. This was Barré's solution to what had been the animator's problem from the very beginning: how to animate a character who operates in a particular environment without having to draw both the character and the environment each time.

In 1915, Barré produced *The Animated Grouch Chasers*, for distribution by Edison. In this series, live action film clips introduce the animated sections: whenever an actor reads a cari-

cature album entitled *The Grouch Chaser*, this comes to life. Here Barré's drawings are sharp and purposely ungraceful.

In 1916, Barré was commissioned by the International Film Service (which will be discussed later) to film seven *Fables*, based on a comic strip by T.E. Powers (other episodes of the serial were created by Vernon George

Fig. 8. Colonel Heeza Liar and the Pirates *by John Randolph Bray (USA, 1916).*

Fig. 9. Colonel Heeza Liar in Africa *by John Randolph Bray (USA, 1914).*

Stallings and Frank Moser). That same year, in partnership with Charles Bowers, Barré successfully produced the animated adventures of Mutt and Jeff, the famous comic strip duo created by Bud Fisher. Work remained hectic until 1919 when Barré, victim of a plot allegedly masterminded by Bowers, abruptly abandoned his business and took up painting in a Long Island country house. He made a fleeting return in 1926–27 as the animator of *Felix the Cat* for Pat Sullivan. Then he went back to Montreal, where he devoted himself to painting and political satire until his death on 21 May 1932.

John Randolph Bray

In the first decade of American animation, a most dominant personality was John Randolph Bray. Resolute, manipulative and far-sighted, he laid the foundations for American animation and gave it direction. Born on 25 August 1879 in Addison, Michigan (he died at nearly one hundred years of age on 10 October 1978 in Bridgeport, Connecticut), he became successful as a cartoonist and an illustrator in New York between 1906 and 1907. He probably moved to cinema in an attempt to emulate Winsor McCay, however, his attitude differed greatly from McCay's creativity. According to Bray, the field of animated drawings was a for-profit enterprise. From the very start he sought ways of rationalizing labour, cutting out unnecessary effort and speeding production time.

The *Artist's Dreams* (or *The Dachsund and the Sausage*, July 1913) tells the story of a drawing which comes alive as soon as the artist leaves the studio. In this case the drawing represents a dog, hurriedly eating sausages until it explodes, exactly as happened to McCay's mosquito. Here Bray experimented with the technique of printing background scenes rather than drawing them repeatedly by hand. The film was received with enthusiasm by Charles Pathé, a leader in world cinematography who at the time was visiting New York. Pathé postponed a trip to Paris, so that he could sign a six-movie contract with Bray, then a 34 year old novice.

The Bray Studios were founded on the basis of competition, commission and the subsequent need for constant production. When the United States intervened in World War I, Bray promptly began marketing government-funded instructional and training films, a move that was later echoed by Walt Disney during World War II. Bray's studios were almost contemporary with the founding of Raoul Barré's group, but their structure was very different. In the Bray Studios, work was divided and compartmentalized. Having become a businessman, Bray laid down his pencil, and employed animators who were responsible for the creation of the movies. In turn, the animators supervised assistants and helpers.

Bray stressed technological development. Within two years, he filed three patents: in January 1914, the use of printed background scenes; in July 1914, the application of grey shades to drawings; and in July 1915, the use of scenery drawn on transparent celluloid to be applied over the drawings to be animated. These patents gave him the leadership in the field and ensured him an effective monopoly over his competitors. Bray was equally prompt in averting the danger posed by Earl Hurd, who had patented an alternative technique in December 1914. In fact, Hurd's process was not only alternative, but ultimately more important than Bray's: it consisted of the cel process, involving the drawing of characters on transparent celluloid sheets, which then were applied over painted background scenes. The transparent sheet was called *cel* in English, and *cellulo* in French (from celluloid). Most animated movies world-wide were to be produced with this technique. At a time in which the animation industry was still developing, the importance of Hurd's discovery was not immediately apparent. For good measure, Bray hired the inventor/moviemaker and made him a partner in the Bray-

Hurd Patent Company, a firm which sold licences for the patented techniques. Until the patents expired in 1932, the company earned healthy profits from royalties.

Innovations did not stop there. In the late 1920s Bray released *The Debut of Thomas Cat*, the first colour animated movie.[1] As the title suggests, the movie features a kitten making its debut at mouse-hunting, finding itself in danger when faced by a large rat. The movie was successful, but the techniques it employed (two colour bi-pack Brewster Color) were considered too expensive. The film itself was too easily subject to scratches and abrasion. The experiment was not repeated and it would be ten more years before colour animation was attempted again.

As for the other movies, the hero of the Bray studios was the comic character Colonel Heeza Liar. A short, bald, nearsighted man, the colonel was a Münchhausen-like character: physically unassuming, but exuberantly daring. His first adventure (January 1914), entitled *Colonel Heeza Liar in Africa*, jokingly referred to the big-game hunting experiences of former US president Theodore Roosevelt, whose expeditions were a popular topic in the media. The colonel went through several changes as, in time, different animators were assigned to draw him (a phenomenon typical in American animation until the 1930s), but he always maintained his place in the comic category of aggressive rascals.

Another protagonist of the Studios was Bobby Bumps, a creation of Earl Hurd, who brought his character along when he joined Bray. Bobby was a little boy who went through his daily-life adventures in the company of his inseparable dog Fido. With the exception of McCay, Hurd (Kansas City 1880 – Hollywood 1940) was probably the best American animator of his time. His well struc-

tured movies display an uncommon visual inventiveness, gentle humour and attention to drawing and scenography.

Other American artists

In the year 1916, William Randolph Hearst's media empire of newspapers, news agencies and movies opened a new branch, the International Film Service. Hearst is known among cinema devotees as the stubborn promoter of his companion Marion Davies's acting career as well as the model for Orson Welles's character of Charles Foster Kane in *Citizen Kane* (1941). The goal was to use the copyrights of several popular comic strips published in Hearst's newspapers for cinematographic purposes. These strips included *Bringing Up Father*, *Krazy Kat*, *Happy Hooligan* and *The Katzenjammer Kids*.

Gregory La Cava[2] was in charge of the service and was able to obtain the participation of old friends such as Bill Nolan and Frank Moser, whom he had met when working with Barré, as well as newcomers, such as Jack King, Grim Natwick, Burt Gillett, Walter Lantz and, from Georgia, the self-taught Vernon George Stallings. Despite its promising beginnings, the International Film Service was forced to close after two years, a victim of swings in the policies of its mother-company. Its productions were not able to surpass those by the competition, and the only relevant achievement of Hearst's foray into animation was to launch talented artists who later emerged on their own.

In 1915, Paul Terry made his debut with the distribution of his *Little Herman*, featuring the caricature of a popular magician. Born in San Mateo, California, on 19 February 1887, Terry studied in San Francisco. In 1911, he moved to New York. After attending a vaudeville performance by McCay he decided to forget his ambitions as a

---

1 To be more precise, even meticulous, this was the first instance in which colour film was used. Since the beginning of cinema, however, many films had been coloured after printing by hand, imbibition or colour change.

2 Gregory La Cava (1892–1952) later pursued a career as a director of live action movies. His masterpiece was *My Man Godfrey*, 1936.

cartoonist and become an animator. A modestly gifted artist (after many rejections his *Little Herman* was bought by a minor distributor for little money), Terry was nevertheless a hard-headed, independent spirit.

was also the author of animated satirical vignettes, which were inserted in newsreels. Similar vignettes were produced, starting in 1913, by Henry 'Hy' Mayer for Universal. Several students of Bray's also became caricaturists. They included Louis Glackens, F. M. Follet and Leighton Budd, who worked for Pathé's newsreels, and John Terry (Paul's older brother) and Hugh M. Shields, who distinguished themselves with some experimental animation work in 1911 in San Francisco. Like Palmer, Wallace Carlson also worked on animated vignettes and serials, creating the character Dreamy Dud (1913) for Essanay. Two important figures, Pat Sullivan and Otto Messmer, will be discussed in Chapter 5.

For the major part of his career, he worked on his own, sometimes accepting commissions from other studios. Despite endless disagreements over the use of animation techniques, Terry did work briefly as a hired animator for John Randolph Bray (in the 1920s an altercation between Bray and Terry led to a lawsuit). Terry's first important character, Farmer Al Falfa, made his debut under Bray's protection. A representative of rural America, Al Falfa was a bald old farmer, bearded and good natured. Although the character was never deeply developed, it survived several changes and lasted until the late 1930s.

Outside the New York area, there is some documentation on the pioneering work of Robert Sidney Smith (1877–1935), a successful cartoonist from Chicago. Smith's first serial dealing with the character Old Doc Yak (a billy goat in human clothes) was distributed by Selig in 1913. Two other serials followed in the next two years. Howard S. Moss, a specialist with animated puppets, also worked in Chicago. His *Motoy Films*, produced around 1917, were based on caricatures of movie stars such as Charlie Chaplin, Mary Pickford and Ben Turpin.

The work of other New York animators is less well documented. Harry S. Palmer, creator of the serial *Keeping Up with the Joneses*, had to give up in 1916 when Bray accused him of using patented techniques without a licence. Palmer

Fig. 10. Old Doc Yak, character by Robert Sidney Smith (USA, 1913).

In the field of puppet animation, Willis O'Brien (Oakland, 2 March 1886 – Hollywood, 8 November 1962) played an important role in the 1910s. After an adventurous youth (he even led a palaeontological expedition in Oregon), O'Brien discovered how to animate clay figurines in the laboratory of a San Francisco marble cutter. Later he substituted india rubber for clay and made figurines equipped with metal skeletons. In 1915, he completed his first short, *The Dinosaur and the Missing Link*; Edison's company bought the movie (which was distributed one year later) and invited the sculptor-director to continue his work in New York.

Besides some animated works, such as *RFD*

10,000 BC; Prehistoric Poultry; The Dinornis or the Great Roaring Whiffenpoof, O'Brien made other films mixing live actors and animated figurines. Toward the end of 1917, he left the economically troubled Edison and accepted an offer by Herbert M. Dawley, a wealthy New Jersey sculptor, to work on *Ghost of Slumber Mountain.* Dawley, who had unsuccessfully experimented on his own with the animation of prehistoric monsters, not only demanded the profits earned by the movie but also attempted to take the artistic and technical credit for it. He was silenced, however, by O'Brien's evident contribution and rising career.

O'Brien's first efforts are excellent for their believable animation of prehistoric animals. As works of art, however, they lack substance and display corny, simplistic humour, clumsy rhythm and uninteresting plots. In a word, they show that, from the very beginning, O'Brien was above all a master of special effects – a quality which returns in his famous contribution to later movies, such as *The Lost World* (1925), *King Kong* (1933) and *The Son of Kong* (1933).

Instruments and language

With the exception of Winsor McCay, who can be considered a case apart, American animation in 1910 was characterized not so much by valuable productions, as by the filmmakers' search for devices, technical processes and language. In 1913, Bill Nolan used the dolly shot for the first time: while the character remained still, the background scene slowly moved under its feet (since the frame by frame technique was used, the character would appear to be moving). Elsewhere, an assistant of Barré and Bowers forgot to insert the background element and filmed the character walking on air. This episode initiated the immortal generation of characters walking into the void and falling only when they become aware of what they are doing. Another time, Stallings, bothered by the difficult task of drawing on a fixed table, invented the rotating panel which allowed the artist to work from every side of a sheet of paper. Many devices were also tried in order to keep the sheets of paper aligned (the most reliable was still Barré's peg system, featuring a standard perforation on the bottom of the paper), although it took years to solve the problem.

The cel was rarely used, and animation was done on paper. Labour was structured in such a way that animators first sketched their drawings with light blue pencils. Since the ortho-chromatic films then in use were insensitive to a light blue colour, light blue pencils reproduced as white, so lines could be changed and corrected over and over again. The drawings were then passed over to assistants for colouring. The assistants were also responsible for adding those details which the animators, concerned with the fluidity of action, did not have time to draw: physiognomical traits, clothing details, etc. Theoretically, the task of the animator involved the creation of stories and gags as well as the animation of characters. Sometimes one individual was responsible for a whole movie or a series, but generally the job was divided and the people who worked on its fragments did not take care to maintain continuity of action. This resulted in unbalanced movies, based on incongruous or even non-existent plots. The underlying principle (which lasted for the next twenty years) was to make the viewers laugh at any cost, even if the movie resulted in an assembly of primitive expedients.

Graphically, none of these movies sparkled. Produced at a frantic pace for distributors who did not understand, or did not care about, the details of workmanship, they were unsophisticated and coarse, featuring rounded, simplified forms which were the easiest to animate. For their part, viewers had low expectations: animation was a curiosity exactly like the many others offered by that popular, populist form of entertainment that was cinema. On the screen, animation mingled

with newsreels, slapstick comedies, endless serials and low quality fiction (with the exception of the works of T. H. Ince and D. W. Griffith). Animators themselves lacked ambitions. They were usually self-taught graphic artists whose education was limited to comic strips and whose commercial craftsmanship was a far cry from fine art. Significantly, their works were called 'animated cartoons' rather than 'animated drawings'.

The early movies were also influenced by vaudeville, a secondary but still significant element.[1] The commonly used formula of the drawing which becomes autonomous after a real life artist has sketched it, derives from the acts of vaudeville artists and magicians. In the following years, popular shows still influenced animated movies, but vaudeville was replaced by live action cinema.

1   Donald Crafton, *Before Mickey* (Cambridge: The MIT Press, 1982), pp. 48 ff.

Chapter 3

The European individualists

A t the beginning of the century, European animation found expression not only through Emile Cohl and the avant-garde painters, but also through the isolated artists who worked in Great Britain, Spain and Russia, establishing a European map of animation even before the 1919 Peace Conference traced the new geographic boundaries of the Old Continent. With almost no exception, animators worked either alone or in small groups. In many countries lacking structure and know-how, animation was left to the enthusiasm and extravagance of a few isolated amateurs, the so called 'pioneers'. Some nations with old cultural traditions, such as The Netherlands, Poland and Czechoslovakia, produced only occasional films. World War I boosted the market by creating a demand for satirical propaganda films; and in several cities, small studios produced advertising reels, film titles and, sometimes, entertainment shorts.

While live-action cinema was evolving prosperously towards the production of its first master-pieces, animation still laboured to emerge from its 'prehistoric' conditions. Unlike live-action filmmakers, animators remained novices in their field even after cinema had entered the sound age. This congenital weakness of the European industry of animation was overcome only in the mid-1930s, with the establishment of a more solid, consistent production in imitation of its American counterpart. With the improvements, however, animation did not always gain in quality; in fact, the animators of the 'heroic' years were anything but negligible, finding their strength in poverty and artistic freedom. An extreme, yet typical, example was Berthold Bartosch, the creator of only one film.

Animation in the Weimar Republic

In Germany, advertising, scientific and technical films were produced along with the most auda-cious of avant-garde cinema, and satirical films appealed to wide audiences. The main centres of production were Berlin and Munich.

Julius Pinschewer began his career in 1910, (Hohensalza, 15 September 1883 – Berne, 16 April 1961), addressing his activity exclusively toward advertising. In *Die Suppe* (The Soup, 1911), he mixed object animation with live-action. Pinschewer's collaborators included some of the most talented artists of the time, such as Walther Ruttmann, creator of the famous *Der Sieger* (The Victor, 1920), Lotte Reiniger, Hans Richter, Guido Seeber, Oskar Fischinger, Hans Fischerkoesen and George Pal. Pinschewer gave an artistic direction to German advertising, which continued for twenty years as the most advanced worldwide. After his escape from Nazi Germany in 1934, he continued his activity in the advertising and educational fields in Berne, Switzerland.

Guido Seeber (1879–1940) was multi-talented as a full-fledged filmmaker, director of photography, designer, editor of technical and trade magazines, inventor, writer of manuals, teacher and producer. As a director of photography, he contributed to many films, including *Student von Prag* (The student of Prague, 1913), several films starring Asta Nielsen and some others directed by Georg Wilhelm Pabst. In the field of animation, Seeber created advertising works such as *Kipho*, or *Du musst zur Kipho* (You Must Go to Kino-Photo, 1925), an abstract film produced by Pinschewer for the Berlin film and photography exhibition. In this original work, Seeber combined a vast range of cinematographic tricks with a constructionist rigour.

The Swiss-national Rudolf Pfenninger, son of painter Emil Pfenninger, was born in Munich on 25 October 1899. A scenographer, designer and animator, his talent emerged more through his inventions than in his films (*Largo*, 1922; *Sonnenersatz*, 1926). He was particularly notable for his synthetic sound experiments, called *Tonende Handschrift* ('sound writing'), which he conducted between 1930 and 1932. Disappointed by a lack of recognition, he made a few more short films (*Pitsch und Patsch* , *Serenade* and *Barcarolle* with the Diehl brothers). With the rise of Nazism, the artist slid into anonymity. He died on 14 June 1976 in Baldham, near Munich.

In the 1920s, theatres showed the series *Kollege Pal* and *Max und Moritz*, as well as films by Hans Fischerkoesen and Harry Jaeger, Kurt Wolfram Kiesslich (who made nationalist propaganda work), Louis Seel (possibly an American) and Toni Rabold of Dean Film. The Diehl brothers began their long-lasting career; Lore Bierling, a specialist in Chinese shadows, also made her debut. In 1928, the prestigious satirical caricaturist George Grosz filmed, for a stage performance by Erwin Piscator, *Die Abenteuer des braven Soldaten Schweijk* (The Adventures of the Good Soldier Schweik). Among production companies, the omnipotent Berlin-based UFA deserves mention as the initiator of the great German cinema, with its future production of special effects, educational films, movie titles and avant-garde work. In the following years of Nazism, World War II and the post-war, the animators' importance steadily weakened and the public lost interest in the very same films it had applauded only a few years earlier.

The matrix

In terms of artistic freedom, Germany and France led the way in Europe. However, it was the avant-garde German film community, unlike its French counterpart, that favoured expressing itself through animated drawings. This preference is perhaps a matter of origins: the French avant-garde was rooted in the Dada and Surrealism movements which drew upon material from real life and turned it inside out. On the other hand, the Germans paid attention to lessons of formal and geometrical rigour taught in part by Suprematism, De Stijl, the Bauhaus and Expressionism. It is not by chance that the German dadaist Hans Richter turned to films with a post-Méliès slant, after having attempted to follow Eggeling's theory of geometry and 'purity'. The pictorial and literary cores of expressionism (represented by Kokoschka, Dix, Toller and Trakl), lacked direct followers in animation, excepting perhaps Berthold Bartosch, who made his only art film in Paris in the early 1930s. Likewise, the experiences of the so called Expressionist Cinema (with Lang, Murnau, Dupont, Pabst) had little influence on the animators of their day.

Hans Richter

Hans Richter (1888–1976) was one of the most consistent, tenacious champions of experimental cinema. (He collected his own numerous works in a long film, explicitly entitled *40 Years of Experiments*). He began his career as a Cubist painter; and later with Tzara and Arp, he contributed to the founding of Dadaism in Zurich. In that ebullient, stimulating environment, he came to feel the emptiness of 'static' painting and the need for something new and rhythmic like music. After having studied the basics of counterpoint under the direction of Ferruccio Busoni,[1] he began painting in black and white in order to reproduce opposites – a fundamental rhythmic principle. Common interests led Richter to befriend the lonely Swedish painter Viking Eggeling, who had moved to Zurich during the reign of Dadaism and was involved in similar research. Together, the two artists continued their experiments, first in Switzerland and later in Germany.

As Richter later remembered, they decided one day to give continuity a definite form by using rolls of paper. They tried to fuse the different stages of evolution as if they were phrases of a symphony or a fugue. The first roll, made by Eggeling in late 1918 or early 1919, was *Horizon-*

tal-Vertical Mass. At the same time, Richter created *Prelude* on the theme of *Crystallization*. Clearly, the rolls involved movement and movement involved cinema.[2]

The logical development of Richter's research is to be found in three shorts, filmed between 1920 and 1925 with the animation of cut shapes: *Rhythmus 21*, *Rhythmus 23* and *Rhythmus 25*. Squares and triangles in motion appear and disappear, attempting to convey a sensation of purely visual rhythm. Technically, the three *Rhythmus* were poorly made, and do not succeed in capturing the viewer's attention.

In 1926, having overcome the difficulties of cine-camera and having learned the secrets of lenses, Richter made *Filmstudie*, a complex, articulate work from the standpoint of language and rhythm. Here he used superimposition, various tricks and geometrical games. For the first time, he also employed a technique which he would use for many years to come: the juxtaposition of live action shots with animation, and of real people with abstract elements. In *Filmstudie*, for instance, Richter gave equal consideration to human subjects and to some ocular glassy globes which rhythmically grouped themselves together and separated in various forms.

Richter wrote:

'The next year was *Inflation*, an introduction

Fig. 11. Rhythmus 21 *by Hans Richter (Germany, 1921)*

1   Pianist, composer and editor of the music of Johann Sebastian Bach.
2   Hans Richter, 'Dreams That Money Can Buy: The Narcissus Sequence', Roger Manvell, ed. *Experiment in Film*. (London: Grey Walls Press, 1949).

to an UFA film, *Die Dame mit der Maske* (The Lady with the Mask), a dance of inflation pictures with the dollar sign in opposition to the multitude of zeros (of the Mark) as a kind of leitmotif ... It was certainly not a regular documentary film. It was more an essay on inflation. ... In 1927–28 I got a little film, *Vormittagsspuk* (Ghosts before Breakfast) done. It was produced for the International Music Festival at Baden-Baden with a score by Paul Hindemith. As it was before the era of sound-film, it was conducted from a rolling score, an invention of a Mr. Blum, in front of the conductor's nose. It did not sound synchronous at all, but it was. The little film (about a reel) was filmed in my artist's studio in Berlin with the Hindemiths and the Darius Milhauds as actors. It was the very rhythmical story of the rebellion of some objects (hats, neckties, coffee cups, etc.) against their daily routine.'[1]

Although 'very rhythmic', *Vormittags-Spuk* was no longer an attempt to make music through images, but instead offered a predominantly narrative film characterized by a subtly absurd humour. As with Richter's previous films, this also was composed of heterogeneous elements and employed various kinds of tricks (the single frame technique was rarely used). Unfortunately, the animation of the hats did not succeed; the 'invisible' threads that made the hats dance were clumsily revealed to the audience.

In 1929, Richter released *Rennsymphonie*, based on a horse race. In the following years, which he spent as an obscure advertising filmmaker, he decided to leave Germany. After short stays in Switzerland and the Soviet Union, he finally settled in the United States. In the 1940s and 1950s, together with old Dadaist friends and other American artists, Richter contributed to the creation of non-animated, experimental films, such as *Dreams That Money Can Buy*, a feature film made in collaboration with Léger, Ernst, Duchamp, Man Ray and Calder.

During this activity, Richter only marginally used animation and is most properly placed among the non-conformist filmmakers who technically experimented with motion picture language. As a director, Richter demonstrated neither original vigour nor a well-defined plan of research; to the modern viewer, his films appear as avant-garde exercises. Still, his work undeniably represents a summary of tendencies and temptations, good and bad, which characterized the artists of his generation and upbringing.

Walther Ruttmann

In *Die Niebelungen* (Part One) by Fritz Lang, the sequence of Kriemhild's nightmare stands out, with flocks of menacing birds flying about in a darkly shaded sky, visiting the queen in her dreams. The author of that suggestive sequence was Walther Ruttmann. Born in Frankfurt-am-Main (28 December 1887), he studied architecture in Zurich and Fine Arts in Munich, while learning to play the 'cello. Between 1912 and 1918 he painted and engraved, flowing through abstraction and from this moving to a theory of abstract cinema ('painting with time', in his words). After being a lieutenant in World War I, and after a subsequent nervous illness, Ruttmann devoted himself to the realization of his theory. On 27 April 1921, in Berlin's Marmorhaus, he presented his *Lichtspiel Opus I*,[2] which featured a musical score expressly written by Max Butting. As the first public presentation of an abstract film, the event was sensationally received by the public and press (newspapers had already reported the praises of previous private projections). *Opus I* is striking not only for its lyrical sensitivity and imaginative capacity, but also for its stylistic maturity in technique and form (see Colour Plates 1

---

1   Hans Richter, same source as above.
2   'Lichtspiel', which can be translated as 'light play', is also the word for 'movie'.

and 2). Amoeboid forms contrast with sharp objects; curvilinear shapes, anticipating those by Oskar Fischinger, cross the screen diagonally, while stripes with a pendulum-like motion seem to beat time. In the following years, Ruttmann produced three other shorts, each called *Opus* and progressively numbered, which were successfully released at home and abroad. The London *Times* wrote in 1925 that Ruttmann's short films would be long remembered.

Ruttmann's contacts within the film industry (besides the sequence for Lang, he created another nightmare sequence for Paul Wegener's *Lebende Buddhas* (Living Buddha), in 1923), introduced him to Lotte Reiniger's team. Ruttmann collaborated with them on a feature film, *Prince Achmed*, but did not find the experience rewarding. The artist was then entering another stage of his creative evolution: the music of imagery should now have links to history. Having put aside Abstractionism, Ruttmann devoted himself to projects (which were improperly classified as 'documentaries'), in which elements of real life combined rhythmically with each other.[1] In 1927, he put his mark on *Berlin, Die Sinfonie der Großstadt* (Berlin, Symphony of a Great City), which began with 30 seconds of abstract

**Chapter 3
European
Individualists
29**

animation – a farewell by the filmmaker to his earlier artistic phase. *Melodie der Welt* (Melody of the World, 1929), and *Wochenende* (Weekend, 1930, a film 'without images', only the sound track was edited) followed. In 1933, Ruttmann went to Italy for the shooting of *Acciaio* (Steel), a hybrid between a documentary and a fiction film based on a text by Luigi Pirandello. Back in Germany, he continued along his path as a rhythmical-documentary filmmaker. He died on 15 July 1941 in Berlin, of wounds he suffered as a war photo-correspondent.

Ruttmann figures as a talented artist and a contradictory intellectual (a follower of the left, he later unconditionally supported Hitler). His contributions to animation were limited in number, but important in their quality as well as in the influence they exerted on other artists. Some elements of the styles of Eggeling, Richter, Fischinger and even McLaren, can be traced to Ruttmann's pioneering films.

Viking Eggeling

Viking Eggeling was born in Lund, Sweden, on 21 October 1880, the son of a German immigrant and a Swedish mother. After having at-

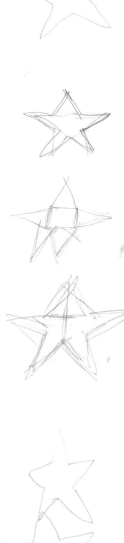

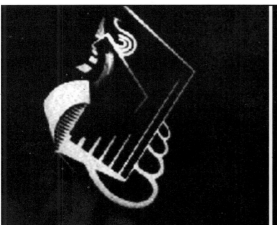

Fig. 12. Diagonal Symphonie *by Viking Eggeling (Germany, 1925).*

---

1   This change was probably influenced by Ruttmann's admiration for Eisenstein's films and for their 'intellectual editing'.

tended public school without distinguishing himself, Eggeling was forced by economic difficulties to leave Lund for Germany, Switzerland and Italy (at the end of the century Sweden was an impoverished country, with a high level of emigration). For six years, from 1901 to 1907, he lived in Milan, working occasionally and attending the Brera Academy of Fine Arts. He returned to Switzerland where he taught in a boarding school, and later spent four years in Paris. In 1916, once again in Zurich, Eggeling established contacts with the newly-born Dadaism, but he never joined the movement. In Richter's company, he returned to Germany and lived first in Berlin, then in Klein-Kolzig, the home of Richter's birth. When his friendship with Richter ended, he moved once again to Berlin.

After filming a few experiments in 'visual music' which had been made possible by UFA, Eggeling decided to continue filming on his own, with very limited means. Loans from relatives allowed him to buy a cine-camera, which he installed in his basement apartment. For three years, he carried on his experiments, filming the drawings of his 'long reel' entitled *Horizontal-Vertikal Orchestra*. A few people saw the film, including the Swedish journalist Birger Brinck who described what he saw as a ten-minute sequence dealing with a rhythmic vertical theme beginning from the top.[1] Reportedly, Eggeling never considered *Horizontal-Vertikal Orchestra (Horizontal-Vertikal Orchestra)* a finished film; unhappy with the results, he abandoned the project and began working on *Diagonal Symphonie*.

With the help of his companion Erna Niemeyer, Eggeling began *Diagonal Symphonie* in the summer of 1923 and completed it one year later, after experiencing financial, as well as other difficulties. Friends and collaborators saw the film on 5 November 1924. On 3 May 1925, the film opened to the public with the support of UFA, which wished to maintain its 'image' as a far-sighted film company attuned to the avant-garde. The stellar programme included Hirschfeld-Mack's experiments, Richter's sequences of *Rhythmus*, Léger's *Ballet mécanique*, Ruttmann's various *Opus*, René Clair's *Entr'acte* (with screenplay by Francis Picabia) and Eggeling's film. Unfortunately, Eggeling was not able to attend the show. Hospitalized a few months earlier, weakened by deprivation, he died of septic angina, at the age of 45, on 9 May 1925, six days after the premiere.

His remaining film, *Diagonal Symphonie*, is based on the movement and metamorphosis of a white abstract form on a black background. While the main movement is diagonal, horizontal and vertical movements also take place, contributing to the film's complex content. There is great artistry in *Diagonal Symphonie*. Eggeling's pure graphics move harmoniously and rigorously for seven minutes. The figuration on which *Symphonie* is based presumes a 'time' dimension. The film is a painting which lives and develops in time and space, and which could not be appreciated when considered in its static fragments.

A hermit with a nearly oriental mysticism, Eggeling thought that art should involve aesthetics and politics, ethics and metaphysics. His search for purity addressed lifestyle as well as pictorial work. Abstract art was valid because it offered an uncorrupted language through which human beings could communicate. The abstract artist, he believed, gave an unlimited amplification of the human feeling for freedom; and the goal of art was to reflect the spirit of every single individual.[2] A tormented artist, slow to mature stylistically and ideologically, he died too early to be able to fully express his talent.

1   Birger Brinck, 'Linjemusik på vita duken. 'Konstruktiv film,' ett intressant experiment av en svensk konstnär,' *Filmjournalen*, Vol. 5, No. 4 (Stockholm 1923), p. 50.

2   L. O'Konor, *Viking Eggeling 1880–1925 Artist and Film-Maker Life and Work*, (Stockholm: Almqvist & Wiksell, 1971).

Lotte Reiniger

Born on 2 June 1899, Lotte Reiniger started to work in cinema at an early age. 'It all began in the year 1919,' she wrote:[1]

'I then was an enthusiastic maiden who could really do nothing at all well but cut out silhouettes, but who desperately wanted to get into films. When I was fifteen years old, I heard a lecture by Paul Wegener, who by this time was the foremost champion for fantastic films in Germany and whose films, the first *Golem* and the first *Student of Prague*,[2] had made a profound impression on me. So I went to this lecture, and that settled it for [the lecture] was dedicated mostly to the fantastic possibilities of "trick" films, of which very little was known. From this moment onward I had nothing in my mind but to get near that man.

'As he was one of the leading actors of the theatre of Max Reinhardt, I persuaded my unfortunate parents to let me go to the acting school attached to that theatre. It was not easy for them for the world of theatre was most alien to them. But they let me go. I was very happy. But as we pupils of the school were not allowed to be present at rehearsals, I did not know how to approach my hero. In order to draw the attention of the famous actors playing there, I began to cut out silhouettes of them in their roles. These silhouettes were very good and the actors liked them immensely. In 1917, even a book of them was published. Even Prof. Max Reinhardt approved of them and allowed me to be on the stage. I tried very hard to get into a play where Wegener was acting. I cut out silhouettes of him like mad – and he liked them. His interest in the visual arts was very great and so he helped me enormously and let me also do

extras for his films. In 1918, he let me do the captions for his film, *Der Rattenfänger von Hamelin* (The Pied Piper of Hamelin)[3] (in this period the films were shown in reels, and the best films had extra captions for these reels).

'In the summer of 1919, when I was in the studio in the garb of a grande dame for *The Galley Slave*,[4] a film of Balzac's novel *Lost Illusion*, Wegener presented me to a group of interesting young men [who] were about to open an experimental animation film studio, as he explained to me, and he said to them "For heaven's sake help me get rid of this mad silhouette girl. She makes very good silhouettes which cry out for animation. Can't you let her make a film with those silhouettes as they make cartoons?" And they did.

'These gentlemen were: Dr. Hans Cürlis, the leader of the group (to be named the Institute for Cultural Discovery) who had studied art history and was often seen in Wegener's surroundings. His friend Carl Koch, studied the same subject, becoming a well-known writer of art books specializing in the Far East. Also present was Berthold Bartosch, an animator who had come over from Vienna where he worked with Professor Hanslick. [Prof. Hanslick] had already founded an Institute like this in Vienna, had made various cartographical films there; these works emphasized the differences between the natural conditions found in Eastern and Western countries. He had come over to form a group with equal ambitions in Berlin. They created an animation table in Berlin and allowed me to have a go there with silhouette tables.

'I first helped Bartosch with some geographi-

---

1   Letter received from Lotte Reiniger, 7 November 1972.

2   *Der Golem, und wie er in die Welt kam* (The Golem, and How He Came Into the World, 1915, directed by Paul Wegener): *Der Sudent von Prag* (The Student of Prague, 1913, directed by Stellan Rye, starring Paul Wegener).

3   *Der Rattenfänger von Hamelin*, 1918, directed by Paul Wegener.

4   *Der Galeerensträfling* (The Galley Slave, 1919, directed by Rochus Gliese, starring Paul Wegener)

cal films to learn the techniques of animation. I made my first silhouette film on 12 December 1919, a kind of *pas de deux* with two figures and a movable ornament, which followed the mood of the dancers. This was called *Das Ornament des verliebten Herzens* (The Ornament of the Enamoured Heart). The re-

Fig. 13. Die Geschichte des Prinzen Achmed by Lotte Reiniger (Germany, 1926).

action of the audience was so favourable that I went on ever since.

'In 1923, a young Berlin banker, Mr. Louis Hagen – who had seen me manipulating my little fairy-tale films in the Institute – asked me whether I would not like to produce a full-length film in this style. This was a big temptation, an unheard of offer we could not resist. Mr. Hagen did not want that work to be produced in the Institute, but offered to construct a studio above his garage, near his house in Potsdam. In the meantime, I had married Carl Koch and we went there and Bartosch went with us, for we had developed a very close friendship to each other and we liked to work together.

'Shortly before these happenings, Ruttmann showed his first films in Berlin and we were enthusiastic about them. To my joy, he liked the silhouette films too and we became friends. We all, the so called avant-garde people, always worked outside the industry and only very occasionally were we asked to do some things for commercial films. Bartosch, for instance, made the titles for Wegener's *Golem*, and I did a little short shadow scene for his *The Lost Shadow*.[1] When we were given the chance to produce that full-length film, we asked Bartosch and Ruttmann for their collaboration. They agreed. It was this collaboration which led to the most striking parts of this film (needless to say, it was *Prince Achmed*), for I played my silhouette bits in black and white only and handed them to Ruttmann who on his own animation table composed and executed the fantastic movements of his magic.[2] As far as I remember, it was the earliest time that two animators of a quite different artistic temperament worked together on the same shot. We had negatives and nobody can imagine the tension with

1   *Der Golem, und wie er in die Welt Kam*, 1920, is a remake of the film identified earlier, directed by and starring Paul Wegener *Der verlorene Schatten* (Lost Shadow, 1921, directed by and starring Paul Wegener).

2   Ruttmann created the background scenery, while Reiniger filmed the action using silhouettes.

which we awaited the marked print.

'Ruttmann was slightly ashamed to work on such a fairy tale ... . "What has this to do with 1923?" he asked me once. I only could say "Nothing", and it had not. [The film] was finished in [1926].'

The feature film (one of the first animation features in the world and the first in Europe), was entitled *Die Geschichte des Prinzen Achmed* (The Adventures of Prince Achmed). The technique used involved a particular type of cut-out animation; the silhouettes, cut from black paper, portrayed backlit people, animals and objects. They were also called 'Chinese shadows'. The film had great success, especially in France, where Jean Renoir and René Clair passionately recommended it. Several fables from *The Thousand and One Nights* were adapted for the film in a way which attempted to maintain their gentleness as well as their drama. Chases and escapes by princesses, love stories, fights between the good spirit of the lamp and monstrous devils are narrated with a refined taste both in figuration and in the movements of filigreed paper actors.[1]

After Bartosch and Ruttmann went their separate ways, Reiniger and her husband Carl Koch worked in Germany, Italy and Great Britain, where they had been invited by John Grierson to contribute to the adventurous Film Unit of the General Post Office. Before World War II, the couple made twenty-six films; among them, *Papageno* – probably their best known work, based on Mozart's *Magic Flute*, and the insert of silhouette animation in Jean Renoir's *La Marseillaise*.

When World War II broke out, Reiniger was in Italy filming *L'elisir d'amore* (The Elixir of Love).

After the declaration of war, she and her husband, who were unpopular with Hitler's regime, had to return to Germany. An attempt to create a film *Die goldene Gans* (The Golden Goose) during the war failed.

In 1948, the couple resumed their activities in Great Britain. In the 1950s, they opened the Primrose Productions company and added about fifteen more works, some of them in colour, to their already rich filmography. One of the first films, based on the silhouette colour technique, was *Jack and the Beanstalk* (1955), followed by *The Star of Bethlehem*. The earlier *The Gallant Little Tailor* won a prize at the Venice Film Festival of 1955.

After the death of her husband, Reiniger did not slow her pace of activity. In 1976, she went to Canada, where she made *Aucassin et Nicolette* for the National Film Board. She also taught seminars for young animators in several cities of the world. She died on 19 June 1981 in Dettenhausen, Germany. The reviewers have unanimously praised the gentleness and precious frailty of her work. The atmosphere which her minute animated silhouettes convey exists as a separate realm that has no relation to a historical perspective, nor to current times (Ruttmann was right in this); her figurines belong to an absolutely calm, abstract world of fantasy which is made nearly dreamlike by the undefinable nature of silhouettes (who can't have facial expressions). Such a choice of figuration may seem eccentric when compared to the major artistic currents of the 1920s. In fact, it belongs to the passage from liberty to modernism to art déco, which had the Frenchmen Bourdelle and Maurice Denis as its most renowned exponents. Reiniger's techniques have inspired several modern filmmakers, particularly the former East Germans. Even so, nobody has ever equalled the fluidity of her ani-

---

1   The events surrounding this film are tortuous. The bombing of Berlin destroyed the negative and all the positives. In 1954, a positive copy was found in the British Film Institute files, but the fine-grain prints made from it did not permit the reproduction of the original colours (which had been obtained by imbibition). Later, a copy of the technical instructions for the colouring process, written in 1926, was found. Finally, in 1970 the film was shown to the public in its original form.

mation and the plastic finesse of her figures.

France's contributions

Lortac

France was not only the first European country to provide a spawning ground for animated cinema, it was also the site of the first organized animation studio. In 1919, Robert Collard, best known under the pseudonym Lortac, founded his own studio of animation in Montrouge. A fine arts student and later a soldier who was wounded and discharged in 1915, Lortac studied under Cohl and worked with him on short films to be inserted in the newsreels of Eclair. Lortac's team included animators such as Cavé, Cheval, Raymond Savignac (in charge of washing cels, he later became a well-known commercial artist) and Emile Cohl himself.

Lortac's business thrived until his peaceful retirement after the end of World War II. The major part of his production was advertising, but in 1922, he became involved in the creation of a satirical supplement to newsreels; its title, *Le canard en ciné*, was a pun referring to the humorous-satirical publication *Le Canard Enchaîné*. Afterward, Lortac worked on a series

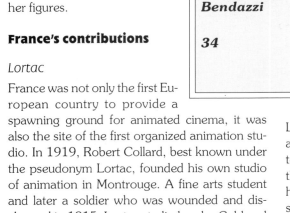

based on the adventures of the professorial character Mécanicas, and then on the episodic film adaptation of *Monsieur Vieux-Bois*, by the famous Swiss designer and humorist of the 19th century Toepffer.

Lortac animated Toepffer's drawing in collaboration with Cavé, using the pasteboard cutout technique; by cutting images and moving them as they were without any physiognomical changes, he respected Toepffer's work and style. This respect emerges also in the choice of a flowing, narrative structure. Vieux Bois is a clumsy character stuffed with Arcadian readings, who lacks any sense of reality. Without fail, he emerges beaten and ridiculed from all kinds of adventures, but never gives up and never learns from his experiences. His unique power lies in his ability to continually summon all his courage to begin anew – by simply changing his undergarments. Lortac and Cavé's series represents an example of European-style comic animation, detached from the American slapstick that was soon to dominate. This kind of humour, not founded on rhythm but on character, and with undertones closer to comedy than to the circus, re-appeared only in the 1950s in *La bergère et le ramoneur* (Mr Wonderbird) by Grimault-Prévert. Lortac died on 10 April 1973, at the age of 89.

Advertisers and illustrators

A large number of artists with different backgrounds created advertising films and more ambitious work. Benjamin Rabier (1864–1939) was a brilliant illustrator and cartoonist, whose work was published in magazines such as *Gil Blas*, *Rire* and *Pêle-Mêle*. A specialist in animal stories, in 1916 he worked with Emile Cohl on shorts, the most famous of which is *Les fiançailles de Flambeau* (Flambeau's Engagement), featuring a dog named Flambeau. After leaving Cohl, Rabier made some other films on his own.

O'Galop (Marius Rossillon, 1875–1946), who made his debut in the 1910s as an advertising

Fig. 14. L'histoire de M. Vieux Bois by Lortac and Cavé (France/ Switzerland, 1922).

poster designer, worked on a series based on the character of Bécassotte (1919) and on a film adaptation of the fables of La Fontaine. In the early 1920s, Albert Mourlan (1887–1946) created a series dedicated to Potiron. In 1923, he devoted himself to *Gulliver chez les Lilliputiens* (Gulliver and the Lilliputians), a feature film which employed mixed technique (live action and animation). After one year of work, however, a fire destroyed the negatives as well as positive copies of the film. Finally, Didier Daix filmed the series *Zut, Flûte et Trotte* (1929), featuring Zut as a good-natured hippopotamus.

The artist who left his mark on this period, however, was a painter, Fernand Léger. His *Ballet mécanique* (Mechanical Ballet, 1924), a potpourri of live action shots, direct painting on film, classical animation and special effects, is one of the most well-known works of avant-garde cinema. (The American Dudley Murphy collaborated on the excellent sequence *Charlot cubiste*, or Cubistic Charlie Chaplin, which apparently dated back to 1920–21). At that time, Léger was interested in objects; he arranged them in his painting in different ways, at times isolated, at other times grouped or contrasting with each other. He wrote:

> 'This film is above all the proof that machines and fragments, as well as usual mass-produced goods, are *possible* and plastic ... The action of giving *movement* to one or many of these goods can make them plastic. There is also the possibility of creating a plastic event, itself beautifuly, without the artist being forced to find what it means. It's the *revenge of painters and poets*. In such an art where image had to be all and everything, and where image was sacrificed to narrative anecdotes, we had to defend ourselves and we had to prove that *imaginative art*, relegated among

accessories, could build a film by itself, with its own strength, without scenario and considering the *moving image the central character*'[1].

Léger's film must be interpreted as a pictorial and dynamic work-in-progress and a linguistic proposal. It had a significant cultural influence (it was circulated perhaps more than any other abstract film of its time) and boosted the development of the French historical avant-garde and of other 'non-aligned' films by Dadaist and Surrealist artists.

Marcel Duchamp also made an animated film, *Anémic Cinéma*, with drawings, and so did the American Man Ray, who filmed the Basque *Emak-Bakia* ('Leave Me Alone') before working on *Mystères du Château de Dès* (The Mysteries of the Castle of the Dice), and *L'étoile de mer* (The Star of the Sea).

Ladislas Starewich

Ladislas Starewich was born in Moscow into a family of Polish origins, on 8 August 1882. Curious by nature, he devoted himself to several disciplines, taking a particular interest in entomology. His first encounter with cinema originated from this scientific passion:

> 'In the mating season, beetles fight. Their jaws remind one of deers' horns. I wished to film them but since their fighting is nocturnal, the light I used would freeze them into total immobility. By using embalmed beetles, I reconstructed the different phases of that fight, frame by frame, with progressive changes; more than five hundred frames for thirty seconds of projection. The result surpassed my hopes: *1910 – Lucanus Cervus* (10 metres long) – the first three-dimensional animated film'.[2]

Although this was Starewich's first attempt with

1   Fernand Léger, *Fonctions de la peinture* (Gauthier, Paris, 1965).
2   Irène Starewich, *Hommage à Ladislas Starewich*. Paris. Unpublished mss provided by the writer. No date (perhaps 1973).

this technique, the film was perfectly animated. Reportedly, he learned the secrets of this frame-by-frame procedure while viewing the Russian performance of *Les allumettes animées* (The Animated Matches), the 1908 film by Emile Cohl. In fact, he acquired enough technical skills to be able to create, a few months later in June 1910, *The Beautiful Leukanida*, a 230-metre film featuring beetles fighting for the beautiful beetle Elena, in humorous, fable-like undertones. Shown in January 1911, the film brought its author much praise. After its English screening, London newspapers wrote that the insects were alive, trained by an unidentified Russian scientist.

Starewich's career in cinema included animated works and live-action feature films. In 1911, he joined the Khanzonkow production company (Khanzonkow, the founder, had gained fame for

having interviewed the ill-tempered Tolstoy shortly before the writer's death). That same year, Starewich won a prize from the Czar for *The Grasshopper and the Ant*. With the live action film, *The Terrible Vengeance*, he again used a talented new actor, Mozhukhin.

In the years preceding the revolution, Starewich continued his frenetic activity exerting a remarkable influence on the world of cinema. He originated a large number of filming techniques and created special effects, such as those used for the tempest in his last feature film, *Stella Maris* (1918).

In 1919, he left his country following economic difficulties and, possibly, disagreements with the regime. He moved to Fontenay-Sous-Bois, near Paris, where he opened his new studio. This new phase of his production, extremely rich and not

Fig. 15. Le roman de Renard *by Ladislas Starewich (France, produced 1930, released 1938).*

yet completely catalogued, dealt exclusively with animated films. Starewich made his first French animated feature film, *Le roman de renard* (The Tale of the Fox) with puppets. Completed in 1930, it was released in this country only ten years later although it received its world premiere in Berlin in April 1937. He died on 26 February 1965, during the filming of *Comme chien et chat* (Like Dog and Cat).

For this last imposing production, Starewich found inspiration in the fable. Genuinely linked to the European tradition of this genre, his animals were definitely animal-like, humanized only at times by their attitudes or clothes. As an heir of Krylov, he kept alive a sense of poetry which sometimes lapsed into moralism and sentimentality. He wrote:

'My film has succeeded when the spectator is

ready to believe that Fétiche is not like all the other stuffed dogs; because its little heart is a mother's tear; with memories of past glory, the old Lion's gaze becomes foggy and rouses emotions. How do I make my films? Just as from an armful of cut flowers, one chooses the ones used to braid a wreath.'[1]

This difficult position, caught in between the sublime and the pompous, generated heterogeneous reviews. 'Notable' Lo Duca said of Starewich and placed him second only to Emile Cohl in a theoretical classification of French animators. Marie Seton, Eisenstein's biographer, defined him an 'Aesop of the 20th century'. As for the 2,100-metre long *Le roman de Renard*, based on the old literary text in *langue d'oïl*,[2] the film appealed to Starewich's contemporaries as 'excellent cinema, and something more. Perhaps poetry' (L. Delaprée). Léon Moussinac praised

Fig. 16. Poucette by Ladislas Starewich (France, 1928).

1 Irène Starewich, *Hommage à Ladislas Starewich*.
2 The Romance language of Northern France.

him; René Jeanne remarked on his ingenuity, while Michel Coissac covered him with compliments.

In their *Histoire du Cinéma*, Bardèche and Brasillach recognized in Starewich, 'Méliès' same genius' and gave him a 'place personnelle' and 'très grande' in the history of cinema. In their own *Histoire du Cinéma*, René Jeanne and Charles Ford wrote:

'It was during the age of sound that his talent rose higher, in *Le roman de Renard*. A great artist and a very gifted artisan, Ladislas Starewich is a unique case in the lineage of cinema, and nobody stands a comparison with him, not even Walt Disney who industrializes, and not even Emile Cohl ...'

Starewich received negative criticism, mainly due to his exaggerated lyricism and extremely slow action. Overall, an extensive analysis of his work (which is today possible, since most of his production has been restored) confirms this sense of contradiction, even if his originality is irrefutable.

Berthold Bartosch

Berthold Bartosch was born in 1893 in Polaun, then Austrian Bohemia (today, Polubny, Slovak Republic). In 1911, he moved to Vienna to study architecture; there he became friends with Professor Hanslick, his teacher at the Fine Art School and a leftist, who exerted great influence on Bartosch. When Bartosch finished his studies, Hanslick suggested a collaboration to create educational animated films 'for the masses'. Bartosch accepted. Some of his earlier works were strictly educational (such as his geograhical films); others, such as *Communism or Humanity*, illustrating Jan Masaryk's theses, were obviously politically oriented. These 'non-artistic' works constituted Bartosch's sole apprenticeship. An individualist with an inborn passion for inventions

– two requirements for becoming a true animator – he did not learn technical procedures from anybody, preferring to manage on his own.

In 1919, he moved to Berlin to open a branch of Hanslick's production company. There he met Eggeling, Richter, Ruttmann, Lotte Reiniger and, later, Jean Renoir, with whom he established a lasting friendship. He also befriended Berthold Brecht, then a young, still unknown writer. In Berlin, Bartosch continued creating educational films; he also collaborated with Lotte Reiniger on *Prince Achmed*. In 1929, he received an offer from Kurt Wolff, the cultured, shrewd publisher who had discovered Franz Kafka. While printing an illustrated storybook by the Flemish Frans Masereel, Wolff thought to turn it into a film.

He chose Bartosch for the task, and Bartosch accepted. Having moved to Paris, Bartosch began working in absolute solitude from a very small apartment above the Vieux Colombier.[1] Masereel's wood engravings, which were beautiful on paper, were too rigid and heavy for the screen and very hard to animate. On his own, Bartosch organized the work and began filming, combining three-dimensional images with the shaded back-lighting provided by a machine of his own invention. In order to create the depth of field which is not offered by simple drawings, he placed the motion picture camera vertically above a working surface formed by several levels of glass plates.[2] On each of them he would arrange scenographic elements or cut-out figures with the illumination coming from below. In an attempt to soften the hard lines of the drawings and the rigidity of the animation, he created a muffled, opalescent atmosphere by blurring the glass plates with common soap, while also making frequent use of superimposition.

---

1 A legendary theatre on the Left Bank, where writer-director Jacques Copeau renovated French theatre at the beginning of this century.
2 This technique is now called 'multi-plane'.

When the film entitled *L'Idée* (The Idea) was finished in 1931, it was a creation by Bartosch, retaining little of Masereel's original mark. The 8 January 1932 issue of *Le Peuple* (The People) reported:

only towards the exploited. Even when her creator is executed by a firing squad, she continues to spread to the stars. The syncopated editing and dramatic superimpositions of the film can still captivate the modern viewer. This is one of the rare films in which political commitment does not conflict with lyricism, similar to other films of the times, such as those by Pudovkin, Eisenstein and Dovzhenko.

'Some of us went to look at *L'Idée*. Born of the brain of a man, worker, artist – it is not known and it is not necessary to know – the Idea, born of love and revolt, dominates. As pure light, it accompanies workers in their painful march toward freedom, and nobody can kill it. Everybody tries, though, since [the Idea] upsets their calm digestion. But neither the industrialist nor the judges in his service, nor the soldiers working for the ruling class are able to destroy it. When the man who generated [the Idea] is shot, the bullets pass through [the Idea] without touching it. How much did I regret that this beautiful work by Bartosch could not have been (will it ever be?) shown to the audience of workers for which it had been conceived. We have censorship. The work is so movingly beautiful that at a second viewing – when attention is no longer so strongly directed toward the surprising novelty of the technical creation – emotions are purified. One is even more moved by the wonderful story, dedicated to all the martyrs of this Idea, which honours the world of labour.'

The plot of *L'Idée* is scanty. A man conceives of 'the Idea' of a beautiful and pure creature, represented by a naked girl. Although the conservatives try to destroy her, dress her (thus making her impure) or coerce her to their ends, the Idea turns

The film, which took months to complete, was not released and Bartosch did not earn anything from it.[1] It was the English critic Thorold Dickinson who, impressed by Bartosch's work, saved the artist by offering him financial help for the creation of another film.

Bartosch's second film was a poem 'against the war', filmed in colour and involving the use of a laborious procedure. Each image had to be shot

Fig. 17. L'Idée by Berthold Bartosch (France, 1931).

1   *L'Idée* (The Idea) was a protest film in the tradition of German socialism. It is not improbable that, in the scene portraying the workers' defeat, Bartosch intended to depict the defeat of the Spartacist rising of 1918. The film had distribution problems, confirmed by the existence of two versions of the title cards, an original version and a second one, cautiously edited by an anonymous Englishman who made an illegal copy of the film. *Original Introduction* (in French): 'Some men live and die for an Idea/but the Idea is immortal./One can persecute her/judge her/prohibit her/condemn her to die/but the Idea continues to be alive/in the souls of men./She is everywhere, she is in our presence/side by side, in misery and struggle./She rises here/and there, She continues/her walk through the centuries./Injustice trembles in front of her./To those who are exploited she shows the path/toward a better future./He whom she penetrates/does not feel isolated anylonger/because she is, above everything else/THE IDEA.' *Counterfeit Introduction.* The female image appearing/as unifying symbol throughout/the film is the Idea/which reaches every creative artist,/to the poet she is inspiration/to the sculptor, form/to the novelist, theme/to the patriot, the ideal.

three times on three film stocks each sensitive to the three colours of the three-colour process. The exposed films were to be developed in London, since Paris lacked a suitably equipped laboratory. When the filming ended, just before the war, Bartosch began editing the 900–1,000-metre film, which was to be released with music by Arthur Honegger (who had also composed the sound track for *L'Idée*). However, all negative and positive stocks were destroyed in the war, with the exception of a few centimetres. Years later, Maria Bartosch, the artist's widow, wrote 'Only three people saw the anti-war film: my husband and I in Paris, and Thorold Dickinson in London'. The work did not even have a final title, being called from time to time *Cauchemar* (Nightmare), or *Saint François*.

Bartosch emerged from the disasters of the war without even a nationality. After obtaining French citizenship in 1950, he began research for a third film about the cosmos. In his small study, he tried to give life to a sort of poem of light ('Light, always this search for light obsessed him,' his wife Maria recalled). Because of his deteriora-

Fig. 18. Matches: An Appeal *by Arthur Melbourne-Cooper (Great Britain, 1899).*

ting health, however, he was not able to work at his machine, which required standing for many hours at a time; in his last years, Bartosch devoted himself to painting. He died in 1968, telling Alexandre Alexeïeff, who frequently visited him in the hospital, about his project for the film:

'It must be very simple. It is difficult to be simple; but it is necessary. I learned much in the years I worked.'[1]

'Bartosch works as a poet who does not even wonder whether he will be read,' wrote André Martin after visiting him in 1959. 'Those who want to know cinema from A to Z must fall into the habit of recognizing the importance of films which have become invisible, of abandoned projects and impossible cinema. In the age of expensive art and sciences, controls, governmental agencies and the hyperbole, Bartosch stubbornly settles down, committing the upsetting crimes of non-conformity, the crime of poetry ... '[2]

Other European countries

Great Britain

As already mentioned, Arthur Melbourne Cooper (St. Albans, 1874 – Barnet, 1961) was the creator of the 'first' animated film ever, *Matches: An Appeal* (1899). Cooper had learned the technique of 'moving pictures' by working with the pioneer of British cinematography, Birt Acres; later, he became a producer, cinema owner and director of all kinds of short films. In 1908, he made another valuable animated film, *Dreams of Toyland*, in which toys, given as presents to a child one afternoon, come alive in the child's dream. The puppets are animated with precision and delicacy, despite quickly rotat-

1   Personal communication to the author by Alexandre Alexeïeff.
2   André Martin, 'Berthold Bartosch immobile,' *ACA* No. 5 (Paris, March–April 1959).

ing shadows which give rise to a somewhat bizarre atmosphere (instead of artificial illumination, the animator still used sunlight, and the frame-by-frame work was affected by the earth's rotation). Other films by Cooper include *Noah's Ark* (1906), *Cinderella* (1912), *Wooden Athletes* (1912) and *The Toymaker's Dream* (1913).

In 1906, Walter P. Booth filmed *The Hand of the Artist*. The camera focused on a hand which draws the dance of a peddler and a girl. In the following three to four years, Booth made other films, including *The Sorcerer's Scissors* (1907). In 1910, the silhouette specialist Samuel Armstrong made *The Clown and his Donkey*, followed by a few other films, no trace of which has remained.

Among the numerous cartoons of the times (it should be said that many of those cartoons were simply still pictures, projected like slides on a screen), the lightning sketches became a true genre, popular not only in Great Britain but also in the United States. During World War I, lightning sketchers such as Harry Furniss and the Anglo-Indian Frank Leah, as well as satirical illus-

trators and comic strip artists brought their drawings to the screen. Ridiculing the Germans, particularly the Kaiser, and raising morale at home and on the battle front, Furniss made *Peace and War Pencillings* (1914) and *Winchelsea and Its Environs* (both 1914). George Ernest Studdy initiated the series *War Studies* (1914); and Dudley Tempest made *War Cartoons* (1914). Lancelot Speed, responsible for the series *Bully Boy* (short satires dealing with current and war events) distinguished himself with *The U Tube* (1917, in which the Kaiser attempts to reach Great Britain by digging a tunnel under the English Channel but goes the wrong way) and *Sea Dreams* (1914) (which ridicules the monarch's aspirations of Naval power). Dudley Buxton's *War Cartoons* included *Ever Been Had?* (1917), a work with an extremely elaborate plot for its time and a disturbing atmosphere (it features the 'last man' on the Earth, which has been burned by war, and a defeated England; only later does the viewer discover that the drama is actually a film in the making).

Buxton is also credited with having introduced his

Fig. 19. Dreams of Toyland *by Arthur Melbourne Cooper (Great Britain, 1908).*

friend Anson Dyer (1876–1962) to British animation. For about twenty years Dyer worked as a painter of stained glass for churches. When he entered the world of animation at 39, he did not have any specific experience in the field; still he worked with animation until 1952 and became the most important English producer of animated films in the 1930s. During World War I, in collaboration with Buxton, Dyer gave life to the war propaganda series *John Bull's Animated Sketchbook.*

By the end of the war, British animators had acquired a trade, learning new techniques (even though they still preferred the use of animated cut-outs) and experimenting with longer films. Buxton, Dyer and a few collaborators made a series entitled *Kiddigraphs,*[1] produced by Cecil Hepworth. Afterward, Dyer worked on adaptations from Shakespeare, while Buxton made two series, entitled *Memoirs of Miffy* and *Bucky's Burlesques.* Lancelot Speed worked on still another series, entitled *Pip, Squeak and Wilfred.* The most successful with the public was George Ernest Studdy, with the adventures of *Bonzo* (begun in 1924), a good-natured puppy which gets into trouble in a middle-class environment.[2]

Despite economic difficulties affecting the small

British film industry, new series were continually in production and more studios were opening. Joe Noble created *Sammy and Sausage,* about a boy and his dog. Sid Griffiths, who learned the basics of animation by analysing the movements of Felix the Cat while working as a projectionist in a theatre, also made a series featuring a dog, entitled *Jerry the Tyke.* Instead of a canine, cartoonist Tom Webster opted for a horse to feature in his *Tishy the X-Legged Horse.* Anson Dyer was the one who left the most noticeable mark in British animation of the 1920s; amidst his several engagements as a set designer and educational filmmaker, he spent two years working on *The Story of the Flag* (which was conceived as a long feature, but was released in six episodes in 1927). As happened for British live action cinema, animation was mostly isolated for domestic exhibition only. The very few films distributed on the Continent did not exert any influence on other filmmakers working in Europe at the time.

Italy

The first animated sequence filmed in Italy with the frame by frame technique was *La guerra e il sogno di Momi* (The War and the Dream of Momi, 1916), which was incorporated into a live-action feature film by Giovanni Pastrone (director of *Cabiria*). In the sequence, a grandfather tells his nephew, Momi, war stories. Slowly the child falls asleep and dreams of a battle among puppets. Eventually he wakes up, pricked by a bayonet, which is actually a rose thorn. This virtually faultless short film, remarkable in its fluid, expert animation, was in large part a result of the collaborative effort between Pastrone and a Spanish cameraman and special-effects expert, Segundo de Chomón.

Fig. 20. Bonzo, character by George Ernest Studdy (Great Britain, 1924).

---

1   Among these fables, two deserve mention: *Three Little Pigs* (1922) and *Little Red Riding Hood* (1922), both by Dyer.
2   This series measured up to the standards of its American counterparts for its fluid animation as well as for the use of graphic and cinematographic language. (For instance, when the character notices an odor, it transforms itself into the corresponding object: a sausage, a hare or an egg).

In 1920, Tiziano Film of Turin produced a few comedy films for children by the Bolognese artist Carlo Amedeo Frascari, known as Zambonelli (1877–1956). Three films featured Baron Münchhausen; a fourth one was entitled *Baby … e la Lucrezia Borgia* (Baby … and Lucrezia Borgia). Also in 1920, an enterprising artist from Genoa, Antonio Bottini (Sanremo, 24 August 1890 – Genoa, 23 July 1981) led the way for Italian animation. Bottini (who later took the French-sounding name Jean Buttin) turned to animation after viewing a cartoon, 'possibly American'. He rediscovered the use of production techniques such as frame-by-frame and the use of transparent paper. After eight months of work, he released *La cura contro il raffreddore* (The Cure for the Common Cold), an approximately ten-minute film, complete with balloons and title cards. Ten years later, Bottini began work on a second film, *La rana dispettosa* (The Spiteful Frog, released in 1933), an attempt at a sound film. Afterward, Bottini left cinema for comic strips, illustrations and scenic design.

Between 1923 and 1931, the Roman scene designer Guido Presepi (1886–1955) created short films for children. Among these, *Il topo di campagna e il topo di città* (The Country Mouse and the City Mouse) stands out in quality. His small studio also produced advertising, scientific and educational films. Presepi was also one of the first to work on an animated feature film, *Vita di Mussolini* (The Life of Mussolini), which remained unfinished.

In 1925, Alberto Mastroianni (born in Paris in 1903), filmed *Avventura in Africa* (African Adventure), by sequentially photo-graphing chalk drawings on a blackboard. After an interruption lasting almost fifty years, he suddenly reappeared in 1972 with *Quella dannata bobina K. 43, Top Secret* (That Damned K. 43 Reel, Top Secret).

Other pioneers, such as Gustavo Petronio from Trieste, and Ugo Amadoro and Luigi Liberio Pensuti from Rome, leaned toward commissioned works, particularly in advertising. Carlo Cossio (1907–64) and his brother Vittorio (1911–84) had long-lasting careers in the field, in spite of interruptions and frustrations; along with Bruno Munari, they 'discovered' the cel, over ten years after it had come into common usage in the United States. In 1932 in Milano, the Cossio brothers, Corbella and Piccardo, filmed *Zibillo e l'Orso* (Zibillo and the Bear), a short film with a sound track, featuring a brat with a chimney-shaped hat. Shortly afterwards the Cossios made a visual representation of two popular songs, *Tango dell'amore* and *Tango del nomade* ('Tango of Love' and 'Nomad's Tango'). In the same year, the twenty-year old Antonio Attanasi from Lecce made his debut with *Il pifferaio di Hamelin* (The Pied Piper of Hamelin), based on Browning's poem.

Spain

One of the finest artists of early animation was the Spaniard Segundo de Chomón (Teruel, Aragon, 17 October 1871 – Paris, 2 May 1929), an excellent cameraman and creator of special effects. His first film, *Choque de trenes* (Train Collision, 1905, approximately sixty-metres) marked the beginning of the use of models in cinema. Chomón's *El hotel eléctrico* (The Electric Hotel, also filmed in 1905) was 'a masterpiece, honourably competing with the animation of real objects, in later years, by masters such as Walt Disney or by McLaren in *Neighbors* (Francisco Macián).

Chomón's contribution to cinema involved not only animation, but filmmaking as a whole. As a film director and director of photography, he worked in Barcelona, Paris (Pathé) and Turin (for Itala Film. His contribution to *La guerra e il sogno di Momi* has already been mentioned.). He was above all a major director of photography and a tireless inventor of devices such as the dolly and of equipment which allowed the motion picture medium to develop its expressiveness. As for the frame-by-frame technique, Chomón considered it one element of the whole language of moving images – no more than one of the many tricks he created or perfected. It is said that he refused offers to direct animated feature films because of the economic risks and the effort involved.

Caricaturist Fernando Marco attempted the path of cinema only once, with *El toro fenómeno* (The Phenomenal Bull, 1917, first screened in 1919). Marco worked on the images, while Luís Tapia wrote the text in nimble verse. Despite its insignificant plot (an accident-filled run by a bull with huge horns), the film became popular because of its entertaining observations.

A few years later, Joaquín Xaudaró filmed *Un drama en la costa* (1933). K-Hito (born Ricardo García Lopez) shot *El rata primero* (The First Rat, 1932) and *Francisca la mujer fatal* (Francisca the Femme Fatale, 1933). Both were praised by critics and audience. Puppet animators Feliciano Pérez and Arturo Beringoli filmed *El intrepido Raúl* (Ralph the Intrepid) in 1930. José Martinez Romano and the caricaturist Menda made their debut in 1935 with *Una de abono* (One for Safety) and the short western *Buffalo Full*. Sculptor Adolfo Aznar (1900, La Almunia de Doña Godina – 1975) filmed *Pipo y Pipa en busca de Cocolín* (Pipo and Pipa in Search of Cocolin, 1936), a puppet film based on characters by artist Salvador Bartolozzi. The Civil War, which began in 1936, drastically reduced the already thin Spanish production to a few inserts for newsreels and documentaries.

Fig. 21. Les cocottes en papier *by Segundo de Chomón (Spain-France, 1908).*

Sweden

From the 1920s on, Swedish animation grew in the field of advertising. Outside the commercial world, the filmmaker Victor Bergdahl (1878–1939) was the outstanding representative of Swedish animation.

A comic artist and a cartoonist, Bergdahl followed the same path as his American colleagues by animating his comic strip characters. During his activity as an animator, which lasted about fifteen years from 1915 to 1930, he focused on the character of Captain Grogg, a sailor-fisherman-seafarer, and developed his naïve adventures brilliantly. With his passion for inventions, Bergdahl enriched his shooting techniques with a whole variety of improvements, but never discovered the advantages of the transparent celluloid sheets. His work, which he carried on in solitude, was characterized by significant manual as well as intellectual effort. Still, he still maintain his inspiration – with wit and humour.

Emile Agren and M. R. Liljeqvist made similar efforts, but their attempts were not organized, remaining merely individual and spontaneous impulses. In 1933, another independent artist, painter Robert Högfeldt, released *How We Tame a Troll*, an entertaining ten-minute film. Born in The Netherlands in 1894 of Swedish parents and educated in Düsseldorf and Stockholm, Högfeldt won fame for his paintings of trolls, the magic wood-dwelling creatures of Nordic fairy tales. He also worked as a book illustrator. *How We Tame a Troll* was his only cinematographic work.

Denmark

Another example of independent production can be found in Denmark, in the work of writer, illustrator and actor Robert Storm-Petersen. The creator of successful comics published in daily newspapers, Petersen also owned a small production company which released animated films from 1916. Storm P., as his fellow Danes called him, displayed a 'baroque' taste for humour, as

well as a crisp and self-confident style of drawing. Actually, Karl Wieghorst, the operator who assisted Storm throughout his cinematographic career, was responsible for the animation. But to those who asked for technical explanations, Storm enjoyed responding with playful answers such as 'Professional secrets are not revealed by magicians nor by lion tamers either'.

The earliest known films were *The Island* (1920), unfinished, and *A Duck Story* (1920), a comical, nonsensical story about three little men,

Fig. 22. Captain Grogg, character by Victor Bergdahl (Sweden, late 1920s).

Fig. 23. A Duck Story by Robert Storm-Petersen (Denmark, 1920). The characters are 'The three little men'.

who later became regular characters in Petersen's films. In *A Duck Story*, the artist portrayed himself in a character who had to deal with the three men during a duck-hunting expedition. Among the comic films which followed, *Rejuvenation: Professor Stejnack's Method* (1921) is notable. In the late 1920s, Storm-Petersen devoted more attention to his advertising activity and, in 1930, abandoned the movies (where he had also made a name for himself as a comic actor). Born in 1882, he died in 1949. Storm-Petersen had only one known competitor in Denmark, Sven Brasch (1886–1970), a caricaturist and commercial artist who made *A Rather Good Intention* (1919).

Finland

Erik Wasström (1887–1958) appears as the first animator in the history of Finnish cinema. In 1914, in an imitation of Blackton, he filmed a 'magic pen' drawing current events. Ten years later, Karl Salén and Yrjö Nyberg (who changed his name to Norta in 1934) made an animated film *Aito sunnuntaimetsästäjä* (A True Sunday Hunter). The film was released by Lahyn Film, a Turku-based production company which also produced animated advertising.

In the late 1920s, caricaturist and cartoonist Ola Fogelberg (1894–1952) shot a five-minute long film based on the character Pekka Puupää (Peter Woodenhead), while animator Hjalmar Löfving (1896–1968) made his debut and continued to create fifteen animated films over the course of his career.

Russia

In the early 20th century, Czarist Russia witnessed the rise of Ladislas Starewich. After the revolution, when Starewich emigrated to the West, several years passed before the reborn Soviet film industry presented new animated works. Two major personalities became involved in animation: Vladimir Mayakovsky (whose Futuristic poetry was compatible with his activity in animation, and who tried to animate political manifestos) and Dziga Vertov.

Despite their contributions, however, plus a unique co-operation among the different artistic fields in one of the most creative periods of this century which they enjoyed, animation played a marginal role in the world of a cinema dominated by Eisenstein, Pudovkin, Dovzhenko and Dziga Vertov. Soviet animation included quality works, but remained a less-developed field than those of real-life cinema, theatre, literature and painting.

> 'The popular tale, the modern tale, the surrealist tale, the musical comedy based on current events, the political and social satire, and pamphlet – these were the themes of Soviet animation in the beginning.'[1]

Soviet animation originated directly from political manifestos and satirical vignettes. Dziga Vertov inserted animated passages in his *Kino-Pravda* newsreel, starting with *Soviet Toys* (1924), by artists Aleksandr Ivanov and Aleksandr Buskin and camera operator Ivan Beljakov. These filmmakers also made other films using the technique

Fig. 24.
Humoresque by A. Ivanov and A. Buskin (USSR, Russia, 1926).

1   Ivan Ivanov-Vano, *Risovannyi Film* [The Animated Film] (Moscow, 1950).

of animated cuttings: *Humoresque*, *In the Face of the Second International*, and *McDonald's Career*. While Buskin (Balasov, 1 April 1896 – Moscow, 5 June 1929) died too young to be able to express his talent in full, Ivanov (Rasskasovo, 5 June 1899 – Moscow, 13 March 1959) organized an animation department within the powerful Sovkino (1928) and had a successful career in the field.

During the same years, painters Nikolai Khodataev (Rostov, 9 May 1892 – Moscow, 27 December 1979), Zenon Komissarenko (Simferopol, 10 April 1891 – ?) and Juri Merkulov (Rasskasovo, 28 April 1901 – Moscow, 3 February 1979) began their experiments in animation. After the unfinished *Interplanetary Revolution*, which was intended to resemble in part Mayakovsky's *Comic Mystery*, and in part a parody of the science-fiction film *Aelita*, by Protazanov, they released *China in Flames* (1925), dedicated to the revolutionary struggle of the Chinese. That same year they shot *1905–1925*, covering the period between the first Russian insurrection and the events of 1925. In 1927, Khodataev directed an all-woman crew with his sister Olga, and Valentina and Zinaida Brumberg; together they created *One Among the Others*, about the dreams of an adolescent girl in love with movies and (American) movie stars. The film, which mixed animated passages with shots of the blonde protagonist, was narrated in a moralistic, yet amused, tone.

Still in 1927, Juri Zheljabuzhsky (1888–1955) filmed *The Skating Rink*, based on a subject by N. Batram, with drawings by Daniel Cherkes and Ivan Ivanov-Vano. The film features an urchin who sneaks into a skating rink and behaves mischievously, but in the end wins a race. The story, entertaining and well-animated, is based on excellent black-on-white artwork, simple, dry, and extremely expressive in its unadorned style. Cherkes (Moscow, 31 August 1899 – 10 June 1971), who had worked as a theatrical set de-

signer with Meyerhold and had collaborated on political films, made two more animated films before devoting himself to painting in the 1930s. Ivan Ivanov-Vano (Moscow, 27 January 1900 – May 1987), instead, pursued a long-lasting career in the field of animation. With Cherkes, he co-directed *Senka the African* (1927) and *The Adventures of Münchhausen* (1928), which helped to launch another branch of animation: the animation of classical texts, stories or folkloric tales for children. An example in this category was Khodataev's *The Samoyed Boy* (1928), featuring folkloric images of the people of North Siberia.

While these events were taking place in Moscow, in Leningrad the painter and book illustrator Mikhail Tsekhanovsky (Proskurov, 6 June 1889 – 22 June 1965) directed *Post Office*, probably the masterpiece of nascent Soviet animation. Based on a popular text for children by Samuel Marshak, the film described mail carriers from all over the world. Filmed in 1929 and re-edited in 1930 in a sound version, *Post Office* also became popular outside the Soviet Union; the American critic Harry Alan Potamkin praised it highly, while architect Frank Lloyd Wright showed it to Walt Disney as an example of thought-provoking animation.

Fig. 25. Post Office *by Mikhail Tsekhanovsky (USSR, Russia, 1929).*

Chapter 4

Argentina: the world's first animated feature film

Argentinian cinema reached its most significant stage primarily in the 1930s. It is a surprising and rare phenomenon that a still little-developed film industry, affected by technological limitations and by import and export troubles, could achieve the prolific rate of inspiration that the Argentines did in the difficult field of animated feature films.

Quirino Cristiani

On the fringes of the main cultural industries and currents of the time, Argentina owed its production of animated films mainly to the Italian-born Quirino Cristiani (Santa Giuletta, Italy, 2 July 1896 – Bernal, 2 August 1984), who moved to Argentina at the age of four. At a very young age, Cristiani attracted attention with his caricatures, published in the daily papers of the capital. When producer Federico Valle (Asti, Italy, 1880 – Buenos Aires, 1960) wanted an experimental political vignette 'in action' for his newsreel *Actualidades Valle*, he hired the then twenty-year old Cristiani. After having learned the basics of animation from a film by Emile Cohl[1] from Valle's collection, Cristiani filmed *La intervención a la provincia de Buenos Aires*, (Intervention in the Province of Buenos Aires) an approximately one-minute sketch which made fun of the provincial governor Marcelino Ugarte.

Following the success of the film, Valle decided to produce a full-length animated political satire. Alfonso de Laferrère wrote the text while Quirino Cristiani took care of animation and of what today would be called the direction; Andrés Ducaud built the models for the impressive sequence of the Buenos Aires fire. In order to attract more publicity to the venture, Valle hired Diógenes 'El Mono' Taborda[2], one of the most famous caricaturists of the time, for the creation of the characters. (In fact, Taborda worked only partially on the film, bored by the meticulous, slow workmanship needed in the frame-by-frame process).

El Apóstol (The Apostle) was first projected at the Select-Suipacha theatre, on 9 November

Fig. 26. Preparatory drawing by Diogenes Taborda for El Apóstol *by Quirino Cristiani (Argentina, 1917).*

1917. Lasting a little more than one hour, *El Apóstol* was the first animated feature film ever made. (No copy of this film exists today and we must rely on a few written sources and Cristiani's memory. Whether or not *El Apóstol* was actually a feature film is still uncertain.) The plot was quite linear, albeit complicated by several digressions: angered by the Argentines' moral decay, elected president Hipólito Yrigoyen[3] dreams of rising to Olympus, dressed as the apostle of national redemption. After several political discussions with the gods, the president obtains Jupiter's lightning and burns Buenos Aires in a purifying fire. He is about to build his perfect city on the ashes of the corrupt one, when he awakes and returns to reality. Although poorly distributed, the film enjoyed great success with the public, and the newspapers of Buenos Aires pointed to it as an example of the progress of the national cinema.

Cristiani took advantage of his success to leave Valle and work on another feature film, based on an episode of the then raging World War I.[4] Entitled *Sin dejar rastros* (Without Leaving a Trace, 1918) the film was shown for only one day; confiscated for political reasons, it disappeared in the basement of some government office. In the following years, Cristiani became involved with a variety of projects, from advertising to educational-scientific shorts, such as *Rinoplastía* (Surgery of the Nose) and *Gastrotomía* (Surgery of the Stomach) of 1925, to institutional and comic shorts. These last were, as usual, linked to current events: boxing matches with heavyweight Angel Luis Firpo (*Fir-pobre-nan* and *Firpo-Dempsey*, 1923), or the visit to Argentina by the handsome young Italian prince Umberto di Savoia (*Humbertito de garufa*, 1924).

In 1928, after the six year interval required by the constitution, Yrigoyen ran again for president

1   The film was probably Cohl's *Les allumettes animées* [Animated Matches], of 1908, since in his old age Cristiani remembered that the film he saw featured 'moving matches' (personal communication to the author).

2   Diógenes Taborda (1890–1926) was a real pillar of Argentine modern humorous drawing and comics. He was nicknamed 'El Mono' (the monkey) because of his ugliness.

3   Hipólito Yrigoyen (1852–1933) was elected in 1916 as the first radical (populist) president, after decades of conservative leadership. His election was received with hope but also scepticism.

4   The German secret service had tried to provoke Argentina's entry into the war as a German ally by torpedoing a merchant ship from Rio de la Plata and accusing the English and the French of the act. Although the mission was supposed to 'leave no trace', (in Castilian, *sin dejar rastros*), it was discovered and became a major issue in Buenos Aires. Yrigoyen expelled the German ambassador but avoided any other action which could have undermined the country's neutrality.

and was re-elected. When the president's senility and the dishonesty of his collaborators became objects of ridicule for the country, Cristiani could not resist the temptation to make fun of him once again. In 1929, he began filming *Peludópolis* from the newly founded Estudios Cristiani. (The title of the film, 'city of Peludo', referred to the radical president's nickname).[1]

The film took two years to complete and was shown at Cine Renacimiento on 16 September 1931. The final edition, however, had undergone radical changes from the original project; history had forced Cristiani to re-edit. One year before the film was released, a coup by General José Félix Uriburu, on 6 September, overthrew the democracy. Cristiani hurried to modify the film in an attempt to save whatever sequences he could, but the result was not well received by the public.[2] More favourably disposed, the critics encouragingly praised the artist. As the world's first *sound* animated feature film, *Peludópolis* was further proof of Cristiani's precociousness.

After suffering from an economic loss from this project, Cristiani took a more careful approach to cinema, limiting his production to advertising. In 1938, he made a brief comeback to entertainment when writer and editor Constancio C. Vigil asked him to make a film from one of his short stories, 'El mono relojero' (The Monkey Watchmaker). For this short film Cristiani used the North American technique of cel drawing[3] and a style influenced by the cinema of the United States. The film was not successful with the audiences. Of average quality, it suffered from the contrast between the filmmaker's comical, playful inspiration and the writer's strictly educational intent. A planned screen adaptation of Vigil's other stories did not take off, particularly because of the difficulty in finding a market. For this same reason, Cristiani gradually abandoned his advertising activity and focused on developing, printing and sound recording in the new studio bearing his name. He returned twice to the creation of comic shorts, working on *Entre pitos y flautas* (Between the Pipes and the Flutes), of 1941, and *Carbonada,* of 1943; afterwards, he retired permanently from the field.

Along with Cristiani, Andrés Ducaud deserves our attention, although there is only scarce and uncertain information on him. After having worked as a scene designer for Cristiani's *El Apostól,* Ducaud continued his collaboration with the producer Federico Valle. In 1918, he directed *Abajo la careta or La república de Jauja* (Down with the Mask or The Republic of

*Fig. 27.
Peludópolis by
Quirino Cristiani
(Argentina, 1931).*

---

1   'Peludo' in Argentinian-Castillian means 'hairy' or 'shaggy'. It also has a slang meaning – 'idiot'.

2   Very briefly, this is the plot: the Ship of State falls into the hands of pirate El Peludo, who lands with his crew in the Quesolandina Republic. After several adventures, a boat appears on the horizon, carrying General Provisional (Uriburu) and Juan Pueblo (the people), who intend to remedy the troubles of Quesolandina. The name Quesolandina (Argentina) derives from the idiom 'le gusta el queso' (he likes cheese), referring to the greediness of corrupt officials.

3   For his previous film, Cristiani had used an original technique for animating cutout figures, which he patented in 1917. *El Apostól, Sin dejar rastros, Peludópolis* were filmed with this method, which was used in other films as well until the early 1930s.

Plenty), a satiric feature film on the old conservative oligarchy. The tepid reaction of the press was justified by the slow action and overall ennui which characterized the film. Shortly afterward (the precise date is unknown), Ducaud filmed another feature-length satire on the high society of Buenos Aires. Entitled *Carmen criolla* (Creole

Carmen) or *Una noche de gala en el Colón* (Gala Night at the Colón Theatre) it was a combination of drawings and puppets, with characters by Diógenes Taborda. The film failed because of its dull, drawn-out pacing and technical imperfections.

Chapter 5

The United States of America: breaking the sound barrier

A nimation grew its deepest roots in the United States, although initially production was limited to the more commercially viable comic animated drawings. It would be wrong, however, to think of animation as a flourishing industry. With the exception of Disney's small group in California, operations concentrated in New York where a few dozen people founded and dissolved production companies, moved from one studio to the other and constituted what in the jargon was called the *cartoon racket*. It cannot be said, either, that the public loved the films produced by those groups: as many veterans later recalled, animated films were more or less considered fillers; whether they were shown or not was of no major consequence to the audience.

The three most prosperous enterprises were the Fleischer group, which underwent a number of organizational changes before ending in a takeover by Paramount; Pat Sullivan's group, which thrived on the extraordinary domestic and European success of *Felix the Cat* and on its clever merchandising strategies; and Terry's *Aesop's Fables Studio*, of which ninety per cent was owned by its distributor, Keith-Albee Theater circuit. From time to time, films served to support the more lucrative field of comic strips by reminding the audiences of their favourite characters. The world of New York animators was a closed group, dominated to a certain degree by a 'ghetto' mentality: the artists who did not belong to 'the racket' were outsiders, branded as lacking in humour and incapable of inventing comic situations. Quality artists were both envied and despised and newcomers were discouraged from attending art schools and pursuing anatomy studies or etching.

The desire for experimentation and discovery also suffered: forms, actions and movements became routine, and learning animation basically meant learning the recipes for what were openly called stock actions. Despite a few exceptions, the industry's assembly-line systemization did not inspire competition between the companies, nor did it instigate demanding consumers;

consequently, this led to inbreeding. Winsor McCay was correct in reproaching his colleagues for their lack of artistic impulses in the mid-twenties.

The advent of sound as well as Walt Disney's extraordinary success completely changed the rules of the game. The older animators found themselves confronted with the choice of either learning up-to-date techniques or retiring. The market expanded and sales revenues and employment increased. In the gloomy years of the Depression, young artists found opportunities in animation, which in turn was enriched by their fresh talent. Overall, it was a giant step ahead for an industry which, according to a 1931 issue of *Popular Mechanics*, could have been bought for US$250,000 just a few years before.[1]

The Fleischer Brothers

Max Fleischer (Vienna, 19 July 1883 – Woodland Hills, California, 11 September 1972) was the second son of an Austrian-Jewish family which left Europe in 1887 and moved to New York. Interested in both drawing and small mechanical inventions, Max invented the rotoscope (around 1915), a device which permitted a live-action sequence to be transferred to drawings frame by frame. His collaborators were his brothers Joe and Dave. Before the patent for the rotoscope became active in 1917, Max showed a short film sample to producer John Randolph Bray, whom he had met ten years earlier when they both gravitated around a newspaper, the *Daily Eagle*. Bray hired both Max and Dave.

During the war, Max worked successfully on military training films. Promoted to director of his own group, in 1919 he created a series featuring Koko, a clown emerging from an inkwell in every new episode (the series was entitled *Out of the Inkwell*). The format was standard for the time: Max, the artist, would create Koko, a character which would live its own adventures in a drawn

world and would play tricks on its creator.

In 1921, the Fleischer brothers left Bray and founded their own studio, which was to be second only to Disney's both in America and world-wide until 1942. The enterprise was largely a family business. Dave (New York, 14 July 1894 – Hollywood, 25 June 1979), always second-in-command, had a position which could broadly be defined as artistic director. Max's other brothers Charles, Joe and Lou, his sister Ethel and his brother-in-law Seymour Kneitel all participated in the enterprise at various times. In 1924, the economic expansion of the *Out of the Inkwell Studio* (as the company had been named) led Max to found the Red Seal distribution company, which was to circulate the short films of the clown, the *Song Car-Tunes*, documentaries and live-action series and comedies. The distribution company lasted only two years, after which Paramount took over distribution of the films. The production company continued its operations and in 1928, after ups and downs among its shareholders, the company was renamed Fleischer Studios.

The *Song Car-Tunes* were short films based on the sing along formula, i.e. a song which was a known classic of American light theatre was sung by the whole audience. In place of a singer on the stage, it was the film which invited the audience to join in the melody. The Fleischers introduced the expedient of the 'bouncing ball': bouncing on the words of the song projected on the screen, the ball directed which word was to be sung. In the finest films, these drawings were much more than a simple ball bouncing on title cards; Koko or another character often appeared on the screen, and the words of the song were visually interpreted by comical drawings. An orchestra or a pianist provided the music except for the few short films which had been synchronized with Lee De Forest's Phonofilm system. Although not

---

1   Leslie Cabarga, *Fleischer Story* (New York: Nostalgia Press, 1976), p. 27.

much is known about this system, at least four or five experiments were produced in 1924–1925, the first of which might have been *Come Take a Trip in My Airship*. While the Fleischers did not actually open a new age, they preceded all other animators in the rush toward sound.

Among other enterprises of this decade of production, two educational-scientific documentaries made Max Fleischer especially proud: *The Einstein Theory of Relativity* (1923) and *Evolution*, (1925, based on Charles Darwin's theory). Only parts of the two documentaries were animated.

Along with the films featuring Felix the Cat by Sullivan Studio, the films starring Koko (who later became Koko) and his dog Fitz were the most lively, clever American productions of that time. Koko does not have a very distinct personality (his main trait is a hilarious insolence clearly borrowed from clowns in the circus), but his stories are marked by a delirious comicality. His world is rigorously graphic: every object can become something different at any time because everything is, after all, nothing but drawing. While this principle was more or less shared by American animators of the 1920s, it found its best expression in the Fleischers' films, in which the character always emerged from the artist's inkwell and returned to it at the end of the adventure.

The Fleischers' style fluctuated constantly, depending on the 'hands' of several animators (the company's organization of labour remained informal even in the highly departmentalized age of sound cinema). A few elements, however, remained from the beginning as a sort of trademark: the 'rubbery' animation of characters, which moved constantly, and a taste for black humour, perhaps distantly rooted in Middle-European influences.

Felix, Pat and Otto Messmer

Until the late 1960s, producer Pat Sullivan was

considered the creator of Felix the Cat, the most important character in American animation before Mickey Mouse. The rules of the studio system, as well as the reserved character of Felix the Cat's actual creator, Otto Messmer, contributed to the longest lasting case of embezzlement in the history of cinema. Otto Messmer was born in Union City, New Jersey, on 16 August 1892 and died in Teaneck, New Jersey, in October 1983. A lover of drawing and cinema, in 1914 Messmer met the cartoonist-animator Hy Mayer, who taught him the basics of the craft. With Mayer, Messmer created some advertising films. In 1915, Pat Sullivan noticed Messmer's skills and hired him for his small, recently opened studio. Their collaboration was to last the next twenty years.

In 1919, in his own time, Messmer created Felix for Paramount's newsreel *Screen Magazine*. The cat was well received and Paramount patented its name and rights. In order to continue to have Messmer draw the black cat, Paramount chose the easiest way, asking the Pat Sullivan studio to produce the episodes. When, in 1922, Paramount newsreel began having problems, Sullivan cannily acquired the rights to Felix. From that time on, Messmer directed a long series of

Fig. 28. How Charlie Captured the Kaiser *produced by Pat Sullivan (USA, late 1910s).*

animators which included, at different times, Bill Nolan, Vernon George Stallings, Raoul Barré, Burt Gillett and Al Eugster. For years, films were produced at a pace of one every fifteen days; they were distributed by Educational Films. Messmer also created comic strips with Felix for the Sunday comic page.

Sullivan, an Irishman whose real name was Patrick O'Sullivan, was born in Sydney, Australia, in 1887. After travelling, and after a stint as a boxer and an artist, he moved to New

York where he discovered animation and produced several advertising films. Winning the approval of the usually very cautious Charlie Chaplin, he created an animated series based on Chaplin's comic character. Even though he was quite occupied with business affairs, he signed every graphic or cinematographic creation produced by his company. He also capitalized on the great success of Felix with one of the first instances of merchandising, a phenomenon which Roy Dis-

Fig. 29. Felix the Cat, character by Otto Messmer, Pat Sullivan Productions (USA, early 1920s). These images are taken from a flipbook made by Otto Messmer for the 1967 Montreal Expo retrospective of animation cinema. Collection La cinémathèque Québecois and John Canemaker.

ney later developed and mastered for the Disney company. Toys, stuffed animals and various objects displaying the image of Felix, increased Sullivan's profits.

Felix disappeared from the screens at the height of its success. Pat Sullivan – who suffered from alcohol-related problems – did not have either the strength or the determination to adapt his studio to the changes which sound cinema required. The death of his wife, in 1932, further undermined his health, and he died the following year on 15 February 1933. The disposition of Sullivan's estate was so intricate that Messmer could not continue with the production of Felix (it was first necessary to determine who owned the rights to the character). Messmer retired from cinema and devoted himself to comics and illustrations.

In the panorama of its decade, Felix was uniquely complex, being at the same time feline, human and 'magical' (to avoid using 'surreal', an improper term here). Its shape cleverly mixed rounded and gracious forms with corners suggesting the character's shrewdness and naughtiness. Felix was probably the only example of a great animated mime which did not need situations or comic accidents to provoke laughter; its habit of walking in a circle when worried or reflexive is still famous. Messmer's work on the animated version of Charlie Chaplin probably helped him to understand how a movement or a typical gesture, used with the appropriate timing, could become by itself a powerful, humorous technique. The smooth use of every element in Felix's graphic world contributed to the character's magic. His tail transformed itself into all kinds of useful objects; exclamation and question marks that the animator superimposed on the character could become baseball bats or fishhooks; and even the door of a faraway house could be used, regardless of perspective, as a hatch in a blank wall.

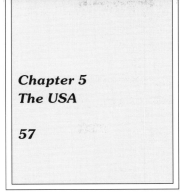

As the creation of a great scriptwriter, artist and filmmaker, who was assisted by a staff of professionals that provided a unique style, Felix was an isolated case in the panorama of American animation of its times. Messmer's animation, sober yet elegant, did not result from an imitation of other animators. It is ironic that Felix's originality cost its creator years of dispossession.

Terry and the Fables

In 1921, Paul Terry began a new series entitled *Aesop's Fables*. Actually, the only common link his fables shared with Aesop's stories was the fact that they both were populated by animals of all kinds and that they had a more or less appropriate moral ('Three thousand years ago, Aesop said ...') concluding the story. Terry's character, the old farmer Al Falfa, as previously mentioned in Chapter 2, was inserted in this new Thespian group. The films, which were produced at the suffocating pace of one every week, did not stand out for quality among the production of the time. They were, however, influential on the then debuting Walt Disney, for they were filled with all kinds of animals and mice, with some of them resembling the Mickey of 1927.

Terry adopted the name *Aesop Fables Studio* as his new logo. Financially, the Keith-Albee Theater Company,[1] which took care of film dis-

Fig. 30. Farmer Al Falfa, character by Paul Terry (USA, 1920s).

1 The group Keith-Albee, later Keith-Orpheum, the largest vaudeville circuit in North America, was the foundation on which RKO, one of Hollywood's major production companies, was later built. RKO stands for Radio-Keith-Orpheum and is the result of the merger of Radio Pictures with Keith-Orpheum.

tribution, held the majority of shares until 1928, when the group sold its shares to businessman Amadée J. Van Beuren. The friction created by the arrival of the new partner ended only when Terry (and the majority of the animators) left the studio in 1929. One of the reasons for the disagreement between Terry and Van Beuren was the advent of sound, which Terry, reluctant to undertake additional expense and innovation, opposed. Ironically, it was one of Terry's productions (*Dinner Time*) that preceded *Steamboat Willie* by a few weeks in becoming the first animated sound short.[1] By the end of this first decade, Terry demonstrated a tendency which was to characterize his career: stylistic and organizational conservatisms striving toward maximum savings, regularity and punctuality in delivery to distributors. Overall, his films were of average quality, with occasional instances of comic creativity.

Bowers unbound

Born in 1889 in Cresco, Iowa, Charles R. Bowers lived a gypsy-like childhood and youth, moving from place to place and from job to job. Fascinated by animation, Bowers collaborated briefly with Raoul Barré, as already mentioned. In 1916, he began working independently on the production of the series *Mutt & Jeff*. Filled with energy and ideas, and with no scruples, he plotted against Barré, but in turn, was expelled by Bud Fisher, who had remained as the company's sole owner. The rich, resolute Fisher owned all rights to the characters he had created for comic strips years before and made successful. Fisher also claimed all credit for himself, demanding the rights to every film made in the studio, when, in fact, he appeared there only sporadically. It did not take long for Bowers to re-enter Fisher's

good graces, and he returned to work again on the production and design of the series, albeit as a sub-contractor, for five or six more years after 1919.

Bowers' most ambitious project (which he planned with unique precision for such an explosive personality), concerned live-action cinema. From 1926 to 1928, he produced, wrote, acted in and directed about fifteen comedy shorts in which animated objects and puppets were his co-stars. As Louise Beaudet wrote:

> 'The dichotomy between the animated films of the *Mutt & Jeff* series and the comic films called "novelty type" of Bowers is startling. Setting aside the surrealist aspect of the two kinds of films, the construction and orchestration, the manner of expression, the spirit and the letter of the two styles do not come together in any way.'[2]

Judging from the few which remain, Bowers' films were extremely fascinating, characterized by a striking originality. According to Beaudet,

> '... he succeeded in bringing about an almost unique kind of marriage of slapstick with frame-by-frame animation. Moreover, he had a mind and spirit too bizarre to fail to delight today's lovers of the fantastic.'[3]

Bowers disappeared from public life after 1928. He died in New Jersey, on 25 November 1945.

Lantz's debut

Walter Lantz made his directorial debut in the 1920s. Born on 27 April 1900 in New Rochelle (died 22 March 1994 in Los Angeles) to a family of Italian origins (the the Lanzas), at the age of fifteen he moved to New York. While working at Hearst's *New York American*, he took a corre-

---

1 With the exception of attempts by the Fleischers.

2 Louise Beaudet et Raymond Borde, *Charles R. Bowers ou le mariage du slapstick et de l'animation* [The Marriage of Slapstick and Animation] (Cinémathèque de Toulouse: La cinémathèque québecoise, 1980), p. 13.

3 Louise Beaudet et Raymond Borde, p. 44.

spondence course in drawing and practiced tirelessly. Impressed by the boy's enthusiasm, the newspaper director, Morrel Goddard,[1] sent him to Hearst's newly founded International Film Service where Lantz, then sixteen years old, learned animation from the twenty-four year old Gregory La Cava. When Hearst's venture ended two years later, Lantz moved to Charles Bowers' group at Mutt & Jeff Cartoons. In 1921, he was hired by Bray. He advanced quickly and in 1923, became responsible for the entire animated production as well as for his own series entitled *Dinky Doodle* about the boy, Dinky Doodle, and his dog, Weakheart. Lantz himself appeared regularly in the films, continuing the formula of 'live-action plus animation'.

During the four years in which Lantz worked in Bray's studio, he was the artistic driving force. When the studio closed, there were few opportunities in New York and Lantz decided to start over in Hollywood. For some time he worked with the legendary Mack Sennett,[2] the 'king' of the pie-in-the-face. Eventually he met Carl Laemmle, the patriarchal leader of Universal who liked the young, rigorously professional animator and put him in charge of organizing an animation department for his production company. Laemmle took the character 'Oswald the Lucky Rabbit' away from Charles Mintz, who had once expropriated it from Disney, and gave it to Lantz in April 1929. Without feeling intimidated by the task, Lantz changed the character, making it more gentle, more graphically detailed and overall more similar to a real 'Bunny Rabbit'.

Bray, Hurd and Sarg

In the 1920s, John Randolph Bray continued expanding and diversifying his company. Busy with newsreels, live-action comedies and educational

films, he left more and more of his artistic responsibilities to others (Max Fleischer first, Walter Lantz later). His enterprises in the field of animation ranged from the temporary resurrection of Colonel Heeza Liar in 1922, through Lantz's *Dinky Doodles*, to the series *Unnatural History*, which had been initiated autonomously by Earl Hurd around 1924. A risky project (a documentary on the Colorado River which endangered the life of the crew during filming and later led to legal troubles due to a delay in delivery to the distributor) accelerated the pioneering tycoon's growing dissatisfaction. In 1927, he closed the entertainment department of his company and concentrated on more modest, but safer, educational works.

Earl Hurd began his own business in 1920, producing aesthetically good but unsuccessful films. After the aforementioned *Unnatural History* series, Hurd created the *Pen and Ink Vaudeville Sketches*, a series of unrelated episodes set in a

Fig. 31. Dinky Doodle by Walter Lantz (USA, 1923; the human actor is Walter Lantz himself). [© MCA Publishing.]

true puppet theatre complete with rising curtains. After he resumed working for Bray, he dropped from sight until the 1930s, when he joined Charles Mintz's studio. In 1934, he moved to Disney, where he worked on films such as *Snow White* and *Fantasia*, and where he remained until his death in 1940.

Finally, Tony Sarg warrants our attention for his work with cut-out silhouettes. An illustrator, he worked in partnership with Herbert Dawley, Willis O'Brien's old producer. Sarg's involvement with animation lasted three years, from 1921 to 1923.

Chapter 6

Walt Disney: The world's most successful animation studio

Walter Elias Disney was born in Chicago on 5 December 1901, the fourth son of the Irish-Canadian Elias Disney, a man of many trades, and Flora Call, an Ohio teacher. The Windy City did not stay long in Walt's memory because in 1906 his father moved the family to a farm in Marceline, Missouri, in one of several attempts to find a better life. The four years spent in the country (the Disneys moved once again in 1910, this time to Kansas City) remained in the future filmmaker's mind as a symbol of childhood happiness. Disney constantly returned to pastoral themes in his films, and he often gave his interviewers nostalgic, detailed descriptions of Marceline's paths, willows and prodigiously large apples.

In 1918, motivated by his desire for adventure as well as by disagreements with his father, Walt decided to volunteer for the Red Cross. Although World War I ended precisely at that time, he was transferred to France with the occupational troops. There, his drawings and caricatures found favour with his fellow soldiers, to the point that, once back home, he decided to become an artist, or more modestly, a 'comic strip artist'. After a brief stay with his family, which had returned to Chicago, Disney moved to the Kansas City of his youth. One of the first people he met was a gifted graphic artist, Ub Iwerks, with whom he would create great things. The two artists, then nineteen years old, began animating at the Kansas City Film Ad Company, a production company of animated advertising reels. They both loved their jobs: Walt was inventive and enterprising, while Ub was a born animator.

In 1922, Disney resigned and founded Laugh-O-Gram Films.[1] Having hired Iwerks and other promising young artists including Hugh Harman and Rudolf Ising, he began producing fables, such as *Cinderella* and *Puss in Boots*, retold in a comic tone.[2] The beginning of what seemed a bright career, however, was interrupted when Disney's bankrupt distributors remained insolvent. Hoping to survive, the young entrepreneur produced the pilot film for a new series, *Alice in Cartoonland*; but soon finding himself without money, he eventually had to file for bankruptcy. In 1923, he took a train for Hollywood with the intention of leaving animation for cinematography. Surprisingly, *Alice in Cartoonland* turned out to be a success; and the New York distributor, Margaret J. Winkler, whose company had already taken the Fleischers' and Sullivan's movies, placed an order with Disney for the continuation of his series. In partnership with his brother Roy, who was to remain as his life-long business advisor, the animator resumed working, this time alone. The series, based on the idea of a live child in a world of animated images, continued for four years.

One at a time, the Laugh-O-Gram veterans joined Disney from Kansas City: Iwerks first, then Harman, Ising and a friend of Harman's, Isadore 'Friz' Freleng.[3] In 1927, Disney created another character, Oswald the Lucky Rabbit, the protagonist of a fully animated production without live actors. The distribution was entrusted to Charles Mintz, Margaret Winkler's husband and successor, and was supported by Carl Laemmle's Universal. Following the success of Oswald the Rabbit, Mintz managed to hire the studio's best animators and to appropriate the copyright for the character. (Mintz's victory lasted only one year, when Universal took Oswald away from him and gave it to Walter Lantz). Once again, Disney had to start anew. The story goes that after his disagreement with Mintz, Disney sketched the figure of a small mouse and that his wife decided to name it 'Mickey', a much more familiar name than the serious 'Mortimer' suggested by Disney himself. In fact, the credit for

Mickey Mouse should be shared equally by Disney, who traced the character's personality, and Ub Iwerks (the only animator who had refused Mintz' offer), who drew the mouse.[4]

The first short film of the new series, which had been produced while waiting, or rather hoping, for a distributor, was *Plane Crazy*. Following Lindbergh's transatlantic flight, an enthusiastic Mickey decides to become a pilot, involves farm animals in the process and even brings his fiancée, Minnie, with him into the sky; they crash, but end up safe and sound. Well directed and entertaining, the film featured some impressive close-ups, although it did not surpass the quality level of the previous productions; in fact, Mickey was no more charismatic than Oswald, and from a purely graphic viewpoint, neither character amounted to much. It did not take long, however, for the mouse to become a giant.

When Al Jolson began to sing and talk in the screen production *The Jazz Singer*, Disney sensed that an industrial revolution, rather than a passing fad, was taking place: cinema was to become irrevocably oriented toward sound. Assisted by Wilfred Jackson, a collaborator of his who had some knowledge of music, Disney set up a make-shift synchronization system and used it for *Steamboat Willie*, the third film of the series featuring Mickey Mouse, entitled after the song *Steamboat Bill*.[5] After several technical and logistical problems (recording took place in New York) as well as difficulties with financing and distribution, the film premiered at the Colony

---

1   The name comes from the Newman Laugh-O-Grams – short films, partially animated, that Disney made in his free time and later sold to theatre-owner Frank Newman, of Kansas City. The films were fairly successful.

2   These films have a certain value still today. Disney, who had not yet been influenced by the works of Messmer, the Fleischers or Terry, displays his skills as a scriptwriter and his expert sense of rhythm and timing.

3   More will be said later about Friz Freleng's career.

4   From Alice or Oswald to Mickey, Disney's style remains uninterrupted. In the series about Alice, the girl had a very small role in the film, while the action focused on several animals, particularly a cat named Julius. As for Oswald, he was a sort of pre-Mickey, albeit less sweet and more adult; he shared Mickey's same gestures, mimicry and even the same ... desire to kiss his girlfriend when possible (*Oh, What a Knight!*, 1928).

5   The second film of the series was entitled *Gallopin' Gaucho*. Originally a silent film, it was released after *Steamboat Willie* in a post-synchronized version.

Theatre in New York, on 18 November 1928.[1] The public was delirious. The success was repeated two weeks later at the Roxy, the largest theatre in the world and the temple of New York cinema. Disney patented Mickey Mouse's name and held on to it tightly.

The plot of *Steamboat Willie* is negligible: Mickey, the pilot of a riverboat, has a difficult relationship with the 'bad guy', Peg-Leg Pete, as well as with Minnie. The story is just an excuse to utilize the effects of sound synchronization. The characters, and even the boat, dance perfectly in time with the music, and even the gags are sound-oriented; for instance, Mickey forces a cow to open her mouth so that he can play the xylophone on her teeth. A brilliant film-ballet, comic and daring at the same time, the movie centred on the music-hall tastes of the American public. Curiously, it was released exactly at the same time in which another musical show set on a river triumphed on Broadway: Jerome Kern and Oscar Hammerstein's *Show Boat*.

Even before knowing the result of his *Steamboat Willie*, Disney had ensured himself the collaboration of a resident musician, Carl Stalling (also from Kansas City, 1888–1974), who wrote the music of the first Mickey Mouse cartoons. The strong minded musician argued immediately with Disney's imposition of rhythms, effects and synchronisation, which often contrasted with the rules of musical composition. The two reached a compromise: while music would remain in the

background in Mickey's comic films, in the series entitled *Silly Symphonies*, it would dominate over images, which were simply used to illustrate it. *The Skeleton Dance* (1929) was the first of the 'symphonies', a sort of danse macabre[2] created by Ub Iwerks[3] for Stalling's music.[4] The most famous of these sketches, or short tales, was *Three Little Pigs*; the theme song, 'Who's Afraid of the Big Bad Wolf?', by Frank Churchill, became one of the most popular American tunes from 1933 on.[5] The film won an Oscar, the second for Disney after the award-winning *Flowers and Trees* (see Colour Plate 3), the first *Silly Symphony* in colour.[6] Disney had won eleven other Oscars by 1943, in several categories, thirty in all by the end of his career.

Fig. 32. Steamboat Willie by Walt Disney and Ub Iwerks (USA, 1928). [©The Walt Disney Company.]

1 It should not be believed that the novelty of sound was the cause, or at least the only cause, of such a sensation. In fact, the Fleischer's had already released sound cartoons; a couple of months before the release of Disney's film, Paul Terry distributed his *Dinner Time*, and Charles Mintz himself was ready to release revised films with Oswald.

2 The music for *The Skeleton Dance* has nothing to do with Camille Saint-Saëns *Danse Macabre* as some books report; it is a composition which used elements of Grieg's *March of the Dwarfs*.

3 As for Iwerks's fate, see the paragraph concerning him.

4 Carl Stalling (not to be confused with animator Vernon George Stallings) left Disney after only one year. He gave the best of himself at Warner's, where he composed more than 600 music scores for cartoons.

5 According to several people, a Roosevelt-inspired optimism was present in both film and song. Disney's biographer Richard Schickel argues instead that they mirrored Herbert Hoover's beliefs: disasters happen because of improvidence, while a solid, traditional house does not crush when the wolf blows. Politically, Disney pronounced himself a Republican.

6 In 1932, Disney signed a contract which gave him the exclusive rights, for three years, over the Technicolor three-colour process.

In just a few years, Mickey Mouse became the object of an incredible phenomenon of collective love all over the world. In 1930, Mickey's comic strips, drawn by Floyd Gottfredson,[1] began publication, followed by the merchandising of handkerchiefs, T-shirts, combs, watches and dolls all bearing the mouse's image. For such a successful animated character, however, Mickey had a surprisingly short life. Born in 1928, he concluded his career in 1953 (with the one exception of *Mickey's Christmas Carol* in 1983), after 121 short movies (in his last appearance, *The Simple Things*, he went fishing with Pluto). Most relevant, his lack of action as a protagonist began in the early 1930s. 'Mickey is not a clown,' Ted Sears, director of the script department re-

marked in a memo directed to his collaborators:

'He is neither silly nor dumb. His comedy depends entirely upon the situation he is placed in. Mickey is most amusing when in a serious predicament trying to accomplish some purpose under difficulties or against time'.

It was soon clear that such a well-behaved and groomed mouse could not include comicality among his qualities. It was necessary to surround him with less respectable co-stars, capable of providing laughter. In the end, these same characters, the hot-tempered Donald Duck, the dull Goofy, and Pluto the clumsy dog, took all the action for themselves, reaching a stardom of their

Fig. 33. Three Little Pigs *by Burt Gillett (USA, 1933). [©The Walt Disney Company.]*

1   For a few months, Disney wrote the scripts while Iwerks sketched in pencil. Floyd Gottfredson drew Mickey's cartoons from 1930 to 1975; he stood out among the other comic strip artists who worked on Mickey for his excellent work. Among the specialists working on Donald Duck comics, the best was Carl Barks, a Disney animator, gagman and scriptwriter who became a comic strip artist in 1942.

own and achieving top billing in their own cartoons, beginning in 1938. It was after this date that Mickey Mouse made less and less frequent appearances. As director Frank Capra once remarked, if nobody has ever succeeded at building or imposing stars, it is because stars are born by themselves – Mickey Mouse was such a phenomenon.

According to Fred Moore, supervising animator, Mickey was the typical boy, clean, happy, polite and as smart as necessary. In fact, Mickey, born a mouse, became a person in his seventh or eighth short film, *The Plow Boy*, because 'the public was willing to accept Mickey, a pseudo-mouse, as a boy, and Goofy, a pseudo-dog, as a man'.[1] These fantastic creatures lived in an equally fantastic environment, a beyond-the-looking-glass[2] caricature world, interlaced with normalcy and magic. The mouse-boy, the dog-man, the duck-youngster became credible because of their acting, which was created using the same principles as actors. Disney focused on his 'drawn actors', which he carefully studied for their facial mimicry, gestures and acting expedients. Each character needed his own personality, a way of gesturing consistent with his appearance and psychology, and a body with properly located bones, muscles and joints. No longer pure graphics, animation had become a real world in caricature, which obeyed logical laws.

'A natural action must be caricatured to constitute acting. Action as a thing in itself has little sustaining interest for an audience. When

action, portrayed graphically, is ordered – caricatured – it becomes a new form of acting.'[3]

In his excellent essay 'Disney Design: 1928–1979', John Canemaker quotes a note written by Disney in 1935: 'The first duty of cartoons is not to picture or duplicate real action or things as they actually happen – but to give a caricature of both life and action ... I definitely feel that we cannot do the fantastic things, based on the real, unless we first know the real.'[4] Disney distanced himself from defining animation as a 'copy of reality' or as exclusively graphic research, opting instead to call it 'plausible impossibility'.[5] Such a concept marked the beginning of what was later defined as Disney's 'realism'. Given this, it is easy to see how the weak point of Disney's movies has always been said to be the human characters which tend to be underdeveloped, such as Snow White, Cinderella, and the Prince.

In later years, Disney's 'realism' became more and more dominant, particularly with the use of the multiplane camera and the narrative requirements of feature length movies.[6] Many sequences became minute, decorative copies of reality, breaking the basic unwritten rule of animation never to challenge live-action cinema in its own territory. Multiple examples can be cited in which the audiences' attraction to the Disney character depends more on the classical dramatic patterns (suspense, choreography, 'romantic moments') than on the dreamlike, imaginative qualities created by the animated drawings. According to Dis-

1   Don Graham, 'The Art of Animation' *TS*, 20 July, 1955. Property of Walt Disney Productions (courtesy John Canemaker). From 1932 to 1941, Graham was the director and the *éminence grise* of the art school founded by Disney inside the company.

2   Perhaps not by chance Disney often returned to the theme of the walk-through mirror and to Lewis Carroll's work.

3   Don Graham, 'Animation: Art Acquires a New Dimension' *American Artist*, December 1940, p. 12.

4   John Canemaker, 'Disney Design 1928-1979: How the Disney Studio Changed the Look of Animated Cartoon,' *Millimeter*. Vol. 7, No. 2 (February 1979) p. 107.

5   As for the aesthetic creed of Walt Disney, see the memo he dictated in 1935 for Don Graham, quoted in its entirety in Shamus Culhane's *Talking Animals and Other People* (St. Martin's Press, New York, 1986), pp. 117–127. It is one of the most remarkable documents in animation history.

6   This massive device was used for the first time in the Silly Symphony *The Old Mill* (1937); it was also used partially in *Snow White*, and extensively in later feature films. Characters and background scenery were placed on superimposed glass planes, so that a three-dimensional composition appeared in front of the vertically-positioned camera.

ney's recipe, in front of a believable character, acting in a believable way and in a plausible environment, viewers feel perfectly comfortable and accept even the most impossible dream as normal behaviour.

Following the success of Mickey, for the first time in his life, Disney had money and used it to expand his projects and his company. From the six people employed in 1928, the enterprise grew to include 187 employees in 1934, and more than 1,600 in 1940. The studio which had been on Hyperion Avenue, Hollywood since 1925, experienced an enormous growth, and throughout the 1930s it expanded to include new buildings and additions. As for his staff, initially Disney wanted to include the best animators available on the market, particularly those in New York. However, it soon became clear that these skilled collaborators had little inclination to adapt to Disney's philosophy of work and to his brand of innovations. Therefore, the company hired and trained beginners. In seven years, it screened 35,000 applicants for a Disney art school which, until 1941, educated animators and introduced them to new stylistic and technical principles.

Disney's new methods of production followed a Tayloristic rationalization of labour: specialized teams worked at either animation, scene design, special effects, lay-outs or scripts; inking, colouring and filming were also separated. The storyboard, a sort of drawn script, helped to keep the theme of a film under control. As a matter of fact, the company's structure was like an extension of its founder's personality. Having hired animators who adopted his method, but had better creative skills than his own, Disney took upon himself the

task of organizing and motivating them, sometimes correcting and reproaching, occasionally giving praise. His employees agreed that he had a difficult, often tart character. He also must have had an extraordinary charm to have been able to manage so many remarkable personalities, some of them for over forty years.[1]

Disney had the same impact on American animation that the discovery of sound had for the rise of the industry of cinema as a whole: all of a sudden, he made obsolete every production created in the old way and put it out of circulation. In fact, much of the praise he received from the critics, especially in the early 1930s, was due to his visual inventiveness as well as to his ability to bring the 'image-sound' relationship into the grammar of cinema (at that time a controversy surrounded sound, which was seen by many as the destroyer of the visual language of silent cinema).

On 21 December 1937, during a gala, Disney showed his latest extravaganza: an animated colour feature film entitled *Snow White and the Seven Dwarfs*. Despite some initial scepticism by those who believed that animation had to be comical, the adventures of the princess, persecuted by her stepmother and protected by the dwarfs, poisoned by an apple and brought back to life by Prince Charming's kiss, conquered all audiences. Stories about the film premiere abound. John Barrymore was said to have tears in his eyes, while Disney, incapable of dealing with the emotion, waited outside, wondering at the first outbursts of laughter, if the audience was laughing at him or with him. It is also said that for once in his life, Roy Disney did not yield when, a

---

1   Beside the artists cited throughout the chapter, the following deserve mention: David Hand, Ben Sharpsteen, Norman Ferguson, Hamilton Luske, Don Lusk, Earl Hurd, Hugh Hennesy, Albert Hurter, Joe Grant, Jules Engel, James Algar, Al Eugster, Cy Young, Ugo d'Orsi, Grim Natwick, James 'Shamus' Culhane, Thornton Hee, William Cottrell, Aurelius Battaglia, Preston Blair, Dick Huemer, Perce Pearce, Zack Schwartz, Charles Philippi, Bill Peet, Vernon George Stallings, Clyde 'Gerry' Geronimi, Hal King, Rudy Larriva, Judge Whitaker, Burt Gillett, Dick Lundy, Charles Nichols, Bill Justice, Rudy Zamora and Isidore Klein. The voice-over artists include Clarence Nash (Donald Duck), Pinto Colvig (Goofy), who also worked as a gagman, and Jim Macdonald (Mickey, after 1946). Among musicians, outstanding were Leigh Harline, Paul Smith and Oliver Wallace.

few days before the release, his brother insisted on remaking a scene which had been spoiled by a small flicker. After a three-year long search for perfection, *Snow White and the Seven Dwarfs* (which began in 1934 with a budget of US$250,000) ended up costing US$1,488,423. The young producer's creativity was clearly motivated by a strange mixture of perfectionism and risk-taking. Disney came close to bankruptcy during the filming of *Snow White*, as he had with *Steamboat Willie* (after the war he even borrowed against his life insurance policy in order to build his amusement park, Disneyland). In a very short time, however, *Snow White* grossed more than eight million dollars. The critics were unanimously favourable, and Disney's love affair with his audiences reached its apex.

Snow White's solid narrative structure was dominated by the classical unities of time and action. To avoid the risk of boring the spectators with a one-and-a-half hour long feature of elementary drawings, Disney painstakingly connected the events of the story to its moods (from romantic to comic, to dark, to pathetic). The songs were given narrative or psychological functions; colours were distributed harmoniously throughout the movie. As for characters, the dwarfs were the best, magnificently animated, each with his own name and personality (in contrast to Grimm's original text, where they were portrayed as an indistinct group).[1] Even years later, *Snow White* can be said to be one of the best musicals in Hollywood history.

Besides *Snow White*, Disney's best remembered feature films are *Pinocchio* (in which the animation is undoubtably superb), and *Dumbo*, a fine, compact work. Among short films, the number of notable works is greater, especially in the first seven to eight years of sound cinema, when the

character of Mickey was rendered more powerful by a certain irreverence, a vague sadism and even a rustic inelegance. The other stars of animation, Donald and Goofy, were at their best in the next decade, under the care of Jack King, Jack Kinney and the genial Jack Hannah.[2]

Mickey was still the best actor. Besides the aforementioned films, other works deserving mention include the precocious *Just Mickey* (1930, featuring the violinist mouse playing solo), *The Brave Little Tailor* (1938, a clever tale) and *The Pointer* (1939). The character's charm was

Fig. 34. Publicity still of Snow White and the Seven Dwarfs by David Hand (USA, 1937). [©The Walt Disney Company.]

1   Much of the credit belongs to Vladimir 'Bill' Tytla, a highly praised New York animator of Greek-Ukranian origin (1904-1968).
2   Jack Hannah should not be confused with William Hanna, of the Hanna & Barbera team. Jack Hannah managed to stop the decline of Donald Duck in the 1950s, by putting him in comic situations and by having him confront other antagonists, particularly the rodents Chip and Dale.

also due to his voice, which until the end of World War II was given to him by Walt Disney himself.[1] As for the *Silly Symphonies*, despite their immediate success, they did not stand up as well to the test of time. To different degrees, they all suffered from the problem of 'cutesiness' which affected a large part of Disney's production from the mid-1930s on. Exceptions to this rule were *Three Little Pigs, The Tortoise and the Hare* (1935, see Colour Plate 4) and *The Country Cousin* (1936).

Disney's most sophisticated work was *Fantasia* (see Colour Plate 5). Created as an illustration to eight pieces of classical music, this full-length *Silly Symphony* was spectacular because of the animators' magnificent virtuosity, but it drowned in its pictorial and graphic choices. Caricature drawings and animation, which would typically accompany popular songs, clashed in a trite manner with music by Beethoven, Bach and Stravinsky (Stravinsky's *The Rites of Spring* became a history of the world with toy-dinosaurs and syrupy lava). The relation between serious music and art-in-movement demanded more powerful artistic temperments (a comparison can be made with the film *Night on Bald Mountain*, the extraordinary gothic world, created seven years earlier by Alexandre Alexeïeff.[2]

Years of expansion, reorganization and, in Disney's words, confusion, followed. In 1940, when the studio produced *Pinocchio* and *Fantasia*, they moved the company to larger, and more impersonal headquarters in Burbank. In the meantime, with World War II, the vital European market was shut. *Fantasia* failed at the box of-fice. In 1941, the company which had always been characterized by a spirit of enthusiasm and collaboration, was severely affected by an animators' strike, spurred by disagreements over contracts and wages, which lasted from 28 May to 29 July. Disney considered it a personal attack; there was even a hint of physical confrontation between him and the strikers. An agreement was reached while Disney was away, travelling in South America. Because of the changed mood inside the company and the American intervention in the war, several excellent artists left, including Art Babbitt, Vladimir William Tytla, John Hubley, Stephen Bosustow, Dave Hilberman and Walt Kelly.[3]

Disney's trip to South America had been promoted by Nelson Rockefeller, then a Washington delegate for Inter-American Affairs. In an international scene dominated by World War II (from which the United States was still abstaining) the American government wanted to reinforce its bonds with its neighbours and counted on the immense popularity of Mickey's 'father'. After the Japanese attack on Pearl Harbor, on 7 December 1941, Disney's studio in Burbank established a very intensive relationship with the Government, the Army and the Navy. Educational, technical and training films were released in a continuous cycle, more than quintupling annual production.[4] This huge effort (which in the year 1943, represented 94 per cent of the company's activity) was considered as a patriotic duty by Disney and was furnished at cost only. In turn, this public service permitted Disney to keep the offices open and his skilled animators active.

---

1   Ollie Johnston, a veteran at Disney's wrote, 'In my opinion, Walt was synonymous with Mickey, and when he lost interest and stopped doing the voice things changed. No one else ever had the ability to project personality into that high falsetto voice that he did. One man did it for many years after Walt stopped and did a great job, but how can you expect anyone to have the same feelings as the creator?'. (Letter received 8 November 1982).

2   In *Fantasia*, the less pretentious sequences are the best; for instance, Dukas's *The Sorcerer's Apprentice* musically accompanies one of Mickey Mouse's most clever performances.

3   Kelly (1912–73) left cinema for comics, starting the comic strip Pogo (1942), Kelly animated the 'Pastoral' episode in *Fantasia* for Disney.

4   It should be kept in mind that these films required limited, simplified animation.

During this war period, the entertainment section continued to produce full-length feature films: *Dumbo* (1941); *Bambi* (1942), *Saludos Amigos* (1943) and *The Three Caballeros* (1943); these last two derived from Disney's visit to Latin America. The production of shorts included anti-Nazi propaganda films, such as *Der Fuehrer's Face*, *Education for Death* and *Reason and Emotion* (all of 1943). *Victory Through Air Power* was another expression of Disney's participation in the war effort. Convinced of the decisive role played by the Air Force, Disney produced, at his own expense, this full-length film supporting Major Alexander de Seversky's drive to build more bombers.

At the end of the war, America went through a time of prosperity never seen before, but for Disney's animators the booming 1930s never came back. Short films suffered with the new fashion of showing two feature films, rather than the usual single feature with a cartoon and a newsreel. Furthermore, animated feature films could not be improved because of skyrocketing costs. Disney began looking towards other kinds of production, such as documentaries on nature, live-action movies for children and television shows, where he became a forerunner among Hollywood producers. Above all, he concentrated on his ever larger amusement park project, Disneyland, leaving more and more responsibility for the production of feature films to his veterans from the golden age, and especially to the 'Nine Old Men' – the old guard of the Napoleon of animation.[1] One year after Disney died, in Burbank on 15 December 1966, *The Jungle Book*, the last film on which he had directly worked, was released. Walt Disney Productions continued operating with large profits, due especially to its amusement parks (Disneyland and the more recent Disney World, in Florida), and more movies were made in the early Disney style under the management of Wolfgang Reitherman (1910–85). Later in the book, the new momentum given to animated feature films in the late 1980s by a completely new group of animators, is covered.

The personal Disney will always be difficult to define (he was 'a very complicated man', in his collaborators unanimous opinion). Some accused him of being a harsh speculator, or just a manager unable to draw. With his employees, he was often impenetrable, distant and brusque, and considered those who left or who opposed his will to be traitors. Conversely, he was a faithful husband and an affectionate father, so nostalgic for childhood that he had a giant toy-train built in his backyard. He was also generous toward his old friends and those who had worked with him during difficult times. Never a rich man, at least by Hollywood standards, he did not demand quantity, but rather quality from his collaborators. His ambitious enterprises kept the company in a perilous state of indebtedness, which lasted until his death, when prosperity came with a more conservative management.

Despite the large investments toward the continuous race for perfecting new and improved technologies, Disney never lost his awareness of the fact that he was just making products directed toward a consumer's world. This commercialization catered to the largest number of buyers, and as a consequence, was ultimately limiting for the film, the producer and the public. Although this 'entertainment' cinema could be made 'artistically', Disney himself recoiled from the idea of 'art' cinema, defending his choice and describing his movies as being made without cultural or intellectual ambition and totally out of place in art theatres ('I sell corn, and I love corn').

As a middle-class, small-town Mid-Westerner (he

---

1   These 'Nine Old Men' were Milton Kahl, Marc Davis, Eric Larson, Wolfgang Reitherman, Les Clark, Ward Kimball, John Lounsbery, Frank Thomas and Ollie Johnston. Disney himself jokingly coined the name, which reminded him of the US Supreme Court, who were also identified by this sobriquet.

always considered himself a Kansas City boy), Disney shared the aesthetic aspirations as well as the social origins of his audiences.[1] *Funny Little Bunnies*, one of the most manneristic Sillies, gave a simple-minded vision of Eden with limpid brooks, green hills and smiling little animals depicted while painting opulent Easter Eggs. Gradually, Disney's 'good' characters acquired ever more rounded forms and newborn-like features with large heads, overdeveloped eyes, short arms and showy buttocks. Their baby-like traits moved adults and reminded children of their dolls and teddy-bears,[2] while the neat lines, mixed with soft nuances, created a look as polished as the most perfectly kept home.[3] (Disney reacted angrily when, during a visit to the studio, architect Frank Lloyd Wright suggested that he film the lively pencil sketches, rather than the buffed cels). In the long run, this kitsch became the worst, most insinuating enemy of Disney and his collaborators.

For a long time, Disney was the only standard: not only did he defeat competition, he also erased it, because in the mind of his viewers, his animation was accepted as the only possible one. On the negative side, his work fed the general public's reluctance to accept alternative proposals for a more cultured, stimulating or simply different animated cinema. Disney, himself, contributed in reinforcing his 'cartoon monopoly' by publicly describing animation and by theorizing about it as if it had never existed in any other forms but those he himself had created – needless to say, his keen sense of public relations assisted him in his quest for animation superiority.

Disney was the important Hollywood producer of animation in the 1930s and the 1940s, on a par with the live-action producers Irving Thalberg and David O. Selznick. As a 'founder of an empire', he belonged to the all-American group of 'emperors' which included: J. P. Morgan; Henry Ford; Thomas A.Edison; William R. Hearst; Florenz Ziegfeld and P. T. Barnum. His cinema is one hundred percent Hollywood – founded on the star-system, oriented toward the luxurious packaging of mass products and based on broad stereotypes. On the one hand, he was hailed as the animator 'par excellence', the Burbank magician, the 20th century Aesop. On the other hand, he was criticized as the one who destroyed the graphic freedom of animation in favour of live-action-style realism or as the sly propagandist of American ideology all over the world. No matter, a critical history of cinema cannot overlook the ideological weight that Walt Disney's work had and still has on audiences and animators alike. (See also Colour Plate 6 from *Mickey and the Seal*.)

---

1   In any industrial sector, dependence on a mass market implies a reduction of creativity. In Hollywood cinema, the caution imposed by 'decency' as well as by the fear of offending ethnic or religious minorities has led to both anecdotes and sociological dissertations. Disney accepted these limitations more than other animators.

2   An ethological analysis of this tendency towards puppy-like shapes has been suggested by Stephen Jay Gould in *Mickey Mouse Meets Konrad Lorenz*, *Natural History*, vol. 88, no. 5, May 1979.

3   What Norman Mailer wrote about Marilyn Monroe, another cinematic myth loved by the same public, can be applied to this phenomenon: '[She had] all the cleanliness of all the clean American backyards.' Norman Mailer, *Marilyn, a Biography* (London: Coronet, 1974), p. 15.

II

Animation in the 1930s

Chapter 7

Europe

Great Britain

In the thirties, the majority of British animators worked in advertising, with only a few involved in the production of entertainment feature films. Anson Dyer returned to animation after some years of activity with live action cinema and documentaries. In 1935, he founded Anglia Film, hoping to compete against American predominance in the area of cartoons. After a first attempt to animate musical works (such as *Carmen*, in 1935, which was released in 1936), he turned to a character which was already familiar to the English public: Sam Small, a foolish little soldier, who often served as a scapegoat for other snappish characters, and whose first adventures had been told by comedian Stanley Holloway on the stages of music-halls, and later, on the radio.

Holloway recorded eighteen monologues for Dyer's films, the first of which was *Sam and his Musket* (1935, see Colour Plate 7). Wanting to make a breakthrough, Dyer decided to work in colour. The result was aesthetically acceptable (although the narrative and the cinematographic ideas did not mesh well with Holloway's skilled yet slow presentation); the film did poorly with audiences. After five episodes, Dyer's backers pulled out; but with unusual generosity, they let the filmmaker keep the equipment, and he was able to reopen a small studio for the production of advertising films. Among these, *The King with the Terrible Temper* (1937) was a funny short with a mere trailer at the end for advertising.

In 1936, Roland Davies, a cartoonist with the *Daily Express*, attempted to animate the adventures of one of his comic strip characters, the horse Steve. The result was a failure in every respect: Davies' graphic style was insignificant, his choice of black-and-white was obsolete and even the inventions and plots were linked to an old-fashioned concept of animated film. The public did not show any interest. While lacking native artists (McLaren's unique talent was still in the making), Great Britain became a stopover for foreign animators, including Lotte Reiniger, Hector Hoppin, Anthony Gross, John Halas and Len Lye.

Len Lye

An eccentric genius, Lye was born in Christchurch, New Zealand, on 5 July 1901. At the age of fifteen, he moved to Wellington in order to attend classes at the local Technical College. It was here during a discussion with his drawing teacher, that Lye suddenly understood 'movement' in plastic art.

'Every painter, every artist, I think, is making a discovery in just trying to isolate images that convey what he thinks is significant. I had my own pet little subject, which was motion. So I was incessantly inventing my own exercises for this kind of development.'[1]

At the age of seventeen, he made his first kinetic sculptures, utilizing pulleys and cranks which he applied to fruit crates. His interest was exclusively directed towards the problems of form; consequently, film seemed to him the ideal instrument to 'control movement'.

In 1921, in Australia, Lye learned the basics of classic animation. He soon abandoned his attempts to paint films directly on stock and went in pursuit of hundreds of other ideas. He dreamed about Moscow and Meyerhold's theatre but moved to the Samoan islands; after two years in paradise, he left the South Seas, moved by the urgency to create. ('I couldn't do much work there', he recalled, 'It was too wonderful for a young person').[2] Still wishing to go to the USSR, he decided to stop first in London, where he planned to learn Russian; in 1927 in London he found a job as a theatrical assistant. As critic and filmmaker Edgar Anstey wrote:

'In his earlier days Len Lye had been something of a rolling stone in art, journalism, poetry and philosophy, a gay troubadour of the intellect, ready and indeed eager to plunge into current aesthetic and philosophical controversy at the drop of his gay check cap, and never known to plunge without returning to the surface with some rare fish, or, at worst, a sizable red herring'.[3]

With financing from the London Film Society, in

1929 Lye shot a nine-minute-long film using traditional animation techniques. Entitled *Tusalava*, which in Samoan means 'things go full cycle', the film received good reviews, but could not stand a comparison to Disney's fireworks; according to Alberto Cavalcanti, it was an out-of-fashion bagatelle. Cavalcanti also recalled how Lye needed all his personal charm to convince John Grierson and Cavalcanti himself, then directors of the General Post Office Film Unit, to produce a film by painting directly on to stock. Lye's charm worked and, in 1936, he released the five-minute-long *A Colour Box*. That same year, Gerald Noxon produced Lye's *Kaleidoscope*, four minutes long and made with the same technique. The two abstract films were acclaimed, albeit only within the limited circle of experimental filmmakers.

'Every film I got from the GPO, I tried to interest myself in by doing something new. Every film I did was something not previously done in film technique'.[4]

In 1936, in collaboration with the great documentary filmmaker Humphrey Jennings, Lye made a puppet film, *The Birth of the Robot*, featuring a very fine abstract sequence of a storm. In *Rainbow Dance* (1936), he used the human image, made abstract by special colour effects. 'This is my most quirky film', Lye wrote later, 'quirky is how it makes me feel – in a kind of pop-art way ... All the stuff was shot in black and white, and transposed into three primary colour separations for the final colour print'.[5] *Trade Tattoo*, of 1937 (see Colour Plate 8), was followed by a series of war propaganda films, made for the British government. A common misconception has arisen concerning Len Lye's *Swing-

1   Gretchen Weinberg, 'Interview with Len Lye,' *Film Culture*, No. 29 (Summer 1963) p. 41.
2   Personal communication to the author, 1975.
3   A. Mancia and W. Van Dyke, 'The Artist as Filmmaker: Len Lye,' *Art in America*, (July – August 1966) p. 101.
4   Gretchen Weinberg, 'Interview with Len Lye'.
5   Len Lye, 'Caption for Rainbow Dance,' mss. Provided by Len Lye to the author in 1972.

ing the *Lambeth Walk*[1] which was sponsored by the British Council for the Travel and Industrial Development Association and which was not war propaganda. In 1940, Lye filmed *Musical Poster*, very dear to him, for which he employed many techniques. The film was used as a 'curtain raiser', attracting viewers to the films produced by the government in order to support the war effort.

In 1944, invited by the production company responsible for the March of Time newsreels, Lye moved to New York. He won an award at the Festival of Brussels in 1958, with *Free Radicals*, a five-minute-long, black-and-white film referring to some electronic particles (free radicals) which according to Lye, moved in a way similar to his painted forms. For political reasons, however, this little film did not please the millionaire from whom Lye had sought financial support. Later that year, Lye resumed his activity as a kinetic artist by making sculptures which moved electrically and produced sounds. In 1979, as he sensed his impending death, he honed and completed *Free Radicals* and *Particles in Space*, (the latter filmed in the 1960s). Lye died on 15 May 1980, in Warwick, Rhode Island.

His films can be classified into three main groups. Some revolve around the exploration of colour and graphics (*Rainbow Dance* was probably the finest, see Colour Plate 9). Others centre on texture, colour transparency, and on the interrelationship between these two elements. (The unusual palette includes unsaturated colours, dusk and periwinkle blue; the masterpieces of this group being *Trade Tattoo* and *Color Cry* (1953).) Finally, a third group, which includes

Lye's last films, makes a masterful use of 'graffiti' on black stock, creating three-dimensional exploration (*Free Radicals*, *Particles in Space* and the posthumous *Tal Farlow* (1981)). The major contribution of this genial New Zealander was his audacious inventiveness, which allowed him to film abstract cartoons (*Tusalava*), to give up the camera (*A Colour Box*) and to combine, as never before, abstract drawing with live action images (*Trade Tattoo*).

'The first breakthrough from the confines of the traditional "I" came in the Renaissance when painters started developing imagery of three dimensions, which is a bodily sensory thing of spatial relationships. ... The early post-Impressionists tried to simulate the everyday physical things of the vibrations of light by juxtaposing little stipples of colour. ... The artists were exhilarated by the sensory exploration of the physical world. You could emphasize it with your bodily senses rather than perceiving it by your brain.

'The film area exists in the sensory side of art. ... There's a whole lot of areas that we experience that we have not words for. ... All these physical things that we do we take for granted and all these are related to movement. ...

'My terms of reference are "individuality". The experience of individual being, of heightened states of being, is what we're trying to get at in art. One of the ways of getting to it is by the process of feeling yourself in the shoes of another image, by empathy ... .

'I don't know what an audience is. It's a whole lot of other people who are basically an unique

1 For a long time, this film suffered from mistaken identity. In a letter to this author (31 July 1972), Lye denied that his film could be confused with the film featuring Hitler and his troops involved in an exhilarating dance (the effect was obtained by reprinting the frame with an optical printer). 'I've never seen it,' he wrote. 'I think it was done by Jack Ellit. My *Lambeth Walk* is an abstract colour film with OK accompaniment for guitar and double bass (neither instruments ever having heard of the madman Hitler).*Lambeth Walk* is named after a district of London. The 'Lambeth Walk' was an exceedingly popular song before and during Wold War II. Both films are distributed non-theatrically in the United States: the Len Lye film, which is described by its filmmaker, is entitled *Swinging the Lambeth Walk* ('Swing' was a kind of big band music of the 1930s). The optically printed film is called *The Lambeth Walk Nazi Style*. In it the goose-stepping Nazi soldiers are optically printed to march forwards and backwards in time to the tune, as if in a dance.

version of individuality like me, so I'm only interested in me. Art is a question of you being me.'[1]

What interested Lye, was the composition of movement: animation techniques are methods of controlling the movement on the basis of its composition. As for the connection between his activities as a filmmaker and as a kinetic sculptor, he wrote that he wanted to communicate nothing, or at least, nothing to the 'new brain'.[2] His images came from the primitive 'old brain' to the body and to its sense of kinetic presence.[3] Lye's films, as Cavalcanti remarked in the 1940s on the occasion of a retrospective, are like Mallarmé's poems or Picasso's paintings: people may or may not like them, but those who like them can understand them. Or maybe there is nothing to understand: one has only to enjoy them.[4]

Lye's production is limited as far as quantity is concerned, and is somewhat episodic due to financial problems which prevented the artist from working in cinema with continuity. Nonetheless, his works are among the best in the history of animation.

France

The popularity of Disney's movies led some animators and producers toward American-style animation. A short-lived example of this was DAE (Dessins Animés Européens) which was founded in Paris (1934), by the Italian designer and painter Leontina 'Mimma' Indelli (Signa, 1909) and Italian immigrant, Giuseppe Maria Lo Duca (Milano, 1905), a journalist and filmmaker.

'DAE began work on La découverte de l'Amérique (The Discovery of America), Dorothée chez les fantômes (Dorothy and the Phantoms), and La conquête de l'Angleterre (The Conquest of England),'[5] wrote Lo Duca. 'The first film was completed. Its animator was Pierre Bourgeon. We will mention neither the operator, nor the colouring process of the film. Together, they caused DAE to go under: the operator did not notice a defect in the camera, while the inventor had not yet perfected his process.'

After the production company dissolved, Mimma Indelli never again had the opportunity to use her remarkable skills as a humorist and an artist. In 1942, she tried again with Le coche et la mouche (The Stage Coach and the Fly, based on La Fontaine's fable, made in collaboration with Paul de Roubaix),[6] but the work was destroyed in a fire. Disheartened, she left cinema for painting.

In France, animation survived primarily because of cinematographic advertising, but other attempts were made. André Rigal (1898–1973) was responsible for the humorous insert of the France-Actualité newsreel which began in 1933 with the title France bonne humeur (France in a Good Mood). During the years of German occupation, he directed some short films including Cap'taine Sabord appareille (Captain Sabord Gets Underway), Cap'taine Sabord dans l'île mystérieuse (Captain Sabord in the Mysterious Island) and V'la le beau temps (Here Is the Good Weather). For many years, Rigal collaborated with Jean Régnier, director of Les joies de l'eau (The Pleasures of the Water, 1932).

Filmmaker and scientist Jean Painlevé animated clay figurines made by sculptor René Bertrand, in

1   Gretchen Weinberg, 'Interview with Len Lye'.
2   Letter received from Len Lye, 31 July 1972.
3   In the cryptic language of Len Lye, the 'old brain' is the one which performs at the level of sensory perceptions; the 'new brain' is the one which actuates conceptual thinking.
4   Alberto Cavalcanti, 'Presenting Len Lye,' Sight and Sound, Vol. 16, No. 64, (Winter 1947–48) p. 136.
5   Giuseppe Maria Lo Duca, Le dessin animé (Paris: Prisma, 1948) p. 40.
6   The original French title of this film is part of a metaphoric idiom. In French to 'act like a fly in a stage coach' means to buzz around, or to be a busybody. Thus the title might very well be rendered The Busybody.

a successful version of *Barbe-bleue* (Bluebeard, 1938). Four years earlier in 1934, Alain de Saint-Ogan created drawings for *Un concours de beauté* (A Beauty Contest), in collaboration with Jean Delaurier.

In 1930, Delaurier (Aurillac, 1904 – Chatillon, 1982) met Jean Varé, an Anglo-Swiss artist whose real name was Maurice Hayward (1914–1940). Together they completed *Meunier tu dors* (Miller, You Are Sleeping, 1931). In 1935, Delaurier made *Couchés dans le foin* (Asleep in the Hay), illustrating a then fashionable song by Mireille and Jean Nohain. The film, which included a few daring scenes, was not liked by Mireille, who prohibited its distribution.

Arcady (Arcady Brachlianoff) made his debut in the field of popular songs too. A Bulgarian from Sophia born in 1912, he wrote the music for some of Charles Trenet's lyrics before moving to animated advertising. In the 1940s, working in the unoccupied part of France, he made some short films, including *Pym dans la ville* (Pym in the City), *Les aventures de Kapok l'esquimau* (The Adventures of Kapok the Eskimo) and *Le carillon du vieux manoir* (The Bells of the Old Manor), all of 1943.

Painter and illustrator André Marty (1882–1974) displayed his elegant style in *Callisto, la petite nymphe de Diane* (Callisto, the Little Nymph of Diana) of 1943. Comic strip artist Albert Dubout (1905–1976), assisted by animator Jean Junca, attempted to make a series based on his character Anatole; *Anatole fait du camping* (Anatole Goes Camping) and *Anatole à la Tour de Nesle* (Anatole at the Tour de Nesle) were filmed during the war and distributed in 1947. Antoine Payen (1902), a veteran from the Twenties, made two short films in 1946: *Cri-Cri, Ludo et le soleil* (Cri-Cri, Ludo and the Sun) and *Cri-Cri, Ludo et l'orage* (Cri-Cri, Ludo and the Storm). Finally, it must be remembered that artists such as Alexeïeff and Bartosch continued working in France

during the 1930s and 1940s.

An important event in this period was the debut of Paul Grimault. Born on 23 March 1905 in Neuilly-sur-Seine (one hundred feet and five years away from Jacques Prevért, who later became his very close friend and artistic collaborator), Grimault attended the School of Applied Arts and later found employment arranging displays for a department store. Pierre and Jacques Prevért, Jean Aurenche and Jean Anouilh all advised him to turn to animation. In 1936, in partnership with André Sarrut, Grimault founded Les Gémeaux, an advertising and technical animated film production company. After working on commissioned films and on *Monsieur Pipe*, an art film project which remained unfinished, Grimault created his first art short film in 1941, by utilizing what was left from an old project financed by Air France. Entitled *Les passagers de la Grande Ourse* (The Passengers of the Great Bear), the film was the first manifestation of the author's vigorous caricature drawings, his sober sense of colour and his delicate touch. Grimault died in Mesnil-Saint-Denis on 29 March 1994.

Jean Image (Budapest, 26 January 1911 – Paris, 21 October 1989) worked briefly in advertising. Born Imre Hajdu, he emigrated to France in his youth. He worked on sponsored films, then he made several shorts on his own including *Sur deux notes* (On Two Notes, 1939), *Le loup et l'agneau* (The Wolf and the Lamb, 1940), *Les noirs jouent et gagnent* (Black Plays and Wins) and *Les aventures de M. Pinceau* (The Adventures of M. Pinceau, 1944). After the war he became the first French author of a full-length animated film.

Anthony Gross

The Englishman Anthony Gross (Dulwich, 19 March 1905 – 8 September 1984) found his artistic homeland in Paris. In partnership with American financier Hector Hoppin, he founded the production company Animat (1932). The company's small but functional staff quickly produced two good shorts: *Jour en Afrique* (A Day in Africa) and *Les funérailles* (Funeral Ceremonies). It was the third work, *La joie de vivre* (The Joy of Living, 1934), which confirmed Gross' skills. An example of Liberty-style floral ballet, *La Joie de vivre* features two girls, a blonde and a brunette, running through a varied countryside; they are chased by a boy who wishes to return the shoe that one of the girls has lost. In the end, all three happily disappear into the sky on the boy's bicycle. After the success of this short film, Hoppin and Gross were invited by Alexander Korda to London, where they animated the brilliant *The Fox Hunt* (1936), in colour. Perpetuating his taste for ballet, Gross played on the choreography between the dull hunters and the smart fox, which manages to escape even in traffic. Back in Paris, the two partners viewed *Le jour et la nuit* (Day and Night), filmed during their absence by the Animat crew under the direction of David Patee.

Fig. 35. La joie de vivre *by Anthony Gross and Hector Hoppin (France, 1934).*

After changing the company name to Société Hoppin et Gross in 1937 they began a new adventure: a feature film entitled *Le tour du monde en 80 jours* (Around the World in 80 Days). Once again, however, events conspired against the birth of the European animated feature film: World War II broke out in 1939, and Nazi troops entered Paris on 14 June 1940. Gross, who escaped to England, lost all trace of his film. At the end of the war, the old 1939 stock was found in the archive of Technicolor and returned to its creator. With the help of the British Film Institute, Gross reorganized his work, adding some transition sequences. The film was thus released in 1955 as a short, entitled *Indian Fantasy*, featuring Phileas Fogg preparing for his trip and the episode in which he saves the Indian Princess from her death at the stake. *Indian Fantasy* was the last animated work by Gross, who then retired from cinema and devoted himself to painting.

A true *joie de vivre* characterizes Gross' work, instinctive and spontaneous, uninhibited and nearly pagan (in a conversation with this writer, the artist defined himself as a 'dionysian'). A refined sense of humour is also present, directed against everything that is pompous and artificial and which opposes free fantasy. As for style, the floral creations of this pliant choreographer move in a lively and graceful manner. The colour, also, is original, emphasizing a game of whites and reds, in contrast to the broad palette used by many contemporaries.

Italy

In 1935, three artists of the comic magazine *Marc'Aurelio*, Attalo (Gioacchino Colizzi), Mameli Barbara and Raoul Verdini, joined forces in an attempt to produce a full-length film, *Le avventure di Pinocchio* (The Adventures of Pinocchio). Musician Romolo Bacchini was the film's director. The effort failed because of internal disagreements as well as problems in the animating process (Attalo confessed later that the eager filmmakers knew almost nothing of the technique of animation). An attempt by Verdini alone, the next year, had no better luck. This

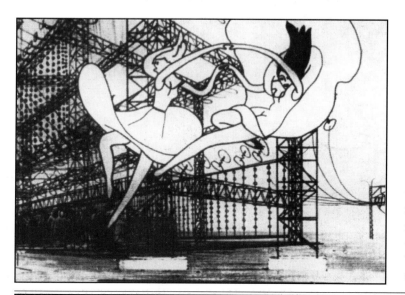

Pinocchio was the most famous, if not the first, of the many Italian attempts to make a film about Collodi's puppet.

In 1937, the Cossio brothers filmed *La secchia rapita* (The Stolen Bucket), based on the playful poem by Tassoni; in 1938, they made *La macchina del tempo* (The Time Machine) based on H.G. Wells' story. In both movies, the artists experimented with colour and stereoscopy, using a procedure devised by Milan engineer Gultiero Gualtierotti. Due to technical reasons (the procedure required very expensive equipment) their work did not continue.

Gino Parenti (1871–1943), an artist and humorist from Modena, created *Il prode Anselmo* (The Valiant Anselmo, probably 1936) practically on his own, with music by Daniele Amfitheatrof (from 1930).[1] Umberto Spano, born in 1902 in Cagliari, found inspiration in American models such as the breakneck chase for his *Barudda è fuggito* (Barudda Has Escaped, 1940), featuring a boy who captures the outlaw Barudda. Still in 1940, the Roman painter Luigi Giobbe (1907–45) made his debut with *Il vecchio lupo di mare norvegese e il vecchio lupo di mare americano* (The Old Salt from Norway and the Old Salt from America). Soon afterward, Giobbe invited the Cossio brothers to Rome and together they made two short films inspired by the classical Neapolitan masque: *Pulcinella e i briganti* (Pulcinella and the Brigands), also known as *Pulcinella nel bosco* (Pulcinella in the Forest) and *Pulcinella e il temporale* (Pulcinella and the Storm).

Comic strip artist Roberto Sgrilli (Florence 1897–1985) released a version of *Il barone di Münchhausen* (Baron Münchhausen, 1941), followed a few months later by *Anacleto e la faina* (Anacleto and the Polecat). In 1941, another comic strip artist, Antonio Rubino (San Remo, 1880 – Baiardo, 1964), made *Nel paese dei ranocchi* (In the Country of the Frogs), giving an original interpretation of the art nouveau. In 1943, Giam-

berto Vanni's *Piccolo Budda* (Little Buddha) was released – an ambitious work for a nineteen year old filmmaker.

Nino Pagot made his debut in the 1940s. An artist characterized by an uncommon vigour, he later became the director of a quite influential team, the first Italian animation establishment. Born in Venice on 22 May, 1908, Pagot moved to Milan, where he began short experiments in animation. In 1938, he founded his own production company and invited his much younger brother Toni (Milan, 16 December, 1921) to join him. During World War II, Pagot managed to keep working, employing his skills on a few war propaganda shorts. In 1946, he released a mid-length film, *Lalla, piccola Lalla* (Lalla, Little Lalla), which was his first critically acclaimed work.

Fig. 36. Il prode Anselmo *by Gino Parenti (Italy, 1936).*

---

1   Contrary to common belief, Parenti never made his own version of *La secchia rapita* (The Stolen Bucket).

Germany

After Hitler's rise to power, the minister for education and propaganda, Joseph Goebbels, nazified culture and cinema. Any kind of 'degenerate' (or 'abstract') art was prohibited. The best animators, who had found their roots and their finest form of expression precisely in abstraction, emigrated, kept silent or worked semi-clandestinely. Production continued in the advertising field, but very little data and few films survive from the twelve years between 1933 and 1945. From the limited information left, one gathers a general impression of a production which tried to compete (especially on the technical level) with American animation, but lacked verve and inventiveness.

Hans Fischerkoesen[1] (18 May 1896–1973), who built his reputation in the 1920s, became a producer and founded a major studio in Leipzig, moving in 1941 to Potsdam. His most famous films were *Verwitterte Melodie* (The Dilapidated Melody, 1942) and *Der Schneemann* (The Snowman, 1943, see Colour Plate 10), both of 1943. In the first film, about a wasp and a record player abandoned on a lawn, the virtuoso camera movement and scene design contrast with the graphically poor characters. The second film is undoubtably better; sad and playful at the same time, it features a snowman who wishes to see the Summer, but ends up melting. His third Potsdam cartoon *Das dumme Gänslein* (The Silly Goose, 1944) was finished just before the fall of Berlin. Fischerkoesen collaborated with Horst von Möllendorff (Frankfurt-am-Oder, 26 April 1906), an excellent cartoonist and humorist who was responsible for the subjects and ideas of the two early films. In 1944, Möllendorff was invited to Prag-Film, in Prague, as the artistic director of the animation department. Amidst the hardship

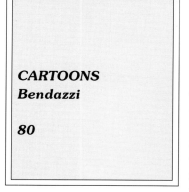

of the war and occupation, he worked with Bohemian filmmakers on *Hochzeit im Korallenmeer* (Wedding in the Coral Sea), about two fish celebrating their marriage in spite of a menacing pirate-octopus.[2] When the war ended, von Möllendorff returned to Berlin and resumed his work as a cartoonist. His original contribution to animation lasted only two and a half years in all.

Ferdinand Diehl (born in 1901) began his apprenticeship in 1927 at Emelka Film. In 1929, he opened a production company with his brothers Paul and Hermann. Their first movie was *Kalif Storch* (Caliph Storck, 1929), based on a tale by Wilhelm Hauff and made with silhouettes. The company specialized in animated puppets: human-like and quite realistic figures, such as those featured in *Die Erstürmung einer mittelalterlichen Stadt um das Jahr 1350* (The Storming of a Medieval City in the Year 1350). Of the brothers, the most involved in creative work were Ferdinand, who was responsible for direction, animation and the characters' voices, and Hermann, who created the puppets. In 1937, they released *Die sieben Raben* (The Seven Ravens), a feature film based on a tale by the Grimms; the film was praised for its beautiful photography and good animation, but was criticized for being too slow. The same year, Mecki the hedgehog made its appearance in the short *Der Wettlauf zwischen dem Hase und dem Igel* (The Race Between the Hare and the Hedgehog). 'We made at least one thousand puppets', said Ferdinand Diehl in 1985, 'but only one was truly successful: Mecki.'[3] In fact, the hedgehog rose to fame in the post-war era as the hero of a comic strip.

Hans Held (born in 1914) founded an animation studio in Berlin-Babelsberg and worked at several

---

1 His, real name was Fischer. In order to distinguish himself from the many people with the same name, the artist followed a common German custom and added the name of his native city, Koesen, (Thuringia) to Fischer.

2 Little information exists on *Wetterhäuschen* and *Klein, aber oho*, which are considered to be two other Prague films by Möllendorff.

3 Cited by critic Rolf Giesen (Letter received 10 February 1986).

projects, specializing in colour cinema. He made the animated sequences for Josef von Baky's *Münchhausen*, a super production commissioned by UFA on the occasion of its twenty-fifth birthday celebration. Another notable animator was the abstractionist Herbert Seggelke, creator of a two-minute-long work, *Strich-Punkt Ballet* (Line-Dot Ballet), drawn directly on film stock (Munich, 1943).

The artist who raised the hopes of those waiting for a local Walt Disney was Kurt Stordel (Morgenroth, 30 July 1901). After a period of industrious apprenticeship and self-instruction, Stordel began making advertising films in Hamburg. Afterward, he moved to Berlin. From 1935 to 1938, he animated fairy-tales, such as *Hansel und Gretel*, *Die Bremer Stadtmusikanten* (The City Musicians of Bremen), *Dornröschen* (Sleeping Beauty) and *Der gestiefelte Kater* (Puss in Boots). He became commercially successful in 1938, with his first colour film, *Purzel, Brumm und Quak*, about a gnome (Purzel) who fights a spider, saves his friends' lives (the spider Brumm and the frog Quak), and gives the king a beautiful bride. Although Stordel was the director of a tiny organization, he displayed the same ambition and attention to detail which were typical of Disney. It is known, for instance, that he made line tests on a regular basis before making the final animation, and that he used the rotoscope in order to study movements. As for aesthetics, here is what the gnome Purzel said in a curious autobiography:

> 'In his films, my father Kurt Stordel looks intentionally for an atmosphere, and not merely for the grotesque; contrary to the Americans, he prefers watercolours to contoured drawing'.[1]

In 1944, Stordel made *Zirkus Humsti Bumsti* (Humsti Bumsti Circus) and in 1945, *Rotkäppchen und der Wolf* (Red Riding Hood and the

Wolf). Wolfgang Kaskeline (who died in 1973) should be mentioned particularly for his prolific production, particularly in advertising. For some time, he directed the animation department at UFA. Among his films, several are worthy of mention: *Zwei Farben* (Two Colours, 1933), *Der Blaue Punkt* (The Blue Point, 1936), and *Der bunte Tag* (The Colourful Day, 1936). As for the Deutsches Zeichenfilm, a large organization promoted by Goebbels, it did not succeed in the original purpose of its founder to compete with American production. *Der arme Hansi* (Poor Hansi, 1942), featuring a canary and its adventures, was meticulously animated, but scarcely interesting.

Hans Fischinger stands out among the representatives of a languishing avant-garde. The younger brother of the more famous Oskar, Hans was born in Gelnhausen, in 1909. Having graduated in Fine Arts, he joined his brother in his Berlin studio in 1931. He collaborated on *Studien* (Studies) *No. 9* and *No. 10*, before filming *Studie No. 12* (1932) on his own. While working on *Studie No. 14*, the filming of which

Fig. 37. Tanz der Farben *by Hans Fischinger (Germany, 1937).*

1   Anonymous, 'Zwerg Purzel heisse ich', *Die deutsche Filmwelt*, No. 52, (23 December 1938).

was never completed, the two brothers were divided by arguments and artistic jealousy. Hans promptly moved to Alzenau, near Frankfurt. In 1937, he filmed *Tanz der Farben* (Colour Dance), a seven-minute long abstract film produced by his family. Despite Goebbels' prohibition laws, the film was circulated and was well received by reviewers and audiences. The filmmaker was working on a new project when the war began, and he had to enlist. The date of his death is uncertain; he probably died on the Rumanian front in 1944. Notwithstanding his adverse fortune, Hans Fischinger was an excellent artist. His style differed profoundly from Oskar's. As William Moritz pointed out, Hans 'preferred slender, hard-edged, streamlined figures, with serpentine, elegant but somehow jazzy movements.' Oskar loved 'working with charcoal and delicately smudging the edges, while Hans preferred to work with ink and paint, mixing gray-shades and painting the forms with brushes'.[1]

1 William Moritz, 'The Films of Oskar Fischinger,' *Film Culture*, No. 58, 59, 60, (New York, 1974) p. 49.

Chapter 8

The United States of America: animation heads west

In the course of a few years, American animation followed in the footsteps of live action cinema and moved its operations from New York to Hollywood. Many animators left the East Coast, attracted by Walt Disney's reputation and expansion. Charles Mintz's studio was relocated; Sullivan also planned to move, although he never actually did so. Other studios were founded directly in California. By the end of the 1930s only Paul Terry kept his headquarters in the East, in New Rochelle, New York. He was joined in 1942 by the survivors of the Fleischer group, which had returned to Manhattan from Florida. Every major Hollywood company had its own animated fillers, to be distributed with its live-action features. These fillers were mainly bought through distribution contracts with small animation production companies. At times, large companies opened their own departments of animation, as Metro-Goldwyn-Mayer did in 1937. This financial link between producers and distributors was an important reason for their geographical proximity.

Animation was thus influenced by its wealthier counterpart, mainstream cinema. The theme of the 'magic', which had been a constant suggestion in the first two decades of the century, vanished suddenly; cartoons became *films*, leaving behind their origins as drawings which came to life under the eyes of their artist-demiurge. Following the rules of the Californian 'dream industry', animation also relied on the star system. Producers directed all their efforts toward creating stellar characters. They also became involved in a race for colour, music, depth of field and a sumptuous animation, but still, characters remained the centre of attention. Only after World War II (with the exception of a few works released by Screen Gems in 1941), did formal and colouristic interests get the upper hand in UPA productions. As for visual style, it lost that graphic stamp which had been its distinctive mark. Camera movements, framing and cutting strove to imitate live action cinema. Comic inventions were drawn ever more often from situations and accidents, rather than metamorphoses or the sudden activation of inanimate objects.

Due to the new market-place, many old animators became scriptwriters and gagmen, leaving the drawing to more artistically gifted newcomers. Other gagmen came from the variety theatres. Although it would not be fair to infer that the comic solutions they invented were inappropriate to animation, their new style was oriented toward *action* and gave rise to a new generation of slapstick comedy in which Donald Duck and Bugs Bunny imitated Charlie Chaplin and Buster Keaton. The time of bell towers kneeling to avoid being hit by planes, or big toes transforming into ballerinas at the sound of a flute had gone forever.

Hollywood cinema influenced cartoons in still another way, by becoming itself a source of inspiration – in satire. Several animated shorts were parodies of famous films, others hosted the caricatures of current stars, and still others comically hinted at the current events in the world of cinema. In some cases, animation even referred to its own internal situations; one of Frank Tashlin's characters, for instance, ate spinach saying that if it was good for Popeye, it should work for him too.

Concurrently, animation loosened its ties with comic strips. In the years preceding World War II, only the Popeye strip moved successfully from the printed page to the screen; the few others had short life-spans. By that time, characters were specifically designed for the needs of animation. If anything, the reverse process took place, when almost every hero of the screen – from Mickey Mouse to Betty Boop, Porky Pig and Woody Woodpecker – was given a second life in print. The evolution of American comic strips into adventure themes, with non-caricatured characters such as Alex Raymond's *Flash Gordon*, did not influence animators, with the exception of an insignificant rendition of *Superman* by the Fleischer brothers.

Following the example of Disney, many companies gradually departmentalized labour. Figures, dimensions, gestures – all the principal traits of characters – were fixed on a model sheet which served as a reference to each animator and director. In this way, the cartoon character would not suffer from changes in physiognomy or personality, even when it was assigned to different teams. The old time anarchy was replaced by an organization in which several teams worked under a director, with separate groups writing scripts and gags. With no exception, the cel process was the chosen technique, as it allowed the distribution of tasks among director, scene designer, chief animator, animator, 'inbetweener' (who did the transitional drawings between two extremes set by the animator) and the departments responsible for colouring and buffing.

The new importance given to 'acting' over simple action decreased the opportunities for ad-libbing and diminished the whimsical development of action during filming; the technique of inbetweening depended precisely on the need to predetermine every detail. In fact, the straight-ahead technique, in which the animated sequence was invented while it was being created, was soon shelved.

One aspect which has been most stigmatized by modern scholars is the lack of veracity in the credits. The names appearing in the head-titles were often chosen not to indicate the people who actually worked on a particular film, but to 'compensate' those animators who were next in line in rotation; sometimes credit was taken by those who had the power to do so (this happened with some producers). This questionable practice, had its own rationale. The screen credit was a privilege reserved for only a few in the Hollywood system; in several instances screenwriters (to mention only one category) did not receive any credit for major works, while smaller contributions were recognized. Furthermore, the production companies, which were large melting pots of talent, produced good, albeit homogeneous if not excellent results. Without dwelling on the theories of mass communication or mass production, assembly-line animation and market demand undoubtedly affected these productions. To a greater or lesser degree, every short was the sub-

product of a greater work created by all the creative people engaged in it at that time. To search for individual creative responsibilities becomes a critic's mirage, more seductive than practical. With no regrets, artists gave up their graphic personalities and reached a sort of common dialect of the pencil, a standardized formula. Their expertise in the trade was such that they were able to switch between tables of animation of different characters, move from one studio to another and work on different projects simultaneously without causing variations visible to the general viewer.

The characters of American animation at that time, whether human or zoomorphic, did not differ much from one to the other, as far as plastic choices were concerned. These last were far from the level demanded by a perfectionist: drawings were elementary and the palette and background took no more from art history than a few suggestions from fairy tale illustrations. In fact, what counted was not the drawing in itself, but animation, or the drawn movement. Norman Ferguson, a veteran at Disney who was considered the best animator of his time by many colleagues, drew only middlingly well, but was able to 'capture' movement like nobody else. Animation meant also to 'create' movements: to invent and hone the mimicry of face and body, set a rhythm, give life to what needed to have life on the screen. Then as now, these characteristics determined who was a good animator.

If drawings were to be uniform for everybody, a higher level was reached with the adoption of a 'common dictionary' of physiognomic traits. In a how-to manual, Preston Blair, an animator for Disney and later for Metro, gave some sugges-

tions: the cute type needed the basic proportions of a child, plus a shy and timid expression; the screwball required exaggerated traits, such as a long head, thin neck and big feet. A goofy character needed a long neck, humped back and curved shoulders; he should also have a beak nose, no chin, long swinging arms and sleepy eyes. The 'heavy' type should be characterized by big chin and jaws, large trunk and chest, long, heavy arms with large hands and short legs.[1] Many protagonists from different series can be easily identified with these archetypes. The animated version of the pie-in-the-face comedy is very close to the ancient *commedia dell'arte*. The dumb, quarrelsome and scatterbrain types are brothers of the smart Harlequin or the greedy Pantalone. They have a well-defined psyche and are ready to jump into a series of adventures, improvised or even suggested by current events. As in the *commedia dell'arte*, this comedy also constantly repeats basic themes, playing on the razor-blade sense of *déjà-vu*. Those who criticize these films for their mediocre drawing should keep in mind that the value of a comic character does not reside so much in its features as in its actions and in the rhythm with which those actions occur. Round contours invited deformations and accidents; in the post-war era, when a more sophisticated drawing prevailed, the impetuous comedy of slapstick began to wane.

The same did not happen for non-comic cinema: not much of the 'pretty' production of that age has survived today's tastes. The Roosevelt years, dominated by economic crisis, social demands and international isolationism, were not markedly reflected in cartoons. A few exceptions include Disney's *Three Little Pigs*, in which the characters have been seen as the representatives of national hope, and the restless bunnies, ducklings, dogs, cats and mice of Warner Brothers and Metro-Goldwyn-Mayer at the end of the 1930s,

---

1   Preston Blair, *Learn How to Draw Animated Cartoons* (Tustin: Foster, 1949).

suggested a frenetic activity ready to burst after a ten-year-long sleep. Those same years were also a time of research, artistic experimentation and stylistic developments for American intellectuals. At this time, American avant-garde artists released their first animated films.

Lantz, from the Rabbit to the Woodpecker

The early 1930s were particularly promising for Walter Lantz. Universal asked him to prepare an animated insert for an ambitious project, *The King of Jazz* (1930), starring Paul Whiteman, which was to be filmed in Technicolor on bichromic (two colour) stock. Although the film was undeservedly unsuccessful, the animated insert (also in Technicolor) was very well received. Lantz, who still had the trust of the company executives, asked Bill Nolan to join him in a partnership. Directing separate teams, the two worked hard at maintaining the heavy schedule of production (including twenty-six Oswald films per year). It was not a time of masterpieces. Oswald was a cute but inconsistent character in need of heavy gags and funny situations to avoid becoming boring; it is not by chance that in his most famous movie, *Depression* (1933), he had only a minor role. *Depression* was a true example of political propaganda, depicting the ghost of the

Depression with its economic and social problems, and showing Oswald running to Franklin Delano Roosevelt for a remedy – the newly elected president offers a dose of trust, which Oswald injects into everybody with a syringe.

In 1934, the colour series *Cartune classics* was introduced with the intention of competing with Disney's *Silly Symphonies*. Wiser than other animators, Lantz halted production after a few episodes. Two troubled years followed. In 1935, Bill Nolan went his own way. In 1936, after the reorganization of Universal, Lantz decided to establish his own business, working with the production company only through a solid distribution contract. Now the sole owner of the rights to Oswald, Lantz changed the character's traits, transforming it from a black rabbit to a white rabbit, and accentuating its physiognomy as a rodent. This expedient served only to delay the wear and tear on the star, which finally disappeared in 1938.

It was necessary to invent a new character. After several efforts (including the three little monkeys Meany, Miny and Moe) it was time for Andy Panda.

'Lantz was constantly searching for animals

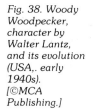

Fig. 38. Woody Woodpecker, character by Walter Lantz, and its evolution (USA,. early 1940s). [©MCA Publishing.]

that had not been used as cartoon stars before. ... The panda was a novel idea, sparked by the national attention given to the donation of a panda to the Chicago Zoo,' wrote Leonard Maltin.[1]

product, a restless character whose manners could be blunted but never completely controlled.) It should be noted that the peak of Woody's popularity concided with the arrival in the studio of Shamus Culhane (Wara, Massachusetts, 12 November 1908), a veteran of many production companies who switched to directing after working on films such as *Snow White* and *Gulliver's Travels*. A person with vast cultural interests and a predisposition for music, Culhane directed the extremely entertaining *Barber of Seville* for Lantz in 1944.

While Lantz's unusual choice may have indeed been rooted in that current event, the long-lasting success of the character was due to the artist's ability to appeal to children. Gracious and polite, Andy was nevertheless always ready to correct his clumsy father, leaving children with a feeling of power. Andy Panda debuted in 1939.

In the 1940s *Knock, Knock*, Andy acted as a host to the first performance of Woody Woodpecker – the foolish bird created by Ben 'Bugs' Hardaway (a refugee from Warner's who had previously worked on Bugs Bunny and Daffy Duck). Distraught, delirious, even dangerous, the very first Woody exhibited brutal features, feverish eyes and two pendulous teeth in his beak. Gradually, his appearance and manners improved, but the character remained a constant pain-in-the-neck, with idiotic laughter which was destined to become famous. Just like Bugs Bunny, Donald Duck, Avery's characters, or like the earlier version of Daffy Duck, Woody embodied an uncontrolled force, typical of the American cartoons of the 1940s.

In his studio, Lantz often directed the films, coordinated the work and hired new people; in short, he functioned as a Disney on a smaller scale, yet with a more affable personality. It is impossible to state the degree of his actual participation in the creative process of production and to point out the amount of credit which other artists deserve. Without any doubt, his films can be easily recognized by their style and elegance, although at times they suffered from poor taste. Quality was sacrificed for speed and the characters' sense of decorum often lapsed into mannerism. (Not by chance Woody Woodpecker was Lantz's best

Ub Iwerks

Ub Iwerks was born in Kansas City on 24 March 1901. Since his original Dutch name, Ubbe Ert Iwerks, did not sound pleasant to American ears, he simplified it when he was in his twenties. In 1919, he held a job as a publicity graphics technician at Pesman-Rubin Commercial Art Studio, where he met Walt Disney. The first part of Iwerks' career developed at Disney's side. The two artists worked almost uninterruptedly together until 25 January 1930, when Iwerks accepted an offer by producer Pat Powers to open

Fig. 39. Flip the Frog, character by Ub Iwerks (USA, early 1930s).

1   Leonard Maltin, *Of Mice and Magic* (New York: New American Library, 1980) pp. 163–164.

a studio in his own name. Aside from the flattering thought of his own studio, Iwerks had several other reasons to split with Disney. Once successful, Disney tended to limit his collaborators' individual creativity, even when they were his oldest, most loyal friends, such as Iwerks. Furthermore, Disney's idea for a 'new' kind of animation clashed with Iwerks', who was strongly anchored to the style developed in the 1920s.

At his studio, Iwerks retrieved a character he had copyrighted in 1928, Flip the Frog. Originally designed with very frog-like features, the frog later became more anthropomorphic because of marketing reasons, to the point that it almost looked like a Mickey Mouse without ears and snout (the fact that the animation of both characters had been the work of the same hand undoubtedly accentuated the similarity). When the anticipated success did not come, Iwerks abandoned Flip after thirty-six episodes. In 1933, he released a new character, Willie Whopper, a child with a blonde forelock and a tendency to tell lies, who only lasted one year. The series *ComiColor Cartoons* followed in the vein of Disney's *Silly Symphonies* and was made with the two-colour technique of CineColor. From 1936 to 1940, Iwerks worked as a sub-contractor for Warner's and for Charles Mintz Screen Gems. In 1937, for Mintz, he directed *Merry Mannequins*, which can probably be considered his best work.

Finally, faced by a lack of opportunities and fascinated more and more by the technical aspects of animation (in the 1930s, Iwerks had created a sort of multiplane camera, built with little money and much ingenuity), Iwerks returned to Disney, working on special effects and new machinery from 1940 until his death on 7 July 1971. In 1959 and 1964, he won Oscars for his inventions. Of the artist's relation with Disney after his return to the studio, there are only rumours; he certainly came back as an employee with no re-

maining evidence of the old friendship.

The failure of Ub Iwerks as an independent artist was due in part to his lack of entrepreneurial skills, and in part to his limitations as a director. He lacked that instinct for stories and plots which was Disney's strength. His films were loosely built, un-entertaining, revolving around characters with weak personalities. Moreover, even his later drawings and gags were clearly products of the 1920s, irretrievably outdated and scarcely competitive. This notwithstanding, Iwerks' talent as an animator, a colourist and a gagman stands out in sequences which often outdo the films of which they are parts.

Mintz, Krazy and Columbia

Universal's requisition of the copyrights for Oswald the Lucky Rabbit did not leave Charles Mintz resourceless. Wishing to make it in the market, he moved from New York to Los Angeles bringing along the best of a small studio which, in the 1920s, had continued to produce average Krazy Kat shorts under the management of Ben Harrison and Manny Gould. Distributed by Columbia, the new shorts bore the Charles Mintz Screen Gems label and featured the cat drawn by the ingenious cartoonist George Herriman. The protagonist of this new series was a far cry from the anthropomorphic lunar cat who wandered in Coconino county, through a constantly changing background, while being struck by the bricks thrown by his beloved Ignatz the Mouse.[1]

The new Krazy Kat was merely one of the numerous imitations of Mickey Mouse, lacking not only a personality of its own, but also those features which characterized the original version of the cat, except for the bow knotted behind the neck. With Krazy Kat, Mintz released another series featuring a little boy named Scrappy, his ever-present dog and his female counterpart.

1   The character appeared in its first cinematographic performance in 1916, under the care of Frank Moser, at Hearst's International Film Service.

Mintz did not involve himself with the artistic aspects of production, leaving his animators full autonomy. This philosophy worked with some productions; the series with Scrappy, for instance, had fine episodes and improved animation in imitation of Disney's. However, Mintz lacked ambition as far as quality was concerned; as a consequence, several artists, such as Dick Huemer, Al Eugster and Preston Blair, left the company at the first opportunity. In the field of colour, Mintz was more eager to succeed; in 1934 he began his *Color Rhapsodies*, characterized by the same imperfections and highlights as the rest of his production.

Mintz died in 1940, shortly after the Columbia distribution company took over his firm. Afterward, the studio was affected by the constant change of artistic directors (seven in eight years). It had a brief golden age under Frank Tashlin, in 1941, who not only imposed his original taste, but also recruited talented artists from Disney who had been disappointed by the strike at Disney and its outcome. The new arrivals included Zack Schwartz, Dave Hilberman and John Hubley, who would later become three of the best talents at UPA. Some productions, particularly *Prof. Small and Mr. Tall* (1943), were forerunners of the graphic and pictorial revolution which took place after World War II. The studio also released a clever pair of new characters: the Fox and the Crow (the fox was the predestined victim of the scatter-brained, spiteful crow). Tashlin's tenure lasted only a few months. Afterwards, the studio showed little promise of profitability and closed in 1948, when Columbia decided to distribute the shorts of the rising UPA.

Van Beuren

Tom and Jerry (not to be confused with the much more famous cat and mouse by Hanna and Barbera for MGM) were the first characters created at the studio of Amadée J. Van Beuren. After 1929, when Paul Terry left with a good number

of animators to open his new company, Van Beuren remained with a reduced staff and with the rights to *Aesop's Fables*. As an entrepreneur, he had made his fortune dealing with peep-show machines (individual viewers for short, sometimes spicy, films mainly destined for amusement parks). Like Mintz, and unlike the typical bosses of American animation, he was a businessman turned filmmaker. An ambitious man, Van Beuren made every effort to develop his company, abandoning the updated *Fables* and hiring Vernon George Stallings and George Rufle.

In 1931, George Stallings and George Rufle helped to create the youngsters named Tom and Jerry, the first tall and dark, the latter short and blond. The debut film, credited to John Foster and George Stallings *Wot a Night* (1931), was a playful, creative mixture of the comical and the horrific, in the best tradition of American cinema, be it live-action or animation. The episodes which followed were less successful, and Van Beuren turned to Otto Soglow's Little King, a well-known character from comic strips. This, however, did not produce much better results since the anima-

Fig. 40. Wot a Nite *by John Foster and George Stallings (USA, 1931). The characters are Van Beuren's Tom and Jerry.*

tors of the studio were only capable of utilizing outdated, ten-year-old styles and techniques. The use of talented but young and inexperienced artists such as Frank Tashlin, Joe Barbera, Pete Burness, Bill Littlejohn, Shamus Culhane and Jack Zander did not help matters, and the films remained substantially poor, in spite of a few good ideas. Still undaunted, Van Beuren attracted Burt Gillett, director of *Three Little Pigs* at Disney, who appeared to be a key player in animation at that time. Gillett's changes and improvements included a rapid conversion to colour, a much more refined animation and the release of *Rainbow Parade*, a new successful series from 1934.

Two major problems, however, weighed heavily on the studio: Gillett's mercurial behaviour, which estranged many employees (much later, Shamus Culhane described Gillett as a man who was just one step away from the madhouse) and the inability to create a character which could effectively appeal to the public. An attempt to

revive Felix the Cat, in 1936, failed. In 1935, Van Beuren, who was in poor health, suffered a stroke which confined him to a wheelchair. When the RKO distribution company withdrew its support from Van Beuren's studio and gave it to Disney in 1936, the studio closed. Van Beuren died in 1937 of a heart attack.

The Terrytoons and Mighty Mouse

Paul Terry (founder of Terrytoons, in partnership with Frank Moser from 1930) is currently referred to as an example of resistance to the innovations taking place after the introduction of sound. Parsimonious and afraid of novelties, Terry was extremely diligent in his productions and in maintaining deadlines (he behaved less properly in 1936, when he managed to kick out Frank Moser in order to remain the sole owner of the company). Favouring independent episodes, the producer yielded with reluctance to the fashion of eponymous characters; only in 1938 did he produce his first one-character series (featuring the silly Gandy Goose, a cross between Donald Duck and Goofy). The first colour short of his studio was released in 1938 and the bulk of production was converted to colour only in 1943. Terry's creations, however, should not be underestimated. Although not particularly attractive in graphics and animation, they often displayed good gags and a sense of non-respectability, which contrasted pleasantly with the simpering of other contemporary productions. As Terry once remarked, with Disney, it was form which counted, with him it was ideas.

Neither Kiko (1936) – a kangaroo who wanted to be a boxer and who walked like a clown, using its tail as a third leg – nor Gandy Goose were able to achieve perennial fame, but Mighty Mouse, a cross between Mickey Mouse and Superman, (1942) became a success. In spite of his being a little more than a unifying element for a series of gags, the character pleased the public, probably because of the contrast between its reduced

Fig. 41. Mighty Mouse, character by Terrytoons, with friends (USA, early 1940s).

dimensions and its huge strength (it should be noted that Terry exclusively addressed an audience of children). Primitive mimicry did not prevent Mighty Mouse from becoming a character of comic strips, nor from having a long career which culminated with TV appearances in the 1960s. The Mighty Mouse shorts had a basic structure, relying on suspense or so-called 'Griffith-style' conclusions: in a dangerous situation, will the super-hero manage to arrive in time to reestablish law and order? How will he do it?

After the attack on Pearl Harbor, in December 1941, Terrytoons contributed to America's role in the war by providing patriotic propaganda films as well as other productions commissioned by the US Government.

The Fleischers: Betty Boop, Popeye and two feature films

A surprising mixture of impetuous growth and stylistic, as well as organizational, carelessness characterized the development of the Fleischer Studios. Despite the fact that the organizational structure of the studio continued to rely more on improvisation than on planning, personalities such as Betty Boop and Popeye enjoyed an extraordinary success. The film *Minnie the Moocher* (1932) became a masterpiece of American animation; Max Fleischer's technique of shooting with a great depth of field preceded Disney's multiplane camera by two years; and his *Gulliver's Travels* (1939) was the second American feature-length animated film.

Still, until the mid-1930s, the studio lacked a story department. When the department was finally opened, it was merely embryonic, and the animators kept creating their own stories. The role of a director, also, was never officially established. Dave Fleischer, who appropriated for himself the right to sign as the director of each film, in fact held the responsibility for motivating

the various teams, insisting on the already outdated formula of attracting the public with a machine-gun-like fire of gags. This inclination was, after all, his very strength; as Shamus Culhane, at that time an employee of the studio, remembers, Dave Fleischer was able to provide his crew with an ever-constant flow of new gags. From 1930 to 1932, characters such as Betty Boop or her dog Bimbo underwent constant unexplained changes, until their features were frozen with a model sheet. Even a technical event such as the invention of sound – which was supposed to reawaken at least the interest of the family inventor, Max – was dealt with casually; for a long time, the Fleischers dubbed the already finished animation instead of following the standard practice of recording the sound track first. Despite these odds, the studio's animation evolved.

Although animators in New York were still far, if not totally alienated, from the attention Disney paid to mimicry and action, they tried to undertake a psychological study of their characters, defining attitudes and mannerisms. Each character acquired its own typical movements, which were kept under control (as opposed to the perpetual motion of the early Fleischers' production). Betty Boop was animated sensitively and with a good dose of realism by Grim Natwick (Wisconsin, 16 August 1890 – California, 7 October 1990)[1] a senior animator who had studied painting and anatomic drawing in Europe and who had become a specialist in female characters (a sort of George Cukor of animation). Betty was the typical flapper of the just-ended Jazz Age. A curly-haired brunette with two deceptively naïve eyes, she wore a black dress which uncovered arms, shoulders, legs, and a garter on her left thigh. Aware of her sex appeal, she was capable of flirtation as well as self-irony. Among the mice, ducks, rabbits, dogs and children crowding the cartoons of the times, she was almost subversive.

---

1   Among other projects, he took care of *Snow White*, at Disney Productions and, after his return to the Fleischer Studio, of Princess Gloria, in *Gulliver's Travels*.

To help mitigate her personality, she was given two companions: first Ko-Ko the Clown, with his buffoonesque comedy, and later Bimbo the Puppy, characterized by infant-like traits.

In 1935, following complaints from some cinema managers who had to face ever more puritanical audiences, especially in small towns, the peppy character was drawn with more chaste clothing, and her attention was turned toward domestic tasks and to loving animals. Thus censored, Betty Boop lost her gloss and disappeared from the screen in 1939. A significant aspect of the character's charm was her voice, a mischievous and childish falsetto given to her by several dubbers, the best of whom was Mae Questel. Betty's voice was precisely the element which prompted the singer Helen Kane (on whose personality Betty had actually been modelled) to file suit for plagiarism against the Fleischers. The case was dropped with the revelation that Kane herself had actually imitated another singer's style.

Minnie the Moocher, featuring Betty Boop, is probably the masterpiece among the productions of the Fleischer Studios. Dense with action and atmosphere, the film is based on a song by Cab Calloway, who appears in person in the opening scene,[1] and revolves around a runaway girl, telling of the ghosts and fears she encounters during her trip into the unknown. Although the film has a conformist ending – the girl and her companion Bimbo return home – the visions and the allusions to danger and sex demonstrate the rare power of a *totentanz*, a dance of death.

Popeye the Sailor (1933) marked the cinematic debut of the character created in 1929 by cartoonist Elzie Crisler Segar. Popeye represented another untraditional choice by the studio. He

Fig. 42 (below). Bimbo, character by Fleischer Studio, in its original shape ((USA, early 1930s). [©King Features.]

Fig. 43 (right). Betty Boop and Bimbo, characters by Fleischer Studio, in their classic shape (USA, mid 1930s). [©King Features.]

---

1 Because of their close relationship with Paramount, the Fleischers were able to use the singers who were under contract to the Hollywood-based company.

was an angular, grouchy, selfish character, difficult to understand, surrounded by a true menagerie of characters: the gluttonous Wimpy, the clumsy Olive Oyl and the primitive giant Bluto. Popeye fell like a stone thrown into the quiet pond of melodies, symphonies, rhapsodies and harmonies. In 1935, a poll taken among American children surprisingly revealed that Popeye was more well-liked than Mickey Mouse. His charm could probably be traced to his innocent, uninhibited use of strength: when faced by a bully or by danger, the sailor would eat spinach, gain a Herculean strength and reverse the critical situation.[1] However, Popeye, too, underwent a gradual process of refinement by Jack Mercer (1910–84), Popeye's scriptwriter and voice-over (Mercer was the one who gave the character his typical mumbling speech).

Among the numerous episodes featuring Popeye, three lush specials, each on two reels, cannot be forgotten: *Popeye the Sailor Meets*

Sinbad the Sailor (1936), *Popeye the Sailor Meets Ali Baba's Forty Thieves* (1937), and *Aladdin and his Wonderful Lamp* (1939). The second film of this group is undoubtedly the best for its inventiveness and richness of drawings and background. The refinement of the quarrelsome sailor occurred when the Fleischers' surrendered to the domineering influence of Disney. In 1934, with *Color Classics* they attempted to imitate the *Silly Symphonies*, by mixing their propensity toward action, the grotesque and the absurd with sentimentality and gracefulness. The result was a hybrid product.

The same hybrid style returned in *Gulliver's Travels* (the first feature film produced by the Fleischers), dumbfounding many viewers. The path leading to this project had been long. In 1937, the Fleischers had to face a strike – one of the first strikes affecting an American studio – which ended after nine months of intransigence on both sides. The event convinced Max that it

Fig. 44. Model sheet of Popeye, character by the Fleischer Studio (USA, late 1930s). [©King Features.]

---

1   The expedient of eating spinach, which had been only episodic in the strips, became a tradition on the screen. Crystal City, Texas, centre of the canned vegetable industry, erected a statue to Popeye.

was time to leave overly unionized New York for a more friendly area. In the same period, Paramount, which did business with the Fleischers, began pressuring the studio for an appropriate answer to the success of Disney's *Snow White and the Seven Dwarfs*. With their characteristic rashness, the Fleischers moved to newly built headquarters in Florida.

While some artists lacking in corporate spirit returned home to the Hudson, the others began working strenuously on *Gulliver's Travels*. The staff of artists grew beyond measure to include about one hundred animators from California, among whom were the prodigal sons Shamus Culhane, Grim Natwick, Al Eugster, veteran Bill Nolan and scriptwriter Tedd Pierce. Young people from the Miami Art School were hired for those tasks requiring less responsibility. The artists, however, not used to working together, produced mediocre results characterized by a few high points (such as the opening scene featuring Gulliver's ship being tossed by the storm) and many clumsy sequences. Gulliver, a character drawn with human features and animated with the rotoscope, stylistically clashes with the Lilliputians, who are represented by caricatures and who, in turn, contrast with the half-realistic, half-caricatured traits of Prince David and Princess Gloria. The plot itself is scarcely enthralling. Overall, the only truly original character is the muddling town crier Gabby (an entire series was later based on him). Presented to the public on 18 December 1939, *Gulliver's Travels* did rather well at the box office even though it suffered from the closing of the European markets due to the ongoing war.

The second feature film by the Fleischers was *Mr. Bug Goes to Town* (UK title: *Hoppity Goes to Town*). The title was clearly a play on Frank Capra's *Mr. Deeds Goes to Town*. The plot revolved around various New York insects searching for a quiet home and a couple (Hoppity, a male grasshopper and his girlfriend Honey Bee) living their love-story, opposed by the rich and cruel C. Bagley Beetle.

This second production, while no worse than the first, was rejected by the public and contributed to the ruin of the studio; although, the actual events which caused the studio to close are not clear. As a matter of fact, the studio was highly indebted to Paramount, which owned and distributed the films produced by the studio. After the flop of the feature film, Max Fleischer found himself in a situation of insolvency, which caused his dismissal and the acquisition of the property by Paramount. Dave Fleischer, who had been in bitter disagreement with his older brother for several years, had left the company before this outcome. Renamed Famous Studios, the production company returned to New York, with a reduced staff under the direction of Izzy Sparber, Sam Buchwald and Seymour Kneitel (Max Fleischer's son-in-law), and continued producing films featuring Popeye and a new star, Superman. Max and Dave Fleischer still attempted to survive in the entertainment world, however, they never again achieved the success they once had.

Warner Brothers: from Harman and Ising through Tex Avery to a republic of equals

After their defection from Disney and a subsequent separation from Mintz, Hugh Harman and Rudolf Ising decided to work on their own. Having invented a character as similar as possible to Mickey, a black boy named Bosko, the two artists made a pilot film, entitled *Bosko the Talk-Ink Kid* and tried to market it. Their best bidder was Leon Schlesinger, chief of Pacific Art and Title, a company specializing in title cards and main titles. Schlesinger also enjoyed a good relationship with Warner Brothers, as they were distant relatives, he had helped financially at the time of their daring conversion to sound. Schlesinger drew up a distribution contract and became instantly a producer of animated films. After Disney, Schlesinger (1884–1949) was probably the most far-sighted American producer of his field. Although his employees described him as a bland person, detached and mercenary, he deserves the credit for having established an extraordinary group of artists in the course of several years, and for having managed it without hindering their fantasy.

In the years of World War II, Schlesinger's studio guided American animation as Disney had done about ten years before. Initially, Harman and Ising were put in charge of the films. In 1930, they began the series *Looney Tunes*, featuring Bosko, who was soon accompanied by a girl named Honey, and by the dog Bruno (the vowels of whose name remind one of Pluto). Although Bosko lacked both personality and mimicry, Harman and Ising themselves had the makings of entertainment moguls: their ambition did not stop with the creation of a standard product, and their sense of comicality went far beyond the usual tricks of animation. The two became successful only after they quit their jobs at Warner's in the middle of 1933, when they had already left their mark on the highly professional *Looney Tunes* and in the sister series *Merrie Melodies* (created along the lines of the *Silly Symphonies*, featuring music that the mother company had already launched in its musicals).

Harman and Ising's request for larger investments in the quality of products led to a clash with Schlesinger, precisely at the time when Metro-Goldwyn-Mayer offered them an advantageous distribution contract. The two artists left, taking Bosko with them. Schlesinger turned to two directors at Disney, Jack King and Tom Palmer, but he soon got rid of them, hiring instead two newcomers with promise, Tex Avery and Frank Tashlin. He also promoted chief animator Friz Freleng to be director. A new character (a boy named Buddy who was nothing more than a

white version of Bosko) temporarily filled the vacuum left in the production.

In the long run, the studio's most profitable idea was the contemporaneous launching of a series of new characters, some of which were short lived, but others became long lasting stars of the animated world. From 1935 to 1940, Porky Pig, Egghead, Elmer Fudd, Daffy Duck and Bugs Bunny made their debut in some of the best films of comic cinema. It would be misleading to attempt to determine the individual creators or the precise dates of birth of these characters, since they developed over the course of years, undergoing many alterations in their physical aspects, manners and personalities. Porky was a stammering piglet, innocent but not without vanity, who was doomed to be a victim of circumstance and of the other protagonists. He soon became a second fiddle to Daffy Duck, a black duckling characterized (in his first phase, which lasted until the post-war era) by a frenzy and an impudence which made him the prototype of the scatterbrain as described in Preston Blair's manual. Daffy's lack of cruelty made him likable: his continual pestering of others was just a consequence of the illogical logic which determined his every action, and which his viewers came to accept. On the contrary, Egghead was a human; after a few years of independent existence, he became Elmer Fudd, the grumpy, foolish adversary of Bugs Bunny.[1]

Finally, Bugs Bunny was perhaps the most accomplished animated version of what nineteenth century Jewish comedy theatre (mother of much humour in American cinema) defined as a *schnorrer* – the loner, characterized by facile speech, a mocking coldness and the irresistible ability to dazzle others with his shrewdness and chatter. As far as his acting was concerned, Bugs Bunny mastered the use of the slow-burn – the

---

1 In spite of its nickname 'Bunny', the character is more of a hare than a rabbit. Supposedly, 'Bugs' comes from the nickname of animator Ben 'Bugs' Hardaway; having received a sketch of the character from Hardaway, a member of his team by the name of Charles Thorson wrote on it 'Bugs's Bunny'.

comical procedure in which a character reacts to the most serious provocations with faultless composure. When threatened by death, the bunny toys with the ever-present carrot while amiably asking 'What's up, doc?'. When provoked, he clarifies: 'Of course you realize that this means war,' before counter-attacking and zeroing in on his enemy. All things considered, Bugs Bunny is a sort of frame-by-frame Groucho Marx.

Tex Avery (Taylor, Texas, 26 February 1908 – Burbank, California, 26 August 1980) subverted the order at Warner's as soon as he joined the company. Having abandoned his ambitions as a comic artist, this talented entertainer spent a few, rather obscure years working for Walter Lantz. Hired by Schlesinger almost by chance, Avery was put in charge of a small team of animators who were too rebellious to collaborate with their colleagues; among them, Chuck Jones, Bob Clampett and Bobe Cannon would later have brilliant careers. The small group settled into a cottage, detached from the main body of the studio, which was renamed 'termite terrace', and started creating. Even though Avery did not reach the height of accomplishment at Warner's that he later attained at Metro-Goldwyn-Mayer, it was here that he developed his original style. A genius at exaggerating and turning things upside down, he pushed the techniques of deformation of a character's physiognomy to their limits, fearlessly risking a fall into bad taste.

In his intellectual understanding of cinematographic fiction, he was second only to the Buster Keaton of *The Cameraman*. Very often Avery broke the conventions of the screen, addressing the audience and commenting on sequences and tricks through either title cards or the characters themselves (years later, Bob Hope developed this same style of humour). As a prophet of the most fantastic paradoxes, Avery created a world in which all that is impossible hangs without expla-

nation like a perpetually hovering cloud – a delirious comicality equalled only by Stan Laurel. Tex Avery was obsessed with speed.[1] With Avery, characters began to disappear suddenly from a frame, leaving behind only their trails. Exactly as Mel Brooks would do decades later, Avery counted on excessive laughter, supreme comicality, a monument to mirth. His overflowing personality served as a lesson to Bob Clampett and Chuck Jones, who were promoted to directors in 1937 and 1938 respectively, and many others, from Friz Freleng to Ben 'Bugs' Hardaway and to Robert McKimson who followed suit.

When Tex Avery left Warner's in 1942, Bob Clampett (San Diego, California, 8 May 1913 – Detroit, Michigan, 2 May 1984) took over the group's leadership. Clampett too, was full of ideas and in love with the absurd. His style, however, was characterized not by a sense of universal folly, as was Avery's, but by a sometimes disquieting mixture of violence and naïveté. A predecessor of the 'sick comedians' of the Fifties, he was the creator of Tweety, the angelically sadistic canary.

Friz Freleng was responsible for Bugs Bunny, which he skillfully developed into the most faceted character and the most experienced actor in the history of the studio. Freleng (Kansas City, Missouri, 21 August 1906) was already a veteran in the 1940s, having started with Disney in the years of silent cinema; in 1929, he returned to his hometown to work in advertising and joined Harman and Ising. He worked for Schlesinger and briefly for Metro-Goldwyn-Mayer. In 1940, he returned to Warner's. He had all the skills of the great cartoon directors: a sense of the comic and of timing, a taste for the characters' personalities, and experience as an entertainer.

As with Chuck Jones, Freleng's golden years came after the war. The years between 1942 and 1945–46 were characterized by a sort of 'repub-

---

1   Joe Adamson, 'Interview With Tex Avery', *Take One*, Vol. 2, No. 9 (1970).

lic' of equals, where each director gave his best, but where no one in particular emerged as a leading personality. Leon Schlesinger, who had always maintained a low-wage policy, compensated his crew with fast careers and the most complete freedom at each stage of creation. With the same foresight, Schlesinger gave his artists, animators and designers the support of two experts in the use of sound: musician Carl Stalling and actor Mel Blanc (1908–89). The latter, gifted in making a surprising number of voices with unexpected caricaturistic powers, gave Warner's animals and people much of their personalities and liveliness.

Of all major companies, Warner Brothers served as a Rooseveltian stronghold, reflecting, in its films, the social and political spirit of the New Deal. With the advent of World War II, the company increased its political involvement, taking sides even in its cartoons. Freleng's *Daffy the Commando* (1943) and *Herr Meets Hare* (1944), and Tashlin's *Plane Daffy* (1944) mocked the Nazis, while Freleng's *Bugs Bunny Nips the Nips* (1944) was a ferociously anti-Japanese film. The Studio also produced films on behalf of the US Government. A series of short comedies (three-to-four minutes long) featuring Private Snafu were exclusively directed to a military audience.

In the filmography of this production company, no single film stands out. *Gold Diggers of '49* (1936), *A Wild Hare* (1940), *Coal Black and De Sebben Dwarfs* (1943) deserve mention for historical rather than artistic reasons. The first film, which marks Tex Avery's debut, shows the artist's developing style; with the second film, Bugs Bunny's adventures began; the third, directed by Bob Clampett, was indeed a good film, a sort of animated *Hallelujah!* starring an all-black cast. As a matter of fact, in the case of Warner Brothers, to search for a masterpiece would be a respectable but short-minded critical approach. Although these films were made by prominent filmmakers, who did excellent creative work, they

were also a series of productions in which quantity counted as much as quality. The repetition of a formula was no less important than the skilled variations in the formula itself, and each episode belonged to a saga without beginning or end.

Series production, having existed for decades in animation and in the other fields of mass culture, became a consciously adopted genre by Warner's, as well as Metro-Goldwyn-Mayer. Basic stylistic choices, such as the one-on-one chase or fight (hunter and hare, cat and mouse, cat and canary, and so on) were no longer straitjackets but rather the aspects of a total narrative. A limited number of facial traits and idiosyncrasies of the characters were manipulated in a virtuoso manner within a unity of time, place and action. Despite a few exceptions (above all, the irrepressible Tex Avery), the style of each film was established by the animated protagonist even more than by the artist-director (whose style could be distinguished from time to time only by an attentive observer). This substantial homogenization (another characteristic of mass production) emerged even when economic pressure did not exert any influence on freedom of expression, as was the case for Warner Brothers' animated films.

Metro-Goldwyn-Mayer: Hanna & Barbera and Tex Avery

From 1930 to 1934, Ub Iwerks supplied animated short subjects to Metro. In 1934, he was supplanted by Harman and Ising, who launched the *Happy Harmonies* series (which lasted only a few years), and reintroduced, albeit not too convincingly, their star from Warner's, Bosko. The two artists' success with Metro lasted three years and was due particularly to the strong personality and intellectual ambitions of Harman (Colorado, 1903 – Chatsworth, California, 25 November 1982). Then, what had happened at Warner's occurred again: the artists' financial requests for a work which would compete with Disney were considered excessive. As the most important film company, Metro-Goldwyn-Mayer at this point felt that it was able to afford its own department of animation, without having to depend on small external production companies. Fred Quimby, an administrator with little originality but a good sense of organization, was named chief of the new department (1937).

As a newcomer to animation, Quimby groped for a few years until, in 1939, he played it safe by returning to Harman and Ising. In 1939, Harman directed *Peace on Earth*, a 'serious', pacifist film featuring a Christmas Night, honoured only by animals since the humans on the earth had exterminated each other in wars. The film was very well received by critics and audiences; Harman was even considered for the Nobel peace price. Meanwhile, Ising (1904 – 18 July 1992) was able to satisfy his old ambition of creating a truly popular character. *The Bear That Couldn't Sleep* (1939) featured the bear Barney, whose popularity would last for the next four or five years. In 1940, Ising became the first, after his former-employer Walt Disney, to win an Oscar for animation. The award-winning film, entitled *The Milky Way*, was a fable taking place in space – a praiseworthy film, but overly drenched with the manneristic loveliness dictated by the taste of the times. The entertainment industry phase of Harman and Ising's career ended around 1942 when Ising was named officer in charge of animation at Fort Roach (Hal Roach Studios). For the next decades the duo concentrated on training and educational films.

The year 1940 was important for Metro as it marked the beginning of the adventures of the cat, Tom, and the mouse, Jerry, in the film *Puss Gets the Boot*. The primary credit for the movie rested with two young animators who had received their training inside the studio: William Hanna and Joseph Barbera. Hanna (born 14 July 1910 in Melrose, New Mexico), studied journalism and engineering. He moved to California in order to find employment as an engineer. As times were hard, he looked into other fields and found a job with Harman and Ising. Barbera (born 24 March 1911 in New York) was a bank employee who soon tired of his job and tried his hand in comic strips. Attracted to animation by the charm of Disney's *Skeleton Dance*, he worked as an apprentice for Van Beuren, when in 1937, he moved to the promised land of California.

Hanna and Barbera worked in the same studio for two years before deciding to form a creative team. The success of their first film strongly influenced their careers and for the next fifteen years the two artists recounted all possible variations of the struggle between the cat and the mouse, winning seven Oscars. Later they founded and directed one of the world's most gigantic companies of animated television series. In the beginning, the grey cat Tom differed greatly from the red mouse Jerry. Tom was ferocious and violent; Jerry represented shrewdness opposed to brutality. Later, when the two characters were more developed, the two roles mingled and Tom and Jerry spent much of their time attempting to hurt each other as much as they could. As a general rule, Tom was the one who suffered the most, since he was not able to hide his wickedness behind an angelic mask as did the small and apparently defenceless mouse. In the end, as with all the pairs of implacable enemies who are incapable of exterminating each other, a sort of solidarity was established: the existence of the one appeared justified by the other, and the reciprocal attempted murder seemed to become a precious common heritage.

The team, soon directed by Hanna and Barbera, achieved Disney-like perfection. Barbera would write the stories, make sketches and invent gags, while Hanna was responsible for the actual direction. Together the two would orchestrate an actual pantomime for each short for the benefit of their animators, and would later be extremely demanding in quality. The series reached its highest level of excellence when its creators found themselves in competition with Tex Avery, who had moved to Metro in 1942. In Avery's work, violence had always been instrumental in an unlimited vision of comicality; its characteristic tendency toward paradox, therefore, combined harmoniously with every other possible exaggeration. Hanna and Barbera captured and reproduced this same concept, but concentrated it into the smallest situations. (In fact, the entire saga of Tom and Jerry rarely went beyond the confines of the dining room and the formal living-room.) So much violence was related in the explicit rule that in animation any catastrophe can be solved in a few frames; Tom (almost always the victim) was thus massacred, twisted, flattened and worked into every conceivable shape. In the long run, the fun disappeared and the formula became mechanical, due to the characters' substantially poor acting.

Tex Avery worked for Metro from 1942 to 1955. His activity will be examined more thoroughly later on; however, it is worthwhile to mention that during World War II, he created Droopy (see Colour Plate 11), one of the most original characters of the time (for Metro). Droopy was a small, wrinkled dog with a sad, inexpressive muzzle and a whining voice; despite his looks, typical of the individual whom everybody could get rid of with a simple blow, Droopy was a true demon, capable of destroying his adversary, usually the 'heavy' character, named simply the 'Wolf'. Giving the most surreal performances of Herculean strength, Droopy moved from inaction to explosiveness, and vice versa, without transition. Each incredible event was emphasized by the character's monotone voice and deadpan face (this latter being another classical procedure used by the comics of silent cinema). As if to confirm the originality and filmic individuality of Droopy as a character, it is noteworthy that among all the animated stars on the screen, this was one of the least successful in comic strips.

Tashlin the Wanderer

Frank Tashlin (Weekhawken, New Jersey, 19 February 1913 – Hollywood, 5 May 1972) was born into a French-German family (the Taschleins). At the age of fifteen, he found a job as an errand boy with the Fleischer Studio in New York and later worked as an animator for Van Beuren. Finally, attracted by the Mecca of cinema and the California sun, he moved to Hollywood (he recounted that he arrived there on the most rainy day of the year without a raincoat).

Once in Los Angeles, Tashlin covered a lot of ground. From 1933 to 1935, Tashlin joined Leon Schlesinger at Warner's; after which, he performed a brief stint with Ub Iwerks. He returned to work for Schlesinger and was promoted to director. From 1938 to 1941, he worked for Disney. He moved to Screen Gems and later, for the third time, he returned to Warner's. About 1945, Tashlin quit animation to become a script writer for live-action feature comedies. Finally, in 1951 he became a film director. His works include *Son of Paleface* (1951), starring Bob Hope; *Artists and Models* (1955), starring Jerry Lewis; and *The Man From the Diner's Club* (1963), with Danny Kaye. In addition, Tashlin drew his own comic strip in 1933 ('Van Boring' was a caricature of his ex-employer Amadée Van Beuren), and wrote and illustrated four comic books.

Tashlin has yet to be honoured with the esteem he deserves; undoubtedly, his fragmentary career makes it difficult to single out a common thread in his work. Still, some elements of his style emerge constantly: a preference for fast, 'cinematographic' editing and difficult framing; a slapstick-like inspiration (it was believed that Tashlin secretly studied the old films of Keaton and his peers); an ironic perspective of everyday superficiality; and finally, a predisposition (as had Avery) to disclosing the filmic facade by involving the spectator directly. A moment of fame came to him toward the end of the fifties with his work with Jerry Lewis. Usually, his live-action films were affected by his training as an animator as much as his animated films showed his ambitions as a movie-director. Tashlin was a well-rounded filmmaker – one of the few; he was also one of the very few artists who left a mark in each field in which he worked.

The American avant-garde

As European cinema absorbed Disney's teachings and tried to appeal to a larger public, European-inspired experimental animation landed in the United States and found room to grow within the independent, non-conformist cinema. These filmed experiments – similar, in their non-conformity, to those of the French movements of the 1920s, were to prepare the road for the 'second avant-garde' of the 1940s, with Maya Deren, Gregory Markopoulos, Curtis Harrington and Kenneth Anger. They were also the foundation for the underground movement of the 1960s. The number of grants offered by 'cultural' institutions to independent artists increased, and a flourishing cultural circuit of 16 millimetre films grew in Universities, museums, libraries and film clubs. Animation offered the most flexible medium to those who wanted to free fantasy and to present views unknown to regular cinema; in such an environment, abstract cinema became ever more important.

Following a course parallel to the Hollywood dream-industry, the avant-garde found expression in films by Robert Florey (*Life and Death of 9413*, *The Loves of Zero*, *Johann the Coffin Maker*), by the Webber-Watson duo (*The Fall of the House of Usher*, *Lot in Sodom*), by photographer Rolf Steiner (*H₂0*) and by poet Emler Etting (*Oramunde*, *Poem 8*).

Painter Mary Ellen Bute (Houston, Texas, 25 November 1906 – New York, 17 October 1983) made her first abstract film in 1934; entitled *Rhythm in Light*, the film was based on Grieg's

Anitra's Dance. Previously, in 1933, Bute had collaborated with the filmmaker and cinema historian Lewis Jacobs on the failed project, *Synchronization*. Later, Bute made *Synchromy No.2* (1935), *Escape* (1938, an illustration of Bach's 'Toccata and Fugue'), *Tarantella* (1939, with music by Edwin Gershefsky) and *Spook Sport* (1940, based on music by Saint-Saëns, with animation by Norman McLaren). Bute's camera operator and, later, producer was Ted Nemeth, who became the artist's husband.

Douglas Crockwell (Ohio, 1904 – Glens Falls, New York, 1968) earned his living as an illustrator and designer of covers for magazines. In 1938, 1939 and 1940 he made *Fantasmagoria* I, II and III, respectively. Here, he adopted a technique used later on by Fischinger, which involved photographing the composition and modifying a painting on glass in its succeeding phases. In 1946, he released his most famous film, *Glens Falls Sequence*, and one year later, *The Long Bodies*, an assembly of the experiments he had made over several years. In his own words, the long bodies are the four-dimensional traces objects leave in space during the course of their existence.

Dwinell Grant (Springfield, Ohio, 1912) moved to abstract animation in 1940, after working as an abstract painter. Until 1948, he produced films with the title of *Compositions*. Then he devoted himself to educational films, returning only sporadically to art cinema. Francis Lee (New York, 1913) made his first film as a reaction to the Japanese attack on Pearl Harbor. Entitled *1941*, the film gave an abstract interpretation of war. After having worked as a cameraman on the European front, Lee filmed *Le bijou* (The Jewel) in 1946 and *Idyll*, in 1948. Later, he devoted himself to studies of painting and Chinese civilization, on which he based the film *Sumi-e*. In 1940, the Californian brothers John and James Whitney debuted in what turned out to be a long and productive career.

Chapter 9

Talent in other pre-war nations

Soviet Union

Toward the end of the 1920s, the Soviet production of animated films increased, but the innovative thrust lost momentum. In 1929, the 'futurist' Lunacharsky quit his position as People's Commissar for Culture. In 1932, an important congress of Soviet writers sanctioned a new current of creative effort, which was to be known as 'socialist realism'. Instead of exploring new territory in the avant-garde, as in the preceding decade, Soviet animators set themselves to the service of national culture by adapting classical texts, producing children's works and utilizing the figurative and plastic suggestions of popular traditions.

The new orientation of animation toward children was evident in the name of the production centre Sojuzdetmultfilm (*det*, or child, and *mult*, which refers to *multiplikatsija*, that is, animation), founded in Moscow in 1936 as a result of a merge of the Sovkino and Mezhrabpomfilm groups.[1] One consequence of this orientation was a propensity for round forms typical of American cartoons, which represented an involution from the creativity that had characterized Soviet animation in its early years.

The first director of Sojuzdetmultfilm was Alexander Ptushko (Lugansk, Ukraine, 19 April 1900 – Moscow, 6 March 1973). An actor, designer and journalist, he had studied architecture in Kiev before devoting himself to mechanical engineering. Among other inventions, he created an adding machine which was used until very recently in the Soviet Union. Eventually, Ptushko was able to concentrate all his technical, pictorial and theatrical interests in the field of animation. He made his directing debut in animation with *It Happened at the Stadium* (1928). A puppet specialist, Ptushko used marionettes in his first important film and the first full-length film of Soviet Animation. *The New Gulliver* (1935), mixes marionettes, the Lilliputians, with live-action cinema, as Petya-Gulliver was played by an actor. A boy, Petya, fascinated by his reading of *Gulliver's Travels*, falls asleep and dreams of himself as the protagonist. Noticing the corruption of Lilliput's aristocrats and the miners' oppression, Petya helps the miners in their armed revolution before waking up.

In contrast to Swift's book, Ptushko's Gulliver is a political polemicist and a supporter of the theories of the October Revolution. His didactic verbosity limits the film, which otherwise stands out for its excellent scenographic configurations as well as for the animators' skilled exchanges of facial elements on the wooden actors. The puppets are very expressive, and their lips are well synchronized with the dubbed sound. The second one, *The Little Golden Key*, based on Aleksei Tolstoy's version of the adventures of Pinocchio, was also directed by Ptushko, in 1939. Afterwards, the filmmaker left animation for live-action cinema.

Between 1930 and 1935, the impetuous Merkulov, Komissarenko and Khodataev (this last one directed *The Barrel Organ* in 1934, and his farewell film *Fialkin's Career*, in 1935), abandoned animation and returned to painting and sculpture. Tsekhanovsky worked sporadically with animation after an unfinished attempt at a full-length film based on Pushkin's work (*The Story of the Lord and His Peasant Balda*). Tsekhanovsky's

student Mstislav Paschenko deserves recognition. His *Dzhyabsha,* of 1938, was a film for children based on the folklore of the Nanaic people, one of the Soviet Union's ethnic minorities living in the far North of European Russia.

Ivan Ivanov-Vano was a prolific director who also turned to children's films (*The Three Musketeers*, 1938) after working in satirical films such as *Black and White* (1932, based on a theme by Mayakovsky), and folkloric films (*The Tale of Czar Durandai*, 1934). The Brumberg sisters were especially active in the field of children's cinema. Valentina (Moscow, 2 August 1899 – 28 November 1975) and Zinaida (Moscow, 2 August 1900 – 9 February 1983), who nearly always worked together, collaborated with Ivanov-Vano in *The Tale of Czar Durandai* and *Ivashko and the Baba Jaga* (1938).

In the same period, the Armenian Lev Atamanov (Moscow, 21 February 1905 – 12 February 1981) made his debut. Atamanov, whose real name was Atamanian, studied under Lev Kuleshov at the State school of cinema. Later, he abandoned his ambition of becoming an actor and director and concentrated on animated drawing. In the 1930s, he distinguished himself by directing a series, *Ink-Spot on the Artic* (1934), *Ink-Spot Hairdresser* (1935) and with the antimilitaristic satire, *The Story of the Little White Bull*. In 1938, he moved to Erevan where he established the foundations of Armenian animation with *The Priest and the Goat* (1941), based on a story by the Armenian writer Ovanes Tumanian.

Eygpt

The small Egyptian animated production was mainly due to the Frenkel brothers. Born into a Jewish family in Jaffa, Palestine, Herschel, Salomon and David Frenkel later established their lacquered-wood furniture business in Cairo.

Fig. 45. Poster of Enjoy Your Food! by the Frenkel brothers, with their character Mish-Mish (Egypt, 1947).

1   The name was later changed to Sojuzmultfilm.

Fascinated by animation after viewing the films of Felix the Cat, the three brothers began studying the frame-by-frame technique. In 1936, they released *Nothing to Do*, featuring the character of Mish-Mish, an Egyptian youngster wearing a fez. Other productions based on the same character followed, including the war propaganda film *National Defense* (1940) and *Enjoy Your Food* (1947). When the political stage in Egypt became too turbulent, the Frenkels left the country. The younger brother, David, moved to France, where he revived Mish-Mish by substituting his fez with a very French *casquette*, and by renaming him Mimiche. These films were not distributed in theatres, but sold for family shows. In 1964, he made *Le rêve du beau Danube bleu* (The Dream of the Beautiful Blue Danube), the only major creation in his European production.

Another Egyptian pioneer was Antoine Selim Ibrahim (Cairo, 11 November 1911), whose *Aziza and Youness in El Sheik Barakat's Book* (1938) was the first animated film with an Arab language soundtrack. Ibrahim made more films in the 1940s (among them *Dokdok*, 1940), then commercials and titles for live-action films. In 1972 he went to the USA and worked at Hanna & Barbera's, then from 1976 to 1980 he worked for De Patie-Freleng. He later retired and devoted himself to painting.

Japan

As soon as the first cartoons by John Randolph Bray were shown in Tokyo around 1910, some local artists wanted to try their own skills as animators. The pioneer of animated films (which were called *doga*, 'moving images,' until the term was replaced with *animation* in the 1950s), was Seitaro Kitayama. In 1913, he made his first experiments with India ink on paper. In 1917, he filmed *Saru kani kassen* (The Crab Gets Its Revenge on the Monkey), *Cat and Mice* and *The Naughty Mailbox*. Kitayama's *Momotaro* (The Peach Boy, 1918) was the first Japanese drawing

Chapter 9
Talent in other
pre-war nations
103

to be shown abroad, in France. In 1921, Kitayama (who had learned the trade by drawing title cards for silent films and who loved traditional children's stories) opened his own studio. His activities were undermined, although not interrupted, by the devastating 1923 earthquake. A very prolific artist, he made up to six films a year, despite his craftsman-style of production.

Another pioneer was Junichi Kouchi (1886–1970), author of *Hanahekonai's New Sword* and *The Lazy Sword* (1917). He had a preference for popular tales. In the early 1920s (simultaneously with his colleagues Kiichiro Kanai and Zenjiro 'Sanae' Yamamoto) Kouchi introduced the use of grey nuances into animated drawings, which up to then had been economically traced with India ink.

A third pioneer of Japanese animation was Oten Shimokawa (1892–1973) who made his debut with *Imokawa Muzuko genkanban no maki* (Imokawa Muzuko the Concierge, 1917). An artist published in daily newspapers, he made several films based on his comic strip characters. Shimokawa tried to introduce the technique of drawing on a blackboard with chalk and correcting the drawing after each frame had been shot.

Fig. 46. The Spider and the Tulipan by Kenzo Masaoka (Japan, 1943).

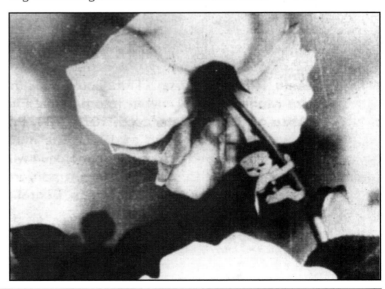

Finally, he adapted to drawing on paper, but was later forced to retire because of an eye disease.

Zenjiro 'Sanae' Yamamoto (6 February 1898 – 8 February 1981) apprenticed with Kitayama before directing *Ubasute-Yama* (The Mountain Where Old Women Are Abandoned) and *Ushiwakamuru* (Ushiwakamuru, the Little Samurai), both of 1925. In 1928, in collaboration with Kiichiro Kanai, he directed *Stakiri susume* (The Sparrows with the Cut Tongues) and *Issunboshi* (The Little Man). He also worked on educational animation. He continued to direct films until the mid-1940s; after World War II, he moved to production.

The Japanese animator most renowned by far in Europe was Noburo Ofuji (Tokyo, 1 June 1900 – 18 June 1974). At the age of eighteen, he became a student and collaborator of Kouchi; in the mid-1920s, he began working on his own. A stern artist, Ofuji did not believe in animation as a comic art, but strove toward a dramatic cinema for adults, including erotic themes. After some undistinguished films, two years later in 1927 he made *Kujira* (The Whale), a remarkable exercise in action and suspense. The film was acquired by a French distribution company and successfully circulated from 1929. For this film, Ofuji used a special technique, cutting figurines out of *chigoyami* (a semi-transparent paper then available only in Japan), and arranging them on different, superimposed glass planes, from the background to the forefront. Filmed in black and white, all this offered an extremely charming world of transparencies and shadows. In *The Whale*, viewers can notice the effort of the perfectionist animator, striving for a fluid 'total' movement rather than the limited animation used at the time. In 1930, Ofuji made his first sound film, *Sekisho* (The Inspection Station), and in 1937, his first colour work, *Katsura Hime* (Princess Katsura).

Yasuji Murata (Yokohama, 24 January 1898 – 22 November 1966) made his debut in 1927; he was the first Japanese animator to use the American-style cel process with the technique of total animation. A prolific filmmaker (from 1927 to 1935 he made no less than thirty films), he used a caricatural style and many zoomorphic figures, such as ducks, monkeys and pigs. His finest film was *Tako no hone* (The Octopus Bone, 1927).

In the 1930s, Japanese militarism grew to dominate the country's politics. With the beginning of the war against China in 1933, movie theatres were required to show educational, documentary and propaganda films in massive doses. When World War II broke out, the small animation companies underwent a process of consolidation aimed at coordinating production. Kenzo Masaoka, a movie actor, and later, director (born in Nishi, on 5 October 1898), suffered this fate but remained leader of his group. Beside the propaganda films dictated by events, he produced shorts based on popular tales. Masaoka made his animation debut around the late 1920s with the excellent *Sarugashima* (The Monkeys' Island, 1930). In 1932, he made his first sound film, *Chikara To Onna No Yononaka* (The World of Power and Women), which told the comic story of a clerk who falls in love with a typist, in spite of his gigantic jealous wife. It was followed by *Benkei tai Ushikawa* (Benkei the Soldier-Priest and Little Samurai Ushikawa, 1939), which was praised especially for its expressive use of music.

In 1943, he created his masterpiece, *Kumo to Chulip* (The Spider and the Tulipan). The film was partially based on a country tale written by a woman writer, Michiko Yokoyama, winner of a literary competition promoted by the daily *Asahi Shinbun*. It told the adventures of a ladybug who was chased by a Don Juan spider and who hid in a tulip in order to escape her pursuer. When the god of thunder caused a storm, only the tulip survived out of all the flowers. The ladybug could then emerge from her hiding place to begin singing anew.

A former assistant of Masaoka, Mitsuyo Seo (26

September 1911) opened a studio under his own name in 1933. Among other productions, he made a series about the monkey Sankichi. *The Assault Troops of Sankichi the Monkey*, 1935, set during the Chinese-Japanese war, featured the Imperial Army efficiently attacking a fortress which was poorly protected by Chinese Pandas. Mitsuyo Seo, too, suffered from the consolidation process and in 1940, his studio became part of the large company Geijutsu Eiga Sha. During the war, besides propaganda films, he managed to make *Momotaro no umiwashi* (Momotaro, the Brave Sailor, 1943) and *Momotaro-umi noshinpei*, (Momotaro, Divine Sailor, 1944), the first Japanese feature film. Imperial sailors with animalistic features build a landing strip, undergo training and eventually conquer an enemy base in New Guinea. Although the film was made for propaganda and recruiting purposes, it has some charm of its own, particularly due to its realistic treatment of action.

Chapter 9
Talent in other
pre-war nations
105

The following made notable contributions to Japanese animation. Among propaganda mid-length films, *Fuku-Chan no Sensuikan* (Fuku-Chan and the Submarine, 1944) should be mentioned. Although credited to Isoji Sekiya, it was in fact made by Ryuichi Yokoyama (Kochi, 17 May 1909), who later became a promoter of post-war animation by founding Otogi and by creating many works for television. Tadahito Mochinaga, who became the founder, ten years later, of Japanese puppet animation, contributed to the movie as a camera-operator and script writer. Wagoro Arai (Kojimachi, 11 December 1907), a dentist with a hobby in animation, was encouraged by constant praise to become a professional. The first of his films was *Kogane no Tsuribari* (The Golden Hook, 1939), made with animated cutouts. Ikuo Oishi also deserves distinction for a comic film, *Ugoki Ekori no Takehiki* (The Fox Versus the Racoon, 1933).

Chapter 10

The masters of animation

George Pal

A world traveller, George Pal defeats any attempt at classification by nation. Born as György Pál Marczincsák (Cegléd, Hungary, 1 February, 1908 – Beverly Hills, California, 2 May 1980), he began his cinematographic career as a scene designer at the Budapest studio Hunnia. He later joined UFA in Berlin, where he made his first puppet film, an advertising short for a brand of cigarettes. In 1934, in Eindhoven, The Netherlands, he worked for Philips Corporation, which equipped a studio for the animation of puppets where he produced the famous *Philips Broadcast 1938*. While in The Netherlands, Pal also made several advertising films for the British market. In 1940, he moved to the United States, where his professional life reached its apex. From that time until 1949, he was under contract to Paramount for the animated puppet series *Puppetoons*. Unique of its kind, the series featured Jasper, a black boy based on the stereotypes of American black vaudeville. Later he became an expert of special effects, winning five Oscars, and finally a producer and director of fantasy films, such as *Doc Savage, The Man of Bronze* (1975, directed by Michael Anderson).

Pal was not so much a great artist in command of his own poetic world, as an inimitable technician of movement and a showman of taste. His elegantly stylized puppets give excellent acting performances, and his films display lively mass scenes, pathos and the style of framing used in live action cinema.

Alexandre Alexeïeff

Alexandre Alexeïeff was born on 18 April 1901, in Kazan, the heart of Russia. The son of a school principal and an officer of the Czarist army, Alexandre moved to the Bosphorus shortly after his birth when his father was promoted to the post of military attaché at the Russian embassy in Constantinople. There, young Alexandre learned French even before Russian and spent several enchanted years until his father's mysterious death during a mission to Germany. The family then returned to Russia. At the age of ten, Alexandre entered St. Petersburg's Military School where he received his first artistic education from an inspirational art teacher who asked his pupils not to copy objects, but to draw from their memories or from impressions of literary works. In 1917, during the October Revolution, the young cadet fervently supported the revolutionary movement, but later withdrew, after witnessing tragedy and injustice – in particular, the jailing and later killing by the Bolsheviks of an uncle of his, a socialist and a defender of labourers and peasants.

As soon as he finished his courses in St. Petersburg, Alexeïeff boarded a military ship, travelling to Japan and then to China, India and Egypt. In 1921, the crew dispersed in Dubrovnik, Yugoslavia, leaving Alexeïeff to land adventurously in Marseille. Dreaming of painting, and possessing a letter of introduction to set designer and fellow Russian refugee Serge Sudekin, he moved to Paris.

> 'At the time', he remembers, 'it was believed that three hundred thousand Russians lived in Paris; among them were the major forces of the theatre. There was Diaghilev's famous ballet, there was Pïtoeff, there was Sudekin, there was Alexandre Benois.'[1]

For a few years, he worked as a set designer, while taking painting and drawing lessons at the Académie de la Grande Chaumière in Montparnasse.

In 1925, he devoted himself to illustrating high-quality books and to etching, an activity which ensured him some economic security. But at the age of thirty, Alexeïeff went through a stage of dissatisfaction:

> 'I had the feeling I had tried everything ... everything I was capable of. I illustrated books, and that gave me money; thus everything was going well. But I kept repeating to myself that this was no longer an art, just a trade like others. That was the time of *Caligari*, *Circus*,

Chaplin's tramp and Eisenstein's films. Cinema certainly deserved the interest which my writer friends gave to it. I told myself: I will make some cinema. By myself. I don't want a large crew, I don't want Eldorado. Mine shall not be a product, but a work of art'.[2]

At that point, the idea of the 'pinscreen' was born. As an engraver, Alexeïeff knew how to express himself through the use of chiaroscuro, nuances of grey and complex images. They were images requiring a unique dynamism compatible with their style, so complicated as to discourage any animator who used traditional animation techniques. It was therefore imperative for Alexeïeff to discover a way to animate engravings:

> 'I had to find a way to work by myself, in my art studio, and to create by myself images exactly as I wanted them'.[3]

He designed a white screen in which thousands of retractible pins were mounted perpendicularly so as to form a mesh. If two light sources were set at the sides of the screen, each pin would cast two oblique shadows on it; the sum of all the shadows together would make the screen completely dark. At that point, if certain groups of pins retracted, their shadows would shorten and the corresponding area would lighten. Full retraction of the pins would produce no shadows, only the white of the surface. In this way, the artist would be able to obtain any figure and to utilize the complete palette of greys. A film of animated engravings would then become possible if the artist gradually changed the images and photographed them frame-by-frame at each new stage.

This idea would have remained in its conceptual stage (Alexeïeff had considered an animated version of Mussorgsky's music), but for Claire Parker (born in Boston on 31 August 1906). Like many

1   *Portrait d'Alexeïeff*. (Post-production script for the television documentary produced by ORTF (French Television), Service de la recherche. Directed by Maurice Debèze, 1971).

2   *Portrait d'Alexeïeff*.

3   *Portrait d'Alexeïeff*.

young Americans of the 'lost generation', Parker lived in Paris. Having seen the books illustrated by Alexeïeff, she wrote to him expressing her admiration, and asking him for lessons. The event marked the beginning of a long lasting artistic and personal relationship. With the support of Parker, Alexeïeff decided to go on with the project.

In 1932, the two artists began shooting *Une nuit sur le mont chauve* (A Night on Bald Mountain) and worked on it uninterruptedly for eighteen months. Having listened again and again in the dark to Mussorgsky's music, Alexeïeff built the film in his own mind, frame-by-frame.[1] With his pinscreen technique it was not possible to make preparatory drawings, and mistakes in shooting could be corrected only by starting all over again. In 1933, the film was completed. When shown to friends and experts, it obtained a great *succès d'estime*, but the distributors objected that the only way to reach profitability was to produce a dozen films per year. Disappointed, Parker and Alexeïeff left art cinema and turned to advertising.

At the time, advertising was still in its infancy, and artists enjoyed a large degree of freedom. Claire and Alosha, as he was called by his intimates, worked with a group of friends, including Alexandra de Grinevsky, Alexeïeff's former wife. Together they produced a few small masterpieces, especially valuable for the precision of set design, the detailing of light tricks, and the use of varied techniques (which, however, did not include the pinscreen). *La belle au bois dormant* (Sleeping Beauty), made for a wine firm, deserves praise; Alexeïeff's contribution to the film is clearly recognizable over those of the other artists.

With the outbreak of World War II, the Alexeïeffs left Paris for the United States, where they en-

countered difficult work conditions. Large animation corporations, with their assembly-line production did not hold any interest for the mastery of the Russian-French emigré. With a larger, more perfected pin screen, Alexeïeff made *En passant* (Passing By, 1943), for the National Film Board of Canada. Based on a song from French-speaking Quebec, this very short film was the first example of 'free work' produced by Alexeïeff after ten years of silence. In America, Alexeïeff also continued his activity as an engraver, developing a technique which allowed him to obtain colour engravings. Shortly after the end of the war, the couple returned to Paris.

In 1951, a period of abstract experimentation began: the animation of illusory solids, that is, of solids which are traced on the frame by a moving light source after a long exposure time. Alexeïeff decided to connect these tracing sources (usually metallic spheres, properly illuminated), to composite pendulums, whose oscillations could be mathematically computed, and which could therefore be planned. By adjusting the various

Fig. 47. Une nuit sur le Mont Chauve by Alexandre Alexeïeff and Claire Parker, detail (France, 1933).

---

1   The symphonic poem in one part, *A Night on Bald Mountain*, evolving around one basic theme, was composed by Mussorgsky in 1876. It referred to the legendary witches' Sabbath, which supposedly occurred every summer solstice (on the night of the 24 June, the feast of St. John the Baptist) on Mount Triglav, near Kiev.

forms traced by the light source, he was able to 'animate' these nonexistent solids. 'This is the second stage of movement', he claimed. Using this technique, called 'totalization', he shot some advertising films, including *Fumées* (Vapours), winner of a special award at the cinema festival of Venice, in 1952.

In 1962 Orson Welles, who had admired one of Alexeïeff's books of illustrations, invited the artist to make the prologue of *Le procès* (The Trial), a film based on Kafka's novel. By using the pinscreen, Alexeïeff created some pictures which he filmed one after the other, without animation. Many reviewers wrote that the prologue was of a better quality than the film itself.

In 1963, Alexeïeff and Parker filmed *Le nez* (The Nose), based on the short story of the same name by Nikolaj Gogol. In 1972, they completed *Tableaux d'une exposition* (Pictures at an Exhibition)[1], a work which was for several reasons connected to *A Night on Bald Mountain*. Based on the music which Modest Mussorgsky had expressly composed to 'suggest images to painters', it was intended as the first part of a trilogy which was to include all the *Pictures* by the Russian composer. Due to practical problems, the project was left unfinished. Then in 1975, Alexeïeff provided drawings and scene designs for *Finist*, a Russian fable produced by Corona Cinematografica of Rome and animated by the Italian Giorgio Castrovillari.

Fig. 48. Le nez by Alexandre Alexeïeff and Claire Parker, (France, 1963).

1   Mussorgsky composed *Pictures at an Exhibition* in 1874. They refer to the paintings of Viktor Hartmann, a friend of the composer, whose work had been exhibited posthumously in St. Petersburg. Originally written for piano, the music was transcribed for orchestra in 1922 by Maurice Ravel. The music, which guides a hypothetical visitor through the exhibition, is divided into fourteen passages, spaced by a *promenade* which is repeated four times in variations.

In 1977, on a new screen of pins built the preceding year, Alexeïeff and Parker began *Trois thèmes* (Three Themes), based on three more *Tableaux* by Mussorgsky. Alexeïeff wrote:

> 'The terms *adagio, maestoso, lento* have not yet found their place in animation, which is limited to *scherzo*, excluding elegy, eclogue and other lyrical terms. This happens because it is difficult – if not impossible – to "slow down" animation. Well, this is what I am trying to do.'[1]

Trois thèmes opened in Milan, Italy, in March 1980, during a triumphant soirée honouring Parker and Alexeïeff. It was also the filmmakers' swan song: Parker died in Paris on 3 October 1981, while Alexeïeff's death followed less than one year later, on 9 August 1982.

> 'You know,' wrote Elie Faure (1922), a French poet and art critic who loved prophecies, 'these animated drawings, still so barren, so stiff, so meagre, that are projected on the screen and that are, if you will, as the forms I imagine a child's graffiti drawn on a blackboard are to Tintoretto's frescoes or Rembrandt's canvasses. Suppose that three or four generations of people are harnessed to the problem of animating these images in depth, not by surfaces nor lines, but by thicknesses and volumes; of modelling, by values and half-tones, a series of successive movements that by long practice would gradually become habit, almost a reflex, so that the artist comes to using it at his pleasure for drama or idyll, comedy or poetry, light or shade, forest, city, desert. Suppose an artist is so armed with the heart of Delacroix, the passion of Goya and the strength of Michelangelo; he will throw on the screen a cineplastic tragedy entirely his own, a kind of visual symphony so rich and so complex, opening, by its rush through time, perspectives of infinity and the absolute which are both exalting by their mystery and more moving by their tangible reality than the symphonies in sound of the greatest musicians. There, that is the distant future which I believe in but which I do not know can be achieved.'[2]

It did not take three or four generations, but eleven years. *A Night on Bald Mountain* was screened in 1933, while Faure was still alive (he died in 1937). In spite of the pompous prose and name dropping, Faure's text was actually prophetic, showing how Alexeïeff's work led to a sudden leap in the art of animation.

A master of the fine arts, a friend of writers such as Soupault and Malraux, a 'careful' participant in the surrealist and advant-garde movements ('careful' because his inborn aversion for clamour and publicity never made him a protagonist), Alexeïeff was considered an experimental filmmaker, whose value had to be judged in terms of the novel linguistic contributions he made to the history of cinema. *A Night on Bald Mountain* was, and still is, considered a solution to the old problem of agreement between the music of sounds and the music of images; Alexeïeff's animated engravings are seen as a proposal of the linguistic potential of the cinematographic medium. The critics are certainly correct, but experimentalism was only a secondary facet of Alexeïeff's prismatic activity. The artist invented the pinscreen not for the sake of invention, but in an effort to make an instrument for himself, the only instrument capable of producing his fantasy.[3]

A Night on Bald Mountain is an exceptional poem of images, an inexhaustible source of lyric suggestion, rich with ambiguous hints. The music

---

1   Letter received from Alexandre Alexeïeff, 14 February, 1978.

2   Elie Faure, *De la cinéplastique*.

3   The painting *Vaste Ocean* of 1964 (Art Institute of Chicago) by German artist Günther Uecker, should be mentioned here. Uecker's painting is a large white canvas on which nails have been affixed to create the appearance of waves. Alexeïeff's procedure was very similar.

functions as a text, to which the fluidity of images continuously refers, but without any mechanical linking of rhythm and timbre. Images enrich music and music enriches images, in an evocative process which allows both artistic expressions to maintain their individual vitality and mutual respect. Looking for suggestions, the filmmaker turned to the musician who was for him a spiritual guide and with whom he shared a common ethnic origin (Alexeïeff always had a place in his heart for great Mother Russia).[1] Alexeïeff's figurations also derived inspiration from Mussorgsky's notes to the musical piece, Gogol's *The Night of St. John*, and some poems by Pushkin. For his creative work, Alexeïeff adopted the following method: he encountered a text, a memory or a word and then liberated his fantasy. The images of *A Night on Bald Mountain* are subtle, voluminous and often intertwined; far from being simple 'animation' or simple 'animated engravings', they are a window open on a fantastic universe.[2] Fantasy takes shape thanks to the infinite shades of greys.

> 'The artists of my time,' Alexeïeff stated more than once, 'used surfaces and lines. I wanted shades. They played the trumpet, I wanted to use the violin.'

Clearly, the attitude of this poet of images differed from that of his friends, writers or painters, who were striving toward less artistic, more cultural and more intellectually oriented research. Perceived as an experimentalist, he was criticized by many reviewers for his lack of self-renewal, for the similarity of his films – particularly his last releases. Such an accusation is valid only as far as technique is concerned. In both *Pictures at an Exhibition* and *Trois thèmes*, Alexeïeff still used the pin screen, exactly as he had done for *En passant* and *Le nez*. But the inner, poetic evolution is very clear. From the anguished, aggressive, 'gothic' vision of the 1933 film, the artist moved to the all-consuming childhood memories as well as Russian legends of *Pictures*. The complex, sinuous rhythms of the two pin screens rotating in front of each other act as mediators for a world which does not exist anymore and for traditions which can no longer be found.

> 'While making *A Night on Bald Mountain*,' wrote Alexeïeff, 'I believed I was showing the struggle between Good and Evil, between Night and Day. Much later, I discovered that I recounted the drama of my father's death and the metamorphosis of my mother, who became depressed. But it was involuntary; I did it without knowing. I understood it twenty years later. I was thirty. I had then to demonstrate that it is possible, for a human being, to make a picture in movement. I am seventy as I start the *Pictures*. I believe that now I have to demonstrate that animation can also be poetic, to prove that cinema can abandon "photography", to look for a certain grammatical form of dialogue: something like a sonata with two themes, on two alternating pinscreens. After all, like every other artwork the *Pictures* are the portrait of their author, Mussorgsky. Clearly, the film will also be my self-portrait. But what the film will be in the end I cannot know, and I will never know'.[3] Shortly afterward, he wrote, 'We saw copy number zero of the *Pictures at an Exhibition*', on 17 December. I believe that this film equals *A Night*, although it is very different. One has to see this film twenty times before understanding it: this is true for good poetry.'[4]

If there is a division between narrative and poetry,

---

1   It is perhaps significant that Mussorgsky was also educated at the Cadets' school in St. Petersburg.

2   It is possible to track down some visual memories of *Faust* (1926) by F. W. Murnau: the flight through the clouds, the flight over reconstructed model countryside, the grey husks, the character who 'takes off his head' when he takes off his hat.

3   Letter received from Alexandre Alexeïeff, 25 October 1971.

4   Letter received from Alexandre Alexeïeff, 19 December 1971.

this is represented by the adjustment of language to the logical principle deriving from daily sensory experience. The narrative medium always keeps in mind a before and an after, reality and fantasy, a cause followed by an effect. Not so for the poetic medium, which substantially is atemporal, having an inner time and space, expressing itself with images liberally created by the poet's mind, then integrating and structuring itself not according to logical laws, but according to the emotional response of the person who enjoys them. Because of the close connection between narrative and the world of daily and sensory experiences, cinema – which is born from the filming of current events and is linked to the sensory world it photographs – absorbs the logical categories of this world and becomes the central place of narrative. After Eisenstein's failed attempt at an 'intellectual editing', (for instance, *October*), the only cinema which could free itself from its obligations to prose was the one which had for its object the intellectual creations of the author rather than the surrounding reality.

This occurred in the cinema of Eggeling and Ruttmann. The rhythmic flowing of abstract images produced something which could equal the rhythmic flowing of abstract sound or music. To create poetry, some images were needed which were figurative, loaded with meaning, and it was necessary to give them a rhythmic formalization. With his delirious figurative fantasy and with his powerful style, Alexeïeff was able to fulfill these requirements. His chiaroscuros were his past recollections, nightmares and visions of the legends of pagan Russia, as well as images of the loved and lost native country. All these were strongly autobiographical elements, as Alexeïeff himself remarked, which made his work into a lyrical anthology.

Up to a certain point, one can speak of decadence, keeping in mind the historical notion of

the term rather than the current pejorative meaning.

'As far as decadence and romanticism have been absorbed by the avant-garde movements of the beginning of the century, Alexeïeff's art can be considered avant-garde' writes Gianni Rondolino.

Referring to the artist's participation in the intellectual movements of his time, he adds that Alexeïeff:

'... observes and learns many things, but seems almost afraid of being overwhelmed by a zeal for research and experimentation which could drain the artistic expression of any human content'.[1]

Alexeïeff's art was strengthened by the artist's isolation, by his quiet awareness of not belonging to any fashionable currents and by his consequent renunciation of the praise of a large public. His art is refined, sometimes aristocratic, but never 'cult'. Hoffmann and Poe, Dostoevsky and Pasternak were travelling companions rather than models for a filmmaker who never had masters other than himself and whose art was not born from his books, but from his life.

Alexeïeff's two poetry works, *A Night* and *Pictures*, contrast with the more lengthy narrative of *Passing By* and *The Nose*. *The Nose* derives from a short story by Gogol about a barber who finds a nose in a loaf of bread, a young man who wakes up without his facial ornament, and the nose itself which seeks a life of its own. The film is related to Alexeïeff's other activity as a book illustrator: without literally following the text, Alexeïeff the illustrator entered the spirit of the book and rewrote it through images. *The Nose* does not repeat Gogol's plot, but creates a poem in its own right, a 'salute to Gogol'. It is an interweaving of the few events making up the story with delicate images of Nineteenth century Russia, flash-like syntheses of space and time, meta-

---

1   Catalogue of the exhibition honouring Alexeïeff. Giannalberto Bendazzi ed. (Milan, Italy), 1973.

morphoses of objects, constructions, living beings, dark mysterious figures rising from the pavement and then disappearing after having communicated nothing but their presence. The film is a splendid example of modern and surrealist narration, created by a man 'who had learned spontaneity' from surrealism.

The prologue Alexeïeff created for *The Trial* can also be connected to book illustration. Images are fixed, following one another on the screen like pages turned by hand. The only changes consist of the passing from a lighter to a darker tone, obtained during the film developing. The value of such experience suggests a careful examination of Alexeïeff's fascinating work as an engraver. It was tightly linked to his activity in cinema, to the point that he theorized and applied a real montage to this artform: in the relation between printed pages and illustrated pages; in the number of consecutive illustrated pages; and in the number of printed pages separating the illustrated ones. Such an analysis, however, deserves a separate essay.

Trois thèmes, created in Alexeïeff's old age, is almost a goodbye and a will. In the first segment, very slow images are superimposed like final memories of the Russian countryside; the second

summarizes several framings from *Pictures*, in a sort of self-quotation serving to reaffirm the artist's own inspiration; and the third segment features Goldenberg and Schmuyl, the former heavy and rich, ready to produce coins by striking his hammer, the latter in the form of a fluttering bird, poor and creative. Schmuyl resembles Mussorgsky and, in Alexeïeff's words, symbolizes 'the artist as opposed to those who own money'. It is impossible not to notice also an autobiographical portrait by Alexeïeff, who throughout his life rigorously rejected the influence of commercialism. Although these observations have stressed Alexandre Alexeïeff's masterful creativity, Claire Parker's role should not be overlooked. An inspirer and supporter, she was gifted with a lively sense of movement – the couple loved to define themselves as 'the artist and the animator'. Able by logic to catalyse the most daring dreams of her companion, Claire deservedly co-signed every film. In the course of friendly conversations, the two wondered, 'What would have happened had we operated separately?'; when asked alone, Claire Parker never had a doubt. 'He is the genius,' she used to say.

Norman McLaren

Born in Stirling, Scotland, on 11 April 1914, Norman McLaren showed a precocious inclination toward the arts. His father, an interior designer, had a natural interest in painting and did not refuse his son's request to study at the School of Fine Arts in Glasgow, in 1933. There, young McLaren discovered cinema; he organized a school film club, tirelessly viewing films by the contemporary masters, the Soviet filmmakers and the German 'expressionists'. Eventually, he discovered a 35mm projector which had been abandoned in the school basement and which was practically out of order. McLaren repaired it hoping to use the machine to project his own film. Not owning a camera, he thought of painting directly on stock. He immersed an old positive film in a water bowl in order to detach the

Fig. 49. Alexandre Alexeïeff and Claire Parker in front of the pinscreen with a scene of 3 thèmes *(France, late 1970s).*

emulsion and after two weeks he began drawing coloured circles and dots on the transparent sheet. Although this work did not result in an actual film worth projecting, it was a promising experiment.

From 1934 to 1936, McLaren made some 16mm films, which obtained praise from the school directors and which stood out in local festivals. They were live action films, enriched with slow motion, special effects and colour; among them, *Hell Unltd.* (1936), a pacifist film that attacked the nationalists with a harshness uncommon to McLaren, took an appealing, direct stance against war and militarism.

In 1937, McLaren joined the General Post Office, in London, under the sponsorship of Grierson and Cavalcanti and worked with Len Lye, the artist who had preceded him in painting directly on film stock. There McLaren created two live action documentaries and two animated *scherzos*, *Money a Pickle* and *Love on the Wing* (both 1938). The latter film contained excerpts which had been painted on the frame; it was McLaren's first official use of this technique.

Having left the GPO, after a brief collaboration with the Film Centre in London, McLaren moved to the United States. He landed in New York in 1939, with three-hundred dollars and the determination to work. After a job-search of several months, he finally obtained financing from the Guggenheim Foundation, for some very short films such as *Dots* and *Loops*. They were short films little more than two minutes long and were painted directly on the film frame. They featured coloured forms attracting and repelling, engulfing and then separating. The sound also was abstract, obtained through mechanical modification of the sound track. McLaren's interest in synthetic sound culminated with *Rumba*, a film without images, composed only of artificially obtained music. *Stars & Stripes* was more traditional, painted directly on film stock with images referring to the American flag, featuring the popular song of the same name.

For his last film in New York, *Spook Sport*, McLaren worked with Mary Ellen Bute, author of abstract films. The effort was, however, faulty, satisfying neither McLaren nor, most likely, Bute. Meanwhile, John Grierson, who had been put in charge by the Canadian government to organize a national office for film production, invited McLaren to renew their collaboration in Ottawa.[1] In Canada, the twenty-seven year old McLaren found favourable ground for his research. For two years, he created short films, with the precise goal of helping the Canadian war effort by moving citizens to buy Defense Bonds, explaining the danger of inflation and promoting savings. Those same films, *Hen Hop* (1942), *Dollar Dance* (1943) and *V for Victory* (1941) were also extraordinary experiments in filmmaking.

In 1943, McLaren was asked to organize a separate department of the National Film Board of Canada that would be dedicated to animation, and to hire the most promising young animators, students of art schools and amateurs. As a consequence, George Dunning (the future author of *Yellow Submarine*), Jean-Paul Ladouceur, René Jodoin, Jim McKay and Grant Munro joined the NFB. In 1944, in collaboration with Jodoin, McLaren made a film with cut paper, *Alouette*(The Lark) which marked the beginning of a second stage for experimentation.

By illustrating three popular songs of French Canada, *C'est l'aviron* (It Is the Paddle, 1943), *La poulette grise* (The Young Grey Hen, 1947), and *La-haut sur ces montagnes* (Up There on Those Mountains, 1945), McLaren perfected two techniques which also represented two

---

1   Still in April 1941, Grierson made an agreement with Disney for five cartoons of war propaganda. Later, he entrusted the job completely to McLaren. It is curious how these two diametrically opposed animators happened to compete at the same time, on the same topic.

styles: the perpetual travelling forward in space (*C'est l'aviron*), and the continuous metamorphosis of pastel drawings (*La poulette grise*). He applied an analogous process – the drawing making itself – to pictorial works, the first of which was *A Little Phantasy on a 19th Century Painting*, an elaboration of Arnold Boecklin's *The Isle of the Dead*. This film, however, was one of the least successful works by the Scottish animator. Similar defects emerged in the second film *A Phantasy*, an elaboration of a painting vaguely inspired by Tanguy.

In 1947, McLaren returned to painting directly on film. This time, he wanted to escape the slavery of frames by painting, instead, lengthwise on the stock. The first attempt at this new technique was entitled *Fiddle-De-Dee*, lasting four minutes. The second, more complex film was the ten minute long *Begone Dull Care* (1949, with jazz music by Oscar Peterson's trio, see Colour Plate 12). *Begone Dull Care* won several prizes, and a praise by Picasso: 'Finally, something new!'

In 1949, McLaren left for China on a mission sponsored by UNESCO, with the goal of teaching visual communication to the local artists working on preventive medicine propaganda. He came back satisfied and spiritually enriched, reassuring his friends who had feared for his safety (at that time, the region of Szechuan where McLaren had worked, had been the stage of the withdrawal of the nationalists and the advance of the revolutionary troops). In 1951, McLaren approached the problems of stereoscopy with *Around is Around*. One year later, he applied the frame-by-frame technique to live actors. In *Neighbors*, his colleagues Grant Munro and Jean-Paul Ladouceur played two neighbours who liked and respected each other until a matter of boundaries (a flower born on the dividing line between their two lots) led to hate, violence and mutual destruction. The effects of the frame-by-frame process on human movement are surprising. The original work was awarded an Oscar. McLaren received the telegram of congratulations in India, where he was involved in a social project. He answered, candidly: 'Thanks, but who is Oscar?'.

Fig. 50. Blinkity Blank *by Norman McLaren (Canada, 1954). [©NFB of Canada}*

In 1954, he made *Blinkity Blank*, by engraving black stock with a pin and a small blade. After the comic *Rythmetic* (1956), *A Chairy Tale* (1957) and *Le merle* (The Thrush, 1958), he returned to abstractionism. *Lines Vertical* (1960) featured the dance of a line which splits in two, then in four and so on, eventually returning to a single line. This pure geometric abstraction takes place on a background of pale colours. *Lines Horizontal* followed: a similar film, transposed on the other Cartesian axis by means of a prism. After *Opening Speech* (1960), *Canon* (1964) and *Mosaic* (1965), McLaren directed *Pas de deux* (1967), probably his masterpiece and certainly one of the best animated films overall.

In 1969, he made the sound track, with music by Bach, for his *Spheres*, a film which had been lying in a drawer for twenty years. He then released *Synchromy* (1971), simultaneously featuring the music of the eye and of the ear, and *Ballet adagio* (1972), using the technique of slow motion – a film in which baroque music (Albinoni's *Adagio*) corresponded to 'baroque' images of unreleased impulses and knotty muscles. McLaren's last work was *Narcissus* (1983), the conclusion to the trilogy about dance. For reasons related to production, health and perhaps lack of inspiration, the completed film differed from the initial project and was unsatisfactory in several aspects, lacking the visual creativity and the figurative precision which had characterized the artist's finest works. The filmmaker died in Montreal on 26 January 1987.

The events of McLaren's life mingled with his work and research, which took place within the economic and social security offered by the Canadian National Film Board. With the very rare position as a 'court artist inside a democratic state', McLaren was a producer of culture, supported and financed so that he could express himself. This privilege was even more unique as his films were never made for a large public, but contrarily, were the work of a tenacious, hermit-

like personality, quite isolated from his contemporaries.

At a first viewing, McLaren's work usually baffles the spectator. The exuberance of the unusual techniques, the absence of a 'meaning', the apparent coldness are difficult elements for an audience used to other means of visual communication. Although many years have passed since Picasso's *Demoiselles d'Avignon*, many audiences have not yet acquired a taste for non-objective art, and therefore, for non-objective cinematographic art. Undoubtedly, McLaren's works, not all of which are abstract, have 'content'. For instance, *Neighbors* and *A Chairy Tale* are two short, enjoyable philosophic tales, and some of his abstract films are rich with figurative or narrative passages. The inclusion of content, however, was McLaren's least concern. In his words, animation is not the art of moving drawings, but of the drawn movement; the key is not what one finds in a drawing, but what is created between drawings linked in a series.

> 'Every film for me is a kind of dance, because the most important thing in film is motion, movement. No matter what it is you're moving, whether it's people or objects or drawings; and in what way it's done, it's a form of dance'.

Once more, we have the distinction between abstract film and music, rhythm of light and rhythm of sound. Abstract films are like a symphony, from which ordinarily one does not require any rational 'meaning', and which often lacks narrative and figurative content (Mussorgsky is the one exception which confirms the rule). McLaren's style consists especially of rhythm and coherence (or even fusion) of the visual rhythm with the rhythm of sound. Just as a musician writes parts for different instruments, McLaren gives rhythm to human figures, objects, drawings and graffiti on film.

The scholar who chooses to evaluate McLaren's opus as if it were the work of a composer will notice that *Blinkity Blank* is more than just a clever discovery by the inventor of the technique of graffiti on black film stock. The film is a passage of visual jazz as it had never before been conceived. The black spaces, the dark moments have the same meaning and the same effect as certain pauses in contemporary music. Conditions of perception are created in which even flashing images, perhaps lasting one frame only, acquire life and strength, and the line of light erupting from the obscure background weaves and dances in tempos which have never before existed.

'I am not simply "un auteur experimental", but also, or even rather, "un auteur experimenté",' said McLaren.[1] His complex personality escapes facile definition; a spiritual descendant of Leonardo da Vinci, he considered science, art, technique and style as one whole, belonging to the same system of values. For him it was important to have a technical challenge; he often researched the technique first and later established the subject of a film. Once he accepted the technical rationale, he accepted the creative challenge with a perfectly 'surreal' method: in the making of a film, he believed, animation is not premeditated, but evolves from day to day, with concrete and imaginary attributes deriving from a subconscious current which the artist himself, by his own admission, does not dare to control. McLaren's work is clearly marked with this perennial dialectic between applied reason and creative feeling. Just as he used graphics and a nearly hellenic structural balance, he was also exuberant in the invention of sounds and images.[2]

Synchromy, the work of his maturity, was a sort of summation of his long research. Here, the same images which produced music on the sound track had been impressed on the visual film by the author.[3] The movement of images *is* the movement of sounds: the ambitious goal of composing a work in which image and sound coincide is reached here more than anywhere else.[4] Paraphrasing Shakespeare, Gavin Millar remarked, 'the eye hears, the ear sees'. With meticulous research and rigorous logical construction, McLaren displays his artistic taste, almost disarmingly unsystematic in the use of colour.

'I did not make this a B&W film, as it would have been less tolerable to look at, and also because I was trying to use the colour functionally wherever possible. True, I kept the decorative aspect in mind, but I used colour also with certain relationships to the sound in mind.

'The *loudness-quietness* gamut was often related to the degree of *colour saturation* and tone-value (luminosity) contrast. For example, for a pianissimo passage I would use colours of low saturation, and low mutual contrast in luminosity. For *fortissimo* I would use maximum saturation, maximum light-value of the colour, irrespective of which hue was used. ... These are my general principles, which I have not theorized about, but only felt intuitively, and which I used *loosely* in many abstract films, such as *Begone Dull Care*, *Mosaic* and *Lines*.'[5]

1   Letter received from Norman McLaren, 22 June 1972.

2   In spite of their diversity, many works such as *Little Phantasy*, *Rhythmetic*, *Lines*, *Canon*, *Pas de deux* and *Synchromy* share the same clear-cut structure 'introductory theme-development-return to theme'.

3   Starting from the fact that the optical track is formed by images (optical translations of sound vibrations, which are read by an electronic instrument and later re-transformed into sound at the time of projection), McLaren researched for years a way to obtain sounds not existing in nature, by drawing images to be inserted in the sound track. He finally obtained six 'synthetic' octaves, on which he composed the music he later illustrated in *Synchromy*.

4   A very similar experiment had been made in 1933 by László Moholy-Nagy: in *Tönendes ABC* (ABC of Sounds). He made letters of the alphabet, silhouettes and fingerprints produce noise on sound track. This experiment did not have any immediate relevance until McLaren started his research. Work on the drawing of sound tracks was performed also in other countries, such as Germany (with Fischinger and Pfenninger) and the Soviet Union.

5   Letter received from Norman McLaren, 9 August 1972.

A loner in cinema, McLaren never forgot his social role as an artist.

> 'I'd always been interested in human problems, but particularly when as a teenager in my late teens and early twenties ... and as an amateur I made an anti-war film[1] ... I sort of drifted off into abstract films and got more and more detached from human problems but ... two months after I went to China the communists took over and I saw what was happening in our village because of them, and a lot of good things happened. ... So I became fairly sympathetic to the new regime. ... When I came back to Canada, it was just at the beginning of the Korean war and I felt myself being estranged to some extent, or being pulled between one culture and another, one side and another side and [with] the tension that built up in me because of this I produced *Neighbors* ... I have sympathy for things that are sat upon ... the exploited, the underdog.'

As to why he did not return often to the theme of *Neighbors*, McLaren explained that it depended on his interest in abstractionism.

> Abstract cinema ... is like music which is an abstraction. It doesn't refer to things outside of itself ... I've been really concerned about exploring the field of abstraction; in other words visual ideas that do not refer to anything outside of themselves.'[2]

The concepts McLaren expressed in his films have various degrees of acceptability: the anti-war indignation of *Neighbors* is sincere, but the fable of human greed and egotism as a source of war is quite simplistic. In fact, McLaren is not a polemicist. If *Neighbors* was a good film, this was due to its cinematographic 'form'.

McLaren also had a comic side, which should not

be overlooked. Subtle and discrete, in a very British manner, his humour filters throughout his productions, from the films which had been painted on stock (*Hen Hop* featured a hen who lost her legs), to the graffiti (as in some sequences of *Blinkity Blank*), to the films made from cut-outs (*Rythmetric* was a small masterpiece) and especially in the films with live actors. *A Chairy Tale* (made in collaboration with the mime and, later, director Claude Jutra) was an enjoyable film close to the style of Keaton and to the 'struggle with objects' characteristic of the Keystone comedians. A different kind of struggle is featured in *Opening Speech* where the rebellious object is a microphone. McLaren himself tries to tame the instrument, which spitefully lengthens and shortens preventing him from saying more than 'Ladies and gentlemen ... '. For an artist who prefers to express himself with images rather than words, the simplest solution is to give the microphone its freedom and to dive into the screen, releasing animated expressions of welcome. (The film was the opening presentation at the Montreal Festival of 1960.)

Fig. 51. Pas de deux *by Norman McLaren (Canada, 1967). [©NFB of Canada]*

---

1   *Hell Unltd.*
2   Gavin Millar, *The Eye Hears and the Ear Sees* (post production script for the documentary, produced by the BBC and ONF, 1970).

McLaren's work is very complex, large and richly faceted, so much so that there still remain several unexplored areas and diverse possibilities of interpretation. André Martin wrote:

'The persistence of themes and motifs indicates something more than a simple interest in the kingdom of the unconscious. It indicates the author's fidelity, which takes into account a personal reality, accurately, obstinately expressed. The criticism of incoherent emptiness which has been sometimes directed at him should have been substituted with diagnoses of schizophrenia or abusive egocentrism, had the value of his films not proven that his art is very different from an imaginative refuge. His images have a biographical starting point and are founded on a personal reality, conscious and unconscious'.[1]

An introspective poet, a delirious dreamer of moving geometric forms, an explorer of the lesser known areas of cinematic art, a man versed in technical research and inventions, McLaren is as versatile as a Renaissance artist. As the prototype of technologically based art of our century, his work is detached from daily problems as well as from active imitation. The artist's goal is the future redemption of the creative man. In a Leonardo-like fashion, he claims the task of interpreting the new age of applied science and technology, becoming a mediator between human beings, who have remained weak, and the machine, which has become dominant. McLaren is one of the few people in cinema who have been able to renovate and update the aesthetic experience.

Oskar Fischinger

Oskar Fischinger was born on 22 June 1900 in Gelnhausen, Hesse (Germany). After secondary school, he moved to Frankfurt and found em-

ployment as a technical artist. In a Frankfurt literary circle he met Bernhard Diebold, a local critic open to novelty. Following Diebold's suggestion, Fischinger painted two rolls of paper illustrating the dynamics of Fritz von Unruh's drama, *Der Platz* (The Square)[2] and Shakespeare's *As You Like It*. When the members of the circle found the experiment hard to understand, Fischinger did not get discouraged, but wondered what elements could have made his paintings clear to everybody. He found the answer in movement, and through cinema he studied the possibilities of moving paintings. In 1921, he designed a machine which enabled him to conduct experiments with abstract films. He placed a parallel piped shaped conglomerate of coloured waxes on a sort of slicer with a rotating blade. He set the camera in front of the device so that the shutter was synchronized with the movement of the blade. Cut after cut, the camera filmed the changing features traced by the veins inside the wax.

In April 1921, Diebold introduced Fischinger to Walther Ruttmann, who was then leaving painting for cinema. In 1922, Fischinger moved to Munich and founded two companies: one, in partnership with Louis Seel, oriented toward the production of animated, conventional short films; and the other, in partnership with a fellow named Guttler, for developing another of Fischinger's inventions, a motor which burned inert gases without pollution. Walther Ruttmann, who also lived in Munich, visited Fischinger a few times, and in November 1922 bought one of his machines for filming the wax cuttings along with the rights to use it for commercial purposes.

After four years of work, Fischinger's two companies closed, submerged by debts, grudges, and lawsuits. Depressed, Fischinger also had to face the fact that Ruttmann and Lotte Reiniger had used his machine to film some scenic effects for

---

1   André Martin, 'i x i = ou le cinema de deux mains (II partie),' *Cahiers du cinéma*, No. 40, 1958, Paris).
2   Second part of the *Das Geschlecht* trilogy (The Generation Trilogy).

their *Adventures of Prince Achmed*. 'Others are lapping up the cream that belongs to me,' he wrote to Diebold – a strong expression of anger, since Ruttman and Reiniger were using a machine which had been legally bought.

In 1930, he gave a copy of his *Studie n. 6* to Paul Hindemith, who intended to use it as an exercise for the students in his Conservatory. Starting from their impressions of the visual rhythm, the students composed several musical scores for the film (which actually featured jazz music by Jacinto Guerrero, synchronized with recordings).

Albeit difficult, the four years Fischinger spent in Munich were not wasted. Demonstrating from the beginning an extraordinary prolificacy, the artist completed *Wachsexperimenten* (Wax Experiments), in which he explored the possibilities of the wax machine, several hand-coloured essays which he had obtained with different techniques, two sample-films (*Vakuum* and *Fieber*) to be shown with five projectors working simultaneously, and finally, *Orgelstabe* (Organ Staffs), a work featuring several rolls of abstract film composed of parallel bars moving with different rhythms. Fischinger also made six traditional animated shorts (the *Münchener Bilderbogen*, or *Picture Sheets from Munich*, created for Seel), special effects for some unidentified full length films, and a charming, original experiment with cutouts entitled *Seelische Konstruktionen* (Spiritual Constructions).[1]

In 1927, tired of Munich, Fischinger decided to move to Berlin. During the trip (on foot!), he shot pictures of people and places he met. Later, he used these pictures for a film, made of very quick flashes: *München-Berlin Wanderung* (Munich-Berlin Walking Tour). In 1928, he accepted a job with UFA, where he created special effects for Fritz Lang's *Frau im Mond* (The Woman in the Moon), but an accident in which he broke an ankle cost him his contract (1929). While in the hospital, he worked intensively in charcoal and decided to devote himself to the creation of abstract films with musical tracks. From 1929 to 1930, he composed eight *Studien* (Studies), accompanying them with different kinds of music, from fandango to jazz to Brahms's *Hungarian Dance No. 5*.

The German public showed an appreciation for avant-garde production, and Fischinger was able to expand his staff. In 1931, he hired his cousin Elfriede, an artist ten years his junior who would later become his wife. Shortly thereafter, his brother Hans joined him for a brief period. *Studie n. 8* remained unfinished for lack of funds needed to purchase the rights to Dukas's *The Sorcerer's Apprentice*. Fischinger asked for his brother's help on later studies. Together they collaborated on *Studien* 9 and 10. Oskar made 11 and 13 (the latter unfinished), while Hans worked on 12 and prepared the drawings on paper for number 14, although he never made them into a

Fig. 52. Oskar Fischinger with his paintings (USA, late 1940s).

---

1   This may be a pun in German on the name of the client for *Münchener Bilderbogen*.

film. Shortly afterward, in 1933, Hans left the partnership.

While working on the *Studien*, Oskar found time to research a purely visual rhythm without any musical support; the result was *Liebesspiel*, (Loveplay, 1931). He also tried other experiments. With Bela Gaspar he explored the problems of colour film. He worked to create synthetic sound – a field which was to be McLaren's. Fischinger designed a series of images which generated special sounds when they were transported to the optical sound track area of the film. Using a procedure he developed with Gaspar (Gasparcolor), he made *Kreise* (Circles, 1933), his first important work in colour, featuring a play of circles in space. One year later, he filmed a colourized version of *Studie n. 11*, with music by Mozart, and entitled it *Studie n. 11 A*. Then he made an advertising film for Muratti cigarettes. Ironically, of all his artistic creations, it was this work which made him famous. With the support of a good commercial distribution system, the short circulated in theatres for a long time. From 1934 to 1935, the artist worked on his most ambitious project: 'rhythmic' animation linked to the third dimension and colour. The film, entitled *Komposition in Blau* (Composition in Blue), with music from the overture to Otto Nicolai's *Merry Wives of Windsor*, was shot in Gasparcolor, utilizing solid forms (see Colour Plate 13).

Meanwhile, abstract art, which in Hitler and Goebbels' dictionary meant degenerate, had been prohibited. For some time, Fischinger managed to continue his activity by defining his films as 'decorative' rather than abstract. Then he accepted an invitation by Paramount, a company which had followed the artist's European success, and decided to cross the ocean. On 11 February 1936, Fischinger left Germany.

Once in Hollywood, the artist was asked to set up a long abstract sequence for *The Big Broadcast of 1937* (1937), a typical Hollywood musical show featuring brief appearances by a large number of stars. Fischinger utilized a jazz score, entitled *Radio Dynamics*, by Ralph Rainger, one of Paramount's musicians.[1] Eventually, the producers decided to make *The Big Broadcast of 1937* in black and white and wanted to transform the abstract short accordingly. Fischinger, who had worked on the short with colour in mind, refused. The contract was broken in September. Following advice from his friends – among them painter Lyonel Feininger – Fischinger decided to simultaneously make his living by painting: a hard choice for an artist convinced that 'oil on canvas' was a thing of the past, an artistic medium inferior to cinema.

Fischinger's Hollywood career continued. In 1938, he made *Optical Poem* for MGM, based on Liszt's *Second Hungarian Rhapsody.*; and in 1942, he was approached by Orson Welles, who was planning a biographical film on Louis Armstrong, although this effort never reached fruition. Afterward, Fischinger took a trip to New York to seek financial support for his projects, which included an abstract feature film inspired by the *Symphony from the New World*, by Dvorak. While this idea failed, personal exhibitions of Fischinger's work opened in two New York galleries.

Fischinger's brief collaboration with Disney began when the German artist contacted orchestra conductor Leopold Stokowsky about the possibility of a film based on Bach's *Toccata and Fugue*. Stokowsky suggested the project to Disney, who started working on *Fantasia* and hired Fischinger. Disney showed the drawings that Fischinger had generated for *Fantasia* to his staff. The German artist's designs were then systematically manipulated by Disney's crew and changed to a more figurative form, more easily accepted by audiences. Eventually, Fischinger left the production and in the film's credits there is no

---

1   Rainger made another attempt at animation by preparing music for a very different project, the Fleischers' *Gulliver's Travels*.

trace of his collaboration.

Throughout the years, Fischinger's house became a meeting place for a large group of intellectuals. The Whitney brothers met there to discuss synthetic sound. Maya Deren, Kenneth Anger and musicians John Cage – creator of aleatory music – and Edgar Varèse also would gather there. Much of the conversation focused on Oriental philosophy, and Fischinger never stopped expounding on his theory of the correspondence between optical vibration and sound vibration. Using one of Cage's musical compositions, he began a new film but soon quit, convinced that the public would have never been able to accept it.

Fischinger's exhibitions, however, increased and so did his contacts with the Guggenheim Foundation. In 1940, the curator of the Solomon Guggenheim Foundation, Hilla Rebay Von Ehrenwiesen, financed a new short film by Fischinger, *An American March*, with the music of *Stars and Stripes Forever*. She also bought the film originally entitled *Radio Dynamics* from Paramount and had it remade. *Radio Dynamics* then came back to life, when the title of the old film was given to a new, complex experiment without a sound track. In 1946, the painter Jordan Belson, impressed by Fischinger's films, wanted to meet the artist and follow in his path. Fischinger himself introduced the painter to the Guggenheim Foundation for the purpose of obtaining finance.

Still in 1946, Fischinger began his last work, *Motion Painting No. 1*, with a musical score from Bach's *Third Brandenburg Concerto*. The film was a novelty for the filmmaker, who renounced his search for strict, mechanical correlations between sound and image. *Motion Painting No. 1* is based on the constant transformation of a painting on plexiglass, a sort of return, twenty years later, to Eggeling's way of making cinema. The extraordinary power of this work, however, was not understood by the Guggenheim Founda-

tion, which considered it disappointing and refused to grant the money necessary to make copies of the film. This episode ended the long period in which Fischinger had been encouraged, but also overwhelmed, by his mentor, Hilla Rebay.

In the following years, Fischinger did not have further opportunities to make films. In 1950, he returned to his inventions, patenting his lumigraph, 'a living-room instrument, large as a big piano, for the production of light shows'. In 1953, due to financial problems, he abandoned his studies on stereoscopic film. Suffering from heart disease, he gradually reduced his volcanic pace of activity, limiting himself to painting and directing a few advertising films. In 1961, he tried to begin *Motion Painting No. 2*, but soon abandoned the project. Fischinger died on 31 January 1967, at the age of 66.

The roots of Fischinger's interest in cinema can probably be found in Diebold's encouragement as well as in the artist's meeting with Walther Ruttmann (later on, Fischinger tried to play down the importance of this meeting and wrote that he had begun his experiments earlier). Thirteen years older than Fischinger, Ruttmann was a prestigious painter and filmmaker, who certainly influenced the young artist. Given Fischinger's indomitable and jealous character, Ruttmann influenced him more by example than direct teaching (Fischinger continued to admire Ruttmann as an artist, even while complaining about him as a person). It seems that Fischinger and Eggeling also became friends, or at least, if they never met personally, Fischinger held Eggeling's work in great esteem. Conversely, he did not appreciate Hans Richter. Fischinger maintained a close relationship with Moholy-Nagy, Kandinsky and with the Bauhaus group as a whole. He was invited to participate in the Bauhaus but because of his individualism he refused the offer.

Only after 1930, did Fischinger question himself about the meaning of his work. He always wrote much about his films to friends and acquaintances, or even to himself. He confessed that in *Composition in Blue* he had wanted to express joy. *Optical Poem* was a digression on the relation between body and movement, between the parts of a whole and the whole itself. *Radio Dynamics* was based on the concept that colours are relative and that their value depends on the way they are perceived.

A person of multiple interests, Fischinger studied astronomy and atomic and molecular science, deepening his knowledge of physics and reading Einstein. He was a friend of the pacifist and Nobel prize laureate Linus Pauling and worked out a series of philosophical-mystical ideas according to which microcosmic and macrocosmic worlds share common laws and relationships. Another of Fischinger's many facets was his love of Goethe, whose philosophy he found very close to his own (particularly the first part of *Faust*). Fischinger's conception of the world and life led him to practice Buddhist philosophy and yoga. He often drew human eyes, including the third eye of knowledge, always changing its colour. His interest in Buddhism increased in his last years and came to involve his lifestyle during a time when Buddhist theories, especially the Zen version, were very popular among American intellectuals.[1]

As for music, Fischinger's attitude fluctuated. Initially, he argued that music was only a means to attract audiences, who already knew a certain 'music', or who, in any case, found it pleasant. In short, music had a merely accessory-like function. Whenever possible, films were to be silent. Later on, he considered music as a teaser (and a very acceptable one from a linguistic standpoint), used to induce the public to concentrate on an abstract film. He even gave up a planned film with the avant-garde composer Cage precisely because the music was 'unpleasant' to the ears of a traditional public. More than any other artist, he kept alive the search for a visual rhythm, meticulously linked to sound rhythm. He loved music and wanted to imitate it, trying to steal its secrets of harmony, melody and counterpoint, and transfer them to the field of images. Fischinger used to say that his dream was to create a new art-form, which he defined as 'Colour Rhythm'. He praised the 19th century composers because, in his opinion, they had created a new world, 'the abstract language of sound'.

Fischinger's production includes at least five major works, the first of which is the group of *Studien*. Sharing the same stylistic and technical choices, the *Studien* can be considered as chapters of one novel. They are composed of abstract elements (dots, geometrical forms), intertwining and moving in correspondence with sound; each of these elements playing an instrumental part in the creation of an optical symphony.

Composition in Blue has more historic than aesthetic importance. Although it is sometimes questionable and pompous, trying too hard to amaze, it is the first abstract film utilizing all three dimensions like a moving set design. Here Fischinger uses not only forms and colours (with a

*Fig. 53.
Komposition in Blau by Oskar Fischinger (Germany, 1935).*

Komposition in Blau   Oscar Fischinger

1   William Moritz, *Oskar Fischinger*, unpublished mss.

primitive though fascinating Gasparcolor), but also space: abstract sculpture, made real through rhythm.

Optical Poem, the film Fischinger made for MGM, has been defined by some as the 'abstract rendition' of the cat-and-mouse chase which the production company was to release in a figurative edition later on. The film is a long travelling pan-shot in the horizontal direction, a long trip across an abstract space in which polychromatic geometric forms intertwine and 'chase' each other following the rhythm of Liszt's music. As in earlier experiments, here also Fischinger builds a distinct physiognomical correspondence: low sounds to round shapes, higher sounds to triangular shapes. Colour is used with a freedom unknown to American animators. The basic tonality of the film is a strident yellow ochre, with the appearance of unusual colours, such as saturated brown.

Radio Dynamics is perhaps the artist's masterpiece. The finesse and complexity of invention are balanced for the most part, and the novelty of visual elements is more advanced than in earlier works. William Moritz, a scholar of Fischinger's films, based his interpretation of this work on yoga-spirituality.[1]

Finally, the most recent effort, *Motion Painting*, was no longer mechanically linked to music but became an interpretation of the music itself. Featuring two different movements and different rhythms interrelating, this is a painting in movement as well as an animated film. As never before, both film and fine art critics are summoned. It is yet another demonstration of the lack of precise boundaries in the visual arts.

1   William Moritz, 'The Films of Oskar Fischinger,' *Film Culture* No. 58, 59, 60 (1974), pp. 156–157.

III

The next three decades (1940–1970)

Chapter 11

The United States of America

The industry

The fifteen years from 1945 to 1960 were a contradictory time for the United States. Victory in the war, together with an extraordinary economic expansion and the simultaneous collapse of the traditional world powers gave the US a position of world leadership. To the world, America presented a picture of prosperity, generosity and optimism – an image reinforced by American financial aid, particularly to Europe. Such splendor, however, was not faultless. The Cold War against the Soviet Union hid psychological disquiet and phobia which materialized in the McCarthyite persecution of the Left. Cinema replaced the portrayal of the bold American, naïve perhaps but always inexhaustible, with new characters and new actors (from Clift to Brando, Dean and Perkins) who expressed anxiety, uneasiness and neurosis. Juvenile crime increased, and the large American middle-class gradually became aware of its socio-cultural fragmentation. Beatnik communities arose to propose an autonomous counter-culture. The consumer age broke out with the popularization of television, modifying decades-old patterns of thought and behaviour.

It was precisely television which helped precipitate the crisis of cinema. Starting in 1946, the sale of television sets increased dramatically; shortly afterward, the networks began broadcasting in colour. This new kind of home entertainment kept huge numbers of spectators away from the theatres. Then, in 1948, with a decision which ended years of litigation, the Supreme Court upheld the ruling in the *United States vs. Paramount et al.* trial, involving all major California movie companies, pursuant to the antitrust law. From that time on the three components of production, distribution and exhibition were to be separated. The verdict terminated the companies' monopoly over spectators and ended the lifestyle and work methods which had characterized the entertainment field – in short, it marked the end of legendary Hollywood. Comedy evolved. Deprived of artists such as Capra, Lubitsch and Stevens, it survived through the work of craftsmen and through the caustic films of Billy Wilder.

In the late 1950s, causticity became a rule outside cinema, with the 'sick comedians' – educated entertainers, well versed in quick political gags and dirty words, who addressed students and intellectuals in the thousands of night clubs which spread like mushrooms after the war. Their favourite topic: the American malaise. The group, which included Lenny Bruce, Mort Sahl and Dick Gregory, exerted its influence for years, spawning artists such as Woody Allen. On the contrary, the old slapstick comedy, with its absurd pyrotechnics, was dismissed as being definitively naïve, as the inheritance of a 'childish' age; Jerry Lewis and Bob Hope, who partially hearken back to it, became isolated phenomena.

In music, beside the experiments of the likes of John Cage, bebop reigned; a form of jazz born in the black ghetto, it was, by its own definition, the expression of an 'alternative' culture. Artists such as jazz musician Charlie Parker, writer Jack Kerouac, poet Allen Ginsberg and painter Jackson Pollock were all heralds of a marginal world and the bearers of stylistically overflowing, rebellious ideas. Initially, what they all wanted was to detach themselves from the mainstream of American culture; inevitably, they were absorbed and embraced by the market (especially Pollock and his colleagues of Action Painting).

Within this background, animation played quite an important role. Still, Hollywood animation shared the fate of the film industry in general; as its most frail branch, it was the first to dry out. Animated shorts, which had always been used as fillers, were eliminated without being really missed when costs rose. Gradually, animation studios shrank and eventually closed. Very few young artists joined studio staffs, and only a few original ideas hatched (one exception was UPA). Disney was the first to reduce production of shorts, concentrating on feature films and later on other projects such as live-action features for children, documentaries on the wonders of nature and the very successful amusement parks. In the meanwhile, avant-garde groups collected the spiritual inheritance of Mary Ellen Bute and

Oskar Fischinger and gave rise to new rich productions of abstract animation which perfectly complemented the stylistic and linguistic research of off-Hollywood filmmakers.

Traditional round shaped drawings (O style) could no longer compare with the drawings of comic-strip artists, fashionable cartoonists and advertisers. Animators found themselves looking with awe at the style of artists such as Thurber and Steinberg, and at the cerebral humour of the corrosive New York magazine, *Mad*. Despite the presence of a few personalities from the Golden Age who continued their artistic careers and even peaked professionally in the period we are now examining (this was the case with Chuck Jones), the 1940s and 1950s belong by right to a small revolutionary studio: UPA.

UPA

In 1944, Dave Hilberman, Zachary 'Zack' Schwartz and Stephen Bosustow, three former-employees of Disney who had left the company during the 1941 strike, joined efforts to produce a short political film for Franklin Delano Roosevelt: *Hell Bent for Election*. Somewhat grandly, they named their company United Productions of America, or UPA.

At first, they devoted themselves to non-fiction productions, including educational and propaganda films. These works already displayed traces of the innovative research which would characterize the years to come, and which was largely due to a newly hired staff of scene designers and lay-out experts John Hubley, Paul Julian, Jules Engel, Bill Hurtz and Herb Klynn), directors (Bob Cannon) and screenwriters (Phil Eastman).

In 1946, Hilberman and Schwartz withdrew from the enterprise, and Stephen Bosustow remained as the only executive producer. It was under his guidance that UPA became famous. Bosustow[1]

---

1   The name, which suggests Slavic roots, is actually from Cornwall.

had a complex, contradictory personality. Born in Victoria, British Columbia (6 November 1911), he moved to California years before his debut at MGM in 1931. A good scriptwriter, he worked for Walter Lantz before joining Disney in 1934. Once at Disney, he collaborated on a Mickey Mouse series and on films such as *Snow White*, *Bambi* and *Fantasia*.

As the leader of UPA he demonstrated good organizational skills, respect for the talent and culture of his collaborators and great energy. At times, he was also naïve and tactless. A basically shy man, he often blamed himself retrospectively for making wrong decisions and for being weak; with admirable modesty, he also downplayed his artistic talent, despite his valuable role within the company. He did not teach anything to his filmmakers, he said, but left them free to express their intellectual needs; he dismantled the assembly-line system of animation and supported the forming of small spontaneous teams of animators.[1] Bosustow died in Los Angeles on 4 July 1981.

The fortunes of the newly founded company turned for the better when Columbia, which was now ready to terminate its contract with Screen Gems, agreed to become a distributor for UPA shorts. *Robin Hoodlum* (1948) and *The Magic Fluke* (1949) featured the same characters (the Fox and the Crow) most recently used by Screen Gems. The films were cleverly spectacular. Characterized by an original, thoughtful comicality, and by already quite stylized drawings, these works were less furious than Bosustow's earlier cartoons. (Years later, the filmmakers at Disney remembered *Robin Hoodlum* when they made their feature film, *Robin Hood*.)

Still in 1949, Mister Magoo, who became UPA's most famous character and a sort of new-gener-

ation Mickey Mouse, made his debut in *Ragtime Bear*. Magoo was himself a novelty. He was human rather than zoomorphic, and an adult rather than a child. Moreover, his psychological and physical traits were far from the typical Hollywood glamour. With his scratchy voice, shabby aspect and baldness, Magoo was a hard-headed grouch, appealing only because of his naïveté and incurable nearsightedness. His adventures developed into a ten-year series – the only one produced by UPA, which preferred individual shorts. Directed at first by John Hubley, Magoo's cartoons were later entrusted to Pete Burness.

UPA's rise to fame, and the success of its new stylistic language, came in 1951 and 1952 with two shorts: *Gerald McBoing Boing* by Bobe Cannon and *Rooty Toot Toot* by John Hubley. The former, an Oscar winner, featured a child who was unable to speak, but could only emit noises, such as the echoing 'boing boing'.[2] The latter was a version of the traditional ballad of *Frankie and Johnny*.[3] The drawings are purposely flat, two-dimensional, with oblong or angular shapes, and the limited animation contrasts

Fig. 54. Gerald McBoing Boing *by Bobe Cannon (USA, 1951).*

1   Personal communication to the author (1973).
2   The character is based on a subject by children's writer Theodor Seuss Geisel, 'Dr. Seuss'.
3   For more information on this film and on John Hubley, see pp. 238–241.

with the *continuum mobile* of the style which was considered 'classical' at that time. Strongly anti-realistic backgrounds are here often limited to a few sketches or to large areas of solid colour. Everything is clearly, deliberately dominated by a visual culture influenced by Matisse, Picasso and Klee: no longer animated comic drawings, or films with drawn actors. These were the works of cultivated art directors who gave drawing and painting a major role.

Two other important films were released in 1953. Bill Hurtz's *A Unicorn in the Garden* was an adaptation of a bittersweet tale by James Thurber, featuring the humorist's own drawings. A compact and clever work, it was probably the most elitist American cartoon ever released to general audiences.

The Tell-Tale Heart was considered innovative by virtue of being a non-comical cartoon. Illustrating a work by Edgar Allan Poe, it emphasized the nightmarish qualities of the story, and was a first example of an animated horror movie. The staff included director Ted Parmelee, scriptwriter Bill Scott and scene designer Paul Julian, who, in 1964, made a screen version of Ogden's poem,

The Hangman, for a Les Goldman production.

Bobe Cannon was a director of rare sensitivity (who was always credited as Robert), who fully understood the possibilities of animation. His works include *Madeline* (1952, from a subject by Ludwig Bemelmans) and *Christopher Crumpet* (1953), featuring a poetic, maladjusted child like Gerald McBoing Boing.

By the mid-1950s, UPA's short life began to dim. The best artists left the company for various reasons (in Hubley's case, blacklisting) and activities were reduced to repetitions of the Mister Magoo series, a TV programme entitled *The Gerald McBoing Boing Show* (broadcast by CBS from 1956 to 1958) and advertising. Other contributors to UPA included Aurelius Battaglia, Thornton 'T' Hee (formerly with Disney), Bill Melendez, abstract animator John Whitney, the young Ernest Pintoff, Jimmy Teru Murakami, George Dunning and Gene Deitch. In 1958, the New York and London branches closed. One year later, *1001 Arabian Nights*, a Mister Magoo feature film, flopped, thereby precipitating a crisis. Bosustow retired in 1961 to work for an educational movie production company carrying his name. In the following years, UPA produced undistinguished television series.

Gerald McBoing Boing and Mister Magoo were forerunners of a comic spirit which broke with the tradition of the pie-in-the-face and breakneck chases. The new characters belonged to small refined middle-class comedies, spiced with cerebral and *blasé* humour. To cinema they were what Charles Schulz's *Peanuts* was to comic strips in the same period, the expression of a restless, somewhat neurotic sensitivity. Nevertheless, these films were always made for entertainment purposes. Despite a production list which included valuable films, UPA kept a constant eye on the market, favouring movies made by art-directors rather than by artists.

The dry angular 'I style' proposed by Hubley and

Fig. 55. Mister Magoo, character by UPA (USA, early 1950s).

friends quickly spread, proving that the time had come to abandon the much imitated Disney style. The new style was not always properly used. Some applied it to old slapstick comedy, hoping to reduce work, but missed the implications of 'limited animation' as a new stylistic solution. In UPA's productions, on the contrary, precise correlations exhisted between humour, drawings and animation. The consequences of this style must be considered over an extended period of time. When John Hubley let colour overlap the contours of his characters and considered both lines and colours as one plastic whole obeying pictorial rather than narrative laws, he claimed his right to a specific language. In short, he did what Jackson Pollock had initiated some time before in the 'unfinished', incidental style of his paintings.

Without exaggeration, it can be inferred that art-animation, in the United States as well as in other countries, was born with UPA. The 'I style' and the narrative solutions based on ellipses were imitated everywhere (even at Disney in the Oscar-winning *Toot, Whistle, Plunk and Boom*, 1954, despite initial scepticism); the thinking behind the stylistic choices had a large following. Afterward, entertainment animation left the exclusive realm of comedy and became the foundation for graphic and pictorial research as well as for diverse styles, themes and 'genres'. In short, it became a medium for the greatest freedom of expression. It should be added that the audiences did not always adapt to the new language. Those who loved tradition criticized stylization as poor drawing, and segmented animation as a sign of incompetence. *Full animation* was later re-evaluated, and today, the two schools still vie for the favour of the public.

Chuck Jones and Warner Bros.

Warner's lost one of its best directors in 1946, when Bob Clampett left to work at Screen Gems

and subsequently, to devote himself to hand-animated puppets for television. (Clampett's TV show *Time for Beany* began in 1949). Friz Freleng and Chuck Jones remained at Warner's, joined by the less creative Robert McKimson. Freleng kept producing excellent works; but it was Jones who underwent a process of artistic growth and significantly renewed Warner's, the one production company which best sustained changes.

Born on 21 September 1912 in the state of Washington, Charles Martin Jones moved to California as a child, and lived in proximity to Charlie Chaplin's studio. Since then he was attracted to comedy and cinema. Having graduated from art school, he worked at a menial job for Ub Iwerks, moved to Screen Gems and eventually switched to Walter Lantz. After a bohemian crisis (during which he drew caricatures on the street for a dollar each), Jones applied for a job with Leon Schlesinger. He joined the group of Clampett and Avery, whom he greatly admired, and soon had a decisive role in developing characters such as Bugs Bunny, Porky Pig and Daffy Duck. In 1938, he directed his first film, *The Night Watchman*.

Jones' creative career took a dramatic turn after the war, when he could count on talented collaborators such as script writer Mike Maltese and lay-out artist Maurice Noble. Among the film-makers not working for UPA, Jones was the most intellectual, favouring the games of the mind over surreal craziness, loving to build his characters and their psychological reactions carefully. He also winked at culture (in his films, background scenes often referred to modern art) and played with the mimicry of his drawn actors. In Jones' hands, Bugs Bunny and Daffy Duck changed radically. Bugs Bunny maintained his absolute self-confidence but lost his cheap, delirious sadism. Daffy Duck became more and more the ideal partner for the rabbit, a sort of jealous would-be Bugs, ready to replace him at the first opportunity but inexorably bound to fail.

Under Jones' guidance, the psychological contest between the two rascals became more relevant and entertaining than situations or gags.

Chuck Jones' most important and original contribution was his Wile E. Coyote series, which he managed autonomously, clearly showing his hand. Begun in 1948, the main characteristic of the series was a sort of atemporality. Without undergoing significant changes throughout the years, the coyote tried any means to capture the Road Runner – a fast bird who dashed along dessert roads and uttered a horn-like beep-beep. The coyote perpetually ended up frustrated and beaten (see Colour Plate 14).

> 'The cartoons always take place in the same dessert setting,' Leonard Maltin writes, 'The Road Runner and Coyote never speak. The Road Runner never leaves the road. The Coyote's injuries are always self-inflicted. No matter what misfortune the Coyote suffers, he always appears intact after the fade-out, ready to try again. His mail-order machines and appliances are almost always from the Acme Corporation. He and the Road Runner are always introduced by bogus Latin names. And finally, the Coyote never catches the Road Runner.'[1]

Despite the overabundance of rules, Jones' comical version of the Sisyphus' myth is actually very terse, arithmetical and basic. Each gag shows a basic structure: a premise, mounting expectations and a surprise ending. Jones played not only with the rules of comicality, but also with the intellectual axiom of the series, which challenged the artist to repeat the same structure over and over again, with only those minimum changes necessary to make repetition exciting rather than tedious.

The Coyote appeared in a second series in which he attempted to capture sheep, always ending up beaten by a sheepdog. The Coyote's efforts took place only during business hours; at the end of the working day, both coyote and dog punched out their time-cards, amicably said good-bye to each other and went their own ways. As in any example of good classic comedy, the rationale of structure produces exhilarating effects only when joined by a solid character, who is humanly interesting and psychologically credible. The Coyote is an extremely refined actor, who skillfully stresses delusions, fears, anger and greed. Although he plays the role of the bad guy (who wants to hurt an innocent bird), he manages to be likable, because he is defeated from the start. His unshakable tenacity is almost sublime. Compared to Daffy and Bugs, who speak relentlessly with regional accents and verbal distortions, and who sing, dance and use theatrical expedients, Wile E. Coyote is surprisingly terse.

Another creation of Jones' was Pepé Le Pew, a male skunk who speaks with a French accent and expertly flirts with a female cat, who is instead disgusted by the difference in species and by the skunk's odour. Perhaps more entertaining are the *Three Bears*, featuring a cyclopic cub who is devastatingly attached to his short grumpy father.

Among Jones' one-shot cartoons – individual films which allowed animators larger creative freedom – the most noticeable are *One Froggy Evening* (1955) and *High Note* (1960). The first tells the amusing but disquieting story of a demolition worker who finds a frog walled up in the stone of an old house. When the frog turns out to be an extraordinarily skilled singer and artist, the man wants to exploit it in the entertainment world; every time he tries, the frog behaves like a perfectly normal animal. The worker has no choice but to wall up the frog again in a new building, and the story is bound to repeat itself over and over again. Characterized by the excellent animation of the protagonist, this film would

---

1   Leonard Maltin, *Of Mice and Magic: A History of American Animated Cartoon* (New York: The New American Library, 1980) p. 261.

have probably pleased Mark Twain. Contrarily, *High Note* is an almost abstract film featuring animated musical notes. A red note (red because it is drunk) upsets the performance of *The Blue Danube*, disrupting the behaviour of the other notes until the conductor (also a note) totally loses control. Jones, Freleng (see Colour Plate 15), McKimson and the others continued working on the same characters and drew new ones, such as Yosemite Sam (the red-mustached cowboy fighting Bugs Bunny, with his brutality destined to result in humiliation), Foghorn Leghorn (a Confederate rooster) and Speedy Gonzales (the supersonically quick little Mexican mouse, shouting war-cries in Castilian).

Above all, there is the rival duo of Tweety and Sylvester (see Colour Plates 16 and 17). Originally created by Clampett, Tweety the canary achieved stardom after Friz Freleng matched him with Sylvester the Cat (in *Tweety Pie* of 1947). The new antagonists basically repeated the MGM-produced cat-and-mouse struggle between Tom and Jerry, but with enough fresh material for a good new series. Tweety and Sylvester displayed richer personalities than Hanna and Barbera's two characters. Tweety is a baby canary, with childish traits and big blue eyes. But underneath his angelic aspect he is sly and often ferocious. Naturally, luck and the many allies he skillfully seduces protect him against Sylvester. As for the cat, he is far from innocent, double crossing and acting mean as often as he can. But fate is against him. Furthermore, he is plagued by the David-and-Goliath rule which grants the weakest – or the one who appears the weakest – everybody's favourite. This contrast between appearance and substance was new to American cartoons, which were until then immune to duplicity. A flavour of malaise and uncertainty, perhaps as a symptom of the new times (the spiteful canary was never punished) was beginning to insinuate itself in animation.

In 1955, Jack Warner closed his studio for the first time, believing that stereoscopic cinema was unstoppable and the costs for producing 3D animated films were too high. Arguing that, in any case, humans were not born with red and green retinas,[1] Chuck Jones joined Disney. Once there, he discovered that Walt held the only good position within the company. When Jack Warner reopened the studio, Jones returned to his old job. In 1963, the studio closed for a second time, after a five-year decline in product quality. Production continued on a very reduced scale throughout the 1960s and 1970s, when the studio re-opened briefly, often working as a subcontractor for other producers, but without attaining further significant achievements.

The resurgence of Terrytoons

In 1946, Terrytoons added the two black crows, Heckle & Jeckle, to its limited number of stars, which included Mighty Mouse. The two birds, self-confident and surly, further proof that the age of good feelings had ended, were well-liked by the public, particularly for the snooty tone they displayed in the face of apparently invincible adversaries or situations. Actually, the New Rochelle-based studio continued to enjoy the favour of the public despite its monotony. Without being rich, the company was financially healthy and productive. Thus, when Paul Terry suddenly sold it to the CBS television network and retired to private life, in 1955, the move came as a complete surprise to his associates of many years, who had expected some acknowledgment for their fidelity and hard work.

It was at that time that Terrytoons experienced an unexpected resurgence. Thirty-one year old Gene Deitch (Chicago, 8 August 1924), who had been trained at New York's UPA, was entrusted with the artistic direction. Deitch created shock waves in the traditionally structured studio, immediately changing its style, neglecting the most

---

1   In order to enjoy 3D, spectators must wear plastic glasses with one red lens and one green lens.

well-developed characters and introducing new ideas by hiring young artists (Ernest Pintoff, Al Kouzel, Eli Bauer and scriptwriter-cartoonist Jules Feiffer among others). *Flebus*, by Pintoff, featuring a human protagonist and a bare graphic style, took UPA's lesson to its extreme. *Another Day, Another Doormat*, by Al Kouzel and Jules Feiffer, featured John Doormat, a little man who changed personality whenever he was far from his virago of a wife. *The Juggler of Our Lady* was the film adaptation of a book by the then not-yet-famous artist R. O. Blechman, who contributed to the project with his own drawings.

Among the characters developed for series, the most promising was Sidney the Elephant, a shy animal who liked to whine and suck his trunk. Deitch also created a good television series featuring Tom Terrific, a blonde child with a magical funnel as a hat. All this, and much more, was accomplished during the two years of Gene Deitch's direction. When Deitch was considered too progressive, the chief-executive of Terrytoons, Bill Weiss, decided to assume the artistic direction himself. In the following years the Terrytoons studio partially returned to the past, reviving some old characters. Despite its limitations, it established itself among the most modern and vital studios.

Walter Lantz's Oasis

The most long-lived of the older studios was Walter Lantz's, which eventually closed in 1972. The studio was quite different from the others because Lantz continued production on a tight budget and remained faithful to his characters. His relaxed work-environment was a peaceful oasis attracting many excellent artists from other production companies. In fact, Lantz's collaborators included more experienced professionals than young, hopeful artists. Among the many who came from Disney, were Dick Lundy, Ken O'Brien, Homer Brightman and Jack Hannah.

Other talented artists included script writer Mike Maltese (formerly of Warner's), Tex Avery, Alex Lovy and Sid Marcus. Among the stalwarts of the studio, La Verne Harding (1905–1984), possibly the only great female animator in Hollywood, deserves a mention. As Lantz later remembered, Disney was an authoritarian, and many favoured Lantz's friendly attitude; while Disney was a prophet, Lantz was a pragmatist.[1]

The Woody Woodpecker series lasted throughout the life of the studio, although the character underwent changes. As often happens in real life, Woody Woodpecker became sober and indulgent in his old age, abandoning his destructive rage, reacting only when provoked and acquiring quiet, middle-class tendencies. Donald Duck and Bugs Bunny underwent similar transformations. Woody Woodpecker's physical appearance also evolved into a more pleasing, smaller, softer form.

The screen adventures of Andy Panda came to an end after the 1940s. A character similar to Mickey Mouse in form and mannerisms, Andy shared the same fate of no longer having a role to play in the world of cartoons. His shorts needed the support of new characters, and Andy became simply a linking device.

Another Disney character, Pablo the Penguin (from *The Three Caballeros*), inspired Chilly Willy, a penguin who is sensitive to the cold. Making his debut in 1953 under the guidance of Alex Lovy, Chilly Willy was Lantz's last significant creation. It was with Tex Avery, however, during the artist's short stay at Lantz's studio, that the character became popular in *I'm Cold* (1954) and *The Legend of Rockabye Point* (1955). Chilly Willy was a small penguin, with a mechanical walk, tormented by the cold and dressed in warm clothes; although he lacked the psychological traits necessary to last, he managed to survive until the studio ceased its activities.

---

1 Personal communication to the author (1986).

Over the years, the studio's comic vein and inspiration ebbed significantly, following a parallel course with the decline in quality of its competitors. Lantz did not disdain television and even made a personal appearance in the *Woody Woodpecker Show* (1957). Finally, when costs rose dramatically, Lantz closed the studio, devoting his time to merchandising his characters, to selling his old productions world-wide and to painting.

MGM and Tex Avery's golden years

Tex Avery worked for MGM from 1942 to 1954, during the most productive years of his career. Although he was meagerly supported by the studio's executive Fred Quimby, who did not understand Avery's sense of humour – preferring the comedy of Hanna and Barbera – Avery found the ideal ground for his creativity at MGM.

One of the dangers in discussing Avery's filmmaking is to intellectualize this spontaneous, popular artist. In fact, the lack of sentimental, political or ideological content in Avery's work forces this critic to consider the artist as he actually was, an extraordinary explorer and manipulator of filmic and comic languages. Avery's poetic content is laughter itself, together with all the available forms of humour, ranging from games of broken logic to denied conventions (such as his habit of addressing the spectator directly), to challenged limits of time (with a frantic accumulation of gags) and realism (with characters becoming hyperbolically huge or deformed).

Undoubtedly, Avery belongs to that very limited group of movie artists (Chaplin, Keaton, Laurel and Hardy) who built this century's visual comedy from scratch, inventing procedures and styles which have since become common knowledge. This is confirmed by Avery's preference for 'single' non-serial films as well as for his lack of interest in continuing characters. Except for Droopy, Avery's characters were short-lived (one of them, the crazy Screwy Squirrel, was even killed on the screen). Furthermore, Avery's dogs, cats, canaries, bears and wolves were not markedly different from the graphics of other characters of their species. As Avery himself stated, the important elements were not so much characters as their actions. In other words, what counted was pure comedy.

Avery separated himself from even his most distinguished colleagues, such as Hanna & Barbera, Clampett, Jones and Freleng, by rejecting generalities and by considering every film as a work in itself, albeit strictly connected to the artist's opus. Instead of focusing on stereotypes as the basic elements of serial movies, Avery preferred to touch on the commonplace which he overturned and used as an occasion for ironic laughter. For instance, he loved to take figures of speech and transfer them literally onto the screen (a formula which he applied to isolated episodes as well as to a whole film). For instance, in *Symphony in Slang*, of 1951, a man tells his life story using linguistic expressions, such as 'the dress fit her like a glove', which are literally illustrated.

An easy critical expedient is to represent Avery as an anti-Disney – violent and surrealistic, just as Disney was sweet and realistic. In fact, Avery learned from Disney's lesson and brought it to completion. It was because of the two artists' combined contributions that *personality animation* – cinema with drawn actors – came to be identified with the Golden Age of American comic animation. Certainly, Avery's drawn characters were not merely graphic signs, but great actors and mimes, despite their living in a distraught, exaggerated world. His histrionic skills emerge most strongly in the six works featuring a voluptuous red-head who performs in front of a lascivious wolf (*Red Hot Riding Hood*, 1943; *The Shooting of Dan McGoo*, 1945; *Swing Shift Cinderella*, 1945; *Wild and Woolfy*, 1945; *Uncle Tom's Cabaña*, 1947 and *Little Rural Riding Hood*, 1949). The extraordinarily anthropomorphic girl, animated by Preston Blair

(*Pinocchio*, *Fantasia*), contrasts elegantly with the behaviour imposed on the stunned wolf, which rolls its eyes and chews its paws.

In 1947, Avery created what could be deservedly considered his masterpiece, *King Size Canary*. In the very ordinary environment of a suburb, four ordinary characters (a cat, a mouse, a bulldog and a canary) confront each other. Their fight becomes paradoxical when a 'Jumbo Gro' potion alternately enlarges the animals, until the cat and the mouse stand on the much smaller terrestrial globe and greet their audience.

After leaving MGM in 1954, Avery worked for a few months with his first employer, Walter Lantz, for whom he directed four good, but not exceptional cartoons. Afterwards, he worked in advertising and spent his last years in the script department at Hanna & Barbera Productions. He died on 26 August 1980.

Avery's colleagues William Hanna and Joseph Barbera, with their creations Tom and Jerry, en-

joyed great success with the public (and with artists as well as the seven Oscars from the Academy of Motion Pictures, Arts and Sciences attest). Tom and Jerry survived the years without undergoing major changes. From time to time, their stories were enriched by the intervention of a big bulldog, or the appearance of Little Nibbles, also known as 'Tuffy', as a third protagonist and a child counterpart to Jerry. Sometimes, an unusual environment was used, such as in the costume film *The Two Mouseketeers* (1952). The substance of the cartoons however, remained the same, and the best movies of the late 1950s did not show fatigue when compared to the productions of fifteen years before.

Just as it was possible to adapt the cast and narrative structure with small modifications, so too was comic style slightly altered from time to time. When the friendly competition with Tex Avery's team was most heated, Hanna and Barbera quickened the action in their movies and adopted exaggerated deformations and violent expedients. Later, they found a compromise between slapstick and screwball comedy, as in the well-known *The Cat Concerto* of 1946 (see Colour Plate 18), in which an elegant pianist (Tom) performs the *Hungarian Rhapsody No. 2* by Liszt and disturbs Jerry, who is sleeping inside the piano. The two animals tease each other without ever interrupting the musical performance, until the finale, when the unlucky cat is forced to hear the opus repeated endlessly. This was probably the duo's best movie, elegantly animated, with expert timing and a tasteful construction of action.

Quite similar was *The Two Mouseketeers*, where the newcomer Little Nibbles directs a good deal of childish mischievousness against the cat. More than all other novelties, Little Nibbles was able to refresh the old formula, as his relation to the other characters (a sort of pesky little-brother for Jerry and another much worse Jerry for Tom) introduces subtle psychological nuances. It

Fig. 56. The Cat Concerto by W. Hanna and J. Barbera (USA, 1946). [©Metro Goldwyn Mayer.]

should be briefly noted that these cartoon heroes left traces in feature films with live actors. Gene Kelly – who embarrassingly asked Disney's studio to design a dance for him with an MGM cartoon character – danced with Jerry in *Anchors Aweigh* (1945). This is the most celebrated sequence of live-action and cartoon mixing. Esther Williams followed in his footsteps with *Dangerous When Wet*, (1953) and it was Kelly's turn again in *Invitation to the Dance* (1953).

In 1955, when Fred Quimby left his job at MGM as director of animation, Hanna and Barbera were invited to be his successors. After only two years, when the company decided to close its animation department, Hanna and Barbera founded their own company and began producing low cost series for television. Their empire is discussed in the coming chapter.

From Fleischer to Famous

Fleischer, once the second largest animation studio in America, continued its activities through its subsidiary, Famous Studios. The new name came from Paramount's Famous Players-Lasky. Having dismissed the Fleischers in 1942, Famous Studios transferred its equipment from Miami to New York, and reduced the overly-large staff remaining from the time of feature films. The studio was managed by three members of the old staff: Sam Buchwald, Seymour Kneitel (Max Fleischer's son-in-law) and Izzy Sparber (who revived Dave Fleischer's habit of taking credit for films on which he had collaborated little or not at all).

The production turned from Superman's adventurous line to comics, such as the traditional *Popeye* films and Little Lulu. This girl, characterized by a static face, had already been a popular comic strip by Marge in the pages of the *Saturday Evening Post*. Lulu lasted five years. Thriving at first and then becoming monotonous, she was another victim of the difficult passage from still drawings to animation.

A more successful character was Casper the Friendly Ghost, introduced in 1945 by animator and script writer Joe Oriolo (1913–85). Casper's series began only in 1950, but lasted and flourished also as a comic strip. Casper is a child-ghost, who constantly seeks friends, but is always rejected. Based on one of the most elemental components of child psychology, the desire for acceptance and the fear of abandonment, Casper appealed to children, although his films never excelled in quality or originality. Due to a complex story of unfulfilled legal obligations, Joe Oriolo did not enjoy any financial gain from the successful goldmine he instituted.

Activities at Famous Studio (or Paramount Cartoon Studio, as it was called after 1956) continued sleepily for several years, scoring more losses than gains. In 1951, Sam Buchwald died. The production of Popeye stopped in 1957 followed by the deaths of Sparber and Keitel. In 1961, the company had a short period of success when it bought an Oscar-winning film, *Munro*, which had been produced externally by Gene Deitch. Later, Shamus Culhane, back for the third time, and Ralph Bakshi attempted to revive the studio by addressing the omnivorous television market, but with scant success. The studio finally closed in 1967.

Bunin's puppets

In the field of puppet-animation, the only distinguished artist of this time was Lou Bunin. Born in Kiev (28 March 1904), the Russian emigre directed a puppet theatre in Chicago and filmed *Bury the Axis* (1937), *Pete Roleum* (1938) and *Homer, the Horse Who Couldn't Talk*, (1941). In the mid-1940s he moved to Hollywood, where, among other things, he created a few animated puppet sequences for an MGM feature film, *Ziegfeld Follies*, by Vincente Minnelli (1945). An alumnus of the Paris academy of Grande Chaumiere, a sculptor, a reader of Brecht and the classics, Bunin had too many intellectual ambitions to feel at ease in Hollywood, and went on working independently.

In 1948, he made *Alice in Wonderland* (a European co-production), a feature film mixing a live protagonist with animated puppets. The movie was shown to the public much earlier than Disney's own adaptation, however it never gained popularity. From an aesthetic viewpoint, it came up short of expectations; rhythmically weak, unimaginative and unoriginal, it should be included in the number of daring but unmemorable works. Later, in collaboration with his wife Florence, a costume specialist, Bunin undertook a successful career in advertising, briefly contributing to fiction films such as *The Sly Little Rabbit and How He Got Long Ears* (1955) and *The Dingo Dog and the Kangaroo* (1956).

Animation in the West Coast: Experimental film movement

In 1946, the first Art in Cinema Festival opened in San Francisco. Sponsored by the San Francisco Museum of Art, it featured ten programmes on the best of 'traditional' avant-garde cinema, animated and otherwise. These included *Diagonal Symphonie*, *Das Cabinet des Dr. Caligari*, *Entr'acte*, Oskar Fischinger's films, *Rien que les heures*, *Le sang d'un poète*, surrealist cinema and the new American avant-garde with, above all, Maya Deren, then Douglas Crockwell, the Whitneys and the James Broughton-Sidney Peterson duo.

To West Coast filmmakers, the Art Cinema Festival became what the New York City gatherings of refugees from the European Surrealists and other pictorial currents had been for painters a few years before. The Festival represented the occasion to cross the vast distance separating provincialism from the avant-garde. Just like Peggy Guggenheim, who exhibited works by Miró, Ernst, Tanguy and Matta at her Art of This Century Gallery but also launched young Ameri-

cans, the California festival's directors, Frank Stauffacher and Richard Foster, presented films by the great and introduced new American artists. This led to a sudden flowering of talent, proposals, novelties and revolutions. In the same way that Action Painting paved the way for Pop Art approximately ten years later, the West Coast Experimental Film Movement gave rise to the phenomenon of Underground Cinema.

The West Coast Experimental Film Movement did not distinguish between live-action and animation. The 'experimental' concept of the filmic image was precisely the unifying element among so many different filmmakers who considered the image as non-realistic, capable of being manipulated in any which way: by expanding the traditional timing of 'live-action' framing, by breaking the convention of scene design or by painting on frames. Authors wished to create more personal films in such a way as to completely separate themselves from (even more than oppose) Hollywood philosophy. Many, including Hy Hirsch and later, Larry Jordan, made both live-action and animated films; others, such as Anger, were more abstract in their live-action works than the openly declared abstractionists. Their cinema was influenced by many elements, from Buddhist philosophies to jazz to Surrealism to Cabala, but was still autochthonous and innovative, following a parallel course with the literary currents of the time and making rich contributions to culture. The Art in Cinema Festivals lasted some years, revealing talented artists in the field of animation, including Jordan Belson, Harry Smith and Hy Hirsch.

Jordan Belson and Mandalic Cinema

A native of Chicago (1926) Jordan Belson graduated in Fine Arts from The University of California at Berkeley (1946). Painting was his major interest since adolescence; his silent black-and-white film, *Transmutation*, made in 1947 under the direct influence of the Art in Cinema Festival, was more a 'painting in movement' than an actual film.

In 1948, Belson made his second abstract work, *Improvisation No. 1*, also a silent, black-and-white film. Meanwhile, he continued creating cinematic paintings, which sometimes were images of the films, detached from their context and reworked. He became affiliated with the New York-based Guggenheim Foundation, which exhibited his paintings in New York and Paris.

Throughout the 1950s, Belson kept a balance between painting and cinema, resuming his camera work in phases. In 1952 and 1953 he made four short colour and sound films, entitled *Mambo*, *Caravan*, *Mandala* and *Bop Scotch*. The first two were 'free' exercises in painting on paper rolls, while the third beautiful film made use of the traditional frame-by-frame animation technique. *Bop Scotch*, instead, was a clever experiment with objects, in which images of paving stones, bricks, tiles and other mineral elements were rhythmically combined through fast editing.

From 1957 to 1959, Belson was the artistic director of Vortex Concerts, a programme of electronic music and abstract images performed simultaneously and live at San Francisco's Morrison Planetarium. Belson used up to seventy coloured projectors, while composer Henry Jacobs took care of the musical aspects of the performance.

In those same years, Belson resumed his cinematographic activity. His 1961 *Allures* marked his passage from a formative stage to maturity. It is a 'mathematically precise' film:

> '... on the theme of cosmogenesis – Teilhard de Chardin's term intended to replace cosmology and to indicate that the universe is not a static phenomenon but a process of becoming, of attaining new levels of existence and organization.'[1]

Cosmogenetic figures of molecules and stars catch the eye at a superficial level, but the transcendent value of the film emerges from its dynamic development. The elegant rhythms dominating its images are not merely illustrative or decorative, but suggest a musical path of transformation; according to Belson, the film moves from matter to spirit. *Allures* is still a graphic film, displaying lines, curves and periods. Belson's successive works, instead, consisted of lights, irises, dawns, gases, opals and flames, based on an uncompromisingly mystical search for spirituality which went beyond art itself and which was joined with other stimuli such as an enchanted wonder of space conquests.

In *Re-entry* (1964) Belson drew his inspiration from the Tibetan book of death *Bard Thodol*, and astronaut John Glenn's first journey into space. The Bard, a Limbo-like form suspended between death and rebirth, is formed by three phases in the film: the rocket leaving the Earth (death), the space flight (karmic illusions) and the return to the terrestrial atmosphere (rebirth).

Fig. 57. Allures by Jordan Belson (USA, 1961).

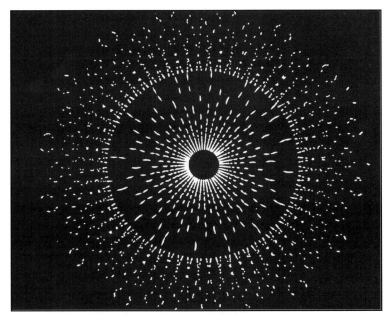

1   Gene Youngblood, *Expanded Cinema* (London: Studio Vista, 1970), p. 160.

The next film, *Phenomena* (1965), displays Belson's growing interest in asceticism. Two extremely rigorous years of Yoga resulted in the 1967 film *Samadhi* (that state of conscience in which the individual soul amalgamates with the universal soul). While filming what came out as a 'documentary on the human soul', Belson became aware of the fact that the soul was a true physical identity, and he was actually surprised not to have died after having run the creative distance. *Momentum* (1969) derived from the impulses left over from the visions of *Samadhi*, which the artist found to correspond with solar effects. In 1969 and 1970, Belson directed *Cosmos*, for which he used videotape; in 1970 he released *World*, which recalls the geometrism of Belson's first works, followed by *Meditation* (1971), *Chakra* (1972), *Light* (1974) (see Colour Plate 19) and *Music of the Spheres* (1976).

A detailed description of Belson's films would be superfluous here as it has already been excellently done by others.[1] It would also be difficult, as the filmmaker's works from 1961 on appear as diverse cantos of an extended, logically connected whole poem on light and spirit. Belson's technique differs from the usual approaches to animation – or even the abstract ones – in that pure light and pure space appear on the screen without visible human contribution. His cinema is made of visions, hallucinations and beatifications.

'I reached the point that what I was able to produce externally, with the equipment, was what I was seeing internally. I could close my eyes and see these images within my own being, and I could look out at the sky and see the same thing happening there too.'[2]

For this reason, his works go beyond technique and should be viewed as audiovisual, spiritual experiences. He threw away hundreds of feet of film when he feared that technique was becoming dominant.

This spiritual component has become an uneasy heritage for the critics to judge, and for the author himself to evaluate during his rare interviews. Considered more important from philosophical or religious perspectives than from the aesthetic standpoint, his films have been interpreted according to Hatha Yoga or the texts of Tibetan Buddhism. Only recently, concluding a lengthy examination of himself and his work, did Belson reevaluate his artistic motivations.[3]

'Right now I think of my films only as works of Art,' he wrote.[4] He also denied the all-embracing influence of Oriental religions and philosophies: 'Over the years I have been interested in, and influenced by, *many* subjects – yoga, Buddhism, mandalas, Indian holy men, Tibetan mysticism, theosophy, Egyptology, Rosicrucianism, Gurdjieff and Rodney Collins, Cabala, Jung, Magic, Tantra, Alchemy, symbolism, Astronomy, Japanese mon design, Arabic patterns, non-objective art, optical phenomena, science imagery, surrealism, visual Art (all kinds, ancient through modern) and Romantic classical Music – to mention a few.'

1 Youngblood, Gene, *Expanded Cinema*; P. Adams Sitney, *Visionary Film* (New York: Oxford University Press, 1974), pp. 300–312; Ernest Callenbach, 'Re-Entry,' *Film Quarterly* (Fall 1965); Ernest Callenbach, 'Phenomena and Samadhy,' *Film Quarterly*, (Spring 1968); William Moritz, 'Non-Objective Film: the Second Generation,' *Film as Film* (London: Hayward Gallery, 1979).

2 Thomas Albright, 'Imagery on Film,' *Sunday Chronicle* (San Francisco: 21 April 1968). Belson also wrote, 'Even if I were to say exactly how my images are produced, would that explain the patient care, attention, and discrimination that goes into every scene (to make sure the technique does *not* show?) Then, of course, much of my style is the result of editing and composing the material – along with sound and synchronization – as smoothly as possible; this process takes longer than the actual photography. Also, my films come out of a wide *variety* of means – all kinds of experiments, some natural phenomena, electronic enhancement, etc., blended together.' (Letter received from Jordan Belson, 5 August 1986).

3 Letter received from Jordan Belson, 2 June 1986.

4 Letter received from Jordan Belson, 5 August 1986.

The most relevant and unifying characteristic in Jordan Belson's films is his obsession with centrality. No matter whether the composition is round or spiral, it always grows from the centre of the frame – an immovable point of movement, converging colours and lights. Belson's films have no camera movements, but are like open windows to the secrets of the eye and soul and develop according to their own rhythm. Echoes and solemn notes constitute the sound track, without reference to traditional musical accompaniment.

This preoccupation with centrality reveals its Mandalic origins. The mandala is a cosmogram – of the universe, considered through its spatial extent and temporal revolution – rotating around a central axis. Mandala is also a psychogram, revealing psychic experiences which flow toward concentration, to find unity of conscience and to discover the ideal principle of things. In this perspective, Belson's 'major' films are mandala, or a unified search for the union between the artist and objects, although a religious reading of Belson's opus should not be exaggerated, as the Buddhist complex magic rite of initiation goes beyond Belson's intentions as well as his results.

Centrality can also be found in *Allures* and in *Raga* (1959), which belong to Belson's formative, or pictorial and graphic stage. The two films recall the designs of a kaleido-scope, combining the need for a central visual pivot with the most absolute chance. In a similar way, Belson joins together visual and spiritual quests, the most subtly significant ritual constructions with the uncontrolled search for chance preached by the surrealists and the painters of Jackson Pollock's school.

Above everything else, his skills as a visionary captivate viewers and lead them into his fluid, delicate colours (seldom does Belson use violent colours). Images of the real world are thrown as dreams into the conscious stream of irridescent nebulae: people, landscapes, a rocket, volcanoes, aeroplanes, a diver. An isolated, almost unapproachable man, Jordan Belson was one of the most original, least publicized masters of postwar avant-garde cinema.

Harry Smith, heaven and earth magician

Harry Smith's first four movies were shown in 1947, at the second Art in Cinema Festival. The dates of the actual filming are unknown, a common trait of the entire production of this hermetic, ambiguous, sometimes indecipherable artist.

Smith was born on 29 May 1923, in Portland, Oregon.[1] From his family he inherited an interest in alchemy and occultism, his skills as a craftsman and a passion for music and films. His parents separation left a less-than-ideal family situation for young Harry, who lived an isolated childhood. While in college he became interested in anthropology and worked as an assistant to an anthropologist. He lived for some time with an Indian tribe and was invited to observe their rites – he was actually one of few outsiders allowed to enjoy such a privilege. There, he experienced halluci-

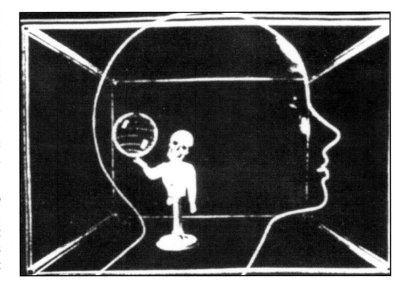

Fig. 58. Heaven and Earth Magic *by Harry Smith (USA, 1950–60).*

1 This date is not certain.

nations which he tried to repeat by using drugs, especially peyote, and to reproduce in his painting once back in San Francisco.

Smith's first films were abstract experiments, directly painted on film. According to the filmmaker (who candidly admitted his tendency to pre-date some of his works), they were made in 1939. More probably, the date should be moved forward five or six years.

The films shown at the Art Festival do not correspond to the ones which have remained today, and which have been numbered from 1 to 4. For more than thirty years, Smith manipulated his films, cutting and discarding, changing their structures or titles, making them fit his idea of a whole opus. As he wrote in the introduction to a 1963 catalogue, his films were to be seen all together or not at all.

Smith's works attained their final form in the mid-1970s. They are surprisingly expressive films, which strike even those who miss the artist's many hermetic references. The works painted on clear film stock (collected in an anthology, *Early Abstractions*, which does not always correspond to the rest of the opus) are worthy of Len Lye or Norman McLaren, although their complexity and intricate references or subtleties are foreign to the more dynamic Lye and McLaren.

Unlike Smith's other films, *Film No. 5* was given a title, *Homage to Oskar Fischinger*; it featured multicoloured circles recalling those animated by the German master in *Kreise*. *Film No. 7* is a masterpiece of Smith's first phase. It contains

'very intricate, multi-layered images rephotographed by repeated rear-screen projection to build up elaborate constructs reminiscent of Kandinsky's later geometric paintings, moving in a vibrant, organic, truly symphonic in-

CARTOONS
Bendazzi

144

terlacing. ... The soft luminescence of the re-photographed images reminds us continually that we are watching a movie of a movie, like reflections in parallel mirrors, opening the aggressively flat screen into a conceptual infinity.'[1]

Film No. 12 (named *The Magic Feature* by Jonas Mekas and conventionally known as *Heaven and Earth Magic*) belongs to Smith's most fascinating and meaningful chapter.

'[It] was originally about six hours long, and then it was edited down, first to a two hour version, and then to a one hour version,' recalled Smith.[2]

Filmed between 1950 and 1960, this black and white work is a story-without-a-story, alternating many images in an inextricable turmoil of references, hints, symbols and metaphors. Bright white cuttings of objects from the last century show up against a black background: wheels, eggs, hammers, portraits, Egyptian mummies, watermelons, syringes, butterflies, crocodile-skin bags, birds, mannequins, drops, skulls, skeletons and wrestlers. The sound track features wind, voices, screams, bells, traffic and water noises. Although the images refer to Max Ernst's collages or to Joseph Cornell's 'boxes', the film narrative resembles the hermetic and symbolist languages of this century's poetry. Smith bases his method and style on free-association and analogy. He is like a poet who skips the passage of similitude and puts two seemingly unrelated elements side by side, so that they can reverberate on each other – or who builds a comprehensive discourse on banalities (T.S. Eliot's objective correlative). Smith's associations of seemingly insignificant images or compositions of apparently clumsy, taken-for-granted actions create a compact poem which is a long journey – an hypnotic experience – into the mind.[3]

1   Moritz, 'Non-Objective Film'.

2   P. Adams Sitney, 'Harry Smith Interview,' *Film Culture*, No. 37 (Summer 1965).

3   For a study of Harry Smith's work and a description of *Heaven and Earth Magic*, see Sitney, *Visionary Film*, pp. 270–300.

In later films, Smith was more inclined toward 'live-action'. His last known work, dating approximately to 1967, is the fifteen-minute long *Film No. 16*, or *The Tin Woodman's Dream*. He admitted to being a magician and an alchemist, as well as the worshipper of innumerable sciences and para-psychology, arts, cults and experiences. This turbulent cultural and intellectual background which provides material for his art is also a whole field for critics to decode. The most appropriate judgment of Smith is probably Carol Berge's. As a poet judging another poet, with a witticism that would please Smith, she wrote:

> 'Flash of Beckett, yes, he is much with Beckett. Joyce a bit. Kafka of course. Bosch, Heinrich Kley. The other viewers are mentioning Jung. I don't give a damn for Jung but I know art when I see it.'[1]

The Enigma of Hy Hirsch

Born in 1911 in Chicago, Hy Hirsch worked all his life as a camera operator and a photographer in advertising. In 1937, he turned to avant-garde cinema and collaborated on a few projects as a comic actor and a camera operator in San Francisco. A friend of Belson's and Smith's, he counselled the two artists during their first experiments, and was inspired by them to create films of his own. In about a twelve year span, Hirsch made a large number of films, in the United States first, then in The Netherlands and finally in Paris, where he died in 1960 of a heart attack.

His disorderly life and his lack of interest in his own works make his filmography very difficult to compile. Many films have been lost, and any conjecture about the actual form of his surviving works is impossible, as some of them have been mutilated. Treating each showing as a happening, Hirsch edited and re-edited his films according to the need, favouring live-music over sound tracks and, at times, choosing multivision. In short, he acted as a choreographer of cinema, refusing to bring his films to completion. What is left shows a genial and uneasy jack-of-all-trades. Gifted with great visual and rhythmic sensitivity, vivacious taste and unrestrained vitality, Hirsch was probably too attracted by the novelty of the next experiment to complete the artistic themes he had just discovered.

Chasse de touches (The Chase of Brushstrokes) is a beautiful, elegant graphic game, marred only by a banal ending of fireworks. The film employs the same technique of drawing on dense oils used in the late 1940s by John Whitney.[2] *Come Closer* is a festive, carnival-like three-dimensional experiment, best viewed with 3-D glasses, which is held together by a sure handed use of form and rhythm. *Scratch Pad* mixes graffiti on film stock and live-action, while *Gyromorphosis* frames the close-up of a metallic structure as a three-dimensional sculpture, and enriches it with superpositions. *Autumn Spectrum* is a 'liquid' film, edited with live-action shots of water effects, reflections and waves; it is similar to *Defense d'afficher* (Post No Bills), a sequence of peeled off walls and pieces of old posters.

Hirsch's finest remaining work is *Eneri* (almost certainly made for 3-D), which recalls McLaren's *Around is Around* or Alexeïeff's *Fumées* (Smoke, 1951); a complex film, it includes a brilliant use of the split-screen and a reappearance of Hirsch's fireworks theme (presented here in a figuratively coherent manner).

Other experiences

Numerous other artists experimented with cinema within the Californian movement. Patricia Marx, an Australian landscape painter, was so

---

1   Carol Berge, 'The Work of Harry Smith,' *Film Culture*, No. 37 (Summer 1956).
2   For more information on John Whitney, see pp. 244–246. When asked about this film by this writer, Whitney maintained that he never told Hirsch about this technique.

influenced by Harry Smith that she turned to non-objective art. She made *Obmaru* (1951) and *Things to Come*, assisted by Jordan Belson who animated her drawings. In *Obmaru*, a film inspired by the traditional culture of New Zealand, she showed hands, feet and ocean symbols in 'sandy' images.

Denver Sutton made some abstract films from 1948 to 1950, of which *Film Abstraction No. 2* and *Film Abstraction No. 4* have survived. Elwood Decker filmed mobile three-dimensional sculptures made of wire in *Color Fragments* (1949). Martin Metal, who studied at Chicago's Institute of Design with László Moholy-Nagy, filmed *Color* (1947, a constructivist film) and *Form Evolution* (1949). Robert Howard, a San Francisco painter, filmed *Meta* (1947), featuring a sequence of fluid forms obtained by dropping oil colours on water. In 1951, La Jolla photographer Lynn Fayman made *Color in Motion* (which was divided into *Greensleeves* and *Sophisticated Vamp* in 1958) and *Red Dot*.

Dorsey Alexander, a painter and graphic artist from Berkeley, began producing silent, black-and-white abstract films in 1947. His first titles were *Mood, Improvisation* and *Dime Store* (this last is considered the best) followed, in 1948, by *Life and Death of a Sphere,* a cycle of forms based on the circle. In 1948, Leonard Tregillus and Ralph Luce made *No Credit*. It was one of the first times clay was used for abstract purposes. In 1949, they repeated the experiment in *Proem*.

Musicians also were attracted by abstract cinema. This was the case with Hal McCormick who showed his *Suite No. 2* at the 1947 Art in Cinema Festival. The film was followed by the interesting *Compendium of Marvels,* divided into a first part of animated comic cut-outs, and a second part of abstract and geometric drawings.

In 1957, Jane Conger, who had been a student at the California School of Fine Arts and who at the time was Jordan Belson's wife, produced *Logos,* a two-minute film based on forms resembling snow crystals and accompanied by music from Henry Jacobs (musician of the Vortex Concerts). In 1959, she experimented again with *Odds and Ends*.

All this happened in San Francisco. In 1954, the soul of the Cinema Festival, Frank Stauffacher, died. With him, the cohesive spirit of young artists discovering new worlds and their use of the festival as a means of sharing their progress in such discoveries, also disappeared. In the mid-1950s, the artists began working with a spirited independence; and an attempted festival comeback did not succeed. By the 1960s, New York became the major centre for experimental animation.

Los Angeles too had a few experimental filmmakers of its own. Charles Eames was a successful advertising artist when he filmed *Blacktop* in 1951, an essay on the reflections of light on water and on the bubbles that water produces upon impact with pavement. *Parade* (1959) features marching animated toys and *Communications Primer* (1953) gave the first proof of Eames' graphic skills.

Art Clokey, a filmmaker involved in other fields of cinema as well, created the abstract work *Gumbasia* (1955), in which he synchronized abstract forms of clay to jazz music. The film was viewed by 20th Century Fox producer Sam Engel, who suggested a commercial adaptation. The result was the television series entitled *Gumbee Gumbee,* also made with the technique of clay animation.

Donald Bevis made *Danse macabre* when he was still a student at the University of Southern California. Later on, with financing from the film collector and distributor Raymond Rohauer, he filmed *Parade* and *String Time,* television interpretations of two *scherzos* by Jacques Ibert, as well as *Whistle Stop*, based on a jazz piece,

Night Train, and featuring abstract animation of objects. *Carnival* followed, with music by Darius Milhaud. Hank Stockert should be remembered for *Scopes 2,* an abstract film made with the oscilloscope technique and an electronic sound track by Henry Jacobs.

The most important among Los Angeles avant-garde animators was Saul Bass, who curiously enough found room for his inventions within the Hollywood film industry. A famous designer and graphic artist, Bass (born in new York City, 8 May 1920) was commissioned by director Otto Preminger to draw credit titles for *Carmen Jones* (1954). One year later, in Preminger's *The Man With the Golden Arm,* featuring Frank Sinatra and Kim Novak, Bass drew attention with his revolutionary approach. Putting aside the informative characteristics of the credit titles, he transformed them into a true preamble to the movie, with its own narrative and figurative importance.

Afterward, Bass produced title credits for in-numerable films, including *The Seven Year Itch* by Billy Wilder, *Around the World in Eighty Days* by Michael Anderson (for whom Bass created a delightful animated sequence), *Saint Joan, Bonjour Tristesse* as well as *Anatomy of a Murder* by Otto Preminger. Bass was also a favourite of Alfred Hitchcock's with *Vertigo* (in which Bass collaborated with John Whitney, responsible for many of the obsession scenes), *North by Northwest* and *Psycho.* In later years, Bass directed one live-action film (*Phase IV,* 1973) and won an Academy Award for one of his short animated films (*Why Man Creates,* 1968).

Bass' avant-garde drawings led to an advancement in Hollywood graphic culture, although his sequences were actually works of art direction as opposed to works of avant-garde cinema. In the 1950s, their influence extended all over the world to those artists who tried to bring animation into the circle of 'serious', more sophisticated, graphics rather than the standard UPA's proposals.

Chapter 12

The Canadian Phenomenon

O ther than Raoul Barré in New York, Walter Swaffield and Harold Peberdy in Toronto, and Loucks and Norling in Winnipeg (on whose work only sketchy information exists), the early history of Canadian animation is best epitomized by Bryant Fryer. A native of Toronto, Fryer developed his skills in Paris, London and New York where he worked for John Randolph Bray. Returning to Toronto in 1927, he attempted to create a series with silhouettes entitled *The Shadow-laughs*. He completed only two episodes, *Follow the Swallow* and *One Bad Knight*. In 1933, Fryer tried again with *Sailors of the Guard*, *Bye Baby Bunting* and *Jack the Giant Killer*. But this time the endeavour was beyond him. Although Fryer never achieved the same heights as Lotte Reiniger, 'the care he put in scanning movements and in the effects of perspective is absolutely remarkable[1].'

The actual birth date of Canadian animation coincides with the arrival of Norman McLaren. Invited in 1941 by John Grierson to the National Film Board of Canada, the Scottish filmmaker initially worked alone, and subsequently with a team of young artists he himself hired and trained including George Dunning, Jim McKay, René Jodoin, Jean-Paul Ladouceur, Evelyn Lambart and Grant Munro. The early films were influenced by McLaren's desire to obtain maximum results with limited means, as well as by the unavailability of means themselves. The young artists devoted their efforts toward sober and inexpensive 'experimental' animation. Aware that he must avoid a heavy-handed influence on his followers, McLaren encouraged them to search for their own individual styles.

Due to the war, the majority of the work was directed toward propaganda films. The small group was also involved in preparing graphics and animation for the Film Board's other projects. When the time came to re-direct production toward peace-time activities, a statute was drawn to address the Board's new priorities: to make Canada familiar to Canadians and foreigners alike, to promote technical research and to act as state consultants for the field of cinema. The animation department was one of many branches of the organization not the most important from the economic and productive standpoint. Whilst it soon became the most acclaimed abroad for its innumerable works of high quality. In 1966–67, so as to meet the demands of the French-Canadian minority, the department split into English and French speaking divisions.

Among the initial members of the group, the most talented was George Dunning. Born in Toronto in 1920, Dunning graduated from the Ontario College of Art and went directly to the National Film Board. After directing a few educational films, he made *Grim Pastures* (1944), *Three Blind Mice* (1945) and his first significant work in collaboration with Colin Low, *Cadet Rousselle* (1946). Based on a popular song, *Cadet Rousselle* was one of the first films using animated cutouts, created with a magnetized base and metal cuttings. In 1948, Dunning went to Paris where he met Grimault, Alexeïeff and Bartosch. Back in Canada, he did not return to the Film Board, but instead co-founded a production company in Toronto with his former colleague Jim McKay. In 1956, after a short stay at Bosustow's UPA in New York City, Dunning went to London to open a local branch of the production company. The following year he opened a production company in London.

Jim McKay (Beaverton, 1917), formerly a caricaturist, worked on a 'popular song' series and gave a good account of himself with *En roulant ma boule* (1943). Having co-founded the Toronto-based Graphic Associates with Dunning, McKay worked on commissioned films after his partner left for London.

Jean-Paul Ladouceur (Montreal, 1921) was one of the two protagonists in McLaren's *Neighbors*. Shortly after completing the movie, he left the Film Board for the Canadian Broadcasting Company (CBC). His co-star in McLaren's film was Grant Munro (Winnipeg, 1923), an expert technician and animator who filmed *The Daring Young Man on the Flying Trapeze*. Munro left the Board but returned in time to be 'animated' in *Neighbors*.

After the stagnation of the 1950s, Canadian animation was able to boast an avant-garde production which was state-of-the-art in style and form. Still, the goal of the Film Board was to perform a public service rather than finance young artists. An anecdote tells of a bureaucrat's furious opposition to *Begone Dull Care* on the ground that the public's money had been wasted on useless experiments. Dissatisfied with the lack of creativity involved in their jobs, some of the most talented artists left the Film Board.

'After the war,' wrote filmmaker Pierre Hébert, 'the style of the animation department at the Film Board underwent radical changes. A sort of professionalization came about. Works became more and more polished and precise, whereas in wartime animation was performed with everything and nothing, and certainly not with the cel process. Some professional standards, as well as the victory of graphic style over "animated style" came about – these were well drawn films, somewhat similar to those of UPA, with accurate scene design.'[2] The Canadian animators, limited in number, joined Californian 'rebels' in their new stylistic directions, as the bearers of a revolutionary message – full creative freedom. In fact, Canada would become a patron of animation in the following decade.

Finally, the 1950s were witness to another milestone, the creation of the first Canadian animated feature film. Entitled *Le village enchanté* (The Enchanted Village, 1955), it resulted from the efforts of Marcel and Real Racicot, young filmmakers who learned their trade at the National Film Board. Based on Quebec legends from the colonial age, the film was amateurish, prompting condescending reviews.

1   Louise Beandet 'L'animation' in *Les cinémas canadiens* edited by Pierre Vérounneau, Paris-Montreal, Lherminier-La Cinémathèque québécoise.

2   Pierre Hébert, *Rétrospective du cinéma canadien – Animation ONF 1947–1959*. (Montreal: Cinémathèque Canadienne, 1967).

Chapter 13

Western Europe

The division of Europe into East and West by the Iron Curtain was reflected more strongly in animation than in live-action cinema or other forms of artistic expression. In the free market economies of Western Europe, the artistic and financial weakness of animated productions relegated animation to a subordinate position within cinema. In the attempt to reproduce Walt Disney's successful formula, animators focussed on feature films for children which were nothing more than frail imitations. Since the production of short films was not encouraged, just as in the United States at the time, only a handful of artists were able to build profitable careers in animation. Little new talent joined the field, and for many years production was sporadic, often amateurish. The only opportunities were offered by advertising, which boomed with the diffusion of television in the mid 1950s. By letting animators educate their audiences, advertising companies spurred constant renewal. Some of them even financed the creative efforts of their artists and made forays into the field of entertainment.

Conversely, in Eastern Europe, all efforts were directed toward the development of national cinemas, and in some cases this meant starting from scratch. All of a sudden, countries which had been almost non-existent on the geographic map of animation leapt into prominenace. Czechoslovakia was the first, followed by Yugoslavia and Poland. Working as the sole producer, promotor and distributor, the State supported only certain kinds of animation, resisting market forces and using cinema for educational purposes. For the first 15 years following World War II, animation in Eastern Europe shared similar characteristics with 1930s Soviet animation: mainly created for children, oriented towards moral and civic teaching, and resistant to stylistic changes.

In the following years, the situation gradually changed on both sides of the Iron Curtain, but the substantial dissimilarities in production, rather than cultural and ideological differences, determined a sharp division between animation in Western and Eastern Europe. One of the few traits common to both cultures was the division – stronger in Europe than anywhere else in the world – between live-action and animation cinema. Countries where live-action cinema had a rich tradition, such as Italy, produced only a few animated films while the opposite was true in Belgium. In Poland, live-action filmmakers such as Wajda, Munk and Has, did not have equivalents in animation, which developed later. Important live-action cinema currents, such as France's Nouvelle Vague or Italy's Neorealism, did not inspire European animators, nor were animators with certain exceptions, extensively influenced by other artistic experiences in literature, music or fine arts.

Great Britain

Propaganda and war-related educational films helped keep British animation alive during the war while advertising, which had traditionally supported production, amost disappeared. The major novelty in 1940 was the founding of two studios, Halas & Batchelor, and Larkins. Both studios worked mainly on commission during their first years of activity. Halas & Batchelor produced more than seventy shorts for the War Office, the Ministries of Information and Defence, the Central Office of Information and the Admiralty. Bill Larkins opened his own business after a short-lived partnership with veteran Anson Dyer; the studio produced many educational works and survived even after its founder left. With Peter Sachs and Denis Gilpin, Larkins created graphically advanced films which led some to claim that the British had preceded UPA in revolutionizing style. As for Dyer, he produced and directed a few anti-Nazi propaganda films and, later on, entertainment movies such as the three part serial *Squirrel War* (1947). He retired in 1951, when his animators left to found their own production company.

In 1944, a group of animators formerly connected to the production company of J. Arthur Rank founded G.B. Animation. The group, which started with few ambitions, quickly expanded into what many saw as the British challenge to Disney. David Hand (1900–1986), director of *Snow White* and *Bambi*, was named head of the studio. A growing number of young people, recently returned from military service, took the company's admission tests which were similar to those given by Disney in the 1930s, and the studio announced its intention to employ two thousand specialists. Through an imposing training plan, Hand undertook the task of teaching artists the secrets of Don Graham's animation, such as design and character acting. But the series *Animaland*, featuring Ginger Nutt the squirrel and its mate Hazel, flopped, despite its high technical achievements. As Hand himself

admitted, these films were not as amusing as the filmmakers had expected. Some animators contended that the group should have continued along the path of British tradition rather than attempting to translate a foreign style. The group dissolved in 1949.

Another American, George Moreno of the Fleischer school, produced some shorts featuring a London taxi driver and his car. Entitled *Bubble & Squeak*, the series lasted only five episodes.

Gerard Holdsworth, a former officer of the advertising agency J. Walter Thompson and a collaborator of George Pal's in the 1930s, worked in the field of puppet animation. With the help of Dutch animators he had brought in, Holdsworth began working on commission. *His Story of Time* (1951), made for Rolex, is still popular today. But a failed screen adaptation of Saint-Exupéry's *The Little Prince* was fatal to the production company.

Among non-professional artists, the Grasshopper Group must be noted. From 1953 to 1968, the group's founder and leader, John Daborn, directed two films with the technique of animating live actors. One was entitled *Two's Company* and *Bride and Groom*), and a parody of a well-known text by Kipling called *The Battle of Wangapore*.

The Hungarian-born Peter Földes made his debut in Great Britain. Born in 1924, Földes emigrated in 1946 and made his first film in 1952, with the financial support of the British Film Institute. Entitled *Animated Genesis*, it was a stimulating, stylistically original film about human life on the Earth. Földes broached the same topic in *Short Vision* (1955), a look at humanity on the verge of a nuclear explosion. In 1956, he moved to France and temporarily devoted himself solely to painting. Földes' major asset was a superb graphic style, which he displayed even in his earliest works.

The Producer and the Bauhaus: John Halas

John Halas (Janos Halász) was born on 16 April 1912 in Budapest. After experimenting with animation in his native city, he moved to Paris and, in 1936, to London. Enterprising and curious, Halas pursued various projects, which had him return briefly to his native country. Just before World War II, he finally settled in Great Britain.

In 1940, he founded the production company Halas & Batchelor, in partnership with the British animator and scriptwriter Joy Batchelor (Watford, 22 May 1914 – London, 14 May 1991) whom he later married. The company was to become the longest lasting production company in Western Europe and one of the most prestigious in the world.

Among wartime productions the series *Abu*, an anti-Fascist, anti-Nazi production addressed to Middle-Eastern audiences, was highly regarded. In 1944–45, the company worked on *Handling Ships*, a feature film for the Admiralty. In 1946–47, it produced the series *Charley*, for the Central Office of Information; the character of Charley, impersonating the average English citizen, explained postwar legislation to the English public. As postwar production in the social information and educational fields was a driving force for the company, Halas had time for only one artistic film, *Magic Canvas*, in 1948.

Animal Farm, the first British animated feature film, led to a jump in quality for the company. In 1951, two years after George Orwell's death, the American producer Louis de Rochemont suggested that the two British partners make a film of Orwell's anti-Stalinist novel. The original intent was for a strong ideological propaganda movie, but Halas and Batchelor insisted on making a movie for all audiences. The result was an adult film, far from the mannerisms which charac-terized some of Disney's animation, but not a film of political propaganda. As Joy Batchelor said, years later, their intent was to make a film about freedom – a task which already implied taking a political stand.[1]

After a two-year effort by more than seventy people, *Animal Farm* was completed in April 1954. British critics acclaimed it as the best film of the year, and the *New York Times* called it a masterpiece. In fact, without straying from the accepted rules of performance, the film displays vivid and dramatic atmospheres, expertly uses a palette of dark colours and shows how it is possible to learn Disney's lesson while maintaining one's own autonomy and character. Much criticism was directed against the happy ending, very different from the gloomy and mocking ending of Orwell's story. Halas objected to the criticism with an anecdote. During a performance in New York City, a lady left the theatre sobbing and threw herself in Halas' arms. To calm her down he reminded her that it was just an animated story. Think what would have happened, commented Halas, if the film was given a dramatic ending.

Fig. 59. Hamilton, the Musical Elephant *by John Halas (Great Britain, 1961).*

1   Personal communication to the author (1981).

From that time on, Halas & Batchelor was able to rely on a solid reputation, and for many years the studio was synonymous with British animation. In 1960, it produced the country's first television series: *Foo Foo* (thirty-three episodes) *Snip & Snap* (twenty-six episodes) and *Habatales* (six episodes). The production of art films included *History of the Cinema* (1956), a feisty, formally elegant film, and *Automania 2000* (1963), an entertaining satire on motorization. In the seven part, *The Tales of Hoffnung* (1964), Halas himself skillfully animated the drawings of Hoffnung. *Ruddigore*, (1967) was a featurette. A 55-minute quasi-feature film, directed by Joy Batchelor and based on the operetta by Gilbert & Sullivan of the same name, it humorously displayed the atmosphere of London at the turn of the century.

In the late 1960s, the production company made a daring move, when it began to operate in the field of computer animation – one of the first studios in Europe and in the world to do so. *What Is a Computer* (1969) and *Contact* (1974) were the first examples, while *Autobahn* (Highway, 1979) and *Dilemma* (1981) were the best productions. In the 1980s, Halas filmed a semi-documentary series on the old masters of painting, from Leonardo to Botticelli.

As Halas admitted, he was a direct disciple of the Bauhaus and, in particular, of the Hungarian László Moholy-Nagy. The goal of the Bauhaus was to reinstate artists inside society after the industrial revolution had alienated them. Consequently, to design a chair was as artistically dignified as to paint on canvas, while the notion of authorship dissolved in the need, or even the opportunity, to share work. Above all, Bauhaus believed in machines and directed its efforts toward building a society in which machines could positively be of service to humankind. This is why Halas put his skills as an animator at the service of the public or rather society. Later, he dedicated himself to the training of other animators, or invited them to collaborate with him. He was ready to spread culture, participating in innumerable public discussions and festivals. Above all, he took upon himself the task, or even the mission, of divulging the advantages of the computer which, in his opinion, was capable of bringing the animators to the highest levels of creativity by saving them the burdensome manual work.

John Halas' skills went beyond his activity as an intelligent producer and director. He brought together the many aspects of the culture of animation and worked in various fields, from writing on theory, criticism and technique, to editing a collection of works on animation, to directing ASIFA (Association Internationale du Film d'Animation). Every step of Halas' career is the consequence of the artistic choices he made in his youth, from his comic, experimental and educational activities, to the diverse applications he found for animation, to the many collaborators and students he taught (Harold Whitaker, Tony Guy, Tony White, Bob Privett, Derek Lamb, Peter Földes, Alison De Vere, Paul Vester and Geoff Dunbar), and who carried on the Halas tradition.

France

While Alexeïeff was quietly researching illusory solids, Bartosch was trying to give life to his cosmogonic dreams and Starewich was continuing his independent activity as a puppet animator, some talented new artists emerged, and others brought to maturity the skills they had developed during the war. Arcady left classic animation for special effects and became known for the instruments he designed to produce unusual images. (An example is the *traceur d'ectoplasmes*, a sketcher of ectoplasms created with an oscilloscope). In 1960, he made a magniloquent but effective abstract film, *Prélude pour orchestre voix et caméra* (Prelude for Orchestra, Voice and Camera). A year later, he completed *L'ondomane* (Wave Spirit).

Henri Gruel (5 February 1923), who apprenticed with Arcady, came out in 1953 with his first work, *Martin et Gaston* (Martin and Gaston). In *Gitanos et papillons* (Gypsies and Butterflies, 1954), he animated children's drawings with the technique of cutouts. Three years later, he made his last film, *La Joconde* (Mona Lisa, based on a subject by Boris Vian). His best film ever, *La Joconde* is an example of playful iconoclasty worthy of a Duchamp.

Jean Jabely (3 April 1921), another student of Arcady's, was a pioneer in the animation of collages, and worked actively in the field of advertising. He distinguished himself with comic films such as *Teuf Teuf* (1956), *Ballade chromo* (Colour Ballad, 1957) and *Lui et elle* (He and She, 1958).

Henri Lacam (1911–1979), master craftsman of classic animation and a long-time collaborator of Paul Grimault, made the clever *Les deux plumes* (The Two Feathers, 1957) and *Jeu de cartes* (Cardgame, 1960). Albert Champeaux (29 November 1922) and Pierre Watrin (1918–1990) joined forces for some successful comic productions such as *Paris-Flash* (1958), and *Villa mon rêve* (The Villa of My Dreams, 1960). Omer Boucquey (17 August 1921) is remembered for his Disneyesque *Choupinet* (1946). Albert Pierru (7 August 1920) was a follower of Norman McLaren, from whom he learned the technique of painting on stock. Pierru's *Surprise boogie* (1957) deserves mention.

Jean Image left an impressive opus, in quantity if not quality. Beside producing shorts, the Hungarian-born Image authored the first French animated feature film, *Jeannot l'intrépide* (Fearless Jeannot, 1950). In her attempts to save other children from an ogre Jeannot, a diminutive child takes a trip to the world of insects, and with the help of bees defeats the wicked giant. The fable is unpretentious, and the characters are hardly charming, but overall the film is entertaining, especially in its description of insect life. In 1953, Image released *Bonjour Paris*, a feature film about two pigeons in love and the theft of the Eiffel Tower. He continued to produce good but not exceptional feature films, shorts and television series.

Grimault and the stories from the front

The foremost representative of French animation is Paul Grimault whose debut has already been discussed. Having returned to Paris from the war in Africa, the artist retrieved the drawings and sketches which he made for a film commissioned by Air France. These were reworked and filmed to create *Les passagers de la Grande Ourse* (The Passengers of the Great Bear). After this first success, Grimault produced and directed *Le marchand de notes* (The Note Merchant), *L'épouvantail* (The Scarecrow), *Le voleur de paratonnerres* (The Lightning Rod Thief) and *La flûte magique* (The Magic Flute), all engaging films.

Grimault was supported by Jacques Prévert, his long time friend, who joined Les Gémeaux studio as a scene designer for *Le petit soldat* (The Little Soldier) in 1947. Immediately afterward, Grimault and Prévert collaborated on the feature film *La bergère et le ramoneur* (Mr Wonderbird). Assisted by an artistic team of more than one hundred people, they worked on the film for more than three years. The film was expected to be the European answer to American-made animated feature films, but the production stalled in 1950 when, despite Grimault's opposition, his partner André Sarrut decided to exploit the film before its completion (one-fifth was yet to be filmed). Lawsuits, criticism from the press and intellectuals' indignation could not prevent the film from being shown in an incomplete version. Discouraged, Grimault interrupted his creative activity; he quietly returned to it later on, working more as a producer than an artist.

In 1967, he got hold of the negative of the unfinished feature film and managed to complete it, while still working on shorts such as *Le diamant* (The Diamond, 1970, a subtle apologue about colonialism) and *Le chien mélomane* (The Music-loving Dog). The film is a biting, well-designed attack against greed and power. Re-released in 1980 with the new title *Le roi et l'oiseau* (The King and Mister Bird, see Colour Plate 20), it won the prestigious prize Delluc. Approximately half of the film consisted of old material while the script, restructured in agreement with Prévert, helped transform the original project into a drier, more mature work and one of the finest feature films in the history of animation. In 1988, the filmmaker collected his short films into a single feature entitled *La table tournante* (The Revolving Table), with the collaboration of Jacques Demy for the live-action sequences. He died on 29 March 1994.

Grimault's originality and artistic personality do not emerge so much in his graphic style as in his narrative structure. The artist's technique is personal, and is linked to the caricatural tradition of curved lines, full animation and realistic settings. The mainstream taste of graphic synthesis or dense syntax are foreign to his cinema which is predominantly narrative and is more influenced by the scenery and camera movements of live-action films than by animated graphics.

It is within this narrative structure that the essence of Grimault's poetics are found. Frequent themes are the fundamental goodness of human beings in the face of power, oppression and wickedness. *Le voleur de paratonnerres* features Niglo, a tiny character (the same as in *Les passagers de la Grande Ourse* and *La flûte magique*) who steals lightning rods simply because they are beautiful, and escapes two insensitive policemen. In *L'épouvantail*, the cat who wants to trick the scarecrow and attack the birds hiding under its hat, is a terrorist opposed to peace and beauty. Therefore, the cat must be defeated. In *Le petit soldat*, a doll's love for a wooden soldier wins out

against the wickedness of a 'devil-in-the-box' is a re-interpretation of Hans Christian Andersen's tale *The Shepherdess and the Chimney Sweep*. As the messengers of love, the protagonists fight the kingdom in which they live – a vertical world (see Lang's *Metropolis*) – dominated at the very top by an effeminate, cruel monarch, and populated in the underground by common people, destined never to see the sunlight.

Grimault joins the 'poetic realism' of artists such as Carné, Renoir, and Duvivier, inside a cinematographic current which had been the pride of the Popular Front of France.

Spain: Catalan vibrance

After the Civil War, animators resumed their activity and established a small-scale golden age of Spanish animation despite the unavoidable scarcity of means and structures. The major centre of production was Barcelona, which also housed the then developing industries of comic strips and children's publishing. The two graphic arts of animation and comics were thus coordinated, with artists moving from one activity to the other, editors founding production companies, and characters appearing both in the press and on the screen. This quite unusual coordination was characteristic of Spanish (or more precisely, Catalan) animation of the time.

In the 1930s, the Baguñá brothers founded the production company Hispano Gráfic Films. Salvador Mestres (Vilanova i La Geltrú, 3 December 1910 – Barcelona, March 1975) was the company's artistic director. After his debut as an amateur filmmaker, he released a series of shorts on the adventures of Juanito Milhombres, a screen adaptation of a successful comic strip character originally called by the Catalan name, Joan Milhomes.

In 1940, publisher Alejandro Fernandez de la Reguera founded Dibsono Films, which released *SOS Doctor Marabú* (1940), directed by Enric

'Dibán' Ferrán, the first animated film following the Civil War. Carlos Fernandez Cuenca praised it as 'one of the most remarkable, brilliant and fluid films of the time'.[1]

Shortly afterwards, Hispano Gráfic Films and Dibsono Film merged into Dibujos Animados Chamartín. The new company, which employed the best Catalan artists, was located in the very central Paseo de Gracia, in Barcelona, in the prestigious Casa Batlló, designed by architect Gaudí. Three series were successfully developed and lasted for some years. The first one, based on the adventures of Don Cleque, was a project initiated by Dibsono Films and was entrusted to Francesc Tur (Barcelona, 1885–1960) and Guillem Fresquet (Barcelona, 1914). Don Cleque, the slow, sedentary protagonist, was the prototype of the average person, but displayed the strongest of wills. The second series, probably more popular, was dedicated to the anthropomorphic bull Civilón; the director was the most talented of the team, Josep Escobar (Barcelona, 1908). The third series was *Garabatos* (Scribbles), a sort of animated variety show which caricaturized the stars of the entertainment world, both foreign (Greta Garbo, Mickey Rooney) and national. Initiated by Ferrán, the series was later continued by Escobar. The good fortune of Casa Batlló ended in 1945, when the company dissolved due to distribution problems and to the financiers' wish to move the studio and business to Madrid. The Baguñá brothers founded Editorial Científico-Cinematográfica and produced educational movies for the next few years.

Among smaller-scale productions, two series deserve mention: *Fáquir González* (Fakir González, featuring a fakir struggling against his own magic), designed in the early 1940s by Joaquím Muntañola (Barcelona, 1914); and *Quinito*

(1943–1947), by J. Pérez Arroyo.

The most memorable enterprise was directed by Arturo Moreno (Valencia, 1909 – Barcelona, 25 June 1993) who had worked in advertising in the 1920s. In 1942, within his own small production company, Diarmo Films, Moreno made the short *El capitán Tormentoso* (The Boisterous Captain). While looking for a distributor, Moreno was invited by the production and distribution company Balet y Blay to make a feature film; the result was *Garbancito de la Mancha* (1945, see Colour Plate 22), the first Spanish animated feature film and one of the first in Europe. Garbancito (in Castillian, small chickpea) was a Quixotesque child fighting as defender of the weak against the child-eating giant Caramanca. Garbancito was helped by the goat Peregrina and by a good fairy, who gave him the power to become a chickpea. Developed from a subject by poet Julián Pemartín, the story was published simultaneously with the film's release.

Following the success of *Garbancito*, the production company entrusted Moreno with another project, *Alegres Vacaciones* (Happy Vacations, 1948), in which the characters of the previous film left their studio in Barcelona and went to Palma de Majorca, Valencia, Andalusia, Madrid or Morocco. The third, and last, feature film produced by Balet y Blay was *Los sueños de Tay-Pi* (The Visions of Tay-Pi, 1951, see Colour Plate 21), directed by Austrian Franz Winterstein after Moreno had moved to Venezuela. This jungle-based story, featuring monkeys wearing tuxedoes and weeping crocodiles, displeased the public and led the production company to bankruptcy.

Meanwhile, the former artists of Chamartín studio, united under the name Estela Films, released *Erase una vez* (Once Upon a Time), based on Perrault's tale *Cinderella*.[2] Alexandre Cirici-

1   Carlos Fernandez Cuenca, *El mundo del dibujo animado* (Festival internacional del cine de San Sebastian, 1962) p. 30.
2   Initially, the film was announced as *La Cenicienta*, the Spanish for Cinderella. Walt Disney Productions, however, claimed international rights over the title (Disney's *Cinderella* was released in 1950). It was thus necessary to adopt the new title, which means 'once upon a time' in Castillian.

Pellicer (Barcelona, 1914–1983) was artistic director, and Josep Escobar director of animation. The film, the best ever made in Spain up to that time, received favourable reviews, was declared to be of 'national interest' by cinema authorities and received praise at the Venice Festival. Remembers Giuseppe Flores D'Arcais, 'A.C.Pellicer's film was much more convincing than Disney's *Cinderella*'.[1] The background design was particularly praised for its links to Catalan architectural and decorative tradition. However, the film was not successful at the box-office.

Outside Barcelona, only Madrid could claim a few

animated works. Fernando Morales made a few films in the early 1940s, including *Un día de feria* (Market Day, 1941) and the colour film *Una extraña aventura de Jeromín* (The Strange Adventure of Jeromín, 1942).

Some puppet films also originated in Madrid. In 1943, Salvador Gijón, who in 1936 had collaborated on Adolfo Aznar's *Pipo y Pipa en busca de Cocolín* (Pipo and Pipa in Search of Cocolín) produced and directed *No la hagas y no la temas* (Do No One Wrong and Fear No Wrong), the first title of a modest but long filmography (Gijon was an active animator until 1970). Another puppet animator was Angel Echenique, whose major work was probably his collaboration with José Maria Elorrieta on *La ciudad de los muñecos* (Puppet City), a film mixing live-action and animation. After this very promising start, Spanish animation lost vigour, resuming activities only in the 1960s.

Italy: feature films and experiments

During the war, two feature film projects were developed[2]. The first, entitled *I fratelli Dinamite* (The Dynamite Brothers, 1949, see Colour Plate 23), resulted from the efforts of Nino Pagot and a few other animators including Osvaldo Cavandoli, Osvaldo Piccardo and Nino's brother, Toni, who had just recently returned from a German prison camp. The episodes of *I fratelli Dinamite*, which are based on the mischievous doings of the brothers, are linked together by a tea party sequence in which the rascals' aunt informs her friends of the children's adventures. Episodes, just to mention a few, are set on a desert island, in hell and the Venice Carnival. The most amusing segments happen at a Carnival, while the episode in hell should be noted for its bizarrely sinister originality and horror film atmosphere. It is a similar feeling to that which

Fig. 60. Civilón and Civilona, characters by Josep Escobar (Spain, early 1940s).

Fig. 61. Garbancito de la Mancha by Arturo Moreno (Spain, 1945).

1   Flavia Paulon ed. Giuseppe Flores D'Arcais, *Il cinema dopo la guerra a Venezia*. (Rome: Ateneo, 1956) p. 79.
2   Both films can claim to have been 'the first' feature-length Italian animated film, since both were first screened at the Venice Film Festival of 1949. Interestingly enough, they also were the first colour feature films of the Italian cinema as a whole.

characterizes Nino Pagot's comic-strips.

The film did poorly at the box office, and the production company soon turned to advertising. Success came to Pagot in the 1960s with her creation of the black chick Calimero, a character who appeared in a popular series of television ads. Calimero later developed into a fiction series. Nino Pagot died in Milan on 22 May 1972.

The other postwar feature film was *La rosa di Bagdad* (The Rose of Baghdad). The movie was first shown in 1949, after seven years of troubled work. The producer and director, Anton Gino Domeneghini (Darfo, 1897 – Milan, 1966), was a major advertising artist in pre-war Italy (see Colour Plate 24). Domeneghini resorted to cinema as a means of keeping his artistic team together during the war. Because of bombings, the group left Milan and moved to Bornato, in the countryside of Brescia.

The film was completed, edited and scored in the following years. Angelo Bioletto, well-known creator of the Perugina figurines, which a popular contest had promoted throughout Italy in the 1930s, designed the characters. Backgrounds were created by Libico Maraja and music was composed by Riccardo Pick Mangiagalli. Domeneghini himself was responsible for the subject of the film. The fable owed something to Snow White and whilst it had an awkward narrative progression it nevertheless boasted some beautiful sequences: Princess Zeila singing as the sun sets, the dance of the snakes, the final celebration with fireworks. Although this film did well at the box office, Domeneghini discontinued the films' production and turned again to advertising.

With these two features, animation gave Italian cinema the gift of colour; the first live action colour film, *Totó a colori* (Totó in colours) arrived only in 1952.

The only other significant animator, in the years immediately following the war, was Francesco Maurizio Guido, known as 'Gibba'. This young independent filmmaker learned the craft of animation while working with Giobbe[1] in Rome. Afterwards, he returned to his native Liguria and began working on his own. Once Nazi occupation ended, he filmed *L'ultimo sciuscià* (The Last Shoeshine). Completed in 1947, this film displays original perspective. Telling the story of

Fig. 62. L'ultimo sciuscià *by Gibba (Italy, 1947).*

1 Giobbe made his last film, *Hello Jeep*, in 1944 (he died in 1945), in collaboration with Niso 'Kremos' Ramponi. The subject and script for the film were created by the then very young Federico Fellini.

a little shoeshiner who has gone to heaven, Gibba intended to abandon the comic tradition. In favour of sentimentality, his desire was to bring animation into the highly-emotional, Neo-realist movement. His effort, however, proved to be unfeasible. He returned to Rome, where he was stifled by the difficult environment and never managed to fully develop his artistic skills as an animator.

The works of two comic-strip artists also deserve attention: *I sette colori* (The Seven Colours, 1955), by Antonio Rubino and *La piccola fiammiferaia* (The Little Match Girl, 1953), by Romano Scarpa who also designed several Donald Duck comics.

In the late 1950s, the decision of the Italian Broadcasting Corporation (RAI-TV) to permit advertising resulted in an explosion of activity. On 3 February 1957 the advertising series *Carosello* was inaugurated. Animators could now build long lasting careers in their field. In short, modern Italian animation was born from *Carosello*.

Luigi Veronesi

The most important artist to emerge during this period was Luigi Veronesi (Milano 1908). One of the major Italian representatives in the field of non-figurative art, Veronesi went through a variety of experiences. Without associating himself with any major international current, he studied contemporary art, travelled widely (especially to Paris), and met the most influential artists of his time. In the 1930s Veronesi became a friend of László Moholy-Nagy and undertook in-depth studies of the Bauhaus. Involved in engraving, photography, stage design and painting, the versatile Veronesi was eventually attracted to cinema.

'I tried to paint anyway, through the means of cinema,' he said. 'In 1936, I painted *Quattordici variazioni su un tema pittorico* (Four-

teen Variations on a Pictorial Theme), and Riccardo Malipiero composed the same number of music variations. In 1938, I made another series; but I was feeling the need for real movement, while the series of painting did not offer anything but fictitious movement.'

Veronesi's first film was non-pictorial.

'It was a documentary filmed in a factory of wooden figures, into which I introduced some object animation, the wooden figures. Once I had begun, I attempted abstract filming. It was a mere experiment: with colours and materials. The film stock was no longer than twenty metres. I called it *Film N.1*. In 1939, I created a *Film N.2* and from 1939 to 1940, I made *Film N.3*. These experiments were extremely rich in colour. *Film N.4* was more disciplined, even though very chromatic. *Film N.5* was bichromatic, based on the complementary colours green and red. Yellow would appear a few times, but only for the optical effect of rapidly substituting red for green. *Film N.6* was based on black and red. Before the end of 1941, I made two other films, *N.7* and *N.8*, in which I returned to some themes of the initial works. Finally, ten years later, I made *Film N.9*, upon request of the director of the Cinémathèque Française, Henri Langlois, a friend of mine. This film was less geometric than the others, it used more free, less precise forms.'[1]

Of Veronesi's overall production, limited but still remarkable in a panorama of non-prolific artists, the only surviving films are the charming *Film N.4* and *Film N.6*, which were stored during the war at the Cinémathèque by Henri Langlois. The others were destroyed in the 1943 bombings of Milan. In Veronesi's opinion, the finest was *Film N.5* (see Colour Plate 25). In 1940, Veronesi made a pre-underground experiment, filming a

1   Personal communication to the author (1976).

woman's face in such a way as to change her expression with lighting. After the war, he abandoned his cinematographic activity for painting, although in 1989 he made *Film N. 13* (without ever making the films *N. 10*, *N. 11* or *N. 12*).

German Federal Republic

Along with the country's fast economic renaissance, West Germany saw the rise of occasional resourcefulness in the entertainment field, and frequent advertising and educational productions.

Hans Fischerkoesen, having escaped from the Soviet-occupied sector of Germany in 1948, founded a successful studio in Mehlem am Rhein which survived even after his death in 1973. Gerhard Fieber (Berlin, 1916), an artistic director at UFA, founded the EOS studio in Wiesbaden in 1948. Two years later, he released *Tobias Knopp, Abenteur eines Junggesellen* (Adventure of a Young Fellow), a feature film of turn-of-the-century tales illustrated by Wilhelm Busch. The film, purposely in black-and-white, preserved Busch's graphic style.

The documentarist Herbert Seggelke, of Munich, made the aforementioned *Strich-Punkt Ballet* (Line-Dot Ballet, 1943), in which he experimented with animation drawn directly on film stock. As these kinds of work were considered degenerate by Nazi ideology, the film was shown to the public only in 1949. In 1955, Seggelke persuaded painters Jean Cocteau, Gino Severini, Ernst Wilhelm May and Hans Erni to attempt to use the same technique with the musical accompaniment of a polonaise. The result was a documentary entitled *Eine Melodie – Vier Mahler* (One Melody, Four Painters) with commentary by Cocteau, in which live-action images of the artists at work mixed with their brief experiments. Curiously, the finest sequences are those by the less famous artists, May and Erni; Severini drew Ve-

ronesi-style vibrating rods, while Cocteau played with asterisks, points and holes in the stock.

The Diehl brothers emerged from the destruction caused by the war with their animated puppet films and with their ever-more-popular hedgehog Mecki. In 1950, they released a feature film, *Immer wieder Glück*, in which the protagonist, Kasperle Larifari (Casper Absurdity), travels to a distant island in search of a magic flower. Their third and last feature film, *Der Flaschenteufel*, (The Devil in the Bottle, 1952), based on a text by Robert Louis Stevenson, again featured Kasperle Larifari together with live actors.

Kurt Stordel also survived the war after many adventures, which included working as an artist for the occupation troops. In 1948, he established his residence in Hamburg and devoted himself to educational films and documentaries. In the 1950s he spent some time in Taiwan; in the 1960s, he made several children's films for German television.

Denmark

In Denmark, where almost nothing relevant had happened after Storm-Petersen, Allan Johnsen produced the feature film *Fyrtøjet* (The Tinderbox, 1943–46) (see Colour Plate 26), based on Hans Christian Andersen's tale. Johnsen was a clothing manufacturer who decided to invest in cinema, like other industrialists whose businesses had been halted by the war. Svend Methling, a stage and live-action cinema director, took on the artistic leadership. The film, shot in Agfacolor and developed in Berlin, was quite an adventurous enterprise. As the story goes, Johnsen caught the last train from Soviet-occupied Berlin, in the spring of 1945, and travelled on the locomotive in order to bring the movie to Copenhagen. The film, which opened exactly one year later, was given tepid reviews, especially by those critics who were used to Disney's style. Re-

released almost forty years later, it was praised as a 'surprising' film, 'stupefying and very well animated'.[1]

The most active studio of the 1950s belonged to stage designer, illustrator and comic-strip artist Bent Barfod (Frederiksberg, 1920). After his 1949 debut with *They Guide You Across*, Barford founded his own studio and produced experimental and documentary films to order, creating and trying diverse techniques. In 1956, he made *Noget om Nordet* (Some Things About the North), based

on a subject by Carl Theodor Dreyer. His best animated film was probably *So Be It Enacted* (1964),[2] which received awards from the European Council and the Danish Cultural Ministry.

Finland

In Finland the war left deep wounds also on cinema, and the brief tradition established by the pioneers of animation was lost. In the 1950s, animation reawakened, particularly in advertising. From 1950 to 1958, Holgar Harrivirta (Nastola, 25 October 1915), who had been active in live-action cinema since 1938, made animated puppet films in collaboration with Vilho Pitkämäki (Helsinki, 13 September 1925). The two animators' main character was Professor Nerokeino. Toivo 'Topi' Lindqvist (born in 1920) created advertising films. The most influential Finnish animator was painter, sculptor and Kinetic artist Eino Ruutsalo (Tiutinen, 19 September 1921). In the 1950s, he made films by painting or engraving directly on stock and continued his experiments well into the next decade with *Two Hens* (1963), *The Jump* (1965), *Plus Minus* (1967) and *ABC 123* (1967). Afterward he quit animation, continuing his work in avant-garde and art cinema.

Fig. 63. ABC 123 *by Eino Ruutsalo (Finland, 1967).*

1 'Scandinavie,' *Banc-Titre*, No. 25 (November 1982) p. 22; letter received by Kaj Pindal, 27 January 1985.
2 Original title in English.

Chapter 14

Eastern Europe

In almost all East European countries, cinema conformed to the same structure: a State-funded cinema which depended on the political leadership and which embraced all areas of production, rental, exhibitions and theatre management. Due to a philosophy of decentralization, in the footsteps of the Soviet Union, production often included one or more teams of animators, and these teams were often located in cities other than the capital.

State cinema aimed to fulfill the diverse needs of citizens of all ages. Because of its popularity among children, animation was usually limited to younger viewers. With time and with the relaxation of ideological control, animation became open to stylistic research and to a larger range of themes. When this happened, at times and in ways varying from nation to nation, production split into 'functional' films and 'prestigious' ones, the latter made by a few selected animators who were allowed to follow their inspiration. Even so, complete creative freedom was never granted, and several films were not released because of their alleged ideological danger.

To give a concise portrait of animation in Eastern European countries is a difficult task because of the many traditions and proposals of this varied world (which, before the revolution of 1989, has often been considered a monolithic block by the West). The most distinctive current of Eastern European cinematographic productions (but not common to all countries) was based on folkloric and popular traditions. Having cut all links to the avant-garde movements of the world (the films produced by the Eastern countries did not contain any reference to the major artistic movements of the century, as they were disliked by the reigning socialist realism), animators looked for inspiration in ageless peasant songs or handed-down legends and tales. While production often suffered from affectation, some artists (such as Jiří Trnka) used mannerism to their advantage. Inspiration found its source in graphics, as in Poland and in illustrations or satirical and comic drawings; as in the countries which formed the socialist republics of Czechoslovakia and Yugoslavia.

Soon after World War II, the production of animated films tended to be uniform and conformist; as the economy improved, facilities became more available and the influence of Stalinism over aesthetic ideology faded; animation in Eastern European countries emerged as one of the most vital and innovative of the world.

The Socialist Republic of Czechoslovakia and puppets

The initiator of Czechoslovakian animation was Karel Dodal, the director and producer of several advertising films, who also made *The Lantern's Secret* (1935, the country's first animated puppet film), and the experimental *Ideas Search for Light* (1936). Dodal moved to the United States shortly before the war; afterward, he worked in Argentina.

In 1941, in the midst of the war, Dodal's wife and collaborator Hermína Tyrlová (born in 1900) filmed the animated puppet film *Ferda the Ant*. Showing Ptushko's influences, this work marked the beginning of a long and fruitful career in the field of children's animation. From Prague Tyrlová moved to Zlin and joined Bata's studio.

Great Czechoslovakian animation, however, was rooted in Prague. In 1935, AFIT (Atelier Filmovych Triku) opened at 33 Stépánská Street. The small studio, which employed about six people, produced tricks for live-action cinema, models, special effects and animated titles. In 1941, during the German occupation, Nazi leader Joseph Pfister took over the studio and decided to transform it into a large production company. The staff quickly expanded to include students from art schools. The artistic direction was entrusted to the inexperienced Austrian Richard Dillenz, who quit after the flop of an amateurish opera-like feature inspired by Orpheus and Euridice. Before the arrival of Dillenz's replacement, Berlin's Horst von Möllendorff became the new artistic director. The animators at the studio produced *Hochzeit im Korallenmeer*, a short film about a fish wedding. The short was finished under von Möllendorff who took credit for it. (This film, as well as the two other films produced by the studio, have been mentioned previously). In September 1944, the studio closed for war-related reasons and re-opened only at the end of the war.

In June 1945, shortly after Prague was liberated

from German occupation, theatres released the advertising short *Sensational Attractions, Marvelous Entertainment*, the first to be produced by independent animators and the first animated film of the new Czechoslovakia. Activities started in earnest. Jirí Trnka, Eduard Hofman, Josef Vácha and musician Václav Trojan began working on their debuting short, *Zasadil dedek repu* (Grandfather Planted the Beet, 1945).

The country was in turmoil. The struggle for power was paralleled by heated debates and an atmosphere of reconstruction and optimism. At the studio, animators were euphoric. 'This is time for experiments,' stated Jirí Trnka in 1946. 'We must take advantage of it!'. From that time on, artists looked for new ways to animate. Even when some conformism of themes took root some years later, the best artists (Trnka, Zeman, Tyrlová) continued to find unusual stylistic solutions and to look forward. Following a witty suggestion by Trnka, the Prague studio was named Bratri v triku ('the brothers in shirt', but also 'the brothers of tricks', referring to animation). The logo, by Zdenek Miler, represented three curly children wearing striped shirts. Jirí Trnka (whose work will be discussed in detail later) was the most influential among Prague's animators. For more than a decade almost every animated puppet movie made in the capital was released by the studio he directed from 1946, and which was renamed after him at his death.

Films with animated drawings had a different course. Many talented artists ventured into production, but the only remarkable works were Jirí Brdecka's first film, *Vzducholod a láska* (Love and the Dirigible, 1948) and Zdenek Miler's *O milionári, ktery ukradl slunce* (The Millionaire who Stole the Sun, 1948). The first, with Kámil Lhóták's drawings inspired by turn-of-the-century illustrations, told the story of two lovers who fulfilled their dreams after the young man built a dirigible and snatched the girl from another suitor. The second film (award-winner at the 1948

Venice Festival) described a rich man who stole the sun for his exclusive enjoyment, leaving the world in darkness until a child saved humanity. Characterized by inventive drawings, it was one of the finest films by Miler (Kladno, 21 February 1921).

In 1947, Stanislav Látal (Samotisky, 7 May 1919) directed the original tale *Liška a džbán* (The Fox and the Pitcher, 1949). Václav Bedrich (Pribram, 28 August 1918), a specialist in children's productions, was a prolific animator. Eduard Hofman (Krakov, 16 May 1914 – Prague, 1987), who also specialized in works for children, displayed his verve and taste with *Andelsky Kabát* (The Angel's Cape, 1948) and *Papírové nocturno* (Paper Nocturne, 1949). In 1950, Hofman was invited to direct the animation studio. Recalled Jiří Brdecka:

> 'Hofman was a great organizer. He was the one who kept animation on its feet after the war. He was also the one who brought Trnka to cinema, convincing him to leave behind illustrations and puppet theatre. Hofman was an exceptional manager from 1950 to 1956, when he directed the animation studio, and also later, when he directed the entire production company of movies for children.'[1]

Despite Hofman's achievements, his years were not the most satisfying. As Jan Horejsí wrote:

> 'Beside negative external influences, which were, in my opinion, the most important reasons, there were also the consequences of a general decay in animation. Together with a growing intellectualism and a tendency to over-illustrate as an end in itself, these led to an ever increasing limitation in the development of animation'.

However, Horejsí added,

> '... production started breathing again after 1956, and the reasons for such a delay were ... social above all. In an atmosphere of gradual openness, the creative courage ... of the postwar reappeared in all artistic fields.'[2]

To conclude on Hofman, it should be added that he directed the first Czechoslovakian feature film with animated drawings, *Jak je svet zarízen* (The Creation of the World, 1957), based on drawings by the Frenchman Jean Effel.

As already mentioned, other animators worked at Zlin, then re-named Gottwaldov; above all, Hermína Tyrlová, who devoted herself to children's animation. Tasteful and sensitive, Tyrlová was 'a woman and an artist of clear, terse and delicate imagination, capable of weaving the subtle, minute events of people and objects which are usually neglected by men'.[3] She preferred modern tales over the adaptation of traditional ones, and never ceased challenging her viewers with unusual materials. Instead of making traditional puppets, she chose balls of yarn, silver paper, pieces of wood, handkerchiefs, towels or toys. By using new materials, she managed to achieve the dual goal of avoiding creative stagnation and showing children the hidden lives of common, close-at-hand objects. Among her remarkable productions are the classic anti-Nazi *Vzpoura hracek* (The Revolt of the Toys, 1946) and *Ukolébarka* (The Lullaby, 1947), both mixing live actors and animated objects, and *Devet kurátek* (The Nine Chicks, 1952), *Uzel na kapesníku* (The Knotted Handkerchief, 1958, with animated fabrics), *Vlacek kolejácek* (Little Coal Train, 1959), *Modrá zásternka* (The Blue Apron, 1965) and *Malovánky* (Paintings, 1970).

1   Personal communication to the author (1977).
2   Jan Horejsi and Jiří Struska, *Occhio magico – Il cinema d'animazione Cecoslovacco 1944–1969*, Ceskoslovensky Filmexport, 1969) pp. 16 and 20.
3   Vladimir Kolman, *Vom Millionar, Der die Sonne stahl – Geschichte des Tschekoslowakischen Animationsfilms* (Frankfurt: Deutsches Filmmuseum, 1981) p. 22.

Karel Zeman

Karel Zeman was born on 3 November 1910 in Ostromer and died on 5 April 1989 in Zlin Gottwaldov. After his 1943 debut with *The Christmas Dream*, he gained popularity among children with his five comic shorts on Mr. Prokouk. In 1948, he directed *Inspirace* (Inspiration, 1948), a lyrical film, and the featurette *Král Lávra* (King Làvra, 1948), a satire based on a novel by Karel Havlicek Borovsky. Featuring a story similar to King Midas', *King Lávra* showed Zeman's self-confident hand at direction and puppet-creation. Afterward, Zeman turned to the production of feature films with *Poklad ptacího ostrova* (The Treasure of Bird Island, 1952). His *Cesta do prevaku* (A Journey into Prehistory, 1954) told the story of four students who ascend the river of time, discovering ancient animals (the only animated elements of the film were the models of dinosaurs, while everything else was live-action).

In 1958, after two years of work, Zeman released *Vynález zkazy* (The Diabolic Invention, 1958), based on Jules Verne's novel *Face au Drapeau* (Face the Flag), featuring animated drawings and models together with live actors. Reviewers praised the technical results of the film and its background design (from illustrations by Riou and Bennet) which maintained Verne's 19th century ambiance.

'The film suffers from imbalance, both in technique and inspiration,' wrote André Bazin, 'but there are innumerable beautiful sequences and frequent comic expedients.' Added Vittorio Spinazzola, 'Not too many critics noticed the decisively modern thesis, dealing with the failure of disinterested science and the tragic end of the researcher, unable to understand whether his conquests will be used to help humanity or will be turned against it.' Local critics proudly claimed, 'Méliès did not die, he is Czechoslovakian and his name is Zeman'.

In 1961, Zeman repeated this success in *Baron Prásil* (Baron Münchhausen, 1961), based on Gottfried Bürger's novel and Gustave Doré's engravings.

'This time, in a way never seen before in live-action cinema, Zeman enters the worlds of Münchhausen, Bürger and Doré. Prásil's journey (Prásil is the Czech name for Münchhausen) from the Moon to Constantinople on a vessel drawn by Pegasus; his entry into the sultan's palace, which Dore's engraving enlivens in all its magic; the romantic kidnapping of princess Bianca from the palace; the naval battle and Münchhausen's glorious victory; the involuntary flight of the Baron in the claws of a huge bird; his return riding a seahorse; his flight on a cannonball … It is not surprising that in his other two films *Blaznová chronika* (A Jester's Tale) and *Ukradena Vzducholod* (The Stolen Airship), the filmmaker builds on his past achievements, although with new twists.'[1]

Fig. 64. Inspirace by Karel Zeman (Czechoslovakia, 1948).

1   All quotations on this page are from André Bazin, 'Bruxelles', *Cinema nuovo*, No. 134 (July–August 1958); Vittorio Spinazzola, 'La diabolica invenzione,' *Cinema nuovo*, No. 139 (May–June 1959), and Horejsí and Struska, *Occhio magico*.

After *Na komete* (On the comet, 1970) Zeman made *Druhá cesta námorníka Sindibáda* (Sinbad the Sailor, 1972), *Krabat Carodejuv ucén* (The Sorcerer's Apprentice, 1977), *Pohádka o Honzíkovi a Marence* (The Tale of John and Mary, 1979) and *Karel Zeman for Children* (1980). Always suspended between marvel and technique, Zeman's subtle, vibrant films do not fit the limiting definition of adventure cinema, but display a playful vitality and faith in progress which are deserving of Verne and Méliès.

Jirí Trnka

'Jirí Trnka was the master. Although he was not directly the master, because he was too modest to teach anybody anything. But the quality of his work was such that all of us tried to equal or surpass it. Trnka had been the first to show us that animation could be an art form. He made art films, and this was somewhat revolutionary at the time. Trnka also taught us discipline: he was self-disciplined and industrious and expected the same from his collaborators. He was very kind but also strict. He did not accept compromises. He encouraged us to be serious.'[1]

This is how Jirí Brdecka described the artist who more than anybody else brought honour to Czechoslovakian animation.

Trnka was born in Pilsen on 24 February 1912, the son of a blacksmith and a dress-maker. His junior-high art teacher, and one of the last great puppeteers, Josef Skupa, encouraged the boy to study art and made him his assistant. From Skupa, Trnka learned the art of carving wooden puppets.

Asked why animated puppets had undergone such a development in Czechoslovakia, critic Jirí Struska answered:

'perhaps because of the tradition of Renaiss-

ance and Baroque popular performances ... perhaps because of the puppet tradition.' Explained Maria Benesová, 'Puppet theatre was adopted centuries ago as a way to substitute for ordinary theatre with live actors. During the Austro-Hungarian oppression, puppet theatres stirred up rebellion against forced Germanization. Toward the 1840s, no fewer than seventy-nine puppeteer families toured

Fig. 65. The Diabolic Invention *by Karel Zeman (Czechoslovakia, 1958).*
Fig. 66. Baron Prasil *by Karel Zeman (Czechoslovakia, 1961).*

---

1 Jirí Brdecka, personal communication to the author (1977).

Bohemia. The musician Smetana composed two graceful overtures to puppet theatres, the artist Ales painted scenes and puppets, the novelist Jirasek dedicated his fairy tale *Mr. Johannes* to puppeteers.'[1]

In the years following World War I, Czech puppets gained even more popularity because of the rise of specialized theatres, new companies and radio programmes. There was no theatrical 'genre' which was not approached by wooden actors, from children's works to vaudeville to classical dramas, comedies and political satire. In Czechoslovakia more than anywhere else, this tradition entered cinema with the greatest spontaneity. There is no visible hiatus between puppet theatre and animated puppet cinema. The transition occurred smoothly, with those minimal changes required by the new means of communication but with the same acting and scene design.

Having made a name for himself as a painter and a satirical illustrator, Trnka still felt attracted to book illustration and theatre. He worked as a scene designer with avant-garde director Jir Frejka, but did not forget his old love for puppets and founded the Wooden Theatre. Except for an isolated episode in the mid-1930s, when Karel Dodal animated Trnka's puppet Hurvinek, Trnka approached cinema at the end of the war. The subject he suggested, *Grandfather Planted a Beet*, was accepted; the result was Trnka's first film with animated drawings, which shows the artist's undisputed skills, but is still far from the level he would later reach with puppet animation.

Darek (The Gift, 1946) is an almost experimental movie, unusually surrealistic for its time. *Zvíratka a petrovští* (The Animals and the Brigands, 1946) is a brisk rendition of an old popular tale. *Pérák a SS* (The Springer and the SS Men, 1946) is a well-made anti-Nazi movie, featuring a chimney sweep who dons two strong springs,

taunts the SS and jumps away from them. All these works were made in 1946. In Trnka's opinion, however, too many middle-men (artists, colour technicians) weakened the originality of the author's drawings, and he made plans to animate puppets. It was autumn, 1946.

Trnka observed:

'With Pojar, we animated one of my oldest wooden puppets, a ballerina. It moved well, but gave an abstract impression. The effect was nice, but did not mean anything. Thus we understood that a puppet film needs concrete situations, or "a story".'

Špalicek (The Czech Year, 1947), the feature film born after this experiment, indeed told a 'story', or rather, many stories. Based on a book illustrated by Mikulás Ales, the film was a type of documentary on Czech customs throughout the year. It already showed the seeds of the poetics Trnka eventually developed: love of nature; a subtle but powerful lyricism; and a deep feeling for popular culture.

Trnka's second feature film was *Císaruv Slavík* (The Emperor's Nightingale, 1948), based on Andersen's tale. Set in the Court of the Celestial Empire and characterized by the porcelain-like softness of aristocratic places and faces, the subject seems very different from Trnka's previous film which featured solid, spontaneous Bohemian peasants. In fact, the underlying theme of this second movie does not differ substantially from the first one, but is approached here through irony. The court, the mechanical toys of the shy little emperor and the elegant headdresses are ridiculed in comparison with the simple life and nature. This theme was already present in the tale by Andersen, an author to whom Trnka felt close.

In 1950, Trnka made his third feature film, *Ba-*

1   Horejsí and Struska, *Occhio magico*; Maria Benesová, 'Il cinema di animazione,' *Il film cecoslovacco*, Ernesto G. Laura ed. (Rome: Ateneo, 1960).

jaja (Prince Bayaya, 1950), about a peasant who becomes a knight, fights a dragon and conquers the love of a princess. With Old Czech Legends, the artist returned, seven years later, to the national popular theme of his first film. The structure itself was similar to Trnka's old work, with various episodes from ancient Slavic popular mythology being presented as parts of one whole fresco. Considered by many as Trnka's masterpiece, *Staré povesti ceské* (Old Czech Legends, 1957) was an example of how heroic or sublime topics could be treated with such unpretentious tools as puppets.

In 1954 and 1955, Trnka undertook an ambitious adaptation of three episodes from *Dobry Voják Švejk* (The Good Soldier Schweik, 1955) by Jaroslav Hašek. As with most literary texts, Hašek's novel does not lend itself to dramatic representation, although several versions have since been made for cinema or TV. Trnka's version was not one of the finest works by the filmmaker; nevertheless, he managed to preserve Hašek's spirit, using characters based on Josef Lada's classic illustrations of the text.

Trnka's last feature film was *Sen noci svatojánské* (Midsummer Night's Dream, 1959), from Shakespeare. Here he let his fantasy go free and created luxurious costumes. The film excels, however, for its portrayal of common people such as the foolish peasants from Athens (Bottom and company) who fall victim to Puck's tricks. Critic Dilys Powell wrote in the *Sunday Times* (11 October 1959) that she was surprised at how powerful puppets could be: Bottom was enchanting, and Snug could not have been more entertaining. Ugo Casiraghi disagreed:

> 'Trnka likes to let loose in a spectacular, tasteful pantomime, rich with choreographic expedients but mixing too many styles (from neoclassic to rococo), displaying somewhat exaggerated refinements and, in the long run,

excessive mannerism.'[1]

Trnka's other works were mainly shorts. 'I experienced all that was possible with a puppet film. I experimented with all genres, from tales and parodies to epics. I still have only one genre left: the civic one'.

Once a fertile and brilliant artist, Trnka entered an increasingly pessimistic stage, his last. *Vášen* (The Passion, 1962) is the bitter story of a youngster who is totally insensitive to the humanistic ideals of Resistance artists, and whose only interest is his motorcycle. *Kybernetická babicka* (The Cybernetic Grandmother, 1962) tells of a child who goes from the loving care of her grandmother to that of a robot granny – an obvious polemic against encroaching technology. Trnka's gloominess culminated in *Ruka* (The Hand, 1965). A potter and sculptor is commissioned to make a monument by a huge Hand. He refuses, and the Hand turns to coaxing and to force. Locked in a golden cage, the man first abides and then escapes and returns to the flower for which he made his pots. However the Hand, a symbol of power, causes the man's death and gives him a grand funeral. *Ruka* was Trnka's last film (see Colour Plate 27), a sort of angry paen to creative freedom just before the artist was forced to interrupt his activity because of poor health, in 1966. As his friends remember, Trnka's last years were sad. Because of a heart ailment, he could not work, and the lack of work worsened his condition. 'My hand is intact, but my mind is empty,' he said, one year before his death, in Prague, on 30 December 1969, at the age of fifty-seven.

Casiraghi wrote:

> 'Trnka shows two tendencies. The most authentic, one might say realistic, appears in a classic manner every time he addresses the popular traditions of his land. The most fantastic, sophisticated, one could even say "de-

1   Ugo Casiraghi, *Il cinema cecoslovacco* (Monza: Quaderni del circolo monzese del cinema, 1962).

cadent" tendency appears when the artist deals with culturally-refined aristocratic legends of other countries.'[1]

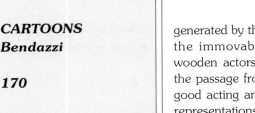

Trnka's role as a national poet actually derives from his being a peasant-poet. 'I belong to the country,' he said, 'I have never felt at home in cities.' Rooted in the peasant traditions of people who have always turned to the land for their resources, Trnka brought to cinema a deep love for nature and a lyric faith in a people's traditions and their eternal spirit, which inspired his full-blooded sense of humour and his faith in life.

A great narrator, Trnka is the ultimate representative of the long line of Bohemian story-tellers and novelists. His work can be compared to a very prolific writer who addresses historic or chivalric novels, tales for children (the short *Arie prérie* – Song of the Prairie, 1949), experimental stories (the shorts *O zlaté rybce* – The Golden Fish, 1951, with drawings, and *Dva mrázici* – 2 Frosts, 1954, with Chinese shadows).

The 'refined' side of Trnka's work is the representation of a well-assimilated culture, but is also the most open to criticism. Trnka is at his best when developing a poetics for animated puppets, creating rules for their acting and structures. Before Trnka, animated puppets clashed with the problem of physiognomy and face-animation; entire files were filled with mouths, eyes and eyebrows ready to be superimposed on the puppets' faces. Trnka discovered that those faces had the same role as theatrical masks, and therefore were to be as fixed and sacred as masks. His puppets, characterized by contained expressions and almost stately movements, artistically surpassed those artists who had tried to loosen their puppets' joints or give them the same contortions as animated drawings. Trnka's puppets received their expressions from framing and lighting rather than gestures. Characters were enlivened by psychological elements, and their mimicry was generated by their drama. With the immovable faces of his wooden actors, Trnka marked the passage from histrionics to good acting and from external representations to internal dramatic experiences. As Bretislav Pojar wrote, 'I often noticed Trnka, while he was painting his actors' heads. He always gave their eyes an undefined look. By merely turning their heads, or by a change in lighting, they gained smiling or unhappy or dreamy expressions. This gave one the impression that the puppet hid more than it showed, and that its wooden heart harbored even more.'

Whenever the theme challenged his expressive skills, Trnka became more subtle, even falling into a precious, but uninspired, style. Culture stifled the artist's spontaneity. This is the case of *Midsummer Night's Dream*. Some sequences of earlier works (*Old Czech Legends* in particular) also suffer from a complacent formal perfection and a smug representation of 'realistic' movements and characters. Not by chance, Trnka's most touching work was the stark *The Hand*.

Yugoslavia: the first stage of the Zagreb School

The man responsible for bringing animation to Yugoslavia was Serij Tagatz, who trained in the Soviet Union and later returned to Zagreb. Tagatz worked on commission, particularly in the advertising field. Also in Zagreb, the Berlin-born Maar brothers, who had left Germany to escape anti-semitic persecutions, founded a new flourishing advertising studio, which lasted until 1940, producing up to two-hundred short films a year.

The war dispersed artists, equipment and films and when the war ended, occupation troops prohibited filming. When, in 1945, Yugoslavia was again free, it did not have any background in ani-

1   Casiraghi, Ugo, *Il cinema cecoslovacco.*

mation. Unlike other socialist nations (from the start Yugoslav socialism differed from that of the Warsaw Pact countries), production was not promoted or supported by the State, but was rather the work of a few Zagreb-based enthusiasts. Fadil Hadzic, was one such enthusiast. As editor of the satirical magazine *Kerempuh*, Hadzic decided to celebrate the detachment of Yugoslavia from the East European countries with a satirical short. *Veliki miting* (The Big Meeting, was filmed in 1949, but dated 1951 in Yugoslav sources), with contributions by artists such as Borivoj Dovnikovic and Walter and Norbert Neugebauer, who were to make names for themselves in later years.

Helped by governmental support, Hadzic founded Duga Film. With more than one-hundred artists, the artistic team included some of the best of Croatian-Yugoslav animation, such as Marks, Bourek, Kolar, Grgic and Kristl. Dusan Vukotic (the master of the first stage of the Zagreb School) headed a unit. Inexperienced in technique, the animators proceeded by trial and error, imitating a bit of Disney here, and a degree of Czechoslovakian films there. Production continued for a couple of years, until the federal government diverted funding toward schools and hospitals rather than animation.

Architect Nikola Kostelac, who had fallen in love with animation, managed to preserve some minimal activities with the help of Zora Film, a producer of educational shorts. By that time, Yugoslavia had become a modified version of a free-market economy, and required some advertising campaigns. The founders of the now defunct Duga Film jumped into this field, creating an independent group which collaborated with Kostelac's team. Around 1955, they developed the technique of limited animation, which saved time, work and money while experimenting with a 'new' style. This trend was similar to the one pursued by the American UPA a few years earlier.

With remarkable success came clients. The distributor for the group was Zagreb Film, which incorporated the group itself as soon as the government ordered the company to reorganize. In 1956, under the white horse logo of Zagreb Film, Vukotic, Marks, Kolar, Bourek and other artists resumed their activity in the field they favoured, fiction films. The first short to be released by Zagreb Film was *Nestasni robot* (The Playful Robot, 1956) directed by Dusan Vukotic, on a subject by Andre Lusicic, with drawing by Aleksandar Marks and Boris Kolar, scene design by Zlatko Bourek and animation by Vjekoslav Kostanisek and Vladimir Jutrisa. Shown at the Pula film festival, the film won an award – the first to be presented to the Zagreb School.

In 1957, Vatroslav Mimica (Omis, 1923) joined the animation section. Writer, critic and journalist, in 1952 and 1955 Mimica had directed two live-action feature films from which he had gained neither money nor popularity. The group co-opted Mimica, who did not know how to draw, as a script writer. Soon Mimica switched to directing and from that time on, his dedication and personality influenced the team. 1958 was an important year for production: Mimica's *Samac* (Alone, 1958) was awarded a prestigious prize at the Venice festival, and the entire animation section of Zagreb Film was praised by critics and spectators alike at the Cannes Film Festival.

The news of this success reached Vlado Kristl (Zagreb, 1923), one of the first-wave of animators, who had migrated without much luck to South America and who was hoping now to return to Zagreb Film. The company, meanwhile, had put a tight rein on its animators.

It was the time when artistic directors were imposed from above. Kristl injected his talent in *Kradja dragulja* (The Great Jewel Robbery, 1959) but the film was credited to the artistic director. In *Zagrenska koza* (La peau de chagrin, 1960), based on Balzac's horror story), Kristl anticipated a revival of Art Deco and created a tense atmosphere, but the film was credited also to Vrbanic as co-director. Finally, Kristl directed *Don Kihot* (Don Quixote, 1961) a difficult, intellectual but very poetic film for which he used state-of-the-art graphics.

In 1962, Kristl began filming *General i resni clovek* (The General-in-Chief, 1962), a satirical

live-action short which put him in trouble with the censors. Annoyed, he moved to Germany, where he filmed several live-action shorts and two feature films, *Der Damm* (The Dam, 1965) and *Der Brief* (The Letter, 1965), in which he made acting appearances. Kristl returned briefly to animation in 1967, with *Die Utopen* (Utopia) and *Das Land des Überflusses* (The Land of Plenty), and in 1982, with *Verräter des jungen Deutschen Films schlafen nicht!* (The Traitors of the Young German Films Don't Sleep).

The system of 'artistic direction' ended after a clamorous press campaign demanded the return of freedom of speech. In the early 1960s, the axiom that animated films must be art films was established.

The Zagreb School is usually thought of as being divided into two periods. The first, from 1957 to 1964, is dominated by such authorities as Vukotic, Mimica and Kristl. During this era, the Zagreb School legitimized its style of limited animation, with its marked tendency toward avant-garde graphic and pictorial techniques (such as collages and assemblages) and its subjects. Yugoslav artists no longer dealt with brief stories of caricatural characters, but rather with anguish, incommunicability and Evil. Films provoking liberating laughter still existed, but Zagreb's films gradually grew into long painful moanings about the horrors of existence. This became the school's trademark. A common inspiration generated by shared experiences, despite different artistic personalities, and thoughts. At Zagreb, exchanging roles and forming new teams for new projects was common practice. Directors would become artists or designers for their colleagues, and vice versa. Nikola Kostelac (Zagreb, 1920) was the first of the distinguished directors. His *Preimijera* (Opening Night, 1957), and *Na livadi* (In the Meadow, 1957) were partially indebted to the best of American and Canadian productions, but still exhibited cleverly incorporated novelties of style.

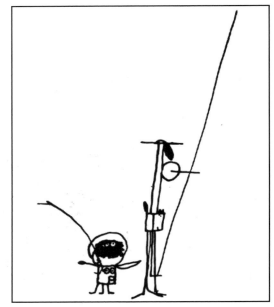

Fig. 67. Don Quixote *by Vlado Kristl (Yugoslavia, Croatia, 1961). Fig. 68*. Substitute *by Dusan Vukotic (Yugoslavia, Croatia, 1961).*

After his debut film, *Alone* (1958), Mimica made *Inspktor se vratio kuci* (The Inspector Comes Home, 1959), *Mala kronika* (Everyday Chronicle, 1962) and *Tifusari* (Typhus, 1963, based on a poem by Jure Kastelana). In 1963, he left animation to devote himself to live-action cinema, his first love, and became one of the most important Yugoslav filmmakers of the new generation, together with Petrovic and Makavejev.

Vukotic (Bileca, 1927) filmed *Koncert za mazinsku pusky* (Concerto for Sub-Machine Gun, 1959) and *Krava na mjesecu* (Cow on the Moon, 1959) in 1959. *Surogat* (Substitute, 1961), his best-known work and one of the finest in the history of animation won him an Oscar. Critic Ranko Munitic wrote:

> 'Vukotic chose simple caricatural drawings moving like arabesques against a white neutral background. He also used colour as the element which best defined his highly decorative concept of surface. As for Mimica, he paid attention to the pictorial aspects of animation. He favoured rich and complex graphic structures over neutral planes or surfaces and bare drawings. In his scene design, space consists of parallel strata of colour which articulate in depth, subordinating figures to a broken, maze-like fabric.

> 'This way of using material, already in 1959, transformed collage into an expressive solution. As a symbolic synthesis of the contemporary concept of absurdity, Mimica's figures are not as natural or mobile as Vukotic's caricatures, but their external rigidity is a poetic metaphor for the desperation of man caught in the web of modern civilization. Mimica uses the expressive value of colour in its entirety. His world is characterized by a keen awareness of the tragic conflict of our times, which

forces man to adapt to the fast technological rhythm at the cost of personal integrity.'[1]

Poland

Polish animation began before World War II. In 1917, philosopher and journalist Feliks Kuczkowski (1884–1970) filmed *The Chairs' Flirtation* and *The Telescope Has Two Ends*. 'They were based on a small number of drawings by his friend, painter Lucjan Kobierski,' Marcin Gizycki said. 'The first film consisted of 38 drawings, which means that it wasn't "true" animation.'[2]

Fig. 69. Inspktor se vratio kuci by Vatroslav Mimica (Yugoslavia, Croatia, 1959).

Fig. 70. Tifusari by Vatroslav Mimica (Yugoslavia, Croatia, 1963).

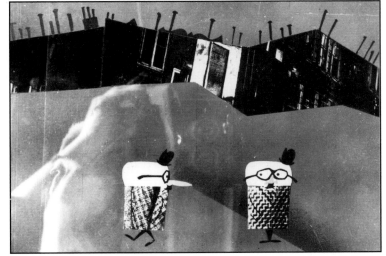

1 Ranko Munitic on Yugoslavia, in *Il film d'animazione d'Europa*, Orio Caldiron and Turi Fedele ed. (Abano Terme, 1971).
2 Letter received from Marcin Gizycki, 1 March 1986. Much of the information on pre-war Poland reported in this chapter is based on this source.

In 1918, Kuczkowski created a film (the title of which has been lost) with animated objects. The work was the practical rendition of what he called 'visual filming', a sort of improvisation in front of the camera. In the 1920s he made *The Orchestra Conductor*, a second 'visual film' using clay.

Another pioneer was Stanislaw Dobrzynski, who made a few films from 1918 to 1924. In the following years, the most active Polish animator was Wlodimierz Kowanko, who worked in Cracow, Katowice and Warsaw. His best films were *Mr. Twardowski* (1934), based on a popular tale, and *The Mice's Expedition for a Cake*. Kowanko's style shows traces of American influence. Jan Jarosz, from Lwow, began his career in the mid-1920s. In 1931, he made the notable *Puk's Adventures*. Later, he experimented with a hand-drawn sound track in an advertising film. In the 1930s, Jaryczewski was active in Poznan; in 1924, he released *Female Stars and Male Stars*.

Stephan and Franciszka Themerson occupy a special chapter in Polish animation with their experimental work (collages, animated objects and direct painting on stock), from *Pharmacy* (1930) and *Europe* (1931–32) to *The Eye, the Ear* (1945, made in Great Britain).

In the field of puppet animation, the finest artists include Karol Marczak (former assistant to Ladislas Starewich in Paris and director of *The Golden Pot*, 1935) and Maksymilian Emmer and Jerzy Maliniak (*Toy Soldiers*, 1938, partially animated). It was precisely a puppet animator, Zenon Wasilewski (1903–66), who represented the only link between pre-war and postwar productions. A poet and a satirical cartoonist, Wasilewski learned the basics of animation in the mid-1930s while drawing for Kowanko. In 1938, he made some advertising films with puppets. The following year he used this same technique in a tale featuring the dragon of Wawel (Cracow's hill); because of the German invasion in September 1939, the film was left unfinished, without a sound-track. Wasilewski spent the war years in the Soviet Union as a representative of Polish Resistance. Afterward, he returned to his country, establishing his residence in Lodz, where he founded a production and distribution company (which would later become the important Se-Ma-For). In 1947, Wasilewski released a second version of his previously filmed tale, renamed *In King Krakus' Time*. In the following years, until his death, he divided his time equally between painting and cinema. His releases include *The Two Little Dorothies* (1956) and *Dratewka the Shoemaker* (1958), for children, and *Caution! The Devil* (1958) and *The Crime on the Street of the Ventriloquist Cat* (1961), for adults.

Poland was worn-out by the world conflict, with its major cities largely destroyed and a razed capital. Lodz and Katowice, two of the least stricken cities, became the very first centres of animation. In Katowice, a group named Slask made productions with animated drawings for the state department of cinema, Film Polski. Later on, a studio in Bielsko-Biala specialized in animated drawings, while the studio in Lodz became pre-eminent in puppet animation. It was in this field that Wlodimierz Haupe and Halina Bielinska distinguished themselves with *Janosik* (1954), the first Polish animated feature film, and four years later, with *Changing of the Guard*, created with animated matchboxes. In the field of animated drawings, only Wladislaw Nehrebecki's films for children are noteworthy.

After 1956, in Poland too there was a gradual thawing in favour of art films. The initiators of this new attitude were the then debuting artists Jan Lenica and Walerian Borowczyk, who made their first films together: *Byl sobie raz...* (Once Upon a Time ..., 1957) *Dom* (The House, 1958) and *Nagrodzone uczucie* (Love Rewarded, 1957), and the two made-to-order micro-shorts, *Striptease* (1957) and *Sztandar mlodych* (Banner of Youth, 1957).

Lenica (born in Poznan in 1928) had studied music, architecture and fine arts before dedicating himself to graphics, where he soon made a name for himself. Borowczyk (born in Kwilcz in 1923) undertook the same kind of studies before passionately applying himself to cinema. He made his debut in the early 1950s with short live-action films. The collaboration between the two artists, marred by their strong and independent personalities, ceased in 1958. Within a few months of each other, both Lenica and Borowczyk emigrated to the West. They never resolved their frictions, but independently they were both able to attain high levels of creativity.

Lenica and Borowczyk's joint works of 1957 made history in Poland, as their sense of absurdity, surrealism and anguished settings became favourite themes of the Polish school.

Hungary

The very first pioneer of Hungarian animation was István Kató, who made his debut with *Zsirb Ödön* (1914), using cutouts.[1] During his long career (he retired in 1957), the filmmaker produced hundreds of animated films for all purposes, from entertainment and advertising to education and newsreels. Kató began in a most empirical way, working from the roof garden of a cinema, using the sunlight and measuring exposure times with a metronome. His adaptation of Sándor Petöfi's poem *Janos the Knight* (1916) and a silhouette film entitled *Romeo and Juliet* (1931) merit acclaim.

In pre-war Hungary, Istvan Walker animated the popular tale *The Miller, His Daughter and the Donkey* (1934). Animation, however, suffered from a diaspora of talent. Among the artists who left for work abroad were: György Pál Marczincsák (George Pal); János Halász (John Halas); Imre Hajdu (Jean Image); and Etienne Raïk (a collaborator of Alexeïeff's and a fine puppet ani-

mator who worked mainly in advertising).

Gyula Macskassy (1912–1972) a former filmmaker in the advertising industry, became the initiator of postwar Hungarian animation. A student of painter and Bauhaus follower Sandor Bortnyk, in 1951, Macskassy directed *The Rooster's Diamond*, the first short of the new generation. Hungarian films had been modelled on the state-sanctioned production typical of other Eastern European countries, favouring children's films and folkloric tales. In 1959 Macskassy and Gyorgy Varnai (Budapest, 1921) made a breakthrough with *The Pencil and the Eraser*. Shown at Annecy in 1960, this film gave outside exposure to the new, sober ideas born in the studios of Budapest, which no longer wanted to address only children. The same year, the two filmmakers made another fine production, *The Duel*, a clever and entertaining reprimand of warmongering.

An innovative, high-calibre film was *The Ball with White Dots* (1961), featuring a little girl who daydreams about the fantastic adventures she might have with her ball. With this film, which won a Gold Lion at the Film Festival of Venice, Tibor Csermak (Kaposvar, 1927 – Budapest, 1965) reached the apex of his brief directing career begun in 1957.

Romania

In the 1920s, Aurel Petrescu (1897–1948) pioneered the field of animation in Romania by working, in solitude, on about forty films, the most famous of which were *Pacala in the Moon* (1920) and *Pacala in Love* (1924). A journalist, graphic artist, director, comic illustrator and the first film critic of his country (he wrote a column from 1915 on), Petrescu remained without imitators or followers. With a few exceptions his films were lost during the war, and his premature death prevented the new generation benefiting from his

---

1   This is the name of the protagonist, the sound of which in Hungarian means 'keg'.

technique and artistic experience.

Another multifaceted, disorderly genius was artist, painter, writer and teacher of film direction, Marin Iorda. *Haplea* (1927), featuring the popular character of the title, was his only animated short. After the war the communist regime promoted state-funded cinema. True professional animation began later in 1950.

Ion Popescu-Gopo and the 'Pill-film'

Ion Popescu-Gopo (Bucharest, 30 April 1923 – 3 December 1989), debuted in 1951 with the first state sponsored film, *The Bee and the Pigeon*, produced by Bucharest Studio. The country's productions gradually increased in number, from the one film in 1951 to ten in 1956. Until then Popescu-Gopo and his colleagues had followed a traditional style, without much fantasy. In 1956, with a sudden change,

Popescu-Gopo got rid of his 'classical' heritage and directed an innovative short, *Scurta istorie* (Short History, 1956). The protagonist is a primitive naked little man, with an oblong head, who goes through all the evolutionary stages of history until he reaches Space and discovers a new life. A philosophical film, cleverly fanciful and characterized by compact editing and by drier-than-usual drawings, it was well-received both in Romania and abroad. *7 arte* (Seven Arts, 1958), *Homo Sapiens* (1960) and *Allo, allo ...* (Hallo, Hallo, 1962) followed, featuring the same character in a series of similar comic, gnomic films. Meanwhile, Popescu-Gopo concentrated on language problems, developing a theory of expressive synthesis which favoured minimal-length films. He entitled his offering 'pill-film' and presented it in a series of lightning-like animated sketches (often no longer than fifteen seconds) which opened the evenings at the Mamaja Film Festival of 1966.

In 1967, Popescu-Gopo released a second anthology of *Pills*, followed by *Kisses* (1969) and *Hourglass* (1972), and by a quite pale production which included some live-action feature films as well as experiments with various materials (pins, hair). Popescu-Gopo's best period was the span between 1956 and 1962, when he filmed the four-part work on the naked little man. A clever essayist, he used the history of human kind, the birth of the arts and the history of communications as themes on which to develop his variations.

Popescu-Gopo's somewhat professorial, pedantic tone emerged whenever he neglected plot to rely exclusively on expedients. Then his humour came out as gratuitous or expected, no longer supporting the subversive and somewhat absurd taste he displayed in his early works. *Kisses* marked a return to the style Popescu-Gopo had displayed in 1956 (although his leading character did not appear in this film). The bare apologue is vaguely moralistic, however it does convey

Fig. 71. Homo Sapiens, a character by Ion Popescu-Gopo (Romania, 1960s).

Popescu-Gopo's point on the subjects of cheating and exploitation.

Popescu-Gopo's theory of making animation the place for cinematographic epigram was certainly prolific. In 1967, the Montreal Expo held a competition with a fixed theme for one-minute maximum films. This confirmed that Popescu-Gopo's revolution had come at the right time, summarizing a need – the detachment from standardization, even in footage – which was greatly felt in the fast expanding world of animation.

Ivanov-Vano's Soviet Union

For fifteen years after the end of World War II, Soviet animation was involved mainly in the production of children's films, favouring the classic technique of drawing on cels and the round American style. This style, however, had sober movements, far from the deformations and contortions typical of slapstick animation; in short, it learned from the lesson of Disney's feature films. Research and experimentation (as well as memories of the avant-garde of the first years), were put aside. Animation of puppets and cutouts resumed with new strength in 1953, with the opening of a specialized section at Sojuzmultfilm.

The 1960s saw a timid renewal in style and theme, which emerged particularly in folkloric representations of the Russians and of the other peoples of the immense multi-racial, multi-national republic. Much time had to pass, however, before Soviet animation, as well as Soviet cinema as a whole, abandoned its conventionality and its lack of creative and intellectual daring. Years had to pass, also, before the Soviet Union produced autonomous artists capable of elitist and personal creative discourses, as happened earlier in other countries with similar communist regimes such as Czechoslovakia or Poland. Unlike Russian live-action cinema, flourishing with Grigori Chukh-

rai's works, Soviet animation did not take part in the thriving period coinciding with Khrushchev's thaw. Notwithstanding the excellent technical, narrative and dramatic knowledge Soviet animators possessed, animation was considered (supported by Ivan Ivanov-Vano) as a public service, responsible for good entertainment and methodical teaching. Beside the traditional shorts, feature and featurette films were also produced. The main artists were well-established professionals Ivan Ivanov-Vano, the Brumberg sisters, Lev Atamanov and Mikhail Tsekhanovsky.

Ivanov-Vano, the most influential personality in cultural politics, became a favourite of the public with an immensely popular feature film, *The Humpbacked Little Horse* (1947). Based on a subject by Ershov and on other popular tales, the film tells the story of Ivanuska the fool, his hump-backed horse, a beautiful princess and a wicked king who wants to marry her. Helped by his little horse, Ivanuska passes a test with three cauldrons containing cold water, milk and boiling water, and becomes a prince. He marries the princess, while the evil king is left to boil forever in the liquid. The film was traditionally structured but well animated and well supported by a warm, competent narration.[1]

Later, the eclectic Ivanov-Vano made innumerable films, displaying his solid taste for good animation and for diverse figurative proposals. His feature films included: *The Story of a Dead Princess and a Brave Family* (1951), a version of *Snow White* as told by Pushkin; *The Twelve Months* (1956), about a capricious queen who wants a basket of snowdrops on New Year's Day and who is punished by the twelve months meeting in a forest; and *The Adventures of a Puppet* (1959), a version of Collodi's *Pinocchio*, made in collaboration with Dmitri Babichenko. *The Left Hander* (1964, also known as *The Mechanical Flea*), featured Leshkov's 19th century story, il-

---

1   As the negative of the original film was lost, Ivanov-Vano made a second version thirty years later.

lustrated with painter Arkadij Tiurin's Lubok images (equivalent to the French 'images d'Epinal'); a good deal of figurative suggestions, from engravings to Napoleonic caricatures to toys contributed to develop a mixed but coherent discourse. In 1969, Ivanov-Vano directed *The Seasons of the Year*, based on Tchaikovsky's compositions *Troika and Fall*, with images referring to embroidery and traditional fabrics. The director died in May 1987.

The Brumberg sisters also worked on feature films. *The Missing Diploma* (1945) tells of a Cossack's dream about a little devil who steals a diploma and gives it to the Czarina. *Christmas Eve* (1951) features a blacksmith who wants a pair of beautiful shoes for his whimsical beloved, and who obtains them at the royal palace. *Flight to the Moon* (1953) is about a boy who participates in an interplanetary trip so as to help the crew of a vanished rocket. In *Wishes Come True* (1957) a lumberjack receives the gift of realizing his every wish and marries a beautiful princess.

The two sisters' mainline production, however, was educational, with attacks against poor study habits and laziness as in *The Girl at the Circus* (1950), *Mistake Island* (1955) and *Stepa the Sailor* (1955). At least one of these preachy films, *Fedya Zaitsev* (1948), was noteworthy for its good drawings and vivaciously rhythmic story telling. Known also as *I Drew the Little Man*, the film tells of a boy who draws a little man on the school wall, lets a schoolmate be accused of the mischief and finally, remorseful, confesses in front of the entire class.

Lev Atamanov chiefly produced adaptations of literary texts, emulating Ivan Ivanov-Vano. An accurate artist, ready to lean toward sentimentalism, Atamanov was, however, less gifted than his colleague as far as inventiveness and directing ability were concerned. The feature film *The Reddish Flower* (1952), based on a subject by Aksakov, told of a merchant returning from far-away lands who, while looking for a gift for his beloved, is captured and kept prisoner by a tyrant, until his sweetheart comes to the rescue. Atamanov's best known films include the feature films *The Golden Antelope* (1954, based on Indian tales) and *The Snow Queen* (1957, based on Andersen's tale). The first tells of a greedy rajah who attempts to exploit an antelope that can produce golden coins from its hooves. The second one is the story of a boy who is kidnapped by the Snow Queen, imprisoned in the ice palace and finally freed by his friend Gerda's love. Although artistically weak, the films were loved by the public and by festival juries, and won several awards. In the 1960s and 1970s, Atamanov continued children's productions but also worked on more ambitious projects, such as *The Ballerina on the Boat* (1969, praising the pure beauty of art), *The Bundle* (1966), *The Bench* (1977) and *We Can* (1970, dealing with political and social events). Atamanov died in Moscow on 12 February 1981.

Mikhail Tsekhanovsky forfeited his old ambitions and devoted himself to children's cinema. In 1954, he made *The Frog Princess*, the umpteenth version of the popular tale. After some short and medium-length films, including *The Girl in the Jungle* (1956), Tshekhanovsky made the feature film *The Wild Swans*, from Hans Christian Andersen. In 1964, he made his last film, a remake of *Post Office*.

Like Tsekhanovsky, Mstislav Paschenko (Jaroslavl, 1 April 1901 – Moscow, 22 October 1958) developed as an artist in St Petersburg (then Leningrad) where he worked at the Lenfilm studio and made *Dzhabsha* (1938) a quite important film. After the war, Paschenko moved to Moscow with his colleague Tsekhanovsky. His films include *When the Christmas Trees will be Lit* (1950), *The Traveler of the Forest* (1951) and the prize-winning *An Unusual Match* (1955). This last film was co-directed by Boris Dioskin (Kursk, 19 August 1914), an artist who for several years worked mainly for other directors, only occasionally making his own creations. In the 1960s he became definitively a director after his internationally successful film *Goal! Goal!* (1964).

Chapter 14
Eastern Europe

Vladimir Degtiarev (Moscow, 18 January 1916 – 6 September 1974) debuted in 1953 with *The Proud Pak*. He ensured his popularity with *Spoiling* and with *Who Said Meow?*, the first successful puppet film made after the war.

Chapter 15

Animation in Asia

China

China has been one of the most restless countries of the century, troubled by civil war, the struggle against foreign invasions and internal upheavals. Chinese live-action cinema felt the influence of these events both in production and, more significantly, in content. The beginning dates back to 1923, when foreigners and Chinese émigrés financed the construction of movie theatres in Shanghai, followed by developments in Hong Kong, Beijing, Nanking and Chengchow.

For a long time China was represented in the field of animation only by the four Wan brothers – the twins Wan Laiming and Wan Guchan (born in Nanching on 18 January 1900, although according to Wan Laiming himself, the year was 1899), Wan Chaochen (1906–1992) and Wan Dihuan (1907). Having been attracted since childhood to figures in movement, the brothers made their first animated film, *Uproar in the Art Studio*, in 1926, followed by *The Revolt of the Paper Figures*, in 1930. The Wans, who were set-designers for live-action cinema, made these films in amateurish fashion, repeating the Fleischers' formula of drawings which come to life independent of the will of a human protagonist. In 1932, their production reached a total of six films, including two tales (*The Race of the Hare and the Tortoise* and *The Grasshopper and the Ant*) and patriotic films inspired by the Japanese attack on Shanghai on 28 January 1932 (*Compatriot, Wake Up, The Price of Blood*).

In 1933, the Wans (now three, as the youngest Dihuan had left the group to devote himself to photography) found some stability within the production company Mingshin, which asked them to develop an animation department. For four years screens were populated with characters such as the little black monkey (which resembled Mickey Mouse) or Miss Lu's father (a little man with a square jaw, who dressed in western clothes). Another series mixed live-action shots (with child actress Zhang Minyu) and animated drawings. Patriotic themes often re-emerged: *The Painful History of the Nation* and *The New Wave* denounced imperialist aggression, while *The Year of Chinese Goods* encouraged spectators to buy national products. In 1935, the Wans made the country's first animated sound film, *The Camel's Dance*.

The brothers did not neglect to divulge their ideas on art. In 1936 they wrote an article for a journal published by the production company for which they worked. In it, they praised American, Soviet and German animation but also maintained the need to find an indigenous Chinese style and humour. They also stated their goal of teaching, not merely entertaining. All these themes would reappear later in the People's Republic of China.

Fig. 72. The Princess With the Iron Fan *by Wan Laiming and Wan Guchan (China, 1941).*

When the Japanese invaded Shanghai (13 August 1937), the filmmakers escaped to the still free city of Wuhan. The events inspired their new

productions, including five films for the *Manifestos of the War of Resistance* series and seven for the *Songs of the War of Resistance* series (featuring the Fleischers' theme of the bouncing ball). Then Wuhan also fell into the hands of the Japanese army. Since it was not possible to work in Chungking, where the Wan's production company was at this time based, the brothers returned to Shanghai. There, Wan Laiming and Wan Guchan established another team of animators inside the unified Shinhwa company and began their most daring venture – the first Chinese feature film.

Work began under shaky diplomatic protection, since the animators' atelier was located in the French concession (which the occupation troops respected, like other foreign concessions, until 1941). The film (shown to the public in 1941) was entitled *The Princess with the Iron Fan* and was based on a chapter from the traditional Chinese novel *Journey to the West*. A Monk, Shwangzang, is accompanied by a pig Zhu Baizhe, a priest Shaseng and the Monkey King Sun Wukong, as he crosses a mountain of flames in search of sacred Buddhist texts. After many adventures, the film's true protagonist Sun Wukong manages to get a magic fan from the Buffalo King's wife and extinguishes the flames. Marie-Claire Quiquemelle wrote:

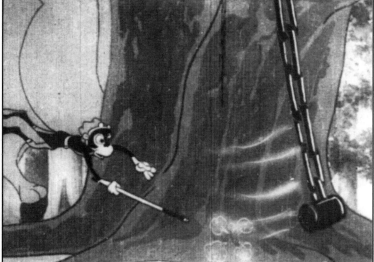

'This production, on the "orphan island" of the French Concession in the middle of the war, was a real feat not only on the artistic level but also on the technical level: seventy artists, in two teams, worked without a break for a year and four months, all in the same room, in limited space, in the cold of the winter, and in the atrocious heat of the summer. To assure the accuracy of the movement, certain scenes were filmed with actors to serve as a guide to the artists.'[1]

1   Marie-Claire Quiquemelle, 'I fratelli Wan, sessant'anni di cinema d'animazione in Cina,' in *Ombre elettriche – Saggi e ricerche sul cinema cinese*, ed. Marco Muller (Milan: Electa, 1982); and *Les frères Wan et 60 ans de dessins animés chinois/The Wan Brothers and 60 Years of Animated Films in China* (Festival d'Annecy, 1985).

The film was well received in China, Singapore and Indonesia. Its success was probably helped by a veiled patriotism, particularly as Sun Wukong's victory over the Buffalo King was obtained with the alliance of the people. From an aesthetic viewpoint, the film made interesting contributions. 'This film, with its many inventions, sparkles with humour, fantasy and poetry. It is a delight to the spectator.'[1] While this statement is probably an exaggeration (the narration often drags, the drawings and the animation of the characters are flawed, and the fusion between American teaching and Chinese artistic tradition is not in sync) the originality and autochthonous strength of the film compensate for its defects.

As the war and the political situation grew worse, production on the following work, a feature film titled *The World of Insects*, was stalled. In the meantime other Chinese artists had turned to animation. In 1941 a group of young Hong Kong artists, founders of the Association of Chinese Animation, released *The Hunger of the Old Stupid Dog*. In Changqing, Qian Jajun (2 December 1912) produced some shorts. In 1946, in Manchuria, the Communist Party sponsored *The Emperor's Dream* (by Chen Bo'er, with animated puppets; screened in 1947) and *The Turtle Caught in the Jar* (1948, by Fang Ming, with animated drawings; Fang Ming was the Chinese name of Japanese animator Tadahito Mochinaga). Both were satirical propaganda films, poking fun at Chiang Kai-shek and his troops trapped in the Northeast by the revolutionary army.

In 1949, twenty-two people, including the caricaturist Te Wei (by his real name Sheng Tewei, born 1915) and the young intellectual Jin Shi (born 1919), assembled in Changchun, forming the core of what would later become the large Shanghai studio. The following year, the animators were transferred to Shanghai and the team expanded to include painters, puppeteers, children's writers and Wan Chaochen himself who in 1946–48 had migrated to Hollywood and had studied the equipment and the methods of American animation. In 1954, Wan Laiming and Wan Guchan, who had migrated to Hong Kong during the war, joined the Shanghai studio. In 1956, the studios included 200 workers and by the 1960s they had grown to include 380. The films were mainly for children. According to Jin Shi, the studio director, films had to be entertaining and educational while at the same time maintaining a national character. These points had already been made by the Wan brothers twenty years earlier. As examples, Jin Shi held up his own animated puppet film *The Magic Paintbrush* (1955) and Te Wei's *The Braggart General* (1957). Within the Maoist climate of ceaseless ideological turmoil, animation as well as all other Chinese intellectual and cultural forces experienced constant mobilization and debate. The politics of the 'One Hundred Flowers' and the 'Great Leap Forward', as well as all other ideological vacillations to left or right, influenced the contents of films (sometimes indirectly, with allusions and allegories, other times by openly imposing propaganda).

The Shanghai studio was closed in 1965. The filmmakers were sent to educational camps and the studio did not reopen until 1972. Until 1965, however, the studio was responsible for a good amount of work. By 1962, almost one-hundred movies had been filmed, some of them excellent. In the area of cut-out animation, the experienced Wan Guchan created *Zhu Baizhe Eats the Watermelon* (1958), an original episode of the *Journey to the West*. Humorous, cleverly ironic and expertly animated, this film was the precursor of many films made with this technique. Wan Guchan's works include *The Little Fisherman* (1959, based on a popular story from the Boxer rebellion) and *The Spirit of the Ginseng* (1961),

1   Quiquemelle, *Les frères Wan*.

about a child who is sold as a slave to a landowner, but who overthrows the tyrant with the help of the spirit of a ginseng plant. Hu Shionghua (29 December 1931 – 14 November 1983) was responsible for *Let's Wait for Tomorrow* (1962) and *More or Less* (1964), while Qian Yunda (21 January 1929) made *The Red Army's Bridge* (1964). Set in the Hunan province at the time of the peasants' revolt, the film forcefully tells of a bridge which is destroyed by landowners and rebuilt by Mao's soldiers. Eventually, the bridge becomes a trap for the Kuomintang troops. The commander of the nationalists is given a sarcastic characterization.

As for animated drawings, the finest short was *The Tadpoles in Search of Their Mummy* by Te Wei and Qian Jajun (1960). From the viewpoint of style, the film deserves mention for its cinematic adaptation of the traditional technique of mixing watercolours and India ink. The animation was so good as to appear almost virtuoso. It was the animation of the tadpoles, however, with its clever developments (the tadpoles do not know their mother's features and must identify her among the various animals of the pond before finally meeting her) which fascinated spectators. In 1963 the same two directors made *The Cowherd's Flute*. More traditional animated drawings appeared in *The Little Carp's Adven-*

tures (1958), by He Yumen (8 May 1928), and in the featurette *The Chwang Tapestry* (1959, from an old legend of the South-western Chwang people), by Qian Jajun. *A Golden Dream* (1963), by Wang Shuchen (4 Septemebr 1931 – 23 November 1991), is about five kings who torment their subjects by drinking their blood and eating gold and diamonds all with the help of villains such as a general, a tax-collector and an intellectual. *The Two Heroic Sisters of the Steppe* (1965) tells of two little girls who when entrusted with a commune's herd, save it from a blizzard. Traditionally styled but ideologically schematic, the film shows hints of the coming Cultural Revolution.

Animated puppets were also a lively genre. One particular type was made of paper folding using a traditional Chinese technique. Yu Zheguang's (1906 – 1991) *The Intelligent Little Ducks* was the first film of this type. The many films using this technique include Jin Shi's *Small Heroes* (1953, the first colour film of this genre); *The Carved Dragon* (1958, from the old tale of a carpenter who carves a dragon in order to defeat a monster raging in his province), by Wan Chaochen, You Lei (11 April 1926) and Zhang Chaoqun (25 August 1920); and the feature film *The Peacock Princess* (1963) also by Jin Shi. Based on an old legend of the ancient Tai (a south-eastern people), this film tells the story of a prince who is given a strong bow that only super-human strength can flex. In troubled 1964, You Lei made *The Rooster Sings at Midnight*, based on the autobiography of Red Army fighter Kao Yupao. The film tells how the protagonist foiled the plans concocted by the exploiter Chen, the 'skinner,' against his labourers.

The most challenging and prestigious work of post-war Chinese animation was *Confusion in the Sky*, Wan Laiming's second feature film. The first part was released in 1961, followed by the second part in 1964. Lasting approximately two hours, the film was also based on *Journey to the West*. Here, Sun Wukong – the Monkey King –

Fig. 73. Zhu Baije Eats the Watermelon *by Wan Guchan (China, 1958).*

takes possession of the pillar that supports the Sky in the palace of the Dragon King, and with it he challenges the Jade Emperor. Once he has become a celestial mandarin, Sun Wukong faces attacks by the one hundred thousand warriors of the Jade Emperor. Sun Wukong personifies the human character, whose courage and shrewdness are superior to any strength. The film is memorable for its rich scene design and animation as well as for its vigour, but is marred by its slow rhythm. Its many sources include Buddhist frescoes and the popular images of the Beijing Opera. Shown at the Locarno Festival in 1965, *Confusion in the Sky* was also well received in the West.

Japan

During the years of reconstruction in Japan, animation attempted to turn from an isolated and craftsman like field to an industrial one. In 1945, about one hundred specialists joined the studio Shin Nihon Doga. Among them were 'Sanae' Yamamoto, Yasuji Murata and Kenzo Masaoka. That associative spirit, however, dissolved in the course of two years. Masaoka and Yamamoto co-founded Nihon Doga and produced Masaoka's *Suteneko Torachan* (Torachan the Kitten, 1947). Other works deserving mention include Masao Kumagawa's *Poppaya-san Nonki Ekicho* (Poppaya-san, the Good-natured Station Master, 1948) and Hideo Furusawa's *Kobito to Aomushi* (The Dwarf and the Green Caterpillar, 1950). When Masaoka retired, Yamamoto reorganized his studio under the new name of Toei Doga.[1]

The company continued along a traditional line of work. Its best artists included Yasuji Mori (Taiwan, 28 January 1925), who directed the delicate *Koneko no Rakugaki* (The Kitten Artist,

1957); Koji Fukiya, who made *Yumemi Doji* (The Child and the Dream, 1958); Sadao Tsukioka (15 May 1939), who later became famous for art-films as well as productions for larger audiences. Sadao Tsukioka debuted in 1961 with *Nezuni no Yomeiri* (The Mouse Marriage). Toei Doga's finest work completed during this period is the production of feature films, beginning with *Hakuja-den* (The White Snake, 1958). Directed by Taiji Yabushita (Osaka 1 February 1903 – 1986), *Hakuja-den* initiated the huge industrial development of the past thirty years in Japanese animation.

In 1953, Tadahito Mochinaga returned to Japan from China. A former assistant of Mitsuyo Seo and a collaborator on the mid-length propaganda film *Fukuchan and the Submarine*, Tadahito Mochinaga had moved to his parents' house in Manchuria for health and war-related reasons. After the war, the Chinese Communist Party had requested his collaboration in opening the Shanghai studio. There, the artist specialized in puppet animation. Back in Japan, he produced advertising, educational and entertainment puppet films. His collaborators included scene designer and playwright Tadasu Iizawa, and Kihachiro Kawamoto (whose creativity and fame eventually went beyond that of his teacher's). Ryuichi Yokoyama, who was responsible for *Fukuchan and the Submarine*, founded Otogi (1955), which later became a major production company. He also made a 'personal' film, *Fukusuke* (1957), featuring the comic story of a frog who goes to the sky to face the God of Thunder.

Noboru Ofuji was the only creator of art films during that period. In 1952, he decided to use coloured cellophane to obtain transparency effects in colour films (he thought chigoyami was obsolete). By applying his old techniques and cut-

---

1   Not to be confused with Toei – one of the six major Japanese production companies of live-action films – which opened an animation studio in 1956, taking over Nichido Eiga, a company which had been involved with animation before World War II. In the 1970s and 1980s, Toei Animation became the most influential Japanese company in the field, producing thousands of hours of TV series, feature films, etc.

ting in new material, the artist made another version of his successful *The Whale*. The film was well received at the 1953 Cannes Festival. In 1955 he made the dramatic *Yurei sen* (The Ghost Ship). When a prince and his peaceful crew are killed by pirates, the victims' ghosts take revenge against their executioners. The film won a prize at the Venice Festival.

Kon Ichikawa

Born in Uji Yamada, in the province of Mie, on 20 November 1915, Kon Ichikawa discovered his vocation while watching Walt Disney's movies. As he recalled later, in them he found everything that interested him: cinema, painting and drawing. In 1936–37 the Jo studio, with a small animation department, opened in Kaiko No Yashiro, near Kyoto, and Ichikawa was hired. Animation, however, turned out to be an economic liability for the studio and was gradually eliminated. Production decreased and eventually, the team dissolved. 'I was the only one left,' recalls Ichikawa, 'and I did everything. I would draw, animate, film and write the scripts.'[1] In

1939 he directed a short, *Kachikachi Yama* (The Hare Gets Revenge Over the Raccoon, 1939); the film, which definitely derives its drawings and structure from the *Silly Symphonies*, makes a remarkable use of music.

When the animation department finally closed, Ichikawa was assigned to the group of assistant-directors for live-action movies. In 1944, the studio (which meanwhile had been renamed Toho Eiga and had moved to Tokyo following a merger with other companies) decided to produce an animated puppet film and promoted young Ichikawa, the only animation expert, to director. The movie, entitled *Musume Dojoji* (A Girl at Dojo's Temple, 1947) was an adaptation from a Kabuki drama. Those who were able to view it said it was excellent, but American authorities commanding occupation troops in defeated Japan prohibited the showing of the film. Still today Ichikawa claims that *Museum Dojo* is his best work.

In the 1950s, the director turned to live-action films. After some comedies, in 1953 he made his first masterpiece, the dramatic *Pu-San* (Mr. Pu). In 1956, he attained well-deserved international fame with *Biruma no Tategoto* (The Burmese Harp). In 1959, he directed his third masterpiece, *Nobi* (Fires on the Plains).

Ichikawa can be considered one of the masters of Japanese cinema, together with Kurosawa, Ozu and Mizoguchi. Although he quit animation, except for a few, sporadic productions, his precious compositions of images and pictorial shot-balance illustrate his figurative achievements and his expertise in the field.

Fig. 74.
Kachikachi Yama
by Kon Ichikawa
(Japan, 1939).

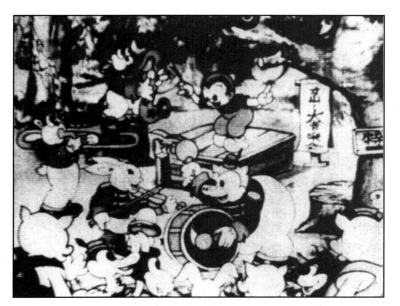

1   Angelo Solmi, *Kon Ichikawa* (Florence: La Nuova Italia, 1975).

Chapter 16

Animation in Latin America

Argentina

After Quirino Cristiani, animators in Argentina were not able to complete major projects. Juan Oliva, a painter and comic strip artist (Barcelona, August 1910) emigrated to Argentina in 1930 and was apprentice to Cristiani for a few years. In 1937, he began animating his own productions. These were brief comic episodes about Julián Centella, a little gaucho, for insertion in the newsreel *Sucesos Argentinos* (Events in Argentina). In 1939, he founded the Compañía Argentina de Dibujos Animados (The Argentine Company of Animated Drawings), with the intention of producing animated shorts that could compete with their American counterparts.

After his trial-production *Desplumando avestruces* (Plucking Ostriches), Oliva released *La caza del puma* (Hunting the Puma, 1940). The movie features the child Rejucilo and his horse Ciclón. They succeed in their hunt for the puma by getting the animal drunk. Despite good quality animation and drawings, at least for the standards of the time, the film didn't have much of an audience, and Oliva was forced to dissolve the company. He worked for a time in advertising before producing two shorts, *Filipito el pistolero* (Filipito the Gunslinger, 1942) and *Noche de sustos* (Night of Fright, 1942). Oliva then retired to drawing, painting and the teaching of animation. Plagued by poor health (for many years he was almost blind), he died on 3 July 1975.

Dante Quinterno (Buenos Aires, 1908) was a comic strip artist, publisher and creator of the famous Indian Patoruzú, a sort of Argentine Don Quixote. A man of vast financial means, in 1939 he planned a feature film based on his own comic strip character. After visiting the Fleischer and Disney studios in the United States, he assembled a good team, managed by his closest comic strip collaborators. For various reasons (such as the choice of the German film *Gasparcolor*, which became unavailable after the outbreak of the war), the piece was reduced to eighteen minutes. It was released unsuccesfully in 1942 with the title *Upa en apuros* (Upa in Trouble). This was the first Argentine colour animated film, and for a long time was considered an example of good animation at the international level.

José M. Burone Bruché began his activities in 1942, when he replaced Juan Oliva at the Emelco advertising agency. Precisely where his predecessor had found little opportunity to produce his art shorts, José Burone Bruché was able to film *Los consejos del viejo vizcacha* (The Advice of Old Man Hare), a free adaptation of José Hernández's national poem *Martín Fierro*. In 1947, he created the series *Refranes populares* (Popular Sayings), each lasting one minute. He also made several educational films before devoting himself exclusively to advertising.

In 1950, a student of Burone Bruché, Jorge Caro, began a series based on a rabbit named Plácido, a cheerful character which became very successful, particularly in *Puños de campeón* (Fists of a Champion). After several similar shorts, Caro moved to Peru where he founded an animation studio.

The 1950s also saw some developments in avant-garde cinema. Filmmaker, cinema critic and organizer of cultural events Víctor Iturralde Rúa (1927) deserves mention for his movies which were drawn directly on film-stock. He had seen McLaren's films, which employ the same technique, at specialized viewings. His productions include *Ideitas* (1952), *Hic ... !* (1953), *Piripipi* (1954) and *Petrolita* (1958). Rodolfo Julio Bardi combined tiles, painted glass, threads and other materials in *Composición* (Composition, 1954). José Arcuri used geometric drawings to make a ten-minute abstract film entitled *Continuidad plástica* (Plastic Continuity, 1958).

Puppet films were also produced, particularly by specialist Carlos Gonzáles Groppa. The most popular, *Trío* (1958), *Franc* (1959) and *Magía* (1960) won awards at a number of international festivals. The previously mentioned Czechoslovakian-born Karel (now Carlos) Dodal also worked with animated puppets, although he devoted himself primarily to educational productions, in collaboration with his second wife Irene, also from Czechoslovakia.

In the 1960s and 1970s advertising underwent extraordinary growth so that, at one time, there were 450 animated advertising minutes produced each year, a number which could make Europe envious. The best artists in the field include Carlos Costantini, Alberto del Castillo and the duo of Gil & Bertolini (who made the much-praised short *Sir Wellington Bones*, 1961).

In the 1960s artist and publisher Manuel García Ferré laid the foundations of a small empire. Born in Almeria, Spain, on 8 October 1929, at seventeen he moved to Buenos Aires and, in 1955, was hired as an animator by Lowe Emelco. In 1959 he founded Producciones García Ferré and produced and directed some of the most successful TV series in Latin America: *Anteojito y Antifaz, Hijitus* (1967–1973), the educational *El libro gordo de Petete* (with hand-animated puppets, actors and animated drawings) and *Las aventuras de Calculín* (The adventures of Calculín). Ferré also made three feature films: *Mil intentos y un invento* (One Thousand Projects and One Invention, 1972), a musical comedy featuring television characters Anteojito and Antifaz; *Petete y Trapito* (featuring the land and sea adventures of a scarecrow and a little bird) and *Ico el caballito valiente* (The Tale of a Foal at the King's Court, 1983, see Colour Plate 28). García Ferré was actively involved in comic strip designing, children's publications, merchandising and television production.

Another multi-talent was Simón Feldman. A writer, essayist and live-action director, he made *Los cuatro secretos* (The Four Secrets, 1976), an animated feature film about three children who are told, during a dream, the four secrets of water, fire, air and earth.

Another animated feature film was made in 1987 by Luis Palomares: *El escudo del condor* (The Condor's Shield). It used puppet animation to tell a science fiction story where circus actors defeat evil robots.

Finally, Jorge 'Catú' Martín deserves mention. Born in San Isidro (2 August 1933), he worked on comic drawings for specialized magazines before moving to animation in the early 1960s. *La pared* (The Wall, 1961) and *Compacto cupé* (The Compact Cab, 1964) are his creations. In the 1970s he directed more than two hundred shorts based on Mafalda, the rebellious little girl by the cartoonist 'Quino' (Joaquín Lavado). Mafalda was also the protagonist of a feature film for which Catú denied any responsibility. He remarked, 'an industrious work of editing which suffers, however, from a basic lack of progression, rhythm, development and plot.'[1] Nevertheless, Mafalda was one of the rare examples of a successful passage from comic strips to animation. Further proof that Argentine comic strips, among the world's best, had much to offer animation.

Brazil

O Kaiser, by caricaturist Seth (Álvaro Marins), is considered the first Brazilian animated movie. First shown in January 1917, this very short satire against the war targets Kaiser Wilhelm II. The German leader first dreams of dominating the world, but is later swallowed by the globe itself. It may be helpful to mention that Brazil sided with France, Great Britain and the United States in World War I. A few months later, on 26 April 1917, Kirs Filme released the country's second animated film, *Traquinices de Chiquinho e seu inseparável amigo jagûnço* (The Escapades of Chiquinho and His Inseparable Friend Jagûnço). The filmmakers were not acknowledged in the film credits. *Avênturas de Bille e Bolle* (The Adventures of Bille and Bolle), by Gilberto Rossi and 'Fono' (Eugênio Fonêca Filho) followed one year later. The film features two characters, Bille and Bolle, who were modeled after Bud Fisher's Mutt and Jeff.

For about ten years thereafter, animation was produced only in advertising, mainly by Seth, who had switched to this field. In 1933 João Sta-

mato, a collaborator of Seth, co-directed *Macaco fêio, macaco bônito* (Ugly Ape, Pretty Ape) with Luiz Seel. In 1938 caricaturist Luiz Sá released the short *Avênturas de Virgolino* (The Adventures of Virgolino), and a year later, *Virgolino apânha* (Virgolino's Troubles). In the 1940s, Humberto Mauro, one of the pioneers of Brazilian cinema, worked briefly with animation. His eighteen-minute *O dragãozinho manso* (The Good Little Dragon) introduced the country to the use of animated puppets.

In 1953, Anélio Latini Filho (Nova Friburgo, 1924 – Rio de Janeiro, 20 April 1986) made the first Brazilian animated feature film, *Sinfônia amazônica* (Amazon Symphony). At the age of twelve Latini made a six-minute animated film. After that he learned technique by incessantly reading manuals and viewing North American movies. While he loved Disney stylistically, thematically he felt close to Brazilian folklore. At twenty-four he asked writer Joaquim Ribeiro for a folkloric subject to transpose into a feature film. Ribeiro gave him seven legends of the Amazon Indians, and from this comes the title *Sinfônia amazônica*. The protagonist's journey through the region served to connect the seven episodes.

Fig. 75. Sinfônia amazônica by Anélio Latini Filho (Brazil, 1953).

1   Letter received from Jorge Martín, 24 May 1982.

Since Brazil did not have any labs for colour film development at the time, Latini made the movie in black-and-white. He wished to show it in light blue tones, but the attempt failed because of technical and production-related reasons. Therefore, he was forced to settle for black-and-white. The movie was released simultaneously in eight Rio theatres; despite good reviews and large audiences, Latini, who was a poorly organized business man, was not able to profit. For a short time he worked in advertising. Later he sold his paintings to tourists in Copacabana. In 1968 he began a second feature film, *Kitan da Amazônia* (Kitan from Amazonia), which remained unfinished.

McLaren's work had a notable influence on Brazilian avant-garde animation. Roberto Miller made his first painted-on-film stock movie, *Rumba* (1957) after a six-month stay with McLaren in Canada. An isolated experimentalist, Miller (1925) continued animating with complete dedication. His remarkable filmography includes abstract works made using various techniques. Among his films are *Boogie Woogie* (1959), *Desênho abstrato* (Abstract Drawing, 1960), *O átomo brincalhão* (The Playful Atom, 1968), and *Fotograma Abstrato* (Abstract Frame, 1985, see Colour Plate 29). Rubens Francisco Lucchetti and Bassano Vaccarini, also abstract artists, began their animation work in 1960 after viewing McLaren's shorts (as Miller had six years earlier).

> 'For a long time I had been looking for an expressive medium which could totally satisfy me, and which I could use to give rise to an art with a new meaning: interpret music through forms, give movement to an abstract painting or simply create 'fantasies', arabesques, whirlwinds of forms, sounds and colours,' Lucchetti wrote.[1]

Lucchetti and Vaccarini's first four experiments were united into a seventeen-minute film, *Ab-*

strações (Abstractions). Beside painting on film stock, the two artists used other avant-garde techniques. Their most valued work, *Fantasmagóricas* (1961) was the animation of a painting. The two artists founded the Cêntro Experimental de Cinema de Ribeirão Preto (in which Miller also participated). The group, however, lasted only a couple of years because of financial problems.

In 1962, Hamilton de Souza (1929) joined with some friends under the name of Grupo Tan Tan and made the short *Uma história do Brazil – tipo exportação* (A History of Brasil – made for export). Later he worked on a feature film, *História da América* (History of America) in three half-hour segments. Only the first part, *A descoberta* (The Discovery) was completed.

Álvaro Henriques Gonçalves (1930) took only forty days to film *Estória do índio alado* (The Story of the Winged Indian, 1969). A filmmaker with a background in television, Gonçalves worked every night for two years on *Presênte de Natal* (Christmas Gift), the second Brazilian animated feature film and the first in colour. The film was released on February 1971 in Manaus, the filmmaker's birthplace. It told a Christmas story about the children João and Miriam, and displayed naïve style and techniques.

Yppe Nakashima (Japan, 1927) emigrated to Brazil in 1956. Nakashima made the TV series *Papa Papo*, and the shorts *Leyenda da Vitória-Régia* (Legend of Victoria-Regia, 1957) and *O gôrila* (The Gorilla, 1958). In 1972, in collaboration with João Luiz Araújo and Sylvio Renoldi, he completed *As avênturas de Piconzé* (The Adventures of Piconze, see Colour Plate 30), the third Brazilian animated feature film. Piconzé is a dark-haired kid who is accompanied in his adventures by the turtle Teimoso, parrot Louro Papo, pig Don Chico Leitão and a blonde girl named Maria. The filmmakers claimed to have created Brazilian characters with Brazilian feelings, op-

---

1   Letter received from Rubens Francisco Lucchetti, 14 January 1974.

posing the cultural imperialism of the United States. Yppe Nakashima died in the mid-1970s.

In 1967, a group of young artists from the School of Fine Arts founded the Cêntro de Estudos do Cinêma de Animação (Center for Animation Film Studies, CECA). The group produced shorts, such as *Nêgrinho do pastoreiro* (Black Child of the Pastures) by João de Oliveira, and Rui de Oliveira's *O palhaço domador* (The Animal-tamer Clown) and *O coêlhinho sabido* (The Shrewd Little Rabbit) before some of its members separated. One year later, the remaining members founded the group Fotogramas, aimed at production as well as divulging avant-garde art. Humorist 'Zélio', who made *No caos está contido o gêrme de uma nova esperança* (In Chaos Lies the Germ of New Hope) planned to work on a feature film. Although that ambitious project remained unfinished, some shorts brought the group to the attention of experts.

João de Oliveira made *A pântera nêgra* (The Black Panther). Carlos Alberto Pacheco and 'Stil' (Ernesto Stilpen) filmed *Status quo*. Stilpen gave proof of his talent in *Batûque*, a film which brought honour to Brasil at the Mamaja Festival, in Romania (1970). In *Urbis* (City) and *O filho de urbis* (Son of the City), Stilpen (born in 1944) dealt with the theme of alienation in the large city. In 1971, he sided with popular culture (as opposed to mass culture) in *Lampião, ou para cada grilo uma curtição* (Street Lamp, or For Each Cricket There is a Whore). In 1974, in collaboration with Antônio Moreno, Stilpen made *Reflexos* (Reflections). Stilpen is undoubtedly an important artist who uses modern drawings and themes to produce forceful and disquieting effects.

In 1968, Jorge Bastos made *A linha* (A Thread), a respectable film. An advertising animator, Bastos tried unsuccessfully to make a feature film, adapting Monteiro Lobato's novel *Journey to Heaven*. In 1975, Clóvis Vieira drew and di-

rected *Amôr mor* (Greatest Love) a somewhat hermetic attack against the politics of government and the ruling class. Some creations, encouraged and financially supported by the newspaper *Jôrnal do Brasil* also deserve mention. Produced from the late 1960s to the early 1970s, these include Pedro Aares' *Semente* (Seed), Walter Hiroqui Ono and Ênio Lamoglia Possebon's *Vida e cônsumo* (Life and Consumption); Enio Lamoglia Possebon's *... pôntos ...* (Dots) and Roberto Chiron's *Sêm título* (Untitled).

José Rubens Siqueira, an inventive artist gifted with a dry elegant style, made *Emprise* (1973), *Sorrir* (To Smile, 1975) and *Hamlet* (1977). Besides being an animator, Siqueira was also a stage and live-action film director. Before collaborating with Stilpen on *Reflêxos*, Antônio Moreno (1949) made *A rapôsa e o passarinho* (The Fox and the Little Bird, 1972) and *Reflexões ou divagações sobre um ponto duvidoso* (Reflections or Ramblings on a Doubtful Point, 1973). He used the same technique of drawing on paper, without cels, in *Ícaro e o labirínto* (Icarus and the Labyrinth, 1975). The highly praised, prize-winner *Eclipse* (1984) was instead completely painted on film stock.

The 1980s was an active period, beginning with Marcos Magalhães' *Meow* which was a highlight at the Cannes Film Festival. In 1986, Magalhães coordinated the work of twenty-eight colleagues on *O planêta terra* (The Planet Earth), in celebration of the International Year of Peace. Other noteworthy films include *Um minuto para a mêia noite* (A Minute Before Midnight) by Flavio Del Carlo; *Um e outro* (One and Another) by Francisco Liberato; *Quando os morcêgos se calam* (When Night Hawks Hold Their Tongues, 1986, by Fabio Lignini (Rio de Janeiro, 1965); *Frankenstein Punk* (1986, see Colour Plate 31), an internationally acclaimed film by Cão Hamburger (São Paulo, 1962); and several films made independently by Eliana Fonsêca (São Paulo, 1961).

Finally, Maurício De Sôusa deserves a special place in this overview. Born in Santa Isabel (São Paulo) on 20 October 1935, this comic strip artist and filmmaker is a true Brazilian Disney. In 1959 he managed to have his first comic strip published in the daily paper *Folha da manhã*. His success was immediate. A few years later, he directed a team of artists involved in the production of children's stories. More than one-hundred characters grouped into different clans were created. The most popular were Mônica and Magali, two little girls inspired by De Sôusa's own children; the country man Chico Bênto; the child-ghost Penadinho; Cascão, the great enemy of water; the little dinosaur Hôracio; and Pelézinho, a representation of the well-known soccer player Pelé as a child. The comic strip adventures of these characters appeared in over 120 Brazilian newspapers, and the comic books reached monthly sales of one and a half million copies. To this add records, stage performances, merchandise and a remarkable success abroad, particularly in Latin America and Europe.

The Maurício De Sôusa studios began the production of animated television shorts in 1979. These included a mini-series of four 25 second episodes connected by a narrator, which were the television equivalent of comic strips. They also created one-to-two-minute shorts addressing educational themes for children such as friendship, cooperation and nature.

The most important activity of the São Paulo-based studio was the production of feature films, all credited to Maurício De Sôusa as director. *As avênturas da turma da Mônica* (Adventures of Monica and Her Friends, 1982) was viewed by almost a million people in the first year of its release. *A princesa e o robô* (The Princess and the Robot, 1983), *As novas avênturas da turma da Mônica* (The New Adventures of Mônica and Her Friends, 1986), *Mônica e a sereia do Rio* (Mônica and the Mermaid of Rio, 1987), and *A turma da Mônica em o bicho papão e outras histórias* (Monica and Her Friends, the Bogeyman and Other Stories, 1987) (see Colour Plate 32) were also very well received. Each of these films are for children, solidly anchored to an entertaining and playful conception of animation cinema. De Sôusa's cheerful and peaceful universe is far from interplanetary wars, warmonger robots, monsters, dangers or challenges to overcome. His smiling world is centred on optimistic themes, and yet it manages to avoid affectation and sentimentality.

Colour Plates

Colour Plate 1.
Lichtspiel Opus 1 *by*
Walther Ruttmann
(Germany, 1921).
See page 28.

Colour Plate 2.
Lichtspiel Opus 2 *by*
Walther Ruttmann
(Germany, 1921).
See page 28.

Colour Plate 7.
Sam and His
Musket *by Anson
Dyer
(Great Britain,
1935).
See page 73.*

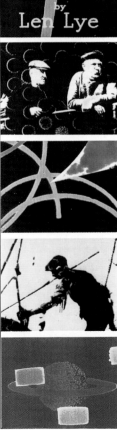
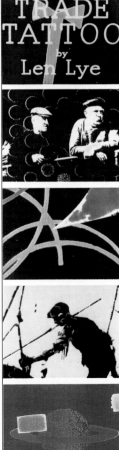

Colour Plate 8.
Trade Tattoo *by Len
Lye
(Great Britain,
1936).
See page 74.*

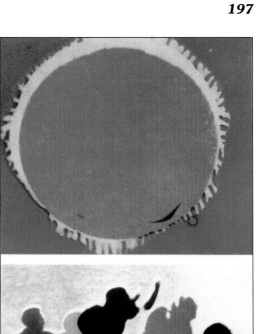

Colour Plate 9.
Rainbow Dance *by Len Lye
(Great Britain, 1936).
See page 74.*

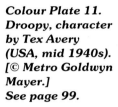

Colour Plate 10.
Der Schneemann by
Hans Fischerkoesen
(Germany, 1943).
See page 80.

Colour Plate 11.
Droopy, character
by Tex Avery
(USA, mid 1940s).
[© Metro Goldwyn
Mayer.]
See page 99.

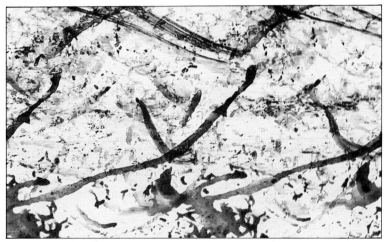

Colour Plate 12
(centre left).
Begone Dull Care by
Norman McLaren
(Canada, 1949).
[© NFB of Canada.]
See page 116.

Colour Plate 13.
Komposition in Blau
by Oskar Fischinger
(Germany, 1935).
See page 122.

Colour Plate 14. Wile E. Coyote and the Roadrunner, characters by Chuck Jones (USA, mid 1950s). [© Metro Goldwyn Mayer.] See page 134.

Colour Plates 16 & 17. Sylvester and Tweety, characters by Warner Bros. (USA, late 1940s). [© Warner Bros.] See page 135.

Colour Plate 15. Show Biz Bugs by Friz Freleng (USA, 1957). [© Warner Bros.] See page 135.

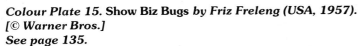

Colour Plate 18.
The Cat Concerto *by*
W. Hanna and J.
Barbera
(USA, 1946).
[© Metro Goldwyn
Mayer.]
See page 138.

Colour Plate 19.
Light *by Jordan*
Belson
(USA, 1974).
See page 142.

Colour Plate 20.
Le roi et l'oiseau *by*
Paul Grimault
(France, 1980).
See page 156.

Colour Plate 21.
Los sueños de Tay-Pi
by Franz
Winterstein
(Spain, 1951).
See page 157.

Colour Plate 22.
Garbancito de la Mancha *by Arturo Moreno*
(Spain, 1945).
See page 157.

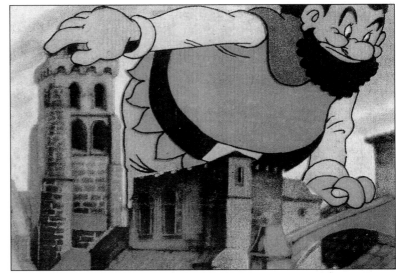

Colour Plate 23.
I fratelli Dinamite *by Nino and Toni Pagot*
(Italy, 1949).
See page 158.

Colour Plate 24.
Poster of **La rosa di**
Bagdad *by Anton*
Gino Domeneghini
(Italy, 1949).
See page 159.

Colour Plate 26.
Poster of **Fyrtøjet**
(The Tinderbox) *by*
A. Johnsen and S.
Methling
(Denmark, 1946).
See page 161.

Colour Plate 25.
Film N. 6 *by Luigi*
Veronesi
(Italy, 1941).
See page 160.

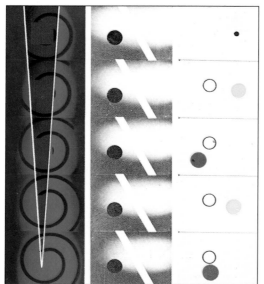

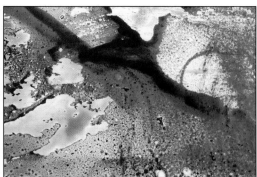

Colour Plate 27.
Ruka *(The Hand) by Jiri Trnka*
(Czechoslovakia, 1965).
See page 169.

Colour Plate 29.
Fotograma abstrato
by Roberto Miller
(Brazil, 1985).
See page 190.

Colour Plate 28.
Ico el caballito valiente
by Manuel Garcia Ferré
(Argentina, 1983).
See page 188.

Colour Plate 30.
Piconzé by Yppe
Nakashima
(Brazil, 1972).
See page 190.

Colour Plate 31.
Frankenstein Punk
by C. Hamburger
and E. Fonseca
(Brazil, 1986).
See page 191.

Colour Plate 33.
**The Pink Panther, character by Friz
Freleng, and its evolution
(USA, 1960s).**
See page 232.

Colour Plate 32. **A turma da Mônica em o
bicho papão e outras historias,** *characters
by Mauricio De Sôusa (Brazil, 1980s).*
See page 192.

Colour Plate 34.
An American Tail *by
Don Bluth
(USA, 1986).*
[© *MCA Publishing.*]
See page 233.

Colour Plate 35.
The Little Mermaid
by John Musker
and Ron Clements
(USA, 1989).
[© The Walt Disney
Company.]
See page 234.

Colour Plate 36.
Aladdin *by John*
Musker and Ron
Clements
(USA, 1992).
[© The Walt Disney
Company.]
See page 234.

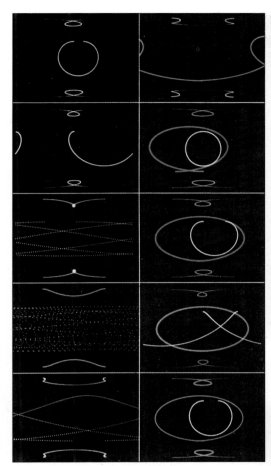

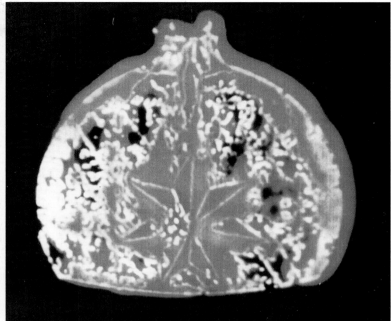

Colour Plate 37.
Arabesque by John
Whitney
(USA, 1975).
See page 245.

Colour Plate 38.
Dwija by James Whitney (USA, 1973).
See page 247.

Colour Plate 39.
Chips in Space by Kenneth O'Connell
(USA, 1990).
See page 250.

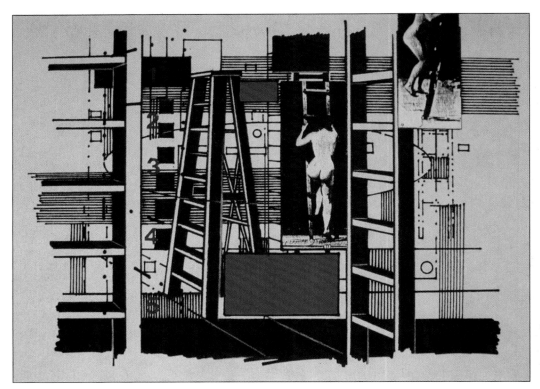

Colour Plate 40.
Ladders: drawing
for the film Object
Conversation *by*
Paul Glabicki
(USA, 1985).
See page 251.

Colour Plate 41.
The Violinist *by Ernest Pintoff*
(USA, 1960).
See page 254.

Colour Plate 42.
Bottom's Dream *by*
John Canemaker
(USA, 1983).
See page 255.

Colour Plate 43.
The Adventures of
Mark Twain *by Will*
Vinton
(USA, 1985).
See page 259.

Colour Plate 44.
The Big Snit *by*
Richard Condie
(Canada, 1985).
[© NFB of Canada.]
See page 264.

Colour Plate 45.
Premiers jours *by*
Clorinda Warny
(Canada, 1980).
[© NFB of Canada.]
See page 265.

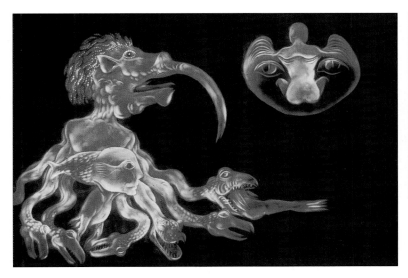

Colour Plate 47.
L'homme qui plantait des arbres by
Frédéric Back (Canada, 1987).
[© CBC-SRC.] See page 272.

Colour Plate 46.
Afterlife by Ishu Patel (Canada, 1978). [© NFB of Canada.]
See page 271.

Colour Plate 48.
The Black Dog by Alison De Vere
(Great Britain, 1987).
See page 276.

Colour Plate 49.
Babylon *by D. Sproxton and P. Lord (Great Britain, 1985). See page 278.*

Colour Plate 50.
Gwen, ou le livre de sable *by Jean-François Laguionie (France, 1984). See page 290.*

Colour Plate 51.
Allegro non troppo *by Bruno Bozzetto (Italy, 1977). See page 295.*

Colour Plate 52.
Il flauto magico *by*
G. Gianini and E.
Luzzati
(Italy, 1978).
See page 296.

Colour Plate 53.
Solo un bacio *by*
Guido Manuli
(Italy, 1983).
See page 297.

Colour Plate 54.
I huvet på gammal
gubbe *(In the Head*
of an Old Man)
by Per Åhlin
(Sweden, 1968).
See page 316.

Colour Plate 55.
**Pelle Svanslös *(Peter No-Tail) by S. Lasseby and J.*
*Gissberg (Sweden, 1981). See page 317.***

Colour Plate 56.
**The Cat, the Bear and the Jocular Dog *by Karl-Gunnar*
*Holmqvist (Sweden, 1982). See page 317.***

Colour Plate 57.
**Flåklypa *(The*
Pinchcliffe Grand
Prix) by Ivo Caprino
(Norway, 1975).
*See page 320.***

Colour Plate 59.
Kunibert *series by Hans O. Sindelar (Austria, 1974). See page 328.*

Colour Plate 58. **Seitsemän veljestä** *(Seven Brothers) by R. Nelimarkka and J. Seeck (Finland, 1979). See page 321.*

Colour Plate 60. **El mago de los sueños** *by Francesc Macià n (Spain, 1966).* ▼ *See page 330.*

Colour Plate 61.
A lênda do mar
tenebroso *by*
Ricardo Neto
(Portugal, 1974).
See page 331.

Colour Plate 63.
The Cat *by Zlatko*
Bourek
(Yugoslavia,
Croatia, 1971).
See page 337.

Colour Plate 62.
Adam *by Jordan Ananiadis*
(Greece, 1986).
See page 332.

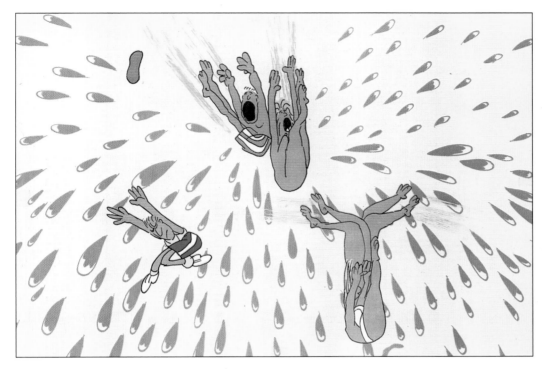

Colour Plate 64.
Neboder
(Skyscraper) by
Josko Marusic
(Yugoslavia,
Croatia, 1981).
See page 339.

Colour Plate 66.
Fehérlofia (Son of
the White Horse) by
Marcell Jankovics
(Hungary, 1980).
See page 349.

Colour Plate 65.
The Blue Ball by Miroslav Kijowicz
(Poland, 1968).
See page 342.

Colour Plate 67.
A Crushed World by Boyko Kanev
(Bulgaria, 1986).
See page 360.

Colour Plate 68.
Alice by Jan Svankmajer
(Czechoslovakia, 1988).
See page 364.

Colour Plate 69.
Krysar (The Pied Piper) by Jiri Barta
(Czechoslovakia, 1985).
See page 366.

Colour Plate 70.
Ceburaska, character by Roman Katsanov
(USSR, Russia, 1971).
See page 367.

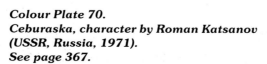

Colour Plate 71.
The Poodle *by Nina*
Shorina
(USSR, Russia,
1986).
See page 369.

Colour Plate 72.
The Butterfly *by Andrei Khrzhanovsky*
(USSR, Russia, 1972).
See page 370.

Colour Plate 73.
The Tale of Tales *by Yuri Norstein*
(USSR, Russia, 1979).
See page 373.

Colour Plate 74. Kikos by
Robert Saakiantz
(USSR, Armenia, 1979).
See page 376.

Colour Plate 76.
Is the Earth Round?
by Priit Pärn
(USSR, Estonia,
1977).
See page 377.

Colour Plate 75.
The Whale Hunter by Rein Raamat
(USSR, Estonia, 1976).
See page 376.

Colour Plate 77.
Umurkumurs *by Arnold Burovs*
(USSR, Latvia, 1976).
See page 378.

Colour Plate 78.
There Was, There Was, Sure There Was
by Zenonas Steinis
(USSR, Lithuania, 1986).
See page 378.

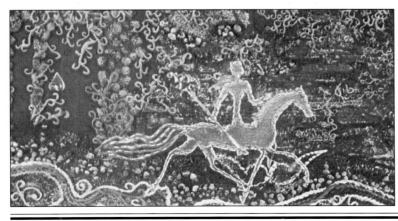

Colour Plate 79.
The Ornamental Tale *by Viacheslav Belov*
(USSR, Kirghizistan, 1981).
See page 380.

Colour Plate 80.
Zana and Miri
by Vlash Droboniku
(Albania, 1975).
See page 380.

Colour Plate 81.
Tlacuilo
by Enrique Escalona
(Mexico, 1988).
See page 385.

Colour Plate 82.
El alma trémula y sola
by Tulio Raggi (Cuba, 1983).
See page 387.

Colour Plate 83.
Elpidio Valdés cóntra dolar y cañón
by Juan Padrón (Cuba, 1983).
See page 387.

Colour Plate 84.
La ventana mágica
series by Isabel
Urbaneja
(Venezuela,
1988–90).
See page 390.

Colour Plate 85.
Adrar
by Mohamed Aram (Algeria, 1979).
See page 392.

Colour Plate 86.
The Weightlifter
by Arapik Baghdasarian (Iran, 1970).
See page 400.

Colour Plate 87.
Nezha Triumphs Over King Dragon
by A Da, Yang Shuchen, Yan Dingsian
(China, 1979).
See page 402.

Colour Plate 88.
36 Chinese Characters
by A Da
(China, 1985).
See page 402.

Colour Plate 89.
The Mermaid,
character from
Soodsakorn
by Payut
Ngaokrachang
(Thailand, 1976).
See page 408.

Colour Plate 90.
Akira
by Katsuhiro Otamo
(Japan, 1988).
See page 413.

Colour Plate 91.
Kataku *(The House in Flames)* *by Kihachiro Kawamoto (Japan, 1979). See page 416.*

Colour Plate 92.
Dot and the Kangaroo *by Yoram Gross (Australia, 1977). See page 423.*

Colour Plate 93.
The Frog, the Dog and the Devil *by Robert Stenhouse (New Zealand, 1986). See page 428.*

Colour Plate 94.
Poster of When the
Wind Blows ...
by Jimmy Teru
Murakami
(Great Britain,
1986).
See page 433.

Colour Plate 95.
Snoot and Muttly
by Susan Van
Baerle
(USA, 1984).
See page 441.

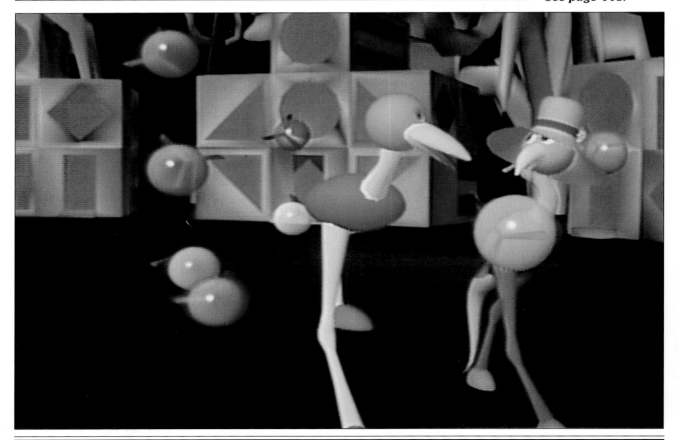

IV

A new wave of animation (1970s and 1980s)

Chapter 17

The United States of America

Fragmentation

Following the decline of the cartoon in movie houses, some studios closed, while others were founded or reorganized specifically for the production of TV series. Although motion picture studies still produced a very small number of shorts (Lantz worked until 1972, and the Pink Panther made its debut in the 1960s), their main concern became an ever-growing number of feature films. The fairy-tale formula created by Walt Disney was continued after his death by his successors, and was widely imitated, at times in an innovative manner (as in the intellectually ambitious *Gay Purr-ee*, directed in 1962 by Abe Levitow on a subject by Chuck Jones). Other artists, instead, like Ralph Bakshi, unhesitatingly took the path of adult feature films.

Animated television productions did not unearth any major new talent. Although they consisted mostly of series, much like Warner's, MGM's or Disney's, they differed dramatically from their cinematic counterparts, for reasons which were not necessarily related to lack of money, reduced creative freedom or time constraints (it would be shortsighted not to acknowledge the commitment by studios and artists alike in the making of professional, prestigious TV products). In fact, structural and linguistic reasons, and a changed audience, marked the difference. Because of their length, television productions were not able to use the same formulas of comic action which had prevailed on the big screen for thirty years. Instead, they had to adopt narrative patterns in which dialogue plays a dominant role (inviting the definition 'illustrated radio'). Moreover, any research into drawing or characterization had to be abandoned so as not to slow down the story. As for audiences, the television format, with its hypnotic, inattentive and fragmentary qualities, created new aesthetic principles and different expectations from viewers. Perpetual repetition, where each actor must reconfirm what is already known, becomes necessary to avoid breaking the story thread through the interruption of commercials, channel switching, etc. TV series became an endless narration, closer to comic strips than to traditional animation.

The most noticeable theoretical contributions were those by independent animators. Among these were the researchers of the effervescent West Coast Experimental Film Movement in

California; the animators spurred on by the Underground or Pop Art movements in New York; and self-financing young filmmakers. New artists' associations were founded, disparate institutions were awarded grants, and art museums helped these new forces financially and by exhibiting their works. There was also a steady flow of made-to-order public relation films, traditionally used as a selling tool during corporate conventions.

Finally, production in American universities increased 360 per cent in only two years, from 1959 to 1961, and still continued developing afterwards. Courses in art animation were offered at the University of Southern California, the University of California at Los Angeles, Harvard and the University of California at San Diego among others. In the 1970s and 1980s, a very high number of University student-films were submitted to the pre-selection juries of international film festivals.

On the big screen

In terms of old-fashioned animation, the only new phenomenon originated in the titles of a live-action movie. In 1964, director Blake Edwards commissioned titles for *The Pink Panther*, a film starring Peter Sellers, David Niven and Claudia Cardinale, from the De Patie-Freleng studio, the new studio born from what had once been Warner Bros. The titles were as well received as the film, and United Artists offered to distribute a series of shorts featuring the pink cat.[1] The first episode, *The Pink Phink*, won an Academy Award in 1964. The director was veteran Friz Freleng, who later entrusted Hawley Pratt and others with the direction of over one hundred further episodes (all with the curious recurrence of the word 'pink' in their titles). The Pink Panther (see Colour Plate 33) is perhaps the last of the old-fashioned animated heroes. Silent, enlivened by action and mime, the character mixes Stan Laurel's tendency to transform good intentions into catastrophe with Buster Keaton's imperturbability.

The De Patie-Freleng studio produced other series for the big screen, such as *The Inspector*, a caricature of Inspector Clouseau, played by Peter Sellers in Blake Edwards' movies; *The Ant and the Aardvark*, featuring the perennial conflict between a purple aardvark and its anticipated meal, a tiny red ant; *Rolland and Rattfink*; *The Tijuana Toads* and *The Blue Racer*. A *Pink Panther Show* also appeared on television.

Friz Freleng had stayed with Warner's until the animation section closed in May 1963. He then became an associate of David De Patie – a younger artist, winner of an Oscar for sound effects in 1951, who had held important positions in live-action cinema. The De Patie-Freleng partnership – basically the only one which continued to produce series of shorts for movie theatres – lasted until 1980.

As for feature films, the most important were those of Ralph Bakshi. Born on 29 October 1938 in Brownsville, New York, into a Russian-Jewish family which migrated to New York from Palestine, Bakshi grew up a troubled teenager and was encouraged to study drawing by a social worker who enrolled him at the Manhattan High School of Industrial Arts. After graduating, he was hired by CBS Terrytoons as an animator, then promoted to director and eventually to studio supervising director. He later joined Paramount, until the ruptures of a New American sensibility, depicted in *Easy Rider* and Robert Crumb's Underground comic strips, motivated him to create an animated cinema for adults. Bakshi made the feature film *Fritz the Cat*, (1972), based on Crumb's character and produced by Steve Krantz.

1 Curiously, in Edwards' films there are no pink cats. The 'Pink Panther' is the much sought-after diamond on which the plot centres.

The movie earned more than thirty million dollars (compared to production costs of one million). *Heavy Traffic* (1973) was also a big box office success, while *Coonskin* (1975) was less convincing and less successful. In this trilogy, animated with care deserving of Disney, Bakshi depicted the hell-on-earth of New York ghettoes and satirized Blacks, Jews and Italians. In his delirious realm, Bakshi, as an 'angry young man' from Brooklyn, mixed sex, violence, and a mockery of Disney's traditional animation and falsely progressive fashions. He belongs to the vast number of New York minority artists who brought their street-life experiences to the 1970s world of entertainment (Martin Scorsese, to give but one example, created live-action representations of a similar ghetto-centred world). To European viewers, Bakshi's Punch-and-Judy style appears uncontrolled and sometimes crass, although enlightened by his distraught talent.

In 1977, the release of *Wizards*, and the making of J.R.R. Tolkien's *The Lord of the Rings* opened a new artistic period. Bakshi looked for inspiration in novels, 'fantasy' illustrations (he collaborated with Frank Frazetta on *Fire and Ice*, 1983) or in pop music (*American Pop*, 1981). The filmmaker demonstrated little imagination in handling his themes, and a culture and taste which did not go beyond the interests and passions of teenagers. Stylistically, his over-use of the rotoscope often led to unpleasant technical results.

Among the directors of feature films, Don Bluth is noteworthy. Born in El Paso, Texas, on 13 September 1937, Bluth went to Disney in 1956, where he worked as assistant to John Lounsbery for one and a half years. After a hiatus from animation which lasted ten years, he returned to Filmation in 1967 as a layout artist, and was re-hired at Disney in 1971. In 1979, he made a sensational departure together with John Pomeroy and Gary Goldman among others, complaining about the decay of Disney's tradition inside the founder's own company. With his colleagues he opened an independent production company which, in 1982, released *The Secret of NIMH*, featuring a little mouse, the widow Brisby, and her anxieties to save her children and house during a series of misadventures. Based on a contorted script and less than appealing characters, the film is, however, redeemed by virtuoso animation.

In 1986, in co-production with Steven Spielberg (the director of *E.T.*) Bluth made the hugely successful *An American Tail*. The film told the adventures of the little Jewish mouse Fievel and his arrival in America – a land without rats and cheese-paved streets (see Colour Plate 34). Set in a meticulously drawn New York circa 1885, sumptuously animated and based on characters more compelling than the ones of Bluth's previous film, *An American Tail* set the box office record for new releases, but once again, this film is more of a punctiliously orchestrated execution than a vital work. In his conservative adherence to Disneyism, Bluth demonstrated his intent to preserve the past rather than a desire to translate Disney's remarkable stylistic lesson into modern terms. In subsequent years, Bluth moved his production company to Ireland.

The most significant animated feature film of recent years, and the one which had the major impact with audiences, was *Who Framed Roger Rabbit*, released in 1988. One more product of Steven Spielberg's entrepreneurial skills, this film was directed by Robert Zemeckis with the animated sections entrusted to the experience of Richard Williams of Great Britain (who will be discussed later). The film is a true post-modern monument to the Hollywood cartoon and detective-story genres built on a dense framework of familiar quotations and joking asides to a knowing audience. This high-quality film introduces two animated characters, gifted with charisma and personality: Roger Rabbit and his seductive wife, Jessica. It offers an interpretation of the

American cartoon tradition (as the place for pure laughter and *joie de vivre*) which is undoubtedly partial, but which is nevertheless sincere and functional.

Roger Rabbit was the first example of complete, plausible coexistence of drawn and live characters in the same frame. A technical achievement that offered Zemeckis and Williams a whole new range of creative possibilities, it also ratified the merger between animation and live-action cinema, a process which had been widely promoted by a decade of special effects and computer animation in science-fiction and fantasy films.

Disney made a dramatic comeback at the end of the 1980s, with feature length fables such as *The Little Mermaid* (see Colour Plate 35) (directed by John Musker and Ron Clements, 1989), *Beauty and the Beast* (Gary Trousdale and Kirk Wise, 1991) and *Aladdin* (see Colour Plate 36) (again by Musker and Clements, 1992). They were luxurious musical comedies, made by a brand-new generation of animators, and were very successful with the public.

On the small screen

Beginning on 3 May 1939, when NBC transmitted its first night of broadcasting (in New York there were a total of two hundred television sets), animation became part of the programme – with the premiere of Disney's *Donald's Cousin Gus*. Immediately after the war, cartoons, such as Van Beuren's *Aesop's Fables* or films by Ub Iwerks, were bought for children's television programmes. These had been available on the market, having appeared numerous times on variety shows and usually introduced by an actor-entertainer. Later, films by Warner Bros. and the Fleischers also became accessible, while CBS bought Terrytoons, and Walt Disney produced and presented his own programmes (*Disneyland* in 1954 and *The Mickey Mouse Club* from 1955 to 1959).

The impact of television on cartoons was felt particularly in the productions conceived and created expressly for the small screen. There was *Crusader Rabbit*, shown in Fall 1949 and produced in San Francisco and Los Angeles by Jay Ward and Alexander Anderson. A series of very brief episodes (four minutes each), it tells of the Round-Table-like adventures of Crusader Rabbit and his friend Ragland T. Tiger. The series had some success, but could not break the ice, as was also the case of *The Ruff and Reddy Show* (1957), the first series produced by the production company Bill Hanna and Joe Barbera founded after leaving MGM. Hanna & Barbera's second production, the series featuring Huckleberry Hound (1958), managed to break through. Huckleberry was a light-blue bloodhound who walked on his hind legs. Inclined to see only the bright side of things, the dog was enmeshed in catastrophic situations from which he always extricated himself with spontaneity. His distinguishing characteristic was the nasal country-accent given to it by voice-man Daws Butler. The *Huckleberry Hound Show* combined three series, the most important being the one featuring the dog. Millions of Americans passionately followed the show, which soon became popular abroad as well. For many years to come, the production was used as a model for TV-made series.

Hanna & Barbera's studio became the unchallenged leader in the field, and remained so for a long time. The company's next success was *Yogi Bear*, the tie-and-hat-wearing bear from the Jellystone National Park who's always accompanied by his little friend Boo-Boo Bear and who makes life impossible for Ranger John Smith.[1] Launched at first as part of the Huckleberry

---

1 Yogi and Ranger Smith derive directly from Fatso Bear and Ranger Willoughby, which Jack Hannah had created for Walter Lantz. In turn, Fatso and Willloughby stem from Humphrey the Bear and the nameless Ranger created by Bill Hanna for Disney.

Hound show, the series with Yogi soon acquired a life and an audience of its own. A feature film, *Hey There, It's Yogi Bear* was also made in 1964.

Next came *The Flintstones* (1960), which imitated the popular live-action TV show *The Honeymooners* starring Jackie Gleason and Art Carney. *The Flintstones* were broadcast in prime-time, as a family programme rather than for children only. The show was an extraordinary success. It was actually the only cartoon to satisfactorily fill that much-coveted time slot. In this case also, ratings soon revealed that youngsters were the most attentive viewers of the show, perpetuating the equation of animation as children's fare. As for its structure, the show was a situation comedy which derived its humour from the anachronisms between prehistory and modern behaviour. The protagonists were Fred and Wilma Flintstone, with their friends Barney and Betty Rubble. All wore animal skins and lived in caves, but used the most modern tools which had been adapted – an electric shaver is a shell containing a bee, and the vacuum cleaner is a little mastodon with a long trunk.[1] The *Jetsons* were also featured in a situation comedy, this time set in a future of technology and space. Although the show flopped on prime-time television, it was immediately successful in Saturday morning children's programming.

Another major series was *Scooby-Doo*, which began in 1969 and starred a cowardly Great Dane and four kids, whose police-horror-comic adventures make light of the dog's hopeless cowardice and of each kid's personality. In 1979, Scooby-Doo was flanked by Scrappy-Doo, a troublemaking puppy.

In the 1970s the company's most successful production was *The Smurfs,* based on the

Schtroumpfs, by Belgian artist Peyo. Already popular in Europe as comic strip and television characters, the Smurfs were launched in the United States on a grand scale.

In the mid-1980s, Hanna & Barbera boasted 800 permanent employees, over 250 children's series in storage, over 4,500 merchandising contracts and an almost twenty-year leadership in the production of series for American audiences, during which the company produced more animation than all its competitors together.[2] This extraordinary success was sometimes bitter for the company's two founders who recalled with nostalgia the days of more careful animation, as opposed to assembly-line production, and who were embarrassed by the quality of their work. 'Actually, I feel like I should crawl under a seat sometimes,' admitted Hanna.[3]

Among the other production companies, Filmation was started in 1962 as a company which specialized in documentaries and advertising. In 1965, it entered Saturday morning programming with a series on Superman. Over the years Filmation has produced *The Archies*, *The Brady Kids*, *Gilligan's Planet* and *Fat Albert*, among many others, displaying business sense and the skills necessary to break into the market. After a crisis lasting a few years, it returned to its earlier vitality in September 1983 with *He-Man and the Masters of the Universe*, a well-received science-fiction story which generated, two years later, the spin-off *She-Ra, Princess of Power*, featuring He-Man's twin sister.

Ruby-Spears Entertainment was founded in 1977 by Joe Ruby and Ken Spears, script writers who had previously worked for Hanna & Barbera, De Patie-Freleng, Krofft and others. This very adaptable company went from a comic-

---

1   The Flintstones also starred in a feature film for movie-theatres, *A Man Called Flintstone* (1967).

2   Figures for the 1980s refer to the joint production by Hanna & Barbera and Ruby-Spears (which, just like Hanna & Barbera, was bought by Taft Entertainment in 1980).

3   Eugene Slafer, 'A Conversation With Bill Hanna,' *The American animated cartoon*, eds. Danny Peary and Gerald Peary (New York: Dutton, 1980) p. 260.

horror story, *Fangface* (its first autonomous production, 1978) to a prehistoric adventure, *Thundarr the Barbarian* (1980), to many other productions; in all, it released twenty-one series and twenty-one special features from 1977 to 1984.

Marvel Productions was founded in 1980 as a branch of the Marvel Comics, a leader in the comic-strip industry. Its creations include *Pandamonium*, *Meatballs and Spaghetti*, *Dungeons and Dragons* and a revival of *Spider-Man*, starring Stan Lee's character which had first appeared on the screen in 1967. Finally, DIC (the American branch of the international company founded by Frenchman Jean Chalopin) opened in 1982. Its best productions include *The Littles*, *Inspector Gadget* and a reprise of *Heathcliff*, a series based on the fat cunning cat created by comic-strip artist George Gately. Heathcliff had already been brought to the screen in 1980 by Ruby-Spears.

The 1990s opened under the banner of *The Simpsons* which is about a middle-class family (two parents, three children) living an everyday conventional ordinary life. Launched in January 1990, the series was an immediate ratings and merchandising sensation, thanks to its irreverent humour. The reasons for the success of the series were not immediately apparent. Ugly (bulbous eyes and yellowish complexion) and extremely vulgar, these characters possibly reassured their televiewers who felt, to their relief, that they were better than the Simpsons. Their creator was underground comic artist Matt Groening, who drew them for his comic strips; producer James L. Brooks convinced animation studio Klasky-Csupo to make a series out of them for Gracie Films, and immediately conquered the coveted space of Sunday prime-time.

There were also several, rarely noteworthy

come-backs in the world of animation brought on by the cathode tube. Old heroes such as Tom and Jerry, Woody Woodpecker, Popeye, Koko the Clown, Mister Magoo, Mighty Mouse, Heckle & Jeckle, Krazy Kat, Felix the Cat and Casper the Friendly Ghost all reappeared in generally poorly animated and tired situations. Old-time techniques and detailed workmanship were lost, but not only for economic reasons. The numerous groups dedicated to the moral preservation and education of children forced producers into self-censorship. For instance, the innate violence between Tom and Jerry was ousted.

In an overview of television programming, Bob Clampett's enterprise should also be mentioned. In his own TV production, Clampett used hand-animated puppets – Beany, an adventurous little boy, and his best friend, Cecil, a sea-serpent which suffered from sea-sickness. The 78-episode series, which saw its characters travel over the seven seas, into space and to every conceivable locale, began in 1962 and was considered one of the best in the field. Another notable series, also 78 episodes long, was the *Bullwinkle Show*, featuring Bullwinkle J. Moose with his large antlers and blank look, and Rocky, a shrewd flying squirrel. George Woolery wrote:

> 'With clean fun for children and sparkling wit for adults, Bullwinkle was one of the most sophisticated, imaginative and humorous of the made-for-TV cartoons.'[1]

Bullwinkle was a creation of producer Jay Ward and script writer Bill Scott. The episodes were directed by UPA old-timers such as Bill Hurtz, Pete Burness and Ted Parmelee.

Even more acclaim was given to Charlie Brown and his court of wise and neurotic friends. The show, however, cannot be described as a true

---

1 George W. Woolery, *Children's Television: the first thirty-five years, 1946–1981 – Part I: Animated Cartoon Series* (Metuchen: Scarecrow, 1983) p. 57.

series, but rather a collection of specials; the first being *A Charlie Brown Christmas* (9 December 1965). Charles Monroe Schulz, who created *Peanuts* for comic strips, collaborated with Lee Mendelson and Bill Melendez to produce these well-made and cleverly written films. The three artists also produced some feature films, but the transposition to the big screen did not help Schultz's characteristically static drawings.

Ralph Bakshi's promotion to head of Terrytoons gave rise, among other things, to *The Mighty Heroes*, one of the most interesting series of the 1960s. The sarcastic and subversive touch of the future creator of *Fritz the Cat* was already evident in this satire of the typical superheroes of American cinema. Leader of the Mighty Heroes brigade was Diaper Man, a child in diapers. He crusaded with his colleagues Cuckoo Man, Strong Man, Rope Man and Tornado Man. Whenever the invincible group set to work, the whole sky flashed gloriously with stars and stripes.

The plethora of true superheroes in adventure series was launched in the mid 1960s by Fred Silverman, then in charge of animation at CBS. As part of an aggressive programme of expansion in the field, in 1966–67 he introduced six action stories, featuring characters such as Superman and Space Ghost. The new trend – largely encouraged by comic strip syndicates and later by toy companies – came to include Captain America, The Incredible Hulk, Iron Man, Batman & Robin, Wonder Woman, Aquaman, Hawkman, Green Lantern and even Tarzan. Overall, these works displayed very low standards from an artistic standpoint. Dramatically powerful episodes were very rare, while the inability to take advantage of individual physiognomy and mimicry (because of the limited animation) led to a lack of identification with the drawn heroes.

While these remarks concern aesthetics and film

criticism, the considerations of business are of a very different nature. In the 1970s and 1980s the market for adventure as well as comic series did not cease to expand, with large-scale operations and investments growing in the field of derived products (most prominently, toys and greeting cards). For instance, much of the popularity of Filmation's *He-Man* (1983) and *She-Ra* (1985) resulted from a close collaboration between the production company and Mattel Toys, whose interest was in promoting the cartoon characters as a new line of dolls. From the late 1970s and the early 1980s, character licensing (the licensing to reproduce characters on products different from the original ones) assumed economic proportions never known before. In 1983–84, this market in the United States went from US$26.7 billion to over US$35 billion, a 30 per cent increase in only one year.[1]

Despite this (or perhaps precisely because of this), the production companies which initiated this phenomenon encountered difficulties. Hanna & Barbera did not survive as an independent company but joined the Taft Entertainment group. The same happened to Ruby Spears, while Filmation was bought by Group W Productions, in turn controlled by Westinghouse. When production costs became prohibitive, a large part of the work was contracted to foreign-based companies. The creative part, including script and story-board, remained in American hands while colouring, 'inbetweening' and sometimes even animation took place in Taiwan, South Korea, Spain, Mexico and Australia. This permitted a 50 per cent saving on production costs, savings which depended largely on the economic situations and the cost of living in the countries involved. To give only one example, at the beginning of the 1980s a painter and an animator would cost an American company $444 and $681 respectively per week plus benefits, versus $50 and $300 for the same employees in

South Korea.[1] The American job market for animators was seriously affected, reducing opportunities for newcomers to the profession. Long strikes did not manage to stop the already entrenched politics, and protectionist regulations demanded by trade unions were either rejected or circumvented. The only company to use exclusively American manpower was Filmation, which established its policy on the basis of ethical and national considerations rather than economic ones. (Filmation's president Lou Scheimer even walked the picket lines during a 1982 strike.)

Due to limited budgets as well as to the repetitiveness of series, production companies have adopted standardized actions and physiognomies. Previously used cels are used again and again with minor changes. (With imprecise albeit likely calculations, approximately 40 per cent of stored material has been reused). With the neutralization of inventiveness as far as movement, graphics, acting and character building are concerned, the series has been a true straitjacket for American animation. This is why this chapter barely touches the immense world of animated series made for American television. A definitive history of this world (as yet to be written) would have to neglect aesthetic factors and focus on economic, sociological and industrial history. In fact, the birth of a series depends on such a large number of converging influences and constraints that the creative aspect is almost insignificant. This topic strays from the goals of this study, whose intention instead is to point out the most refreshing, original intellectual contributions, and belongs to the history of television not animation. Likewise, sitcoms belong to the history of television, not cinema. The same rationale can be applied in the discussion of television series produced in other countries, particularly in Japan.

Independent artists

It is impossible to know just how many independent artists were working in animation. It is not possible to mention actual 'movements', although the tendency to associate with something close to a cultural current was alive in the 1970s in New York, spurred on by filmmakers such as the highly active George Griffin. New York was the major centre for artists who practiced free personal creative production in their spare time outside their advertising, television or teaching jobs. However, many animators worked in other states, which had perhaps never before housed cinematographic productions. Among these independent filmmakers (the number increased massively starting in the 1960s), some were fairly traditional animators, others embraced the mission of the abstract avant-garde, often experimenting with computer animation, and still others tried to translate into cinema the results of research into plastic art. A diversification of themes and techniques was the main characteristic of this wave of animators. Everything was subject to experimentation, from drawing on simple sheets of paper to clay puppets, to computer animation, to collages, to retouched photographs, to object animation. There were exchanges of influence, along with complex and intricate associations amongst diverse groups and stimuli.

John and Faith Hubley

John Hubley was born in New York on 21 May 1914 into a British family with artistic traditions (his grandfather was a renowned English painter). When he was a teenager, the family moved to Michigan where John won a drawing contest sponsored by the local newspaper. With the twenty-five dollar prize, he bought an old Ford from his father, a car dealer, and spent so much time on it that he stopped drawing.[2]

---

1   *Emmy Magazine*, Vol.5, No.4, July–August 1983.
2   Personal communication, as are all quotations by the Hubleys in this section (1973).

During the Depression young Hubley moved to Los Angeles, to live with an uncle, a well-off insurance agent who supported him throughout his studies but whose greed was frequently the target of his nephew's scorn. After graduation, Hubley applied successfully to Disney, which was then in its most lively and enthusiastic stage. From 1935 on Hubley was one of the best layout artists at the studio on Hyperion Avenue. He later remembered that experience as a happy one, when Disney did his best to encourage product quality and to help animators develop their skills (they were able to attend free technical courses). This ended in 1941 with the strike at Disney; Hubley left for the war.

Even during 'the best years', Hubley showed his dislike for being part of a flock. While working on *Snow White* he had formed a small group with some colleagues with whom he shared the need to change style and to leave the money-making business which had been the goal of Disney (just as it had been the goal of Hubley's uncle). Toward the end of 1944, Hubley worked for the first time with the newly founded UPA, to make the aforementioned campaign movie for Roosevelt. The collaboration continued in an ever more exciting environment. Hubley convinced Bosustow, who in turn convinced distributors at Columbia, to make a project of 'counter-current' non-serial films a reality.

It was in one of Hubley's movies that Mister Magoo debuted as an uncle (Hubley's despised uncle) who went to the mountains with his nephew and had to deal with a bear. While Columbia suggested a series featuring the bear, UPA made a counter-offer for a series based on the human character. This was one of the principles of Hubley and his colleagues: they wanted human characters, closer to their times and experiences. They also wanted to destroy romanticism and the syrupy style of earlier animation and to focus in-

stead on human comedy and social issues. For their music, they chose the likes of Stravinsky, whose work would normally not have been accepted for contemporary feature films. Their feeling was that Magoo, a Babbit-like colonel and the portrait of blind authority (before evolving into a gentler character), would have pleased young Americans.

In 1952, Hubley made a landmark film, *Rooty Toot Toot*.[1] The subject came from the traditional ballad of Frankie and Johnny. Betrayed by Johnny, Frankie kills him. She is acquitted, but after the trial, she kills her lawyer, again out of jealousy. Ironic, brilliant and disenchanted, the film made revolutionary use of drawings and colours – pure spots of colour or colours overflowing carelessly from the characters' contours. The ballad, moreover, belonged to the adult-only poetry most suitable for a tavern or brothel.

Meanwhile, as McCarthyism and the Committee for House Un-American Activities rampaged, California had become stifling for those who had a reputation as leftists. During the witch-hunt, UPA, which had grown into a big organization with its own economic and opportunistic interests, did not intend to buck the current and thus forced Hubley to resign, despite his 20 per cent share. That difficult period coincided, however, with Hubley's happy second marriage to Faith Elliott (New York City, 16 September 1924) , a script writer as progressive as her husband. In New York, the couple founded a new specialized production company which dealt with advertising and educational movies. It was 1955. New York boasted privacy and a cultural environment which in Hubley's opinion, was totally lacking in California. The two artists collaborated on *The Adventures of* *, an experimental art film financed by the Solomon Guggenheim Museum. The film was clearly influenced by McLaren, whom Hubley had met a few years earlier. *Moon-*

1   The title comes from the fifth stanza of the ballad, where it has mere onomatopoeic value.

bird (1959) was the result of rigorous stylistic research and was the starting point of a rich and coherent period. This fantastic story of two children chasing a bird in the night demonstrates great inventive freedom. In 1962, in collaboration with Harlow Shapley and with the organizational structure of a co-operative, the Hubleys made *Of Stars and Men*, a poetic educational feature film dealing with man in the universe, space and time, matter and energy.

Politics, nuclear explosions and racism were the themes of *The Hole* (1962). The film visualized the dialogue between two construction workers who were drilling a hole in the ground. This was a line that the Hubleys would follow in their more mature works and that gives a preponderant role to spontaneous, often improvised dialogue on important issues. The sound track in these films is often a small miracle of verbal music and conceptual tension. Analogous themes appear in *The Hat* (1964), dealing with problems of man-made borders between countries. Two border guards converse incessantly. While one guard does not let the other cross the border, even for the instant necessary to retrieve his hat, animals cross it undisturbed. These films featured the voices of artists like Dizzy Gillespie, Dudley Moore and George Matthews. In *Windy Day* (1968) the Hubleys used voices of two of their daughters for two drawn girls talking with the fascinating logic and abstract thought typical of children.

The movies that followed include *Of Men and Demons* (1970), *Eggs* (1971), *Cockaboody* (1972) and the feature film *Everybody Rides the Carousel* (1976). *Eggs* is a freshly fantastic and ironic essay on life and death and God's existence or non-existence. *Cockaboody* follows, more or less, the same line as *Windy Day*. It tells of the evening of two children engaged in a free-wheeling conversation, with a logic of their own dictated by childhood fantasies. The Hubleys' children were again protagonists in the sound track. One of the couple's best movies, *Cockaboody* is a rare example of adult comprehension and reinvention of the world of children. *Everybody Rides the Carousel*, filmed for CBS and based on a subject by Erik H. Erikson, takes the spectator through eight rotations of a Carousel which symbolize life. Every turn, or age, is characterized by psychological problems of its own. This poetic educational film was the last made by John Hubley, who died on 21 February 1977 in New York. Faith continued animating on her own. In 1977, she released *Second Chance: Sea*, in the creation of which John had a minor role.[1]

Fig. 76. The Hole by John Hubley (USA, 1962).

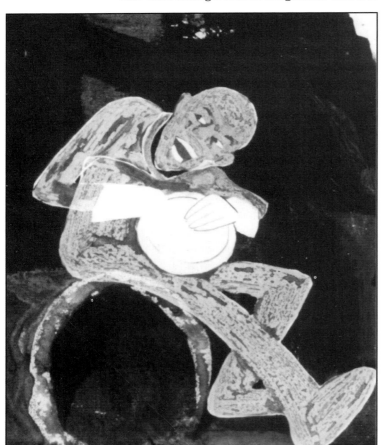

---

1   The many films directed by Faith Hubley after her husband's death are more notable for the causes they embraced (peace, tolerance, spirituality) than for their artistic achievement.

John Hubley, a man of the image more than anything else, directed this specific interest into ever newer and more suggestive figurative inventions. John confirmed that he and his wife had always worked together and that Faith had a tremendous influence on him, also at the artistic level. Having made her debut as a screenwriter and novelist (she also worked on *12 Angry Men* (1956), Sidney Lumet's renowned movie), after her marriage to John Hubley she addressed the problems of figurative art and attended art school. Even though she felt the need to express her inner world, she strongly believed, along with her husband, that cinema needed to have social content. This philosophy was reflected in the couple's last films which carried a less ambitious tone than the earlier ones. As they maintained, an honest representation of life and addressing social issues is as socially relevant as a film on a grand scale of nuclear annihilation, and that even the most fantastic films find their source of inspiration in daily life.

Jules Engel was born in Budapest on 9 March 1918 and at a very young age moved to the United States. His education, as he himself recalled, centred on painting, music and dance. He began as a painter and sculptor, but soon became involved in animation at Screen Gems. Later at Disney, he worked on the choreography for some parts of *Fantasia*; the most often cited part of the film, the mushroom's Chinese dance, is his creation (although the actual animation was executed by Art Babbitt). Besides his knowledge of choreography, Engel was a colour expert and a lay-out man. When UPA was first established, he found himself culturally in tune with the other innovators and became one of the group's foremost personalities. As already mentioned, he contributed to films such as *Gerald McBoing Boing* and *Madeline*. In 1956, he founded his own production company, Format Films which made many productions for television (including a popular series, *Alvin and the Chipmunks*, produced by Ross Bagdasarian in 1960–61). He also created and had his directorial debut with *Icarus*

Fig. 77. Windy Day *by John Hubley (USA, 1968).*

Jules Engel

'[Engel's] abstract films remain like unset gems, brilliant fragments that shine from the screen. If they were brought together in harmonious union the resulting work could be the crowning statement on minimalist animation,' wrote Camille J. Cook.[1]

Actually, Jules Engel's works do not need a setting to express their value in full, but are like a collection of poems or paintings which are born for different occasions and which need no linkage between them. Cook's observation is instead perfectly legitimate in that abstract animator Jules Engel lacks an opus. This versatile artist's many commitments to both dynamic and static visual arts prevented him from focusing on animation alone.

1   CJC (Camille J. Cook), cards on Jules Engel. *Trickfilm Chicago '80*, eds. Camille J. Cook, Frances Gecker, Sharon Russell and Carol J. Slingo (Film Center, School of the Art Institute of Chicago) 1980.

(1960) based on a subject by Ray Bradbury.

All the while, Engel's interest in the arts prevailed over his cinematic production. In 1962 the filmmaker returned to painting and lived for four years in France. During this period, he made the animated short *The World of Siné*, and *Coaraze*, a poetic documentary with strongly contrasting photography set in Coaraze, a town in the Maritime Alps. The film was a recipient of the Jean Vigo award. He also made *Ivory Knife*, winner of an award for best film on painting at the Venice Festival, and *Torch and Torso*, winner of an award at the Edinburgh Festival. In 1992 he was the recipient of the Norman McLaren Heritage Award for his entire work.

Back in the United States, Jules Engel alternated between making short and very-short abstract films and teaching, but did not neglect the fine arts. Since its opening in 1969, he headed the department of animation and experimental film graphics at the California Institute of the Arts – a position which he found satisfactory and productive because of the many young artists who graduated from the courses with technical skills and open minds. The Institute's files contain several first works of high quality, which testify to Engel's progressive and stimulating teaching. As he once told this writer, he was interested in animation when it offered the opportunity to make poetry, and when it pivoted around the imagination.[1] On another occasion, he said that the most important element of a film was rhythm, and that had to come from the artist.[2] These statements frame the work with abstract animation that Engel began in the late 1960s. *Train Landscape* (1975) is a journey by train described using big black shapes with strong edges – both an optical and spiritual experience. *Accident* (1973) was an exciting de-construction of real images reduced to drawings and then to graphic elements. *Shapes and Gestures* (1976) and *Wet Paint* (1977) are based instead on thin thread-like lines, which chase each other sinuously against a white background, meet other coloured elements and at times form figures. Of the two movies, the second one is the most stimulating and most material, as it is drawn on blotting paper. *Landscape* (1971) is one of the best 'pure' films ever made. In it, pulsating colours rhythmically replace one another, and in this way resemble a dance. *Rumble* (1977) features again a geometry of sharp edges: four large black quadrangles on a white background (and vice versa) collide and shake to the rhythms of percussion. Finally, *Play Pen* (1986) is a pastel work with figures and colours chasing each other and waltzing. The film features a dramatic sequence with negative images.

Fig. 78. Accident by Jules Engel (USA, 1973).

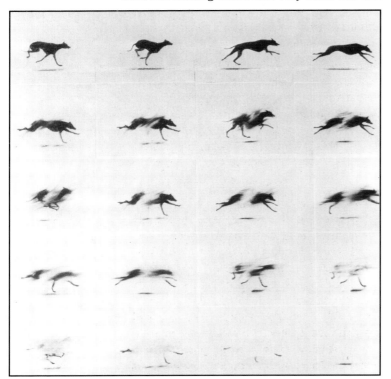

1   Personal communication to the author (1986).

2   Daniel Schillaci, 'Evolution of an Art Form – A Conversation with Film Graphics Artist Jules Engel', *Articles* (Valencia, Ca: 1985). See also 'Experimental Animation … Art in Motion' by Jules Engel, in *Asifa Canada*, vol. 21, No. 3. December 1993.

Engel's various and composite experiences deserve, perhaps, to be deepened and used to a greater extent. Still, Engel adopted one of the most stimulating approaches to abstract animation. Engel's work emerges as being particularly strong in terms of balance and intellectual control, taste and rhythmic invention.

Robert Breer

Robert Breer (Detroit, 1926) began his cinematographic experience in Paris, where he had moved in 1949 to participate more closely in the artistic avant-garde movements. At first, his were simple studies on the action of painting. They can be identified as an animated documentary on figures developed by the brush. The first significant titles were *Form Phases I, II, III* and *IV* (from 1952 to 1954). At the time, Breer had associated himself with the post-Bauhaus group rotating around Denise René's gallery. Following Mondrian's lesson, Breer painted geometric figures with sharp edges. In 1954, he made what would remain his most publicized stylistic innovation and the basis for his credo. For the four films grouped under the title *Images by Images*, Breer chose to make each frame different from the other. Basically, he radicalized the idea that a film is made of different static images which are then seen by the eye for one twenty-fourth of a second each. 'The single frame is the basic unit of film, just as bricks are the basic unit of brick houses', he said.[1] In *Recreation I* (1956), he substituted geometric figures for real images, and each frame became a sort of *objet trouvé* used to machine-gun spectators. In this way Breer acted as a chemical corrosive agent for the structure of filmic communication, pointing out the fundamental characteristic of his artistic activity – the co-existence of construction (of a work) and deconstruction (of working methods and language).

The same reading can be applied also to *A Man and His Dog Out For Air* (1957). An apparently traditional film with animated drawings, it is actually a cognizant re-presentation of Emile Cohl linear style, but presented in a bare and demystifying, although somewhat affected, version.

In 1959, Robert Breer returned to the United States and settled in New York, where the developing Pop Art and minimalism had much in common with his own project (particularly minimalism with its simplified and intentionally inexpressive geometry). Not by chance did Breer make the live-action film *Pat's Birthday* (1962), a sort of happening in collaboration with Claes Oldenburg. J. Hoberman wrote that:

> '... during the mid-sixties' heyday of minimalism, [Breer] reworked the austere geometries of his early *Form Phases* with a consummate authority and sophistication.'[2]

It was during this period that films like *Blazes* (1961) were produced which featured quick appearances and superimpositions of abstract paintings and drawings accompanied by an asynchronous sound track. Another example of this period is the beautiful *69* (1968) in which geometric bi-dimensional and three-dimensional geometric figures move freely in a space which has been 'complicated' by pulsating colours.

Breer began a new stage in 1972 with *Gulls and Buoys* where he used the rotoscope to explore the relationship between live-action shots and the production of animated images. His rotoscope does not give him the pretext for an animation which simply imitates life; rather, one feels the constant presence of the artist's organizing intelligence. Often bits of live-action seem related superficially, approaching animation in their clarity while at the same time the figures seem to dissolve into pure abstract design. Beside *Gulls*

1   J. Hoberman, 'Robert Breer's Animated World,' *American Film*. (September 1980) p. 48.
2   Hoberman 'Robert Breer,' p. 48.

and *Buoys*, he used this technique in the excellent *Fuji* (1974) the report of a train trip in the Fujiyama area, with stylization and abstraction obtained by tempera or spray-gun; and *Rubber Cement* (1975). The following films, *77* (1977), *LMNO* (1978), *T.Z.* (1979) and *Swiss Army Knife With Rats and Pigeons* (1980) are less easily grouped into a homogeneous opus, as they appear to be a celebration of formal and thematic anarchy.

Among modern animators, Robert Breer is perhaps the one who has maintained the most contacts with the artistic avant-garde of post World War II. In animation he is an isolated and lonely master, an experimentalist of language and form who has tried to translate plastic art research into action and movement. As for his inspiration, spectators have always felt it to be colder and more intellectual than it actually is. In fact, Breer filters all the stimuli that today's world offers an artist through watchful intelligence and attentive eyes; at the same time, he asks himself the question of how to offer his product to the viewer. He is certainly apart from the group of visionaries such as Fischinger or Belson. As his biographer Lois Mendelson wrote:

> 'Breer, whose roots lay in the traditions of Constructivism, the Bauhaus and Dada, as well as in the traditions of European graphic cinema, was not influenced by the lyric or mythopoeic modes, even after his return to America. He proposed a cinema without links to literary or poetic traditions, without Romantic or surrealist connotations: a cinema of speed, of pure images and pure rhythm, a cinema of structure.'[1]

John Whitney

Born on 8 April 1917 in Altadena, California,

John Whitney switched from humanistic interests (such as twelve-tone music) to scientific ones (such as astronomy) in his youth. Never the studious type, he had only a fleeting contact with his school curriculum, later recalling how he had to re-learn maths in order to build computer images for his films.

It was thanks to his love for astronomy that Whitney approached cinema, and more precisely, frame by frame cinema – when he recorded the evolution of an eclipse, in single frames and with an 8 mm movie camera.[2] Later on, when the outburst of World War II rendered impossible any cultural trips to Europe (John was then visiting France and Germany while his brother James was in Great Britain), abstract cinema became his intellectual ground for discovery. The two Whitney brothers opened a small experimental laboratory, mixing John's musical interests and James' pictorial ones. In this period John demonstrated his aptitude for inventing and adapting machines by building an optical printer for their 8 mm equipment. The brothers made several experiments (never linked into any conclusive form) and a short film, the graphically constructivist *Twenty-Four Variations* (1940), based on the themes of a circle and a rectangle.

It was with *Film Exercises* (numbered from 1 to 5 and made in 1943–44) that the two artists obtained their first substantial result. The *Film Exercises* are among the most stimulating and complete abstract films ever made – a composition in which each new image offers a subtle variation of the original plan. (The filmmakers' contributions to the movies are basically indistinguishable, although John is the actual author of the first and fifth and James of the other three.) The Whitneys put light itself, rather than lit images, in front of the camera, with drawings deriving from masks placed above a light source.

1   Lois Mendelson, *Robert Breer: A Study of His Work in the Context of the Modernist Tradition* (Ann Arbor: UMI Research Press, 1978) p. 105.

2   During his investigations, William Moritz found abstract experiments which might have been made in earlier years.

Sound is created with a system of pendulums invented by John Whitney, who 'wrote' artificial music on the sound track. This way images as well as sounds have an original, primitive purity.

From then on the two brothers parted. Among his other inventions, John developed a technique which allowed him to film rapidly. He complained about the slow work needed for frame-by-frame shooting and optical printer procedures (as compared to composing in real time). His discovery was ingeniously simple consisting of covering a luminous surface with more or less dense oil and tracing on it images with a finger or stylus. When the fluid closed up, it erased the image. This soft making and unmaking of lines and curves was filmed by the camera. The artist used this technique for, among other films, *Mozart Rondo* (1949), *Hot House* (1949) and *Celery Stalks at Midnight* (1951) – all fascinating and rigorous films, in which colour was added for decorative purposes during printing (particularly beautiful is the light green/light purple of *Celery Stalks at Midnight*).

With the 1950s, John Whitney went through a period of weariness, during which he focused mainly on graphic works and special effects. He came to doubt the value of abstract filming:

'I began to see that these kinds of animation techniques were, if anything, a kind of anachronism ... They resembled the faulty efforts that were made to make a flying machine ... before they had the slightest understanding of aerodynamics ...'[1]

It was then that his interests took a marked direction toward experimentalism. Starting with *Catalog* (1961), each of his films was an attempt to compose visual music as well as to explore the possibilities of harmony and counterpoint offered by the computer. Whitney became concerned with studying, at the moment of creation, virgin territory for cultivating beauty – even more than creating new works (intended as compositions with a coherence of their own). For a long time the artist did not consider *Catalog* as a film to be shown in public but rather as the 'catalogue' of the visual effects obtained with his first computer (an analogue computer which had served during the war to direct anti-aircraft guns). He returned to this topic in 1986 when he wrote that his dream to create music and graphics at the same time was becoming a reality, thanks to the computer. He believed that a new art was being born: abstract architecture, which would combine the two separate artistic expressions of music and painting.[2]

Permutations (1968) was the first film Whitney considered a complete work. The film was made after he was hired, in 1966, as a consultant for a large research programme at IBM, which gave him a 360 digital computer and a 2250 console for graphic display. *Permutations* resembles a rose window, using soft kaleidoscopic movements. Colours have been added at the optical printer with a traditional procedure; whereas, the series *Matrix* (three films, 1971–1972) uses computer generated lines, moving in space, and quadrangular figures. *Arabesque* (1975) is as complicated as the façade of an oriental temple (see Colour Plate 37) and at the same time continues the fluid visual discourse the artist had begun with his oil technique. *Permutations II* is newly structured editing of the cinematographic material already used in *Permutations*.

In articles, interviews and in a book[3] Whitney constantly drew the attention of spectators, scholars and artists alike to the possibilities the computer offers composers (he always considered

1   Richard Brick, 'John Whitney Interview,' *Film Culture*, No. 53, 54, 55 (Spring 1972), p. 51.
2   Personal communication to the author (1986).
3   John Whitney, *Digital Harmony: On the Complementarity of Music and Visual Art* (Peterborough: Byte Books/McGraw Hill, 1980).

himself a composer of visual music). As an author, he felt 'unsatisfied'[1] but his work is extremely important in establishing a language and a grammar for the cinematography of the future.

edged pure textures and thick, irregular, hand-wrought solarized textures induces a contemplation of the self and reality, identity and universality.'[2]

James Whitney

For the first part of his career, James Whitney collaborated with his brother John. The first tests resulted from their joint efforts. Younger than John (he was born on 27 December 1921, in Pasadena), and interested in painting and craftsmanship rather than music and technique, he devoted himself to autonomous poetic research, following the influence of oriental philosophies, Ramana Maharishi, Jung's psychology, alchemy, Yoga, Tao and quantum physics. He withdrew early from the world, retiring to a life of serene meditation in a small wooden, linear, Japanese-like house that he and some friends adapted so that it was possible to watch the seasons change in the garden from inside.

From the early 1950s to his death (Los Angeles, 8 April 1982), James Whitney made only five movies, but of such a high quality as to make him one of the best representatives of non-objective cinema and one of this century's great visionaries. For a long time he considered the possibility of using a visual alphabet, until he finally adopted the point – the basic element of all forms. *Yantra* (1955) derives its title from the Sanskrit 'sacred machine' – be it the instrument for meditation such as the mandala, or the great orderly machine that is the Universe. The film is made entirely of points, which collect and separate with the light of intense colours and of entire sections of film which had been solarized. William Moritz said:

> 'This range of quasi-musical variations of implosions and explosions, light and dark, hard-

Like all other films by James, *Yantra* was conceived as a purely optical and spiritual experience, complete in itself without the need for a sound track. Shown in the most absolute silence, the film is a vivid experience which allows, more than if there were music, a better appreciation of its innumerable visual subtleties. For distribution-related reasons this film as well as the following ones were ultimately given sound tracks. These attachments, however, did not affect the communicative strength of the images (contrary to what happened, just to give an example, with Harry Smith's first films).

Yantra required patient manual work which lasted for five years, perhaps longer (reworking did not end before 1957–58). Afterwards, James Whitney underwent a period of 'white wait', as he described it with a Chinese expression indicating an artist's use of a different creative activity to gain strength and inspiration. For some years he made paintings which largely recalled his films. In 1965, he released *Lapis*, named after the Latin 'stone' and referring particularly to the philosophers' stone of alchemy. Whitney worked on the movie for three years, with his brother John's computer to help him guide camera equipment. It should be made clear that, despite what has sometimes been suggested, the film was not influenced by computer graphics. Each image was created manually on a cel and only a part of the shooting was guided by the computer (hundreds of tiny points had to be superimposed and moved in very small gradations).

Lapis is a perhaps a more vivid and sensual representation of the themes and modules of *Yantra*

---

1   Personal communication to the author (1986).

2   William Moritz, 'James Whitney Retrospective,' *Toronto 84* (Catalog of the Canadian International Film Festival, 13–18 August 1984) p. 11.

– a sort of hypnotic machine representing actions and metamorphoses of swarms of points and colours. Here (as in all other films by James Whitney and in the not too dissimilar ones by Jordan Belson), it is easy to perceive the author's substrata and intent, from mysticism to meditation, to magic and symbolism, to speculation on artistic expression, to the imaginary representation of physical phenomena. While artistically educated spectators feel enriched and stimulated, the mere viewing of the film is a rewarding experience. The film was followed by another 'white wait', during which the artist created ceramics and pots of Far Eastern inspiration.

James Whitney's last cinematographic project was a trilogy, or rather a tetralogy in which the first work served to introduce the other three. The introductory film, *Dwija*, was supposed to correspond to fire, *Wu Ming* to water, *Kang Jing Xiang* to air and *Li* to the earth, in a representation of the four primary elements of the Universe according to ancient tradition. Because of the artist's premature death, the project remained unfinished. He directed *Kang Jing Xiang* but did not edit it (the current version was completed by his nephew Mark Whitney and by critic and filmmaker William Moritz, who followed instructions left by the artist in his last days). At the time of his death, James had only begun work on *Li* .

Dwija (1973) (see Colour Plate 38) derives its title from another Sanskrit word, with the double meaning of 'twice born' and 'bird' (since the bird is born twice, once when still in the egg and then outside). In alchemic terms, the bird represents the essence of the soul, which at first is enclosed in its own container and, after the ultimate purification, is free to escape into the ether. The film images precisely represent eight alchemic drawings which show a bird imprisoned in a sort of alembic, undergoing a purification process until it

is free at the end. The film – formed by a cyclic repetition of those drawings, with solarizations and superimpositions – results in a source of liquid light which grows and flows harmoniously.

Wu Ming comes from the Chinese 'no name' found at the beginning of *Tao Te Ching*:

'At the beginning of Sky and Earth there was no name. Names created million of things. Without desire there is mystery; but with desire, there are only things. Everything starts equal, but names make everything different'.

After the spectators' souls and minds have been purified by viewing *Dwija* they are ready to see the first composition of the trilogy – a sort of dialectic action (action and reaction) between particle and wave during which the particle disappears into infinity and returns in the form of expanding waves. The apotheosis of this film (here abstract cinema manages to achieve grandiosity, perhaps for the first time) resides in the finale, where the centre of the film and the action are represented by a black circle which gradually decreases for five minutes, until it disappears in white. When *Wu Ming* opened in New York (1977), Jonas Mekas praised the film:

'What a relief, and what a feast to see a work where one can feel the many years of intense living, feeling, thinking. So that there is always somebody, working almost in total silence, who comes in to restore Cinema with a work that looks like it's made by gods.'[1]

On *Kang Jing Xiang*, William Moritz, one of the filmmakers who completed the film, wrote:

'The Chinese characters that make up the title are philosophically ambiguous: They could mean 'like an empty mirror' as well as 'what is seen during a lustrous religious ecstasy.' The lovely images would support either interpreta-

1   Jonas Mekas, *Soho News*, 7 May 1977.

tion. Half of the sequences are soft and misty (this would be the 'air' film); but some have a star-like scintillation, such as the splendid scarlet mandala, which can, in turn, dissolve into the white wait of the cosmos.'[1]

Finally, the unfinished *Li* was planned as fields of spot-like elements in contortion. The Chinese word Li means 'granular organic model', however, James Whitney referred to the movie also as *Wu Wei*, 'non resistance'.

Visionaries and avant-garde artists

The Whitneys' contribution to cinema was not limited to John and James. When John began working with the IBM computer, his old computer equipment was put to good use by his wife and three children – John Jr. (born in 1947), Michael (1948) and Mark (1951). John Jr. greatly upgraded the equipment, and all made new films. For about two years the three brothers toured the West with their own production, a one-hour abstract film shown on multiple screens. At the Montreal Expo of 1967, John Whitney Jr. showed the synthesis of one of his previously released works, *Byjina Flores*. The new untitled version was seventeen minutes long. In the 1980s he was in demand as an expert on computer special effects. As for Michael Whitney, in 1969 he made the refined, precious *Binary Bit Patterns* using an Information International computer.

Van Der Beek (New York, 1931 – Columbia, Maryland, 19 September 1984) began making comedies and political satires among other non-objective films in 1955. Involved in technological experimentation for artistic purposes, he worked with the most diverse techniques, including graphic experiments, projections on multiple screens, or cinematographic murals as he called them, computer-aided works for an international chain of satellite-connected Movie Dromes (movie theatres where spectators are surrounded by a continuous flow of images), dance film for ballet accompaniment, and much more. His approach to computer-aided filmmaking was helped by Bell Laboratories engineer Kenneth Knowlton,[2] the inventor of the computer language Beflix, used for creating films as well as static images (Beflix derives its name from Bell and flicks).

Van Der Beek's films, animated mosaics or tapestries, were collected under the name *Poem Fields* (1964–1970). Using Beflix and an IBM 7094 computer, he made *Collisdeoscope*. After 1970, with the help of grants from institutions, large universities and computer corporations, he improved his technology to make *Symmetriks* and *Ad Infinitum*.

John Stehura (Chicago, 1942) put several years of work on the computer into the making of *Cibernetic 5, 3*, with abstract images in a supposed three-dimensional field. Stehura continued his experiments without completing any major film and developed a computer language which unifies musical and graphic systems.

Ed Emshwiller (Lansing, Michigan 1925 – Valencia, California, 1990), painter and illustrator, made his debut in animation cinema in 1959 with *Dance Chromatic* and *Transformations*. In 1966, with a grant from the Ford Foundation he made *Relativity*, a 'film poem'. Afterward, without neglecting the traditional camera, he adopted videotape and computer, creating *Scape-mates* (1972), a mix of live-action dancers, electronically distorted images and animation on magnetic tape. For animation, Emshwiller used the *scanimate*, a video-synthetizer which permits animation in real time while looking at a monitor.

Peter Kamnitzer's résumé includes a directorship

1   William Moritz, 'James Whitney,' *Sightlines*, Vol. 19, No. 2 (Winter 1985–86) p. 27.

2   Knowlton (born in 1931) continued his experiments throughout the 1970s in collaboration with painter Lillian Schwartz: *Pixillation* (1970), *Olympiad* (1971) and *Apotheosis* (1972).

at UCLA's Urban Laboratory and a collaboration on a NASA and General Electric project for the computerized simulation of moonscapes. In 1968, he made *City-scape* using the NASA II computer at the Guidance and Control Division of NASA's Manned Spacecraft Center in Houston, Texas. Drawn directly by the computer with a coded mathematical input but without any input of pre-existing images, *City-scape* is more interesting conceptually than artistically.

Scott Bartlett (Atlanta, 1943 – San Francisco, 1990) debuted in 1966 with *Metanomen*, financed by San Francisco State College where he was a student. Live-action images, printed with high contrast, became pure stylized forms. In his following works, Bartlett used optical as well as computer techniques. *Off/On* (1967), *A Trip to the Moon* (1968), *Moon 69* (1969) resulted from the use of complex and expensive techniques.[1]

On the contrary, Dennis Pies (Indianapolis, 1947) made use of very traditional equipment. With financing from the California Institute of the Arts, the artist made some 'atmospheric' films. *Nebula*, *Merkaba*, *Aura Corona* and *Luma Nocturna* (these titles come either from Latin or Hebrew, with some creative input by the author) follow the same visionary and cosmological path already explored by Belson or James Whitney, although at much lower levels of discipline and taste. Pies has also performed on stage, dancing and acting during his film projections.

The artistic work of Carmen D'Avino (Waterbury, Connecticut, 1918) followed an unusual course of evolution. His first films were abstract and pictorial, and followed the artist's long-lasting apprenticeship as war cameraman, Fine Arts student in Paris and curious traveller in India. *Patterns for a Sunday Afternoon* (1954, which he made three years after his return to the United States), *Theme and Transition* (1956) and *The Big O* (1958) were instead the products of a painter, showing the strong influence of an Indian colour sense. In *The Room* (1959), the artist made a radical change in style, adopting the so-called dimensional, or environmental, animation. An environment, or in this case, a room, as the title itself suggests, undergoes diverse metamorphoses. This second-phase D'Avino (a sort of ahead-of-the-times land art) also characterized *Stone Sonata* (1962) in which stones move and are magically coloured in a forest, *Pianissimo* (1963), *A Finnish Fable* (1965), *Tarantella* (1966) and *Background* (1973). In 1980, the artist made *Clock*. D'Avino worked also for television and made public relation films.

A former mathematician and musician, Tony Conrad (Concord, New Hampshire, 1940) owes his fame to *The Flicker* (1965), in which he alternated simple black-and-white frames, with different widths. This projected different illusions of colour, manipulating the diffusion of light into imaginary forms. An introductory title card warned the audience against the films' possible negative effects, such as a photogenous epilepsy. Afterward, Conrad used the same technique in *The Eye of Count Flickerstein* (1966), *Straight and Narrow* (1970) and *Four Square* (1971). He also experimented with non-animated cinema.

Larry Jordan (Denver, 1934) took his first steps in cinema with his high school friend and future Underground artist Stan Brakhage. Jordan made his more mature works starting in 1959, after having experimented with filmed psychodramas (1954), 'cineportraits', and his first animations. In the area of animation, Jordan worked on eleven animated films, concluded in 1974 under the collective title *Animated Works, 1959–1974* and on other individual projects, such as *Masquerade*

1   This survey does not include those artists who go beyond the classical terms of 'cinema' and 'animation' – namely, 'videotronic' artists who work with videotapes, creating special effects and distortion. This fascinating topic deserves a study of its own.

(1982). In *Animated Works* – which include *Duo Concertantes* (1964), *Hamfat Asar* (1965), *The Old House, Passing* (1966), *Gymnopedies* (1968), *Our Lady of the Sphere* (1969), *Orb* (1973) and *Once Upon a Time* (1974) among others, he used the technique of animated collage. A collector of 19th Century illustrations, metal engravings, figures from ancient anatomy and magic books, Jordan filmed these elements, creating a dreamlike and disquieting atmosphere.

A self-declared surrealist, Larry Jordan explored the continents of the mind, developing craftsmanship to its maximum potential while leaving open ground for his mental associations. His style is reminiscent of Joseph Cornell's poetic 'boxes' containing found objects as well as the artist's own creations. Actually Jordan and Cornell knew each other personally and collaborated.

Paul Sharits' approach to cinema follows the same line as Tony Conrad or Robert Breer. As a student at Indiana University, Sharits (Denver 1943) made *Ray Gun Virus* (1966), alternating images which lasted a few frames each. The film was followed by *Peace Mandala/End War* (1967), by the notable *N:O:T:H:I:N:G* and *T,O,U,C,H,I,N,G*, and by *Razor Blades* (all 1968). In 1970, he released *S:TREAM:S:S:EC-TION:S:ECTION:S:S:ECTIONED.* Sharits makes great use of colour changes so as to suggest a flashing impression of images (such as the positive and negative chair in *N:O:T:H:I:N:G*), and to turn real people or objects into abstractions. In this, his efforts seem linked to the experimentalism of a Léger or a Man Ray, despite his obvious ties to Oriental philosophy.

Ken O'Connell (Ogden, Utah 22 January 1945) animation teacher and historian, made over 12 short films and videos, using various techniques including computers. Best remembered are *Strings* (1979) which takes abstract patterns from ordinary observations, *Chips in Space* (1984, see Colour Plate 39), a computer film reminiscent of Fischinger and McLaren, and *Oregon Country* (1990), a lyrical 'painted documentary' on this state.

Photographer and sculptor, Pat O'Neill (Los Angeles, 28 June 1939) made his debut in the 1960s with *By the Sea* and *Bump City*. His first important work was *7362* (1967). The film included prisms, solarizations and very high photographic contrasts. Black and white were predominant (the title refers to the black-and-white Kodak film used), with colours – particularly magenta – playing a highlighted role. Despite the appearance of real images (a female figure) the film was substantially abstract.

Downwind followed in 1972 – a 'frontier' film, mixing animation and live-action with a great use of time-lapse photography and an optical printer. *Saugus Series* (1974) was a collection of seven very short films, of which the first, sixth and seventh are quite special. The film (for which the optical printer was largely used) refers intentionally to Jasper Johns, one of the artists O'Neill respected the most. Plastic arts also influenced *Let's Make a Sandwich* (1982), which recalls Pollock and Lichtenstein, and which dismantles or 'de-contextualizes' the dramaturgy of regular live-action films.

An intellectually rigorous artist, who always handled technology with the greatest self-confidence (he made almost virtuoso use of the optical printer), O'Neill is very close to research in the contemporary plastic arts. His films have been described as:

'... widely variegated works, composed of overlappings of perceptual data from different sources and categories, which demand constant shifts of attention by the viewer. As straight photography alternates with optical printer manipulation, black and white with brilliant colour, desert landscapes with abstract compositions or subtle nuance with gaudy shrillness, aesthetic distinctions of widely divergent nature seem to be introduced and abandoned within a few feet of film.'[1]

Al Jarnow (Brooklyn, New York, 1945) is noticeable for his interest in the graphic and architectural nature of animation. His academic background (he studied at Dartmouth College) emerges in *Rotating Cubic Grid* (1975) and *Four Quadrants Exercise*, both displaying very elegant geometric effects. *Auto Song* (1976) is also a geometric film, a trip through street scenes and unreal landscapes. Jarnow's finest work is perhaps *Shorelines* (1977), where the designer's sophisticated taste finds life in the real and ordinary items used (marine objects, mainly shells). The film is very fresh and creative, with objects moving and combining to form abstract images.

Also of great interest is the formal-minimalist research by Paul Glabicki (Pittsburgh, 17 January 1951). Glabicki's career, which began in 1975 with *Gameshow*, reached its maturity with the trilogy *Diagram Film* (1978), *Five Improvisations* (1979) and *Film-Wipe-Film* (1983). The latter, approximately thirty minutes long, is a complex stream-of-consciousness work which develops in both image and sound track, at times with a mental lucidity and at others with gentleness. An original filmmaker who draws his inspiration from many sources, in 1985 Glabicki focused on objects in *Object Conversation* (1985) (see Colour Plate 40), a series of visual and verbal dialogues created between, about and with a series of source objects: a pair of scissors, chairs, an hourglass, a bar-bell, an arch, ladders, and so on. *Under the Sea* (1989) is a complex, multi-layered film structured on narratives extracted from *Madame Bovary*, *Frankenstein*, *20,000 Leagues under the Sea*, *Gulliver's Travels* and *The Voyage of the Beagle*. Text from the books is used in graphic form throughout the film, as well as in vocal performances in English, German and a North American indigenous language.

Another complex author is David Ehrlich (Elizabeth, 14 October 1941), who goes from geometric drawing to colour research, to calligraphy, to technical experimentation. His most convincing films are *Precious Metal* (1980), *Dissipative Dialogues* (1982) and *Precious Metal Variations* (1983). Ehrlich is also the artist who has obtained the finest results with holography, in *Oedipus at Colonus* (1978), *Ranko's Fantasy* (1983), *Phallacy* (1983), *Stabila* (1984) and *Dryads* (1988).

'From my early experiments in 1978 which resulted in *Oedipus at Colonus*,' wrote Ehrlich, 'a 360 degree integral animated hologram of a slowly transforming sculpture, I moved to a series of experiments in 1983–1984 which explored the sculptural interaction between foreground solid and

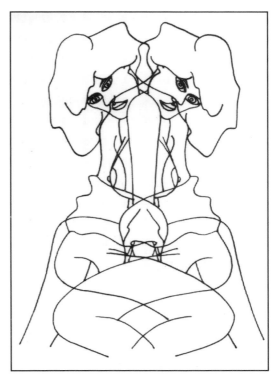

Fig. 79. *Dryads* by David Ehrlich (USA, 1988).

1   Christine Noll Brinckmann and Grahame Weinbren, 'The O'Neill Landscape: Four Scenes From Foregrounds', *Millennium Film Journal*, No. 4–5, Summer-Fall 1979.

background relief. ... The magical movement of mass through the air from foreground to background and back lent itself to the sense of mystery inherent in the holographic form.'[1]

Among the youngest talents who have used the computer as a tool for abstract art is Larry Cuba (Atlanta, 17 September 1950), who began by collaborating with John Whitney. His works include *First Fig* (1974), *3/78* (1978) and the delicate, exquisitely rhythmic *Two Space* (1979). These films are 'austerely beautiful explorations of space, movement, and design, in which point of light move in complicated, cogent patterns'.[2] In 1984, he made *Calculated Movements*.

Richard Protovin (New York, 5 May 1945) created several films on his own, but gave his best when collaborating with Franklin Backus (Seattle, 30 August 1940 – New York, 5 July 1988). Their finest work is a trilogy of cityscapes, which includes *Manhattan Quartet* (1982), *Southern Images* (1984) and *Battery Film* (1984). These attractive films occupy the no-man's-land between animation, environmental and documentary films. The same, but with different premises, can be said of Gary Beydler's *Pasadena Freeway Stills* (1974), where pictures of the highways are put in front of the camera and then gradually animated. Finally, Skip Battaglia should be mentioned for *Parataxis* (1980), made by processing the film stock with a Xerox copier.

Jane Aaron

Jane Aaron's first film, *A Brand New Day* (1974) told the story (entirely drawn on paper) of a young woman who wakes up in the morning, opens and closes her window on new and fascinating landscapes, until the last image – the wall of the opposite building – brings her back to blunt reality. Jane Aaron (New York, 16 April 1948) studied drawing, painting and sculpture at Boston University. She chose animation upon her discovery of films by New York's independent artists, with whom she identified. *A Brand New Day* was a 'small' film which displayed all the characteristics of New York movement: technical economy, non-sumptuous style and an autobiographical theme. A study of the relationship between imagination and reality – between the perceived reality and the invented one – the film was a sort of manifesto of the author's poetics, which were to be gradually and coherently laid out in her subsequent films.

In Plain Sight (1977) is the first time in which Aaron mixed animation and live-action in the same frame. She later described the making of this film:

'I did a series of loose, easy drawings, took them outside and shot them pinned to a tree, on the windshields of a car, or on a stick simply stuck in the ground. There was no conscious effort at that point to have a completed film. I then started shooting these experiments in 16mm and eventually strung them together to make *In Plain Sight*.'[3]

The film is filled with successful scenes (such as the dance on the background of a tree) but it is still technically raw. In general, the pleasantness of the visual expedients outstrips the artistic results. The film, however, opens the door to research into the perception of things by the eye, by the camera and by the visionary intervention of drawing. The landscape and the drawing inserted into it are filmed at the same time, frame by frame. This results in a 'loss of reality' for the landscape (the rhythms of which have become distorted because of speed) and an 'increase of

1   Letter received from David Ehrlich, 5 December 1986.
2   Charles Solomon, *The Complete Kodak Animation Book* (Rochester: Eastman Kodak, 1983), p. 93.
3   Letter received from Jane Aaron, 27 September 1986.

reality' for the drawings (which are characterized by soft and 'believable' movements). The spectator is led to perceive that both worlds are possible and to consider an easy interaction between them.

Aaron obtained excellent results in her following movie, *Interior designs* (1980). Here technique is mastered, the camera moves fluidly, and drawings, landscapes and interiors merge or appear in sequence, developing the visual and dramatic possibilities of each situation. As in the previous film (and in future ones), this is a notebook of sketches, compact, even if not linked by narration. The drawing is alternately a frame for live-action images or the framed part inside live-action images. At times, drawings occupy the entire field, even becoming abstract. Action moves from the filmmaker's bedroom and studio to the desert and mountains, and finally returns to the house, with drawings greeting the spectator. Here Aaron's seemingly larger concerns develop into a cinematographic Land Art, in which the artist's interventions are not permanent on the landscapes but are indelible on the resulting work – a Land Art where nature is not modified, but rather invited to act and assume attitudes and meanings. Another remarkable element of the film is its frugal and suggestive sound track, made by recording real sounds and often using them in an imaginative way. *Interior designs* was shown at the Neuberger Museum, at an exhibition entitled 'Soundings: The Visual Artists' Use of Sound' (1981).

Remains to Be Seen (1983) is a sort of filmic Land Art. Drawings run through the live-action image, tracing its contours or integrating it by introducing characters or narrating bits of life (toys appear on a beach, a person opens a window, some people have their picture taken on a terrace, a fireplace lights itself). The entire work is dominated by a two-dimensional, white, stylized female figure which appears at the beginning, the end and throughout the film. Although a continuation of the previous film, this work has an added lyric quality in the presence of the artist, who fantasizes or remembers, enriching the visual creation with human warmth and softness. Landscape and drawing are here as one. In some passages, the drawing even seems to be an interpretation of the opportunities offered by the landscape itself – for example indicating that the now deserted beach was, or will become, a playground; or that the now empty chairs can accommodate chattering people. In a sense, the already living landscape receives, in addition, a soul.

Traveling Light followed in 1985. A very short film, it featured the light passing over various objects and domestic locales, until it is revealed that the light was only a special effect achieved with tiny pieces of paper. Compared with the two previous films this is certainly a minor work, but it is made with great sensibility and cleverness. Jane Aaron maintained that with this movie she finally discovered the appearance of light – a phenomenon which had always fascinated her. *Traveling Light* was yet another evolutionary step. Besides exploring reality and its appearance, each film by Aaron is also like a journey into research, leading from drawing to three-dimensionalism, that is, scene-design to sculpture. This was precisely the ending point of *Set in Motion* (1986), an example of sculpture and environment in motion which, at some points, resembles a work by Rauschenberg which has been enlivened and animated.

'Coming out of the rigidity of *Traveling Light*, I wanted to make a film that was more spontaneous and less representational,' she wrote. 'I had elaborate ideas (and still do) about the paper defining the surfaces of the objects (again very sculptural), but basically I think the film is just wild and fun to look at.'[1]

1   Letter received from Jane Aaron, 27 September 1986.

Innovators of tradition: the independent par excellence

As already mentioned, independent animators are artists who operate outside the production-distribution system, whether in the field of abstract, visionary, plastic research, or within the broad confines of traditional animation and its techniques. In *Frames* (1978), a collection of drawings and statements by sixty-nine independent animators, George Griffin brought together artists such as James Whitney and Jane Aaron, Larry Cuba and Sally Cruikshank, Carmen D'Avino and David Ehrlich – people who did not necessarily share poetics or styles, but who preferred to work alone, responsible only to themselves and their limited audiences. It should be added, though, that the expression 'independent animators' has been commonly used to define those artists who have looked for the new within the techniques of traditional animation; while visionaries and abstract artists have usually been given their own autonomous space. For these reasons, and for convenience, this chapter will discuss these traditional innovators, mostly from New York.

A common characteristic of these filmmakers was the wide variety of techniques (often dictated by economic factors, such as drawing on paper to replace cels), and their use of a drawing style which no longer had to do with traditional Hollywood cartoons, but referred to contemporary graphics. Themes were often autobiographical, including drawn free-thought or line effects with very little narration. There were also erotic themes, a novelty which would soon appear in other countries as well. Overall, there was a wave of 'private' films, the aim of which was not to entertain (at times entertainment was explicitly disavowed). Rather, filmmakers chose simple daily formulas and often had the tendency to include a description of, or reflections on, the procedures used to complete the film. Not by chance did Thelma Schenkel – a scholar who paid attention to these animators' experiences – speak of 'self referential animation'.[1]

Ernest Pintoff (New York, 1931) can be considered the harbinger of this phenomenon. A former jazz musician and painter who had been employed by UPA (1956) and Terrytoons (1957, where he directed the original *Flebus*), he decided to work on his own. In 1959, he began a brief but sparkling period, during which he made shorts like *The Violinist*, (see Colour Plate 41) *The Interview*, *The Old Man and the Flower* and *The Critic*. The latter (1963), written and narrated by Mel Brooks, the future director of *Young Frankenstein*, won an Oscar. A totally abstract film, *The Critic* is made comic by Mel Brooks who mumbles commentary of what happens on screen, with the common sense of an ignorant spectator who tries to understand the 'meaning of it'. With his sharp humour and an intelligence open to reality, Pintoff was one of the first and best epigrammatists of animation. After 1963, he devoted himself to advertising and theatre. He did continue to make some more live-action features, such as *Harvey Middleman, Fireman* (1965) and *St Helen's* (1981) but they did badly at the box-office.

The duo of Bob Mitchell and Dale Case won an award at the 1971 Annecy Festival with the brilliant and irreverent *Further Adventures of Uncle Sam*, which has the flavour of underground comic strips. Mitchell also released the excellent *Free* (1973).

The promising career of Californian Adam Beckett, born in Los Angeles in 1950, was cut short by his death (Val Verde, 1 March 1979). *Evolution of the Red Star* (1973), *Sausage City* and *Flesh Flows* (both of 1974) feature cyclical repetitions of drawings, which undergo sequential changes. The results are suggestive atmospheres

1   Thelma Schenkel, 'The Circle of Illusion: Self-Referential Animation,' *Trickfilm Chicago '80*.

and innovative images. After *Kitsch in Synch* (1975), using animated cutout figures and the optical printer, Beckett had just time to create some optical effects for George Lucas' *Star Wars*.

thirty-minute long allegory on the liberating power of fantasy.

John Canemaker (Waverly, NY, 28 May 1943) is a multi-faceted artist. A historian of animation (he wrote essays and made documentaries on Otto Messmer and Winsor McCay and has interviewed artists such as John Randolph Bray), a critic and popularizer, a teacher of animation at New York University, an author (of, among others, *The Animated Raggedy Ann and Andy*, which followed Richard Williams from sources to the actual work and the world-respected *Felix, the Twisted Tale of the World's Most Famous Cat*) and speaker. He is a rare example of a specialist who can be an author and critic at the same time. After an adolescent interest in animation, he became an actor, but returned to animation during a long stay at the Disney studio (in 1973) where he was involved in meticulous research. His artistic films, which are in addition to the many works he made-to-order, include *Confessions of a Stardreamer* (1978), *The Wizard's Son* (1981) and *Bottom's Dream* (1983, see Colour Plate 42). The first is based on an interview with actress Diane Gardner, who spoke about her work and her psychological reactions. The images are very inventive, often ironic and tender. The second is an almost classic cartoon, with characters displaying well-defined personalities and communicating through pantomime. Although the author declares it unsatisfactory, it is an original and tasteful work.

James Gore deserves mention for *Dream of the Sphinx* (1971) – a technically imperfect but ingenious film, based on linear drawings. Mary Beams (Chicago, 30 March 1945) began with a graphically similar work, *Tub Film* (1972), featuring a female figure sucked down the drain while lying in the bath tub. The film was followed by *Seed Reel* (1975), a trilogy of brief, finely drawn, erotic episodes. In *Going Home Sketchbook* (1975) and *Whale Song* (1980) she made clever use of the rotoscope. To pursue her career as a designer and computer graphic artist, Mary Beams turned away from her promising creative activity.

Frank Mouris (Key West, 1944) had a blazing start with *Frank Film*, a creative and shrewd autobiography made with animated collage which won several awards. His following films, made in collaboration with his wife Caroline Ahlfors (Boston, 1946) are less satisfactory.

Eliot Noyes Jr. (Washington, DC, 1942) is one of the most conscientious and coherent artists in justifying artistic autonomy. Admitting that animation was a means of self-expression, he made films not to entertain others but for himself.[1] Noyes made his debut at the age of twenty-two with *Clay* (1964), in which he used clay animation to tell the story of Evolution. In 1966, he used another economical technique, marker drawings on opaque glass, for *Alphabet*; for *In a Box* (also of 1966), he used drawing on paper. *Sandman* (1973) was one of the first examples of animated sand (drawings were formed by sand spread on a sheet of clear glass and photographed against the light). A technical experimentalist but not without poetic vision, he demonstrated his skills in *The Dot* (1975), a

Finally, *Bottom's Dream* is certainly the finest of John Canemaker's films. A sarabande inspired by Shakespeare's *Midsummer Night's Dream*, the film is a *tour de force* – a summary of the lessons of Disney and the post-Disney age, with constant changes of style and colours. The work is subtly vague and rich in suggestion. Donald Spoto wrote:

'In this fanciful, limpid rendering of the funny and frightening dream of a midsummer night,

1   *The American Film Institute Report*, 5, No. 2, Summer 1974.

Canemaker shows that he is not only a first-rate artist, but a sensitive reader of our premiere poet, a sensible listener to music and himself a dreamer whose creative instincts seem to have unerringly found their mark.'[1]

In 1986, Canemaker filmed the short *John Lennon's Sketchbook*. A posthumous salute to the former Beatle, the film uses sketches made by the rock singer.

George Griffin (Atlanta, 1943) also did more than create films. He was in a way the driving force behind the independent New York artists. In several essays and interviews he sided with the refreshing independent animators and against the studio system. He collected the aforementioned *Frames*. In 1980, he worked on another project – a collection of six flip books[2] by different animators, including himself. He represented the paradigm of the independent animator, spending many years at work on each stage of his films (eighteen in twelve years) without concern for audience response and distribution problems. In the 1980s, he partially backed away from his extremist position, admitting that in a market driven economy it is necessary after all to keep an eye on finance, selling and production. Although he produced true animated drawings, such as *L'age door* or *The Club* (both of 1975), Griffin has more often dealt with the theme of a film-within-the-film, showing the actual animation process. This is already clear in *Trikfilm III* (1973), in which the making of a flip book is described. It becomes more complex and articulated in *Block Print* (1977) and in the thirty-minute *Lineage* (1979), certainly his most ambitious project.

George Griffin's cinema is analytic, at times cerebral. It is also ingenious, vulnerable in a naïve way, always vivacious and even extravagant. This is the cinema of an artist who, while researching his work, searched inside himself as well.

Howard Beckerman (New York, December 1930) started his successful career as an animator and scriptwriter at Terrytoons. In addition to advertising and educational works, he worked on art films such as *Boop Beep* (1984), a farcical but subtle movie focusing on events as seen in the strobed illumination of a rotating spotlight. Beckerman also wrote extensively about animation.

Kathy Rose (New York, 1951) draws her characters as intentionally ungracious little human-monsters, similar to doodles (not by chance, one of her films is entitled *The Doodlers*, 1975). Her cinema gives prominence to simple lines and continuous metamorphoses, playing on the absurd and the unconscious. In order to reach an even greater detachment from reason, Rose draws her characters upside down and then films them with their heads up. In *Pencil Booklings* (1978), the writer makes a self-portrait, first with the rotoscope and later as a simple drawing, in the company of her animated creatures, with whom she develops a dialogue. More recently, she has performed on stage with her animated drawings.

Maureen Selwood (Dublin, Ireland, 1946) debuted in 1969 with *The Box*, mixing live-action and animation. Selwood's finest work is *Odalisque* (1981), a gentle, lyric and erotic film based on pure lines (as are other films by independent animators such as Gore, Beams or Rose). Maureen Selwood's drawings are sinuous and delicate, with suggestive, almost dreamlike statements.

An erotic theme also characterizes the award winning *Asparagus* (1978), the best-known, and certainly the finest, film by Susan Pitt (Kansas City, 1943). This complex and fascinating work

---

1   Donald Spoto, *The World According to Canemaker*, mss, 1983.
2   The flip book is a small book containing a sequence of images which are animated by leafing quickly through the pages with one's thumb.

mixes cel with three-dimensional animation. The film presents a trip into the unconscious by a faceless woman who at the beginning of the movie defecates the asparagus of the title, and in the finale performs fellatio with the phallic vegetable. The film's sensuality emerges not only in its sexual allusions but also in the variety of materials and objects. The obsessively detailed drawings, make the spectators aware of the intense pleasure of looking at and enjoying things. In her previous works, Pitt had demonstrated promising drawing and painting skills, and a particularly good aggregation of disquieting environments (interiors as well as cityscapes), but had been unable to transpose the painting experience into film. Among her creations are *Bowl, Theater, Garden, Marble Game* (1970), *Crocus* (1971) and *Whitney Commercial* (1973).

Another viewpoint on sex is expressed by Californian Victor Faccinto (1945), whose films, featuring mutilated figures, half-beasts, sometimes masked figures, express black humour, violence and death. After a period of technically traditional animation (with drawn characters), he worked with live-action frame. His finest creation is *Book of Dead*. Barbara Scharres wrote:

> '*Book of Dead* is Faccinto's most developed work, continuing the exploration of death apparent in all his films. Through the stream of violent actions, the ominous markings on characters' bodies and faces, and the unnatural lights in their eyes, he seems to indicate that everything that lives is marked for death. ... We are faced with death images combining singular beauty and horror.'[1]

Sally Cruikshank (Chatham, New Jersey, 1949) is perhaps the only example of an artist who has taken up the Hollywood cartoon of the 1930s, adapting it to a modern sensibility. Her best films, *Quasi at the Quackadero* (1975) and *Make Me Psychic* (1978) are examples of cel animation

and display well-finished water-colour backdrops. Two animal characters, the ducks Quasi and Anita, operate within an embryonic series, and yet they could not be farther from the worlds of Disney or even Chuck Jones. The drawing show many influences, from Art Déco to the Underground comic-strips; characters are not easily identified (they could very well be reptiles or deformed humans); and topics, including sexual fantasies and couple's neuroses, go beyond mere diversion. Nevertheless, Sally Cruikshank's works can be considered glowing and vibrant entertainment films.

The same brilliant characteristics apply to Barrie Nelson's *Opens Wednesday* (1981), the finest product of this Canadian-born American animator who has spent many years working for others (particularly John Hubley). An example of classical animation on cel, the film features a theatre rehearsal which is actually anti-theatrical, made by nonsensical drawings that generate more drawings in a hilarious liberation of fantasy.

Michael Sporn (New York, 1946) became famous in the 1980s with his refined adaptations of children books, including *Doctor De Soto* (1984, from a subject by William Steig), the musical *Lyle, Lyle Crocodile* (1987, from a subject by Bernard Waber) and *Abel's Island* (1988, also from Steig).

Jimmy Picker, a clay puppet specialist, released *Jimmy the C* (1978, an entertaining caricature of former President Jimmy Carter singing *Georgia On My Mind*) and *Sundae in New York* (1983), a funny, Oscar-winning variety show featuring caricatures of New York personalities.

Finally, other artists of note include Bill Plympton (Portland, Oregon, 30 April 1946), who combined a paradoxical, lively humour with unpretentious crayon drawings in films such as *Your Face* (1986) and *One of Those Days*

1   Barbara Scharres, 'Victor Faccinto,' *Trickfilm Chicago '80.*

(1987); Cathy Karol (Miami, 1951), author of *Shapes* (1979) and *Robots* (1983); Paul Fierlinger (Japan, 1936), winner of an Oscar for his *It's Nice To Have a Wolf Around the House* (1977); Tim Burton (Burbank, 1958), who made the comedy-horror movie *Vincent* (1983) before working on live-action films such as *Batman* (1989); Kirk Henderson, director of *Cat & Mouse at (the) Home* (1982), in which the traditional comic struggle between cat and mouse takes place with very old characters in a nursing home (animation by Mark Kausler); D.J. Short, author of *Bird's Eye view*; Flip Johnson, whose *The Roar From Within* (1983) won much praise; Vincent Collins, whose finest works are *Gilgamish* (1973), *Euphoria* (1974) and *Fantasy* (1976); Ruth Peyser and Jo Bonner, who made the finely dialogued *Random Positions* (1984); Michael Patterson, whose almost neo-realist *Commuter* (1981) tells of a New York commuter's day; Sara Petty, author of *Furies* (1977); and Kathleen Laughlin, author of *Madsong* (1976), 'one of the few films about women today that succeeds in being intensely personal and universal at the same time.'[1]

Will Vinton

The small enterprise of Will Vinton – the best representative of the new three-dimensional clay animation – and his team falls somewhere between independent and industrial production.

Born in 1947 in McMinnville (Oregon), Vinton was directed to cinema by his father, an enthusiastic amateur filmmaker. While studying at Berkley, Will Vinton made many shorts, particularly live-action ones, and approached three-dimensional animation as a way to use the models he made as a student of architecture. As he explained to an interviewer, he had always been interested in classic, Disney-like animation.[2] On other occasions, he mentioned how he had acquired an interest in a mould-able and harmonious architectural cinema after studying the works of Catalan architect Antoni Gaudí.

Upon graduating in 1971, Vinton worked as a freelance film-maker. In collaboration with architect Bob Gardiner, he made his first animated clay short, *Closed Mondays*. The film was an immediate success and won an Oscar in 1974. A fascinating work, which at times shows the limits of its virtuosity, it tells of a drunk who enters a closed museum and who reacts in a disorderly manner to the exhibited paintings. To his eyes, as well as to those of the spectators, objects become alive or undergo metamorphoses, in an amusing, original, unreal atmosphere. The film marked the birth of 'claymation', a technique that Vinton patented and perfected. For the first time after many unsuccessful attempts and limited uses, clay found a place in animation, to which it brings its malleability and the freedom of interpretation it offers. On one hand, clay ousted the whole tradition of wooden puppet animation in which puppets 'acted' through complex changes of face traits (although great animators such as Jirí Trnka and Bretislav Pojar followed the opposite path). On the other hand, three-dimensional clay animation presented the same opportunities for metamorphosis and surreal invention that animated drawings had always offered to an author's fantasy.

Closed Mondays already shows an exuberance of absurd inventions (such as the speaking computer which becomes a glove with a face, an apple, Albert Einstein's portrait, a television set broadcasting the usual programming, and so on). The film displays a virtuoso use of the new medium and its possibilities; its demands on the acting, however, have a tendency toward excess.

Having left his partnership with Gardiner, Vinton founded his own company in quiet Portland, Ore-

---

1   Thelma Schenkel, 'Poets of the Single-Frame,' *Millimeter*, February 1977.
2   Pierre Veck, 'Will Vinton,' *Banc- Titre*,

gon, producing shorts and mid-length films. The twenty-seven-minute *Martin the Cobbler* (1976) is based on Leo Tolstoy's story of a man who loses hope and then miraculously finds it again. Amazingly real characters and scene design show a perfectionism similar to Disney's; yet the visual inventiveness goes beyond reality, rather than imitating it. The same can be said for *Rip Van Winkle* (28 minutes, 1978, based on Washington Irving's classic). The film displays freedom of invention as in the memorable flying kite scenes.

The artist reached his maturity, with a taste for experimentation and unrestrained fantasy, in *The Little Prince* (27 minutes, 1979, based on Antoine de Saint-Exupéry's tale). Vinton entrusted one of his closest collaborators, Joan Gratz, with the task of creating two-dimensional scene-designs using clay as a palette colour. These airy effects, together with a subtle poetry, made *The Little Prince* one of the best works released by the Portland studio.

Gradually, the studio took shape as a large craftsman's shop with approximately twenty people including producers, animators and technicians. The raw clay material is melted, coloured and moulded inside the shop, since what is available on the market does not come in all the necessary nuances of colour and ductility.

> 'I like the freedom of being an independent filmmaker,' he said, adding 'I like to think of our production company as an extended family. It's really a good group.'[1]

From 1979 to 1985, Vinton made mainly short films. Among them, *The Great Cognito* (1982) is a small masterpiece which received an Oscar nomination. The film features a nightclub comedian who undergoes a frantic series of unexpected metamorphoses, from Hitler to John Wayne, as he delivers a monologue on World War II.

A major project was the feature film *The Adventures of Mark Twain* (see Colour Plate 43), which required three and a half years of patient shooting. At its release in March 1985, the herald of American entertainment magazines, *Variety*, praised it as 'immensely imaginative'. Written by writer and director Susan Shadburne, Vinton's wife, the film tells of the American writer Mark Twain who wishes to reach Halley's Comet aboard a strange flying vehicle – a mix between a balloon à la Jules Verne and a Mississippi riverboat. Three stowaways also manage to get aboard – the three Twain characters, Huck Finn, Tom Sawyer and Becky Thatcher. The long journey offers the occasion to re-present some of the best pages from Twain's books, from *Extract from Captain Stormfield's Visit to Heaven* to *The Diary of Adam and Eve*, to *The Mysterious Stranger* to *The Adventures of Tom Sawyer*. In the end, Twain reaches the Comet and gets lost, not without having left a spiritual will praising laughter as the human race's best weapon against its misery. The clay actors' subtle movements are well directed, becoming surprisingly refined and powerful in the episode of *The Diary of Adam and Eve* – undoubtedly the best part of the film. Despite some fragmentation, which is inherent in the project itself, this feature film is probably Will Vinton's finest work. It displays a self-assured sense of performance, a flowing well orchestrated rhythm and high quality visual inventions.

Vinton's contribution to animation was not limited to technique and performance: his use of clay cleared the trail followed by many others (among them, Jimmy Picker), dramatically reviving the field.

Joan C. Gratz (Los Angeles, 6 April 1941), after having for a long while collaborated with Will Vinton, created her own films. Her Oscar-winning *Mona Lisa Descending the Staircase* (1991) is an animated history of 20th century painting, with works by everyone from Vincent Van Gogh to Andy Warhol: working chronologi-

cally she animated the paintings so that they metamorphose into each other.

Chapter 18

Canada

The National Film Board

The National Film Board of Canada, a government sponsored organization, underwent remarkable developments in the 1970s; not only did it achieve its goal of spreading Canadian culture within Canada and abroad, but it also contributed to forming a uniquely Canadian culture, particularly in the fields of documentary cinema and animation.

The production facilities in Montreal had long been considered by animators all over the world as a safe haven where one could work on educational productions as well as art films, all the while enjoying economic stability and support. Under the patronage of the Board, a large number of artists were able to pursue their careers as filmmakers, helped by full-time wages and short-term contracts for individual movies. Many foreigners enjoyed privileged working conditions and were able to contribute, from the Czech Bretislav Pojar, to the Croatian-Yugoslav Zlatko Grgic, to the Dutch Paul Driessen.

Within this conducive atmosphere, talent emerged at the management level. As already mentioned, the French-speaking studio was established by René Jodoin (Hull, 30 December 1920), who directed it from 1966, when he made *Notes sur un triangle*, until 1977. Jodoin, a follower of McLaren's, was one of the first animators with the Board.

After 1977, the managerial and production responsibilities were given to Derek Lamb. Born in Great Britain (Bromley, 20 June 1936), Lamb worked as a producer, director and teacher at home, in Canada and in the United States (Harvard University). His finest work was *The Last Cartoon Man* (1973), a perfect example of a comedy of the incongruous, which he created in collaboration with Jeffrey Hale.

Under Lamb's management, the Board enjoyed its last golden years. The crisis began in 1978, when the Canadian government reduced its budget by 17 per cent. From that time on, polemics, restructuring plans, feelings of betrayal and a reduction in programming affected the quality of films as well as the work place. In the mid-1980s, the number of filmmakers supported by the Board had been dramatically reduced. At the same time, thanks to a new policy of decentralization, the Board opened up new offices and greater opportunities for animation in cities such as Winnipeg, Moncton, Vancouver and Edmonton. It should be noted that Canadian animation, independent of the Board in the fields of advertising, education, entertainment and TV series, underwent a surprising development beginning in the 1960s. The largest production centres

Fig. 80 (top). Syrinx by Ryan Larkin (Canada, 1965).
Fig. 81 (left). Walking by Ryan Larkin (Canada, 1968).
Fig. 82 (right). Op Hop, Hop Op by Pierre Hébert (Canada, 1965). [©NFB of Canada.]

were based in Montreal and Toronto, but experienced teams of animators also worked elsewhere.

One of the finest artists within the National Film Board was Ryan Larkin (Montreal, 1943). Larkin made his debut with the short exercise, *Cityscape* (1964), composed of drawings undergoing constant changes in front of the camera. He employed the same technique in *Syrinx*, about the Greek myth of the Nymph Syrinx. The sound track features a short solo for flute written in 1919 by Claude Debussy. This film displays soft movement, rich sensual drawings and self-irony, but is hampered by an inadequate ending. *Walking* (1968) shows how the animator's perceptive eye can capture mannerisms in people's walks and movements. Finally, the fine *Street Musique* (1972) is based on the passerbys' reaction to the street performance of some musicians. This was the last film by Larkin, who has since devoted himself to painting and drawing. Gifted with an inborn sense of movement, colour and image, he was highly praised by artists such as Alexandre Alexeïeff and Norman McLaren.

Yvon Mallette (Montreal, 1935) joined the Board in 1959 and became an animator in 1964. He made his directing debut with *Métrofolle* (1967), a documentary on the history of North America and on the problems of modern technology. *The Family That Dwelt Apart* (1973) is an ironic film about progress. When helpful urbanites attempt to assist a family living on an island, they manage to destroy their idyllic existence.

Laurent Coderre (Ottawa, 1931), a jazz trumpet-player, painter, sculptor and graphic artist, broke into cinema in 1960. After many educational films he made *Métamorphoses* (1968), a vivacious exercise with cutouts and music by Luiz Bonfa. *Les fleurs de Macadam* (1969) is a distinct film based on a song of Quebec by Jean-

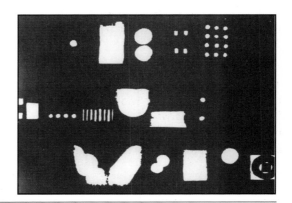

Pierre Ferland. *Zikkaron* (1971) is a short poem on humanity, made by animating thousands of pieces of linoleum. The same subject returns in *Déclin*, but with different, more ambitious tones: against a sandy background, objects resembling nails represent the last people left on the Earth.

Pierre Hébert (Montreal, 19 January 1947) was an amateur filmmaker while a student majoring in anthropology.

After graduating in 1965, he was hired by the National Film Board. That same year, he made *Op Hop, Hop Op*, an experimental film about optical perception which constituted a true assault on the human retina with black and white forms appearing as lightning. Later, he became involved in the teaching and producing of educational and scientific films.

Bernard Longpré (Montreal, 2 January 1937) began his artistic career with educational movies. For *Test 0558*, he used the computer for artistic purposes. Longpre was one of the first to do so. In *Dimensions* (1966), he combined animation and live-actors. For *L'évasion des carrousels* (1968), he filmed a horse race and transformed it using an experimental colourization technique which he obtained with an optical printer and several strips of negatives. His other films include *Tête en fleurs* (Head in Flowers, 1969), a strictly graphic illustration of a song by Jean-Pierre Ferland; *Monsieur Pointu* (1975, in collaboration with Andre Leduc), also combining actors with animated special effects; and *Les naufragés du quartier* (Shipwrecks of the Neighbourhood, 1980).

André Leduc (Verdum, Quebec, 27 November 1949) directed or co-directed numerous films in the 1970s. The most significant is still his very first work, *Tout écartillé* (1972), an original film made by elaborating live-action shots. Basically, Leduc employed the same technique of pixilla-

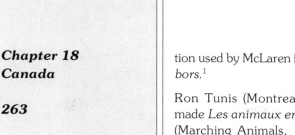

tion used by McLaren in *Neighbors*.[1]

Ron Tunis (Montreal, 1937) made *Les animaux en marche* (Marching Animals, 1966) in collaboration with Grant Munro, and *Le vent* (The Wind, 1972). His finest work, *Le vent* is characterized by a large display of techniques but is of questionable taste.

Pierre Moretti (Montreal, 15 March 1931) directed educational works and films for large audiences, including *Un enfant, un pays* (A Child, A Country, 1967), a well-animated documentary made with a split-screen, still rarely used at the time. After 1970 he was given administrative and production-related responsibilities.

One of McLaren's closest collaborators, Evelyn Lambart (Ottawa, 1914), began producing her own films in 1968. *Paradise Lost* (1970), an enchanting ecological pamphlet made with cut-outs, is her most interesting work. Maurice Blackburn (Quebec, 1914 – Montreal, 1988) was an original composer, responsible for the sound tracks to many films by McLaren as well numerous documentaries sponsored by the Board. In 1966, he was one of the promoters of the French-speaking studio. In 1969, he made *Ciné-crime*, an unintriguing but valuable film in which he employed a small pin-screen similar to the one used by Alexeïeff.

Alexeïeff's actual screen, which the Franco-Russian artist sold to the National Film Board in the early 1970s, was used by Jacques Drouin (Mont-Joli, 28 May 1943) in *Trois exercises sur l'écran d'épingles d'Alexeïeff* (Three Exercises on Alexeïeff's Pin Screen, sub-titled *Le piège, Entr'acte, Le temps passe*, with music by Denis La Rochelle and Maurice Blackburn). This imaginative film, which was considered an essay and had limited distribution, was actually better than the more official *Le paysagiste* (The Landscape Painter, 1976). *Le paysagiste* was made

---

1   The term is a combination of pixilated and animation. This technique consists of filming people frame by frame during their daily activities, so that they will look frantic and awkward during projections.

using the same technique and incorporated good visual ideas, but was spoiled by academicism. In 1986, Drouin's pinscreen joined Pojar's puppets in *L'heure des anges* (The Time of the Angels).

Jacobus Willem 'Co' Hoedeman (Amsterdam, The Netherlands, 1940) entered the world of cinema while still a teenager, paying his dues and working at every possible task at Multifilm in Harlem. Upon graduating in Fine Arts as an expert filmmaker, he began directing in a country that could offer him more than his native The Netherlands. As soon as he moved to Montreal, he found work at the National Film Board. After completing his first major film *Maboule* (1969), he became Canada's leading expert in animated puppets. An original creator of movements and characters and an effective narrator, he covered a large range of topics including Eskimo legends in *Le hibou et le lemming* (The Owl and the Lemming, 1971), *Le hibou et le corbeau* (The Owl and the Crow, 1973), *Lumaaq* (1975), *L'homme et le géant* (The Man and the Giant, 1975); entertainment films for children, such as *Tchou-Tchou* (1972) which was made with wood blocks, and an underwater tale called *Le trésor des Grotocéans* (The Treasure of the Grotoceans, 1980). His best work is *Le chateau de sable* (Sand Castle, 1977) which features strange sand-born creatures who attempt to build their own sand castle. *Le chateau de sable* won an Oscar and an award at Annecy.

During World War II, Kaj Pindal (Copenhagen, Denmark, 1 December 1927) collaborated on the feature film *The Tinder Box*. While risking internment in a concentration camp for siding with the anti-Nazi struggle, Pindal continued his work in drawing and cinema. From 1947 to 1957, before joining the National Film Board, he worked in advertising in Denmark, Sweden and Germany. In the 1970s and 1980s he taught

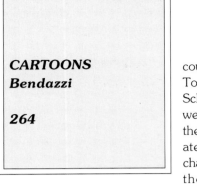

CARTOONS
Bendazzi

264

courses at Sheridan College in Toronto, with colleagues Zack Schwartz and Zlatko Grgic, as well as in other countries. For the National Film Board he created the 'Old Lady', a comic character that surged to fame as the spokesperson for the Board's civic campaigns. A comic animator in the finest tradition, gifted with a strong sense of timing and creativity, Pindal contributed his talent to educational projects and other artists' productions. He also worked on art films of his own, obtaining exhilarating results in *Caninabis* (1979), a film about a trained drug-sniffing dog who ends up doped.

Sidney Goldsmith (Toronto, 1922) is another original talent. From his debut in 1949 to his retirement in 1984, he applied his technical and artistic expertise exclusively to educational projects. *Fields of Space* (1970), *Satellites of the Sun* (1974), *Continuum* (1979), *Starlife* (1983) and *Comet* (1984) have all become classics of the non-fiction genre.

Richard Condie (Vancouver, 21 October 1942) studied art and sociology before becoming an animator. In 1972 he received a grant from the Art Council of Canada, and in the mid-1970s he joined the Board. He directed two remarkable shorts: *Getting Started* (1979) and *The Big Snit* (1985, see Colour Plate 44). The former, appealing to any viewer who has ever had to undertake a challenging task, features a pianist who makes excuse after excuse in order to avoid playing[1]. The film displays Condie's unique humour, his timing based both on fast and dead rhythms and his delirious description of the most unpretentious daily life. Mundanity returns also in *The Big Snit*, this time with a middle-class couple dragging out a domestic afternoon amidst banal, surreal skirmishes, while nuclear war rages outside. More subtle than superficially apparent, *The Big Snit* confirms Condie's singular style with

---

1   Condie said that he had wanted to make a film about procrastination, a topic he researched by spending several hours doing nothing and by studying the problems of one's attention span. In his film, the character's problems with his attention span may be caused by all kinds of reasons, from laziness to fear of failure (undated letter received from Richard Condie in May 1987.

extravagant inventions and lyrically drawn characters.

Condie's style, as well as Chuck Jones', has been picked up by Cordell Barker (Winnipeg, 10 September 1956), director of the hilarious *The Cat Came Back* (released in 1988).

The Canadian Film Board nurtured and spawned a host of women artists. Janet Perlman (Montreal, 19 September 1954) made her name with *Lady Fishbourne's Complete Guide to Better Table Manners* (1976), an engaging catalogue that pokes fun at Victorian etiquette. In 1978, in collaboration with Derek Lamb she directed *Why Me?*. On the psychological stand of patients who are informed that their illness is terminal, *Why Me?* treats this dramatic and arduous subject tastefully and humorously. The *Tender Tale of Cinderella Penguin* (1982), the upteenth adaptation of the popular story, is a vivacious and detailed version of the fairy tale set among penguins.

Lynn Smith (New York, 9 November 1942), studied fine arts and animation at Harvard University and the University of Wisconsin before moving to Montreal in 1975. Skillful at fusing social messages with artistic creativity, she achieved her finest results in *This Is Your Museum Speaking* (1979). The film demonstrates the many reasons why museums are important within a community. *This Is Your Museum Speaking* excels in drawings and narrative ideas.

Clorinda Warny (Ghent, Belgium, 25 June 1938 – Montreal, 5 March 1978) is best known for *Premiers jours* (First Days, 1980, see Colour Plate 45), which was completed by Suzanne Gervais and Lina Gagnon and released posthumously. Within the time-span of the four-seasons and with the use of sensitive pastel drawings, the film describes the relationship between nature and life, world and human being, scenery and physiognomy.

Fig. 83. The Tender Tale of Cinderella Penguin *by Janet Perlman (Canada, 1982). [©NFB of Canada.]*

Suzanne Gervais (Montreal, 26 May 1938) creates subtle sensitive films, such as her first works *Cycle* (1971) based on the line; *La plage* (The Beach, 1978) and *Trève* (The Truce, 1985). Bettina Matzkuhn-Maylone (Vancouver, 1956) introduced a new genre with *The Hometown* (1978), in which a nostalgic visit to an old house was told through animated, 'self-sewing' fabric figures. In 1982, she used the same technique in a similar but less rigorous film, *Distant Islands*. Ellen Besen (Chicago, 23 July 1953) made *Sea Dream* (1979), about a little girl who dreams of going underwater and having tea with an octopus. Viviane Elnécavé (Cairo, Egypt, 20 May 1945) rose to fame with the ambitious *Moon, Moon, Moon, Moon* (1980). Gayle Thomas (Montreal, 28 January 1944) is best known for *Sufi Tale* (1979) with interesting figurative choices based on black, white and red, and *The Boy and the Snow Goose* (1984) a tale of friendship.

For the most part, Joyce Borenstein (Montreal, 19 March 1950) worked independently from the Board. Her films include *Opus 1* (1972), *Revisited* (1974), *Traveller's Palm* (1976) and *The Man Who Stole Dreams* (1988). A creative and stylish artist, she taught animation in Montreal and Toronto.

Before finding employment at the National Film Board from 1966 to 1974, Michael Mills (London, Great Britain, 1942) worked in Great Britain, Germany and Italy. His collaboration with the Board continued even after he founded a production company of his own. Mills managed to combine his own creativity with made-to-order films. In the deservedly popular *Evolution* (1971), for instance, he discussed how species emerged on this planet in a humorous tone with fanciful characters and without scientific pretence.

John Weldon (Belleville, 1945) made his debut with *None for Me, Thanks* (1972). He rose to fame with *Special Delivery* (1978), a gruesome but comic tale of a man who neglects shovelling the snow in front of his house, causing a mailman to slip and die. Thereupon, the man tries to hide the corpse in an atmosphere similar to Alexander Mackendrick's *The Ladykillers*.

Jean-Thomas Bédard (Roberval, 12 April 1947) also owes his fame to one film, *L'age de chaise* (The Age of the Chair, 1979), an allegory of modern society and its struggle for success and power. This evocative work, enriched by a successful choice of set design and visual technique (animated cuttings from photographs), won an

Fig. 84 (top). Distant Islands *by Bettina Matzkuhn-Maylone (Canada, 1982).* Fig. 85 (bottom). Evolution *by Mike Mills (Canada, 1971).* [©NFB of Canada.]

award at the 1979 Annecy Festival.

Pierre Veilleux (Montreal, 31 July 1948) made his debut with *Dans la vie ...* (In Life ... , 1972). He had his finest results ten years later in *Une ame à voile* (Soul at Sail, 1982) and *Champignons* (Mushrooms, 1983), a noteworthy film for its warm colours. Sheldon Cohen (Montreal, 1949) made *The Sweater* (1980) and *Pies* (1983).

Outside the National Film Board, animation had been fervently active, undergoing an evolution in recent years.

From Vancouver, self-taught animator Al Sens (Vancouver, 1933) brought his ironic qualities as a caricaturist to the screen in *The See, Hear, Talk, Think, Dream, Act Film* (1965). For this film, Sens employed a technique of his own called the 'spit technique', which consisted in drawing and erasing directly in front of the camera. Ken Wallace (1946), who is also from Vancouver, directed the technically imperfect, but extremely clever *Thanksgiving* (1973). *Thanksgiving* features a plucked turkey as a somewhat repulsive little monster.

Vancouver's most brilliant animator was probably Marv Newland (Oakland, California, 9 March 1947). Educated in Los Angeles, where he studied design and made a few live-action films, Newland hoped to become a film-director.

Attracted to television advertising, he put his artistic skills to work in comic strips and animation, perfecting his style which arose from his contact with the world of underground comic strips – one of the most vital post-war artistic phenomena which flourished in the 1960s. Robert Crumb, the creator of *Fritz the Cat*, Pete Millar and Bob Zoell were among those who influenced him the most by retrieving the old-style cartoon and bringing it to new life.[1] In 1969, Newland made his first animated art film, the 90-second *Bambi Meets Godzilla*, which became a cult classic of American animation. In 1970, he moved to Canada, first to Toronto and later to Vancouver. There he found that the Canadians, who were relatively recent immigrants from Europe, Japan and Russia, were far more open-minded than the Americans. He also discovered the National Film Board. Although he did very little with the Board, he learned from its lesson on art cinema. In 1980, he made *Sing, Beast, Sing*, a nine-minute cartoon in which popular American comics are revisited in a new way, partly inspired by the underground and partly by Beckett. The film features a monstrous pianist-singer intoning the song *I'm Mad*, and a series of absurd events, such as a man walking a cactus as if it were a dog, or a domestic view of a character who does nothing and displays no personality whatsoever, but who is filmed with three dolly shots. *Sing, Beast, Sing* is a seductive film, particularly for its mood

Fig. 86. Poster of Hooray For Sandbox Land by Marv Newland (Canada, 1984).

1   Marv Newland, personal communication to author (1985).

of delirious black humour.

In 1984, Newland released *Anijam*, an animated version of the surrealists' *cadavre exquis* (exquisite corpse) technique. Twenty-two animators from all over the world contributed to the film making a short passage each, but ignoring what preceded and followed their sections. The only element of continuity was the main character created by Newland. The result was a surprisingly compact film, made all the more pleasing by the inventions of each artist, as well as by the successful hiccoughing rhythms which accompanied Newland's strange creature throughout its adventures. Also in 1984, Newland presented *Hooray! For Sandbox Land*, a well-drawn film for children without the syrupy tones which often affect this genre. As a producer, he sponsored films by some of his friends and collaborators, including Dieter Mueller's *The Butterfly* (1983), Dan Collins' *Dry Noodles* (1983) and Danny Antonucci's *Lupo the Butcher* (1986).

One of the most active animators in Toronto was Al Guest, who directed one of the world's largest production companies of television series in the 1960s. A native of Winnipeg, Guest began working in the field in 1951. In 1955, he moved to Toronto where he produced and directed fifty-two half-hour episodes of *Rocket Robin Hood*, 26 half-hour episodes of *The Hilarious House of Frightenstein*, 20 episodes of *The Sunrunners*, 78 episodes of *The Adventures of Captain Nemo* and numerous other films made in collaboration with Jean Mathieson.

Gerald Potterton (London, 8 March 1931) spent 15 years with the National Film Board before starting his own production company in Montreal (1968, Potterton Productions). Throughout his career, Potterton displayed genuine qualities as a versatile artist, a gifted filmmaker of both live-action and animation movies, and a humorist, drawn to surreal devices and the observation of human behaviour. He made his debut with *Huff & Puff* (1954), produced by the Board under commission for the Royal Canadian Air Force. Potterton's first success, however, came with the satirical *My Financial Career* (1962) which was based on a subject by Stephen Leacock. Highly praised by reviewers, the film was nominated for an Oscar. *Christmas Cracker* (1963) also received an Oscar nomination. Potterton's live-action film, *The Railrodder* (1965), was Buster Keaton's last comic film.[1]

After founding his own company with Peter Sander and Murray Shostack, Potterton addressed his efforts to entertainment and commercial projects, without compromising his artistic integrity. *Pinter People* (1968), a one-hour-long television special, is an original production on British playwright Harold Pinter's work, sprinkled with animated sketches and savvy documentaries. One of the sketches, *Last to Go*, won an award at the 1971 Annecy Festival. In the following 20 years as a producer, supervisor and director, Potterton was responsible for a vast number of works, including feature-films such as *Tiki-Tiki* (1970, which included live-action and animation) and *Heavy Metal* (1981), television productions such as *The Smoggies* (1986) and the Christmas special *George and the Star* (1985). He directed *The Awful Fate of Melpomenus Jones* (1983, with text by Stephen Leacock) during a brief return to the National Film Board. The film is a well-balanced cinematographic piece that features the tale of a grotesquely pathetic man who is too shy and polite to understand reality.

In 1973, a group of young artists founded the production company Les Films Québec Love. Financed by government grants, for a while, they

---

1   *The Railrodder* is a 27-minute long public relations film for the Canadian National Railroad company. It features Keaton crossing the country from coast to coast on a service hand-car. The comic style of Potterton and Keaton's comicality are far from being perfectly compatible, but the film is a pleasant reminder of Keaton's masterpiece, *The General* (1927). Keaton died on 1 February 1966, one year after the release of *The Railrodder*.

released films based on tradi-tional Quebec songs. Later, they became involved in standard professional work, including advertising. The group's most interesting artist is Francine Léger (Montreal, 10 September 1944), maker of *Réveille* (1979), is a rendition of an old song by the French-speaking Canadians against the English invaders.

Caroline Leaf

Born in Seattle, Washington (12 August 1946), Caroline Leaf became involved in animation in 1968 when studying visual arts at Harvard University. Having little interest in free-hand drawing, she found her own personal stylistic avenues with the guidance of Derek Lamb, director of the animation laboratory. She experimented with an unusual technique – the animation of sand resting on an opaque glass which is lit from below. The result is a film called *Sand – Or Peter and the Wolf* (1968/69). Despite the title, it did not have anything to do with Prokofiev; the music, characterized by a quite harsh tonality, was by David Riesman. The film was a captivating, albeit still unripe exercise of black and white, metamorphoses and self-assured movements which won the artist a fellowship from the University and the means to work on a second film, *Orpheus* (1971).

Later, as a freelance animator in Boston, Leaf made *How Beaver Stole Fire* (1971).[1] In 1972, she was invited to join the National Film Board, for which she made her most important work, *The Owl Who Married the Goose* (Le mariage du hibou, 1974), a film of animated sand.[2] The two main characters, an owl in love with a wild goose, stand out in black against a white background.

A foreigner in Canada, Leaf reacted to her estrangement by throwing herself into a traditional,

local topic. Choosing an Inuit legend, she went far north twice to record tapes among the Eskimos. The film itself was made in Montreal. *Le mariage du hibou*, just like her later films, is characterized by dry and sharp narration. Even more than a creator of images, Leaf is a storyteller who prefers making a point rather than emphasizing details and is more concerned with plot than style. That her cinema comes from a literary rather than a visual school is even more evident in her scripts. With her plain narrative style, she pays scarce attention to the rules of performance. Her films lack true finales, and films simply close when their narrative arc ends.

The Street (1976) launched Leaf on the international stage, making her one of the most appreciated artists of the 1970s across the world. The film is the choral tale of a family – grandmother is dying, and the grandchild has been promised her room. It is a common drama shared by many families when one member is departing and the death is experienced by the others, amidst all kinds of feelings. Based on a subject by Montreal's Jewish writer Mordecai Richler, the film is textured with small, true-to-life observations and

Fig. 87. The Street *by Caroline Leaf (Canada, 1976). [©NFB of Canada.]*

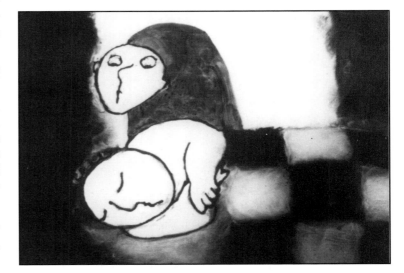

1   Later Caroline Leaf disowned this film, as she was not able to edit the sound track.
2   Caroline Leaf, personal communication (1979).

insignificant daily expressions which create an intimate relationship with the audience, such as rarely occurs in animation. As for style and technique, the film was made with another approach favoured by Leaf – animated painting on glass. Sober, flat colours dissolve one into the other with daring, unconstrained landscapes. The shaded but incisive drawings have a pleasant Picasso-like aura.

In 1977, Leaf returned to sand animation for *The Metamorphosis of Mr. Samsa*, based on Franz Kafka's famous short story. It is a rigorous black-and-white film that neglects the usual contrast between the two colours in favour of rich nuances of grey complementing the sinister theme of a man who becomes an insect. The dark domicile of the man-insect is shown with suggestive realistic tones, closer to *The Street* than to *The Owl Who Married the Goose*. Far from being a horror film, *The Metamorphosis* is a short drama of diffused visions and sounds (the sound track has a specific, primary role, as always in Leaf's work). It is a rewriting-for-the-screen of a classic text on the anxiety of modern life. The animation is masterful with a constantly changing perspective, focussing at times on the protagonist's subjective understanding of his new condition.

Curiously, *The Metamorphosis of Mr. Samsa* was for quite a long time the last animated art film by Caroline Leaf. Afterward, as if exhausted by animation, she turned to other projects. Her subsequent films were mainly documentaries in which she showed her ever increasing interest in social themes, but she made a comeback to her original inspiration in the 1990s with *Entre deux soeurs* (Two Sisters, 1990) and *I Met a Man* (1991).

Ishu Patel

Ishu Patel, born and educated in India, worked primarily in Canada and it is thus appropriate to consider his production in such a context. Born in Jalsan, near Ahmedabad, on 20 April 1942, the son of small landowners, Patel studied fine and applied arts in Baroda and Ahmedabad, and later specialized in Switzerland, Canada and the United States. During a first stay with the National Film Board, he made his first movie, *How Death Came to Earth* (1971), an ancient Indian legend illustrated with vivid colours and folkloric images. The animation shows the influence of the Italian Giulio Gianini, who had been Patel's teacher. It was a very promising first work, mature albeit lacking in its pacing.

During a brief return to his country as a manager of a department at the Ahmedabad institute of graphic arts, Patel directed *The Three Gifts* (1972), the story of a poor family which obtains three wishes from the Goddess Kali, but wastes them and remains in poverty. In 1973, Patel moved permanently to Montreal. As a staff member of the National Film Board, he directed *About Puberty and Reproduction* (1974) and *About VD* (1974). The trilogy on sexual education also included *Conception and Contraception* (1972) filmed during the artist's first stay in Montreal. *Perspectrum* (1974) was the first of a series of creative works made by Patel in Quebec, and the most 'experimental' and 'abstract'

Fig. 87. Le mariage du hibou by Caroline Leaf (Canada, 1974). [©NFB of Canada.]

among his films. It is an essay on colour, obtained by making different impressions on one coloured square with different exposure times which, in turn, causes colours to change. The result is a soft dance of geometric lines and transparencies, comparable to McLaren at his best.

Typically though, Patel's works were born of narrative and a message. *Bead Game* (1977) was conceived from a political event – the experimental detonation by the Indian Government of its first atomic bomb. In his film, Patel showed the perpetual propensity of people toward belligerence. Another current event, his own trip to the Baffin region to teach his drawing techniques to Eskimo artists, gave him the materials for animating the apologue – coloured glass beads, commonly used for crafts.

Expertly animated against a black background, the beads contributed to the creation of a short poem of vivid colours and shininess, remarkable both for its visual charm and its anti-war purposes. The sound track beats a rhythm of Indian drums.

Afterlife (1978, grand prize at Annecy, see Colour Plate 46) is a new experiment with language and technique, on the subject of the afterlife as it is imagined by several cultures, highlighting Indian beliefs. Patel sculpted his own nightmares and dreams in plasticine which had been spread on an opaque glass and illuminated from below; then he played with the translucent colours. With its powerful captivating images, *Afterlife* is probably his finest work.

His subsequent films, *Top Priority* (1981) and *Paradise* (1984) are less satisfactory and show the opposite excesses into which he risks falling. In *Top Priority*, set in a developing country, farmers desperately needing machines for irrigation witness instead the arrival of soldiers who install weapons. Despite its noble intent, the message takes over the film and transforms it into a sermon.

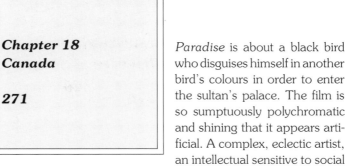

Paradise is about a black bird who disguises himself in another bird's colours in order to enter the sultan's palace. The film is so sumptuously polychromatic and shining that it appears artificial. A complex, eclectic artist, an intellectual sensitive to social issues and to his responsibilities toward the culture of his homeland, Patel looks into animation for new visual means to communicate with the viewer. His most valuable skill is his use of colour (including light blue, nuances of yellow and ochre and the palette of red), but he is also an excellent narrator, clear at times and at times allusive.

Frédéric Back

Born in Saarbrucken, Germany (8 April 1924) to an Alsatian family, Frédéric Back lived and studied in Strasbourg, Paris and Rennes before moving to Canada in 1948. He joined Société Radio-Canada (CBC) in 1952, when the company began TV broadcasting and was interested in his skills as a graphic artist and art director. For years, Back was responsible mainly for still drawings; in his free time, he worked on painting on glass with a technique of his own. In 1968, when the broadcasting company opened its animation studio, Back joined it, having the luck to find a cultivated and far-sighted producer in Hubert Tison. In the 1970s, he directed some shorts for children, beginning with *Abracadabra* (1970, in co-direction with Graeme Ross), about a little girl who retrieves the sun from a wicked sorcerer. *Inon ou la conquête du feu* (Inon, or the Conquest of Fire, 1971) tells the Algonquin legend of how humans and animals conquered fire from Inon, the God of Thunder. *La création des oiseaux* (The Creation of the Birds, 1972) is an adaptation of another native legend, this time of the Micmacs, about the miraculous changing of the seasons. *Illusion?* (1975) denounces the ugliness of urban development, the destruction of nature and the false allurements of consumerism, ending with the illusory hope that children can bring back the ancient harmony. *Taratata* (1976) describes a parade and the feelings of a child, who recreates it without pomp but with love. *Rien tout rien* (Nothing everything nothing, 1978) features the undernourished relationship between humans and the world since the Creation. These films belonged to the first season of the director's production. Back's hand as an artist and painter and his direction were admirable, but he was still a champion of theses, almost a preacher, lacking the humanity which would later become his strength.

In 1981, he directed *Crac*, a hymn to the traditions and culture of French Québec. The linking point is a rocking chair built in 1850 by a jolly woodcutter on the occasion of his wedding. The chair, often broken and repaired, ends up in a museum of modern art as the custodian's chair, but at night relives its past, inviting the modern paintings of the museum to join in a dance.

The film is intertwined with influences from Europe (especially Degas and Monet) and Québec ('... simple painters of the times who, with their often anonymous works, have passed on the history of Québec').[1] Far from falling into chauvinism or folklorism, *Crac* is an invigorating and touching film, which synthesizes past and present, culture and nature, all to a personal scale.

L'homme qui plantait des arbres (The Man Who Planted Trees, 1987, see Colour Plate 47), a 30-minute adaptation of the short story by Jean Giono,[2] with the unedited text read by Philippe Noiret (Christopher Plummer in the English version), was released after five years of work. It tells the story of Elzear Bouffier, a solitary, dignified

shepherd from the Maritime Alps, who perseveres in planting trees, reforesting the mountains and transforming a heap of stones into a blessed land. This is a sincere, honourable work, and undoubtedly Back's ultimate effort. The music by Normand Roger, Noiret's narration and Back's own drawings (evoking Brueghel, Goya, Monet, Cézanne, Renoir and Chagall) lead the viewer on an emotional journey, from the initial desolation to a respectful appreciation of the solitary mountain man, to a finale of hope and joy. Despite its narrative frame, it is an unmistakably lyrical film in which impressions are determined by the author's sensitive palette, including shades from grey and ochre to green and light blue, to a triumphant chromaticism. Here the moralist and the environmentalist have given way to the poet who gives voice to emotions and virtues. *Le fleure aux grandes eaux* (The Mighty River, 1993) is a poetic animated documentary about the St Lawrence River, its animals and how people have threatened them over the centuries. It has sequences of pure beauty but overall is less captivating than *Crac* and *L'homme*.

Back's work lends itself to an ideological debate, particularly by those who oppose environmentalist claims.[3] Artistically, beyond the levels of quality achieved, it should be underlined that his focus is not so much nature as humankind. He hopes that humanity will regain the true meaning of its being and its values, within a world which is not a mythic, middle-class Eden nor a simulacrum of the good old times, but a livable place, marked by authenticity.[4]

---

1 Frédéric Back, *Supplement*, XVIèmes Journées Internationales du Cinéma d'Animation d'Annecy (28 May – 2 June 1987).
2 Among French writers, Jean Giono (1895–1970) was one of the most sensitive to the 'return to nature', which he described beautifully in his writings.
3 Back was an active member of several Canadian and International environmental, pacifist and humanitarian groups.
4 Back once said that violence is often mistaken for virility in today's cinema. He believed that feelings of love and goodness were proof of nobility and virility, and this was reflected in the protagonists of his films (Frédéric Back, personal communication, 1987).

Chapter 19

Western Europe: the new generation

At the end of the post-war age, European animators no longer had much in common. When Disney ceased to be a model and animation became an autonomous discipline drawing inspiration from all cinema and all experiments in graphics, the animators made full use of their creative freedom, even though they had to compromise with the expectations of audiences, market demands and lack of financing. While no single country nor genial artist took the lead in the field, Western European animators contributed dramatically to developing and promoting animation. It was in Europe that frame-by-frame cinema became theorized as a cultural phenomenon.

Great Britain: the good years

Beginning in the 1960s, Great Britain became an active centre of animation. Due to a low demand for entertainment shorts – a common situation in market-driven economies – animators found opportunities elsewhere and developed a diversified production of feature films, series, educational cinema and public relation spots. High standards of quality put British advertising at the top world-wide, and well-organized, peripheral enterprises were founded, such as schools of animation, children's workshops and amateur associations. Because of its individualism and fragmentation, British animation did not exhibit recognizable national traits, but was one of the richest in creative freedom, novelty and variety of themes and motives.

In the field of feature films, after Halas' *Animal Farm* and Dunning's *Yellow Submarine* (which became a cult movie from its inception) two works struck a particular resonance. The first was *Dick Deadeye or Duty Done* (1975, by painter Ronald Searle and American animator Bill Melendez), an elegantly drawn but commercially unsuccessful musical, inspired by Gilbert & Sullivan's operettas and Joy Batchelor's *Ruddigore*. The other British film of note was *Watership Down*, created by American producer Martin Rosen from Richard Adams' best-selling novel. Here the war among the rabbits is described with a fine sense of performance and the astute decision not to 'humanize' the rabbits, avoiding the easy anthropomorphism of American cartoons. Initially directed by John Hubley, producer Martin Rosen fired him. Work started again on the film with Rosen and Tony Guy receiving animation direction credit, this feature film was

completed by director Tony Guy. At its release in October 1978 it received a tepid reception from the critics, who yielded to the questionable temptation of comparing it to the novel. Nevertheless, it was commercially successful, especially abroad.

While these films were unique works, the major portion of production came out of small or medium-sized companies. After the sale of the Halas & Batchelor studio, Halas founded the Educational Film Centre. Richard Williams and Bob Godfrey pursued projects which will be mentioned later; TVC, founded by George Dunning and John Coates in 1957 and wisely directed by Coates, kept producing successful works even after Dunning's death, with films such as *The Snowman* or *When the Wind Blows*. In 1965, Ron Wyatt and Tony Cattaneo founded a company bearing their names, which became one of the most important in the advertising world. Biographic Films thrived from 1955 to 1985 with such talent as Vera Linnecar, Keith Learner, Nancy Hanna and, for a shorter time, Bob Godfrey, producing television, advertising and public relations works. Cucumber, founded by Annabel Jankel and Rocky Morton, used the computer to create original designs. Cosgrove Hall, in Manchester, specialized in cartoon (*Count Duckula*) and in puppet animation (*Wind in the Willows*) while Cardiff-based Siriol Animation, founded in 1982, produced the successful series *Superted* (written by Mike Young and directed by Dave Edwards) and other similar creations. Tony Barnes and Naomi Jones' Fairwater Films, also based in Wales, made its debut with the series *Hanner Dwsin* (in Gaelic, half a dozen), about the adventures of a teenage rock group. Other studios include Oscar Grillo and Ted Rockley's Klacto, Matt Forrest, Film Garage, English Markell Pockett, Ralph Hibbert, Animus and Stuart Brookes.

A distinguished representative of British animation was Richard Taylor (London, 16 June 1929). The son of a well-known advertising painter, Oxford-educated Taylor decided to follow in his father's footsteps. Hired by the Larkins Studio, he became director of production in 1957 and executive director in 1960.

In 1965 he founded his own production company. Throughout his career, Taylor made only one art film, the subtle political satire *The Revolution* (1967). His other works include *Earth Is a Battlefield* (1957), about farming automation; *Put Una Money for There* (1957), made for Barclays Bank branches in Nigeria and Ghana; *Some of Your Bits Ain't Nice* (1981), about hygiene and cleanliness for children; and over 70 minutes for the BBC course *English by Television* (1984–86). A champion of the artists' involvement with political and economic realities, he focused on what he called 'useful' rather than spectacular productions, and transformed them into stylistically daring works.

In 1986, the year of his election as president of British animators, Taylor gave an interesting portrait of British animation. In 1953, at the time of his debut, only two studios and a few independent artists operated in the country, with a work-force of no more than two hundred people, including artists and technicians. In 1987, there were over thirty studios in London alone, and others opened in Bristol, Cardiff, Glasgow, Manchester and Leeds. In all, thousands of people found employment in the field. While the studios multiplied in number, they became smaller, with no more than thirty employees apiece. Unlike their predecessors Larkins and Halas & Batchelor, which employed forty or fifty people, the studios of the 1980s preferred to rely on freelancers, occasionally joining forces with other teams for special series or feature films. According to Taylor, production depended largely on a market which offered limited opportunities to animators. Even television broadcasting companies preferred to buy cheaper foreign films, mainly from the United States. As a result, British studios had to rely on advertising work, and animators like Bob Godfrey depended largely on distribution abroad. In more recent years the situation began to change once again as commercial television supported, or virtually owned, animation production companies. Thames Television financed Cosgrove Hall, Harlech and the Welsh station S4C founded Siriol and financed the series *Hanner Dwsin*, and Channel 4 began offering opportunities to animators. However, even this new interest in animation had its drawbacks, as animators began catering to the educated public of film festivals and elitist TV stations rather than to general, more demanding audiences.[1]

Channel 4 was founded in 1981 as a result of parliamentary legislation and began broadcasting in 1982. A curious compromise between public

and private sectors, the new television channel was aimed at encouraging innovation and experimentation. It was also required not to produce its own programmes but to commission them from outside companies. The result was a patronage system of co-productions (only rarely were works completely financed by Channel 4) which helped animation.

'... the bulk of Channel 4's commissioned animation was intended for adult audiences, and quite deliberately so. That policy was formulated on the basis of trying to be different from other television channels. Animation for adults was scarcely seen on British television.'[2]

In fact, Channel 4 was instrumental in the production of some remarkable films of the 1980s, from the works of Sproxton and Lord to those of

Fig. 89. Mr Pascal *by Alison De Vere (Great Britain, 1979).*

1   Letter received from Richard Taylor, in September 1987, not dated.
2   *Animation and Channel 4* (1987), TS by Paul Madden, animation consultant at Channel 4.

the Quay brothers, to Murakami's *When the Wind Blows*, to Alison De Vere's *The Black Dog* (see Colour Plate 48).

Alison De Vere was born on 16 September 1927, near Peshawar (in today's Pakistan), and moved to London at the age of three. A fine arts student, she paid her dues working as a colourist in a small studio. Later she joined Halas & Batchelor (until 1956), where she was given responsibility for lay-out work and was eventually promoted to director. She remained with the studio until 1956. Her activity in the following years included advertising, documentaries and special effects, as well as a collaboration on *Yellow Submarine*. In the 1980s, she founded a production company.

De Vere's first 'personal' film was *Two Faces* (1969). *Café Bar* (1975), a finely drawn, subtly structured story about a man and a woman meeting at a café, gave her fame at home and abroad. With *Mr. Pascal* (1979) she won an award at Annecy; the film is a lay parable about a simple shoemaker who helps save a crucifix, told with restrained emotion and without excessive sentimentality.

> 'Long ago at school I could never bear the image of the Crucifix and I longed to undo it,' wrote De Vere. 'Over years I had struggled with the idea of the innocent iconoclast, and had written scripts which I discarded as being too obscure. The apartment where I lived for the past 14 years is near a convent which has a crucifix attached to the wall and a bench nearby arranged almost as in the film. For many years I went to an old shoe-mender's shop, whose family finally had grown up and gone away. This man had a sweet face. His name was not 'Mr. Pascal', that came from

CARTOONS
Bendazzi

276

another shop – but it holds, of course, the meaning of the film. These things all came together finally, and a truly magical thing happened when I met the two musicians playing in Hyde Park Underground Station. They played their own music for the sound track, and the drawings depict them. In fact, even the street people are characters I have known, and nothing in the film is by chance. I was really scared to make a cartoon Jesus, and many drawings finished up in the waste-bin.'[1]

After the less satisfactory *Silas Marner*, a mid-length film based on George Eliot's novel, De Vere released another success *The Black Dog* (1987). It features a woman accompanied by a black dog with red-hot eyes – initially menacing, but later protective toward her – during a dreamlike journey of initiation through a desert, a city inhabited by three siren-like monsters, the Great Pyramid and maternity. Intertwined with Egyptian mythology (the dog resembles the God Anubis), cabal studies and Martin Buber's philosophical distinction between Fate and Destiny, *The Black Dog* is an autobiographical, lyrical work about discovery and sensitivity.[2]

Twin brothers Stephen and Timothy Quay (Philadelphia, USA, 17 June 1947), first came to London in 1969 to attend drawing courses at the Royal College of Art. In the following three years they made some amateur animated films. Not finding a congenial environment upon their return to the United States, they moved back to London in 1978 and with the exception of a short stay in Amsterdam,[3] established their residence in the British capital. Their true debut came in 1979 with *Nocturna artificialia*, produced by Keith Griffiths, their partner and mentor, and financed by the British Film Institute. The

---

1 Letter received from Alison De Vere, 17 November 1986.
2 The autobiographical innuendos are clear from the title itself, *The Black Dog*, which refers to the condition of psychological depression which Vere describes together with her fantasies of liberation.
3 On this occasion, the brothers changed their last name to Quaij, in order to facilitate its pronunciation by the Dutch. This spelling appears sometimes in articles and film head titles.

film features a man who imagines himself driving a trolley car in a city at night. Although it suffered from affectation, revealing the animators' inexperience, it offered original suggestions in the field of puppet animation. Here the Quays began showing the core of their artistic material: claustrophobic environments dominated by dark colours, expressionistically deformed images and a focus on the smallest details of daily life which are transformed into Kafkaesque delirium and dream. This search for what is marginal and negligible is probably the main trait of the brothers' inspiration, emerging also in their 'animated documentaries'. '[We] want to flee to ... themes like the "diary", or the "footnote". It's the latter which inevitably opens up entire chapters of the imagination)[1] said the brothers, and in their works they made a point of exploring ambiguous, inner microcosms while putting aside any responsibility to 'narrate'.

Another characteristic of the Quays' art was a link with the Middle European culture, particularly of the 1930s: their second film, *Ein Brudermord*[2] (1981) was based on a subject by Kafka, while the 'animated documentaries' which followed were inspired by Flemish playwright De Ghelderode (*The Eternal Day of Michel de Gelderode, 1898–1962*, 1981), on Czechoslovakian composer Janácek (*Leos Janácek: Intimate excursions*, 1983), Igor Stravinsky (*Igor – The Paris Years Chez Pleyel*, 1983) and the Czechoslovakian filmmaker Švankmajer (*The Cabinet of Jan Švankmajer – Prague's alchemist of film*, 1984). *Street of Crocodiles* (1986), their most poetic, powerful film, was based on a little known subject by Polish writer Bruno Schulz (1892–1942). The only film rooted in a different environment was *Little Songs of the Chief Officer of Hunar Louse, or This Unnameable Little Broom* (being a largely disguised reduction of the epic of Gilgamesh)

Tableau II (1985), based on the Sumerian poem of Gilgamesh. In fact, the source is a mere excuse, as the setting and atmosphere are close to those of the other films. In 1988, they made *Rehearsals For Extinct Anatomies*, a hermetic, perhaps too elegantly complacent exercise inspired by a Fragonard sketch.

With their anti-narrative, ungracious films, the Quays often worried their reviewers, who complained about obscure meanings. In fact, works such as *Street of Crocodiles* or *Leos Janácek* are so intense and visually original that they have an immediate impact on viewers. In other films, the brothers' vast and unconventional culture (music, dance, cinema, painting, literature, constant references to the bizarre and the peripheral) may indeed limit communication with a differently educated audience; but this remark can be said of other filmmakers as well, from Buñuel to Borowczyk to Alexeïeff.

Peter Lord (Bristol, 4 November 1953) and David Sproxton (Liverpool, 6 January 1954) began working together as high school students on an amateur film which was eventually bought by the BBC. After a short separation (the two

Fig. 90. The Street of Crocodiles *by Stephen and Timothy Quay (Great Britain, 1986).*

1   Irek Folaron (interview with the Quays), Galerie Kontakt (Poznan, September 1986). Unpublished mss, in English.
2   Original title in German.

attended different universities), in 1972 they founded Aardman Animation, in Bristol, in order to fill the demand of the BBC for children's series. Their character Morph, a plasticine creature always prepared to undergo metamorphoses, appeared on the small screen in 1976. In 1978, the two filmmakers participated in a rare, pre-Channel 4 project of animation for adult audiences: *Animated Conversations*, an anthology of six short films produced by the BBC. For the project, Lord and Sproxton created *Confessions of a Foyer Girl* and *Down and Out*, which was shown at the Zagreb festival and brought its authors international recognition. Structured around a true dialogue recorded without knowledge of the speakers in a Salvation Army shelter, *Down and Out* features plasticine puppets with most expressive features. For a long time this was the trademark of Aardman: realistic films with unscripted live sound tracks and a taste for witnessing daily life in the tradition of British documentary and Free Cinema. A good example of this is *Sales Pitch* (1983, from the series *Conversation Pieces* produced by Channel 4), which features a street vendor chatting with a client at the doorstep. In their films, the two artists also displayed abstract and paradoxical tendencies and a preference for the world of ideas rather than human beings, as in *Babylon* (1985) (see Colour Plate 49), an anti-war film, winner of many awards, which is perhaps too openly polemical but certainly effective. Nick Park (Preston, 1958) joined Aardman in 1985, and won an Academy Award in 1991 with *Creature Comforts* featuring plasticine models of zoo animals holding 'real' human conversations which had been pre-recorded. The animals have the 'coathanger' mouths that are one of the director's trademarks. Daniel Greaves (born 1959) won the next year's Oscar, with *Manipulation*, where a drawn character undergoes every kind of torture and contortion (even three dimensional). Nick Park won another Academy Award in 1994 with a film entitled *The Wrong Trousers*.

Terry Gilliam (Minneapolis, USA, 22 November 1940) worked both on animation and live-action cinema. When still very young he showed an interest in comics and learned the trade volunteering in a studio. In 1967 he moved to London where he worked as a comedian; in 1969 he co-founded Monty Python, with Britons John Cleese, Graham Chapman, Eric Idle, Terry Jones and Michael Palin. Beside several television series, this group of surreal, fantastic clowns created numerous feature films, which Gilliam co-wrote and co-directed; he was also responsible for animated inserts. As a director of live-action films, his finest work was *Brazil* (1985), an Orwellian fresco, genial and grotesque. In animation, beside the aforementioned inserts, Gilliam became known for the short *The Miracle of Flight* (1974) and *The Crimson Permanent Assurance, a Tale of Piracy on the High Seas of Finance* (1983), a prologue to Monty Python's *The Meaning of Life*. Overall, this production was less-than-remarkable and did not show the artistic qualities he had expressed elsewhere. Curiously, his fantasy seemed better served by the less-malleable live-action cinema; he publicly declared a lack of interest in animation and little faith in the artistic value of its discourse. A specialist of cutout figures, he did not hide the fact that he had chosen this technique because of its practicality and economy.

Geoff Dunbar (Abington, 25 March 1944) made an artistically successful adaptation (1978) of Alfred Jarry's *Ubu*. His 20-minute-long version, finely drawn and scratchy, powerful and as subtly vulgar as the original, won an award at the Ottawa Festival of 1980. This was a rare incursion into fiction cinema by Dunbar, who was a successful advertising artist.

Other filmmakers deserve mention. Kathleen 'Spud' Houston (Edinburgh, 10 January 1911) made her debut animating Anthony Gross's *The Fox Hunt* in 1935. She also worked for Anson Dyer, John Halas and Joy Batchelor. Between her numerous collaborations, she found time to direct *Petunia* (1968) and the colourful tale from New Zealand, *How the Kiwi Lost His Wings* (1980). Oscar Grillo (Buenos Aires, Argentina, 1943) moved to Europe in the early 1970s and lived in Spain and Italy before establishing his residence in Great Britain. As an animator of advertising spots he was original and a perfectionist. In 1979, in *Seaside Woman* he used explosive colours to illustrate a song by Linda McCartney.

Vera Linnecar (London, 1923), was a pillar at Biographic Films. Her works include *Springtime for Samantha* (1965), *The Trend Setter* (1969), *A Cat Is a Cat* (1971) and *Do I Detect a Change in Your Attitude?* (1980).

Ian Moo-Young (Jamaica, 29 December 1943), a renowned advertising artist, directed *The Ballad of Lucy Jordan* (1975), *The World of Netlon Trebor Dandies* (1980) and *Der Falschspieler* (1980, in collaboration with the German Joachim Kreck).

Sheila Graber (14 June 1940) made her amateur debut in 1970 and became a professional ten years later. In 1981, she directed a series of ten *Just So Stories*, based on Kipling's works.

Dianne Jackson (1944–1992) began her career as an animator on *Yellow Submarine*; she obtained great success directing *The Snowman* (1982), based on a children's story by Raymond Briggs. Produced by John Coates' TVC and by Channel 4, this good, but not extraordinary mid-length film was highly praised world-wide by audiences as well as film festival juries.

Tony White (Barking, 27 August 1954), founder and leader of the production company Animus, authored an educational book on animated drawings as well as several commercials. His works include *Hokusai: an animated sketchbook* (1978), a tribute to Japanese artist Hokusai which includes about sixty of his thirty thousand drawings.[1]

Lesley Keen (Glasgow, 10 December 1953) did her apprenticeship in Prague at Bratri v Triku from 1975 to 1978; afterward, she returned to Glasgow and founded Persistent Vision Animation. In 1983, she directed *Taking a Line For a Walk* which is an homage to the work of Paul Klee.

Director and designer Alan Kitching (Morecambe, 16 August 1945) made his name in computer animation, developing Antics – software which was introduced world-wide in 1973.

Among other artists, Ian Emes created ambitious videos for music groups, particularly for Pink Floyd. Philip Austin (18 November 1951 – 24 January 1990), and Derek Hayes (8 June 1952) directed the science-fiction tale *Skywhales* (1984) and the anti-war movie, *The Victor* (1985), with drawings based on comics. Paul Vester (Cambridge, December 1941) made his debut with *Repetition* (1967), followed by *Football Freaks* (1971) and *Sunbeam* (1980). Joanna Quinn (Birmingham, 4 February 1962), made an excellent debut in 1987 with the sarcastic *Girls' Night Out*, about some Welsh girls, factory workers, who go to a male strip-tease joint.

Fig. 91. Ubu *by Geoff Dunbar (Great Britain, 1978).*

1   From the press release for the film.

George Dunning

After his first years of activity in the field, which have been mentioned previously, the Canadian-born Dunning moved to London and founded a production company to compete in the remunerative fields of advertising, education and industrial cinema. Still, he did not abandon an artistic discourse, beginning with the graphic conciseness of *The Apple* (1962) and gradually acquiring moods and colours from the avant-garde currents of the time. *The Apple* (the story of an apple, a man and an attempt to imitate William Tell) concluded Dunning's first period, in which he focused on segments and sharp corners, polemically opposing Disney's style. With *The Flying Man* (1962), an animated watercolour, he began a major pictorial research which culminated with the 'psychedelic' feature film, *Yellow Submarine* (1968), *Moonrock* (1970), *The Maggot* (1973) and *Damon the*

Mower (1972). In these films Dunning mixes suggestions from various contemporary artistic and graphic currents and gives life to an uneasy, hallucinating theatre of his own. In *Moonrock*, for instance, he deals with the monsters of mass society and mass media, under the cover of a science-fiction theme and a game of bright white hues.

Dunning's most relevant work (although less perfect than some of his short movies) is *Yellow Submarine*. The film originated when the rock group The Beatles created a cinematographic activity revolving around their own myth; having founded a finance company, Apple Productions, they produced and starred in some live-action films. When they planned an animated movie, scriptwriter Lee Minoff suggested basing it on one of the groups' most celebrated songs. The idea was transformed into a script by a young

Fig. 92. Yellow Submarine *by George Dunning (Great Britain, 1967).* [©*King Features/ Suba Films.*]

professor of classic literature at Yale, Al Brodax (who was also an executive producer of the film) with the help of some friends (including Eric Segal, who later wrote the best-seller *Love Story*). Heinz Edelmann, a newcomer to animation who had dramatically influenced advertising graphics in Europe and America by mixing Pop Art with the floreal decorativism of Neo-Liberty and psychedelic hallucinations, was responsible for the drawings. Other collaborators included the American director of animation Bob Balser and the then neophyte Dutchman Paul Driessen. f*Yellow Submarine* is a long, colourful 'trip'. Its thin plot (the enemies of joy and colour invade the country of Pepperland and establish a grim dictatorship which the Beatles, after an adventurous journey, overturn with their love songs) is an excuse for all kinds of pictorial references, explicit or obscure symbolism, amazing fantasies and inventions. A complex, almost redundant film, *Yellow Submarine* is an example of the balance between artistic creation and marketing. It also offered an alternative to Disney-style feature films and deserves respect from a formal standpoint, although conceptually it is quite gratuitous – a mere spark of intelligence with no point of reference. This weakness can be traced to the ambivalence which characterized the Beatles and their imitators as a phenomenon – with love, brotherhood and joy presented in a deluxe package. Rather than being the banner of the protest generation, this film is its commercial symbol. Nevertheless, Dunning redeemed it with his expertise, introducing elements of self-irony and an environmental theme. Indeed the film can be considered a documentary on the environmental, physical and psychological (but not political) condition of its times. Dunning wrote:

> 'The film, apart from story and plot, was designed as an "experience". Feature film audiences want this "sensation" or "experience".

'Since the film was made of drawings and paintings, we decided to bring in all the images familiar to the popular mind that we could.

'My opinion about long or short animated films is complex. Many subjects, ideas and designs have limited qualities for a general audience, and therefore the film should be limited or short as well. The artistic validity of long animated films is often a question of their relative vulgarity. Distributors give backing to vulgar films. In the last year I have made a three-minute film, *Damon the Mower*. This demonstrates that I still believe in short films.

'It is always a joy to work on a film which is worth making. This standard of "worth making" eliminates most films we see. The public is forever optimistic, and when it sees a film that was worth while they are quite ready to forget all the bad films they have seen before.'[1]

When he died (in London, on 20 February 1979), Dunning had just begun a feature film based on Shakespeare's *The Tempest*; he left a few, fascinating sequences.

Richard Williams

Born in Toronto, Canada, on 19 March 1933, Richard Williams made his debut with the company founded by George Dunning in Montreal; when Dunning emigrated, Williams also moved to London in 1955. His work for television advertising allowed him to finance *The Little Island*, a more than half-an-hour long film which was highly praised by reviewers at its release in 1958. It is the reversal of a traditional Romantic allegory featuring Truth, Beauty and Goodness; here, the three figures are ugly, pear-shaped little monsters, each bringing the value it represents to its worst conclusion. In the end, Beauty and Goodness fight ruthlessly while Truth precipitates nuclear war.

---

1   Letter received from George Dunning, 25 September 1971.

Afterward Williams founded his own studio, putting together his own team of collaborators, and reinforcing his artistic reputation with *Love Me Love Me Love Me* (1962, based on a subject by the inventive Stan Hayward) and *A Lecture on Man* (1962). The creation of the main titles and animated inserts for Tony Richardson's *The Charge of the Light Brigade* (1968) solidified his reputation. At this point, Williams surrendered his stylized, simplified animation and felt the need 'to go back to school', hosting conferences and courses at his studio by veterans from Disney such as Milton Kahl, Art Babbitt and Grim Natwick. The results of this evolution are clear in *A Christmas Carol* (1971, based on Dickens' story and produced by the American Broadcasting Company under Chuck Jones's supervision); here movements, which are calibrated to perfection, are guilty of Disney's own sin – a pervasive realism. Indeed, Williams aspired to succeed Disney although he was proudly conscious of his own creative personality (he loved animation but hated comic cartoons). His most ambitious project was a feature film about Mulla Nasruddin, a

children's character by writer Idries Shah, which Williams had already illustrated as a painter. Begun in 1964, the film was still in the works at the time of this writing. Another feature film for children, *Raggedy Ann & Andy*, was completed in 1976. Directed by Williams in the United States, it was based on the two rag dolls created in 1918 by American writer and illustrator Johnny Gruelle (1880–1938); this film suffered from production problems and was not a box office success. Afterward, the filmmaker refocused his attention on advertising work. We have already mentioned his remarkable contribution to *Who Framed Roger Rabbit*.

Williams' style of filmmaking differs from the contemporary style as, in his own words, he prefers slowness rather than speed.

> 'Slower than life: out of time ... ' Accordingly, he considers animated drawings as a creation very similar to 'serious painting'. 'Whether I'm good or bad as an artist, Goya is my master,' he said. 'I'm in the same business as Goya and Rembrandt: I may be rotten at it with nothing of the same quality or talent, but that's my business.

> 'I painted for six years solidly before doing *Little Island* ... I can marry the two media: the painting and the animation. I have enough technique now.'[1]

Bob Godfrey

Born in Horse Shoe Bend, West Maitland, Australia (27 May 1922) but brought to London as a baby, Godfrey learned the trade in the British capital. He first displayed his talent in *Watch the Birdie*, created by him and Keith Learner in their own time while they were working at the Larkins Studio. It was distributed in 1954 which was the year that, in partnership with Vera Linnecar, Keith Learner and Nancy Hanna, he founded Biographic Films, a production company

Fig. 93. A Christmas Carol by Richard Williams (Great Britain, 1971).

1   Philip Crick, 'The Need to Draw 80,000 Bug-Eyed Men,' *Film*, No. 40 (London, 1964).

devoted to made-on-commission work. As the company thrived, Godfrey was able to pursue personal films such as *Polygamous Polonius* (1959), the first of the line – a misogenous vaudeville act, characterized by concise editing and

surreal inventions, revolving around some staple material of Godfrey's later productions: sex and the absurd. With this film Godfrey comes out as one of the few animators to share some common traits with the Free Cinema of his contemporaries Lindsay Anderson, Tony Richardson and Karel Reisz.

The Rise and Fall of Emily Sprod (1964) displayed good ideas and much farrago; *Do It Yourself Cartoon Kit* (1961) was a merely entertaining (but fascinating to a film buff) parody of cartoons by a cartoonist. *Alf, Bill & Fred* (1964) was the finest film of Godfrey's first period; a pleasantly comic work, it features a little man, a dog and a duckling who share a passion for skipping and jumping in a story without rhyme or reason.

Having left his partners, Godfrey opened a new studio and with *Two Off the Cuff* (1967) entered a new phase of sophisticated humour, characterized by sarcasm rather than fantastic exuberance. *Henry 9 'til 5* (1970) featured the erotic obsessions of an insignificant clerk, a true face-in-the-crowd. Godfrey's interest in sexual themes reached its peak with *Kama Sutra Rides Again* (1971), featuring the various techniques which a middle-aged couple learn from manuals of eroticism.

Great (1975) was a sparkling, half-hour-long musical about British engineer Isambard Kingdom Brunel (1906–1859), creator of the Great Western, a railway and steamship line connecting London to New York in the time of the first steamboats. With this ironic look at Victorian customs, so resistant to any form of progress, Godfrey displays his taste for performance as well as

his usual scratchy humour. Other films with erotic overtones include *Instant Sex* (1979), about sex ... in a box, *Dream Doll* (1979, a collaboration with Croatian Zlatko Grgic), about a serious gentleman's love for an inflatable doll, and *Bio-Woman* (1981), about a husband who wants to replace his wife with an artificial woman. The Godfrey Studio also produced made-on-commission films and series such as *Roobarb*, about a crazy dog, and the more successful *Henry's Cat*. Godfrey considered his life as a long-lasting ambition to make people laugh.[1] And indeed, he is a very modern, biting humorist, whose work can be likened to that of a Wolinski or a Feiffer; Jarry and Rabelais, to whom he has also been compared despite their different statures, are not far from his unhinibited, fantastic, exuberant inspiration. Godfrey should be mentioned in connection with scriptwriter Stan Hayward, another native of Australia who moved to Great Britain. Their several projects together include *Polygamous Polonius*, *Alf, Bill & Fred* and *Kama Sutra Rides Again*. Hayward wrote also for Dunning and Williams, collaborated with Halas & Batchelor and was among the first to use computer-aided-animation for non-experimental films.

France: from craftsmanship to ambition

Film criticism and film historiography, as well as a passion for cinema (testified to by many film clubs and art theatres) were more alive in France than almost anywhere else. Animation was also touched by this fervor. *Le dessin animé*, by Italian-born Giuseppe Maria Lo Duca, published in 1948, was the first attempt at a historical organization of the subject. In 1956 three young cinema-lovers, André Martin, Michel Boschet and Pierre Barbin, organized the first Rencontres du cinéma d'animation at the Cannes festival. Later they helped launch the Annecy Festival and created the Association Internationale du Film

---

1   'Bob Godfrey par Bob Godfrey,' *Nous mêmes*, Elvira Anitei ed. (Bucharest, 1973).

d'Animation (ASIFA). French film culture had always been attentive to the phenomenon of frame-by-frame cinema, and film magazines devoted special issues to animation. Over the years, the Annecy Festival became second only to Cannes among French film festivals. This interest of intellectuals in animation, however, was not always matched by successful production. Throughout the 1960s and 1970s, French animation maintained its traditional characteristics – it was craftsmanlike, depended on a small advertising and institutional market and was based in Paris. In the 1980s, however, animation underwent a clear industrial revolution and became decentralized.

As for artistic results, Jean-François Laguionie, Piotr Kamler and Walerian Borowczyk, whose works will be addressed later, were the most remarkable personalities. Numerous other filmmakers, however, should be mentioned as the creators of notable works. These artists include painter Robert Lapoujade (Montauban, 3 January 1921– Saincy, 17 May 1993) who began making films in 1960. An enthusiastic explorer of new visual possibilites, he has often worked with black-and-white film. His productions include *Prison* (1962), *Trois portraits d'un oiseau qui n'existe pas* (Three Portraits of a Bird That Doesn't Exist), and two live-action feature films, *Le Socrate* (Socrates, 1968, partly animated) and *Le sourire vertical* (The Vertical Smile, 1972). In 1974 he returned to animation with the cerebral *Un comédien sans paradoxe* (An Actor Without Paradox).

René Laloux (Paris, 13 July 1929) was already a well-known painter when he was invited to open an experimental atelier in a psychiatric clinic, where he made his first film, *Les dents du singe* (The Monkey's Teeth, 1960), with the patients' drawings. Afterward, he abandoned clinical experiments, devoting himself to art works in colla-

Fig. 94. La planète sauvage *by R. Laloux and R. Topor (France, 1973).*

boration with talented post-surrealist painter and writer Roland Topor (born in Paris on 7 January 1938, of Polish parents). Their films include *Les temps morts* (Idle Time, 1964), *Les escargots* (The Snails, 1965) and the feature film *La planète sauvage* (The Wild Planet, 1973). The first is a black and white film, characterized by a slow, gloomy rhythm. The second is a more vivacious and narrative story, in colour, of a peasant whose tears help lettuces grow in his vegetable garden, until snails eat them. Both films are powerful and full of pathos, while the much-anticipated *La planète sauvage* does not rise beyond the mere rendition of uncommon, fascinating settings, created primarily by Topor. In 1982, this time in collaboration with comic-strip artist Moebius, Laloux made the science-fiction feature film, *Les maîtres du temps* (The Masters of Time). Just like the previous *La planète sauvage*, this film displayed beautiful images and attractive worlds, but suffered from little action and weak direction. In 1988 he made his third feature film, *Gandahar*, based on Philippe Caza's drawings.

The aforementioned André Martin (Bordeaux, 31 December 1925) and Michel Boschet (11 September 1927), enthusiastic promoters of animation, founded their production company in 1959. Boschet participated actively in the creative process. Martin was the company's scholar and organizer; he lived for some years in Quebec, and on his return to Paris became involved in visual computer language. The duo worked on several advertising pieces, such as *Patamorphose* (1961) and *Mais où sont les nègres d'antan?* (Where Are the Blacks of Time Past?). On his own Boschet made *Le pays beau* (The Beautiful Country, 1973), a scratchy film based on Wolinski's drawings.

Actor and animator Jacques Espagne (Paris, Feburary 8, 1933) is responsible for the charming *La chanson du jardinier fou* (The Song of the Crazy Gardener, 1963), about a character who

believes all he sees and sees everything he believes in. The film is based on a poem by Lewis Carroll.

In the early 1960s, special effects expert Julien Pappé (Rzesom, Poland, 3 January 1920), made some interesting films, such as *Un oiseau en papier journal* (The Bird in the Daily Paper, 1961), *La mare aux garçons* (Boys Pond, 1963) and *Sophie et les gammes* (Sophie and her Scales, 1964). Later on he collaborated with film critic Michel Roudevitch on *Dog Song* (1975).

Jacques Vausseur (16 April 1919 – London, 1974), a collaborator of Paul Grimault, made his debut as a director in 1962 with the entertaining *Le cadeau* (The Present), about the problems of a man who wants to give his beloved a trumpet. The film was followed by *La porte* (The Door, 1964) and *L'oiseau* (The Bird, 1965).

Italian-born Stefano Lonati (Milano, 1925) and Italo Bettiol (Trieste, 1926), who moved to Paris in 1952, had productive careers as advertising and children's animators. They were particularly successful with *Berthe aux grand pieds* (Berthe and Her Big Feet, 1962), *Un touriste en France* (A tourist in France, 1963) and *Le jongleur de Notre-Dame* (The Minstrel of Notre-Dame, 1965). From within their own company, Bélokapi, the two produced innumerable series for the small screen. These include *Pépin la bulle* (Pepin the Bubble), *Chapi-chapo* and *Albert et Barnabé* (Albert and Barnaby).

Jacques Rouxel (Cherbourg, February 1931) also created a TV series, *Shadoks*. Produced in three stages, from 1967 to 1975, the series became France's best-known production of its kind. The Shadoks are stylized birds who get involved in deliciously offbeat adventures. Created by an original artist and an excellent writer, the series was very close to a drawn, absurd collection of literary essays. After this exploit, Rouxel founded the production company AAA, which became the sponsor of several young artists, and devoted himself to educational films.

Spanish-born Jean Hurtado (Barcelona, 30 November 1933) was a civil engineer with a passion for cinema. His occasional but high-quality production displays a caustic taste and includes works such as *14 juillet* (14th of July, 1961), *Sirene* (Siren, 1962), *Captain' Cap* (1963), *Corinne* (1972) and *Ubu roi* (King Ubu, 1977). In 1983 he completed a challenging feature film, *Les Boulugres*. Jacques Colombat (Paris, 6 January 1940) was the first artist sponsored by Paul Grimault at the beginning of his activity as a producer. Using the quick, inexpensive technique of paper cutouts, he became successful with *Marcel ta mère t'appelle* (Marcel, Your Mother Is Calling, 1961), where he displayed his skills as an incisive artist with some Chagall-like qualities. *Calaveras* (1969), with its aggressive colours, was another example of his excellent drawing, while *La montagne qui accouche* (The Mountain Who Gave Birth, 1973) was a more modest effort. In 1991, his long-awaited feature film *Robinson & Cie* won a prestigious award at the Annecy Animation Festival.

Manuel Otero (Esponella, Spain, 6 December 1938), a student of Henri Gruel, and Jacques Leroux (Paris, 22 October 1922 – 12 February 1982), a former animator for Paul Grimault, co-founded the Cinémation studio in 1964. The two artists had begun their partnership two years earlier with *Maître* (Master), a subtly ambiguous work, half realist and half delirious, based on a subject by Ionesco. Together they worked on numerous educational and technical projects, while each pursued his own artistic vision separately. Before leaving the company in 1965, Leroux made *Pierrot*; afterward he contributed to feature-films such as Pierre Alibert's *La Genèse* (The genesis, 1974). Otero became very productive in the 1960s with *Contre-pied* (The Wrong Way, 1965), *La ballade d'Emile* (Emile's Ballad, 1966), *Arès contre Atlas* (Ares Against Atlas, 1967) and *Sec et debout* (Dry and Standing). Characterized by a tendency to grotesque inspir-

ations and an 'unfinished' style (the finale to his antimilitaristic *Sec et debout*, for instance, appears more truncated than concluded), Otero was probably influenced by the rebellious, creative environment of the students of the Latin Quarter; these were the students who were to be involved in the France of May 1968. Later, Otero worked mainly as a producer, sponsoring numerous talented young artists.

As for institutions, one of the most noteworthy was the Service de la recherche of the French broadcasting company, ORTF (as it was called before its reorganization in 1975). Directed by Pierre Schaeffer, the founder of *music concrète*, the service financed projects by Lapoujade, Espagne, Földes, Kamler, Colombat, Martin & Boschet and Laguionie, and produced *Shadoks* by Jacques Rouxel. This research service was a kind of public financing given to high quality proposals.

In the private sector, a prominent studio was Idéfix, which at its peak was Europe's most modern and influential. Its founder, writer René Goscinny (Paris, 14 August 1926 – 5 January 1977) was the successful co-creator, with artist Albert Uderzo, of the character Astérix le Gaulois (Asterix the Gaul). After two feature films based on Astérix and produced by the Belgian Belvision, Goscinny founded Idéfix in Paris, hiring artists such as Pierre Watrin, Henri Gruel and Jacques Leroux. The studio produced the feature films *Les 12 travaux d'Astérix* (The Twelve Labours of Asterix, 1976) and *La ballade des Dalton* (The Ballad of the Daltons, 1978). Idéfix closed after the founder's death.

A wave of new artists arose in the 1970s. Paul Dopff (Colmar, 1948) worked as a filmmaker as well as a distributor and promoter. His company, Pink Splash Production, released several animated art films. Dopff's films include *Le cri* (The Cry, 1970), *Sourire* (The Smile, 1972), *La rosette arrosée* (The Watered Rose, 1976) and *Le phénomène* (The Phenomenon, 1977).

Bernard Palacios (29 June 1947) was actively involved in the Annecy festival. He directed *Le cagouince migrateur* (The Migratory Cagouince, 1971) with Francis Masse, the intense *Vol de nuit* (Night Fly, 1974) and *Les trouble-fêtes* (The Kill-Joys, 1979), where an atmosphere of subtle malaise is created by apparently simple drawing.

Michel Ocelot (Villefranche-sur-Mer, 2 June 1943) became successful in 1980 with *Les trois inventeurs*, an elegant statement on intolerance made with cuttings of embossed paper. The more traditionally styled *La légende du pauvre bossu* (The Legend of the Poor Hunchback, 1982), also an apologue on narrow-mindeness, is set in the Middle-Ages and is based on that age's engravings. *La princesse insensible* (The Insensitive Princess, 1984), a mini-series of five episodes lasting five minutes each, is yet another discourse on the lack of communication among people: the princess's many suitors are unable to win her despite their deeds, not because she is heartless but because she is near-sighted. This film confirmed Ocelot's refined style and inventiveness. With his delicate touch, he manages to tell sensitive stories with originality and without affectation.

Another original, focused filmmaker is Jean-Christophe Villard (Tamatave, Madagascar, 1952), whose works include *L'E motif* (The Motif E, 1979), *Le rêvoeil* (The Dreaming Eye, 1980), *Conte à rebours* (The Tale of the Cantakerous One, 1981), *Morfocipris* (1981) and *Néanderthal* (1983). Villard enthusiastically developed an analysis of line and drawing by subjecting images to constant transformations and by continuously changing perspective. He borders on the limits of impossibility: a true virtuoso (to the point that he draws with both hands simultaneously), he creates a fascinating graphic reality, with equally original sound tracks.

The twin brothers Paul and Gaëtan Brizzi (Paris, 24 December 1951) made *Un* (One, 1973) and *Fracture* (1978), after having won the much sought-after Prix de Rome, which awarded a stay at Villa Medici in Rome. In 1982 they released *Chronique 1909* (Chronicle of 1909), a fantastic, enigmatic essay about two turn-of-the-century aeroplane pilots who, after an accident, meet strange masked figures and face various adventures. In 1985 the brothers released their first feature film, *Astérix et la surprise de César* (Asterix and Caesar's Surprise) which joins the other films based on the Goscinny and Uderzo characters.

André Lindon (Neuilly-sur-Seine, 1951) authored the intriguing feature film *L'enfant invisible* (The Invisible Child, 1984), which tells of a boy on vacation who meets a transparent girl and falls in love. Previously, Lindon had directed *Jardin public* (Public Garden, 1974), *En voyage* (Travelling, 1977), *Les mers du Sud* (South Seas, 1978) and *Je quitte l'Europe* (I'm Leaving Europe, 1979).

In collaboration with Mireille Boucard (La Laigne, 1954), Bruce Krebs (Rabat, Marocco, 1951) filmed numerous short films in his studio in La Rochelle. These include *Cinq doigts pour el pueblo* (Five Fingers for the People, 1984), about the last moments of the Chilean singer Victor Jara, who was murdered during the Pinochet regime, and *2 ou 3 choses que je sais de la Bretagne* (Two or Three Things I Know About Brittany, 1985).

Fig. 95. L'E motif by Jean-Christophe Villard (France, 1979).

Television actor and scriptwriter Pierre Barletta (Paris, 1959) animated *Harlem nocturne* (1979) and *Au delà de minuit* (After Midnight, 1985), making interesting use of computer-aided scene designs.

Jacques Cardon (Le Havre, 30 September 1936), who made his debut in 1965 as a comic-strip and satiric artist, presented his first work of animation in 1974 with *L'empreinte* (The Impression). Although the drawings and atmospheres are finely interpreted, the quality of the film is compromised by a moralistic tendency (the film is a sort of parable, in which children are born with the mark of power stamped on their skulls).

Claude Rocher (Chateau-Gontier, 5 December 1955) made *Un point c'est tout* (A Point Is All). Caught in between surrealist poetry and games of optical illusion, the film is a salute to Filippo Brunelleschi, the discoverer of perspective.

Some puppet animators became successful in the late 1970s and early 1980s. Olivier Gillon (born in 1947 in Thorigny-sur-Marne) released *Barbe-bleue* (1978) in the tradition of Trnka. Jean-Manuel Costa (Arras, 1954) aimed for the sublime with *La tendresse du maudit* (The Tenderness of the Damned, 1980), featuring the struggle between good and evil in a cathedral spared from a destructive war. Jean-Pierre Jeunet (Roanne, 1953) a freelance journalist belonging to the group which published the speciality magazine *Fantasmagorie* in the 1970s, directed *L'évasions* (The Flight, 1977), *Le manège* (Horsemanship, 1979) and *Le bunker de la dernière rafale* (The Bunker of the Last Burst of Gunfire, 1981), in collaboration with Marc Caro. Thierry Barthes (Fontanay-sous-Bois, 1960) and Pierre Jamin (Paris, 1960) tried to describe the world as it might appear after the nuclear holocaust, in *Râ*. Guy Jacques (Paris, 17 August 1958) created an interesting game of 'cinema within cinema' in *L'invité* (The Guest, 1984).

Organizational changes began in 1983. During the Assises du film d'animation in Lyon, the outlook for animation seemed quite bleak: there were few studios, technological delays, a lack of a true industry and an unemployment (or semi-employment) rate of 70 per cent among professionals. The ministry of culture responded by founding OCTET, a state organization which functioned as an intermediary between animators and entrepreneurs, sponsors and new technologies. Minister Jack Lang presented a well-intentioned plan to support animation; extensive public financing was provided to fuel technological development along the lines of computer-aided animation and to launch French TV series on the international market. In November 1983 the production company IO (Image Computer) opened in Angoulême. In May 1984 the shareholding company France Animation (partially foreign-owned) was founded with the goal of setting the standards for production companies in France and Europe. In the meantime, a plan was laid for the decentralisation of production. The Fabrique of Saint-Laurent-le-Minier opened in 1984 at the foot of the Cevenne, as the first regional centre for animation, under the direction of Jean-François Laguionie.

These initiatives did not always give excellent results, partially because of the fall of the Socialist Government which had promoted the cultural renovation, but they contributed to the diffusion of new technologies and French-made series. France Animation produced *Les mondes engloutis* (The Story of a Journey of Initiation Into the Future, beginning at the centre of the Earth and going through different strata and populations). The director was Michel Gauthier (Paris, 1946), an expert professional who had already made a name for himself with animated documentaries such as *Un matin ordinaire* (An Ordinary Morning, 1980) and advertising spots, such as *Mr. Jerry et Dr. Debyll* (1979). Gauthier also headed the Ys project, a television series and a feature film for movie-theatres about the Celtic legends of the 5th Century A.D. in Britain.

Ys (1983) was produced by Bélokapi, the society founded in 1968 by Lonati and Bettiol, with Nicole Pinhon in charge of administration. Earlier Bélokapi had produced many television series directed by Lonati, Bettiol or Michel Gauthier, or co-directed by Gilles Gay (Caen, 1942) and Jean-Louis Fournier (Arras, 1938). The latter made the series *Ma vache Noiraude* (My Cow Noiraude) featuring pleasant child-like drawings. In 1987–88 the company suffered through hard times.

One of the major producers of television series was DIC, which operated mostly in the United States and in Japan. Its founder, Jean Chalopin (born in 1950) made his debut at Tours in 1975, when DIC was still a small company, producing animation for local advertising. Having moved to Paris, Chalopin became more ambitious. His series *Ulysse 31*, created in France and filmed in Japan, was very successful. Even more outstanding was *Inspecteur Gadget*, a French-American co-production. DIC moved its operations to Los Angeles, transferring many French animators there. DIC's pride is the quality of its animation, a far cry from the savings-oriented animation of its competitors. The series *Minipouss* (translated in America as *The Littles*) and *Heathcliff* conquered American audiences.

Jean-François Laguionie

In 1963 Jean-François Laguionie (Besançon, 4 October 1939) was introduced by Jacques Colombat to Paul Grimault, who admired the young man's drawing and his taste for performance (Laguionie was then attending the Centre d'art dramatique and would have become an actor but for his shyness). Grimault put his equipment and staff at Laguionie's disposal and, with financing from French television, ORTF, acted as his producer. The resulting film was *La demoiselle et le violoncelliste* (The Young Lady and the Cellist), an idyll of a girl and a musician at a seaside resort.

Based on music for 'cello by Edouard Lalo, the film possesses overtones of a fairy-tale and drawings which recall both naif painting and Magritte. Some reviewers even compared it to Emile Reynaud's *Pantomimes lumineuses*. *La demoiselle* won the grand prize at the 1965 Annecy Festival, marking the beginning of a successful artistic career. Still, Laguionie's success was always inversely proportional to his willingness to exploit it. A reserved man, he has always refused fame, and works on his own or with a few close friends.

From the seaside world of *Demoiselle*, Laguionie went to the snowy mountains of the *L'arche de Noé* (Noah's Ark, 1967); some explorers, looking for the lost ark, find the patriarch Noah still alive and ready to embark before a second deluge. In 1968, the artist made *Une bombe par hasard* (A Bomb By Chance), his finest film for many years to come. Here he dealt effectively with the theme of destruction and war, using a minimum of dramatic effects. An empty city, in the stillness of summer is as if suspended, waiting for an imminent danger which eventually occurs. The film is a brief poem of images where delicacy and elegance mix with a muffled sense of damnation.

After two excursions into live-action cinema with *Plage privée* (Private Beach, 1970) and *Hélène et le malentendu* (Helene and the Misunderstanding, 1972), the filmmaker returned to animation with *Potr' et la fille des eaux* (Peter and the Mermaid, 1974), telling of the love between a sailor and a siren; *L'acteur* (The Actor, 1975), about an actor who looks for his true identity in the mirror; and the Corsican set *Le masque du diable* (The Devil's Mask, 1976, in collaboration with painter Kali Carlini, Laguionie's companion).

In 1978, he made another successful film, *La traversée de l'Atlantique à la rame* (Rowing Across the Atlantic). Set at the turn of the cen-

CARTOONS
Bendazzi

290

tury, it tells of two people leaving on a boat for a journey into the unknown. The two, who play duets with a harp and a clarinet, protect their lives from any external intervention, even that of shipwreck victims. Surviving a ferocious fight with each other, they continue their journey, grow old and finally dance with death.

In 1979, from what once had been a fabric factory in Saint-Laurent-le-Minier (Cevenne), Laguionie began an original feature film project. His small team of artists, named La Fabrique (The Factory), included Bernard Palacios, Nicole Dufour, Kali Carlini, Claude Luyet, Emile Bourget, Henri Heidsieck and Francine Léger. In June 1984 they completed *Gwen ou Le livre de sable*, (see Colour Plate 50) an attempt 'to make a feature film having the same artistic qualities as an art film.'.[1] It is the year 3200 AD. In the desert, the nomads hide at the passage of Makou, a force which leaves behind strange, unknown objects: mattresses, teapots, boots and armchairs. One night, a thirteen-year-old girl named Gwen who had been adopted by the tribe, does not hide, and Makou kidnaps her playmate. Accompanied by an old woman, Rosaline, Gwen goes to challenge Makou in a city where twin priests keep a sacred book – the last vestige from the time of the Gods. While the images and setting are beautiful, the script is less successful, with a rather erratic explicative finale. The film also lacks the magic of Laguionie's finest shorts. Nevertheless, it is a significant work in the demanding field of animated feature films.[2]

Laguionie's delicate and elegiac films, made with a rhythm which adapts to the viewers' receptiveness, are deceptively simple.[3] An in-depth study unveils diverse levels of interpretation and complex themes, ranging from political and moral invective to meditation on life, to an analysis of feelings, to a vision of solitude.

'I like false realism,' Laguionie said during an interview. 'I like everything which is false. I like *trompe-l'oeil*, false perspectives and everything against which one could break one's face, but which also displays a sincere intention to represent reality'.[4]

The artist was referring to style, not to message. For him the act of creation is a great work of translation or 'falsification,' which leads to the truth by less aggressive means than portraying the truth itself. In his works, ideas and judgements can be inferred from the events or the characters' behaviour (as in the relationships in *Potr'* or *La traversée*), while his search for the truth and for deep feelings undergoes a masking treatment, as though bare topics were too strong and blunt to be represented just as they are. Accordingly, Laguionie's best film is *La traversée*, a metaphor for human life, which hides its heavy allegorical essence under the appearance of a fairy-tale. Laguionie's cinema is a Voltaire-like interpretation of human worries and feelings, and *L'acteur* can be considered the artist's ideal self-portrait:

'The actor as a mask, the mask as the human condition, the tragic game of reality and fiction, of appearance and essence, as is the game of life itself.'[5]

Animation is the lens which permits a study of the

1 *Catalogo del Dodicesimo festival internazionale del cartone animato* (Catalog of 12th International Festival of Animation), (Asolo, April 1985) p. 20.
2 Besides his activity as a filmmaker, Laguionie wrote two collections of short-stories: *Les puces de sable* (1979) and *Image-image* (1981).
3 'Laguionie is enclosed in a very personal *Weltanschauung* of his own, which does not permit easy interpretation (although it may seem elementary, even child-like).' Gianni Rondolino, 'Jean-François Laguionie', *Visuel*, No. 6 (Turin, February 1983).
4 Pierre Lambert, 'Gwen ou Le livre de sable', *Banc-Titre*, No. 47 (January 1985), p. 31. (Interview with Jean-Francois Laguionie).
5 Gianni Rondolino, 'Jean-François Laguionie.'

world, so that the world can be rebuilt. Laguionie said in a smiling but clever self-analysis:

> 'I remember my father who tried, when I was a child, to build a boat in our garden, and who never finished it. We even bought nautical maps of the Pacific. But the true trip was to build the boat. Perhaps that's why I set about animating.'[1]

Piotr Kamler

Along with Walerian Borowczyk and Peter Földes, Polish-born Piotr Kamler represents the new generation of émigrés who, in the 1960s and 1970s, followed in the footsteps of pre-war animators such as Alexeïeff, Bartosch and Starewich.

Born in Warsaw (on 30 June 1936) Kamler studied at the Academy of Fine Arts. In 1959 he continued his studies in Paris. In 1960 he began working in the field of single-frame and made his debut with *Conte* (Tale). This was the first of some fifteen films which he patiently produced on his own, often financed by ORTF's Service de la recherche. All these works were stimulating for a variety of reasons, although sometimes they suffered from a lack of confidence and inspiration.

Kamler's first interesting film was *Hiver* (Winter, 1964), based on Vivaldi's *Inverno* and characterized by the use of heterogeneous but well-combined materials. In 1966 he revealed his interest in science-fiction in *La planète verte* (The Green Planet), followed in 1968 by *L'araignélephant* (The Spider Elephant), an amusing and apparently less serious film starring a gentle new animal, the spider-elephant of the title. *Délicieuse catastrophe* (Delicious Catastrophe, 1970) featured the strange surrealist theatre of some unexplainable figures, most prominently a small-headed man wearing a horizontally-striped shirt. *Coeur de secours* (Heart of Rescue, 1973)

displayed the elegance of filigree and excellent lighting, which enriched this blue-and-white story-without-a-story. Also very good was *Le pas* (The Step, 1974; grand prize at the 1975 Annecy festival), where a skillfully precise sound track and a few vivid colours underscored the rigidity of figures and movements. The film was visually dominated by a ream of paper – or are they metal sheets? – which was leafed through and then rearranged again.

In 1982, after five years of work with an old 1920 Debrie camera and a few other machines (in very different fashion from the electronic magic of some of his science-fiction colleagues) Kamler returned to the topics of the future and space with *Chronopolis*, his first feature film, which was presented at the Cannes Festival. As Kamler himself wrote in the explanatory brochure:

> 'The film narrates the story of Chronopolis, an immense city lost in space. The only occupation, and the only pleasure of its inhabitants, is to build time. They create instants of all kinds, with which they devote themselves to enigmatic games.'

The plot of the film is impossible to describe, as Kamler proceeds through mental associations. Enigmatic characters, similar to pre-Columbian priests, are engrossed with equally enigmatic spheres, which they control through microphone-like objects. A man, who falls while mountain climbing, meets one of these spheres and begins dancing... With its delirious sculptures and white chalks, its elliptic and dream-like narration, *Chronopolis* acts as a conclusion to, and a fusion of, Kamler's previous experiences. If the film cannot be considered Kamler's masterpiece, it is because of how he paced himself; faced with the problem of length (seventy minutes), the artist was not able to find any rhythmic or dramatic solution, but lost himself in the ecstatic pleasure of building beauty and mystery.

1   Jean-Francois Laguionie, personal communication (1985).

Kamler likes to compare his art to surrealist works – a comparison which can be easily understood in the light of the artist's strong intellectualism, but which is contradicted by his calligraphic, refined style. Formalism appears through Kamler's less inspired films, while in his finest works a rigorous technique is matched by a sure-handed taste.

Walerian Borowczyk

Walerian Borowczyk's Polish debut has already been mentioned. In 1958 he emigrated to France where he completed all his mature works. Although he is one of the masters of animation, he was also an illustrator, commercial artist and director of live-action films, overcoming the barriers between various media. Not by chance do his animated films display all kinds of photographic devices. His *Goto, l'île d'amour* (Goto, the Isle of Love, 1968) and *Blanche* (1971) are considered among the finest achievements of cinema in the 1960s.

Borowczyk made a large number of animated shorts which reveal the richness of his disturbing life: from *Les jeux des anges* (Angels' Games,

Fig. 96. Théâtre de M. et Mme Kabal *by Walerian Borowczyk (France, 1967).*

1964), to *Gavotte* to *Le dictionnaire de Joachim* (Joachim's Dictionary). He is best known for *Théâtre de M. et Mme Kabal* (1967) – probably the only animated feature film to date which is completely successful in both rhythm and style. This film – uneasy, difficult to view – has no traditional plot or simple message. Its essence can be found in the feeling of exhaustion it delivers. With this movie, Borowczyk has dramatically solved the problems of feature films: animated drawings are concise forms, in which concepts and events must be condensed into a few minutes to avoid boring the audience. Borowczyk exploits precisely this exasperating tedium felt by the spectator during a very slow performance and conveys a sense of decaying historic reality through obsessive, almost hypnotic suggestions. For more than seventy minutes, the *Théâtre de M. et Mme Kabal* leads spectators into the bare, moon-like world of the Kabal couple – he small and frail, she enormous. This world, inhabited by unpleasantly coloured butterflies and small hybrids of pigs, dogs and crocodiles, symbolizes the horror of an oppressive life without feelings.

Such an existential concept of life appears throughout Borowczyk's animated works in his obstinate search for man-made objects:

> 'It is difficult to find the traces of a man's hand. Perhaps there are traces of his brain, but not of his hand: craftsmanship is dying. I hate a mechanical society, which is the society of the atomic bomb and concentration camps'.[1]

It appears also in his accusations against the 'bourgeois' order and in his obsessive focus on the nightmarish tendency to 'concentrate'. This refers particularly to *Les jeux des anges*, *Renaissance* (1963) and *Diptyque* (Diptych, 1967), but applies also to the live-action feature film, *Goto, l'île d'amour*, in which all elements of realist narration contribute to create an obsessive environment.

1   Walerian Borowczyk, personal communication (1971).

Borowczyk objectifies reality to the maximum extent, tranforming it into unreality, nightmares and hallucinations. With the help of logic, his world acquires disquieting aspects, resembling a living being deprived of the features and movements which make it familiar. In his films objects dominate as much as they do in real life, conditioning people and becoming the protagonists of the 20th century: from cameras to cars, from atomic bombs to spaceships. This dominance is not negative. As Borowczyk stated:

'I have very positive feelings toward objects. I build little machines which move and even wooden objects. All very simple things, which do not need electricity to move. I also like to collect old objects, crafts, from the 19th century'.

As for the political theme in his films, he says:

'One cannot be apolitical. Cinema and journalism are mistaken when they believe that workers are stupid. It is not true at all: they are simply more interested in their surrounding world than in their everyday lives. Thus, it is ridiculous to expect that once the workday is ended, they still discuss factory work, or that they see and appreciate films about workers. I know they appreciate my films because [these films] bring them to different worlds; this even though they do not understand my language (which, after all, is not understood by the educated viewers either).

'The fact is that a language has to be learned, and to do that one has to contact the speaker of that language. Who would learn Chinese, if nobody went to China? And who could understand my films before having seen them? To go back to the topic of politics, I believe that artists build dreams; true art cannot be educational, cannot explain things. Surely, it has a content, and it is the artists' task to choose between damaging and constructive content. I would hate a good film which praised Hitler'.

And he adds, on the topic of content, 'I particularly thought about Nazi occupation while making *Les jeux des anges*. In the sound track one can also hear the sound of a train: it was exactly like that, trains would come, people would be closed into them and nobody knew if they would come back. But now also there is evil and fear. When I am on the verge of falling asleep, I often have the feeling of being surrounded by the Germans, and of being in a concentration camp. After all, aren't ID cards what numbers were at Auschwitz? Everybody says that I make sad films. I do not make sad films because I hate life, but because I love it. Because I found it wonderful, and therefore I complain against evil and death. I also want the spectator to receive a message of hope: having viewed a sad movie, one leaves happy that it was just a pretence, and having the satisfaction that life is better. And one is more optimistic'.

In the 1970s and 1980s Borowczyk's career evolved around live-action cinema, developing erotic-sexual thematics and a formalist style.

Italy: *allegro non troppo*

The demand for Italian animated films began to match the potential supply in 1957, when state-owned television opened the small screen to advertising. The advertising programme entitled *Carosello* (Merry-go-round) was a children's favourite. Broadcast between the news and prime time, *Carosello* often employed animation for those products which children might love or ask their parents to purchase after viewing the show. Despite limitations, this was a fortunate period for animators, lasting until the mid-1970s when the programme was replaced by more modern forms of advertising. *Carosello* was a strange mixture, following strict requirements which divided each spot into an entertaining central body and a very short advertising 'tail'. Many animators considered the entertaining part of the show a true mini-series, in which they could experiment with their graphics and timing techniques. In many instances, small gems were produced, rich in humour and originality.

On the contrary, movie theatres remained hostile to shorts. A 1965 law rewarding quality shorts drew some producers toward animation, however, the excessive minimum length required (no less than 11 minutes) and a reduction in the value of the remuneration due to inflation, rendered the law less effective. Unlike live-action cinema, for which the production centre was Rome, animation developed mainly in Milan (where many industries, the buyers of advertising, had their headquarters), and to lesser degrees in Rome, Florence, Genoa, Modena and Turin.

Bruno Bozzetto

Born in Milano (3 March 1938) into a well-to-do family from Bergamo, Bruno Bozzetto first became interested in cinema while still an adolescent. In 1958 he had a significant success with *Tapum! La storia delle armi* (Tapum! The History of Arms), a 16 mm film which was nominated for awards at several international festivals and was loosely inspired by Disney's *Toot, Whistle, Plunk and Boom*. By 1960, Bozzetto laid the basis for his studio, which has since then constantly produced animation for the entertainment and advertising worlds.

In 1960 he made *Un oscar per il signor Rossi* (An Oscar For Mr. Rossi). The protagonist, an irascible and neurotic little man, became Bozzetto's most successful character, starring in other shorts, the finest of which was the hilarious *Il signor Rossi compra l'automobile* (Mr. Rossi Buys a Car) of 1966. Mr. Rossi made television appearances in a popular series which later served as the basis for three feature films, was marketed as a doll and was featured in a comic book.

In 1965 Bozzetto released *West and Soda*, the

first Italian animated feature film in sixteen years. The story revolves around two characters, Johnny and Clementina, and the vexations they suffer at the hands of Cattivissimo and his two helpers Ursus and Smilzo. At the end, the self-conscious hero Johnny finds his old self and wipes out the insults. Despite a somewhat flawed narration, this wild parody of American Westerns is lovable for its inexhaustible, paradoxical fantasy.

Vip, mio fratello superuomo (Vip, My Superhuman Brother, 1968), a parody of adventure comic-strips, is Bozzetto's second feature film. Marketing pressures forced changes in the original project, imposing the personality of Super-Vip and the insertion of songs. Nevertheless, the film is interesting, particularly in the long satirical digression on advertising. (MiniVip and Super-Vip, last of a lineage of supermen, land on an unknown island where a virago, Happy Betty, owns a city-factory. The small, weak Vip is the one who defies her plans to condition humanity to her will).

Besides the films featuring Signor Rossi, the Milan- based studio released other interesting works. The lyrical A–Ω/*Alpha-Omega* (1961) and *Una vita in scatola* (A Life in a Box, 1967) convey vivid, albeit still young, feelings on the meaning of human existence. *I due castelli* (The Two Castles, 1963) was a significant novelty for its time, with its bare style (the drawing is pure lines and framing is fixed) and clever comedy.

After the almost experimental *Ego* (1969), made with a notable contribution by scene-designer Giovanni Mulazzani, Bozzetto made *Sottaceti* (Pickles, 1971), a collection of 'film-pills' on the most diverse topics such as hunger, war, conquests, electricity. In 1973, in collaboration with Guido Manuli, he made *Opera* – a brilliant, at times moving divertissement on lyric opera. *Self-Service* followed in 1974; this allegory, set among mosquitoes was about the exploitation of the Earth by the human race.

In 1977 Bozzetto completed his third feature film, *Allegro non troppo*, (see Colour Plate 51) repeating the formula used by Disney in *Fantasia*: the illustration of musical scores (including Debussy's *Prelude to the 'Après-midi d'un faune'*, Dvorak's *Slavonic Dance No. 7*, Ravel's *Bolero*, Sibelius's *Valse Triste*, Vivaldi's *Concerto in C Major* and Stravinsky's *The Firebird*) is connected by a live-action frame starring comedian Maurizio Nichetti, who was also assistant director.

Here the drawing does not attempt to visualize the music. Loath to overdo, Bozzetto develops his own themes, using music as a deluxe accompaniment. The stories differ widely in graphics, animation (almost sumptuous in *Bolero* but very dry in the *Slavonic Dance*) and inspiration. While the faun of the *Prelude* is the most typical Bozzetto character, moving like Signor Rossi, the large-eyed, sad cat of *Valse Triste* introduces a genre which was totally new to the director. Overall, *Allegro non troppo* is a fresh, well-balanced film, exuberant and imaginative. In the following years, Bozzetto devoted himself mainly to works of scientific popularization and live-action cinema, for which he also made a feature film, *Sotto il ristorante cinese* (Under the Chinese Restaurant, 1987). *Mister Tao* (1988), terse and mystical, won a Golden Bear at the Berlin Festival; *Cavallette* (Grasshoppers, 1990) a satire of violence and bellicism, was nominated for an Oscar.

Bozzetto's humour is rooted in American comedy, but with a softened rhythm and a tendency to merge a taste for surrealism with ethical themes. At the centre of his work are the neuroses of a society based on consumerism and machines, and the loss of natural, human purity. His comedy, however, is never sulphurous; far from being polemic and slashing, it displays a clever, sharp spirit. Thus he becomes often ironic, donning a lucid pessimism for the human race. The most evident characteristic of Bozzetto's work is a superb sense of showmanship. Each of his films captures both the eye and the intelligence with rhythms of colours and action, timing of comic expedients and original fantasy.[1]

Gianini and Luzzati

In 1960, the internationally famed scene designer, decorator and potter Emanuele Luzzati (Genoa, 3 June 1921) joined forces with another talented designer and director of photography, Giulio Gianini (Rome, 9 February 1927), one of the first in Italy to use colour. The two made their debut in cinema with a short, *I paladini di Francia* (The Paladins of France) in which Luzzati's colourful creativity combined with Gianini's technical expertise. *Castello di carte* (Castle of Cards, 1962) was followed by the two artists' first significant achievement, *La gazza ladra* (The Thieving Magpie, 1974), which won an Oscar nomination and an award at the Annecy Festival.

Other films included *L'italiana in Algeri* (The Italian in Algiers, 1968), *Alì Babà* (1970) and the beautiful *Pulcinella* (1973), which Luzzati had planned for several years. For RAI, the Italian Broadcasting Corporation, the two artists created *Turandot* (1975) and *L'augellin bel verde* (The Beautiful Green Bird, 1976). In 1978, they made a short feature, the fifty-four minute long *Il flauto magico* (The Magic Flute). Other works followed, the most interesting of which is probably *Il libro* (The Book, 1984). Gianini also collaborated with Leo Lionni on works such as *Swimmy* (1969) and *Cornelius* (1986).

---

1   The artists who contributed at various times to this spectacular enterprise were Guido Manuli (Bozzetto's *alter ego* for over fifteen years before doing independent work), Attilio Giovannini (co-director of the first two feature films), set-designers Giancarlo Cereda, Giovanni Mulazzani and Antonio dall'Osso, Giancarlo Rossi (sound and editing), animators Giuseppe Laganà, Sergio Chesani, Franco Martelli, Giorgio Valentini, Massimo Vitetta and Edo Cavalli, musician Franco Godi, camera operators Roberto Scarpa and Luciano Marzetti, and scriptwriters Sergio Crivellaro and Maurizio Nichetti.

An entertainer with strong ties to theatre, Luzzati often staged his films dramatically, enriching his creations with intentionally unrealistic curtains, scenes and backdrops, and transforming his films, which were trips to the world of fairy-tales, into drawn choreographies. Luzzati and Gianini's films (at least until *L'italiana in Algeri*) contained precisely this – drawn choreographies in which the music suggested and supported action and plot; colours and figures matching music (by Rossini) or nursery rhymes (by Luzzati or Gianni Rodari); and a pacing which evokes the gentleness of a ballet.

Later films are more specifically narrative. *Pulcinella*, (see Colour Plate 52) one of the finest works, summarized many artistic expressions, from puppet theatre to lyric opera, to ballet. *Il flauto magico* is undoubtedly Gianini and Luzzati's most ambitious and finest project – a tribute to scenography, with curtains, revolving stages, puppets, the costume of a real-life actor and fixed images, and to photography, with lights, shadows and figures appearing in silhouettes. Luzzati's extraordinary pallette – one of the most precious elements in the two artists' works – includes tones of filigree in gold and silver amidst the elegant grey scenery.

For their films, Gianini and Luzzati drew from a vast popular tradition of fairy tales, lyric operas, street theatre and puppets, which they interpreted at times with amused irony. Their narration does not suffer from any cerebral or archeological attitude, since the artists feel close to this tradition. Their pulcinellas and paladins bring to the screen the spontaneity and strength of contemporary characters.

Osvaldo Cavandoli

Born in Maderno, on Lake Garda (1 January 1920) but raised in Milan, Osvaldo Cavandoli joined Pagot Film in the 1940s. There he contributed to the first Italian animated feature film, the aforementioned *I fratelli dinamite* (The Dynamite Brothers). In the 1950s, Cavandoli began working on his own in the field of advertising with a specialization in animated puppets. Success came to him, however, with an animated drawing, *La linea* (The Line), which he created in 1969 for a *Carosello* advertising spot. *La linea* features a man who is formed by, and lives on, an infinite horizontal line. While walking along the line, the man is faced with graphical as well as situational adventures. Each time he ends up calling upon the artist's hand which, like a demigod, solves his problems. The man's incomprehensible mumbling serves as a comic thread running throughout the piece.

Soon Cavandoli left the limited world of advertising and turned his creativity to internationally acclaimed TV series (1975, 1977, 1979 and 1984), some films, and two comic books published in 1973 and 1985, all featuring 'the Line'. The artistic qualities of these productions reside in the acting, mimicry of gesture and a sense of rhythm. The main character – who is reduced to the bare essentials, being shown in profile and lacking facial features – displays vivid reactions and psychological traits. Although the graphic choice is

Fig. 97. La linea, character by Osvaldo Cavandoli (Italy, 1970s).

la linea by osvaldo cavandoli equipos

anti-Disney (Cavandoli eliminated any additives, choosing a
simple line on a homogeneous
background), this cinema has
fully absorbed Disney's lesson
that animation is a performance
by actors. With an elegant
graphic scheme, Cavandoli's

finest and most mature works
are: *Solo un bacio*, in which an
artist falls in love with the Snow
White he has drawn, but ends
up beaten by the seven dwarfs
and poisoned by the wicked
witch; *Incubus*, featuring a
common little man who is no

creation returns to the old basic relationship between image and the artist's hand as it had appeared in the very first lightning sketches. In the
two-dimensional, flowing world of 'the Line', the
Hand has the amusing, and amused, role of reminding spectators of the filmic artifice.

longer able to distinguish between reality and his
dreams; and *+1 –1*, about the effects of
somebody's presence or absence in the course of
events.

Guido Manuli

Guido Manuli (Cervia, 11 June 1939) was one of
the most influential artists at Bozzetto Film. As
part of the team, he displayed his skills as a scriptwriter, gagman and director of animation. In
1973 he took his first step toward autonomy,
collaborating with Bozzetto on *Opera* – a whirl-
wind of absurdly humorous expedients on the
theme of lyric opera. Still with Bozzetto he made
Strip Tease (1977), a short scherzo revolving
round the erotic theme of a live stripper's effects
on her drawn audience.

Later, as a busy freelance animator, Manuli produced a body of quite original works which have
been praised by specialists world-wide: *Fantabiblical* (1977), *Count-Down* (1979), *SOS* (1979),
*Erezione (a ciascuno la sua) (Erection: to each
his own, 1981), Solo un bacio* (Only a Kiss,
1983, see Colour Plate 53), *Incubus* (1985) and
+1 –1 (1987).

Opera is still very much the work of a gagman,
despite its brilliance. A fragmented, disjointed
work, it makes spectators wish to see its expedients put to a better use. *Fantabiblical*, a science-
fiction interpretation of the Old and New
Testaments, has some very original comic sequences, but lacks cohesiveness. The same can
be said for *SOS*, where a scientist discovers that
women are extra-terrestrials, and *Erezione*, featuring a parade of male members, differing according to their owners' personalities. Manuli's

A very aggressive, original comic filmmaker, and
a lover of hyperbole and the unexpected, Manuli
has much in common with some American artists
of the 1930s and 1940s, particularly Tex Avery.
Like Avery he shows a propensity for erotic
themes, to the point where eroticism seems his
most congenial topic. Actually, Manuli's films go
beyond the simple development of themes, being
characterized by a deeper, more coherent perception of things than what is shown at first
glance. His cinema deals lucidly with the absur-
dities and the dark forces which loom over daily
life. His is an exuberant cinema, controlled, however, by an underlying bitterness.

Manfredo Manfredi

A Sicilian educated in Rome, Manfredo Manfredi
(Palermo, 6 January 1934) began his movie
career in 1965. A talented painter and scene designer, he worked on social and neo-realistic
themes with Guido Gomas (Valdagno, 1936).
The two artists' finest films were *Ballata per un
pezzo da novanta* (Ballad For a Boss, 1966), a
beautiful fast-paced film on the Sicilian Mafia, and
Su sambene non est aba (Blood Is Not Water, in
the Sardinian dialect), on the reasons for banditry
in Sardinia. Having parted with co-director
Gomas in 1970, Manfredi continued developing
political and social themes, albeit more indirectly,
giving priority to his pictorial research. After
some initial works he achieved excellent results
with *Sotterranea* (Underground, 1973) and *Dedalo* (Daedalus, 1976).

Manfredi is a dramatic director and painter. On

several occasions he made the mistake of abandoning his dramatic tension to become polemical; other times the minimum-length required to obtain state financing affected his works, making them repetitive and slow. On the whole, Manfredi's films from 1965 to 1973 are like a work in progress in which it is possible to recognize some moments of excellent cinema and some of the finest expedients. *Sotterranea* and *Dedalo*, instead, are perfectly completed works; the latter, filmed under optimal conditions, won an award at the Ottawa Festival of 1976 and helped ratify the filmmaker's success abroad. With this film, Manfredi confirmed his role as the most original creator of visionary settings in Italian animated cinema.

Cioni Carpi

Eugenio 'Cioni' Carpi, son of painter Aldo Carpi, was born in Milan on 16 November 1923. After an initial phase in which he was influenced by his father's painting, Carpi found original inspiration of his own abroad. In 1950 working with French television in Paris, he experimented with the visualization of concerts. From 1955 to 1957 he was in Haiti. One year later, in Canada, the artist developed his approach to cinema.

> 'On the one hand, to animate has been a way for me to continue my work as a painter', he maintained, 'on the other, a way to start making cinema. I loved cinema very much. In Canada I saw McLaren's films, and they were a revelation.'[1]

Carpi began making films at the National Film Board with the encouragement of McLaren himself. In 1960 he released his first work, *Point and Counterpoint* (a five minute, twenty-four second long film, directly painted on stock), which he had started in 1959. Although it shows McLaren's influence, the film exhibits the elements of an ingenious personality. Colours are used with rig-

orous originality and a thematic development is visible in the struggle between the individual (the point) and the mass which crushes against him. *Spots*, also of 1960, rhythmically alternates dark sequences with sequences drawn on stock. Both these works are accompanied by synthetic music, which Carpi himself composed, inscribed on the sound track and mixed with real music.

Forty very brief films followed, for Montreal's CBC-TV. Next Carpi made the *Cromogrammi* series (1 to 4), *The Bird Is Good* (with mixed techniques) and *Je veux je veux pas* (I Wish, I Don't Wish), 'a draft for a more ambitious film on human behaviour, indecision and the progressive substitution of reason by destructiveness.' 1961 was the year of *The Maya Bird*, a creative animation of original drawings by the ancient Maya.

In 1962, after making his fifth *Cromogramma* and *The Cat Here and There*, Carpi returned to Italy to film *Un giorno un aereo* (One Day a Plane), using the complex technique of making collage directly on film stock. The film, which dealt with the problems of war and destruction and referred to the plane which bombed Hiroshima, was unanimously praised at the Tours Festival. Still in 1963, Carpi made *Through the Three Layers*, the last of his experiments on stock, using another new and difficult technique. The startling colour effects were obtained by working with the three very thin, photo-sensitive layers of emulsion in colour film.

In 1964 Carpi abandoned true animation for other, still very complex creations. Using a diverse range of techniques and inspirations he made 'integrated' films for theatrical works by Kipphardt, Weiss and Cappelli and for music by Manzoni, Berg, Maderna and Paccagnini. In 1970 he made the excellent *Repeat*. More recently he has moved from the limited fields of painted films and animation, probing ever more deeply into visual research.

---

1   Cioni Carpi, personal communication (1973).

'McLaren's example opened a new path for me, but also risked closing it. I would not have been able to continue repeating certain things'. After a stint with kinetic art, Carpi devoted himself to conceptual art.

'I have seen many films by Italian and foreign kinetic artists. They are not convincing because their work is nothing more than photography, the documentation of kinetic objects [these artists] have created. Cinema instead must be something else: a dynamic discourse, a continuous relation between one frame and the next, between one scene and the next. I believe in cinema as a rhythmic entity, having a development and an end.'

As for inspiration, Carpi confesses his surrealist origins, although he admits he tries to control them with reason. Although his personality has been inspired by other artists and by several artistic currents, he has always made a point of his independence.

Results and promises

For some years, the scene in Milan was industrially dominated by Gamma Film, particularly in the advertising field. The company's success lasted about fifteen years. When at its peak, in the mid-1960s, Gamma Film was one of the largest animation studios in Europe. Beside high-level advertising creations, the company produced *La lunga calza verde* (The Long Green Stocking, 1961), an entertaining mid-length film, with a script by Cesare Zavattini. The film was made for the occasion of the centennial of Italian unity. The director was the owner of Gamma Film, Roberto Gavioli (Milan, 1926) who collaborated with brother Gino (Milan, 1923) and Paolo Piffarerio (Milan, 1924). In 1968, the same team released *Putiferio va alla guerra* (Putiferio Goes to War), about the adventures of a yellow ant which foils an attack by the red ants.

Giuseppe Laganà (Milan, 1944) worked inde-

pendently after having been one of the best animators of Bozzetto's group. Among his films, one of the finest is *L'om salbadg* (The Bogeyman, 1974), a pleasantly human, well-narrated and well-drawn tale from the Po region. In 1982, Laganà released *Pixnocchio*, Italy's first film made with computer animation.

Experimental artist Giulio Cingoli (Ancona, 1927) used mixed techniques for an interesting short, *Relax* (1968), made in collaboration with Giancarlo Carloni, Nicola Falcioni and Giovanni Mulazzani among others.

Pierluigi De Mas (Padua, 1934), active in advertising since 1955, produced and directed twenty-six episodes of the children's series *Tofffsy* (1974), in collaboration with designer Gianandrea Garola. Tofffsy (with three f's) is an elf, who possesses a magic herb which exposes liars. In the 1980s De Mas began to produce films for adults. Using new technologies to make videoclips of notable formal exactitude, such as *No tengo dinero* (I Have No Money, 1983), *Fireworks* (1984) and *Fuffy* (1985), De Mas was perhaps the Italian artist most open to novel techniques, and the most ready to apply them to creative works.

Pagot Film, which had dissolved after Nino Pagot's death in 1972, was revived in various forms and produced some series featuring the black chick Calimero, a character originally created for advertising purposes. Nino Pagot's children, Marco (Milan, 1957) and Gina 'Gi' (Milan, 1954), an art director and scriptwriter respectively, worked with foreign companies on several series of above-average refinement and craftsmanship. Marco Pagot specialized in series in which he displayed taste and expressive animation. After his debut with *Adamo e l'acqua* (Adam and the Water, 1977) he directed *L'ispettore Nasy* (Inspector Nasy, 1980–82), *Il fiuto di Sherlock Holmes* (Sherlock Holmes's Intuition, 1983–85, a Japanese co-production), *I viaggi di*

Fig. 98. Un giorno un aereo *by Cioni Carpi (Italy, 1963).*

Ty Uan (Ty Uan's Travels, 1984–86), and *Reporter Blues* (1986–88, a Japanese co-production).

The veteran Osvaldo Piccardo (Genoa, 1912), who worked in animation in the 1930s with the Cossio brothers, made art films such as *L'onesto Giovanni* (Honest Giovanni, 1961) for Rome-based Incom. Having established his residence in Como, he made *Egostrutture 1* (Egostructures 1, 1970), based on a personal mystic-existential perspective, and the sardonic *La rivoluzione* (The Revolution, 1973).

Advertiser and graphic humorist Marco Biassoni (Genova, 1930) made several good spots for Carosello and a seven-minute long film entitled *Re Artu* (King Arthur, 1977). Romano Gargani (Florence, 1934), also an advertising animator, made a gentle silhouette fable, *Il mugnaio e l'asino* (The Miller and the Donkey, 1975). Japanese sculptress Fusako Yusaki (Tokyo, 1937), who moved to Milan in the 1960s, made some nice advertising films using clay, working with Rodolfo Marcenaro, Paolo Villani and Massimiliano Squillace. Still using clay she made *Ama gli animali* (Love the Animals, 1983) and *Convergenza uomo* (Convergence-man, 1984).

The talented free-lancers Giovanni Ferrari (Ferrara, 1936) and Walter Cavazzuti (Milan, 1946) collaborated with Guido Manuli on *Jay Duck* (1982), an entertaining parody of Busby Berkeley's musicals. On his own, Cavazzuti drew and directed *Tunnel* (1987), an enigmatic, Buñuel-style film. Nedo Zanotti (Ferrara, 1936) has paralleled his advertising career with the production of many personal films, the finest of which was *Un uomo sbagliato* (A Wrong Man, 1967).

In Modena the main animation activity in the 1960s was at Paul Film, owned by multi-faceted animator Paolo 'Paul' Campani (Modena, 1923–1991). Many quality advertising spots were produced there. Secondo Bignardi (Modena, 1925), an employee of Paul until 1965, founded his own production company and released *Ogni regno*

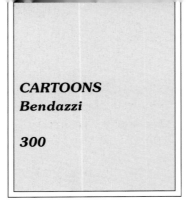

(Each Kingdom, 1970), a fable about discord with brilliant drawings by Czechoslovakian painter and animator Stepan Zavrel. Another former employee of Paul Film, Giancarlo Marchesi (Modena, 1939) drew and produced *Baby Crockett* (1977), a traditionally styled children's series.

In Florence a team of animators began a project on Pinocchio in 1966. The group's leading personality, as well as the film's director was painter Giuliano Cenci (Florence, 1931). Released with the title of *Un burattino di nome Pinocchio* (A Puppet named Pinocchio, 1971), the film crowned decades of effort by Italian animators to create a feature film which was truly faithful to Collodi's text. The result, however, was unsatisfactory, forcing the group to dissolve. Still in Florence, art director Lanfranco Baldi (Florence, 1938–1990) produced children's series with the help of scriptwriter Francesco Misseri (Florence, 1928). Quaquao features a little goose of folded paper; *Mio e Mao* (Mio and Mao) is centred on two clay kittens; and *Il rosso e il blu* (The Red and the Blue) revolves around two humanoid characters, of red and blue clay. These works are often little gems, made even more pleasing by Baldi's clay scene designs. *AEIOU* is another beautiful film, displaying the original technique of animating with wet sand (a different procedure from the dry sand animation done in Canada, the United States and Switzerland). Gianni Boni (Florence, 1939) also worked at productions for children. His *Zig e Zag* (Zig and Zag) and *Gli amici dell'universo* (The Friends of the Universe) deserve mention.

Studio Limite was another Florence-based studio. One of its artists, Filippo Fantoni (Florence, 1950) made the refreshing *Autoritratto disognato* (1983, Dreamed/Drawn Self-Portrait).

Turin is known for the activity of Cooperativa Lanterna Magica, an educational production company. In 1984 the cooperative's technicians helped a group of children from junior high school make *L'importante è partecipare* (It's How You Play the Game), an internationally praised animated film on the Olympics. Vincenzo Gioanola (Casale Monferrato, 1955) also works out of Turin. He is the maker of an entertaining, profane film scratched on black stock, entitled *Garybaldy Blues* (1983).

Giorgio 'Max' Massimino-Garniér (Turin, 7 October 1924 – Rome, 21 December 1985) co-founded the Modena-based Paul Film together with Paul Campani and worked in Milan and Rome. An expert in mass-communication, a theorist and a director of ASIFA, he played a basic role in freeing Italian animation from its provincialism and initiating a cultural debate. He directed some tasteful, one-minute long mini-films with drawings by Campani (an initial series of four in 1968 and ten more in 1973). Afterwards he worked as a scriptwriter and co-director with other European artists. His finest work is undoubtedly *Metamorpheus*, co-directed with Jiří Brdecka. Filmed in 1970, the work supports an artist's duty to testify to the truth, in the face of political pressure.

In Rome, producer Ezio Gagliardo (Cairo Montenotte, 1919 – Rome, 1976) founded Corona Cinematografica, which underwent a remarkable expansion during the 1960s. Gagliardo's finest undertaking was the creation of *European Fables*, for which several European countries entrusted their best artists with the task of transposing each country's traditional fables into shorts. After Gagliardo's death, his enthusiasm and organizational skills were missed, but the project reached completion with forty-one titles by ten nations.

Gibba, who had moved to Rome in the 1950s, was not able to recapture the inspiration he had displayed immediately following the war. He made several shorts and two feature-films, *Il racconto della giungla* (Story of the Jungle) and *Il nano e la strega* (The Dwarf and the Witch), both

released in 1976.

After having worked for Manfredo Manfredi, Guido Gonzo, known as Guido Gomas, made some satirical shorts on his own, among which is *Mio padre brav'uomo* (My Father, a Good Man, 1970).

The well-known satiric cartoonist, Pino Zac (Giuseppe Zaccaria, Trapani, 1930–Fontecchio, 1985) made some grating films such as *Raccomandata R.R.* (Registered Letter With Return Receipt, 1962) and *Il mondo è delle donne* (The World Belongs to Women, 1965). Afterward he became artistically involuted and repetitive. In 1969 he made a feature film, *Il cavaliere inesistente* (The Nonexistent Knight), from Italo Calvino's novel, combining animation and live-action. The film confirmed the artist's shaky inspiration.

Scriptwriter Paolo di Girolamo (Rome, 1927) made his directing debut with *Venezia ... un sogno* (Venice ... a Dream, 1972, in collaboration with Gomas). *L'incontro de li sovrani* (The Meeting of the Kings, 1973) and the colourful Sicilian tale *'An ... 'nghi ... 'ngo* (1975) followed. His brother Vittorio worked in Chile; in 1970 he made the sober *Erase una vez* (Once Upon a Time).

Painter Stelio Passacantando (Rome, 1927) made a name for himself with *Il generale all'inferno* (The General in Hell, 1984), based on a poem by Pablo Neruda. Among younger artists, Maurizio Forestieri (Palermo, September 1961) trained with Giulio Gianini before making *Orpheus* (1986), an upbeat film about a convent where nuns, tempted by the devil, dance to Offenbach's music.

The artists who contributed at various times to this spectacular enterprise were Guido Manuli (Bozzetto's alter ego for over fifteen years before doing independent work), Attilio Giovannini (co-director of the first two feature films), set-designers Giancarlo Cereda, Giovanni Mulazzani and Antonio dall'Osso, Giancarlo Rossi (sound and editing), animators Giuseppe Laganà, Sergio Chesani, Franco Martelli, Giorgio Valentini, Massimo Vitetta and Edo Cavalli, musician Franco Godi, camera operators Roberto Scarpa and Luciano Marzetti, and scriptwriters Sergio Crivellaro and Maurizio Nichetti.

Ireland

The major animation organizations in Ireland had foreign origins. Jimmy Teru Murakami (who will be discussed later on) founded his studio in the early 1970s; the studio operated mostly in advertising. The Sullivan Bluth Studios Ireland had a greater impact; opened in 1985 with a few Irish animators who began working on *An American Tail*, by November 1986 the studios expanded to include one hundred employees. This happened after Bluth had moved to Dublin, reducing his former Californian headquarters to a mere agency; Bluth's move was supported by the Irish Industrial Development Authority, which provided the American with the necessary facilities.

As for native-Irish initiatives (beside minor advertising work) the only major animator was Aidan Hickey (Dublin, 1942), who integrated his production of television series for children with more creative works such as *A Dog's Tale* (1981) and *An Inside Job* (1987). The latter is a well-structured example of comic sadism, featuring an over–10-minute-long sequence of a wide-open mouth in which a fake dentist leaves explosives.

Another timid approach to art animation was Timothy Booth's *The Prisoner* (1983), an unresolved illustration, in modern-key, of a subject by Yeats.

Belgium

The history of Belgian animation began in the 1920s when the Houssiaus, a Brussels-based father and son team, produced some advertising films. In 1932 Ernest Genval directed *Plucki en*

Egypte, in collaboration with A. Brunet, Leo Salkin and M. Van Hecke. From 1935 to 1937 Roger and Norbert Vanpepestraete made *Tout va très bien, madame la marquise* (Everything Is Well, Madame la Marquise) and *Couchés dans le foin* (Asleep in the Hay), puppet films disliked by the censorship committee for their 'licentious' themes. Edmond Philippart also made puppet films: *Chansons de Charles Trenet* (Songs of Charles Trenet), *Style imagé* and *Images mouvantes* (Moving Images).

In 1940, during the German occupation, journalist and photographer Paul Nagant founded a studio, the Liège-based CBA, which produced *Zazou chez les nègres* (Zazou With the Black People) and *Ma petite brosse à rimmel* (My little Mascara Brush, 1940–42). When the building which housed the studio was destroyed by fire, Nagant built another one in Brussels, where he produced *Le chat de la mère Michel* (Mother Michael's Cat, 1943) and *Le petit navire* (The Little Boat, 1944).

In Antwerp producer Wilfried Bouchery in collaboration with Marc Colbrandt and Henry Winkeler, completed *La naissance de Pim (Pim's Birth*, 1945) and *Le forgeron Smee* (Blacksmith Smee, 1945), while two feature films in progress were destroyed by fire in July 1945.

Liège was also home of Albert Fromanteau (born in 1916), director of *La captive de Frok Manoir* (The Captive of Frok Manor, 1944), *Le voyage imprévu* (The Unexpected Trip, 1944) and *Wrill écoute la BBC* (Wrill Listens to the BBC, 1945).

Immediately after the war, Claude Misonne (already well-known as a writer) began to produce puppet films. In 1948 the Misonne studio released the first Belgian feature film, entitled *La crabe aux pinces d'or* (The Crab With Golden Claws). Based on Hergé's comic strip character Tintin, this slow-paced movie had little success at the box office. The studio however continued production, in collaboration with the newly born state-funded television.

In 1955 the publishing house Editions du Lombard, represented by Raymond Leblanc, founded Belvision, a production company devoted to cinema and television productions featuring the comic-strip characters of *Tintin* magazine. Originally Belvision consisted of a small team, but after Leblanc imported American production techniques, it expanded to include eighty employees. In 1960 the studio began work on *Aventures de Tintin*, 104 television episodes, each five minutes long.

From 1959 to 1965 the company's art director was Ray Goossens (Merksem, 26 October 1924), who made his debut in 1939 and later worked with Bouchery. With him in the lead, Belvision produced a fairly good feature film, *Pinocchio dans l'espace* (Pinocchio in Space), in which the wooden marionette created by Collodi still becomes a real child, but only after adventures such as a trip to Mars in the company of a tortoise-like extra-terrestrial, and an escape from a space whale.

After Goossens left in 1965, Belvision continued with a hectic but anonymous production, which included the feature films, *Astérix le gaulois* (1967), *Astérix et Cléopatre* (1968), *Tintin et le temple du soleil* (Tintin and the Temple of the Sun, 1969), *Lucky Luke* (1971), *Tintin et le lac aux requins* (Tintin and the Lake of Sharks, 1972), *Les voyages de Gulliver* (Gulliver's Travels, 1973) and *La flute à six Schtroumpfs* (Smurfs and the Magic Flute, 1975). Goossens went on to free-lance work and teaching; in 1984, he returned to direction with the film *Trompo*.

Following in Belvision's footsteps, the comic-book publishing company Dupuis (publisher of the *Spirou* magazine) founded its own TVA Dupuis (1959). Eddy Ryssack (Antwerp, 1928) was

the company's art director for about ten years. Production was mostly based on television series featuring the Schtroumpfs,[1] the blue elves from the comic strips created by Peyo (Pierre Culliford). Ryssack also released some interesting art shorts: *Teeth Is Money*[2] (1962), *Le crocodile majuscule* (The Great Crocodile, 1964) and *Cinémaman* (1966). After Ryssack, the studio looked to Goossens for guidance until Dupuis handed over the audiovisual development of its characters to SEPP.

The true production of art shorts began only in the mid-1970s, when the ministries of French and Flemish cultures began sponsoring 'cultural' films. Three filmmakers distinguished themselves by using the technique of direct drawing on stock. Louis Van Maelder (Uccle, 30 December 1929) made his debut with *Daily Rhythm* (1958), followed by *Un visiteur* (A Visitor, 1962), *Le canard géométrique* (The Geometric Duck, 1966) and *L'oiseau qui dort* (The Sleeping Bird, 1972). In the following decade, he continued with *Three Cinematographic Fairy Tales* (1980), *Le canard importune* (The duck is a nuisance, 1982) and *L'oiseau singulier* (The Singular Bird, 1987), displaying originality and elegant graphics. Aimé Vercruysse (Puurs, 1923) took up filmmaking in 1970 with *Sijke e Bijke*, followed by *Sir Halewijn* (1978) and *Dinky Toys* (1979). Yvain Lemaire (Verviers, 17 January 1934) drew directly on stock in *L'homme, cette dualité* (1958) and *La danse du sabre* (Sabre Dance, 1958). He later used the technique of cel drawing for *Strip-tease* (1963) and *Le faux mutant* (The False Mutant, 1968); in 1973, he returned to the experimental genre with *Trilogie*. Raymond Antoine (Brussels, 12 September 1934) made a significant debut with *Les huit dames* (The Eight Ladies, 1965) followed one year later by *La chambre* (The Room).

---

1   'Smurfs' in English.
2   Original title in English.

Jean Coignon (Brussels, 1927) did his apprenticeship in Paris with Paul Grimault. Later he created *Le poirier de Misère* (Mysère's Pear Tree, 1962), an animated movie with a dramatic, unusual theme based on a medieval legend. *La pluie et le beau temps* (Rain and Good Weather, 1969), an apologue about technology and economic exploitation, and *Democratia* (1979). Robbe de Hert (born in 1942) a renowned live action filmmaker, had a brief stint in animation with *A Funny Thing Happened on My Way to the Golgotha*[1] (1968), an award winner at the Oberhausen festival.

Among this mid-generation of artists, the most talented was Gerald Frydman (Brussels, 1942), whose vast experience ranged from from live-action films to script-writing for comic books. According to Philippe Moins, Frydman's films take the nervous language typical of action cinema and adapt it to a graphic universe derived from Surrealism.[2] His major films include *Scarabus* (1971), which clearly displays literal and visual influences from science-fiction; *Agulana* (1975), set in an imaginary city where its residents suffer from awkward, wood-related accidents; *Alephah* (1981), about death; and *La photographie* (Photography, 1983) and *Le cheval de fer* (The Iron Horse, 1984), which are surprised, nostalgic looks at the world of the nineteenth century. For the enigmatic, frozen traits of his work, Frydman was compared to such painters as Magritte; in fact, he is above all a composer of disquieting settings, dominated by notes of waiting and destiny.

The opening of professional schools gave rise to positive results. In 1966, Ray Goossens began teaching at the Rijksinstituut voor Toneel en Cultuurspreiding (Flemish for State Institute for Theatre and Cultural Development); Gaston Roch taught at the Ecole nationale supérieure des

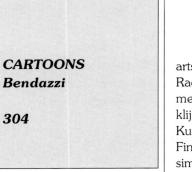

arts visuels de la Cambre, while Raoul Servais founded a department of animation at Koninklijke Academie voor Schone Kunsten (the Royal Academy of Fine Arts), in Ghent. In 1970, a similar department was founded in Genk, at the Stedelijk Hoger Instituut voor Visuele Kommunikatie en Vormgeving (Commercial Institute of Higher Studies in Visual Communication and Design), directed by Walter van Welsenaere and Véronique Steeno. These schools produced good 'dissertation' films and equally good professional works. Another official organization devoted to help young artists was the Ghent-based Belgisch Animatiefilm Centrum, founded in 1976 with the goal of promoting animation. Although the centre achieved only part of its goals, it helped finance many a debut.

As for filmmakers, the first representative of the younger generation was a student of Servais', Daniel Schelfthout (born in 1949), who won an award for *Ego* (1973), his first work at the Annecy festival. Among his later works, the finest were *Awake* (1975) and *Crepusculum* (Twilight, 1979). Paul Demeyer (born in 1952), also a student of Servais's, created a masterful first film, *The Muse*[3] (1976), winner of the award for best student film at the American Academy of Motion Pictures Arts and Sciences.

The aforementioned Véronique Steeno (Mechelen, 10 April 1950) displayed her skills in *La colombe blanche* (The White Dove, 1981), with drawings inspired by the stained-glass windows of medieval cathedrals. Josette Janssens (Antwerp, 15 February 1949 – 22 March 1985) disclosed her artistic qualities in *La maison de campagne* (The Country House, 1982), an exquisite example of pencil-drawing animation. Katrien Alliet (Libenge, Zaire, 1952) directed *Hyde Park* (1981), a beautiful fantasy. The same year, Dirk Depaepe (Bruges, 1951) released *Under Gambrinus's Influence*, an effective, albeit

1   Original title in English.
2   Philippe Moins, 'Le cinéma d'animation en Belgique', *Animafilm*, No. 6 (Turin 1985) p. 15.
3   Original title in English.

somewhat heavy, film about a factory worker's alienation. Etienne De Bruyne (Sleidinge, 1950) stands out for *Gasparazzo* (1979). Suzanne Maes made a name for herself on the international stage with *Birds At Springtime in Oleandra* (1982). Nicole Van Goethem (Antwerp, 1941) released the short *Een griekse tragedie* (A Greek Tragedy), an art film she made after extensive professional production. *A Greek Tragedy* was a comic, clever film featuring three caryatids trying to support the facade of the Greek temple entrusted to their care (the film had great, even disproportionate success, winning the grand award and the audience award at the Annecy festival in 1985, and an Oscar in 1986). The subsequent film, *Full of Grace* (1987), about two nuns who discover masturbation, was less good.

Production companies included Kid Cartoons, founded in 1976 and involved with children's series directed by Raymond Burlet; Pen Film, which released Jef Carriers' *John Without Fear* (1985) – the first feature film from the Flanders region; and Politicalfilm, with an often politically oriented production and a management structure featuring collective decision-making. Atelier Graphoui, founded in 1978 by former students of La Cambre, was also based on the equality of all of its members. Its releases, from television series such as *Yakari* (1981–83, for Casterman consisting of 52 episodes, each five minutes long) to art films such as *Quatre à voyager* (Four to Travel, 1983) had no individual credits. Beside film productions, the group (which grew to include twenty people in the early 1980s) promoted several events: animation courses for children, film shows, publications and so on.

Finally, 'Picha' (Jean-Paul Walravens, born in Brussels on 2 July 1942) deserves mention. A renowned satirical illustrator with publications in *Hara Kiri*, *Time Magazine* and *The New York Times*, Picha directed a feature film without having to go through the apprenticeship of shorts. Entitled *Tarzoon, la honte de la jungle* (The

Shame of the Jungle, 1975), the film was a not always aristocratic mockery of the Tarzan myth. After this success, Picha tried again with *Le chaînon manquant* (The Missing Link, 1980, about the world of troglodytes) and *Le big bang* (1987, featuring the earth after a nuclear disaster); in both films, vitality somehow counterbalanced the heavy comicality and sophomoric sexual jokes, gaining an unconditional acceptance by audiences.

Raoul Servais

Born in Ostende (1 May 1928), Servais graduated in 1950 from the Ghent Academy of Fine Arts. A sensitive artist, he had to overcome many market-related obstacles before becoming famous. His first film was *Havenlichten* (Lights of the Harbour, 1960), a work which he later criticized as being weak and technically raw, but which displayed some good inventions. In 1963 he made *De Valse Noot* (The False Note), a somewhat dewy tale – the subtitle reads, 'an old legend from the 20th century' – about a street musician. *Chromophobia* (1965), his first mature work, is the comic-symbolic story of a colourful, joyful country invaded by an evil army.

Fig. 99. Goldframe by Raoul Servais (Belgium, 1969).

Everything becomes literally grey, but a red little jester mocks the invaders and provokes a revolt. (*Yellow Submarine* clearly owes something to *Chromophobia*).

In 1968, Servais made *Sirène*. In an industrial harbour, menacing, dragon-like cranes kill a figurehead, shaped like a siren, that had come alive. A fisherman is the sole witness to the cruelty of the machines. *Goldframe* (1969) is a brief satire featuring a film-industry tycoon, powerful and arrogant, who is defeated by his own shadow.

To Speak or Not To Speak (1970) is a mocking, ironic short poem on mass communication and the exploitation of brains. *Operation X–70* (1971) is a pacifist space-opera while *Pegasus* (1973) points out the labourers' frustration at the

intrusion of machinery. The film features a blacksmith who creates a steel horse head and then worships it as if it were a god. The head grows in size and multiplies, leaving the man alone and dismayed in a forest of metal horses. An enigmatic, powerful work denouncing alienation, it was also, in Gilbert Verschooten's words,

> '... a personal salute by Servais to the pictorial school of Flemish expressionists. ... [His] style purposely reminds one of works by Gustave de Smet, Constant Permeke and Frits Van den Berghe.'[1]

Harpya (Harpy, 1978), probably Servais' finest film to that time, features a man who witnesses an aggression, intervenes to save the victim and discovers that it is a harpy. Having taken it to his own house, he soon learns about the creature's imperiousness and voracity. Made with a laborious technique mixing live-action shots and three-dimensional animation, *Harpya* is an ironic and tragic film, visually suggestive in its settings which derive from horror movies and chamber theatre.

A tasteful artist, gifted with a strong personality, Servais is a skilled conveyer of incisive situations and the creator of a 'fantastic' world which, especially in *Harpya*, develops as an ironic, nightmarish discourse on the human soul and behaviour. Above all, Servais is a civil poet dealing with themes such as tyranny, power and the use of science against humanity; having overcome the excessive pathos of his first works, he was able to deal with these themes in a forceful but sober manner. Although he left his personal style on all his works, he used a variety of animation and figurative techniques – *Chromophobia* was the work of a pure graphic artist, *To Speak or Not To Speak* was inspired by avant-garde cartoons, *Pegasus* was made with animated cutouts; he did this in such a way that graphic choices are merely instruments in the service of the film itself.

Fig. 100. Harpya by Raoul Servais (Belgium, 1978).

1   Gilbert Verschooten, 'Raoul Servais', *Fantasy Film* (Leuven, VZW, 1986).

The Netherlands

Traditionally, the history of Dutch animation is considered to have begun with *De moord van Raamsdonk* (Raamsdonk's Assassination, 1930), a film of animated silhouettes made by Otto Van Neijenhoff (1898–1977), in collaboration with puppeteer Frans ter Gast. The film tells of the atrocious crime described in a popular song.

During the 1930s, Dutch frame-by-frame cinema was represented with honour by the Eindhoven-based group directed by George Pal. After the Hungarian-born Pal moved to the United States, the studio closed and the group dissolved. In 1941, Johan Louis 'Joop' Geesink continued the Dutch tradition of animated puppets. An ingenious businessman and a great organizer, Geesink (Aja, 12 April 1913 – Amsterdam, 13 May 1984) founded a small advertising company shortly after the beginning of World War II. In 1941 he made *Pierus*, his first animated film, commissioned by the railroad company, followed in 1943 by *Serenata nocturna* (Evening Serenade), Geesink's first work with puppet animation. After this film, the electronics giant Philips commissioned some animated works from him, happy to fill the void left by George Pal. Geesink was thus able to hire a staff, which primarily consisted of former artists of the Eindhoven studio. In the 1950s and 1960s his production company, which in 1947 had been called Dollywood, made numerous films taking advantage of the development of television. Productions included *Kermesse fantastique** (1951),[1] *Prins Electron* (1954), *Philips World Parade** (1954), the series *Dutchy* (1955), *Piccolo, Saxo & Co.*, (1960), *The Travelling Tune* (1962) and *Philips Cavalcade, 75 Years of Music** (1966). Dollywood was terminated in 1971 when, to avoid bankrupcy, Joop Geesink sold it to the studio Cinecentrum. The company's misfortune was due mainly to poor performance of Geesink's

other ventures, particularly the Holland Promenade-Projekt, which he had envisioned as a Disneyland of the Netherlands.

One of the very first associates of Geesink was Marten Toonder (Rotterdam, 2 May 1912), who worked in the field of comic strips – famous for his character of the cat, Tom Poes, he is actually considered the father of Dutch comic strips. In 1943, Toonder left his partner and turned to animation. During the German occupation, he made a few films (among them, *Tom Poes en de laarzenreuzen*, Tom Poes and the Giants in Boots), before going underground as a partisan. In 1945 he reopened the studio and initiated what became a prolific output, mainly in advertising. Among the studio's creative works are *De gouden vis* (The Golden Fish, 1951), *Moonglow** (1955) and *Suite tempirouette* (1956). In 1967, Cinecentrum bought the Marten Toonder Studio and moved it to the Nederhorst castle. Four years later, it was joined by Geesink's group. In 1973–74, the studio produced the television series *Barbapapa*. In 1983 producer Rob Houwer achieved Toonder's old dream of animating his comic strip characters in *Bumble & Co.*, the first Dutch animated feature film.

Among those who made major contributions to Toonder's company were the Briton Harold Mack (London, 6 March 1918 – Haarlem, 25 December 1975), who directed *De gouden vis* (The Golden Fish), and who later became the owner of his own production company, through which many young animators got their start; Henk Kabos (Amsterdam, 1912–1984), who began working for Toonder in the 1940s; Harrie Geelen (Heerlen, 10 October 1939), a creative director; and the distinguished 'three Danes' – Borge Ring (Ribe, 1921), Björn Frank Jensen (Grena, 1920) and Per Lygum (Odense, 1933).

Dutch art cinema developed in the 1970s and 1980s. Besides Paul Driessen, who will be dis-

---

1   The asterisk indicates the original title in German, French or English.

cussed later, some independent animators distinguished themselves.

Ronald Bijlsma (Rotterdam, 1934) made several films for various purposes, including advertising and institutional ones. His finest creative film is the science-fiction apologue with the explicative title *Brainwash** (1973). Talking about himself, Bijlsma said:

> 'I feel inspired by Dutch painters of previous centuries, but in spirit rather than in style. Although I live in a country which is, politically and socially, one of the best in the world, I feel life's malaise and I try to convey it.'[1]

Gerrit van Dijk (Volkel, 5 December 1938), one of the few political polemicists in world animation, directed an even more radical criticism against society. *CubeMENcube* (1975) was a general apologue on hate and war. The twelve short films made in 1978–79 for Jute-Projekt (in which four artists from the city of Haarlem took stands on current events) were true invectives against repression in Northern Ireland (*Queen**), for the release from prison of a black American

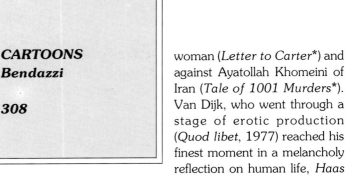

woman (*Letter to Carter**) and against Ayatollah Khomeini of Iran (*Tale of 1001 Murders**). Van Dijk, who went through a stage of erotic production (*Quod libet*, 1977) reached his finest moment in a melancholy reflection on human life, *Haas teen hand* (1982, known also as *He Almost Clutched His Hand**) in collaboration with Jacques Overtoom, Peter Sweenen and script writer Herman van Run.

Niek Reus (De Bilt, 12 June 1949) made a name for himself in 1974 with *Tekenfilm* (Animated Drawing), *Lijn* (Line), where he displayed a spare drawing style, and *A Taste of Happiness* (1977). The specialists of animation on pictures, Jacques Verbeek (Steenbergen, 1947) and Karin Wiertz (Venlo, 1946) made *Reversals* (1972), *Time Takes a Cigarette** (1973), *Between the Lights** (1975) and *The Case of the Spiral Staircase** (1981) among others. In Tjitte de Vries' words, the last two films seem to derive directly from the De Stijl movement of the 1920s.[2] Leo Hofman (Venlo, 1922–1986) displayed a gloomy but lively taste for what is dilapidated, as in *Ondergang der Monumenten* (Decline of the Monuments, 1973) and *Renaissance* (1976). Monique Renault (Rennes, France, October 1939) is the author of feminist films such as *A la votre** (To You, 1975), which features a man as a soluble tablet, and anticlerical ones, such as *Salut Marie** (1978). Borge Ring (mentioned among the collaborators of the Marten Toonder studio) received an Oscar nomination for *Oh My Darling** (1978). He won an Oscar for *Anna & Bella* (1984), a comic, dramatic and sentimental story of two elderly sisters who reminisce while looking at a photo album. In the rather avant-gardist environment of art animation, this film brought back interest and pleasure to full animation and curvilinear drawings. An indulgent, unpretentious study of simple feelings, it was universally praised.

Fig. 101. Anna and Bella *by Borge Ring (Holland, 1984).*

1   Roland Bijlsma, personal communication (1973).
2   Tjitte de Vries, 'Ten Years of Holland Animation,' *International Holland Animation Bulletin*, (Den Haag, 1983).

Hans Nassenstein (The Hague, 1939) made *Troost* (Solace), his first independent film, in 1976. In 1982 he caught the experts' attention with *Nog Eens* (One More Time), a gloomy vision of the immediate future, obtained through a laborious technique combining animated objects and pictures. Ellen Meske (Los Angeles, 1952) devoted herself mainly to children's films. One of her finest is *The Inflatable Alphabet** (1979), a playful animated alphabet book drawn on paper. Evert de Beijer (Velsen, 1953) became reknowned abroad with *De Karakters* (The Typefaces, 1986), a nightmare, with undertones reminiscent of Picasso, about a couple attacked by typesetting characters.

Paul Driessen

Paul Driessen was born in Nijmegen on 30 March 1940. Fascinated by drawings when he was still a child, he developed his own graphic style, learning little from the traditional instruction he had at the Utrecht Academy of Fine Arts.

His long-time dream of animating his own creations came true when he found work at the advertising company Cinecentrum, in Hilversum, and had Californian Jim Hiltz as a teacher. Years later, Driessen remembered his debut:

> 'At that time (it was 1964 or 1965), advertising still granted a filmmaker some freedom. Once I learned the craft, I had a chance to write my own subjects and create them. Today it would be unthinkable. I remained with Cinecentrum for two and a half years.'[1]

During a visit to The Netherlands, George Dunning had the opportunity to view the promising young artist's work, and invited him to London. Driessen arrived precisely the day before work on *Yellow Submarine* began. Months of activity with storyboards and animation followed. In Lon-

don, the Dutch filmmaker – who had been drawn to animation almost by instinct and, quite curiously, without the usual background of Disney films viewed in childhood – began to acquire an education in animation.[2] It was particularly his viewing of McLaren's work, together with George Dunning's memories, which directed his artistic ambitions and eventually led him to join the National Film Board of Canada. Driessen did not immediately cross the ocean. First he returned to his native country where, in 1970, he produced his first independent work with a grant from the government. *Het verhaal van Kleine Yoghurt* (known also as *The Story of Little John Bailey*) was already typical of Driessen in its choice of framing and a heterodox use of colours, but did not yet display the 'tremulant' line which would later become the artist's most distinctive trademark. The film tells of an inexperienced child who causes a forest fire but is helped

Fig. 102. An Old Box *by Paul Driessen (Canada, 1975).*

---

1 Paul Driessen, personal communication to author (1981).
2 Driessen liked to say that it was precisely because he had seen only a few films in the past that he was able to find a language of his own and his own way to animate and edit (personal communication to author, 1981).

by a friend of his, an elephant.

The two films Driessen made at the National Film Board of Canada, when he finally joined its French section, were also ecologically oriented. *Le bleu perdu* (The Missing Blue, April 1972) and *Air!* (July 1972) dealt with the topic of air pollution. Driessen's true inspiration, however, was not in the presentation of issues, no matter how strongly he felt about them.[1] In fact, the film which launched him on the international scene, *Au bout du fil* (Cat's Cradle, 1974), was the pure play of unrestrained genius. The film is a collection of graphic inventions and actions, starting with a spider and its web and including witches, chases, hooded knights and even the Holy Family. Here Driessen appears in the full maturity of his expressive abilities: an original, incisive style of drawing (which on the surface might appear sloppy), an anti-naturalistic animation and ideas based on the most rarefied abstraction. A graphic artist more than a painter, in this film he used a broad chromatic palette, favouring unusual colours such as amaranth and ash. In these initial works in colour (a fact which theoretically could help the sense of three dimensions) Driessen's world is rigorously two-dimensional, the place for graphics as well as implausibility.

In his following movie, *Une vieille boîte* (An Old Box, 1975), Driessen returns to a more accessible narrative style, leaving room for what he himself described as his own 'poetic side'. The protagonist is a lonely old man who uses a box as a symbol for Christmas. The characteristic style which had already emerged in *Au bout du fil* is joined here by a dreamy but sincere touch of melancholy.

In 1976, Driessen returned to The Netherlands. From that time on, he divided his activities equally between the two countries. In his many subsequent films he managed to maintain a high level

of quality, with few weaknesses and some excellent results. *David* (The Netherlands, 1977) features such a tiny protagonist that ... he cannot be seen. David makes his presence felt through his constantly speaking voice and in several other ways as well – for instance, his hair is visible, waving in the wind – but the screen often remains empty. The film is a true dramaturgic challenge.

'This was what I wanted to do: to show spectators an empty screen without losing their attention. It worked fine,' stated the author.[2]

Jeu de coudes (Elbowing, Canada, 1979) is a metaphoric tale, featuring many men in a line, who elbow each other so that the last one falls into a precipice. Then they take one step forward and would repeat the action forever but for a non-conformist, who disrupts the scheme of things. *Une histoire comme une autre* (The Same Old Story, Canada, 1981) is a game of Chinese boxes, in which a man who reads a book lives the same story narrated by the book, but with a few changes which raise issues among the spectators. The story goes beyond the boundaries of animation to live-action cinema. *Het Treinhuisje* (Home On the Rails, The Netherlands, 1981) is another example of absurdity, featuring a series of daily banalities in a house where the door opens every now-and-then to let a train pass through. *Het scheppen van een koe* (Spotting a Cow, or *Les taches de la vache*, The Netherlands, 1983) displays an unusual animation of black-on-white and has an original structure – the off-screen voice of a fictional author explains how difficult it is to find ideas and style for a new story, and the film shows his sketches.

Tip Top (Canada, 1984) and *Spiegeleiland* (Sunny Side Up, or *L'île miroir*, The Netherlands, 1985) played on the differences of perceptions and on the graphic, narrative and conceptual overturning of reality.

---

1   In several interviews he stated his support for environmental movements.
2   Léo Bonneville, 'Paul Driessen (entretienne),' *Séquences*, No. 21 (Montreal, January 1978), p. 35.

'In my films there is no auto-biography,' the author maintains, 'and there are no observations about life and people. There is only fantasy. At times other filmmakers' works or everyday reality suggest ideas; but I'd rather not use them. I sit down, close my eyes and concentrate. Thus my films are born. At first, for practice, I used to think of ideas for a cartoon every night before falling asleep. And in that exercise, I always succeded.'[1]

Driessen is undoubtedly a distinguished creator of philosophical comedies (*Jeu de coudes*) or lyrical ones (*Une vieille boîte*). He provides the spectator with material on which to reflect – from ecological subjects to his preference for the weak, to a melancholic, 'metaphysical', even maliciously cruel perception of life. All his work, however, is based on his lucid day-dreaming, detached from reality and translating into uniquely intellectual films. Driessen seems to constantly challenge creative procedures and filmic language – and conversely the spectator's perception – within a cerebral game. *David, Une histoire comme une autre, Het scheppen van een koe, Tip Top* and *Spiegeleiland* are only some examples of this philosophy. In an interview, Driessen explained his relationship with his audience:

'I like to have people imagine and participate ... I have developed this imaginary world, in which the spectator has to fill the gaps.'

One way to call upon spectators is to provoke them on language and their perception of language, as in *David* and *Het scheppen van een koe*.

Driessen's research into the boundaries of his creative medium relates him to his countryman, painter Maurits Cornelis Escher.[2] Finally, and above all, he is a comic filmmaker. In Michel Ciment's words, Driessen:

'... achieves a fusion of the Hollywood cartoon with its manic rhythms, and the Zagreb studio with its more philosophical concerns.'[3]

German Federal Republic: an uncertain awakening

In the 1960s a new cultural climate swept the German film industry. The Oberhausen Manifesto of 1962, subscribed to by twenty-six film directors, became the starting point of the new German cinema, which would attain international fame ten years later. Among the signers of the Manifesto, two were involved with animation: Wolfgang Urchs, producer and director; and Boris Von Borresholm, who would later produce Jan Lenica's *Die Nashörner*. The Manifesto's goals of putting an end to 'daddy's cinema' and opening new avenues was shared by German animation, which saw a limited renaissance. Hamburg and Munich became major production centres, while smaller teams and independent filmmakers were based in other cities. As in most western countries, advertising and television offered the greatest opportunities to animators, including many foreign artists (especially Poles, Hungarians and artists from the former Yugoslavia and Czechoslovakia, such as Kristl, Sajtinac, Lenica and Csonka), who moved to Germany to fill an unusual scarcity of young native animators. From 1978 on, technical schools were founded in Stuttgart, Kassel and Offenbach, while special courses were offered in other cities. Such activity spurred interest and enterprise, culminating in

1   Paul Driessen, personal communication (1981).
2   His preference for linear drawings indicates his desire to explore. He was interested in the line, Driessen said, precisely because 'with the line one never knows what it will lead to. One can play with it in all possible ways.' He added, 'For me, it's a way to give shape to a thing which cannot be recognized until it reaches its final form. It is only at the end that one can see results.' Léo Bonneville, 'Paul Driessen.'
3   Michel Ciment, 'Situation de l'animation', *Positif*, No. 297 (Paris, November 1985).

the creation of an international festival in Stuttgart (1982).

A forerunner to this renewal of German animation was an outsider's film, *Die Purpurlinie* (The Purple Line, 1960), by Flo Nordhoff. A film for adult audiences, *Die Purpurlinie* suffers at times from a lack of taste, but was still an original and stimulating example of graphic research. It was also Nordhoff's sole experiment in this field.

The first animator of the new generation was Wolfgang Urchs (Munich, 7 September 1922). His *Die Gartenzwerge* (The Garden Gnomes, 1961) was a parable about the aberration of affluence, featuring the legendary good gnomes who become monuments to themselves – or garden statues, as the title suggests. *Das Unkraut* (The Weed, 1962), the pacifist *Die Pistole* (1963) and the sour anti-bourgeois satire *Kontraste* (1964) followed. *Maschine* (1966) told how homo sapiens was forced to think, and how, while improving his ideas, became a prisoner of his own discoveries. In his first movies, Urchs displayed more of a polemic spirit than a mature creativity or well-mastered style; his accusations often sounded superficial. In *Nachbarn* (Neighbours, 1973), however, he managed to deal expertly with the rather worn theme of a fight between neighbours. In 1988 he released *In der Arche ist der Wurm drin* (The Worm Is In Noah's Ark), an acclaimed feature film about Noah's Ark and a little worm living in it. A sarcastic, mocking observer of reality, Urchs deserves the title of heir to the tradition of German journalistic satire.

Helmut Herbst (Escherhof, 2 December 1934) influenced many of his colleagues. A director of fiction films, documentaries and television work as well as a film historian, graphic artist and painter, Herbst was first of all an animator; he also produced animated films directed by others. His first work, *Kleine Unterweisung zum glücklichen Leben* (A Little Introduction to a Happy Life, 1962–63) was a short film with animated cutouts, based on a poem by Peter Ruhmkorf. Herbst also used cutouts for his best known film, *Schwarz-Weiss-Rot* (Black-White-Red, 1964). A violent, polemic attack against the newspaper *Bild Zeitung* and its right-wing director Axel Springer, the film portrays Germans under the leadership of the Kaiser, Hitler and Springer.

> 'Herbst's film is subtle, precise and at the same time, a commentary which could not have been formulated in a sharper manner,' a critic of *Die Zeit* wrote.[1]

Der Hut (The Hat, 1964), a mix of live-action and animation, is a creative comedy about a young woman who carries an egg under her hat. After several experiences as a film director, Herbst made an avant-garde film, *Drei Versuche über Anton von Webern Opus 5, fünfter Satz* (Three Essays on Anton Webern, Opus 5, Fifth Movement, 1979), a filmic attempt to visualize the act of listening to music with abstract and almost-abstract sequences. In the early 1980s he returned to animation with *Dappi-Film No. 1* (1982), featuring little monsters with long ears

Fig. 103. Schwarz-Weiss-Rot by Helmut Herbst (Federal Republic of Germany, 1966).

1   Uwe Nettelbeck, *Die Zeit* (14 February 1964).

and spears in place of arms. The film was inspired by stories Herbst heard in Kingston, Jamaica, during a stay as a cinema teacher. *Sieben Einfache Phänomene* (Seven Simple Phenomena, 1983) was a graphic game on the hatched image of a man attempting to perform simple actions, such as lighting a cigarette or sneezing. *Das Knarren im Gehäuse* (The Creaking of the Clock, 1984) features a basket filled with flies which activate old theatrical machines. In this suggestive film, the figures are inspired by copper prints from the nineteenth century.

Herbst's most famous collaborators from the 1960s were the husband and wife team of Franz Winzentsen (Hamburg, 10 January 1939) and Ursula Asher (Hamm, 4 August 1939). Together they made *Staub* (Dust, 1967), one of the best shorts of the decade, featuring two clouds – one, a dark harbinger of tragedy, and the other a white

bearer of good things. Since 1971, they co-produced and co-directed many television films for children, including the series *Geschichten vom Franz* (Stories of Franz, 1971–75) and *Geschichten vom Flüsterpferd* (1976–78); *Als die Igel grösser wurden* (How the Hedgehog Got Bigger, 1978–79), *Kanalligator* (1981) and *Telefonfieber* (Telephone Fever, 1985).

On his own, Franz made *Verfolgung* (Progress, 1964), *Erlebnisse einer Puppe* (Experiences of the Doll, 1966, winner of several awards), *Der Turm* (Rapunzel, 1974), *Flamingo – aus meinem Animationstagebuch* 1980–82 (Flamingo – From My Animation Diary, 1982) and *Die Königin des schwarzen Marktes* (The Queen of the Black Market, 1989). Ursula Asher Winzentsen made *Der Fuss* (Fussfilm, 1979). In the 1980s she devoted more attention to art films, such as *Der Fährmann denkt an den Schmied*

*Fig. 104.
Erlebnisse einer Puppe by Franz Winzentsen (Federal Republic of Germany, 1985).*

(1982), *Die Rinde* (The Rind, 1984) and *Unter – Wegs* (On the Way, 1987) – the latter a film of painted impressionistic, delicate images which were strengthened, at time weakened by sound.[1]

Katrin Magnitz (Potsdam-Babelsberg, 16 February 1943) followed in the footsteps of her mother, an animator at DEFA. After ten years as a free-lancer, in 1975 she opened a studio in Hamburg producing educational, industrial and television films. She also worked on art films such as *Teestunde* (Tea Hour, 1978), *Also sei es so ...* (So Be It, 1981, her most famous film – plotless, based just on visuality) and *Die gar nicht ungewohnliche Geschichte der Erlose D.* (1985).

Joachim Kreck (Frankfurt, 11 July 1935) was journalist, film critic, producer and director. His most interesting short, *Der Falschspieler* (The Chord Sharp, 1980, co-directed with Britain's Ian Moo-Young, with script and music by jazz and rock musician Volker Kriegel) is the sarcastic story of a guitarist who owes his fame to his off-key music.

Jorg Drühl (Lübeck, 21 February 1947) described the pros and cons of city life in the ten episode series, *Bilder aus der Stadt* (Pictures From the City, 1976). Hayo Freitag (Wilhelmshaven, 19 November 1950) and Jürgen Heer (Husum, 16 September 1950) co-directed *Mein Bruder* (My Brother, 1985), a grotesque, anti-militarist film about an old man's love-hate relationship with his pilot brother, who is also his alter ego.

Raimund Krumme (Cologne, 5 June 1950) made his film debut with *Les phantomes du château* (1980)[2], but achieved international fame with *Seiltänzer* (1986). Here, the tug-of-war between two characters becomes an excuse for refined choreography, an allegory about power and an imaginative use of optical illusions – the rectangle in which the game takes place keeps changing shape according to the circumstances. Solveig von Kleist (Wurzburg, 1956) worked in the United States and in France as well as in Germany; she made a name for herself with *Criminal Tango* (1985, engraved on black stock), a well-structured salute to traditional detective films.

Jochen Kuhn (Wiesbaden, 1954), director of *Der lautlose Makubra* (1981) and *Brief and die Produzentin* (1986), attained his finest results with *Hotel Acapulco* (1987), a pastiche of photographs, animated paintings and live-action.

Thomas Meyer-Hermann (Cologne, 1956) focused on the themes of city life, alienation and mass communication. His best films include *Dauerlauf* (1981, about the power of television messages), *Eiszeit* (1982, featuring a view of Stuttgart as a desert glacier), *Flammender Pfeil im Reich der schnellen Bilder* (1984) and *Flugbild* (1988).

Bettina Bayerl (Nuremberg, 11 August 1960) began her prolific career with *Moralmord*

Fig. 105. Mein Bruder *by H. Freitag and J. Heer (Federal Republic of Germany, 1985).*

1 From the press release for the film (1987).
2 Original title in French.

(1982), producing a constant flow of provokingly sarcastic films often aimed at sexual taboos. In this line are *Oder, was ist* (1984), *Kehrwoche* (1984) and *Sexapill* (1985), three chapters of a single, mocking project.

Christoph and Wolfgang Lauenstein made *Balance* in 1989 which won an Oscar in 1990. This puppet film made by these twins (born in 1962) shows five puppets rotating around a floating platform: their equilibrium depends upon everybody's good will.

Among the animators who preferred to approach larger audiences, the most successful was Ulrich König (Munich, 3 April 1949) who was born into a family of filmmakers including his father, a director, and his uncle, a producer. König made a name for himself with *Meister Eder und sein Pumuckl* (Master Eder and his Pumuckl, 1980), a television series of one-minute-long episodes and 25 minute-long chapters, which was also released as a feature film for movie theatres. One day, Master Eder finds the elf Pumuckl glued to the glue box; Master Eder is the only human able to see the elf, and this premise generates various adventures. All these series were not made in Germany but at the Budapest-based Pannonia. Curt Linda (Budweis, 23 April 1928) also addressed broad audiences with three feature films, *Die Konferenz der Tiere* (The Conference of Animals, 1969), *Shalom Pharao* (Greetings, Pharaoh, 1982) and *Harold und die Geister* (Harold and the Spirits, 1988). He was also very active in television, particularly on series such as *Sensationen unter der Zirkuskuppel* (Sensations under the Circus Tent), *Spass an der Freud* (Joke on Freud) and *Zauber der Magie* (Wonderful Trip to the Past).

Finally, German production companies include Berlin Film & AV, which developed two Iraqi television series: *Die Wiederkehr der Wunderlampe* (1981–82) and *Wundersame Reise in die Vergangenheit* (1983–84); and Film & AV,

headed by Eugen Alexandrow (Zaporozhie, Ukraine, 20 January, 1938) and Hans J. Glauert (Minden, 17 July 1938).

Sweden: growth

For several years Swedish production was limited. In the 1940s, the only notable work was an unsuccessful attempt at a feature film: in 1941, Einard Norelius (who collaborated with Robert Hogfeldt on *Bam-Bam, or How to Tame a Troll*) filmed some minutes of *Nils Holgerssons underbara resa* (Nils Holgersson's Wonderful Journey), on a popular subject by children's writer Selma Lagerlöf. The project failed due to lack of funding. In the following decade, educational and advertising productions by animators such as Hans Arnold (Sursee, Switzerland, 1925), Torsten Bjarre (Madesjo, 1915) and Åke Skiöld (Halmstad, 1917) increased. Some successful groups were founded during these years, including Gunnar Karlsson's GK Film (founded in 1953 from the ashes of Puck Film, which in turn had been created from a company of the 1930s, Sagokonst) and Stig Lasseby's Team Film (1956). Beside its feature films, GK Film should be recognized for the animated series *Patrik and Putrik*, directed by Alvar Eriksson (1895–1968, one of the country's few specialists in puppet animation).

The most popular animator of the 1960s was Rune Andreasson (Lindome, 1925), creator of the six episode series about Bamse, a bear cub

Fig. 106. Balance by Christoph and Wolfgang Lauenstein (Federal Republic of Germany, 1989).

which becomes superpowerful by eating a special kind of honey (1966). The character was very popular with children and made a return with new episodes in 1972, 1981 and 1986.

In 1984 painter Per Ekholm (Ingatorp, 8 September 1926) and actress Gisela Frisen Ekholm (Trier, Germany, 23 March 1927) released *It Was Year Zero*, a twenty-minute-long film of animated drawings made by children. In the following years the couple released other films, including many animated works: *The Angry Film* (1976), *Tago* (1977, an elegant example of science-fiction with an ethical message), *The Film of the Dark Night* (1980) and the noteworthy *Alfred Jarry Superfreak* 1873–1907 (1987, a twenty-three minute long film dedicated to the founder of pataphysics).

In the 1970s, motivated by an increasing demand for children's productions, Swedish television and the Svenska Filminstitutet provided opportunities to young animators and independent filmmakers. Specialized university courses were also taught in the departments of Fine Arts. As the market proved to be receptive, Sweden was finally able to count on a strong production of its own.

Like many of their colleagues throughout the world, Swedish animators disdained large studios, even when working on challenging projects such as feature films. This fragmentation of production was compatible with the country's many techniques and styles, pro-Disney as well as anti-Disney groups, specialists of cel animation and promoters of the cut-out technique. While it is not possible to trace a 'Swedish' style, Swedish animation shares common elements: an almost exclusive focus on children's films; attention to the educational value of styles, themes and settings as well as social issues; and little interest in avant-garde or art films.

The country's very first feature film was *I huvet på gammal gubbe* (In the Head of an Old Man,

1969, see Colour Plate 54) a mix of live-action and animated drawings produced by GK Film and directed by former illustrator Per Åhlin (Hofors, 1931). While not a masterpiece, it does display some good comic live-action scenes and elegant animated passages, such as a grotesque scene in a brothel which can be considered one of the first examples of erotic animation in Europe. In 1973, the founder of GK Film, Gunnar Karlsson (1924–1985) asked Åhlin to work on *Dunderklumpen*, a second feature film with mixed techniques, released in 1974 and based on a subject by poet and actor Beppe Wolgers. The story takes place during a summer night in the Northern regions, where the sun does not set; a good gnome, Dunderklumpen ('Thundering Fatso'), takes some toys from a child who is vacationing with his parents, and gives rise to all sort of adventures involving a goat, a bee and the adults.

Afterward, Åhlin founded a production company of his own, Penn Film. In 1975 he made *Karl Bertil Jonsson's Christmas Eve*, about a boy who takes presents from the rich and gives them to the poor, followed by the series *Alfons Åberg* (1978, based on the books by children's writer Gunilla Bergström) and *Cold Cuts in Bloom*. In 1989 he completed a new feature film, *Resan till Melonia* (Journey to Melonia) a fantastic 'ecological' variation on Shakespeare's *The Tempest*.

Stig Lasseby, also, was a producer and feature film director. Born in Malmberget, Lapland (5 March 1925), he studied Fine Arts in Stockholm and made his animating debut as an amateur. In 1956 he founded the group Team Film, which produced industrial, educational and public relation films as well as works for television. In the early 1970s, Team Film released television series for children, including the very popular *Agaton Sax and the Max Brothers* (1972), which featured small-town detective Agaton Sax created by mystery writer Nils-Olof Franzén. Sax returned in a feature film, *Agaton Sax och Byköpings gäs-*

tabud (Agaton Sax and the Byköping Fair), released in 1976, in which two British criminals unsuccesfully attempt to eliminate the computer files on them which detective Sax keeps in his native Byköping. Three television specials featuring the detective were also released in 1976: *Agaton Sax and the Band of Silent Explosives*, *Agaton Sax and the Colossus of Rhodes* and *Agaton Sax and the Scotland Yard Mystery*.

Team Film's prolific production includes the feature film *Pelle Svanslös* (Peter-No-Tail, 1981, see Colour Plate 56). Pelle, a cat, leaves the countryside to encounter many predicaments in the city of Uppsala. Ultimately he conquers a place as the leader of the cats and wins the heart of the belle. Adapted from two stories by Gösta Knutsson, the film was very successful, with box office earnings of one million dollars in Sweden alone; its positive, often enthusiastic reviews even rated it above Walt Disney's movies. In fact, it was a well animated, well structured work enhanced by an unbridled yet sensitive humour and by fine 'acting'. In 1985 the production company, which in the meanwhile had lost many of its finest employees and had been forced to commission part of its animation work abroad, released a less attractive sequel, *Pelle Svanslös in Amerikatt* (Peter-No-Tail in Americat, 1985).

For a long time, Team Film's leading artist was Jan Gissberg (Stockholm, 13 August 1948), director of animation for *Agaton Sax and the Byköping Fair* and co-director in Lasseby's *Peter-No-Tail*. Gissberg made his directing debut with the series *Totte* (1972). One year later, he became responsible for another series, *Young Lady at Home Alone*, which was followed by the series *How Mommies and Daddies Do* (1976) and *Journey into Eternity* (1977). In 1978 he directed the entertaining, lively *The Pirates' Film*. In 1982, Gissberg left Team Film to found Cinémation with his brother Peter (Stockholm, 5 February 1952) and Lars Emanuelsson (Stockholm, 21 June 1956). The company's first

production, *Bill and Bolla's Secret* (1984), a mid-length film about the relationship between a child and his handicapped little sister, was followed by *Kalle Stropp the Cricket and Boll the Frog* (1987).

Lennart Gustafsson (Stockholm, 1947) also made a feature film, *Ratty* (1986). Although the story takes place among rats, the film repeats the structure of *Peter-No-Tail*; (see Colour Plate 55) here also the protagonist, Ratty, must overcome various tests before achieving a secure life and love. Especially interesting are the scenes featuring juvenile gangs amid the noise of motorbikes and rock music, which Gustafsson represents with the gloomy atmosphere which he had illustrated more incisively in earlier works. An amateur animator since his youth, Gustafsson put aside a degree in engineering for a career in cinema. After his 1972 debut with *The Astronauts*, he made *Perhaps* (1973), and the two series *The H and G* (1978) and *Aber* (1983–84, featuring the middle-class misadventures of an average man). Among his finest works is the trilogy *Damn It!* (1980), *By Night* (1981) and *Christmas Movie* (1984), in which he described, with pathos and at times expressive violence, the sadness, solitude and anger of young people in a society of distorted values. His style inspired Anna Höglund and Stina Berge in the gloomy but humorous *The Walk* (1988).

Karl-Gunnar Holmqvist (Spånga, Stockholm, 1952) was probably the Swedish animator who focused most on the art film. He made his debut with *Company Party in the Candle Factory* (1975; a remake was released ten years later), followed by *The Tale of Pirates in Skafto (1978)*. *Alban* (1981), based on a subject by Barbro Lindgren, was a delicate story about the youth of a stray dog with a torn ear; the film won several international awards. Holmqvist achieved his finest results in *The Cat and the Bear and the Jocular Dog* (1982) (see Colour Plate 56), *The Solitary Wolf and the Cruel Cat* (1984) and *Johnny Katt and the Waltz of the Pirates* (1986). He wrote the subjects and dialogues of these original modern tales, featuring characters with unconventional personalities and realistic behaviour; he was also responsible for drawings, direction and animation. Although his graphics are not faultless, he is nevertheless an excellent animator, and, above all, a narrator who knows how to insert profound observations on human behaviour and lively moments in quiet stories. His films are often characterized by pale, hand-painted photographic settings.

Johan Hagelbäck (Stockholm, 1946) had a long, eclectic career, from his first work, *Boxning* (1968) to the abstract films he created in London and Amsterdam, to the numerous children's films he made in the 1970s. A lively humorist, he is especially well known for his adaptations, such as *But Who Must Pamper the Little Thing?* (1979, on a subject by Tove Jansson), and *Historien om lilla och stora kanin* (The Story of the Little Rabbit and Big Rabbit, 1981, on a subject by Nils Dardell), as well as for extravaganzas such as *Fish and Chips*, 1984, completely based on *trompe l'oeil* effects) and *Precisely Every Morning* (1984).

Gilbert Elfström (Göteborg, 1929) specialized in television series. *Matulda and Megasen* (1971, co-directed with Hans Arnold), was his first and most famous television series, featuring an ugly but kind witch and her faithful dog which became favourites with children. Other works include *A Strange Man* (1975), *The Hole* (1976) and *Ulme* (1986).

The production company POJ revolved around art director and producer Peter Cohen (Lund, 23 March 1946) and artist and animator Olof Landström (Turku, Finland, 9 April 1943). They made their debut in 1972 with *The Crow's Funeral*, a short based on a song by Georg Wadenius, with words by Barbro Lindgren. Some series followed,

characterized by good scripts and basic, stylized graphics and animation: *Kalle's Climbing Tree* (1975), *The Man Who Did Not Like to Be an Adult* (1979), *Maestro Fugue* (1984) and the short *Mr. Bohm and the Herring* (1987, about a man who decides to tame a fish).

A newer production company was Filmtecknarna Celzqrec,[1] founded in Stockholm in 1981 by Jonas Odell, Stig Bergqvist, Lars Ohlson (all born in Stockholm in 1962) and Martti Ekstrand (Stockholm, 1963). Beside advertising and educational work, it produced some intriguing short films, such as *The Man Who Thought with His Hat* (1984), the story of an autocratic king who gets into trouble when he loses his thinking hat, and *Dawning* (1985).

Birgitta Jansson (Öregrund, 1944–85) balanced her career between animation and direction. Trained in Munich, Germany, and The Netherlands, she animated several films, such as *Dunderklumpen*, then turned to direction with *Where Happiness Lives* (1978, partially created with spray paint). In 1981 she used plasticine in *Vacation House*, a sort of animated documentary featuring the real dialogues and sounds 'captured' in an institute for the handicapped; this compassionate and socially-oriented film won an award at Annecy in 1981.

In 1984, Jansson changed technique once again, this time using cel animation in *A Cow's Journal*, based on a subject by Beppe Wolgers; the film features a cow dreaming of a brilliant career which will culminate with a peace speech delivered to the United Nations.

Björm Jernberg (Karlstad, 1938) began animating in the 1960s, producing made-on-commission works. In 1977 he made an entertainment film, *Maggan's Seeds*, followed by *The Garbage Dump* (1978), *The Baby Carriage* (1979) and *Housing* (1980).

---

1   This second name, a neologism, sounds like the Swedish word cellskräck (claustrophobia).

Peter Kruse (born on 17 August 1941) put his name to only one film, *One Armed Bandit* (1974). Using dry, unconventional drawings, he told the story of a comic, but hellish relationship between a gambler and a slot machine – in which the former was bound to succumb. Also hellish was *One Hundred Years* (1984) by Max Andersson (Karesuando, 25 December 1964). Featuring a Mickey Mouse in line with other similar look-alike mice, it told an anguishing story in the style of Lennart Gustafsson, about loss of personality.

Lars-Arne Hult (born in 1942) directed several shorts in the 1970s, the finest of which is *The Statue* (1979). In 1981 he made the simple but curious *Striptease*, based on a succession of disguises by a creature who gets undressed.

Claes-Goran Lillieborg (Stockholm, 1953) made 'personal' films, based on adult cultural references, such as the poetry of Rimbaud, Baudelaire or Apollinaire, jazz music and nostalgia for Hollywood cinema of yore. He often worked with his mother, Irma. His films include *I Conquer the World Together with Karl and the Marx Brothers* (1978), *Boddy Bolden Blues* (1981, on the origins and history of jazz) and *Saturday in North Carolina* (1985, with puppets animated by Birgitta Jansson, featuring the childhood of Swedish-American singer Cindy Peters).

Jan Gustavson (Ludvika, 1952) made a name for himself with *Bella and Gustav* (1985) in collaboration with children's book illustrator and writer Eva Eriksson.

Kenneth Hamberg (Backe, 1945) made very simple films for younger children: *Rulle in the Stone Age* (1975), *Water in Autumn* (1976) and the series *Bobbo* (1979) and *Goliat* (1980).

Marja Seilola (Kuorevesi, Finland, 1948) made a trilogy based on the Tavasland Tales: *The House of Smoke and the Castle* (1975), *Citizens* (1978) and *The Neighborhood to be Razed* (1982). Erling Eriksson (Varberg, 1938), whose

main interest was education, developed many programmes to teach children the art and techniques of animation. Among his works the most famous is the television programme *What Is It That Makes Noise?* (1976–78), featuring films that young viewers were invited to complete.

Owe Gustafson (Eskilstuna, 1940), an artist with a very simplified drawing style, collaborated with animator Bryan Foster on animated inserts for television programmes such as *Svenska Sesam* (Swedish Sesame). In 1985 he made *Four Stories* by Ingemar, based on subjects by author Ingemar Leckius.

Other filmmakers led interesting but more sporadic careers in the field. Olle Hedman (Stockholm, 1940), one of the rare specialists in avant-garde cinema, made *A Semiotic Study of the Non-Logical Modifications of Drawing* (1973), *Dialogue* (1975), *Oremus* (1976), *Coca* (1981) and *Instant Movie* (1982) among other works. Theatrical director Ann Granhammar (Stockholm, 1948) made the interesting *Man Under the Table* (1984). Lars-Erik Håkansson (Karlshamn, 1937) made several inserts with animated cut-outs for television programmes, beginning in 1978. Peter Larsson (Vaggeryd, 1967; he later changed his name to Peter Markenvard) directed *The Old Clock* (1986), about an abandoned grandfather clock which comes back to life. Jan Loof (Trollhättan, 1940) and Lars-Åke Kylén (Trollhättan, 1939) co-directed the animated puppet series, *Skrot Nisse and His Friends* (1979–80).

Norway

The origins of Norwegian animation date back to the 1910s with Sverre Halvorsen who worked with chalk on a blackboard, filming each image and then erasing it (*Oskar Matiesen the Skater*, and *Roald Amundsen to the South Pole*, both 1913), and Ola Kornelius who filmed drawings on paper (*The Devil in the Nut*, 1917). Also in

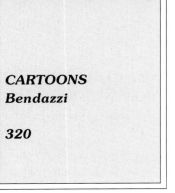

1917 Thoralf Klouman made *Admiral Palads*, a caricature of the USA president Woodrow Wilson. In 1925, Walter Fürst (born on 6 July 1901) made an advertising short, *Teddy*, which is the oldest film of Norwegian animation still existing today. Afterward Fürst worked successfully on live-action cinema.

Wilfred Jensenius (born in 1910) made his debut in 1936 with a political advertisement. For the next fifty years he worked on educational films and television projects.

Trygve Rasmussen (Ålesund, 15 September 1919), a former organist and composer who later produced music for his own sound tracks, made numerous advertising films and commissioned works. He directed only one creative work, *The Golden Coin* (1971), which gained praise from reviewers but was a box office flop.

Björn Tystad Aronsen (born 26 February 1926, died in April 1994) learned the craft at Disney. Having returned to Norway, he opened his own studio, which produced many advertising films before closing in the 1960s. Anna Tystad Aronsen (20 April 1935), Björn's wife and collaborator, continued her activity as an animator working for television and making some shorts for children, such as *The Butterfly* and *Gertrud's Bird* (both of 1984).

The most important filmmaker of the 'old' generation was Ivo Caprino, born in Oslo (17 February 1920) into a family which predisposed him toward the arts. His Italian father, Mario, was a craftsman known throughout Norway for his furniture (the street on which Ivo's animation studio opened was named after Mario). Ivo's mother, a caricaturist, was the niece of Romantic painter Hans Gude. Toward the late 1940s, she made a series of puppets for a theatre which closed soon thereafter and Ivo, then a young man, decided to use them in a film. He invented (and patented) a device to move the puppets and then showed the product to an influential cinema manager, obtaining his financial support. Caprino's first advertising film with animated puppets (1949) became quite popular. His film for children, *The Magic Violin*, won first prize in its category at the 1952 Venice festival; *The Tenacious Tin Soldier* (1954) collected nine international awards. This optimistic, dynamic, eternally young puppet animator became a national treasure.

> 'I enjoyed an easy, quiet life of work. The government has always supported me financially. They say that it is difficult to animate in Norway; well, it has not been so for me.'[1]

Caprino's masterpiece was *Flåklypa Grand Prix* (The Pinchcliffe Grand Prix, 1975) (see Colour Plate 57), a feature film with animated puppets, which the author preferred to call 'models'. Reodor Felgen, a bicycle shop worker and inventor, and his friends the hedgehog Ludvig and the bird Solan Gundersen are challenged by the evil Rudolf Blodstrupmoen in a Grand Prix auto-race. The film's greatest attraction is the incredible car invented by Reodor – a golden flash with an Italian name – Il Tempo Gigante (Giant Time). The feature film was the most successful ever in Norway, with four million spectators (almost the whole of the country's population), and was also praised abroad. For fun as well as for advertising purposes, Caprino commissioned a perfectly working copy of Il Tempo Gigante, almost seven metres long and capable of travelling at 120 miles per hour.

Caprino's puppets, which appeared in more than fifty films throughout the artist's career, are of the traditional, pre-Trnka type.

> 'My foreign colleagues have always told me that I grant realism too much. I have always answered that, in cinema, it is not a matter of keeping one's own style current with fashion,

1   Ivo Caprino, personal communication (1983).

but of making quality work. Obviously, there is a limit beyond which the puppet loses its nature, but I try not to pass it. In my television programmes, puppets discuss policy or current events. Their abstract nature makes them interesting. If the same topics were discussed by actors, they wouldn't have the same meaning at all', said Caprino, and added, on the topic of feature films, 'A puppet-animated film should not last more than 20 minutes. A feature film must have exceptional scriptwriting in order to succeed; in fact, we worked a lot on scriptwriting. It was a huge relief to find that the public didn't leave the theatre before the intermission. When I say to make quality work I mean quality in each component of the film.'

A younger generation of filmmakers appeared in the 1980s. Advertising artist Gro Strom and ASIFA's director Inni-Karine Melbye worked abroad. Among the artists who remained in the country, Knut Eide (Bodo, 18 April 1948) made *The Tie* (1980) and *Star* (1984) in what he properly defined as 'the northernmost studio in the world' (Bodo is north of the Artic Circle). Morten Skallerud (14 July 1954) displayed his unusual techniques in *Winter Solstice* (1984), utilizing time-lapse with a frame of a seascape taken every 15 seconds on the shortest day of the year. The four hours of sunlight are thus reduced to forty-five seconds. Kine Aune (10 March 1943) who worked mainly with live-action cinema, made *Jacob and Johanna* (1981), a sensitive animated film about a phocomelic girl. In 1984 she made *Story of Who Is Afraid of the Dark*, about a man who overcomes his fears with the help of people close to him. Thor Sivertsen (29 July 1950) made his debut in 1980 with *Arne at the Garbage Dump*. He became successful internationally with *Zwisch* (1983), a one-minute long cartoon about a man's life from birth to death.

Finland: reserved and serene

The mid-1960s saw the establishment of a constant, quite significant amount of production. On the one hand, the government initiated a politics of financing, making it possible to produce entertainment animated movies (mainly for children); on the other hand, there was an increase in advertising and educational films. Finnish animators favoured the use of cut-outs, which were appreciated by their young audiences and were relatively economical. Themes were often based on the country's rich narrative and oral tradition. The lack of leading animators was compensated for by a commonly shared orientation: as critic Juho Gartz remarked, Finnish animated cinema mirrors Finnish mentality, which is reserved, serene, gentle and overall a bit grey.[1]

Particularly significant was Riitta Nelimarkka (born on 6 July 1948), who came to animation with a multifaceted background, including painting, illustration and journalism. In 1972–73 she directed *The Story of Sampo*, a six-part series on Sampo, the amulet of wealth based on the national epic poem *Kalevala*. Intentionally naïve drawings and an emphasis on dramatic tones gave life to a theme which could have easily become 'official' or pedantic. In 1979, with co-direction by her husband Jaakko Seeck, the filmmaker released the first Finnish animated feature film, *Seitsemän veljestä* (Seven Brothers, 1979) based on Aleksis Kivi's classic novel (see Colour Plate 58). The film, which was made with cut-outs, told of seven hard-headed brothers on a journey of self-discovery in 19th century Finland. Not without humour, and with some beautiful scenes, it received accolades but also some criticism for its dramatic weakness.

Heikki Partanen (Helsinki, 29 January 1942) began specializing in children's series in 1964 (the year of *Cackle and Whine*). With his wife Riitta Rautoma (13 June 1944) he made *Tales of*

---

1   Juho Gartz, 'A Short History of the Finnish Animated Film,' *Plateau*, Vol. 2, No. 2 (Ghent, Belgium, Summer 1981), p. 10.

Power (1970–72) and *Tales of Finnish Animals* (1973–76), with child-like drawings. Afterwards, the two filmmakers turned to live-action cinema.

Camilla Mickwitz (Helsinki, 22 September 1937) made a name for herself with two series: *Jason* (1973–76) and *Emilia* (1979) – this latter based on a little girl and her father constructing fairy tales.

The kangaroo Kossi was the most popular character brought to the screen by journalist, caricaturist and filmmaker Heikki Prepula (born in 1939). Prepula's linear, two-dimensional bare drawing was inspired by the post-UPA graphics of the mid-1960s. Particularly pleasant is *The Locomotive* (1978), where Kossi enganges in a duel with a stubborn locomotive.

Seppo Suo-Anttila (Luumäki, 9 September 1921) was the Finnish animator best known abroad, particularly after having won an award at the Mamaia Festival with *Impressio* (1967). This was a black-and-white story featuring lively and dramatically animated bottles. His later works include the series for children *The Courtyard* (1968–70), *Impressio II* (1973, a colour reprise of the original film), and the traditional tale *The Death-Tamer* (1981).

Antti Peränne (Helsinki, 14 February 1928) was also internationally active. He began animating in the early 1950s and opened his own studio in 1960. His films (usually animated drawings on cel) include *Farce sans equilibre** (Farce Without Balance, 1965), *Le chien imbécile** (The Crazy Dog, 1968), *The Blue Story** (1971), *My Secret Life* (1972), *Wage* (1981), *Earnings* (1983) and *Father and Son* (1986). His speciality was advertising (over eight hundred works) and educational and industrial films, which he made with a personal touch of irony and humour.

Tini Sauvo (born in 1946), already well-known as an artist, made his debut with *I have a Tiger* (1979), a tale of friendship and tolerance. Antti Kari (born on 4 April 1949) collaborated with musician Jukka Ruohomäki on a trilogy based on poet Eino Leino's texts. The films, entitled *The Slave's Son* (1979), *The Lost World* (1982) and *The Eagle and the Will-o-the-Wisp* (1982), were made with special effects and the aid of computers.

Kari Leponiemi (born in 1954) became a professional animator with *The Wolf and the Fox in the Jaws of Death* (1978). Marjut Rimminen (born in 1944) made her debut with *Vivante* (Alive, 1972, co-written with Lemmikki Nenonen), an advertising film which won an award at the Zagreb festival. Afterward, she moved to Great Britain where she worked in advertising and made the ironic, polemic *I'm Not a Feminist, But ...* (1986). Elina Katainen (born in 1943) worked with animation (*The ABC Gift*, 1970, *Jalmari and Hulda*, 1971, and *Series of Drawings*, 1971) as well as live-action cinema. Heikki Paakkanen (Helsinki, 1948) made *1984* (1985), an ambitious but confused protest film, mixing traditional and computer techniques.

Martti Jännes (Tampere, 18 March 1936) began making educational animated films in 1961, the finest being *Elements of Animation* (1973) and

Fig. 107. Impressio by Seppo Suo-Anttila (Finland, 1967).

Equality (1983). Finally, Sauli Rantamäki (born in 1936) and Martti Utriainen (born in 1939) deserve mention for their activities, predominantly in the field of advertising.

Denmark

In the 1960s, art shorts (including animated films) received state support through the Kortfilmradet Foundation. This attracted newcomers and spurred a production which reached its maturity one decade later, with independent work and television productions even after Kortfilmradet dissolved in 1972. Danish animation of the 1960s, 1970s and 1980s shared some characteristics with the animation of other Scandinavian countries: it used low-cost, unsophisticated techniques, such as cut-outs, focusing more on the concept of creation than entertainment; it paid much attention to children, avoiding evasive, syrupy or indoctrinating language; and it dealt often with social or civic themes.

While veteran Bent Barfod continued his eclectic, professionally unassailable activity, Jannik Hastrup (Nestved, 4 May 1941) had a rapid rise to prominence. A potter and a jazz trumpet player, he turned to animation in 1959, when he joined Barfod's production company. After four years he left and, with partner Flemming Quist Møller, refined the technique of animated cut-outs. Their films include *Erotica Concert* (1964), *Slambert* (1966), *Good Morning* (1968) and, especially, *Benny's Bath Tub* (1971), a mid-length film acclaimed by audiences and reviewers, which became a cultural reference point for later Danish productions. Hastrup also worked on television series *Cirkeline* (1965–71) and *How to Raise Your Parents* (1966), in collaboration with his wife Hanne.

In the 1970s, Hastrup focused on political, social, economic and ecological themes and took more radical positions as a militant leftist. In

Fig. 108. The History Book *by Jannik Hastrup (Denmark, 1972–74).*

1972–74 he directed nine 20 minute-long episodes of *The History Book* in collaboration with Li Vilstrup and Tonnes Nielsen. Here history from the Middle Ages to the 1973 independence of Guinea-Bissau (which is seen as the Third World's symbol of freedom from colonialism) is rewritten from the perspective of the exploited classes. Visually, the artists employed several techniques including vintage etchings, cut-outs, and documentary reels.

The Thralls (1977–80), a series of nine (45 minute long) episodes based on the books by Swedish author Sven Wenström, was another historical film narrated from the viewpoint of the oppressed. The history of Sweden, from the year 1,000 A.D. to the nineteenth century, is told with the assumption that Swedes have always been in a state of rebellion, and that the country has never enjoyed peace until the 20th century.[1]

In 1984 Hastrup completed *Samson & Sally*, a feature film about a whale (Samson) who sets out to look for Moby Dick. While doing so, the whale must escape the dangers of the modern world: radioactive waste, polluted oceans and ruthless whaling. This was more than a polemical film, as Hastrup wanted to make his viewers cry and laugh at the same time,[2] with characters such as an insolent, comic seagull and two walrus musicians. *Strit og stumme* (Subway to Paradise, 1987) was also a feature film; in a futuristic subterranean society two children struggle to reach the surface, seeking the light of hope and a future. Finally, two satiric films deserve mention: *Better Rich and Healthy Than Poor and Sick* (1978) and *New Adventures of the Ugly Duckling* (1982).

Flemming Quist Møller (Copenhagen, 19 May 1942), already mentioned for his collaboration with Hastrup, pursued other projects as well. A writer, painter, musician, actor, director and producer, he made two popular works with Anders Sorensen: the series *The Indiscrete* (1981) and the short, *The Invisible Child*, for a campaign against alcohol abuse. According to Danish reviewers, Møller's films owe much of their charm to the filmmaker's narration and voice – characteristics which cannot be appreciated by non-Danish-speaking audiences.[3]

Lejf Marcussen (Aabenraa, 27 February 1936) joined the television department of Danmarks Radio as a draftsman, in 1972. At first he produced and financed his avant-garde films, but later he found a niche inside the TV production group and was able to continue his research on 'non verbal' films. Rejecting plots as well as the concept that a film is the *mise-en-scène* of a script, he found inspiration in music and created combinations of sounds and images. Marcussen's first noteworthy work is *Orchestra Director* (1978), a divertissement with figurative-caricatural drawings about an orchestra conductor who could control his arms. *Stills* (1979) is a non-figurative film, a chaotic but also harmonic mixing of images and synthesizer music. The less convincing *Duality* (1981) was followed by *Rocks* (1982) and *Tonespor* (1983) – two works marking the highest achievement of this research. *Rocks* is a succession of metamorphoses based on photographs of stones and accompanied by a composition for Celtic harp by Alain Weber. *Tonespor* (known also as Visual Polyphony) was a visual version of musical counterpoint – a search for correspondence between sound and images that nobody had attempted after McLaren's *Synchromy*. Overall, Marcussen's opus is a large work-in-progress, original and stimulating but not always convincing in taste and creativity.

Svend Johansen (born in 1948), a live-action

---

1   Sven Wenström, from the press release for the series.
2   Niels Plaschke, 'Samson et Sally,' *Animafilm*, No. 4 (Turin, October–December 1984).
3   'Scandinavie,' *Banc-Titre*, No. 25 (Paris, November 1982), p. 23.

filmmaker and producer, directed the ecologically-oriented *Perch Lake* (1980) and several works for children. In the early 1980s, the aforementioned Anders Sorensen (born in 1950) founded Tegnedrengene ('Little Designers') in partnership with

Per Tonnes Nielsen. In 1986, he directed the mid-length film *The Story of the Wonderful Potato*, a lively recreation of the history of the potato, from its American origins to European tables. Inni-Karine Melbye (Oslo, Norway, 25 January 1937) worked in France and Canada before moving to Denmark in 1979. Her work includes *Journey to Planet Nazar* (1983), an elegant adaptation of a work by Seventeenth Century dramatist Ludvig Holberg. Jeffrey J. Varab (Cleveland, Ohio, 25 February 1955) trained at Disney, where his colleagues included the Dane Jorgen Klubien (born in 1958). Varab later joined Klubien in Denmark, where they founded a studio. Varab's most popular work was *Valhalla* (1986), a feature film which he co-directed with Peter Madsen (born in 1958). An epic comedy based on comic strips by Madsen (who was also scriptwriter and art director), it featured the gods and giants of the ancient Nordic tradition. Despite its average quality, it was well received by the public.

Finally, Jorgen Vestergaard (Aarhus, 10 April 1939) deserves mention for his independent production. Having studied journalism, in 1962 he turned to documentary cinema, simultaneously developing an interest in the world of puppets and its traditions. He directed some short fiction films with marionettes and in 1968 visited the Jirí Trnka studio in Prague. The following year he founded a production company, first in Copenhagen and later in Thisted, North Jutland. His films, all made in co-production with Danmarks Radio, were well written, well animated adaptations of traditional tales or legends, with characters and sets displaying the dreamy realism of Trnka's tradition. *The Nightingale* (subject by Andersen; produced in 1969 and distributed in

1970) was followed by *The Telltale Heart* (on a subject by Poe, 1971), *The Travelling Companion* (Andersen, 1972); *The Shadow* (Andersen, 1975); *The Story of a Mother* (Andersen, 1977, probably Vestergaard's finest work) and *Thumbelina*, (Andersen, 1983). *Sigurd Fafnersbane* (1980–81) and *Miseri Mo* (1985) were based on traditional legends. Vestergaard also continued his activity as a documentarist.

Switzerland

In the 1960s and 1970s, Switzerland suddenly became host to a rich group of talent, in both live-action cinema (including Goretta, Tanner, Soutter and Schmid) and animation. Previously, activity in animation had been limited. In the 1920s the Frenchmen Lortac and Cavé animated the aforementioned adventures of Monsieur Vieux Bois – a local production filmed in Geneva. Later, in Germany, Swiss-born Rudolf Pfenninger experimented with synthetic sound. In 1934 the German anti-nazi refugee Julius Pinschewer moved to Berne, where he made advertising films. In 1938 Montreux Color Film was founded. The company produced advertising films and an abstract experimental short entitled

Fig. 109. The Story of a Mother by Jorgen Vestergaard (Denmark, 1977).

Chromophony (1939), which attempted to blend music, visual rhythm and colour. The director of the film and leader of the company was Charles Blanc-Gatti (Lausanne, 26 January 1890 – Riex, 8 April 1966), who had first been recognized in Paris during a congress of Musicalist painters. *Chromophony* was neither a technical nor an artistic success, nor was it the first film to attempt a combination of rhythmic images and music. This, however, did not stop Blanc-Gatti from complaining to Walt Disney when he heard about the making of *Fantasia*.

In the 1950s the market for made-to-order films expanded. There were also some experimental works, such as the painting on stock by the Haas, a husband and wife team. A turning point came in the 1960s, when F.G. Rindlisbacher (Berne, 21 November 1930) and Bernhard Meyer (Berne, 8 August 1930) made *Flug zum Mond* (Flight to the Moon), a first example of classic Swiss cartoons to be used as a filler in movie theatres. In the same period, Edmond Liechti (Geneva 5 April 1927) was commissioned to make some spots for television – a genre in which he later specialized. Ernest and Gisèle Ansorge became popular for *La danseuse et le mendiant* (The Dancer and the Beggar, 1958), using animated puppets. Studios, sometimes of the smallest dimensions, were gradually founded all over the confederation, with a striking decentralization for such a small country. Animators worked in Zurich, Berne, Basel, Lausanne, Geneva, Fleurie, Sion and Lugano.

Erwin Huppert (Baden, Austria, 23 October 1923) made half-a-dozen animated pamphlets, such as *Les inutilitaires* (The Useless Ones, 1966) and *J'aime je déteste* (I Love, I Hate, 1969). He established the record for the shortest film ever, with the three-frame *Honte* (Shame, 1970). Gérard Vallet (Geneva, 24 April 1932) made *A + B = Boum* (1966), Switzerland's first cinemaScope animated film. Santiago Arolas (Barcelona, Spain, 19 May 1930) was particu-

larly praised for *Chimères* (Chimeras, 1970). Experimentalists Guido (Berne, 8 November 1931) and Eva Haas (Berne, 31 July 1933) made several films starting in 1958 with *Abstract No. 1*. Their finest work is perhaps *Eine Linie ist eine Linie ist eine Linie* (A Line is a Line is a Line, 1971). Their son Gordon won an international award for *Die Abenteuer von Hick und Hack* (The Adventures of Heck and Hack, 1970), which he made at the age of thirteen.

Painter Gilbert Vuillème (Berne canton, 1924) turned to cinema with *Sarabande et variations* (1964), a high quality abstract illustration of classical music. Robi Engler should be mentioned for his teaching activity, carried out also in developing countries, later authoring the interesting *Métro-boulot-dodo* (1972).

Daniel Suter (Geneva, 19 November 1943), Claude Luyet (Geneva, 9 May 1948), Gérald Poussin (Geneva 13 August 1946) and Georges Schwizgebel (Reconvillier, 28 September 1944) made their collective debut with *Patchwork*, sponsored by Parisian Manuel Otero. Afterward they worked independently. Suter made *Chewing-go-home* (1971) and *Le macaque* (1972) before filming his finest work, *Un jour comme un autre* (A Day Like Any Other, 1974). In 1984, he made *Grimaces*. Luyet filmed *Ricochet* (1973), *Marché noir* (Black Market, 1977) and *Question d'optiques* (A Question of Optics, 1986). Gérald Poussin made the three-and-a-half minute long ballad, *Alphon au pays des merveilles* (Alphon in the Land of Marvels, 1972). Schwizgebel made *Le vol d'Icare* (The Flight of Icarus, 1974, with an original animation of colour bulbs), *Perspectives* (1975) and *Hors-jeu* (Beyond the Law, 1977). At times he falls into cerebralism, as in *Le ravissement de Frank N. Stein* (Frank N. Stein's Delight, 1981), at other times he generates delicate pictures such as in *78 tours* (78 R.P.M, 1985, about a man listening to a waltz, and the images that the music suggests to him). Overall, with his vivid sense for rhythms and atmospheres and his knack for exploring unusual formal solutions, Schwizgebel can be considered the leader of the middle-generation of Swiss animators.

The most interesting works are by Ernest Ansorge (Lausanne, 28 February 1925) and his wife Gisèle (Morteau, France, 9 February 1923–Lausanne, 17 December 1993). Authors of educational films and documentaries, the two artists made their animation debut, as mentioned above, with *La danseuse et le mendiant* (The Dancer and the Beggar). After a ten-year interval they released *Les corbeaux* (The Crows), a gloomy, disquieting work which won several prizes and served as a premise for the more mature, more complex *Fantasmatic* (1969). Here, an unrestrained fantasy creates a hallucinating landscape, with profiles and hands coming out of the ground. The protagonist is transformed into a centaur but becomes a man again before being swallowed by the ground. In 1970 the filmmakers released *Alunissons*, a mockingly clever science-fiction tale which constituted the third ring of this trilogy-of-the-absurd.

The Ansorges pioneered a technique of sand animation which was soon employed by other artists. By working on sand that has been placed on a horizontal plane below the camera and by gradually moving it with special instruments, the animators created films with an unreal charm not far from that of Alexeïeff's animated engravings. What distinguishes these original artists is the sense of mystery brought on by sudden metamorphoses. Their dramatic films (particularly *Alunissons*) display a peculiar humour of the absurd. The Lausanne-based couple also made *Le chat caméléon* (The Chameleon Cat, 1974), *Smile 1 et 2* (1975) and *Smile 3* (1976). In 1977 they released *Anima*, an evocative, erotic movie which was mostly Gisèle's work, and in 1986, *Les enfants de laine* (Woolen Children).

Austria

Austrian animation is rooted in the experiments of Richard Teschner (1879–1948), an avant-garde puppeteer who had worked in live-action cinema in the 1920s; as well as in the avant-garde painting and music which, in the years between the two World Wars, focused on intense formal research. In the 1950s some independent Viennese filmmakers founded Wiener Formalfilm, a movement influenced by the structure of twelve-tone music and studies of perception. In contrast to other movements, such as the American 'West Coast', Wiener Formalfilm did not specialize in visionary graphic or colouristic research, but its underlying principles of the movement were close to animation, considering cinema as a language which could be broken down into smaller units (frames) and later re-assembled through editing.

'Material-artistic elements of motion [are] provided by the intervals (the transitions from one movement to another), but not movement itself', claimed Peter Kubelka, perhaps the principal representative of the group, with a statement which echoes McLaren.[1] Many Wiener Formalfilm artists, including Peter Kubelka, Kurt Kren,

Fig. 110.
Alunissons by Ernest and Gisèle Ansorge (Switzerland, 1970).

1   Peter Weibel, 'The Viennese Formal Film,' *Film as Film*, (London: Hayward Gallery, 1979), p. 110.

Marc Adrian, Valie Export, Hans Scheugl and several younger followers, made films which could be considered animation, strictly speaking, but are actually part of a broader, more articulate and coherent research which cannot be properly treated within the scope of this text.

Traditional animation in the 1960s and 1970s was represented by artists such as Hans O. Sindelar (Vienna, 15 January 1921), an expert in children's films (particularly animated puppets), whose active career began in 1965 and included 107 films. A musician, photographer, producer and director, Sindelar worked for Austrian public television, ORF, and did sporadic advertising work. He officially retired in 1980, but continued animating. His first film was *Circus Sindy* (1965), his ORF creation was *Der Retter* (The Rescuer). Other works by Sindelar include *Weltraumcircus* (World Dream Circus, 1973), the series *Kunibert* (1974, with animated cutouts) (see Colour Plate 59) and *Die Vogelscheuche* (The Scarecrow, 1977, with animated drawings).

The first movement in the tradition of the Viennese school was founded in the early 1980s with the guidance of Maria Lassnig, a teacher at Vienna's Hochschule fur Angewandte Kunst and her assistant and successor Hubert Sielecki. Lassnig (Kappel a. Krappfeld, 1920) worked in Austria, Paris (1961–68) and New York (1968–1979). In the US, she produced her own animated films: *Encounter* (1970), *Chairs* (1971), *Self Portrait* (1972), *Baroque Statues* (1970–74), *Palmistry* (1974), *Shapes* (1975) and *Art Education* (1976). Invited to teach at the Hochschule in 1980, she organized a small animation studio in her class.

Hubert Sielecki (Rosenbach, 6 November 1946), a fine artist, photographer and filmmaker, joined Lassnig in 1982. With his initiative and teaching, the movement – which in 1984 was named ASIFA-Austria – took off. Sielecki and his student-colleagues supported low-technology ani-

mation, oriented toward creative and formal research and used all the low-cost techniques available to single artists. They opposed the established forms of animation, above all cel-made cartoons and the comic film. Sielecki's works include *Countdown* (1982), *Die Suppe* (1983) and the fine *Nachrichten* (1983), and *Festival* (1985, the ironic diary of a participant in an animation festival). In 1987 he collaborated on the collective feature film, *1 x 1 des glücklichen Lebens*, an anthology which served as the manifesto of ASIFA-Austria, and which was the result of a joint effort by James Clay, Sabine Groschup, Dana Herlitzka, Guido Hoffman, Irene Hohenbuchler, Gudrun Kampl, Renate Kordon, Mara Mattuschka, Bady Minck, Hans Werner Poschauko, Susi Praglowski, Roland Schutz, Stefan Stratil, Gerlinde Thuma and Annette Wirtz.

On their own, Sielecki's collaborators had fruitful careers. Susi Praglowski (Vienna, 11 October 1947) made *Bett* (Bed, 1985) and *Sand* (1986). Renate Kordon (Graz, 30 June 1952) displayed her colouristic, graphic skills in *Tageblätter* (Newspaper, 1980), *Hors d'oeuvre* (1981), *Passepartout* (1983), *Buntes Blut* (Coloured Blood, 1985) and *Tonfilm* (Sound Film, 1986). James Clay (Kufstein, 28 June 1958) made *Das Schlangengebirge Wald* (The Wood on Snake Mountain, 1984) and the notable *Das Gespräch* (Conversation, 1985). Mara Mattuschka (Sofia, Bulgaria, 22 May 1959), an extremely prolific filmmaker, also starred in her films as the character 'Mimi Minus'; her works include *Untergang der Titania* (Sinking of the Titanic, 1985). Bulgarian-born Jurislav Tscharyiski (Tolbukhin, 26 November 1956) directed *Movimento* (1986). Sabine Groschup (born in 1959) made the stimulating *Messer* (Knife, 1986).

Spain

The 1950s were meagre years for Spanish animation which produced little more than advertising movies. From this period only *Nausica*

(1958), made with animated yarn by Barcelona-based Josep Serra Estruch (Bráfim, 1921) is worth mentioning. In 1960 Serra Estruch and Angel García (Barcelona, 1923) founded ICA Films, which released such films as *Pancho y Pincho en los infiernos* (Pancho and Pincho in Hell, 1961) and *La gatita blanca* (The White Kitten, 1962).

It was mainly because of advertising that Spanish animation survived. In 1955, the Estudios Moro, which had just been founded in Madrid by brothers José Luis and Santiago Moro, joined the advertising distribution company Movierecord. While retaining a sort of monopoly over movie theatres, Movierecord allowed filmmakers a large range of activities, which soon extended to the newly-born Spanish television (1956). The Estudios Moro were among the most prolific producers of animated advertising films in Europe. Eventually they expanded to producing television series (*Cantinflas*, based on the popular Mexican comedian), to opening an American branch in Miami (1980) and to feature films such as *Kati la oruga* (Kati the Caterpillar, 1983), made in collaboration with Televicine Messicana. The company's most successful work was *La familia Telerin* (The Telerin Family), by José Luis Moro, an animated spot featuring six children who every night sang a goodnight song to their young spectators.

The Estudios Vara, founded by Rafael Vara (Madrid, 1936) were also based in Madrid. Although the company specialized in live-action cinema, advertising and documentaries, it released a pleasant animated adaptation of *Mortadelo y Filemón*, characters from artist Francisco Ibañez' comic-strip. Initially created for television, the films were eventually developed into entertainment series for cinemas and feature films.

In 1964 Cruz Delgado founded a production company under his own name. Born in Madrid on 12 December 1929, he worked at the Estudios Moro and later at Belvision, in Brussels. He was most prolific in the field of entertainment productions. After his debut with *El gato con botas* (Puss-in-Boots, 1964), he released several shorts featuring Boxy, the boxing kangaroo or Molecula, the child inventor (the latter was featured in a thirteen-episode television series in 1968). In 1973 Delgado made his first feature film, entitled *Mágica aventura* (Magic Adventure) about two children visiting the world of fairy-tales. His second feature film was *El desván de la fantasía* (The Attic of Fantasy, 1978), a semi-educational work with José Ramon Sanchez as artist and director. A third film, *Los viajes de Gulliver* (Gulliver's Travels, 1983), featured Swift's classic character in the land of the giants, Brobdingnag. The production company achieved international success with *Don Quijote de la Mancha*, a series of 39 episodes, each lasting 26 minutes, which was an admirable attempt to adapt Cervantes' masterpiece to television.

Other notable Madrid-based studios include BRB International, which has churned out many works for television in recent years (with animation produced in the Far East for economic reasons); Pablo Núñez Story Film, whose owner made the mixed *Día tras día* (Day After Day, 1977), a combination of animation and live-action; and the Estudios Castilla, which produced animated tales for movie theatres in the late 1960s and early 1970s.

In Barcelona – the traditional capital of Spanish animation – the powerful Buch-Sanjuan group was active in the advertising field until it was dissolved due to disagreements between its founders, José Maria Sanjuan and Manuel Martínez Buch. Buch (Barcelona, 1930–78) continued working under the name of Publivisión until his death.

Francesc Macián's work was particularly significant. At a young age Macián (Barcelona, 1 November 1929 – 23 October 1976) was attracted to caricature drawings, music and comic strips. In

1955, after having worked for Balet y Blay on *eLos sueños de Tay-Pi* (The Visions of Tay-Pi), he opened his own animation studio. He made advertising spots, travelled extensively in Europe, the United States and South America and worked on several ambitious projects. These include a documentary on Gustave Doré (1962), a series for the American market (Stan Laurel and Oliver Hardy came back to life thanks to his pencil), and the development of a new technique, M-Tecnofantasy, which Macián described as 'cybernetic' but was unwilling to divulge. In 1966, after three years of work he released the feature film *El mago de los sueños* (The Magician of Dreams) (see Colour Plate 60), based on a tale by Hans Christian Andersen and on the Familia Telerin television characters, for which he had obtained the authorization from the Estudios Moro. Glowing with colours, accurately animated, well-built and well-directed, the film was considered a masterpiece of Spanish animation. 'The experts who have viewed this film unanimously claim that it is the best animated feature film made in Europe since the war,' says feature film expert Bruno Edera.[1] Macián's premature death put a stop to other projects already in the works.

Jordi 'Ja' Amorós (born in Barcelona, 1945) was a distinguished comic-strip artist who learned the trade at the Buch-Sanjuan studio. In 1975 Amorós founded the Equip studio, which produced advertising work but also shorts, such as *Gu-Gú* (1981) and *Prima donna* (1983). The studio's most creative work was a feature film for adults, *Historias de amor y masacre* (Stories of Love and Massacre) finished in 1976 but distributed four years later. The film was a collection of sketches based on famous satirical artists including Amorós himself, Oscar, Perich, Ivá and Fer. Despite the celebrities involved, the film was not a box-office success. In 1986 the Equip studio produced a series (thirteen episodes, each thirty-minutes long) entitled *Mofli, el último Koala* (Mofli, the Last Koala).

The Pegbar studio, directed by Robert Balser (Rochester, U.S.A., 25 March 1927) and Julio Taltavull (Barcelona, 1924), was active in several fields. Balser is one of the most brilliant globetrotters of international animation. He worked in Denmark, Finland, Great Britain (where he was animation director of *Yellow Submarine*) and in Spain where he authored *El sombrero* (The Hat, 1964), an excellent short made for the Estudios Moro. As for Taltavull, in 1974 he directed *La doncella guerrera* (The Warrior Maiden) for Pegbar Productions.

Barcelona-based Manuel Rodríguez Jara ('Rodjara', born in 1958) made the feature film *El pequeño vagabundo* (The Little Vagabond, 1986), about a child lost in the forest, who is found by monks, ends up in a circus and finally joins his parents in heaven. This film, which Rodjara began at the age of twenty-one, was the fruit of seven years of work in complete solitude.

One more feature film deserving mention is the Basque *La calabaza encantada* (The Enchanted Pumpkin), released in 1985 by the San Sebastian-based production company Jaizkibel. Directed by Juan Bautista Berasatégui, the company owner, the film features many elements of Basque mythology and folklore.

Finally, independent production cannot be ignored. Painter José Antonio Sistiaga (San Sebastian, May 1932) founded 'Gaur', a group of Basque artists. He conducted research on style and studied the connection between education and art. In 1968 he conceived an experimental film in three parts: anecdotal, static and dynamic. When the first two parts won an award at the Bilbão festival, he was encouraged to complete the work by expanding the third part to a one-hour and ten minute long film (altogether, the first two parts were ten minutes long). Released with

1   Bruno Edera, *Une rareté cinématographique: le long métrage d'animation*, unpublished mss (1971).

the abstract title of *Ere erera ba-leibu icik subua aruaren* (1969), the film was the first CinemaScope feature to be completely painted on film stock – a task which took the artist and his collaborators eight months, at an average of twelve-hours a day. The film is completely silent and consists of a constant flashing of colour bubbles.

Rafael Ruíz Balerdi (San Sebastian, 1934), a friend and colleague of Sistiaga's and a member of the painting group Gaur, made *La cazadora inconsciente* (The Unknowing Huntress, known also as *Homenaje a Tarzan* or Homage to Tarzan), his first and up to now only film. Using the technique of gouache painting, Balerdi evokes the myth of Tarzan and the luxuriant forest, but a sketchy, unconcluded plot (a woman in danger and a rescue attempt) leaves the film open-ended.

Gabriel Blanco made two shorts, *La edad de la piedra* (The Age of Stone, 1965) and *La edad del silencio* (The Age of Silence, 1978), drawn by Chumy Chúmez and Ops respectively. Jaime Pascual directed *Déco* (1977) and *El bosque blanco* (The White Forest, 1981). Cisco Bermejo made *La caza del monstruo* (1981) and *Para qué una pistola* (1982). Raúl García Sanz was internationally praised for *Mujer esperando en un hotel* (1982). Also deserving mention are Anna Miquel for *Gnochi el inconformista* (1977); the duo of Joan Baca and Toni Garriga for *Blanc negre* (1974); Miquel Esparbé for *Incubo rosa* (1973); and Montse Ginesta, Toni Batllori and Josep Maria Rius for *Ploma daurada* (1981). Finally, among independent experimental artists, Jordi Artigas i Candela (Ciudad Real, 7 July 1948) should be remembered. A filmmaker, artist and historian of animation, he made several avant-garde films and documentaries, including *Metamorfosi* (1979) and *Picasso, l'alegria de viure* (1981).

Portugal

Portuguese animation cinema coincided with the

careers of Artur Corrêia (Lisbon, 20 April 1932) and Ricardo Neto (Lisbon, 18 November 1937). A respected cartoonist, Corrêia learned animation at the advertising company Telecine Moro, where his work earned him an award at the Annecy Festival in 1967. In 1970 he was allowed to utilize his breaks between advertising jobs to make a creative film. The result was *Eu quêro a lua* (I Want the Moon, 1970), an entertaining sketch about a man's never-ending attempt to satisfy his woman's whims, even offering her the moon. In 1973 Corrêia and Neto (who also had learned the craft at Telecine Moro) joined Topefilme. Along with the usual made-to-order pieces, they directed several entertainment films.

In 1974 Ricardo Neto directed *A lênda do mar tenebroso* (The Legend of the Dark Sea, see Colour Plate 61), a traditional Portuguese tale about a spell cast by seven necromantic bishops on the Atlantic Islands, during the Arab invasions of the Iberian peninsula. In 1976 he developed an Alentejo tale, *Os dez anõezinhos de tia Verde Água* (The Ten Little Dwarfs and Auntie Green-water), in which an old wise woman teaches a young bride that ten dwarfs – the ten fingers of the hands – can 'magically' help her with her housework. For the same series of traditional tales, financed by the Portuguese Institute for Cinema, Corrêia directed *O caldo de pedra* (Stone Soup, 1976), about a clever friar who manages to make a soup for himself at the expense of the village's egotists.

Neto and Corrêia co-directed *As duas cômadres* (The Two Women, 1977), about a rich, greedy woman and a poor, generous one; *O grão de milho* (A Grain of Millet, 1979), about a child born on a kernel of millet, and the made-for-television *O papagaio de papel* (The Paper Parrot, 1986). This solid, average-quality cinema represents one of the few cases, outside Eastern European countries, in which national folklore has been brought to the screen.

The meagre ranks of Portuguese animators also include José Carvalho (Lisbon, 1955), author of *Uma história de lêtras* (A Story of Letters, 1980), and Álvaro Graça de Castro Feijó (Braga, 1956), author of the avant-garde *Oh que calma* (What Calm, 1985) and the political *A noite saíu a rua* (The Night Comes to the Street, 1987).

Greece

The first Greek animated film was a 1962 puppet-animation insert made by Ghiorghios Thisikirikis, to be used in Vassilis Gheorghiadis's *Marriage, Greek Style*. This first attempt remained unique until 1969, as Greek animators worked solely on advertising films. In 1969 Thodoros Marangos made Tsou*Tsouf*, with animated drawings and photographic collages; it was a spirited but inconsistent satiric film on money as the engine of all things.

In 1970 Marangos gave a better performance with *Sssst!*, poking fun at politicians' speeches and at their illusory promises to workers. Here also the filmmaker alternated drawings and photos. Still in 1970, Christian Surlos made his debut with *The Hair*, about a man whose hair stood on end every time he was afraid a war might break out. Finally, in 1973 *The Line* by Jannis Kutsuris and Nassos Mirmiridis was shown

at the Zagreb Festival and brought Greek animation into the international arena. The characters had fingerprints as bodies, and a line symbolized the development of human life.

In the feature film *Bio-graphia* (1975), director, movie critic and publisher Thanassis Rentzis used the uncommon technique of moving the camera over the motionless drawings. Based on a subject by the Spanish artist Chumy Chúmez,

> '... [the film] is entitled *Bio-graphia*, because it features a myth of life (bios), using the representation (graphia) of the historic model of man of the last century, which was believed to be universal but which now does not exist anymore'.[1] The film narrates the myths of the 19th century, through the most popular mass-media of the time: print and popular drawing. As Rentzis explained, 'I used colour only for popular effects. The film appears as if it were shown through the lampscope, a slide projector of fixed images of the last century'.

As for Jordan Ananiadis (Salonika, 21 June 1944), his best film was *The Hole* (1983), a brief satiric essay on loneliness. The artist's career began in 1971 with *Banquet*, followed by *Zachos the Masochist* (1979) and *The Circle* (1981). In 1986 he released *Adam* (see Colour Plate 62), a scorching comment on human shortcomings.

---

1 Thanassis Rentzis, personal communication (1977).

Chapter 20

Eastern Europe

Beginning in the 1960s, animation in almost all Eastern European countries underwent artistic and quantitative growth. While many individual artists achieved international recognition, inspired communal spirits did exist, with currents or 'schools' being founded around choices of style or philosophies. This happened most dramatically in Yugoslavia and Poland and in the countries of the former Yugoslavia. In the 1980s, just a few years before the demise of the Soviet Union, animators in the Soviet Republics were finally able to exploit their potential, thanks to the new decentralization of production. Soviet artists were able to abandon the politics of 'service' they had to follow for a long time and to start a period of autonomous work.

Yugoslavia: the new Zagreb film

In 1963, the Zagreb school remained without leaders. Kristl had emigrated to Germany, the politically involved Vukotic[1] was rarely seen in the artistic world, and Mimica had returned to directing live-action films. Another leader, Kostelac, had resumed his advertising career. The solution to this problem was found by promoting the veterans who had worked with the masters of the 1950s, and by searching for new talent.

This 'second phase' of the Zagreb school was characterized by art cinema and by the filmmakers' propensity to write, direct and draw their own films. This notwithstanding, a 'Zagreb style' prevailed and was easily identifiable. According to Ranko Munitic, it was a style which avoided what was collective and strived toward individual models. Within the formula 'uniformity on the basis of individual differences',[2] Zagreb's animators acknowledged that figurative solutions were inimitable outside each artist's system of values.

Spurred by the new generation, the production company, Zagreb Film, gained prestige as one of the major artistic powers in world animation. It did not neglect economic interests, as it favoured international contracts of series productions (such as the well-known *Professor Balthazar* by Grgic-Kolar Zaninovic), advertising assignments and agreements with local television stations for the production of mini-films. During the following decade, the Croatian school maintained its position, timidly renewing its ranks, but faded in the 1980s. Still, due to its influence as well as the work of travelling animator Branko Ranitovic (*Novi becej*, 1925), animation spread to other major Yugoslav cities – Ljubljana (Slovenia), Sarajevo (Bosnia), Belgrade (Serbia) and Skopje (Macedonia) – with new authors and films rising to international attention.

Nedeljko Dragic

Born in Paklenica in 1936, Dragic is one of Zagreb's most acclaimed artists. A well-known cartoonist, he based his first film, *Elegija* (Elegy, 1965), on a subject from one of his comic books. Prior to this, he worked as a designer on short films. He completed his first important work in 1966, directing the screenplay for *Krotitelj divljin konja* (Tamer of Wild Horses) written by Mimica. In 1968, he filmed *Mozda Diogen* (Diogenes Perhaps, 1967), surprisingly innovative and imaginative, and in the following year, *Idu dani* (Passing Days, 1969), just as worthy as its predecessor. Dragic showed his influence in other films as well, as a scene designer in *Ljubitelji cvijeca* (The Flower Lovers, 1970) by Dovnikovic, and as a script-writer in *Covjek koji je morao pjerati* (The Man Who Had to Sing, 1971) by Blazekovic. In 1974, he won the grand prize at the Zagreb Festival for *Dnevnik* (Diary, 1974), a superb example of style which nevertheless owes something to Saul Steinberg's graphic model.

Still, pure graphics are the least important element for Dragic, though he himself is an excellent designer. His cinematic innovation lies in the suppression of believability, and in the creation of a continuously moving and mocking universe as in *The Day I Quit Smoking* (1982), where the environment is highlighted by 'erasure' in contrast to the character's contour. Dragic's world changes its physical appearance, events are tied together by graphic syntheses or simply by separation. Nothing can be considered a reference point for human beings, be they the peaceful little man who is brutalized without reason in *Passing Days*; or the protagonist of *Diogenes Perhaps*, who sees the sky and the stars drip down on him from a window; or the viewers of *Diary*, immersed in a flowing graphic documentary. The uneasy atmosphere created by these images mirrors an unsentimental, desperate view of life.

Zlatko Grgic

Just as Dragic has the humour of grief, Zlatko Grgic (Zagreb 1931 – Montreal, 1988) has the humour of comedy. Grgic made his debut in animation in 1965 at the age of 20 directing *Davolja posla* (The Devil's Work, 1965). Next came *Muzikalno prase* (The Musical Pig, 1965), a snappy film about an unlucky little pig with a gift for singing. *Mali i veliki* (Little and Big, 1966), *Izumitelj cipela* (The Inventor of Shoes, 1967), *Klizi-Puzi* (Twiddle-Twiddle, 1968), the very fine *Optimist i pesimist* (Optimists and Pessimists, 1974), *Ptica i crvek* (The Bird and the Worm, 1977), *Dream Doll* (1979, in collaboration with the Briton Bob Godfrey) and many other films

Fig. 111 (top). Diogenes Perhaps by Nedeljko Dragic (Croatia, Yugoslavia, 1968). Fig. 112 (bottom). Klizi-Puzi by Zlatko Grgic (Croatia, Yugoslavia, 1968).

---

1   During his periodic returns, Vukotic produced at least two major works: *Opera cordis* (1968) and *Ars gratia artis* (1968).

2   Ranko Munitic, *Retrospektiva animiranog filma/Retrospective Animated Films* YU, 6, s.l., s.d. (Zagreb, 1980)

ensued. In the 1980s, he moved to Canada, working in advertising and teaching college courses.

A creative inventor of absurd situations, Grgic is an old-fashioned gagman (not coincidentally, his favourite animator is Tex Avery). *Little and Big*, for instance, is a continuous sequence of hilarious expedients, united by the sole narrative thread of a chase. His entire production as a filmmaker, over a period of about fifteen years, is one of the most imaginative and consistent within the Zagreb school, and structurally, one of the purest. This high quality, however, is diminished by the lack of a pivotal work, and his viewers are left with the feeling that he has never actually proven himself.

Grgic generates liberating laughter which, however, is very different from the classic laughter of comedy's golden age. While his style follows in the wake of Chaplin or Avery, he finds comedy in people's worst feelings, hostility and tension. As other Slavic humorists, he makes fun of the least flattering events of life and avoids happy endings.

Borivoj Dovnikovic

Borivoj 'Bordo' Dovnikovic (born in Osijek in 1930) began working as a comic artist in his youth. One of the oldest members of the school, he was a draftsman in the 'Kerempuh' group and went through the agonizing beginnings of Croatian animation. He made his debut in 1961 with *Lutkica* (The Doll, 1961). Like his fellow countryman Grgic, Dovnikovic displays gagman tendencies in probably his most accomplished work, *Bez naslova* (Without Title, 1964). Winner of several awards, *Without Title* is about a tiny character who attempts to give the best of himself in a movie, but is dislodged by the beginning and end titles which constantly occupy the screen. When the meticulous and exasperating inscriptions finally end, the film ends as well. Another

award winner is *Ceremonija* (Ceremony, 1965): a group of men try to find the best pose for a picture to be taken during a ceremony, which then turns out to be their execution by firing squad.

Usually, Dovnikovic's films are not so much a collection of comic expedients but rather the development of a central idea with variations. For instance, in *Znatizelja* (Curiosity, 1966) the action revolves around a bag of which everybody would like to know the contents, against a moving background of strolling people, the arrival of a boat, etc. Although the bag proves to be empty, the film has built a vivacious, surreal mosaic of events and behaviour. Dovnikovic's humour, noted Ronald Holloway, is combined with an understanding of human psychology.[1]

Among Dovnikovic's films the most successful are *Krek* (1968), *Ljubitelji* (The Flower Lovers) (1970, about the invention of explosive flowers, which begin as a fad but in the end blow up everything and everybody), *Putnik drugog razreda* (The Second Class Passenger, 1974), about a train trip, midway between Kafka and Buster Keaton, *Walking School* (1978, about well-

Fig. 113. Little and Big *by Zlatko Grgic (Croatia, Yugoslavia, 1966).*

1   Ronald Holloway, *Z Is for Zagreb*, (London-Cranbury: Tantivy/Barnes, 1972)

wishers attempting to teach a little boy to walk until the lad finally realizes that his way worked perfectly fine anyway) and *A Day in the Life* (1982, where a factory worker, stuck in a grey and monotonous life, briefly finds enthusiasm while celebrating with an old friend).

Dovnikovic is the herald of the common people and their daily trials. In the world he describes, incomprehensible and unsympathetic, human beings are merely pieces in a puzzle, striving to find a logical justification for being.

Boris Kolar

Kolar (born in Zagreb, in 1933) worked as a member of the 'Kerempuh' group and at Duga Film before beginning a long collaboration with Vukotic as a set designer and a draftsman. He painted scenes for shorts made by his colleagues

and wrote ideas for other works. As an auteur he is known particularly for *Vau, Vau!* (Woof, Woof!, 1964). Despite its simple plot centred on a dog, a cat and a mouse, *Vau, Vau!* contains graphics far ahead of its time, translating every physiological trait into pure charcoal hints. In 1968, he attracted notice with the brilliant *Otkrovitelj* (The Inventor, 1968). Kolar distinguishes himself from other artists by his graphic inclination; for him, animation is above all a means to create expressive, avant-garde drawings.

Zlatko Bourek

Born in 1929 in Slavonska Pozega, Bourek began his career in animation in 1957, after graduating as a scene-designer from the Fine Arts Academy of Zagreb. In 1961, with *Kovacev segrt* (Blacksmith's Apprentice, 1961), he began making his own movies while still collaborating on other artists' works. He was responsible for the splendid scene designs in Dragic's *Krotitelj divljin konja* (The Tamer of Wild Horses). Only in 1968 did Bourek become famous in his own right with *Kapetan Arbanas Marko* (Captain Arbanas Marko, 1968).

More than an animator, Bourek is also a theatrical scene designer and a painter who holds a prominent position among the contemporary painters in the former Yugoslavia. His needs as a figurative artist emerge through his obsessive and lucid graphics in his cinematic creations. As the spiritual successor of Vlado Kristl, Bourek has brought the art direction of the Zagreb school up to date.

Bourek finds inspiration from legends, enriching his palette with the colours of icons and traditional art. With his inclination, he has brought to Zagreb that attention to popular traditions which was a characteristic of socialist countries and which had been less developed in Yugoslavia than elsewhere. *Captain Arbanas Marko* is the quintessential setting for an Albanian ballad. *Becarac* (Dancing Songs, 1966) is a clear display of

Fig. 114. Walking School *by Borivoj Dovnikovic (Croatia, Yugoslavia, 1978).*
Fig. 115. Vau, Vau! *by Boris Kolar (Croatia, Yugoslavia, 1964).*

Bourek's involvement with tradition. The excellent *Macka* (The Cat, 1971, see Colour Plate 63) is a more creative work, although it suffers from an inadequate sound track (with a song by the Italian Franco Potenza).

Ante Zaninovic

Born in Belgrade in 1934, Zaninovic attended the Academy of Fine- Arts in Zagreb and began his artistic career as a draftsman. In 1964, he made his debut as a director with *Truba* (The Trumpet, 1964). The major achievements of his productive career include many of his early movies, such as *Zid* (The Wall, 1965) and *O rupama i cepovima* (Of Holes and Corks, 1967). *The Wall* is a moral parable about two kinds of men: the one who kills himself trying to open the wall blocking his path, and the one who goes through the hole opened by the first man. *Of Holes and Corks*, showing the struggle between a series of small volcanoes and a man who hopes to plug them, is a movie about destiny.

Although Zaninovic is often the animator of his own movies, his role as a narrator should be emphasized. Only in the most recent works, such as *Allegro Vivace* or *The Representation* (both of 1983) has he focused more on the formal or spectacular aspects of production. Among his Croatian colleagues, he can be defined as the most gifted scriptwriter, and it is this quality which has contributed heavily to the success of the aforementioned Professor Balthazar series.

Marks & Jutrisa

Aleksandar Marks (Cazma, 1922) and Vladimir Jutrisa (Zagreb, 1923–1984) found a mentor in Vatroslav Mimica, for whom they worked respectively as draftsman and animator. When the director of *Everyday Chronicle* left the country, Marks and Justrisa joined efforts. In 1966, they released their first important production, *Muha* (The Fly, 1966), a nightmarish movie about a

man obsessed by a fly which assumes gigantic dimensions, finally approaching him and taking up a dangerous co-habitation. In 1967, the duo made *Sizif* (Sisyphus, 1967), about the struggle between objects and man, from a subject by Kolar. Three years later, they released *Pauk* (The Spider, 1970) – another tormented story of a man imprisoned in a dark basement with a horrid spider. *Ecce Homo* (1972, a collaboration with the Italian Max Massimino-Garnier), *Homo 2* (1973), *The Nightmare* (1977) and *Opsesija* (The Obsession, 1983) followed. The two artists' production is dominated by an atmosphere of

Fig. 116. Zid by *Ante Zaninovic (Croatia, Yugoslavia, 1965).* *Fig. 117.* Muha by *A. Marks and V. Jutrisa (Croatia, Yugoslavia, 1966).*

horror, fear and decay as well as by themes from Poe, Hoffmann and Kafka. The excellent drawings by Marks, inspired by the Viennese Secession, are finely animated by Jutrisa, possibly one of the major European creators of animated movement.

Pavao Stalter

Considered among the best scene designers of the Zagreb school along with Zlatko Bourek, Pavao Stalter (Karanac, 1929) was a restorer of ancient paintings until Bourek himself introduced him to animation in 1957. Overall, Stalter had directed his efforts to painting scenery for other artists' films; consequently, his work as a director is quite minimal. One such effort, co-directed with Branko Ranitovic, is the exceptional *Maska crvene smrti* (Mask of the Red Death, 1969), based on the story by Edgar Allan Poe. The movie shines for the plastic qualities of painting, complementing the original text, and can be properly defined as a masterpiece in the genre of animated horror movies. In 1984, Stalter made *House No. 42*, another excellent although stylis-

tically very different film, describing customs in the early twentieth century with a slow, light rhythm and ballet-like qualities.

Zdenko Gasparovic

The best film ever to come out of the studio on the Sava river is the result of the uneven career of Zdenko Gasparovic (Pakrac, 1937). Coming to animation in 1957, for several years Gasparovic worked as an animator of series. In 1966, he directed the unpretentious short *Pasji zivot* (A Dog's Life, 1966); whereupon he moved to North America, dividing his life between California and Canada and his interests between advertising and series. Among others, he worked with Hanna & Barbera. Returning home, he continued to work on series, working on *Kisobran* (The Umbrella, 1972) – a 1972 first episode of a series which never took off – and some episodes of *Professor Balthazar*. Finally, in 1978 he released *Satiemania*, where piano music by Erik Satie acts as the connecting

Fig. 118 (left). Maska crvene smrti by P. Salter and B. Ranitovic (Croatia, Yugoslavia, 1969). Fig. 119 (right). Satiemania by Zdenko Gasparovic (Croatia, Yugoslavia, 1978).

link for images of women in love, bored women, the Grand Canyon and Montparnasse, bars, brothels and supermarkets, breasts, butchered beef and boats in the rain. Grotesque and sensual, the film is a long voyage inside the subconscious where the influences of Otto Dix or George Grosz mix with those of underground comics, Reginald Marsh, Covarrubias and Ralph Steadman. *Satiemania* won the grand prize at the 1978 Zagreb festival, and innumerable awards all over the world.

Josko Marusic

Born in Spalato, Dalmatia (1952), Josko Marusic studied architecture at Zagreb University. Quite early he distinguished himself for his satirical drawings. In 1977 he filmed his first short animated movie, *From Inside and Out* followed by *Perpetual* (1978), *Riblje oko* (Fisheye, 1979), *Neboder* (Skyscraper, 1981) (see Colour Plate 64) and *The Face of Fear* (1986). *Fisheye*, about the nocturnal revenge of the fish against a fishermen's village, is a horror movie. Characterized by few colours with a predominance of black, *Fisheye* is weakened solely by an excessively anthropomorphic rendition of the animals. *Skyscraper* is a funny, paradoxical depiction of the events which take place in a big housing complex with no front walls, so that the spectator can view all the events simultaneously (in a sort of split-screen device achieved within the drawing). *The Face of Fear* depicts the fantasies of a child on the verge of falling asleep, with familiar objects taking strange shapes. *Home Sweet Home* (1988) is a biting comedy on domestic life.

One of the best among Zagreb Film's new generation, Marusic is an eclectic artist who enjoys devoting his talent and style completely to each project. As with the majority of his peers, Marusic also seems to prefer the themes of absurdity and power, and directs his richest inspiration toward laughter and the grotesque.

Other Artists

Dragutin Vunak (Pitomaca, 1929) distinguished himself with *Krava na granici* (A Cow on the Frontier, 1963) and *Izmedu usana i case* (Between Lips and Glass, 1968). Zvonimir Loncaric (Zagreb, 1927), an architect, painter and potter, is responsible for the set design for several movies, such as the remarkable *Sagrenska koza* (La peau de chagrin) by Vrbanic-Kristl; and as a director he is remembered for *1 + 1 = 1*. Milan Blazekovic (Zagreb, 1940) has amused and upset spectators with *The Man Who Had to Sing* (1971) about a little man who repeats the same tune obsessively, even after his death. Draftsman Zlatko Pavlinic (Zagreb, 1944) made, among other films, *Happiness* (1976). Finally, musicians Tomica Simovic (Zagreb, 1931) and Igor Savin (Zagreb, 1946) should also be mentioned together with Zelimir Matko (1929–77), the studio's director who was for many years a wise, hard-working and farsighted producer.

Beyond Zagreb

Besides the studios of the Croatian capital that were mainly involved in the advertising or educational fields (such as in the case of Filmoteka 16), numerous individual artists and groups have distinguished themselves in other states of the old federation. First among them was Neoplanta Film, in Serbian Novi Sad, with the talented Borislav Sajtinac (Melenci, 1943) and Nikola Majdak (Valjevo, 1927) who worked for the studio in the 1960s and 1970s. Sajtinac, an excellent satirist with a gift for black humour, released his first film, *Analiza* (Analysis), in 1968. In 1969, in collaboration with Majdak, Sajtinac made *Izvor zivota* (The Spring of Life, 1969) about the healing powers of a biblical spring. Afterward, he released *Nije ptica sve sto leti* (Not All That Flies Is a Bird, 1970), *Nevesta* (The Bride, 1971 – first prize winner at the Festival of Annecy) and *Don Kihot* (Don Quixote, 1972). Having moved to Germany, first to Essen and later to Munich, he continued producing short films, such as *Befreiung der Hauptperson* (The Liberation of the Principal Person, 1973), *Wir sind viele* (We Are Many, 1975), *Der Meister* (The Master, 1981) and feature films such as *Nicht alles was fliegt ist ein Vogel* (Not Everything That Flies Is a Bird, 1978, which shares the same title as the 1970 short)[1] and *Harold und die Geister* (Harold and the Spirits, 1982). Described by critic Ranko Munitic as one of the most interesting animators, Sajtinac creates a poetically absurd world of his own, with dark colours, gloomy spaces and grotesque drawings. His films are characterized by sequences showing different degrees of intensity, by speeded-up or slowed down rhythms and a visionary mood within the style of black humour.'[2]

Zoran Jovanovic, director of *Zastave* (The Flags, 1973) and the Nikola Rudic–Rade Ivanovic team *Crni dan* (A Gloomy Day, 1969); *Rat i mir* (War and Peace, 1970); *Jednakost* (Equality, 1973), also worked at Novi Sad. In 1970, the studio released a live-action film, *Gastronauti* (The Gastronaut, 1970), directed by Branislav Obradovic with drawings by Borivoj Dovnikovic. As for Nikola Majdak, he produced several valuable movies, such as *The World of Silence* (1979) and *The Last Ray of Sun* (1980). In Belgrade

during the early 1960s, he directed *Solista* (Soloist, 1963), *Covek od krede* (The Chalk Man, 1963) and *S.O.S.* (Letter From the Sea, 1964). In 1971, in collaboration with Belgrade-born Dusan Petricic, he filmed *Vrijeme vampira* (The Time of Vampires, 1971) his finest movie, a horror-comedy produced by Zagreb Film and the Belgrade based Dunav Film.

Still in Serbia: in the field of animated puppets, some work was done in Belgrade, in the 1950s. Later on, this line of production expanded, particularly for made-on-commission movies. Among production companies, Dunav Film rose with the help of the already mentioned animators from Novi Sad and other Belgrade-based artists. Vera Vlajic *Uvo* (The Ear, 1975); *She*, 1975; *Chiromancy*, or *As I Read Myself*, 1985) deserves a special nod for *The Moustache* (1980), a fanciful, lively work despite its lack of compactness. The movie's drawings are by the aforementioned Dusan Petricic (Belgrade, 1946), who gained international recognition as the director of *Romeo i Julija vilija sekspira u izvodenju trupe 'Monstrumi i Druzina'* (Romeo and Juliet, 1984), a very comical and intelligent version of the classic text, with terrifying monsters as protagonists. Rastko Ciric (Belgrade, 24 May 1955) made *The Tower of Lalel*, the extravagant tale of a man whose life passes before his eyes when he falls from an immeasurably tall tower.

Miki Muster, a Disney-inspired cartoonist who is very popular in his native Slovenia, made Ljubljana's first animated movies: *Puscica* (The Arrow, 1960), *Kurir Nejcek* (Nejcek the Courier, 1961), *Zimska zgodba* (Adventure in Winter, 1962) and *The Activist* (1977). Zagreb-born animators (Ranitovic, Gasparovic, Grgic) and Polish ones (Kijowicz, Giersz) also worked in Ljubljana. As for experimental films, Crt Skodlar (*Jutro,*

Fig. 120. Vrijeme vampira *by Nikola Majdak (Croatia-Serbia, Yugoslavia, 1971).*

---

1   *Nicht alles was fliegt is ein Vogel* is a hybrid, made out of original short and several other shorts plus some original material.
2   Ranko Munitic, 'Off Zagreb, Yugoslav Animated Film 1960–1980', *Animafilm*, No. 8. (Warsaw, 1981) p. 21.

jezero i vecer v Annecyju (The Morning, the Lake and the Evening at Annecy, 1965) and *Sinteticna komika* (Synthetic Comedy, 1967)) was much admired alongside Zvonko Coh, whose *Kiss Me, Gentle Eraser* won at the 1984 Zagreb festival.

In Bosnia's Sarajevo, animated works were quite sporadic, with some exceptions in the early 1960s such as *Nokturno* (Nocturne, 1964) by Vafik Hadzismailovic. In Skopje, Macedonia, the two predominant artists were Petar Gligorovski and Darko Markovic. Gligorovski (*Embrio No. M*, (1912); *Adam*, 1977; *Phoenix*, 1977; *The Last Window* 1979, and *The Hand*, 1980 among others) invented an aerograph technique which makes colour vibrate. Markovic distinguished himself for *Oats*, a 40-minute production for Macedonian television.

Poland: the poetry of pessimism

In the early 1960s, Poland joined the small group of countries which were world leaders in quality animation. Polish production increased greatly (up to 120 animation movies per year) due to the quasi-official decision to devote 20 per cent of production to experimental work. After the turmoil of 1965, Polish authorities allowed forms of artistic expression beyond socialist realism. As a consequence, the lessons drawn from Lenica's and Borowczyk's works of the 1950s were combined with the seemingly unlimited suggestiveness of contemporary Polish graphics – one of the most creative and advanced in the world. Thus, the Polish 'school' became a centre for all kinds of audiences.

One of the school's foremost characteristics is a preference for dark-toned images (black, nuances of grey and fogs) and gloomy themes, mostly marked by existential questioning and a sometimes heavy, sometimes scorching pessimism. Gianni Rondolino wrote:

'This basic pessimism ... reflects the unique historical-political situation which in the mid-1960s in Poland took a different course from that in the other socialist countries. The artists and intellectuals reacted to the inconsistencies of the bureaucratic state and its consequent delusions with negative criticism, pessimistically emphasizing the tragic events within a hopeless individual and social reality. Political denunciation broadens to involve the human being, and the representation of daily life becomes the drama of humanity, enclosed in a universe with unrecognizable boundaries. Hence, the symbolism of these films, the bitterness of their images and slow rhythms and their dry, anti-entertaining style which does not leave anything to more facile figurative or narrative seductions.'[1]

The Polish school has not been immune to internal imitations, mannerisms, exercises in formality and decorativeness. As a whole, however, the more than 20-year contribution to world animation by Polish artists has been one of the most incisive and stimulating of the post-war age.

Miroslaw Kijowicz

Kijowicz was born in Leningrad (St Petersburg) in 1929, the son of a general in the Austro-Hungarian army who was captured by the Russians in 1915, defected to the Bolsheviks after the Revolution but was harshly persecuted under Stalin. The filmmaker still remembers when, as a child, he brought soup to his father, an immate in Stalin's prisons.[2] In 1937, he returned to Poland. During World War II he fought with the Partisans and witnessed other atrocities. When the hostilities ended, he graduated in fine arts from the University of Warsaw, worked as an art critic and a painter and, in 1957, became involved in animation as an amateur. In 1960, he made his professional debut in the field. His first

---

1   Gianni Rondolino, *Storia del cinema d'animazione*, (Torino: Einaudi, 1974), p. 239.
2   Miroslaw Kijowicz, personal communication (1971, 1986).

notable work, a criticism of contemporary society entitled *Miasto* (The Town, 1963), was released in 1963.

In 1965, Kijowicz made *Sztandar* (The Flag, 1965). In this film everybody is made to march in line during a parade, holding identical flags, except for one man who has no flag and searches for it frantically. In the end, this antisocial character finds his flag and returns to his line. *Usmiech* (The Smile, 1966) shows the unsuccessful efforts of a sculptor trying to carve a smile into a statue. *The Blue Ball* (1968, see Colour Plate 65) is an allegory of the human being who, like Sisyphus, aimlessly pushes a blue ball until it falls into the sea. *Klatki* (Cages, 1966) is a beautiful aphorism for oppression, showing the long-lasting, ambiguous relationship between an immate and his warden, who will later discover that he also is somebody's prisoner, who is somebody else's prisoner, and so on.

In 1971, he filmed *Which Way*, another disquieting aphorism for human destiny, followed by the sarcastic *A-B* (1979, on the tight-lipped consensus obtained through power) and the meditative *Conversation On the Train* (1984, on the repetitiveness of human life). The most committed of the Polish filmmakers, Kijowicz nevertheless believed that the artist should 'seldom judge, never accuse'.

Kijowicz's films are packed with doubt. In his words, an artist's task is to inculcate doubt in the spectators and let them come up with a solution. As for animation, he maintains that it is:

> '... a plebeian artform, a popular one; just as theatre, which in Poland has a very ancient tradition. But "popular" does not imply "simplistic". The language of animation is recent, not easily understood by everybody, but this does not prevent artists from expressing themselves in the way they find the most advanced. I try to make a *commedia dell'arte*,

CARTOONS
Bendazzi

342

to tell the limited audiences of Polish animation movies the story of their lives, just as troubadours used to tell villagers the stories of the hamlet. Then, if these small things become symbols of a universal way of being, so much the better.'

Stylistically, Kijowicz 'does not consider animated drawings as animated plastic art. He is not interested in forms. The plastic value of his films can be found in relation to the values of their subject matter.'[1] Among techniques he favours the animation of cut outs and has frequently combined baroque settings (often cityscapes from old prints) with linear, caricature-like figures.

Daniel Szczechura

Conflicts (1960) is the first movie by Szczechura (Wilczogeby, 11 July 1930). A more important work is *The Machine* (1962), where many people are busy building a huge machine, which turns out to be ... a pencil sharpener. Based on a subject by Miroslaw Kijowicz, who was also responsible for the setting, the film shows a still immature Szczechura. An even better work is *Fotel* (The Armchair, 1963), a bitter satire on careerism. In a large conference room, shot constantly from above, a savage fight takes place among the contenders to the president's chair.

Progressively, Szczechura dampened his ironic fire to a sadder, more meditative tone. This second stage in the artist's career began with *Hobby* (1968), about a diabolic woman's attempts to trap and cage winged men. A finer work is *The Trip* (1969). From the window of a train, a man watches the telephone poles go by, in a monotonous, exasperatingly protracted sequence. Once arrived, the man (whose face is never shown), finds his village empty and his house abandoned. Returning to the train, he continues his obsessive trip. In 1978, Szczechura directed *Skok* (The Jump, 1978), about the domestic life of a man who plans to kill himself. In 1983, he made *Dip-*

1   Andrzey Kossakowski, 'Miroslaw Kijowicz,' *Projekt* l, No. 80 (Warsaw, 1971).

tych – *Morgana the Fairy I, Morgana the Fairy II*, probably his best work, where the moving images of buildings and surf interact in a silent exchange creating an atmosphere of sadness and expectation. *XYZ* (1987) shows the surreal trip of a man reading a newspaper.

Szczechura displays an achingly Nordic sense of evil. His dramatic works differ from his satiric ones only in style, while the inspiration and themes follow a logical order in the artist's production. Instead of sharpening his humour, he has become more sorry for himself and his peers, and has reached a melancholy, detached contemplation – *Diptych* – where still unresolved tensions seem like evanescent images.

Stefan Schabenbeck

Schabenbeck (Zakopane, 1940) emerged from anonymity in 1967 with *Wszystko jest liczba* (Everything Is a Number) which he directed and for which he created drawings, script, subject and

photography. The film tells the tale of a man who wanders around in a world of numbers, geometry and figures. Despite his efforts to resist, he too becomes a number – a 'number one' which marches in line with other 'number ones'.

In 1968, Schabenbeck used a similar theme in *Exclamation Mark*, where a swarming mass of people try to push a huge ball onto a pedestal. The ball falls, leaving a track of crushed bodies shaped like a large exclamation mark.

One year later, the Polish artist filmed his most vibrant work entitled *Schody* (The Stairs, 1969). Made with animated plasticine, the film features a little man climbing a series of intersecting steep, white-washed stairs. When the man reaches the top, exhausted, he himself becomes a step. After *Susza* (The Drought, 1970), on a similar theme, Schabenbeck had a second success with *Wiatr* (The Wind, 1970). A film characterized more as 'painted' than 'drawn', *The Wind* is a slow, moving poem about the fight for knowledge. Nobody

Fig. 121. The Trip by Daniel Szczechura (Poland, 1969).

can catch a letter which is swirled around by the wind; and when a man eventually manages to grab it, the wind pulls it away. Still, the man doesn't give up. Also in 1970, Schabenbeck made *Inwazja* (The Invasion, 1970), which is a statement against the dangers of technology.

Schabenbeck is one of the greatest but least known authors of contemporary Polish animation. Taking a polemical stand against de-personalization and the coldness of technology, he portrays the struggle of human beings to defend their values as individuals (*Everything Is a Number*) and members of a society (*The Exclamation Mark*), and in the hope of a better future (*The Wind*). As the film *The Stairs* clearly indicates (is the man at the top a winner or a loser?), the

painful act of research is what touches the artist the most: to him, human grandeur resides in suffering, not in results.

Ryzsard Czekala

Czekala (Bydgoszcz, 5 March 1941) became a renowned director of animation films with *The Bird* (1968), a remarkable work with a thesis (the protagonist saves money to buy a bird, which he eventually sets free), but still far from the level Czekala would later reach.

The Son (1970) is the story of a man who returns to his father's farmhouse and finds that he no longer has anything in common with his parents, thus establishing a co-existence of two solitudes. In 1971, the director made his best animated work, *The Appeal*. Set in a Nazi prison camp, it

Fig. 122 (right). Everything Is a Number *by Stefan Schabenbeck (Poland, 1967).*

Fig. 123 (below). The Stairs *by Stefan Schabenbeck (Poland, 1969).*

is a scorching drama dealing with oppression, violence and dignity. The same year he made his debut in live action films with *The Accident* followed by *The Day* (1973), *Zofia* (1976) and other live-action works. This interest in live-action absorbed him almost completely for years, but still he found time for *Autopsia* (1973), an animated story about a murder committed by a woman and described retrospectively, *Water* (1975), about a man fishing in a bath tub, and *Till the Heads Roll* (1987).

Czekala is a creator of moods. His lumpy, out-of-focus images emerge from the fogs of memory and evoke chilling times. Stylistically, with his use of foregrounds, details, long pauses and unusual shots, he owes more to live action cinema than to graphics. His elliptical discourse is often difficult for spectators to follow (as in the arduous narrative of *Autopsia*, a manneristic, involuted work). Whenever he does manage to capture the core of a problem, though, (as in *The Son* and *The Appeal*) these choices yield surprising results. Czekala is not aided by the use of colour. His mists or gleams of light thrive with a palette of greys, whereas the pale tones of *Autopsia* largely deprive the movie of its evocative power.

Jerzy Kucia

Jerzy Kucia (Soltysy, 14 January 1942) directed his first animated film, *The Return*, in 1972. A passenger alone in a train compartment reflects on memories of his youth. Eventually, he joins other people as they begin their daily activities. The film was followed by *The Elevator* (1974), *In the Shadow* (1975, a delicate portrait of a girl on a swing), *The Railway Crossing* (1976), *The Circle* (1978), *The Window* (1979), *Refleksy* (Reflections, 1979), *Springtime* (1980), *The Spring* (1982), *Chips* (1984) and *The Parade* (1987). All these works are characterized by an extraordinary precision of form and an almost ascetic style (not by chance was he called the 'Bresson of animation').[1] They strike the viewer with their compact inspiration, their imagery and their coherence, independent of which technique was used – simple drawings, special effects or the use of live action images. Kucia's cinema describes moods, recollections and the ghosts of the mind, without neglecting even the most routine, least important objective realities. (The example

which comes to mind is *Refleksy*, the tragic story of an insect's birth, struggle and death, overwhelmed by the flat soundtrack of a Sunday in the outskirts of the city.)

With journalistic precision, Kucia depicts even banal phenomena, but holds back from colouring them with an author's intention. As he himself acknowledged during an interview, his experiences are of the 'sensual', perceptive kind,[2] and for good reasons his films have been described as 'impressionistic'.[3] Such an attitude should not be interpreted as cold rationalism.

> 'I've always displayed an emotional attitude toward problems, and I want to attract viewers emotionally ...'

he said, and indeed, his viewers perceive a doleful feeling of estrangement and the awareness of being nothing more than witnesses. An example of this can be found in *Wood Shavings*, a film dominated by darkness from which the images of simple household activities and memories emerge sporadically as in a useless autobiography.

> 'I am witness of my times,' Kucia said on another occasion, 'and some of my films can be my own personal notes on life, although they seem to refer to insignificant problems'.[4]

In fact, the entire meaning of his production goes beyond the poetics of small things; he gives an existential dimension to suffering which surpasses the generic pessimism so frequent among Polish filmmakers.

A master of black and white, who sporadically chooses to employ colours and does so with originality (as the green in *Springtime*), Jerzy Kucia

1   Marcin Gizycki, 'Jerzy Kucia: Between Reality and Dream/ Jerzy Kucia: entre le rêve et la réalité', *Animafilm*, No. 8 (Warsaw, 1981).
2   Alina Terechowicz, 'It Takes Quite a Bit of One's Life to Make One Film/Chaque film demande un morceau de ma vie', *Animafilm*, No. 8 (Warsaw, 1981).
3   Marcin Gizycki, 'Kucia'.
4   Alina Terechowicz, 'It Takes Quite a Bit'.

is attracted by both the images of live action and the techniques of animation. Formally, he is the bearer of an autonomous style which manages to solve syncretically the distinctions of cinematic genres.

Experiments, craftmanship and sarcasm

Among the other Polish animators, Witold Giersz (Poraj, 26 February 1927) broke with conventional style. After a few years of training and an unremarkable debut (with *The Mystery of the Old Castle*, 1956), in 1960 he released *Little Western Movie*, which laid the foundation for the development of Polish animation. Giersz experimented with oil paint as a material to be animated; colours became characters who, in turn, made comic gags (the most popular was the yellow figure mixing with a blue one and giving life to a green character).

Within the course of a productive career, Giersz made purely professional works as well as art films such as *Czerwone i czarne* (The Red and the Black, 1963) with two spots of colour acting out a bullfight. In *Kon* (The Horse, 1967), the animation of oil paint reaches the highest levels of formality, with a suggestive atmosphere. Featuring tissue paper ballerinas, *The Wait* (1962) makes an elegant show of puppet animation. *Be My Guest, Elephant* (1978) is a traditional feature film.

Kazimierz Urbanski (born in 1929) is also an experimentalist who has transposed his own experiences and curiosity as a painter into animated works. Although his productions revolve around a theme, he used them mostly as media to express a formal discourse. His main achievement is probably *The Charm of The Two Wheels* (1967).

Another painter and set designer was Jerzy Zitzman (Wadowice, 1918). His production also is characterized more by an interest in figure and

colour than plot as in his *Bulandra and the Devil* (1959), *Don Juan* (1962, a demystification of the famous seducer) and *Romeo and Juliet* (1969).

The most experimental among Polish filmmakers in recent years has been Zbigniew Rybczynski, who won a grand prize at the Annecy Festival and an Oscar with *Tango* (1980). Rybczynski (born in 1949) is more of a magician in a Georges Méliès vein than an animator in the traditional sense of the word, as the majority of his films testify. An example is *Nowa ksiazka* (The New Book, 1975), a live-action film made using the split-screen technique, with actions taking place simultaneously in the nine sections of the screen. In the 1980s he moved to the U.S., where he has been working on rock videos. *Tango* is based on the 'loop' concept – the constant repetition of the same movie excerpt. A ball is thrown through a window. A boy jumps over the window sill, enters the room, retrieves the ball and leaves. An instant later, the ball is thrown again, the boy returns and everything is repeated. But now a second character enters the scene to perform his own activity, which he will repeat incessantly. A third character follows, then others, until there are thirty people, minding their own business without caring for the others and without even stepping into each other despite the crowding. This absurd dance or tango ceases when everybody leaves. A spiritually rich artist who extracts from his inventions all the spectacularity they can possibly offer, Rybczynski is mainly a magician. As his collegue Daniel Szczechura wrote, 'his art films show the vision of cinema typical of the operator, for whom filmstock and creation, the camera and its possibilities, the laboratory and the work of art hold no mystery, but rather allow for unsuspected effects'.[1]

Other specialists should be noted for their professionalism, even wprking in mass production. A

---

1   Daniel Szczechura, 'Rybczynski: un nouveau regard sur le cinema,' *Banc-Titre*, No. 17 (Paris, December 1981), p. 5.

teacher and educational direc-tor, Jerzy Kotowski (1925–79) worked also as an animator of puppets and cuttings. His films include the anti-fascist *The Shadow of Time* (1964), *Horizon* (1970) and *A Razor in the Glass* (1974).

Wladyslaw Nehrebecki (1923–1978), already mentioned, obtained some success with *The Tournament* (1959), a knightly tournament like a game of chess, and *Beyond Woods, Beyond Forests* (1961). He attained notoriety, however, with the two little brothers Bolek and Lolek, protagonists of a series of more than one hundred episodes, sold to over eighty countries. In 1977, he made a feature film entitled *Bolek and Lolek's Long Trip*.

Edward Sturlis (1927–1980), assistant to senior animator Zenon Wasilewski and formerly a movie actor, put his acting experience into the animation of puppets. His characters give remarkable performances in many films, including the Greek trilogy *Damon* (1958), *Bellerofonte* (1959) and *Orpheus and Eurydice* (1962), *The Little Quartet* (1965) and *The Man and the Angel* (1966).

A new group of talented, albeit not always genial, artists swept Polish animation from the 1960s to the 1980s. Zdzislaw Kudla (Wesola, 1937) received praise for *The Paving* (1971) and *The Noises of the Forest* (1975), a mix of horror film and surrealism. Krzysztof Nowak (1940) and Zbigniew Kaminski (Poznan, 1947) released *The Kerbstones* (1972), where an anguishing, dim atmosphere is depicted with the minimum use of material. Ryszard Antoniszczak (Nowy Sacz, 1947) has brought a cheerful note to the generally gloomy production with *Fantamobile* (1976) and *Sexy Lola Automatic* (1979). Ewa Bibanska also has made relaxed, light-hearted works such as the refreshing, partly autobiographical *Unfaithful Portrait* (1981). Marian Cholerek (born in 1946) made *Night Flights* (1978), an ironic example of social denunciation told through the story of a lover forced to escape by hanglider from a house of adultery. Jerzy Kalina (Garwolin, 1944) is renowned for *The Bermuda Triangle* (1979), where the mystery of the Triangle is shown as documentary, fiction and science-fiction.

Andrzej Warchal (Krakow, 1943) made *The Pigeon* (1977) and *Retrospection* (1977), followed in 1980 by the touching *Anna*, about the letter written by a prisoner to his lover (in actuality the letter written by the filmmaker's father from a Nazi concentration camp in Oswiecim).

Finally, Bronislaw Zeman and Piotr Dumala have distinguished themselves within a current of grotesque movies, characterized by the humour of cruelty. Zeman (Starawies, 1939) is author of the excruciatingly amusing and ferocious *Och! Och!* (1972), on the construction of a bridge over a newborn island. In *Jokes In the Park* (1982), a bully's abuse of a little man and the revenge of the latter serve as pretext for an excellent comedy and political agenda. Dumala (Warsaw, 1956) made his debut with *Lycanthropy* (1981), followed by the sadistic comedy *Little Black Riding Hood* (1983), where the elegant black and white drawings of unbridled imagination are enough to excuse the lack of good-taste and poor rhythm.

Hungary: art and entertainment

From the production of the first Hungarian art films by the Macskassy-Varnai duo in the 1960s, Hungarian animation has undergone a constant artistic and industrial evolution. One of the principal authors of this development was György Matolcsy (Kecskemet, 9 May 1930), an iron-fisted manager, scholar and critic of animation movies. In the 1960s, under his leadership the national studio Pannonia diversified its production, continuing with traditional children's shorts, but giving more space to adult cinema. Senior animator Gyula Macskassy was one of the best artists, dominating the field of animation for adults until his untimely death in 1971. His works include *A Romantic Story* (1964), *The Great Man* (1968), and three films made in 1970, *The Success*, *Assistance* and *Behind Bars*.

In 1961, production began for the first episode of *Arthur*, a series in eight episodes, under the direction of a group of new artists led by Attila Dargay. The series *Gusztav* was created in 1964. From a successful short by Jozsef Nepp, it revolved around a typical ambitious and unlucky comic hero. Jozsef Nepp, Attila Dargay, Marcell Jankovics and Bela Ternovszky among others, worked on the more than 120 episodes. The first series with animated puppets, *Memories of a Hunter*, was released in 1968 with direction by Otto Foky and Istvan Imre.

In 1968 the economic reforms in Hungary ended the rigid state planning of Stalin's communism. With new laws giving more autonomy to businesses (or even independence in the mid-1980s), the production company Pannonia had to deal with issues of quality as well as profitability. The results were an admirable balance of commercial and experimental works, with an overall production of clever films. Pannonia strove to find consonance with the taste and culture of audiences rather than adapting to their most superficial preferences. This can be seen in the 26 episodes of the series *Magyar népmések* (Hungarian Popular Tales, 1977–79, coordinated by Marcell Jankovics) – a colourful production influenced by folkloric culture and early 19th Century art. Another of Pannonia's accomplishments was the successful feature film *Lúdas Matyi* (Matt the Gooseboy, 1976) by Attila Dargay, which was viewed by over one fifth of the country.

Feature films were a new frontier for Hungarian animators in the early 1970s. The very first one was *Janos the Knight* (1973) by Marcell Jankovics. In the following 15 years, a special section of Pannonia devoted exclusively to feature films released a record 18 works. Some of these were international co-productions, as part of the entrepreneurial plan adopted by management at the production company. As confirmation of this prosperity, two branches were opened, in Kecskemet (1971) and in Pecs (1979).

Beside Pannonia, small production establishments devoted mainly to advertising thrived in the mid-1980s; some animators were also lured abroad by good contracts and abandoned their creative work. Animation still flourished, although less methodically. One of the most distinguished artists was Marcell Jankovics (Budapest, 1941), who put his hand to a wide range of works, some more, some less ambitious. He alternated a busy career as a professional (he produced a series of children's movies and worked as an art director) with the creation of art films, including the caustic *Hídavatás* (Grand Opening, 1969). The satirical humour of this film was later reprised in *Az élet vize* (The Water Of Life, 1971), the story of a very important person who, unable to cut the ribbon during the ceremonial opening of a bridge, destroys the bridge itself. *Mélyvíz* (SOS, 1970) displays beautiful black-and-white drawings in repetitive motion which represent a drowning man's floundering. In *Sisyphus* (1974), made with the same style of drawing, human efforts are directed toward setting a

Fig. 124. Sisyphus by Marcell Jankovics (Hungary, 1974).

boulder on top of a mountain. The boulder grows in the process; once it is in place, other boulders must be pushed onto the mountain.

In 1973, Jankovics completed the feature film *János Vitéz* (Johnny Corncob, 1973), in which the folkloric style of Hungarian drawing merges with reminiscences of the Viennese Secession. Based on a famous story by poet Sándor Petöfi (whom the film intended to honour on the one hundred fiftieth anniversary of his birth), *Johnny Corncob* moves from the description of daily life to the narration of wartime events, to myth and fairy-tale.

> 'I am certain that a true renewal of animation films is not possible without leaving the restricted world of caricature, toward more poetic, more philosophic contents,' Jankovics said. ' ... Without poetry, I feel today's animated drawings are meaningless.'[1]

Son of the White Horse (Fehérlofia, 1980) (see Colour Plate 66) is a successful amalgam of various pictorial styles (particularly Art Nouveau and Art Déco), popular legends and mythical structures (Jankovics wrote an extended essay on fairytales in preparation for the film). The white mare is the incarnation of one of three thoughtless queens who had freed the Devil. Her Herculean son is destined to defeat the Evil One and bring Good back to the Earth. Jankovics knows how to organize a vast culture and blends it with technique and original inspiration. A curious and eclectic talent, he dealt with a variety of styles and themes.

Sandor Reisenbüchler (Budapest, 1935) studied languages and philosophy in Budapest. From 1961 to 1964, he attended classes at the Hungarian Film Academy, and in 1964 he joined the Pannonia studio. Originally a live-action filmmaker who treasured the teachings of Eisenstein, he became an animator after an illness prevented him from shooting outdoors. His first film, the 50-second *The Struggle* (1967), was shown at a competition for less than one-minute films, during Montreal's World Exposition. One year later, Reisenbüchler proved his skills in *The Kidnapping of the Sun and the Moon*, based on a poem by the young poet Ferenc Juhasz. A horrible monster, symbolizing the war, destroys the Earth and empties the sky by devouring the sun, the moon and the stars. It is humankind which fights the monster, forcing it to spew the stolen stars from its jaws. The film won the highest award at the 1970 Mamaia festival.

When I Was Little (1969), a mix of animation and live-action, was a repetition of previous works. Dissatisfied, ('My style was becoming mannerist,') he undertook the filming of *The Age of Barbarians* (1970), the second part of a trilogy begun with *The Kidnapping Of the Sun and the Moon*. Made with picture collage, the film deals with famine and death. Bruno Edera judged it:

> '... a masterful film ... perhaps the first short

Fig. 125. Year 1812 *by Sandor Reisenbüchler (Hungary, 1972).*

1   *Hungarofilm Bulletin*, No. 5 (Budapest, 1983), p. 6.

drama in animation history'.[1]

The third part of the trilogy, *Year 1812* (known also as *War and Peace*), was completed in 1972. Reisenbüchler writes:

'One beside the other, the three films reflect the major concerns of the human mind: myth and religion in the first; progress, technology, pollution in the second; self-destruction in the power struggle for the conquest of empires in the third.'[2]

Subsequently, with apparently diminishing inspiration, he has produced interesting works which, however, are devoid of his original biting qualities. These include *Flight To the Moon* (or *Jump Into the Impossible*, 1975), *Panic* (1978)

and *Aviation Chronicle – The Unveiling of a Mechanical Bird in New York City, in the Year 2895, As Imagined by Old Jules Verne* (1981). He was again equal to his best in 1992 with *Allegro Vivace*, a film based on a Tchaikovsky theme, and which vibrates with a joy for youth, hope and springtime. A lonely, isolated artist, a self-taught draftsman and a music lover (as the quality of his sound tracks show), Reisenbüchler captured the meaning of epos and human pain with a powerful and refined style.

György Kovasznai (Budapest, 1934–83) had remarkable graphic, pictorial and musical skills. His excellent *Double Portrait* (1964) was a stylistic novelty for its time, displaying the portraits of a

Fig. 126. Foam Bath *by György Kovasznai (Hungary, 1979).*

1   Bruno Edera, 'A l'est du nouveau ... l'animation hongroise'. Unpublished. Excerpts printed in 'Le cinema d'animation aujourd'hui, petit tour du monde dans le désordre: Hongrie,' *Ecran 73*, No. 11 (Paris, January 1973).

2   Letter received from Sandor Reisenbüchler, 15 July 1973. Later, during a conversation he further explained on *Kidnapping*, 'The actual theme is the war, with the human struggle to eradicate it. But it is dealt with in a magic-mythological way. I wanted to demonstrate how historical events are often presented in legendary and eventually religious manners'.

man and a woman which become animated with the technique of the 'self-making oil paint'. The enthralling sound track includes baroque music and vocal performances in a peculiar mixture of Italian and Venetian dialects.

Wave Length (1971) displays the same technique (with oil colours having bright, abstract, almost greasy qualities), while the sound track is a rich texture of songs and operatic arias, as well as foreign and Hungarian radio broadcasts. From this abstract film one gets the feeling that Kovasznai is in touch with the reality of his times and portrays it in the most figurative way. The same can be said of *Memories of Summer '74* (1974): oil paint blends with traditional animation, and the pleasures of summer, the beach, dances, the Danube and its bridges in Budapest are entangled in a nostalgic reverie to the rhythms of the rock group LGT Hungaria.

Kovasznai's most ambitious work was the feature film *Foam Bath* (1979), a musical comedy portraying common people and events in contemporary Budapest. Shown are a groom-to-be who would like to cancel his wedding, the bride's best friend who is falling in love with the groom, the wedding and, overall, the disillusionment of a generation. In this atypical musical, the drawn characters do not 'act' but are graphic elements against a rich setting, made with the technique of collage and skilfully lighted. Although the film was a box-office failure, according to György Matolcsy it was 'the most innovative Hungarian feature film'[1] which introduced contemporary life and customs to animation.

Ferenc Rofusz (Budapest, 1946) acquired celebrity-status in 1981 with his Oscar-winning *The Fly* (1980), a short movie on the killing of a fly as seen through the fly's own perspective. In 1982, he described another killing in *Dead Point*, with the 'first-person' description by a man con-

demned to die by firing squad. Two years later, he released the third part of this theoretical trilogy, *Gravitation*, about an ambitious, energetic apple that tries to gain freedom from its tree but ends up crushed against the ground. Made with scarce means and few colours, these short movies have a rich atmosphere and invite multiple interpretations.

Attila Dargay (Mezonyek, 1927), a bright humorist and a director of series and popular feature films, achieved a double success with the previously mentioned *Matt the Gooseboy* and *Vuk* (The Little Fox). The latter is an excellent example of personality animation revolving around an orphaned baby fox who grows up learning about life and how to defend itself against humans. Dargay's artistic skills emerge also in *Variaciok egy sarkanyra* (Variations On a Dragon, 1967) and *Go, Go Little Train* (1973, a political apologue unappreciated by censors).

Ottó Foky (Sarhida, 1927), a veteran of the Pannonia studio, gained popularity with *Babfilm* (Scenes with Beans, 1975), with animated objects) which describes the entertaining life on the planet of beans as seen through an interplanetary visitor's eyes. Everything is similar to earth, but in a culinary version. Even the Moon is a croissant.

Jozsef Nepp (Csepel, 1934) made his debut with *Szenvedély* (Passion, 1961). An excellent humorist, he worked on series such as the aforementioned *Gusztav*, as well as individual films such as the funny *Öt perc gyilkosság* (Five Minute Thrill, 1966). In 1984, he filmed *Hófejer* (Snow White, 1984), a remake of the traditional tale in which the little princess is a brawny girl.

Other artists deserving recognition for their comic inspiration include: Béla Ternovszky (Budapest, 1943), brilliant creator of *Modern edzés-módszerek* (Modern Sports Coaching, 1970, an anthology of gags on the theme of sport), *Tart-*

---

1   György Matolcsy, Different Points of Aesthetics in Hungarian Animation Cinema. MSS in English for the conference 'Teorie e forme dell'animazione' (Animation Theories and Forms), Lucca, Italy, October 1986.

sunk kutyát (Let us Keep a Dog, 1975) and the feature film *Macskafogo* (Cat-Trap, 1986);

Tibor Hernadi (Budapest, 1951), author of *Animalia* (1977, comic spots on zoological subjects); and Csaba Szórády (Keszthely, 1950), who displayed a pungent, epigrammatic humour in *Rondino* (1977). Bela Vajda (Kisujszallas, 1935), also a humorist, won a prestigious Golden Palm at the Cannes festival for *Moto perpetuo* (Perpetual Motion, 1980, a little man strives to enter an elevator on which the most astonishing things occur). The non-comic *Strip-Tease* (1970) attaches special effects to a live-action strip-tease.

Zsolt Richly (Sopron, 1941) made his debut in 1966 as the director of *In India*, based on a text by poet Attila Jozsef. In 1972, he released the poetic *Anna Molnar*, inspired by a popular song and animated with photographic elaborations of the stock.

Jozsef Gemes (Budapest, 1939) was successful in the late 1960s, with *Concertissimo* (1969), *Diszlepes* (Parade, 1970), and *Event* (1970). The feature film *Heroic Times* (1985, with animated painting set in the late Middle Ages) was highly acclaimed by reviewers, despite low box-office popularity.

Csaba Varga (Mezocsokonya, 1945) favoured two techniques, drawings and clay animation. He used drawings to represent the constant metamorphosis of images. His first successful work was *Erased By Time* (1980), followed by *Waltz* (1984), a kaleidoscope of bodies, objects and memories which was unfortunately spoiled by an artificial anti-militaristic finale. *Aszél* (The Wind, 1985) is based on recurring 'cycles' of drawings. A pure creation of black on white (with drawings by Ferenc Banga), the film does not have a plot, but only drawings which multiply and become more complicated to the rhythm of an obsessive soundtrack, like a hymn to perpetual change.

Varga's other work is comical, expressed through clay animation. His major character is Augusta, a funny, clumsy housewife who first appeared in *The Dinner* (1980). The finest film in the series is *Augusta Dresses Up* (1984), winner of several international awards. Varga, who admits to being influenced by American classic comedy, refers also to his background as a scholar and teacher of mathematics to prove that laughter is a matter of logic and the contradiction thereof.

Hungary gave birth to a host of skillful animators who deserve mention. Peter Szoboszlay (Diosgyor, 1937), an expert set designer, directed several quality films, such as *Salted Soup* (1969) and *Hey You!* (1976, an original humorous movie about aggressiveness). Kati (Katalin) Macskassy (Budapest, 1942), daughter of the founder of modern Hungarian animation, favoured working with children. In the highly praised *Life Is a Lot of Fun For Me* (1976), she directed a team of Gypsy children. Painter and set designer Peter Molnar (Budapest, 1943) is notable for *In the Plains* (1984), which stands out for its figurative qualities. Maria Horvath (Pecs, 1952) directed *Miracles of the Night* (1982) and two episodes of a grotesque series entitled *The Doors* (1983). Pal Toth (Pecs, 1952) directed *How To Scare A Lion?* (1981), a gently comical short which was later developed into a series with elegiac undertones and which became one of the world's most inspired television series. A young and talented scriptwriter for the series, Bela Weiss, also made a name for himself as a director (*Sprinkling*, 1989). Ivan Kiss (Budapest, 1950) made a salute to Bach with *B.A.C.H.* (1986), an abstract, black-and-white film characterized by solid rhythms and style. Gyula Nagy (Sajoszentpeter, 1961) animated real fingers moving to a jazz beat in the ingenious, pleasant *Wave Of Fingers* (1986). Sandor Bekesi (Budapest, 1954) sympathetically described the life and art of Emile Reynaud in *Fenyek virradat elott* (Lights Before Dawn, 1985, with animated cut-outs).

Romania

In the 1960s and 1970s, the only production company of animated films was Bucharest-based Animafilm, which favoured entertainment and children's cinema (especially series) over art films. In the late 1970s and early 1980s a group of young artists presented more ambitious proposals in which the redefinition of Romanian style was a major issue. At this time, continuity with tradition was maintained by veteran artist Ion Popescu-Gopo, who had lost some of his original vitality, but was still driven by ambition and intellectual curiosity.

Adrian Petringenaru (Bucharest, 19 October 1933 – 29 May 1989) was a historian, critic (author of a valuable book on sculptor Constantin Brancusi), screenwriter and live-action director. He made his debut in animation with *Brezaia* (1968). Afterward, he directed numerous films using a vast range of styles, but mainly focusing on philosophical meditation or political-humanistic messages. His finest is *The Long Road* (1976), a grotesque, dramatic work in black-and-white, in which commoners, attired in tragicomical hats and coats, march toward progress. *The Principle of the Field* (1979, a strong pacifist plea) and *Art Expertise* (1980, a satire against false values) also should be noted.

Painter Sabin Balasa (17 June 1932) specialized in the technique of oil or acrylic images on glass, in constant change, and he used it in some suggestive, brightly coloured films, including *The Drop* (1966, on a subject by poet Marin Sorescu), *Fascination* (1969) and *Exodus Toward the Light* (1979). Painter Laurentiu Sirbu (29 April 1936), worked on children's films as well as on more ambitious projects. He made almost fifty movies including *The Skylark* (1969) and *Window* (1977), and *Games and Toys* (1980), which, as Dana Duma wrote:

'... contain the characteristic traits of Laurentiu Sirbu's cinematographic style: stylized lines, a sensitivity for colour, the suggestion of an idyllic mood.'[1]

Mihai Badica (Constance, 1941) joined Animafilm in 1970 as a puppeteer. He directed his first film, *Icarus*, in 1974, followed by *Genesis* (1975). *Metaphor* (1980) is his finest work, where he attempts:

'to solve a purely artistic problem ... the integration of two seemingly disparate elements of line and mass, transparency and opacity.' Badica 'courageously sets about weaving this process of artistic integration between two characters; one of clay, heavy, a bit clumsy, the other of wire filament, finer, smoother, more flexible.'[2]

Illustrator Ion Truica (Caracal, 16 November 1935) favoured working on adaptations such as *Carnival* (1972, from a subject by H.C. Andersen), or *The Grand Opera* (1974, from a Balkan legend on the sacrifice behind a work of art). In *The Revolt* (1984) he described the Romanian peasant riots of 1907 which were crushed with artillery fire.

Olimp Varasteanu (Gratia-Ilfov, 1929) made his debut in 1955 with *The Fox's Misadventures* and maintained an interesting narrative level. In 1981, he directed *Let's Not Forget*, a film inspired by the terrorist attack at the train station of Bologna, Italy, and recalling the spectre of Nazism.

Victor Antonescu displayed his comic vein in short movies such as *The Ant and the Grasshopper* (1969), in numerous series and in the feature film *Robinson Crusoe* (1971, an Italo-Romanian production co-directed with the Italian Gibba). Virgil Mocanu (Bucharest, 3 June 1931) had a long career as a director, culminating with

1   Dana Duma, 'A New Look at the Romanian Animation/Nouveau regard sur l'animation roumaine', *Animafilm*, No. 7 (Warsaw, 1981), p. 29.

2   David Ehrlich, 'Focus on Four Romanian Animators,' *Animafilm*, No. 3 (Turin, July–September 1984), p. 13.

The Little Tambourine (1982), a salute to Flemish painter Pieter Brueghel. Bob Calinescu, a Romanian pioneer of animation with puppets and objects in the 1950s, deserves mention for *Romeo and Juliet* (1968). Here, the story of the Verona lovers is told with animated stones.

Possibly the first to support the Romanian renewal was Zoltan Szilagyi (Chiochis, Bistrita-Nasaud province, 1 September 1951). A lover of music and drawings, he graduated from Cluj's academy of fine arts in 1976 with the highest grades in the entire country. After three years with Animafilm in Bucharest, he released *The Gordian Knot* (1979). Made of delicate pencil drawings, characterized by an elegant 'micro-physiognomic' animation, the film was innovative for its hermetic plot (the knot waiting to be cut). In fact, Szilagyi is more concerned with the meaning of images as artistic creations than with a dramatic rendition of the plot. This attitude is even stronger in *Arena* (1981), which depicts the fight between monster and knight as it might be seen on television. This original work is characterized by enthralling drawings (particularly the

Fig. 127. Arena *by Zoltan Szilagyi (Romania, 1981).*

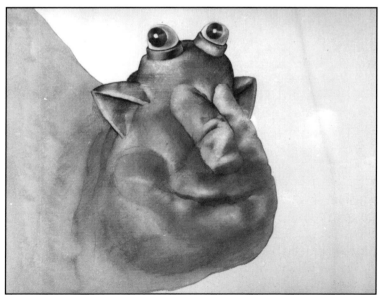

monster), and a development which follows the logic and needs of the graphic-pictorial forms. Here Szilagyi wanted to play on the simultaneity of two actions or, in his words, 'on the simultaneity of different spaces and times which interact casually, as when television transmits into a room where another action is taking place'.[1]

The filmmaker's third movie, *Monologue* (1983), also revolves around parallel events: a railway worker's solitude which is described with the split screen technique, and the development of two different monologues. Szilagyi's movies make difficult viewing, particularly for Romanian audiences which have always demanded certainties, not doubts, from animation. Yet,

> '... the artist plies between this world and the other. Coming back from the other, he marks it on paper or stock so that other people can learn about it. The journey is dangerous because the artist, who returns and is misunderstood, becomes just as alienated as those who live in the other world – the lunatic's.'

During the mid-1980s, Szilagyi (a member of the Hungarian minority in Romania) was allowed to leave the country and established himself in Hungary's Kecskemet. Here he continued his career with films which were more free and colourful: *Origin* (1989), *Pure Image* (1988), *Cultur-Historical Manoeuvre at Night* (1992).

Other artists released their first art movies in 1979: Nicolae Alexi with *The Kite*, Ion Manea with *Grandparents' House* and Stefan Anastasiu (Sibiu, 1950) with *Three Difficult-To-Swallow Pills*. Anastasiu also directed *Relation* (1980) and *The Gray Planet* (1981) before moving to Canada where he made *Chameleon* (1984), a meticulously formal movie on solitude which owes almost too much to Szilagyi's lessons. Szilagyi's influence clearly emerges in other young artists' works, such as *Family Pictures*

---

1   Zoltan Szilagyi, personal communication (1983).

(1984) by Radu Igaszag, or *House* (1986) by Zeno Bogdanescu (Timisoara, 5 September 1955), a film created with pencil drawings, in which the memories of an old ruined house mix with visions of a future mansion.

the country was characterized by a general stillness, when compared to the impetuous innovations taking place elsewhere, and particularly in neighboring countries. The animators, born in the 1920s, who had worked in the field since the foundation of the DEFA studio, were not replaced by a middle generation, and only in the 1980s did some young talent emerge, gifted with new inspiration and a different kind of sensitivity. The quality of animation produced in Dresden depended on the ambitions and the spirit of artists who were hardly stimulated by progressive experiences, and who were conditioned by the tastes of an audience little inclined to abandon tradition.

German Democratic Republic

The devastation left by the war, as well as complex international and domestic circumstances, weighed heavily on the first years of the Democratic Republic which was formed in 1949 from the Eastern section of Germany. Culturally, the emptiness left by Nazism and the new isolation from abroad contributed to this hardship. The only charismatic personality capable of organizing new cultural talent and initiating new projects, Bertolt Brecht, died a few years after his return from exile.

Against this background, live action cinema was revived by the works of filmmakers such as Dudow, Staudte, Maetzig and Wolf, while animation had to be reinvented all over again. In the early 1950s, the Studio für Popularwissenschaftliche Filme, in Babelsberg, released a few animated works, and so did the Dresden-based production company DEFA, which specialized in documentaries. In 1955, the DEFA studio for animation was officially founded by decree of the Department of Culture. The studio remained the centre of national production for many years; only later did a small animation group form for television work. Production was primarily meant for children, but occasionally included some satirical and political films for adult audiences. Innovative works were also released, which separated the Eastern German style from the most fashionable currents of the time and gave it an autonomous character (although Trnka's influence could be found in animated puppet films).

Throughout the years, the overall production of

The first artist to find a style of his own was Bruno Böttge (Halle, 11 December 1925 – 1981), a former camera operator and assistant director of documentaries. In 1953, he directed his first film with animated silhouettes, *Der Wolf und die sieben Geisslein* (The Wolf and the Seven Kids) followed by *Die Bremer Stadtmusikanten* (1954, The Musicians of Bremen), clumsily animated but with good musical gags. In 1957, he directed his first mature work, *Die Geschenke des Graumännchens* (The Gift of the Devil), the tale of a king who steals a magic loaf of bread from a woodsman, but is ultimately defeated.

Böttge made 46 films with animated silhouettes, characterized by good taste, refinement and often, benevolent compassion, as in *Die kleine Hexe* (The Little Witch, released postumously in 1982). In keeping with the German animated film tradition initiated by Lotte Reiniger, he honoured this technique and left it as his inheritance to his younger colleagues.

Two major animators from the initial years of the DEFA studio were Klaus Georgi (Halle, 22 October 1925) and his wife Katja Heinitz Georgi (Lengenfeld, 28 August 1928). They made numerous films together and collaborated on the creation and scripts of each other's works. Klaus directed the first successful cartoon released by the production company, *Blaue Mäuse gibt es nicht* (Blue Mice Aren't Possible, 1958). This is the tale of a blue mouse, ostracized by a couple of snobby grey mice, but accepted by their children. At the end, it turns out that the blue mouse is not really blue, but is covered in paint. The narration is playful and sarcastic, and the modern, stylized drawings are in line with the most advanced currents of animation of the time. *Karli Kippe* (1961), also an avant-garde film, is a well drawn animated piece that warns about the dangers of smoking. *Guten Tag, Herr H.* (Good Day, Mr. H, 1965, co-directed by Klaus and Katja Georgi) is a satire directed against the Federal Republic of Germany, evoking the ghost of Hitler through an interesting mix of styles. In 1980, Klaus directed *Varianten* (Variations), an apologue against hostility among neighbours. He has also worked on series and environmentalist films.

Katja Georgi's productive career ranged from animated drawing to puppet films, and from fairy tales to political protest. Her most renowned work is the pacifist *Die Musici* (The Musicians, 1963), a mix of animated drawings and live-action shots that show musicians playing wonderful tunes, while cannons rage outside. Her numerous animated puppet films include *Die Prinzessin auf der Erbse* (The Fussy Princess, 1959), influenced by Trnka but with personal touches; and *Das Feuer des Faust* (Faust's Fire, 1980–81), on a script by Jiří Brdecka, which elicited mixed opinions by audiences and reviewers. In 1970, she and her husband co-directed the mid-length *Ein junger Mann namens Engels* (A Young Man Called Engels, 1970), in collaboration with the Soviet Union, using drawings made by Engels in his youth.

Kurt Weiler (Lehrte, 16 August 1921), director of animated puppet films, is author of some of the best Eastern German productions. In 1939, to escape Nazi persecution, he emigrated to Great Britain, where he studied at Oxford's City School of Arts and Crafts and later worked at Larkins studio. Back in Germany, he was open to Brecht's influences, which are often reflected in his films.

In 1964, he directed *Das tapfere Schneiderlein*, a fine rendition of the brave little tailor tale, with a setting of miniatures and a soundtrack of ancient French music. The Brecht inspired *Heinrich der verhinderte* (Henry Who Was Hindered, 1966), with stylized masks, posters and explicit references to the use of the stage, is one of the most original animated puppet films in its time, breaking away from the predominant Trnka school as well as from the more caricatural and meticulous cinema of George Pal. *Norgel und Sohne* (1967) is a tastefully ironic history of civilization and invention, starting from prehistoric times.

In 1976, Weiler made what can be considered his finest work, *Die Suche nach dem Vogel Turlipan* (The Search for the Bird Turlipan). While looking for the bird Turlipan, a scientist finds diamonds, and wanders above the clouds, changing the world, but the bird Turlipan is nowhere to be found. Weiler constructed an excellent setting and an original atmosphere, playful and lyrical, with the help of such objects as brushes, crocks, cups, and with the creation of a sea which would make the Fellini of *Amarcord* or *Casanova* envious.

Günter Rätz (Berlin, 30 May 1935) was one of the youngest founders of animation in his country. His first important film was *Der Wettlauf* (The Race, 1962), a comic short with animated puppets, depicting a running competition between a short man and a tall one, intertwined with several surreal complications. Rätz's best work (and probably the masterpiece of East German production) was *Leben und Thaten des berühmten Ritters Schnapphanski* (1977). Set in the 1840s and based on a text by Georg Werth, the film is about a false hero, womanizer, dandy and coward, who moves his ridiculous existence from Germany to Spain. The work, dominated by an ironic look at Prussian customs and the shortcomings of the protagonist, displays excellent ink drawings in black-on-white, with only rare touches of colour. In 1981, Rätz directed *Die fliegende Windmühle* (The Flying Windmill), a science-fiction feature film.

Otto Sacher (Bystre, Czech Republic, 1 December 1928) was a prolific filmmaker, a teacher, and a leader of young animators, with an inclination to satire. His witty films include *Die Falle* (1979), on the topic of seduction; among his productions for children, one of the most entertaining is *Rotkappchen* (Riding Hood, 1977), Little Red Riding Hood retold as in a fairy-tale book (with framed illustrations). The original *Am Fenster* (At the Window, 1979), made in close collaboration with the art director of the studio, Marion Rasche, is a game of free association, combining Rasche's paintings with fade-outs, blurred images, shadows, rock music and Chagall-like touches.

Finally, Lothar Barke (Berlin, 22 January 1926) deserves mention for *Alarm im Kasperletheater* (Alarm in the Kasper Theater, 1960), a popular film for children about a little devil who steals a cake and is chased by other toys. Werner Krausse (Dresden, 19 May 1923) made the award-winning *Wer bist du?* (Who Are You, 1970) with animated puppets; a dog in search of its identity impersonates a peacock, a duck and a hedgehog, but barks as soon as it sees a fox. Monika Anderson (Tallinn, Estonia, 3 December 1929) directed, among other films, *Meta Morfoss* (1979), an entertaining, modern tale about the little girl of the title, who has the magic power to change her features.

Among the animators of the new generation, Lutz Dammbeck (born in 1948) graphic artist and painter directed *Die Entdeckung* (The Discovery, 1982–83), a grotesque tale about a wasp and a toad trying to escape boredom. Narrated

with a clever sound track, the film displays good design, greyish colours and an atmoshpere pervaded by a subtle malaise.

Bulgaria

In the 1920s and 1930s, the whole of Bulgarian animation consisted only of sporadic works by Vassil Bakardjiev (Ruse, 1 January 1906 – Sofia, 5 April 1980), an artist involved with advertising and education (one of his best films, made in 1931, taught about the fight against insects). At the end of World War II, in the wake of renewal and reconstruction, several painters joined forces and made two short experimental films. Under the leadership of Alexander Denkov, a renowned illustrator (Prague, Czech Republic, 10 September 1925 – Sofia, 31 March 1972), they produced *A Sick Person* (a political caricature, 1946) and *The Little Thief* (1946).

Dimitar Todorov-Zarava (Sumen, 21 September 1901) inventor of a sort of phenatisticope, convinced the authorities to open an animation section within the new state-run cinematographic industry. The studio was started in May 1948, but because of scarce means and lack of experience, the first films proved quite unsatisfactory. Todorov-Zarava directed *He Suffers in His Mind* (1949), *Wolf and Lamb* (1950) and *The Republic of the Forest*. Aron Aronov (17 April 1921 – Pleven, 17 April 1987) was a puppet animator, starting in the 1950s (*The Man from the Other World*, 1956; *The Robot Uprising*, 1960). Dimo Lingurski also worked with animated puppets, making his debut with *The Terrible Bomb* (1951) and directing *Master Manol*, the first colour film (1951). He was joined by Stefan Topaldjikov (Carigrad, Turkey, 26 March 1909) director of *Event in The Nursery School* (1953), *The Little Painter* (1954) and several other films of the 1950s and 1960s. As an animator of puppets, Topaldjikov followed the lead of Karel Zeman rather than Trnka, thus taking a direction opposite to that of Lingurski.

True professional animation was first produced in Bulgaria by art director, painter and satirist Todor Dinov, who is considered the father of Bulgarian animation. Dinov (Alexandropoulis, Greece, 24 July 1919), had attended Ivan Ivanov-Vano's courses in Moscow; upon returning home he directed *Marko the Hero* (1955). Besides authoring more notable works, Dinov became an active teacher and promoter. As a filmmaker, his trademark was an optimistic humour:

> 'His most genuine world was a vision of life striving toward a more fair, happy, human society,' Sergio Micheli wrote.[1]

One of Dinov's most famous works is *The Daisy* (1965), characterized by simplicity of drawings and narration (a daisy does not let a man pick it, while it is willing to end up in the hands of a little girl). *Prometheus XX* (1970) and *Chain Reaction* (1971) have dramatic and philosophic structures; *Chased from Paradise* (1967) is the pleasant tale of a flautist who enters Paradise by mistake and turns the Celestial choir topsy-turvy.

Since its beginning, Bulgarian animation developed its own style; careful not to copy major models, it strived to retrieve popular traditions and to develop its own native taste. This was evident in themes and plots, even while the drawing and paintings did not dramatically depart from those of other European countries. In influencing script writers, the oral tradition of humour (particularly that of the Gabrovo region, which has become legendary) mingled with the goals of education and reconstruction of a new society. The result is a cinema in which laughter goes along with moralism, and message prevails over form. In the 1980s, with a new, prolific generation of young artists, drawing has become the core of aesthetic research.

In the 1960s, the animation studio of Sofia was divided into two branches, guided respectively by Donio Donev and Stoyan Dukov. Donev (Berkovitza, 2 June 1929) made his directing debut with *Duet* (1961, in co-direction with Todor Dinov). His style of drawings is playfully caricaturist, and his inspiration aims at laughter. It can be inferred that his sense of humour, free from educational or moralistic worries, is unmatched among Bulgarian animators. His most original inventions, the *trimata glupazi*, or the 'three fools', appeared as protagonists in a film of the same title (1970) and returned cyclically in productions and comics. These three peasants, clad in calf-length pants, who speak with guttural sounds and who regularly get into trouble because of their inability to confront reality. With them, Donev goes back to the core of the original comic character, the stupid peasant (or colonus, in Latin, from which the word 'clown' derives). The spirited *The Intelligent Village* (1972) is yet another study of human stupidity (this time, disguised as shrewdness); the same vivacity characterizes *De Facto* (1973), a play deserving of popular theatre, about the universal search for scapegoats. In 1985, Donev completed his country's first ani-

Fig. 128. The Blackest Mouse *by Stoyan Dukov (Bulgaria, 1971).*

---

1   Sergio Micheli, *Cinema di animazione in Bulgaria* (Bologna: Cappelli, 1975), p. 104.

mated feature film: *We Called Them Montagues and Capulets*, a comic version of *Romeo and Juliet*, Bulgarian-style.

Stoyan Dukov (Sofia, 25 September 1931), also a student of Todor Dinov, directed *The Fortified Houses* (1967), a film on egotism, followed by *The Don Quixote Case* (1968), the excellent *The Blackest Mouse* (1971) and *Requiem* (1982, against intolerance). Contrary to Donev, Dukov stressed the formal aspects of animated drawings, which became the focus of his research as an illustrator. *The Blackest Mouse*, for instance, is a refined study on movements within graphic choices which emphasize two-dimensionality and the use of lines. Among the first generation of Bulgarian animators, Dukov is probably the most complex, conceiving film as a plastic whole rather than the illustration of a script. In 1986, he drew and directed *March*, a playful, caustic peasant comedy about the upsets caused in a village by an itinerant sex-shop. An example of good graphic evolution, the film displays 'unfinished' drawings.

Ivan Vesselinov (Levski, 23 February 1932) has gained attention for his sarcasm and his interest in the alienating aspects of the human condition. His finest work, *The Devil in the Church* (1969), is about the hypocrisy of those who wrap themselves in sanctity. *The Heir* (1970) and *Fear* (1973) also deserve mention.

Penco Bogdanov (Gabrovo, 27 September 1923), who began animating in the 1960s, had a background in journalism and medicine. His most successful film was the internationally acclaimed *The Jovial Ones* (1969), which features, with typical Balkan humour, shepherds defeating the wolf to save their sheep, and later killing the sheep to celebrate the event. Christo Topuzanov (Sofia, 11 June 1930), a former director of live-action films, has been mainly interested in the animation of cutouts. His numerous high quality films, characterized by a strong ethical commit-

ment, include *The World of Chicken* (1972) and the joyful *The Wednesday Before Tuesday* (1988).

Two women animators during this early period were Radka Bacvarova and Zdenka Doiceva. Radka Bacvarova (Sofia, 19 March 1918 – 12 September 1986) was among the founders of Bulgarian animation. She actively worked on productions for children. As she was not a graphic artist herself, she collaborated with several artists at the studio, particularly with Ivan Vesselinov. Ivan Bogdanov made drawings for her most well-known film, *The Snowman* (1960), an apotheosis on self-sacrifice in the name of friendship, written by live-action script writer Angel Wagenstein. Zdenka Doiceva (Terezin, Czech Republic, 22 August 1922) moved to Bulgaria in 1955. She made her first film, *The Mouse and the Pencil* (1958) in collaboration with Radka Bacvarova. While she worked on children's movies, she also undertook more ambitious projects, such as *Passion* (1971), *Gunpowder* (1972) and *Aquarium* (1973).

Gheorghi Cavdarov (Sofia, 29 July 1934) made *The Three Apples* (1971), *The Carefree Man* (1983) and *Panta Rei* (1977). Proiko Proikov (Pernik, 1927) made *Summer* (1970) and *Adventure in the Woods* (1971, introducing the successful character of the little boy Joro); Asparuh Panov (Kiustendil, 1930) made *Once Upon a Time There Was a City* (1972) and *Save the Forest* (1972); Konstantin Peronoski (Sofia, 1931), a specialist in animated puppets, made *Tale Without Words* (1970) and *The Owner* (1972). This generation of filmmakers should also include Ivan Andonov (Plovdiv, 3 May 1934), author of *Melodrama* (1971). An actor and director of live-action cinema, he worked on several occasions with cartoons, which had been his first love.

The link between the old and the new generation of Bulgarian animators was Rumen Petkov

(Sofia, 1948), director of the harsh, ironic *The Monkeys* (1981). With *Treasure Planet* (1986), Petkov contended with Donev for the honour of making the country's first feature film.[1]

Slav Bakalov (Sofia, 1945), an excellent script writer and an artist with a dry, ungracious style, brought a modern note of existential uneasiness to the humour of Sofia-made animation. His films include *Pastoral* (1980), *Zoo* (1983) and *The Fog* (1985). He left his recognizable trademark on numerous movies made by colleagues. Velislav Kazakov (Sofia, 1955) displays his scratchy drawing and his original comic taste in *Cuckoo* (1983).

Two major artists of the new generation were Anri Kulev (Sumen, 1949) and Nikolai Todorov (Sofia, 1952). Kulev attracted the experts' attention with *Hypothesis* (1976), a powerful, black-and-white film with a pessimistic vision of life. In 1978, he directed *Representation* followed by *Ride* (1979), about the creative, vital impulse which brings freedom. Other films followed, including *Labyrinths* (1984) and *Safari* (1985). His work is known for its excellent pencil drawings and the desire to try atmospheres and visual regions never explored before.

This taste for research and an attention to form in drawing are shared by Kulev's younger colleague Todorov, with whom he co-directed several films.[2] *Megalomania* (1979) was a test bed for new solutions, shown in the black-and-white drawings, although a traditional 'moral' provides the foundation (the film jeers at those who still imitate the poses of the famous). *A Day As a Flower* (1981) describes the events surrounding a child's birthday, and *Successful Test* (1984) is an elaborate apologue about human aspirations and results.

Spurred by Kulev and Todorov, Bulgarian animation headed more decidedly toward films for adult audiences. An example of this is *A Crushed World* (1986, see Colour Plate 67), by Boyko Kanev (Sofia, 16 October 1939), winner of Bulgaria's first grand prize at the international festival of Annecy (1987). The film has an interesting stylistic thesis; made with puppets of crumpled paper, it admirably balances traditional puppet animation, cutouts and drawings. In this subtle work, tender and comical at the same time, Kanev refers constantly and ironically to the material he uses (the paper), distancing himself from excessive involvement and identification with the characters.

Czechoslovakia: Trnka's heirs

A stage of feverish growth began in the late 1950s. Trnka returned to animated drawings *Proc UNESCO?* (Why UNESCO?, 1958) after spending many years with puppets. In his debut, Frantisek Vystrcil (Olomouc, 9 November 1923) released *A Place Under the Sun* (1959); Bretislav Pojar, Trnka's first assistant, directed the satiric *Bombománie* (Bombmania, 1959) and the lyrical *Lev a pisnicka* (The Lion and the Song, 1959); and Jirí Brdecka, who had spent a long time as a film critic and scriptwriter of live-action cinema, set out again to direct animated movies *Jak se clovek avcil letat* (How Man Learned to Fly, 1958) and *Pozor!* (Warning!, 1959).

While Trnka had already reached the apex of his career, his younger colleagues were quickly approaching theirs. This resulted in a large number of productions (ranging from children's and television films to adult films, to made-on-commission and educational works) and the discovery of new talent. An American artist, Gene Deitch, also came unexpectedly to help. As mentioned earlier in the section devoted to Terrytoons, Deitch was the typical UPA graduate, having studied with John Hubley, Bobe Cannon and Bill

---

1   Petkov's film was completed before *We Called Them Montagues and Capulets*, but was released later.
2   In Bulgaria, as in many countries where animated cinema is state-funded, teamwork was common practice. Script-writers, scene designers and art directors exchanged roles frequently.

Hurtz. In 1958, he founded his own New York-based production company which, two years later, was absorbed by Rembrandt Films. With Rembrandt, Deitch made *Munro* (1960, in collaboration with Jules Feiffer) and won an Oscar. He went to Prague with the goal of sub-contracting a television series to the Bratri v Triku studio and became fascinated by the spirit he found. Prague's animators were true artists, he later said, rather than assembly-line workers, and were striving to give the best of themselves. Unhappy with the constraints which he felt were influencing his work in the United States, he decided to collaborate with the animators of the studio; eventually, he married a colleague.[1]

In fact Deitch worked almost exclusively on American productions while living in Prague and directing local animators. From 1961 to 1964, he turned out the *Tom and Jerry*, *Popeye* and *Krazy Kat* television series. From 1965 to 1967, he directed a series featuring his own character, Nudnik, an extraterrestrial which lands on our planet and has communication problems with our civilization.[2] Often bitingly comic, the series suffered from the world-wide recession which affected short films produced for movie theatres. In 1968, Deitch began a collaboration with the Weston Woods Studios, the world major production company of scholastic films. For the following 20 years, he produced book adaptations for children. These valuable works, faithful to the contents of the originals, were devoid of Deitch's best inspiration.

After the 1968 Prague Spring, Czechoslovakian cinema experienced unhappy times as intellectual life reflected, and suffered from, political events. In the case of animation, the deadlock

derived also from the most absolute acceptance of Trnka's model, an acceptance accompanied by high professionalism and admirable technique, but without innovation, at a time when the development of plasticine was revolutionizing the sector all over the world. Only in 1982 (with Jiri Barta's *Zanikly svet rukavic* (The Lost World of Gloves) did the school look for new approaches to the animation of three-dimensional figures. With the 1980s, filmmakers found new ground for inspiration and started what could be called a new era.

The country had five active centres of production: The Bratri v Triku and the Jiri Trnka studios, specialized in drawing and animated puppets respectively, in Prague; Hermina Tyrlova and Karel Zeman's studio in Gottwaldov (formerly Zlin); the studio assembled in 1965 around Viktor Kubal, in Bratislava, Slovakia; and the smaller Prometheus, founded in 1971 in Ostrava, Moravia.

Jiri Brdecka

Jiri Brdecka was, in Ranko Munitic's words:

> 'the John Ford of animation – each of the many films he created contains a bit of ingenuousness, sentimentalism and romanticism (and also nostalgia, in his last years), while Brdecka's overall work displays the wisdom of an artist without naïveté, who has seen much in his life and has gone through many experiences.'[3]

Brdecka (Hranice, 24 December 1917 – Prague, 2 June 1982) was a writer, journalist, screenwriter, film critic and painter; he never made the drawings for his films, but engaged the artist who, at that particular time, seemed to him the best to

---

1   Gene Deitch, personal communication (1973).
2   As Deitch explained to Walter M. Brash, a nudnik (Yiddish, from the Polish *nudny*, meaning tedious) was a nuisance, someone who could never do anything right. Deitch himself did not know this word at the time of the film, and his character was to be called Schlemiel (a klutz) or Schlimazl (badluck). *Cartoon Monickers* (Bowling Green, Ohio: Bowling Green University Popular Press, 1983), p. 56.
3   Ranko Munitic, 'Jiri Brdecka, le maestro n'est pas mort,' Annecy 83 (Catalogue of the Annecy Film Festival, June 1983), p. 24.

express his ideas – he was a director in the most traditional sense of the term. During the war, he was a member of the group which laid the foundations of the future Czechoslovakian school. As a script writer his skills were useful to Jirí Trnka.

Fig. 129. Let's Go Hunting in the Woods *by Jiri Brdecka (Czechoslovakia, 1966).*

His production includes some already-mentioned films, such as *Love and the Dirigible* (1948), a compassionate and ironic essay about literary characters; *How Man Learned to Fly* (1958) a humorous look at the history of aviation; and *Warning!* (1959) an anti-war film, on behalf of wisdom and civility. *Rozum a cit* (Reason and Emotion, 1962) and *Spatne namalovana slepice* (Gallina Vogelbirdae, 1963, the tale of an ornithologist who mistakes a child's scribble of a hen for an unknown species) dealt in a subtle and elegant manner with the themes of modern living and knowledge, while *Slovce M* (The Letter M, 1964) and *Let's Go Hunting in the Woods* (Do lesicka na cekanou, 1966) were based on ancient popular songs. The latter is a refined film about a man who accidently kills his fiancée during a hunt, with paintings by Frantisek Braun. His last masterpiece was *Lááááska* (Looooove, 1978), about a lonely man who befriends a spider, but betrays it when the opportunity arises.

In his works, Brdecka went from humour to elegy, to satire, to the simple pleasure of telling a story; he displayed a constant inclination toward constructiveness, love, life and civilization, and a firm dislike for illusions and sentimentality. An illuminist and a humanist, he did not stay away from the cultural and social stage of his times and took a brave stand for freedom when his country's events required it.

Bretislav Pojar

Born in Susice, South Bohemia, on 7 October 1923, Pojar moved to Prague at the age of nineteen, to study architecture. There he found work with AFIT. After the war, he was one of the founders of the Bratri v Triku studio; and later, in 1947, he joined Jirí Trnka at the Prague studio for puppet animation. Remember, Trnka could not animate. Thus, the extraordinary puppet movements in his films are the work of Pojar, who learned cultural and ethical lessons rather than technical ones from the master. One of the finest works by the Trnka-Pojar duo is the sequence in which fearful prince Neklan is stricken by terror and doubt (*Old Czech Legends*). Here, Pojar moves the character with the psychological subtleties of a real actor.

Pojar's rich, diverse production as a director includes children's films, political apologues, animated drawings and puppets, documentaries and live-action films. Even as he became a director (1952), he continued collaborating with Trnka. Trnka himself contributed to Pojar's sets or puppets with his expertise as a painter and sculptor.

Pojar's first important film was *O sklenicku víc* (One Glass Too Many, 1953), which today's viewer might find melodramatic and artificial (it was meant as a propaganda film against alcoholism), but which displayed a rare cleverness in its camera movements, expressionist illumination and visual invention (after the protagonist dies, the picture of his fiancée keeps rolling along the wet ground). Just as *One Glass Too Many* was openly realistic, *The Lion and the Song* (1959) was symbolic. The song is played by a musician in the desert who is eaten by a lion. Later, when the lion dies, the song finds a new interpreter in a young musician. *Bombmania* (1959) is also a humanistic film against nuclear war.

At times Pojar was inconsistent in his themes and his results did not do him justice. His finest works, however, through lyricism or satire, come down to praising positive principles such as peace, freedom and creativity: *Biliár* (Billiards, 1961), *Uvodni slovo pronese* (Opening Speech, 1962, with 'two-dimensional' puppets), *Romance* (Ballad, 1963) and three movies made with the National Film Board of Canada, *To See or Not to See* (1969), *Balablok* (1972), and the excellent *E* (1981). Even more than a filmmaker, he must be considered an entertainer, capable of infusing style and energy into every genre he undertakes (not by chance, his movies for children are the best of their kind). Animation is like hypnosis, he maintained, except that in the film it is the wood that must be the hypnotist, and it takes a good hypnotizer to give life to the puppet.[1] This is the

statement of a great director speaking about his actors.

Jan Švankmajer

The animator most isolated from the Czechoslovakian school and, stylistically, the most striking, is Jan Švankmajer. An autonomous filmmaker oriented toward surrealism, his inspiration shows some traces of the likes of Borowczyk, Buñuel or, partly, Jan Nemec. His production includes animated works as well as live-action films, and an imposing opus as a designer, sculptor and etching artist. In 1974, outside of cinema, he directed an experiment with 'tactile objects', interpreting the visual sensations derived from blindly touching those objects.

Švankmajer (Prague, 4 September 1934) studied Dramatic Arts at the Academy of Fine Arts in the capital. He was first a painter, sculptor and engraver. In 1964, he moved to cinema, with *Poslední trik Pana Schwarcewalldea a Pana Edgara* (The Last Trick, 1964). These early works already displayed the stylistic choices he would pursue during the course of his career: an accumulation, or an overflow of the estranged reality and disparate objects, each with the charm of its own individuality. *Spiel mit Steinen* (Game with Stones, 1965), created in Austria, was mainly a stylistic exercise; while *Byt* (The Flat, 1968), perhaps his first notable film, was a true intellectual drama, featuring the struggle of a man against his inimical furniture. *Tichy tyden u dome* (A Quiet Week in the House, 1969) shows the animated visions of a man who peeps into a room from holes in the door. *Don Sajn* (Don Juan, 1970), a 30-minute film with actors dressed as puppets, is based on an old Czech text for puppet theatre. *Jabberwocky* (1971), on a subject by Lewis Carroll, makes an ironic, delicate use of old toys. One remarkable film is the trilogy *Moznosti dialogu* (Dimensions of Dialogue, 1982), with the first part featuring two heads, one made of food and the other of metallic

---

1   'Bretislav Pojar,' Retrospectives (Zagreb Film Festival, 1974).

objects, fighting each other. In the second part, two plasticine torsos are consumed by ever more destructive love; in the last part, two clay heads give each other objects, in a harmonious relationship which becomes more and more frantic. *Do piv-nice* (Down to the Cellar, 1983) tells of the misadventures of a little girl who goes down into the cellar to get some coal, but is attacked by hostile creatures. *Alice* (1988) (see Colour Plate 68), a feature film, is a very personal reading of Carroll's novel, as thrilling as the original.

As Švankmajer himself acknowledged, his work is marked by the somewhat opposing influences of Surrealism and the 16th Century Mannerism. The film *Historia Naturae* (1967) was dedicated to Rudolf II, the mentor of Prague's Mannerists. Švankmajer's films are filled with objects which show signs of age and are placed in uncomfortable settings such as ruined houses, slovenly rooms or buildings with opaque walls. They display devotion to a world suspended between reality and sleepwalking, between what exists autonomously and what is animated by fantasy.

Švankmajer unfolds his minimalist chronicles with irony at times and with astonished contemplation at others. Within his attitude of constant delirium and provocation (the artist joined the Prague Surrealist Group in 1969), it is impossible to trace a thematic unity which could eventually reveal a 'message'. His only recurring, even obsessive, element is an exploration of the universe of objects, which he often sees as creatures with a will, with independence of movement and even a history of their own.[1]

His opus (inclusive of his other non-cinematic activities) must be analysed in the light of his intent as an author, an intent which he has often explained and claimed, where the act of research prevails over achievement, and attempts are more significant than the finished products. Because of his fertile, subtly disquieting research, Švankmajer has been looked upon with suspicion by some promoters of orthodox aesthetics, while becoming a source of inspiration to younger colleagues, such as the Quay brothers.

Besides the Masters

Frantisek Vystrcil has already been mentioned for his notable debut with *A Place under the Sun* (1959), a linear film about egotism. He continued to achieve excellent results with *Start* (The Departure, 1964) and *Nuzky* (The Scissors, 1970, about love). Vladimir Lehky (Brno, 19 July 1921) made the acclaimed *Parazit* (The Parasite, 1960), with excellent drawings, and *Ptaci kohaci* (Strange Birds, 1965). Josef Kabrt (Lomnice nad Popelkou, 14 October 1920) displayed a more complex figurative and graphic taste in *Rozmary lásky* (Love's Whims, 1969), based on an old eastern tradition. Zdenek Smetana (Prague, 26 June 1925) became renowned for *Destnik* (The Umbrella) and *Voda cerst vosti* (The Water of Life, 1966).

In the 1950s, Zdenek Miler began specializing in children's films and directed an imposing number

Fig. 130. What Have We Done to the Chickens by V. Jiranek and J. Hekrdla (Czechoslovakia, 1977).

1   In 1982, Švankmajer released the following statement to the Prague-based magazine *Film a doba*: 'To my eyes, objects have always been livelier than human beings. More static but also more telling. More moving because of their concealed meanings and their memory, which beats the human memory. Objects are keepers of the events they have witnessed ... In my films I have always tried to extract content from the objects, to listen to [the object themselves] and to put their stories into images.'

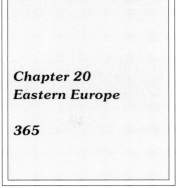

of them, including a long lasting, successful series featuring a little mole. In *Ruda stopa* (The Red Sign, 1963), he made an episodic return to the ideological tone of his famous debut, *The Millionaire Who Stole the Sun*, a film for adults. Vaclav Bedrich also worked extensively for children, but his finest work was a clever series for adults entitled *Smrtící vune* (The Deadly Perfume, 1969, also the title of the first episode). This was an amused re-evocation of the Belle Epoque, in a pleasant Magritte-inspired style which is particularly evident in the best episodes, such as *Nedokonceny víkend* (The Unfinished Weekend, 1970). In collaboration with script writer Jirí Kubicek (Prague, 6 February 1944), he created *Black and White* (1983), a well animated apologue against opportunism, set in the world of sheep.

A major gain for animation cinema was born of Bedrich's collaboration with humorist Vladimir Jiranek (Hradec Kralove, 6 June 1938). Their first film together, *Automatic* (1973), won several international awards. After *Pivo pres ulici* (To Find Some Beer, 1974), the trilogy *Dobré jitro* (Good Morning, 1975), *Excursion* and *Ššš* (Shhh!, 1975), and *Dekujeme, pánové* (Thanks, Gentlemen, 1976), Jiranek moved on to direct his own films. With Josef Hekrdla (Brtnice, 9 December 1919), he co-directed *Co jsme udelali slepicim* (What Have We Done to the Chickens, 1977) and *Zpráva o stavu civilisace* (Report on the Status of Civilization, 1981). With his taste for caricature and lively observation of customs, Jiranek brought to cinema his stylized, linear drawings, in the tradition of a Copi, a Wolinsky or a Blechman. His typical character was the hen, witness to and victim of the misdeeds of contemporary society.

Vaclav Bedrich introduced another renowned humorist and illustrator to animation, Adolf Born

Fig. 131. Black and White *by Vaclav Bedrich (Czechoslovakia, 1983).*

(Ceske Velenice, 12 June 1930). Together they created *Az já budu velky* (When I Grow Up, 1963, puppet animation) and *Dvojnik* (The Double, 1965, animated drawings). For some years Born produced drawings and ideas for all kinds of films, by directors such as Stanislav Latal, Vaclav Bedrich, Frantisek Vystrcil and Jirí Brdecka. In 1972, he joined script writer Milos Macourek (Kromeriz, 2 December 1926) and animator Jaroslav Doubrava (Litovel, 2 February 1921) in the creation of shorts and series episodes for child and adult audiences. *Co cdyby* (And If, 1972) was their first release, followed, among others, by *Ze zivota ptáku* (About Birds' Life, 1973), *Cirkulace* (Circulation, 1976) and the very clever *Complex* (1981), the trio's masterpiece, a tongue-in-cheek tale about a college-educated dog and its ignorant, ill-fated owner. Born and his colleagues have touched the highest levels of sarcastic comedy, playing on exaggeration, paradox and eccentricity in the wake of the Czechoslovakian tradition of Lada and Capek.

Vaclav Mergl (Olomouc, 24 August 1935) deserves mention for *Laokoon* (Laocoon, 1970) and *Krabi* (The Crab, 1976), and Ivan Renc (Litovel, 2 February 1921) for the television series *Track Events* (1975–77), and the effective short with animated puppets, *The Tower of Dalibor* (1978). Viktor Kubal (born 20 March 1923, near Bratislava) demands more attention. A filmmaker and a cartoonist as well, he began animating in the 1940s and since 1965 has been a major personality of the Slovakian studio. His most important films include *Sach* (Check, 1973), *Rebrik* (The Stair, 1978, about careerism) and *Zbojnik Jurko* (Jurko the Outlaw, 1976), a feature film based on the popular tale of rebel Jurko Janosik, who fought for honour and love against the oppression of the lords. The adventures of this Central European Robin Hood had already been brought to the screen, however this fourth version constituted the first Czechoslovakian animated feature film.

Jaroslav Bocek (Ulovice, 25 May 1932), a reviewer, historian and film theorist, became an animator in the 1970s. His finest work is *Tri etudy pro animátora s dohrou* (Three Etudes for Animator with Epilogue, 1977), a tasteful divertissement on the characters from *commedia dell'arte*, in three sections plus epilogue.

Lubomir Benes (Prague, 7 November 1935) had a long apprenticeship at the Bratri v Triku studio; afterward, he directed some highly praised movies, including *Homo* (1969), *Racte prominout* (Excuse Us, Please, 1974), *Akórat* (Precise, 1977), *Král a skrítek* (The King and the Gnome, 1980) and *Unfair Duel* (1982). His talent emerged undisputedly in 1979 with the series ... *And This Is How Much!*, one of the few examples in which slapstick comedy successfully entered the world of puppet animation.

Jirí Barta (Prague, 26 November 1948), formerly a theatrical art director and a graduate from the Prague University for Applied Arts, was the herald of the new generation of animators. He began directing at the Jirí Trnka studio, proving his talent and creativity from his earliest films: *Hádanky za bonbon* (Riddles for a Candy, 1978), *Diskzokej* (Disc-Jockey, 1980) and *Projekt* (Projection, 1981). *Disc-Jockey* is an original work employing animated cutouts, about the tumultuous daily life of a disc-jockey; *Projection* is animated directly on the architectural drawings of modern apartment buildings so as to show their inhospitality and uniformity.

In *Zanikly svet rukavic* (The Extinct World of Gloves, 1982), Barta used object animation (gloves as puppets) to describe a lost civilization, where only a few archeological finds remain, including vintage film. The gloves become protagonists of brief memories in the genre favoured by Buster Keaton, Greta Garbo or Federico Fellini. Despite some self-congratulatory tones, it is a creative, meaningful film, which owes much to the animation of Vlasta Pospisilova (the masterful animator in Švankmajer's *Dimensions of Dialogue*). In 1985, after two years of work, Barta completed *Krysar* (The Pied Piper, 1985) (see Colour Plate 69), a version of Browning's tale of the Pied Piper of Hamelin. A mid-length film (53-minute) with animated puppets and a mix of techniques, it was the most ambitious production released by the Prague-based studio since Jirí Trnka's *A Midsummer Night's Dream* (1959). Barta showed off his excellent directorial skills with a powerful stylistic concoction of Medieval Art, the Flemish School and German Cubism.

Another representative of the generation of renewal was Dagmar Doubkova (Prague, 13 October 1948) who brought women's liberation themes to the screen with *Sbohem, Ofélie* (Bye Bye, Ophelia, 1979). *The Tinder Box* (1986) marked a return to the traditional tale with animated puppets. Igor Sevcik (Trencianske Mtince, 1951) made his debut with *Siesta* (1977), after a rich production as an amateur filmmaker. He also released *Vztahy* (Relations, 1978), *Ráno po flámu* (The Morning after the Party, 1979), *Akce* (Action, 1980) and *Evolution* (1981).

Petr Sis (Brno, 11 May 1949) gave a complex portrait of the stages of human life, its values and pseudo-values in *Hlavy* (Heads, 1979). Frantisek Skala (Prague, 7 February 1956) debuted with the internationally praised *The Eyes*, about a sailor and his dream of sailing to far away seas. Julius Hucko (Bratislava, 1956), after a long experience as an amateur filmmaker, moved on to professionalism with *The Last Stone* (1982) in collaboration with Jaroslava Havettova. Pavel Koutsky (Prague, 1957) debuted with *Violin Concerto* (1981), followed by the valuable *Laterna musica* (Musical Lantern, 1984) and by *Curriculum Vitae* (1986), an amused, sarcastic look at the artistic, philosophical and scientific notions one accumulates in school.

Soviet Union I: Russia

Anatoly Karanovich's first successful film, both on the national and international stages, was *The Cloud in Love* (1959), based on a text by Turkish poet, Nazim Hikmet. A puppet animator, Karanovich (St. Petersburg, 1911 – Moscow, 5 July 1976) had previously made *The Tale of the Pope and Baldo His Servant* (1956).[1] He also brought Vladimir Mayakovsky's play *The Bathhouse* to the screen, an endeavour he felt at ease with because of his own background in theatre. This film (released in 1962 and co-directed with live-action veteran Sergei Yutkevich) was far from satisfying, but succeeded in bringing back into fashion Mayakovsky's acerbic, fantastic, 'adult' spirit, and in reviving figurative suggestions from the constructivist and futurist movements.

Roman Katsanov (Smolensk, 25 February 1921) collaborated with Karanovich on *The Cloud in Love*. After years as a draftsman and a puppet animator, Katsanov made a breakthrough with *The Mitten* (1967), award-winner at Moscow, Annecy, Gijon and other festivals. This film, a small treasure in its genre, features a little girl who cannot have a dog and therefore, walks her mitten as if it were a pet on a winter day. While avoiding any sentimentality, Katsanov creates a delicate atmosphere and stresses the problems of dialogue between adults and children. *Ghena the Crocodile* (1969), a film about solitude and friendship as a balancing act, introduced Ceburaska, a pleasant, fantastic creature halfway between a child and a teddy bear who later returned in the more successful *Ceburaska* (1971) (see Colour Plate 70). *A Letter* (1970) describes the relationship of a child with his father, a sea captain. *Mother* (1971) is a parable on maternal love; *Dawn* (1973) describes the ageless symbols of the revolution as mainstays of popular consciousness. Based on understatement and without trite effects, Katsanov's cinema focuses on

---

1   This was the third animated version of the tale, following Tsechanovsky's unfinished film of the early 1930s and a second one made in 1939 by Panteleimon Sasonov (Grodno, 27 May 1895 – Moscow, 3 October 1950).

nuances and simple things without losing its forcefulness.

Boris Stepantsev (Moscow, 7 December 1928 – 21 May 1983) worked with both puppets and animated drawings, but achieved his best results with the latter. In 1960, he won an award at Annecy with *Petia and Little Red Riding Hood* (best children's film) and at Karlovy Vary with *Murzilka on the Sputnik*. The favourite, most ambitious work is *The Nutcracker and the Mouse King*, based on the tale by E.T.A. Hoffmann and Tchaikovsky's music.

Nikolai Serebriakov (Leningrad, 14 December 1928) had a promising original start as a director of puppet films. Having studied at the art institute in Leningrad, in 1963 he made *I Want to Be Important*, co-directed by Vadim Kurchevsky. *The Life and Suffering of Ivan Semenov* (1964) and *Neither God Nor the Devil* (1965) followed, also in co-direction with Kurchevsky. In *I Am Waiting for a Little Bird* (1966), which Serebriakov directed alone, he already displayed the modern, quick rhythm which was to characterize his more mature works like *Not in the Hat Is There Happiness* (1968) and *The Yarn Ball* (1968). *Not in the Hat Is There Happiness* shows the director's love of detail and attention to contemporary art (the film explicitly refers to Chagall). *The Yarn Ball* is a more laconic, compact film about two opposite attitudes toward life, one energetically creative and the other bourgeois and egotistical. In later years, Serebriakov settled on the production of highly professional, academically oriented works, such as *The Separation* (1980). The film is about two children of a king, the boy raised by acrobats, and the girl in an artificial, aseptic environment.

After his collaboration with Serebriakov, Vadim Kurchevsky (Kolomna, 14 April 1928) made a name for himself with *My Green Crocodile* (1966) and especially with his first important work, *The Legend of Grieg* (1967), a combination of realism and the baroque. His masterpiece

was *The Teacher of Clamecy* (1972), based on Romain Rolland's *Colas Breugnon*. Inspired by Brueghel's imaginary world, this puppet film paid attention to figurative values as well as 'acting' by the characters. Kurchevsky's later films include *The Rich Sadko* (1975), *The Mystery of the Domestic Cricket* (1977) and *Salieri's Legend* (1986). A director with a solid, even though not striking presence, he paid attention to humanistic themes such as the relationship between the artist and the authorities, the nature of talent and the immortality of Art.

Eduard Nazarov (Moscow, 1941), an art director who became a filmmaker only late in his life, exhibited an original humour mixed with amused self-irony. His seemingly simple style pays sophisticated attention to detail, as in *Once There Was a Dog* (1982) and *Adventure of an Ant* (1984).

Aleksandr Tatarsky (Kiev, 11 December 1950) was the first comic of the Absurd among Soviet animators. At times, Tatarsky's work shows some similarities to that of Croatian Zlatko Grgic's. *When It Snowed Last Year* (1983), *The Dark Side of the Moon* (1984) and *Wings, Legs and Tails* (1986) form a sort of trilogy in which comedy is intended as the free will of intelligence and a break with logic. An example of this tendency is *When It Snowed Last Year*, Tatarsky's most interesting film in which traditional elements are revitalized with intellectual humour.

Stanislav Sokolov (Moscow, 18 May 1947) made his debut with *Dogada* (1977). He attained international praise with *Black-and-White Film* (1984, award winner at the Zagreb Film Festival), a 20-minute puppet film with a delicate although somewhat precious description of unfashionable feelings such as melancholy and nostalgia.

Garri Bardin (Orenburg, 11 September 1941) was an innovative director of lively animated object and puppet films. After the sarcastic *The Conflict* (1984), he directed *Break* (1985), the umpteenth but amusing rendition of a boxing match and *Banquet* (1987), an ironic, lightly elegiac tale about ghostly table companions stuffing themselves. In 1990 he made a brilliant interpretation of Perrault's fable with *Seri volk end Krasnaya shapochka* (The Grey Wolf and Little Red Riding Hood), a musical where the girl goes from Moscow to Paris to visit her granny, the wolf sings Kurt Weill songs and eventually eats the Seven Dwarfs, and so on, in a hilarious way.

Anatoly Petrov (Moscow, 15 September 1937), a good but not outstanding director of animated films for children, found his unique inspiration in *Mother Will Forgive Me* (1976) and *Polygon* (1977). The first film (the tale of a little boy who, having misbehaved with his mother, daydreams about a trip to Siberia and other heroic actions which might move his mother to forgive him), displays photographic, poster-like illustrations. *Polygon* is an action-filled, suspenseful science-fiction story based on a script by writer S. Gansovsky. On a desert island in an unidentified ocean, a new tank, capable of reacting to mental waves of fear and hate, is being tested. The new weapon is extremely effective in avoiding enemy strikes, but it becomes deadly when it reacts to the waves of fear from its own builders. Beyond the pacifist message, the film is enriched by realistic visual choices which had also characterized *Mother Will Forgive Me*, and which nearly make it a film of live actors (in fact, Petrov used the features of famous stars such as Jean Gabin, Mel Ferrer, Yul Brynner and Paul Newman).

> 'I was looking for masks which could help me convey the atmosphere of the world I wanted to present, its human content and its psychological aspects,' Petrov said.[1]

Nina Shorina (Moscow, 10 March 1943), the director of several puppet movies, rose to the international stage with *Poodle* (see Colour Plate 71)

and *The Door* (both of 1986). Two sarcastic, even gloomy films for adults in which the narrative tradition of Russian tale mixes with the purest lesson of German expressionist set design. *The Door*, the most acclaimed of the two films, features people entering a house through passages other than the door, even though a child has proven that the door is not locked. The monotonous voice of the radio forces this symbolic tale into an ominous contemporary setting.

It is not possible to mention here the innumerable Moscow filmmakers, except perhaps for Viacheslav Kotenochkin (Moscow, 20 June 1927), whose career took a peculiar turn. After a long apprenticeship, he became very popular in 1969 with the series *Just Wait!*, a cartoon featuring a wolf and a hare. The series, which ran for years, was loved by audiences in the Soviet Union and abroad. An unusual example of openly comic Soviet animation, this is the Slavic version of American action films in the tradition of *Roadrunner & Coyote*; it is a quieter account, less violent, less fanciful and lacking refined animation, but characterized by a sure feeling for performance.

Fedor Khitruk

The major Russian animator of the 1960s was Fedor Khitruk (Tver, 1 May 1917). Before becoming a director himself, Khitruk spent 24 years as an animator at Sojuzmultfilm. 'The animator's work demands enormous effort,' he said. 'When I became aware that my physical strength was diminishing ... I became a director.'[2] His first film, *History of a Crime* (1961) had a neorealist flavour. Why does the quiet, reserved clerk kill a noisy little lady? Because he is a victim of the many people who, at all times of the day or night, make noise and do not let him sleep; he is eventually pushed over the edge and kills the boisterous woman. Khitruk's graphics were innovative for the times and especially for Soviet

1   Anatoly Volkov, 'Anatolij Petrov,' *Animafilm*, 2 (Warsaw, 1980), p. 20.
2   Fedor Khitruk, personal communication (1974).

animation. He developed this film with sympathy for the man's misadventures, and without the manneristic optimism typical of the films produced in the Eastern block countries. *Boniface's Vacation* (1965), a delicate film for children, was a rare example of non-rhetorical work.

In 1968, he directed *Film Film Film* an apt satire on filmmaking, from creation to directing, which annoyed Soviet bureaucracy. Khitruk was an expert, clever craftman who liked to keep up-to-date and concerned.

> 'Modern topics require a modern acting style,' he said about his characters, adding 'I do not believe there is an art which does not deal with social problems; and everything which deals with man is, by itself, a social problem.'

Still, he is well rooted in tradition and is not a revolutionary ('My master is still the great Cha-

plin,' he said. 'A director is impoverished if he does not turn to children's tales from time to time.')

The Island (1973) and *Icarus and the Wisemen* (1977) have a somewhat more preachy tone than his other films; *Icarus*, however, is an intelligent and cleverly indignant film (Icarus attempts to fly despite the derision of the establishment and intellectuals who will later bury him with a eulogy). Another sincere film is *The Lion and the Bull* (1983), a warning against war (including nuclear war) which threatens to break out between the two giant animals after they both have been betrayed by a maleficent creature.

Andrei Khrzhanovsky

The family environment had a large role in Andrei Khrzhanovsky's artistic vocation. Born in Moscow on 30 November 1939,[1] he was the son of a painter and lover of books who passed on his interests in art and narrative (in his mature years the filmmaker would often work on screen adaptations of literary works). After graduating from the Moscow State Institute for Cinema with Lev Kuleshov, Khrzhanovsky made *Once Upon a Time There Was Koziavin* (1966), a parody of the conforming, insensitive bureaucrat who is a classical figure in Russian (and not only Russian) culture. In this case, the bureaucrat is ordered to head in a particular direction while looking for a person; and so he does, taking a trip around the world and treading on everything and everybody before returning to his starting point.

In *The Crystal Harp*, Khrzhanovsky used a mix of different styles, even to excess, to narrate a tale of freedom and hope repressed by despotism. In *The Closet* (1971), a Kafkaesque tale, he describes a man's passion for his closet, and how the closet becomes the man's own world. Other films followed: *The Butterfly* (1972, see Colour Plate 72), *In the World of Tales* (1973), *A Day*

Fig. 132. Film Film Film *by Fedor Khitruk (USSR, Russia, 1968).*

1   The filmmaker gave this date. Other sources report either 30 October 1939 or the year 1930.

of Marvel (1975) and two screen adaptations of English poems translated by Samuel Marshak entitled *The House That Jack Built* (1976) and *Miracles in a Sieve* (also known as *Nine Days of Marvel*, 1976), and a collection of children's rhymes such as *Robin Hood, Visiting the Queen, Impossible* and *Three Wise Men.*

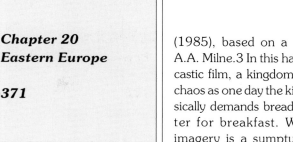
Afterward, Khrzhanovsky undertook an ambitious but less creatively oriented trilogy of mid-length films, based on drawings, notes and poems by Aleksandr Pushkin. The three films were entitled *I Fly Toward You in My Memories* (1977), *I Am Still with You* (1980) and *Autumn* (1982). Although being a state-sponsored poet laureate weighs heavily on the project and the filmmaker's creative freedom, Khrzhanovsky's visionary skills remain intact, and his literary knowledge safely leads the viewers through Pushkin's world.

> 'The central episode of the film, *The Poet and the Czar*, a sort of film-inside-the film, and the best of the trilogy, consists of an ironic dialogue based on a draft of *Imaginary Conversation with Alexander I* (December 1824),' Sergei Asenin writes. 'The visual presentation of this episode uses only one drawing: a humoristic self-portrait drawn by the poet that same year. In a way which is made possible only by animation, the film shows what Pushkin imagines being an emperor must mean. The animator (Yuri Norstein) undertook this complex role) plays the scene so skillfully that the one drawing seems to multiply. The result gives the impression of a totally new vision and of a specific contact with Pushkin's incomparable personality, the journeys of his soul and the creative process behind his ideas.'[1]

Khrzhanovsky returned to a more personal cinema with *The King's Bread and Butter* (1985), based on a script by A.A. Milne.[3] In this happily sarcastic film, a kingdom falls into chaos as one day the king whimsically demands bread and butter for breakfast. While the imagery is a sumptuous synthesis of styles, the paradoxical humour of the film is harshly ironic toward the use of power for personal purposes (symbolized here by the king and his bureaucratic apparatus).

> 'It is necessary to build a meaningful frame, which demands of viewers the highest level of participation,' Khrzhanovsky wrote on his art. 'The free structures of composition and the combination of various stylistic elements must aim at one sole goal: obtaining a direct, pregnant expression, a balance between emotions and the logical order of things'.[2]

Beyond their captivating exteriors, his films are rich in cross-references and offer different levels of interpretation. Cultivated but not cerebral, they show the expert hand of a director who can create a new, independent visual universe from several artistic suggestions. (It should be stressed once more that Khrzhanovsky himself did not draw, but co-ordinated the efforts of different artists, that he chose specifically for each film; among them, Natalia Orlova). Khrzhanovsky's contemporary use of ironic and lyrical themes are typical of late 20th century intellectuals: power and its degeneration, freedom and spiritual search. Like the work by his colleague Yuri Norstein, Andrei Khrzhanovsky's animation is clearly linked to the human, psychological and imaginative avenues explored by Russian cinema as a whole and, at its best, in the live-action works of Andrei Tarkovsky and Nikita Mikhalkov.

Yuri Norstein

Yuri Norstein was born on 15 September 1941 in Andreevka, a small village north-east of Mos-

1   Sergei Asenin, 'Andrej Khrzanovsky,' *Zagreb 86 Retrospectives* (Zagreb 1986), p. 59.
2   Sergei Asenin, 'Andrej Khrzanovsky.'

cow where his Moscow- based Bielorussian family had found refuge from the war. After a childhood that he curiously described as being 'happy, because of its being dramatic', he lost his father at the age of fourteen. He learned cabinet-making and later attended a drafting course at Sojuzmultfilm. At the age of twenty he joined the staff at Sojuzmultfilm, working as artist or art director on innumerable films, including *Who Has Said Meow?*, *My Green Crocodile* and Ivan Ivanov-Vano's feature film *The Left-Handed*. He made his directing debut with *The 25th: The First Day* (1968, in collaboration with Arkady Tiurin). A commemoration of the October Revolution, this captivating, incisive film featured paintings by Petrov-Vodkin, Filonov and Malevich and music by Shostakovich. Directed with full respect for these avant-garde artists (the only accompanying colour was an explicitly symbolic red), it won fame for Norstein, despite its being a project of execution rather than invention.

The Battle of Kerzhents (1970, a 70 mm film co-directed with Ivanov-Vano) used ancient frescoes, icons and miniatures of the 12–14th centuries to describe the Tartar invasion and the Russian soldiers' victorious resistance at the walls of Kerzhents. The style and images were worthy of an Eisenstein epic, although a couple of scenes are not up to par with the rest. The central theme comes from a fragment of Rimsky-Korsakov's *History of the Lost City of Kitez* (an old legend often represented in Russian culture by such artists as Sergei Esenin). *The Battle of Kerzhents* enjoyed a great success and won, among other awards, the highest recognition at the Zagreb Festival of 1972. Norstein deserved much of the credit, but the charismatic and popular Ivanov-Vano eclipsed him in film-reviews.

In 1973, a solo Norstein directed *The Fox and the Hare*, the tale of a fox which is evicted by a hare and makes an alliance with a rooster. Although the film was in tune with the requirements of Soviet animation of the time (it was a children's

film based on folkloric themes), its originality and strength confirmed Norstein's atypical qualities as a director. The tasteful drawings were by Franceska Jarbusova, Norstein's companion, who became his most trusted artistic collaborator.

The Heron and the Crane (1974), with a script by Norstein and Roman Katsanov, was similarly based on a popular tale, but did not have anything to do with films for children. A Chekhov-like succession of proposals, rejections and vexations, between a heron and the crane he would like to marry ('her beak is similar to mine, and she has long legs') constitutes the plotline. Behind a light exterior, a romantic setting (columns with creeping ivy and a delicate but corroded architecture), graceful drawings and veiled colours by Jarbusova, the film tells a tale of solitude and miscommunication, unexpressed hopes and unsolved egotism.

The Hedgehog in the Fog (1975), from a subject by S. Kozlov, was an almost actionless film which provided Norstein with the opportunity to utilize his skills as a visionary and a creator of settings.

> 'One night, the hedgehog went to meet a bear cub, to drink tea and count the stars. The stars on the right belonged to the hedgehog, the ones to the left belonged to the cub … '.

A creature used to talking to himself (' … and I'll tell him, I brought you some strawberry jam …') and to seeing the world through stupefied eyes, the hedgehog is surprised by the fog while in the woods. Out of the fog's ethereal mist come animals, leaves, a snail, an owl, a large tree, a stream, and a white horse which remains impressed on the little traveller's imagination. In the end, the bear cub finds his friend, sits down with him and talks and talks, while the hedgehog still cannot keep the white horse out of his mind. From such a thin plot, Norstein creates a brief poem on the relation between dream and reality and on the role of imagination as an approach to life. The charm of this film relies, above all, on its visual characteristics: the viewers forget that they are seeing just drawings and start living in a three-dimensional environment of opaque lights, humidity and presences coming out of the depths. The multiplane camera is used masterfully.

Norstein's masterpiece (and the masterpiece of Soviet animation) is *The Tale of Tales* (1979) (see Colour Plate 73), a film based on mental associations. Images flow in a 27-minute, all-consuming fantasy: memories of childhood and war, Pushkin's drawings, references to Picasso, a tango in the outskirts of the city, Bach's *Well-tempered Clavichord* and Mozart's *Concert No. 5 in F minor.*

> 'Sleep, sleep, or the grey wolf cub will take you away in the woods ...', a famous Russian lullaby says.

In the film, the wolf cub resembles a stuffed animal and is the unifying element, representing the sweetness of childhood, nostalgia and the truth of feelings. Some sequences are unforgettable, such as the dance hall in wartime, from which the men leave one by one for the front, with only the women remaining; the garden under the snow, with a child, apples and crows; a wolf cub who steals a baby, believing it is a roll of paper, and then tries to rock the crying infant to sleep. Like the *The Mirror* by Andrei Tarkovsky, a film which is in many ways similar, *The Tale of Tales* is an elegiac reading of a man's soul, his research (and rediscovery) of the emotional and spiritual roots of a generation and a time.

Norstein developed inspiration and motifs while a film was in progress, and from film to film, as if his talent needed to crystallize around slowly maturing themes.

> 'A film begins to develop while it is in the

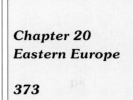

**Chapter 20
Eastern Europe**

373

works, during filming,' said Norstein. 'This may be detrimental from the standpoint of production, but from the standpoint of creation I think it allows for a more transformable content than if everything had been pre-planned.'[1]

Such a statement on the creative process explains the reasons for Norstein's limited production. It also testifies to the position of artist laureate he held in his country. His own methods constrained him with prolonged time and constant retakes. Within a rigorously organized production company, he was able (albeit with some oppostition) to unbridle his fantasies, having to compete only with himself. Years before, John Hubley had followed an analogous process, being first a master of a pictorial, cinematographic form, and later becoming the founder of his own poetics.

Norstein's repeated criticism of experimental art, which he identified with formalism, should be viewed in this perspective: to him, artistic research was the deepening of sensitivity and analysis (including, formal analysis of emotional and human conditions, in a 'classical' manner; whereas avant-garde art existed in a totally different cultural background.

> 'Style is the plastic moment through which we are forced to go, ' he said.[2]

Since Norstein's journey and research are ongoing, a final portrait of his vision is not yet possible. One element, however, can be identified now – the powerful, original interpretation of Russian culture (which so many films have explored only on the surface) by an artist who acknowledged influences from the Chinese shadow theatre, adored Jean Vigo, paid a tribute to the Fellini of *Amarcord* in *The Hedgehog in the Fog*, and admitted 'with no haughtiness' that his films 'lack a deeply Russian spirit'.[3] Norstein

1   Michel Kampolski, Derrière l'image visible sur l'écran,' *Positif* (Paris, November 1985), p. 48.
2   Michel Kampolski, 'Derrière l'image.'
3   Philippe Pierre-Adolphe, 'Youri Norstein: Histoire d'un entretien,' *Banc-Titre*, 23 (Paris, September 1982), p. 36.

shows ties to Pushkin and Chekhov (whose settings and drawings appear in his films), Tolstoy, and post-revolutionary lyrics, while his shy, spiritual hedgehog who counts the stars reminds viewers of Aleksandr Dovzhenko's dreaming peasants, or the woodsman who follows a star in Mikhalkov-Konchalovsky's *Siberiad*.

A sometimes unpopular filmmaker with Soviet cultural authorities because of his hint of bourgeois individualism ('What kind of viewer do I have in mind in my work? As paradoxical as it may seem, I have myself in mind ... ',[1] Norstein offers constant retellings of the psychological and spiritual realities, the culture and the experiences of Russia.

Soviet Union II: Animation in the Federal Republics

Ukraine

In Odessa, Viacheslav Levandovsky made the first Ukrainian short, *The Tale of the Straw Bull* (1927). Immediately afterward, he organized a permanent studio in Kiev, where he was joined by Semen Guyetsky, Evgeny Gorbach and Ippolit Lazarchuk. The most important work of this period was the satirical *The Prohibited Parrot*, by Lazarchuk (Kiev, 1903–79). Because of high costs, the studio suspended production in the 1930s after six films and became involved with educational and scientific films, although it still released a few animated works. In 1959, the studio returned to its original purpose with Lazarchuk's *The Little Pepper's Adventure*.

Irina Gurvich (Letitchev, 30 June 1911), a skilled film and art director, made about thirty films, including *The Ballad of the Fire Heart* (1967, on a subject by Gorky) and the pacifist film *March the Twentieth* (1969). *How the Wives Sold Their Husbands* (1972), probably her master-

piece, is an amusing impertinent film, with references to popular cross-stitched embroideries; based on an old Ukrainian song, it tells how some women brought their husbands to the market in order to sell them to the highest bidder. The film was counterbalanced by *How Husbands Taught Their Wives a Lesson* (1976).

David Cherkassky (1932) distinguished himself with the quasi-feature film *Comic Mystery*, an enlightened interpretation of Mayakovsky's text which suffered, however, from a clearly anti-cinematic structure. Evgeny Sivokon (1937) made his directing debut with *Splinters* (1966). Years later at the 1980 Zagreb Festival, he received international praise for *Laziness* (or *Castling*, 1979), a suggestive symbolic film with allusions to Oblomov. Vladimir Dakhno (born in 1932) owes his popularity to a series about a comical trio of Cossacks. Starting with *How the Cossacks Made Gulash* (1967), the three protagonists (a shrewd one, a calm one and a strong one) went from playing soccer to fighting the pirates, to purchasing salt, to the Olympics and so on. The characters also became popular outside their native Ukraine. Cesar Orshansky (1927) made *The Magical Freezing* (1974), a graceful tale about the Northern regions in ancient times. As the story goes, words freeze and take the shape of beautiful lace. Once a foreigner buys them and takes them away, they melt into songs. The film's images were inspired by the crocheted lace of Voloeda. Overall, the Ukranian studio employed 150 people, including several directors, and produced an average of twelve films a year.

Belarus

The filmmakers of Minsk were the last to appear on the international scene. The key films are *The Last One* (1990) by Alexandre Chepetov (born 1963), *The Wings* (1990) – the first work of Alexandre Lenkine, and *Dreams of an Autumn*

---

1   Mieczyslaw Walasek, 'Just Art: L'art tout court,' *Animafilm*, 5 (Warsaw, 1980), p. 42.

Evening (1990) by Tatiana Jit-
kovskaia.

Georgia

In the early 1930s, a branch of
the Tbilisi-based film institute
produced political and satirical
animated films. In 1936,
Vladimir Mudgiri (1907–53) directed *The Argonauts*, where the Ancient Greek myth on the
conquest of the Golden Fleece was a pretext to
praise the reclamation of Colchian marshes.
Until his death, Mudgiri continued his limited production, which includes *Cora* (1939) and some
films of anti-Nazi propaganda.

In 1957, Vakhtang Bakhtadze (Tbilisi, 26 December 1914), editor of *The Argonauts*, gained
notoriety with *Samodelkin's Adventures*, about
a man-like robot which was loved by audiences
and returned in three sequels. Afterward, Bakhtadze directed *Narcissus* (1964), *Oh Fashion,
Oh Fashion* (1968, his best film) and *More on
Fashion* (1969).

Animation attracted also directors of live-action films, such as
Arkady Khintibidze's *Hostility*
(1959) or the reknowned live-
action director Mikhail Chavreli,
who began animating in the
1960s. In the 1970s, production was given a new boost. Mik-
hail Bakhanov (1942–1974) directed *Ranina*, a
fine film with effervescent pictorial and narrative
styles. A character sings the popular song
Ranina, while other individuals, each representing a region of Georgia, stop him and correct
the song according to the versions of their regions. Josif Samsonadze (born in 1935) filmed
The Wise Man and the Donkey (1978), based
on traditional fables by Sulkhan-Saba Orbeliani
and artistically derived from Georgian illuminated
texts.

Ilja Dojashvili (born in 1938) reached his heights
with *Optimistic Miniature* (1978), a pacifist
manifesto exalting the work of patient, hard-
headed farmers versus the destruction brought by

Fig. 133. The
Argonauts by
Vladimir Mudgiri
(USSR, Georgia,
1936).

a warplane. Vladimir Sulakve-lidze (1957) made *The Land Takes Back Its Own* (1983), a rich but cold tale of a boy looking for a country where death does not exist. David Takaishvili (born in 1959) displayed a suggestive pictorial taste. His first film, *The Crow* (1981), is a work full of subtle references and atmosphere, although it may owe too much to Norstein's lessons. His second film, *The Plague*, (1983), won a Golden Palm at the Cannes Film Festival.

Armenia

In 1937, Lev Atamanov, of Armenian descent, moved to Erivan from Moscow. After *The Dog and the Cat*, he made a second film, *The Priest and the Goat*, which was not released because of the war. Atamanov quit and returned to Moscow. Armenian production started again in the late 1960s with Valentin Podpomogov (Erivan, 1926), whose first film was the pacifist *A Drop of Honey* (1968). Afterward he directed *The Violin in the Jungle* (1969, on the immortality of art), *Parvana* (1970) and *That It Won't Happen* (1976). In 1972, Robert Saakjantz (Baku, 1950) directed *Lilith*, the first work of his large filmography. With images inspired by illuminated codices, the film tells of the creation of the first woman from fire. The happily fantastic *Kikos* (1979, based on a tale by Ovanes Tumanian, see Colour Plate 74), was a very different movie – of the joyous and creative kind. In the even more playful *Who Narrates the Incredible* (1982), a king tries uselessly to steal money from his subjects, challenging them to narrate such unbelievable tales that will cause him to exclaim, 'It is not true!'. Ludmila Saakjantz (Robert's wife), a celebrated script writer, showed her skills as a film director in *The Mouse Meeting*; Elena Prokorova's dark colours serve as a background to this sarcastic tale of mice, incapable of reaching an agreement even when threatened by a cat. Stepan Galstjan (Erivan, 1951) directed *Fanos the Unlucky*, based on a subject by Tumanian, about

a character whose stupidity is defined as bad luck. Aida Saakian (Erivan, 1958) directed *The Wooden Bowl* (1984), based on Leo Tolstoy's tale about respect for the elderly. Aleksandr Andronikian (Moscow, 1960) made his debut with the lively, comically original *Hare Hunt* (1985).

Estonia

The Estonian studio Tallinnfilm opened in September 1957, under the direction of puppet animator

Elbert Tuganov (born Baku, 22 February 1920). Tuganov, who studied cinema in Berlin before the war, directed the studio's first release, *Little Peter's Dream* (1958). Equally interested in puppet films and animated drawings, during his distinguished career he dealt with themes for children as well as for adults. His filmography includes: the satiric *Talent* (1963), about pedagogy inside the family; *The Last Chimneysweep* (1964) a lyric tale in which the traditional chimneysweep is replaced by the more modern technician installing TV antennas; and *Bloody John* (1974), a comic-heroic tale about a pirate, tyrannized by his shrewish wife.

Heino Pars (Mustla, 13 October 1925) made his debut with *The Little Scooter* (1962), the tale of a little scooter which saves a woodpecker and a squirrel from a hunter. In 1964, with the film *Kops, the Cameraman in the Land of Mushrooms*, he began a children's series to spread the love of nature (Kops, a puppet with his camera, is the filmmaker's self-portrait). *The Snow Mill* (1971) was a tale about the beautiful landscape of Northern regions; *The Nail* (1972), featuring a simple nail which became a comic actor, was followed nine years later by *The Nail, Part 2* with variations on the theme.

Rein Raamat (Tjuri, 20 March 1931), a puppet animator and a live-action filmmaker, founded a section devoted to animated drawings at Tallinnfilm, in 1971. An iron-fisted director with a gift for the dramatic, he adapted his own taste as a painter to the artistic qualities of his collaborators and gave way to an eclectic production. In his first important film, *The Flight* (1973), dealing with the human aspiration to rise both physically and spiritually, he coordinated the work of art director Aili Vint and draftsman Avo Paistik. *The Whale Hunter* (1976, see Colour Plate 75), another symbolic film but with faster images and rhythm, depicts the struggle between a hunter and his prey, his fall into the sea, and his ultimate alliance with the animal when they are both in danger, struggling to survive.

For *The Field* (1978), one of Raamat's finest films, the artist used his own drawings as well as Rein Raidme's. The result was, in Sergei Asenin's words:

> 'an epic poem on how the individual's daily labour requires perseverance, will-power, persistence. All this is represented by a plowman, who assumes metaphorical meaning.'[1]

With *The Great Toll* (1980), Raamat rose to international fame. Featuring drawings by Juri Arrak, Heiki Ernits and Valter Uusberg, this film retells the medieval tale of the giant Toll, a symbol of the Estonian people. The colossal Toll combats invaders, and dies in the fight, but returns to life every time his land needs him. Characterized by elegant pictorial solutions, with opaque tints based on amaranth, lilac and brown, and by Lepo Sumera's music in the sound track, the film was internationally praised. Finally, Ramaat's *Hell* (1983) is a powerful choral film on the dissolution and decadence of an epoch and its customs, based on three popular engravings (*Cabaret, The Preacher* and *Hell*, Paris 1930–1932) by Estonian painter Eduard Viiralt (1898–1954). The sound track of this film, also, features the pressing music of Lepo Sumera.

Avo Paistik (Tallinn, 1936) a former electronic engineer whose drawings have appeared in Raamat's *The Flight*, made his debut as a director with a film for children, *The Pastel Pencils* (1973), where the good guys are red, yellow and green pencils and the bad guy is a black pencil. His major success is *A Sunday* (1977), a satirical depiction of a representative of modern civilization, spending a mechanized, consumeristic, inhuman holiday. After a short series featuring Klaabu (a monster with an egg-shaped body, born from a water drop and capable of changing its own features), Paistik made another acclaimed film, *High Jump* (1985, award-winner at the Stuttgart festival, 1986) about an athlete whose emphasis on training, in the end, cannot guarantee his victory.

Priit Pärn (Tallinn, 1946) put aside his degree in biology from the University of Tartu, and chose instead to write and draw. Unlike some of his colleagues, he wanted to be the absolute author of his movies, being responsible for script, drawings and direction. His decidedly sloppy but aggressive graphics were appreciated for the first time in *Is the Earth Round?* (1977, see Colour Plate 76), about a man's journey around the earth that finishes at the point of departure (a journey which corresponds to the man's life). In 1988, he won the grand prize at the Zagreb festival with *Picnic on the Grass*. Taking Manet's painting as a starting point, the film is in fact a libel against Soviet bureaucracy and society, with an hostile perspective which recalls the angst of George Grosz.

A Green Bear Cub (1979) is about a cub who loves to perform in front of the animals of the forest, and can take the shape of a variety of creatures and objects when doing so. As an artist, the cub is a disruption to quiet living, but in the end, it is clearly needed by its society. Pärn's finest, most complex work is *Some Exercises for an Independent Life* (1980), about the contrast between a grey, methodical adult – a true crea-

---

1 Sergei Asenin, *Etüüde eesti multifilmidest: Ja nende loojatest* (Tallinn: Perioodika, 1986), p. 278.

ture of habit – and a playful, creative boy. Gradually the two evolve into one another. This film is a metaphorical work, but with a less schematic message than previous efforts.

In *The Triangle* (1981), Pärn dealt with the problem of family relations, and in *Stories in the Air* (1985) he told the tale of a happy, absent-minded cat.

Other Estonian animators include Ando Kesskula (Tallinn, 1950, *Tales About a Little Rabbit*, 1975); Aarne Ahi (Tartu, 1943, *Does It Move? Yes, It Does!*, 1977); Tonis Sahkai (Tallinn, 1943, *Bedtime Stories*, 1977); Mati Kutt (Tallinn, 1947, *The Monument*, 1981); Kalju Kivi (Tartu, 1947, *A Sheet of Paper*, 1981 and *The Knot*, 1983); Rao Heidmets (Parnu, 1956, *The Lady of the Pigeons*, 1983); Valter Uusberg (Keila, 1953, *The Ox*, 1984); Kaarel Kurismaa (Parnu, 1938, *A Young, Featherheaded Trolley*, 1983); and the duo of Riho Unt (Tallinn, 1956) and Hardi Volmer (Parnu, 1957), who made such films as the subtly disturbing *The Magic Christmas Eve* (1984) and the sarcastic *The Springtime Fly* (1986), an adult tale characterized by an airy, incisive style.

Latvia

The production of animated works in this Baltic republic began in 1965 thanks to the initiative of four professionals with the Puppet Theatre of Riga: director and set designer Arnold Burovs, puppet maker Anna Nollendorf, actor Arvid Norins and theatre operator Valentins Jakobsons. The spiritual leader of the group was Arnold Burovs, who devoted himself exclusively to the animation of puppets. Burovs, (Riga, 23 April 1915), a musician, set designer and the director of the Puppet Theatre (from 1945), authored a remarkable number of films, such as *Cock-a-Doodle-Doo* (1966), *Pygmalion* (1967), *The Tale of the Copper Coin* (1969), *Umurkumurs* (1976, see Colour Plate 77) and the trilogy inspired by O. Henry including *The Dream* (1983), *The Last Leaf* (1984) and *The Princess and the*

Puma (1985). Burovs was a highly reputed artist and one of the most influential puppet animators (Ion Popescu-Gopo praised him with the famous words: 'I have never seen anything as genuine as this since Trnka'). But in fact, his films seem guided by technical expertise rather than poetry and his characters lack personality despite fascinating sets, care for detail and consummate camera movements. An example is *The Dream*, a salute to Charlie Chaplin, where the protagonist puppet is just a pale imitation of the original.

Other directors of the group include the aforementioned Arvid Norins, who directed a series featuring a dog named Caps (or 'catch it'), Peteris Trups' *Springtime Song* (1984) and Janis Cimermanis' *The Live Friend* (1987).

As for animated drawings, the specialist was Roze Stiebra (Riga, 1942), who in 1969 became responsible for the animation department at the Latvian telebroadcasting organization. For several years, she worked with the cutout technique; her best effort was *Journey to the Daughter of the North* (1980) a somewhat disquieting tale about the call to adventure – a call which is initially suppressed with laziness and discouragement, but later resurfaces. Afterwards Stiebra became involved with animated drawings. In 1984 she made the delicate *Sister Dear*, the *leitmotif* of which is a traditional song about cross-stitching. Ansis Berzins (Riga, 1940), co-director for several years with Stiebra, who later became a director in his own right, and Ivars Osins also deserve mention.

Lithuania

In 1984, a production company opened in Vilnius, with a small group of technicians and artists. Painter Nyole Valadkeviciute, an expert at recreating gloomy, menacing sets, directed *The Enigma* (1984) and *Space Tale* (1985). Ilja Bereznizkas (Vilnius, 1948) surprised critics with *The Bogeyman* (1986), a comic, fast-paced tale about a little girl and a bogeyman – the only member of her family that pays attention to her. Renowned caricaturist Zenonas Steinis (Kybartai, 1946), made his animation debut with *There Was, There Was, Sure There Was* (1986, see Colour Plate 78), a dynamic nonsensical tale, in the comical style of Tatarsky. Finally, a forerunner of Lithuanian animation, Antanas Janauskas is remembered for *The Stamp* (1986) and the home production *Initiative* (1970).

Azerbaijan

In this republic on the Caspian Sea, work on animation began in the late 1960s. Aga Nagi Akhundov directed *Girtdan* (1969) and *Fitne* (1970), a fine film based on native poet Nizami's *The Seven Wonders* and traditional images. *The Fox's Pilgrimage* (1971), Girtdan's *New Adventures* (1972) and *Giugialiarin* (1975) followed.

Formerly a collaborator of Akhundov's, Maxud Panakhi made his directing debut in 1973 with *Why Does the Cloud Cry*, inspired by oriental miniatures. He also directed *Play, Play, My Saz* (in collaboration with A. Akperov, 1976) and *The Virgin's Tower* (1978). N. Mamedov, also a collaborator of Akhundov's, directed *Toplan and His Shadow* (1977), *The Little Donkey* (1978) and *The Jar* (1979).

Uzbekistan

A Tashkent-based studio opened in 1965 with Damir Salimov's *In a 6 x 6 Square*. Salimov (1937) also directed *The Golden Watermelon* (1977), a nice tale with animated puppets about a farmer who is helped by a magic crane, and *The Drop* (1984), with animated drawings, about a thirsty man who is staring so hard at a water drop that he can not see the water gushing out nearby. Zinovy Roizman (1941) made his debut with *The Little Swindler* (1968); he reached his apex by animating the puppets in *The Tale of the Shepherd and the Beautiful Princess* (1974).

In the late 1970s, animation was given a new boost, and many young artists joined in. Irina Krivoseieva (1946) made her debut by co-directing *The Most Disobedient* (1976) with Zinovy Roizman. After several other collaborations, she directed *Live Clay* (1982) and *The Queen of the Mice* (1983, about a woman whose daughter is so beautiful that even the sun does not deserve to take her as its wife). Mavzur Mahmudov (1947) vivaciously retold the adventures of the clever Hogia Nasruddin, a traditional character who starred in four films (1982). Musrad Bajmukhamedov (1939) directed *The Last Wonder* (1980) and *The Magic Flute* (1982) The story is taken from a traditional tale about a flute which becomes magical only when played by its legitimate owner, a shepherd.

Nikolai Smirnov (1950) animated ceramic toys in *The Tale of Clay* (1983), about a dragon who wants to make friends rather than be ferocious. Nazim Tuliakhogiaev (1951), the son of a writer and playwright, was original in that he did not draw solely from traditional legends and tales (a common tendency of animation in Central Asia), but also from contemporary texts. After his debut with *The Lake in the Desert* (1979), he showed his skills in *The Idol* (1982), the story of a haughty man who creates an idol in his image, and is then struck by lightning. In 1984, Tuliakhogiaev directed *There Will Come Soft Rains*, a film based on a tale by Ray Bradbury (from the collection *The Martian Chronicles*). Set in the year 2026 after a nuclear catastrophe, it shows a house of the future, emptied of human beings, and inhabited by surviving appliances. Although the film does not do justice to Bradbury's text, it is still rich with evocative charm.

Kazakhstan

Amen Khaidarov (Alma-Ata, 1923) inaugurated the animation activity in this large republic, with *Why Do Swallows have Forked Tails?* (1967). The film, which remained this artist's best work, features a dying dragon which needs fresh young blood to regain its terrible strength, and a swallow which saves humankind but loses the central feathers of its tail to the dragon.

Viktor Tchugunov (Alma-Ata, 1935) also had his best results in his first film, *The Flea and the Wise-man* (or *The Transformation*, 1969). The wise-man's decision not to kill its tormentor (the flea) but to throw it back in the street holds terrible repercussion,s and the conclusion that when a wise man makes a mistake, the whole world suffers for it.

Gani Kistauov (Alma-Ata, 16 December 1944) directed *Kadir's Happiness* in 1977, a comic apologue against laziness, and in 1994 *The Dragon's Island*, a dramatic story about a killer of a dragon who is tempted by jealousy (for his daughter) to become 'a dragon himself'. The images of the film were inspired by the cracked enamel of Japanese vases.

Other works from this region include Tamara Mendeseva's *The Silk Brush* (1977), an Altai tale about a beautiful girl transformed into a snowball.

Kirghizistan

Saghinbek Ishenov (Burana, 1934), former set designer of live-action films, became director of Kirghizfilm in the mid-1970s. He made his directing debut with *The Numbers Fight* (a still-unfinished work filmed with assistance from Kazakhstan). In 1983, he made a tasteful film, rich in pathos, with plasticine and animated puppets entitled *Tolubai, Horse Expert*. It is about a horse trainer who has a knack with stallions, and his fight against the powerful Sara-Khan.

The Ornamental Tale (1981, see Colour Plate 79) by Viacheslav Belov (Frunze, 1953) is another notable work, filmed in the capital city of Frunze. It features the ornamental patterns of local rugs, that have been encoded throughout the millennia into artistic and aesthetic principles.

The film unravels these patterns through the tale of a princess who is kidnapped by a wizard, and then freed by a prince who understands the language of ornamental drawings.

Tajikistan

One of the major artists from the Dusambe-based studio was Munovar Mansurkhogiaev (Dusambe, 1951), director of *Guldor The Little Fish* (1981). The film is about a boy who must give the Shah his fish, and then conquers the beautiful princess Zumat. Mansurkhogiaev also directed other films, including *The Princess of the Goats* (1985).

Turkmenistan

The first film from Ashabad was the comic *Air Bubbles* (1975), written, drawn, animated and directed by Medzek Tchariev (Bairam-Ali, 1944). In 1981, Cariev directed *The Flying Carpet*, the umpteenth variation on the magic object which brings bad luck to anyone attempting to use it, except the legitimate owner.

Moldavia

The activity of Natalia Bodiul (Kishinev, 14 July 1949) stands out from the limited Moldavian production. Her movies include *Melody* (1973) and *The Stairs* (1974), featuring environmentalist and pacifist concerns, and *Elegy* (1975).

Albania

Animation in this republic, which existed secluded both from the capitalist and the communist world from the end of World War II to the fall of the Soviet empire, began in 1975 with *Zana and Miri* (see Colour Plate 80) by director Vlash Droboniku (Berati, 5 February 1945), released by the state-run production company, New Albania. This colour film made with cutouts, featured a boy and a girl playing ball without concern for the flowers. Afterward, the production of animated movies consistently increased to an average of more than fifteen shorts a year during the mid-

1980s, many of which were directed by debuting young artists. The majority of these works were addressed to children and revolved around tales or moral, patriotic and educational themes describing children's lives. The technical shortcomings were counter-balanced by the search for new solutions and improved style and technique.

After *Zana and Miri*, Droboniku directed *Spring Holiday* (1977), *Sokol and the Eagle* (1978, about a boy and a girl who, aided by an eagle, the symbol of the country, give the partisans a flag), and *Edi and Number 4* (1980, an award winner at the Balkan festival in 1981). In 1983, he began work with puppets and released *The White Chick*, which led to a series.

Bujar Kapexhiu (Tirana, 22 May 1944), a re-

nowned actor and caricaturist, was one of the most productive filmmakers of his country. His first film was *The Water Drop* (1976), a fine work characterized by a pleasant use of colour, featuring a water drop during its journey through Albania. *Scribbles* (1977), about a child who drew on walls but then repents, was the country's first animated film on cel. Other films by Kapexhiu are: *Mi-Re-La* (1978), featuring three notes and a little girl, Mirela, who cries easily; *The Moving Haystack* (1980), about a child in wartime who finds the enemy hidden in a haystack; and *Pipiruk at the Palace* (1985) about the adventures of a popular character at a pasha's palace.

Tonin Vuksani (Tirana, 23 August 1954) distinguished himself with *The Shoeshiner* (1979),

Fig. 134. A Bullet in the Forehead *by Gazmend Leka (Albania, 1985).*

featuring a little boy who writes antifascist slogans during the Italian military occupation of Albania and manages to escape from a *carabiniere*. Other films by this director include *The Snowman* (1982) and *The Firs* (1984).

Boris Ikonomi (Tirana, 16 April 1956) employed several techniques. His finest film, *Ilira* (1983), about a boy who learns about the glorious tradition of the Albanian region of Ilira and chooses that name for his newborn sister, combines animated drawings and live-action backgrounds.

Esperanca Konomi (Tirana, 16 January 1959) made her debut with *Stop! Traffic Violation!* (1982), followed by the ironic *Strange Boldness* (1984) and *The Whole City Is Laughing* (1987). Jani Zhonga (Tirana, 5 April 1957) used puppets as well as live-action for *Miri and Her Toys* (1981), and the technique of collage for *The Wind and the Kite* (1984). Other artists include: Gjin Varfi (Tirana, 10 May 1954, *The Log*, 1987); Majilinda Agolli (Tirana, 1 May 1960, *Elkana and the Swallow*, 1984); Robert Qafezezi (Tirana, 26 October 1956, *When the Feathers Falls*, 1985 and *Castles in the Air*, 1986) and Artur Dauti (Tirana, 13 November 1957), director of *The Lie* (1981), *The Call of the Land* (1985) about a brother and sister's relationship during the Ottoman occupation, and *The Last Blow* (1986).

Gezim Qendro (Tirana, 22 December 1957) directed *Inspiration* (1986) and *Pipiruk in the Granary* (1987); Artur Muharremi (Pogradeci, 2 June 1958) created *Winter and Children* (1985) and *The Presumptuous Soldier* (1987). Artan Maku (Tirana, 11 August 1954) invented the character of Pik the dog which was first featured in *Not Like This, Pik* (1983) and several other adventures.

Other Albanian artists include Suzana Varvarica (Tirana, 19 July 1955), director of *The Frivolous Cherry Tree* (1983) and *The Ant Race* (1984); Josif Droboniku (Fieri, 21 December 1953), director of *The Anger* (1983) and *Harvest Days* (1984); and Xhovalin Delia (Puka, 29 April 1959), who co-directed *The Bee and the Dove* (1987) with Niko Anagnosti. Sokol Xhahysa followed common trends in works such as *The Child and the Brush* (1983) about the humility and patience needed when learning the basics of painting, but also created adult films such as the collection of gags entitled *Variations on a Theme* (1986) and *Robinson and Those Who Saved Him* (1986). Finally, Gazmend Leka (Tirana, 11 October 1953), painter, illustrator and engraver as well as the art director of the national studio, has left stimulating works, including the black-and-white antifascist film, *A Bullet in the Forehead* (1985) – a sarcastic, angry work with incisive pencil drawings on paper.[1]

---

1   The original title, *Plumb ballit*, contains a pun referring to the Albanian organization Ballit Kombëtar which collaborated with the Nazi and Fascist forces before and during World War II.

Chapter 21

Latin America

Beyond the aforementioned efforts of Brazilian and Argentine artists (and Cuban animators, also, who will be discussed later in this chapter), the production of animated work in Latin America was generally difficult, and therefore, scarce. In Nicaragua, during the Sandinista regime (1979–1990), the Arlen Siu workshop produced in two years some short films made by Nicaraguan animators who had learned the trade from the Danes Jannik Hastrup and Brigitta Faber. The films were: *El cristal con qué se mira* (The Crystal With Which You Watch, 1984, about elections during the previous Somoza dictatorship); *Panchito* (1984), *Tío Coyote y tío Conejo* (Mr Coyote and Mr Rabbit, 1984), *Vigilancia* (Vigilance, 1984, by Maria MacDalland, about civil defence groups), *Trazadora* (Jig Borer, 1985, by Carlos González, about how to react to foreign aggression). The films, with the latter two exceptions, were not signed because they were considered the work of collective endeavour.

In Puerto Rico some TV series were made, mainly Northern American runaway productions. In Costa Rica, EMK Producciones was founded by Emilio Madriz and grew to include more than 25 employees by the late 1970s, reaching a production volume of 600 advertising spots by the late 1980s. Animated films or spots for TV were made in Ecuador and in Chile (where Vivienne Barry made the short *Nostalgias de Dresden* – Homesickness for Dresden – in 1990).

Uruguay nurtured some good filmmakers who found greener pastures elsewhere. Alberto Monteagudo will be discussed in the section on Venezuela. Walter Tournier made in Uruguay *En la selva hay mucho por hacer* (In the Jungle There Are Many Things To Do, a well designed film which is unfortunately undermined by poor musical accompaniment), then in Peru he devoted himself to the cut-outs (*El condor y el zorro* – The Condor and the Fox – 1980) and to plasticine animation (*Nuestro pequeño paraíso* – Our Little Paradise – 1985). The latter film, a brilliantly derisory apologue on television's hypnotic and consolatory effect, gave Tournier fame and awards. Back in Uruguay, he made TV series, such as *Los cuentos de don Veridico* (Don Veridico's Tales) and *Los escondites del sol* (The Shelters of the Sun). Another Uruguayan was Eduardo Darino, who moved to the United States in 1972. Darino (Montevideo, 6 February 1944) did some interesting work in his country, including *Creación* (1962, drawn directly on film stock). His American works include *Homomania* (1973), *Hello … ?* (1977, a history of the telephone) and *The Legend of the Amazon River* (1978).

Mexico

Animation gained popularity during the golden age of Mexican cinema in the 1940s when film directors and film stars such as Julio Bracho, Emilio Fernández, Gabriel Figueroa, Maria Félix, Cantinflas and Pedro Armendáriz became famous. Engineer José Vergara founded Caricolor, a small company devoted to animated advertising and occasional experimental productions, while José Galicia and Claudio Baña founded Cinemuñecos which was not devoted to puppets as the name implies, but competed directly with Caricolor.

In the 1950s, the American R.K. Thompkins moved to Mexico City and initiated a well-financed and well-managed company that employed such animators as Ernesto Terrazas, Ernesto López and Rodolfo Zamora. Later these three artists moved to a new company, the short-lived but highly professional Gamma Producciones.

In the next decade, with a whole new range of opportunities offered by television, new groups were founded including Daniel Burgos' company, the group started by the American Disney veteran Dan McManus, the Canto brothers' Producciones Kinema, and Caleidoscopio, which was founded by the North American Harvey Siegel. One of the most interesting animators was Fernando Ruiz. Born in Mexico City (19 December 1941), he studied music and voice, and graduated in film direction at the Spanish-American University. From 1961 to 1962 he worked as an animator at Disney in Burbank, California. Having returned to Mexico, he founded Producciones Fernando Ruiz. His *El músico* (1965), winner at the Guadalajara's short-film festival, is based on Grieg's *Peer Gynt* suite and features an entire orchestra of instruments that play without musicians. An abstract interpretation of the lessons taught by *Fantasia* or *Make Mine Music*, the film was followed by many television shorts, such

Fig. 135. Los tres reyes magos *by Fernando Ruíz (Mexico, 1976).*

as *La historia de los juegos olímpicos* (The Story of the Olympic Games), *La familia Tele-miau* (The Tele-Miaow Family), and *La bruja Chirilola* (The Witch Chirilola).

In 1976, after two years of work, Ruiz released the first Mexican animated feature film, *Los tres reyes magos* (The Three Wise Men from the East). The film is a children's version of the Biblical story of the three wise men, narrated with pure simplicity and enriched by fairy tale characters (such as the little devil Murcio, who has the power to become a bat, or Olbaid, the prince of Hell).

> 'In making the feature film, we have been very conservative,' said Fernando Ruiz. 'We'd rather try experimenting in short films, which are economically less risky. As for inspiration, we kept close, as much as possible, to Mexican themes. Joseph and Mary are typical Mexicans, the landscape, music and animals are Mexican, and the characters, even the caricatures, come from the clay figurines of pre-Columbian folklore.'[1]

Enrique Escalona, a documentarist and film editor born in Chicago (USA) on 21 July 1939, made a very interesting film in 1988 entitled *Tlacuilo* (see Colour Plate 81). It was a medium length feature of 56 minutes which led the viewers to the discovery of the world and the philosophy of the inhabitants of pre-Columbian Mexico, through the deciphering of their illuminated manuscripts. 'Tlacuilo' means 'he who writes by painting', i.e., the author of such manuscripts.

The film, wrote Escalona,

> '... is not an academic report aimed at professional anthropologists. It is rather an illustration of the values that are at the basis of our Mexican identity, both social and cultural. I wanted to describe the Náhuatl culture, typical

of the Aztecs, by using their writing, one among the most important and most under-valued of their manifestations.'[2]

Cuba

The very beginnings of Cuban animation were marked by *Napoleón, el faraón de los sinsabores* (Napoleon, the Pharaoh of Troubles, 1937), a two-minute, black-and-white film by cartoonist Manuel Alonso. Based on a comic strip series published in the Sunday issue of *El país gráfico*, the film was quite successful, but not enough to support Alonso's work in animation. Shortly thereafter, artists Roseñada and Silvio failed in their attempt to animate the character Masabi.

In Guantánamo, Luis Castillo made *Coctel musical* (Musical Cocktail, 1946), which is a silent film despite its title, and *El jíbaro y el cerdito* (The Farmer and the Little Pig, 1947). Meanwhile, a group led by César Cruz Barrios was founded in Santiago de Cuba. After some experimental work, they released the first Cuban-made colour short, *El hijo de la ciencia* (The Son of Science, 1947). The film was not a great success; however, the group continued to focus on documentaries, newsreels and live-action movies.

In the 1950s, a few works were completed during a limited period of growth in advertising and television. The advertising agency Agencia Siboney hired some young artists who would later produce the first Cuban animated films of quality.

On 24 March 1959, after the Castro revolution, the Instituto Cubano de Arte y Industria Cinematográficos (ICAIC) was founded, and a small section of the institute was devoted to animation. The section's leader was Jesús de Armas, who worked with illustrator Eduardo Muñoz Bachs and other collaborators. The first film released at this time was *La prensa seria* (The Serious Press,

---

1   Personal communication to the author (1976).
2   Enrique Escalona, *Tlacuilo*, Universidad Nacional Autónoma de México, Mexico, 1989, p. 21.

1960), a political satire directed at an adult audience and intended as an:

> '... open denunciation of the slanders and lies published by the private press and a statement of the need to keep it under control. Aesthetically, the film employed the graphics typically used by United Productions of America (UPA)'.[1]

Jesús de Armas began production on activist films aimed at finding support to rebuild a new society. *El tiburon y las sardinas* (The Shark and the Sardines, 1961) discussed the conflict between imperialism and revolution; *La raza* (1961) evolved around the absurdity of racism; *La quema de la caña* (The Fire of the Cane Field, 1961) and *Remember Girón* (1961) illustrated the threat of aggression by the United States. De Armas also directed the first 'narrative' animated movie, *El cowboy* (1962). In 1967, he retired to painting and graphics, but remained in contact with the world of animation he helped to create in Cuba.

The most interesting work of this period was *Los indocubanos* (1964), directed by Modesto Garcia Alvarez (Matanzas, 1930). A historical film made with elegant pen drawings, it sympathetically depicts the peoples of Cuba before the arrival of the Europeans. The drawings used in the film were later incorporated into a book on the same topic. Spaniard Enrique Nicanor's *El gusano* (The Worm, 1963) was also a striking film made during this period.[2]

In the mid-1960s, Cuban animation declined due to a variety of reasons. Foreign influences, first American and later Czechoslovakian and Polish, dampened the original spontaneity of Cuba's animated works. Also, educational films, which had always been produced in Cuba, such as *El realengo* (The Royal Patrimony, 1961), or Jesús de Armas' *AEIOU* (1961), took precedence over other political or artistic works.

In 1965, Luis Rogelio Nogueras's *Un sueño en el parque* (A Vision in the Park, 1965), a pacifist film influenced by Cubism was criticized for being too sophisticated and intellectual to satisfy the needs of the audience. In the more traditional, nationalistic vein, Hernán Henríquez adapted a folk legend in *Osaín* (1966), and was praised for *Oro rojo* (Red Gold, 1969), a film which was also inspired by folk themes. Leinaldo Alfonso became popular with *Quiero marinero ser* (I Want to be a Sailor, 1970), based on a traditional song. In the educational sector, a major personality was Australian artist Harry Reade, maker of the anti-imperialist pamphlet, *La cosa* (The Thing).

In the early 1970s, the animation division of ICAIC was re-structured and re-launched. Wanting to produce works for children, Cuban authorities turned to animation. Conferences were held in several parts of the country to define what was and was not appropriate for children. While animation had to maintain its educational purposes, its expressive choices were to be adapted to the needs of children. Two categories were established. The first was to include 2 to 7 year olds and the second, 8 to 14 years old. The films addressing the first group were to develop fantasy by bringing plants and animals to life, and containing limited dialogue. Films for the older children were to focus on action and adventure with well-developed characters and plot. Tulio Raggi (Havana, 1938) and Mario Rivas (Santa Clara, 19 January 1939) produced works mainly for the younger group, while Juan Padrón (Cárdenas, 29 January 1947) specialized in works for the older children.

These artists' contributions continued well into the 1980s when Cuban animation began experimenting with style and developing themes for adults. Raggi, who made his debut in 1964 with

---

1   Roberto Cobas, 'Notas para una cronología del dibujo animado cubano,' *Cine Cubano*, No. 110 (Havana, 1984).

2   *Gusanos* (worms) was the name given to anti-revolutionary Cubans who supported the United States.

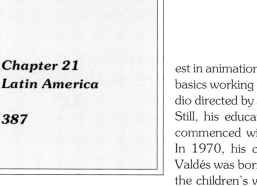

El profesor Bluff, released entertaining educational films such as *El cero* (The Zero, 1977, on mathematics), *El tesoro* (The Treasure, 1977, on geography), and three movies based on Cuban history titled *El negrito cimarrón* (The Little Black Fugitive Slave, 1975), *El trapiche* (The Cane-mill, 1978) and *El palenque de los esclavos cimarrones* (The Shelter, 1978), which is based on a revolt by black slaves and their escape into the mountains. In 1983, Raggi made *El alma trémula y sola* (The Quivering Lonely Soul) (see Colour Plate 82), a film made with still-drawings on an adult subject concerning the exile of the country's father José Martí. The title itself is a verse from a poem by Martí. Set within the dense atmosphere of New York in 1890, the film depicts Martí's chores and memories while preparing the insurrection.

Mario Rivas made his debut with *Parque forestal* (Forest Park, 1973). His many films for children include *Feucha* (Ugly Little Girl, 1978) and *La guitarra* (The Guitar, 1978). In 1981 he directed *El deporte nacional* (The National Pastime), about the development and diffusion of the extremely popular baseball game in Cuba. A serious educator, Rivas displayed his biting humour in episodes of the series *Filminuto* (a collection of short films by different authors from the Havana studio), and in what can be considered his masterpiece, *El bohío* (1984, The Palm Hut). The palm hut, destroyed over and over again by the country's invaders, is constantly rebuilt by one family, until the day of independence proclaimed by Castro. Rich with gags and rhythms, this concise essay on Cuban history is a skilful mix of ideology and entertainment.

A contribution to animation was also made by comic strip artists such as Manuel 'Lillo' Lamar (with his character Matojo), Cecilio Avilés (with Cecilín and Coti) and above all Juan Padrón. Since the age of fifteen, Padrón showed an inter-

est in animation. He learned the basics working briefly in the studio directed by Jesús de Armas. Still, his education as an artist commenced with comic strips. In 1970, his character Elpidio Valdés was born in the pages of the children's weekly magazine *Pionero*. Valdés is a 'mambí', or a nineteenth century Cuban patriot who fights for independence against the Spanish colonialists. After extensive research on customs, objects, uniforms and even food, Padrón offered children an historically accurate view of their ancestors' lives with a long 'novel', narrated with comic strips, as well as animation.[1]

Padrón made his directing debut with *Elpidio Valdés contra el tren militar* (Elpidio Valdés Against the Armoured Train, 1974), which was followed by similar episodes. In 1979, on the occasion of ICAIC's 20th anniversary, he made the first feature film ever in Cuban animation entitled *Elpidio Valdés*. In a second feature film, *Elpidio Valdés cóntra dolar y cañón* (Elpidio Valdés Against Guns and Dollars, 1983, see Colour Plate 83), the amiable rebel is still fighting for independence, this time against arms dealers and Spanish spies. Created with caricatured drawings and a good dose of humour, these adventure films are very popular among youngsters as well as scholars.

A prolific artist, Padrón worked on other projects as well, including the award-winning shorts *La silla* (The Chair, 1974) and *Las manos* (The Hands, 1976). In 1980 he initiated *Filminuto*. In 1985, in collaboration with Argentine comic strip artist and humorist Joaquin 'Quino' Lavado, he started the series *Quinoscopio*. That same year, he released his third feature film, *Vampiros en la Habana!* (Vampires in Havana!), a hilarious story about an invention that allows vampires to live by day. A marriage of the horror and gangster genre, it was saluted by *Variety* as a 'delightfully broad caricature'. A remarkable humorist, Pa-

---

1   Padrón also published a book, *El libro del mambi*, with more than 100 illustrations of the Cuban and Spanish armies.

drón has combined and balanced the requirements of culture and the need for entertainment in his vast productions, whilst providing leadership for Cuban animators of his generation.

Colombia

In the 1960s, the advertising company Cora Film, founded by French-national Balaboine, invited another Frenchman, Robert Rosé, to open an animation department in Bogotá. Rosé trained the first Colombian animators; the result was a new advertising production which soon competed with Cinesistema, Alberto Badal Producciones and Producciones Nelson Ramirez.

As for animated shorts for entertainment, cartoonist Ernesto Franco made some initial attempts, although little information exists about them. He was followed by Luis Enrique Castillo, an animator whose work in advertising was critically praised. Castillo's shorts include *Renacuajo paseador* (The Walking Tadpole, 1976), *Simón el bobito* (Simon the Little Sparrow, 1978) and the gentle, ecological tale, *Toche bemol* (Bird Flat, 1987). In the 1980s, Philip and Magdalena Massonat made *Emmanuella no tiene quien la escuche* (Nobody Listens to Emmanuella, 1981), *¿Donde hay papagayos?* (Where are the Parrots?, 1984) and *Canto a la victoria* (Song of Victory, 1987). In 1986, Carlos Eduardo Santa and Mauricio Matamoros made *El pasajero de la noche* (Night Passenger), an adult short balancing science fiction, horror and surrealism.

The major Colombian animator was Fernando Laverde, a specialist of animated puppets. Born in Bogotá on 17 December 1933, he quit his college studies in agriculture to become a director of photography and a documentary filmmaker, an activity he never abandoned even when his life took a different course. He had his first experiences as an animator in Spain working for Madrid-based television with the team lead by Enrique Nicanor. When he and his family returned to Colombia, he founded a production company, specializing in children's works. He made several shorts, including *El país de bella-flor* (The Country of Beautiful Flowers, 1972, a satirical tale criticizing demagogy, poorly managed economic development and foreign intervention), *La maquinita* (The Little Engine, 1973), *La cosecha* (The Harvest, 1974), *Un planeta llamado Tierra* (A Planet Named Earth, 1979) and *Pepitas Rojas* (1979).

It was his feature film production, however, which made Laverde popular. In 1978, he released *La pobre viejecita* (The Poor Old Woman), based on a rhyme by Rafael Pomo. *Cristóbal Colón* followed in 1983, a children's

Fig. 136. Martín Fierro *by Fernando Laverde (Colombia, 1988).*

rendition of Colombus' voyage to America. *Martín Fierro*, made in co-production with Argentina and Cuba, is probably his most outstanding project. Released in 1988, *Martín Fierro* follows Laverde's philosophy: 'I always strive for simplicity, in narration as well as language'. *Martín Fierro* is a nineteenth century poem by the Argentine poet José Hernandez.

Peru

A truly original production by Peruvian animators was born in the mid-1970s, after Act 19327 of 1971 encouraged and financially supported Peruvian-made films. In earlier years, animated drawings were limited to advertising and followed the models of American cartoons. Only a few of the professionals involved in the old-style production decided to take advantage of the new law, leaving animation divided into two different branches. One major exception was Rafael Seminario, whose *Pacto andino* (Andean Treaty) and *Balanza comercial* (Balance of Trade– both 1976) were the first non-advertising shorts made in the country.

The majority of young artists were trained abroad, such as architect Ferdinando Gagliuffi, who can be considered the founder of a small school of filmmakers in Lima. A fan of animated drawings since his childhood, he made his first short, *Facundo* (1976) in London where he was pursuing graduate studies. In 1983, he released *La misma vaina* (The Same Sheath) followed by a work with painting directly on film stock (albeit with results he himself admitted were unsatisfactory), entitled *Chicha n. 1*.

In the early 1980s, Uruguayan Walter Tournier brought to Peru a modern, open-minded style, giving new models to filmmakers who, up to that point, had faithfully used the technique of cell-drawing. *El cóndor y el zorro* (The Condor and the Fox, 1980) made with cut-outs, and *Nuestro*

pequeño paraíso (Our Little Paradise, 1985) with animated clay, became popular at home and abroad (especially the second film, an acid, critical portrait of Latin American Television), winning several awards. Another interesting artist was Gonzalo Pflucker, a respected painter whose only attempt in animation was the critically appraised *El perfil de lo invisible* (The Outline of the Invisible Things, 1987).

Other animators include Mario Acha (*Mito de Inkarri*, 1977), Pedro Vivas (*El capitán justiciero*, 1981), Carlos Vale (*El combate contra Koatán*, 1981, *El camello sin joroba*, 1988, and *Pequeños consejos para niños y ancianos*, 1989), filmmaker and critic Nelsón García (*El chicle*, 1982), Victor Sarmiento (*Un mundo para dos*, 1983, and *Obscuridad colorida*, 1985), Ubaldo Ramos (*El señor Gallinazo vuelve a Lima*, 1983), Augusto Cabada (*Omagua el niño amazónico*, 1986, and *Pedro Paulet Mostajo*, 1989), Máximo Geldres (*La caza del puma*, 1988), and Edmundo Vilca (*Los primeros hombres de América*, 1988).

Among production companies, Antarki was founded in 1984 by Benicio Vicente and soon became one of the most industrialized, covering 80 per cent of Peruvian animated production. In 1982 and 1988, the company released, respectively, *Pre-natal* and *Animatógrafo* (on animation techniques). These two 'art' shorts were made and signed as collective efforts by the entire Antarki staff.

Venezuela

'To analyse the history of animation in Venezuela is difficult,' scholar and filmmaker Félix Nakamura writes, 'due to the numerous groups of immigrants in the country. A structure of foreign professionals has formed which includes a few natives. Advertising, in turn, has moulded a conventional animation, which had been imported time ago from pre-Castro Cuba'.[1]

Nakamura himself is a Peruvian immigrant, who studied in Argentina in the 1950s. Other talented foreigners throughout the years, were Argentine Jorge Prandi, Zagreb-born Luís Radilovich, Cuban Angel González, Ukrainian Malyna de Koval, Spaniard Juan Queralt, French Georges Lebret, Uruguayan Alberto Monteagudo and Colombian Vargas Codazzi.

The earliest Venezuelan works have not left much of a trace, although experiments in animation go back to the late 1940s. In 1955, Bolívar Films, owned by Luís Guillermo Villegas Blanco, opened the first suitably equipped studio in the country, employing

Mauricio Anteri and Luís Mejías. In 1963, Anteri became head of Animación, the most successful company involved in the production of animated advertising. Mejías became popular for his own television programme, *Mejías y sus muñecos*.

Advertising flourished in the 1980s, creating a strong market but also categorizing the already thin society of animators as either advertisers or artists. Alberto Monteagudo was one of the few who managed to cross the line and succeed in both sectors. He arrived in Venzuela in 1969 and soon became popular in advertising as well as in children's television. In the late 1970s, he made *El cuatro de hojalata*, perhaps the most popular short of Venezuelan animation up to now. The film, which Monteagudo defined as his 'greatest personal challenge', introduced clay animation to

an audience accustomed to the American-style cell animation.

Félix Nakamura made *La historia de la moneda*, *Tu cerebro*, *Historia de Venezuela*, *Vida natural* (in collaboration with Monteagudo) and his most famous work, *El árbol que da corales*, an eight-minute short with animated clay.

Armando Arce made his debut in animation in 1975, after years of work with drawings and graphics. His films include *Karina* (1975), painted on stock and featuring pictographs by Venezuelan native artists. *Desanimaciones* (1975) was a collection of ironic vignettes on politics, religion, art and sport. *Tres cuentos infantiles* (1977) was devoted to children, while *Manzanita* (1978), with animated clay, took place in a world of fruit and dealt allegorically with such problems as national identity and foreign invasions. Finally, *Wanady* (1981) and *El sueño de los hombres* (1986) were inspired by the Makirittanes Indios who live in South Venezuela. The first film narrates the birth of the Odosha, the Evil Spirit, which is impersonated by European colonizers, while the second one describes the creation of the first man and woman by a shaman.

Isabel Urbaneja (Caracas, August 1949) directed *Un cuento a la orilla del mar* (A Short Story on the Seashore), a nine-minute film with animated clay and drawings. Besides her work as an advertiser, she created over 14 micro-programmes for the television series *La ventana mágica* (The Magic Window, 1988–90, see Colour Plate 84).

1   Letter to the author, 12 November 1990.

Chapter 22

Africa

After the struggle against colonialism and the formation of new nations, African cinema underwent an interesting development in the 1970s, both in quality and quantity. Production was especially rich in Egypt, which had enjoyed a much longer tradition of independence than other African nations. As if to confirm the separation between the two forms of cinema, African animation did not thrive as did live-action cinema, but was characterized by isolated production.

Eygpt

The 1950s and 1960s were years of expansion only as far as quantity is concerned. Egyptian animators produced a good deal of advertising, many cast and credit sequences for live-action features, many contributions to TV shows (Egyptian television was born in 1960, and its animation unit, which consisted of Noshi Iskandar, Reda Gobran, Mohamed Hassib, Maher Nassar, Zakaria Agmane, Deawar Hosny, Hussam Mohib and Ali Mohib, was born one year later). More interesting, in terms of quality, were the 1970s and 1980s. In 1958 Hassan Hakem (1929), Mustafa Hussein (1936) and Halim Berguini (1934) made the short *Titi and Rashouane*; in 1963 the abovementioned Ali Mohib directed for the Egyptian television *The White Line*; in the same year Alfred Mikhail and Mohamed Hassan made *The Little Magician*.

Ihab Shaker (Cairo, 15 August 1933) was a painter, illustrator, caricaturist, puppeteer and certainly the best-known abroad among Egyptian animators. In 1968 he made *The Flower* and *The Bottle* in his country, then moved to France where he met Paul Grimault. With his help he made *Un, deux, trois* (One, Two, Three, 1973), a collection of three stories entitled *La douche* (The Shower), *L'oiseau* (The Bird), and *La machine* (The Machine), in which he used non-anthropomorphic drawings (in Shaker's own words, the main characters had 'amoeba-like features'), with an anecdotal taste for the absurd. In 1987 he made two shorts entitled *Chansons d'animaux* (Animal Songs) for Jean-Francois Laguionie's production house, La Fabrique: the first was *Le crocodile* (The Crocodile), the second *Le corbeau* (The Crow). His production of 1993 was called *Love Dance*. The other important Egyptian animator was Noshi Iskandar (Cairo, 5 November 1938), a member of the early TV team for animation and a renowned caricaturist and comic artist. His first film was *One to Five* (1969) which was followed, in the same year, by *Is That True?* and *Question*. In 1974 he made *Room No. ...* and *Where?*; in 1975 *Excellent*; in 1980 *Narcissus*. In 1982 he became head of the Special Effects Department at Egyptian Television.

Among the many other Egyptian animation filmmakers, there is an important woman, Mona Abo El Nasr, who has a very personal graphic style. She made the award-winning *Survival* (1988) during her stay at Cal Arts in the USA, then the TV series *Once Upon A Time* (1992).

Tunisia

In 1968, Mongi Sancho directed *Le marchand de fez* (The Fez Merchant). French educated Nacer Khemir (Korba, 1 April 1948) directed *Le bucheron* (The Woodcutter, 1972) and *Le mulet* (1975) before working on live-action feature films such as *L'ogresse* (1978) and *Les baliseurs du désert* (1984). Mahjoub Zouhair (Tunis, 11 March 1945) released *Les deux souris blanches* (The Two White Mice, 1974, with animated cutouts) from a Tunisian mediaeval tale, *Le petit hibou* (1982, also with animated cut-outs) and *Le guerbagi* (1984, with animated puppets), about a water vendor who was killed by the police during the country's struggle for independence from France in the 1950s.

In 1992 Mahjoub made *Fleur de pierre* (Stone Flower) and the 12 episodes of the TV series *Les Aventures de Hatem, le courageux cavalier Zlass* (The Adventures of Hatem, the Courageous Horseman of the Zlass), about old legends of the North African region of the Zlass.

Samir Besbes (Sfax, 6 May 1949) made two shorts *Les aventures de Jahjou 1* (Jahjou's Adventures 1) and *Les aventures de Jahjou 2* (Jahjou's Adventures 2, 1992) based on Jahjou, son of Jha, mythical character of Northern Africa. Other films include: *Secourez-la, elle est en danger* (Help Her, She Is In Danger, 1988) by Mustupha Taieb; *La cigale* (The Balm Cricket, 1986) by Erzeddine Harbaoui; *Petite histoire d'oeuf* (Little Egg Story, 1975) by Mohamed Charbagi; *Trip* (1977) by Claude Ballare and Jean-Jacques Le Garrec.

Algeria

The country's first animated film, *La fête de l'arbre*, was released in 1963 by Mohamed Aram (Hussein Dey, Algeria, April 1934), the founder of Algerian animation, just one year after Algeria had attained its much-fought-for independence. Aram taught himself the techniques of animation, built his own equipment, and directed in his spare-time from his job as an assistant set-designer at the national broadcasting company. His early works were black and white films made for educational purposes: *La fête de l'arbre* was an invitation to replant the forests destroyed by napalm; *Ah, s'il savait lire* (If He Knew How to Read, 1963) fought illiteracy; and *Les microbes des poubelles* (Microbes of the Garbage Cans, 1964) discussed health problems in the city.

In 1964, Aram formed his own team at the Centre National du Cinema and began working with colour. In 1967, he returned to television and in 1976 opened his own studio. Despite the number of productions released (approximately thirty titles from 1963 to 1988), his activity was not trouble-free, mainly because of the lack of support given to him from the country's cinematographic authorities. Aram focussed on themes which respected Algerian sensibility and tradition, and used characters, both human and animal, that could be recognized locally. His other works include *H'Mimo et les allumettes* (H'Mimo and the Matches, 1965), *H'Mimo et le baptême* (H'Mimo and the Baptism, 1966), *Douieb au Sahara* (Douieb in the Sahara, 1967), *Fertoh et le singe* (Fertoh and the Monkey, 1971), *Les couleurs du diable* (The Devil's Colours, 1975), *L'olivier justicier* (The Olive Tree Who Loved Justice, 1978), *Adrar* (1979, see Colour Plate 85) and *Sema* (1983).

Among his collaborators were Mohamed Mazari and Menouar 'Slim' Merabtene who worked as directors as well as comic strip artists, as did Aram. Mazari directed *Le mariage* (The Marriage, 1966), while Slim directed *Le magicien* (The Magician, 1965), followed by *Gasba et Galal* and *Bouzio dans le train* (Bouzio on the Train). Another Algerian animator worthy of mention is Mohamed Toufik Lebcir who made *Rami,* (1991, from *1001 Arabian Nights* and *Atakor,* (1993, 'pilot' of a series of the same title).

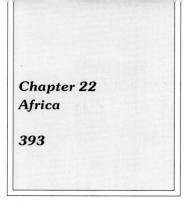

Giant Rock and the Super Rocks).

Zambia

Production began in 1982 in television, with Fordson Mobi Kolala deserving mention for animated works such as *Life Cycle of a Butterfly*, *Faces* and *Tube*.

Niger

Moustapha Alassane (N'Dongou, 1942) was one of the first filmmakers in his country who adopted 'primitive' techniques, such as drawing directly on film stock, to make up for the lack of equipment. He spent time in Paris and Montreal and, although he attained recognition for his work as an animator, he directed ethnographic documentaries and live-action fiction films too. His first animated work, *Le piroguier* (The Pirogue Paddler, 1962), was followed by *La pileuse de mil* (The Millet Grinder, 1962), *La bague du roi Koda* (King Koda's Ring, 1963), *La mort de Gandji* (Gandji's Death, 1965, award-winner at the black art festival in Dakar), *Bon voyage, Sim* (Have a Nice Trip, Sim, 1966, a somewhat ironic pacifist film), *Samba le grand* (The Great Samba, 1978, with animated puppets) and *Kokoa* (1985, on a wrestling match between chameleons and leopards).

Liberia

In this country, which has enjoyed a long tradition of independence, animation was introduced via television. A department of graphic arts, under the leadership of Jefferson Abruzi Zeon (Buchanan, Grand Bassa County, 28 December 1958) operated within the Liberian Broadcasting System. Other than the usual productions for the small screen, Zeon directed several educational and entertainment short films, displaying energy and ambition. His works include *Avoid Accidents*, *The Greedy Magician* (about a voracious man who eventually loses all his food) and *Don't Be Too Anxious* (about the struggle between

Mali

This country's leading animator was Mambaye Coulibaly (Mali, 2 May 1955), filmmaker and musician, who spent his life between his motherland and Paris, where he studied cinema under the guidance of Jean Rouch. His film *Le geste de Ségou* (Ségou's Deed, 1989) which tells the story of a child who menaces the wisdom of the king of Ségou, won a prize at the festival of Ouagadougou. Besides him, animation was represented in the country by a woman, Ouattara Oumou Goita, who told a children's story with *La poule et l'épervier* (The Chicken and the Sparrow-Hawk, 1993).

Senegal

The only animator having made a film in the country was probably Soko Mehelo, with his *Histoires de dettes* (Stories of Debts, 1978). In Montreal, at the National Film Board of Canada, Babacar Camara made *Les mésaventures de Bath* (Bath's Misadventures), and in Geneva Ernest N'Goran, Simon Kassi and Noel N'Goran made, with the advice of Robi Engler, two short films in 1977: *Tam Tam* and *Mensonges d'un soir* (One Evening's Lies).

Burkina Faso

In 1984 the National Film Board of Canada organized a workshop in this country under the direction of Gaston Sarault. This brought to the screen *The Eagle and the Chameleon*, signed by Burkinese Sanou Kollo and produced by the NFB.

Ivory Coast

Only African filmmakers working abroad represent this country in the field of animation. Marcellin Brou and Abdoulaye Touré made, in Switzerland, *L'orphéline et la marâtre* (The Little Orphan Girl and the Stepmother) about a girl, her bad stepmother and the genius of the river. G'noan M'bala made at the National Film Board of Canada, *Kacou* (1984). Kacou is a small stylized character who can't match with his shadow. Annick Assemian Laurence, one of the few African women involved in animation, in 1975 made *Agression* (Assault) and in 1983 *Métro*, a film on female sensuality.

Ghana

The National Film and Television Institute, established in 1980, produced some animated educational films during the 1980s: *Road Safety Campaign*, *Drug Abuse*, *National Mobilization and National Building*, and above all *From Genesis to Zero* (directed by Victorine T. Broohm) and *Trees for Life* (directed by Angelina Kotey). Some former students of the Institute became professional animators, devoting their endeavours to advertising films but making 'personal' films as well. Alex Bannerman made *Windfall* about two men and two pots: the moderate guy takes the small pot and is happy to see it's full of gold; the greedy guy takes the big pot and discovers it contains a snake. *Don't Waste Water* was an educational film. In collaboration with Kofi Sarpong, Bannerman eventually made the pilot of a longer work by the title of *Ananse*, featuring a traditional character who is very popular across Africa (1988).

David Ababio took this character for his film *Ananse Story*. It is worth mentioning that a third Ghanaian animator, John K. Ossei, had directed in Montreal, in 1973, the fable *Ananse's Farm*, under the aegis of the National Film Board of Canada.

Togo

The only animator in Togo was Clem Clem Lawson, whose best known film is *Voyage en Métropotamie* (Journey in Metropotamia, 1982), a satire of the Paris tube.

Cameroon

Jean-Marie Téno, born in Bafoussam in Cameroon in 1954 but living in France, made all of his films in this European country, among which the only animated one was *Hommage* (1985). It is about two friends who meet after many years and confront their lives, one very traditional and the other one oriented towards modernity.

Zaire

The first animated films were made in this region when it was still a Belgian Crown colony and was called the Congo. Alexandre Vandenheuvel and Roger Tamar produced, between 1951 and 1956, seven films of about ten minutes each, under the general title of *Les palabres de Mboloko* (Mboloko chatter). They were still being broadcast by Zaire Television as late as the 1980s. The titles were: *Malafu – le vin de palme* (The Palm Wine); *Ekolo – Le panier* (The Basket), *Bokasi – La force* (Strength), *Etalaka – Le gué* (The Ford), *Motambo – Le piège* (The Trap), *Kanda – La colère* (Anger), *Mekana – Le concours* (The Competition).

In 1990 Jean-Michel Ndjaie Wooto Kibushi (Lubefu, Zaire, 3 August 1957) made his first film, *Le crapaud chez ses beaux parents* (The Frog Visits Its In-Laws) in Brussels with the Atelier Graphoui. It was the story of a frog who meets every kind of character on his way to his relations, and invites everybody to the party. In 1992 the director made a sequel, with the title *Le crapaud chez ses beaux parents – L'orange blanche* (The Frog Visits Its In-Laws – The White Orange), and also a completely different, committed film denouncing the atrocities of the military regime during the riots in the Zaire capital, *Kinshasa, Septembre Noir* (Kinshasa, Black September). Another Zaire filmmaker (but living in Switzerland) was Mohamed Soudani, whose only foray into animation was *Le secret du baobab: Le petit griot* (The Baobab's Secret: The Little Sorcerer, 1993).

Mauritius

In this island, famous tourist paradise and native land of the extinct Dodo bird, animation is represented by Veerasamy Galen Parianen (born in 1951), a professional live-action cameraman. His first animated film, three minutes long, was *Sow and You Will Reap* (1986), where plasticine animation is used to tell an educational story about diligently preparing for the future. His second film, entitled *La magie des fleurs* (The Flowers' Magic, 1987) is a eulogy to beautiful Mauritian flowers.

Mozambique

Two animated films are known. *Na Estrada* (On the Road, 1984) is about a wounded guerrilla lying on the road for days until his comrades rescue him; *A lua e a filha que não sabia pilar* (The Moon and the Girl Who Couldn't Pound, 1984) is a legend about a man who goes to the moon and asks for her daughter as a bride – he can have her provided he doesn't ask her to pound. Both are signed by Mendes de Oliveira, the second one in collaboration with Anna Fresu.

Burundi

Joseph Bitamba, head of the Children and Young Adults Department of the national television station Radio TV Bujumbura, was the director of *I comme image* (I for Image, 1989), a 'pilot' of a never-made TV series. In 1991 he organized a workshop for children with the Belgian Atelier Graphoui, where many very short films were created and later edited together in an

anthology with the title *Histoires Burundaises* (Burundi Stories).

The South African Republic

In 1947 Denis Purchase went to South Africa from Great Britain and began producing animated commercials for Alpha Film Studio, where he worked until 1963. In 1975 the local Television (South African Broadcasting Corporation) started producing programmes for children, and charged Butch Stolz and Gerard Smith to make animated productions such as *Wolraad Woltemade*, *Bremenstadtmusikante* (The Musicians of Bremen), and *An Introduction to Dickens*. Gerard Smith entered into a partnership in 1978 with pioneer Denis Purchase and both worked for Rentastudio, where many animators came and went. The series *Bobby The Cat* and the special *Rachel de Beer* were the most significant exploits of this group. Dave McKey Studio is also significant, for its commercials as well as for shorts like *The Story of the Bath*. The most interesting personality in the small circle of South African animation was probably William Kentridge (Johannesburg, 1955), artist, film, TV and stage director, animation filmmaker. After *Pastry* (1985) and *Exhibition* (1987), he made the 'Soho Eckstein tetralogy' *Johannesburg – The Greatest City After Paris* (1989), *Monument* (1990), *Sobriety, Obesity and Growing Old* (1991) and *Mine* (1991). Soho Eckstein, his wife and Felix Teitelbaum are the characters of a strange saga where greed, power and politics intermingle and interact, in a sort of animated *théâtre de l'absurde*. Glenn Coppens (Gent, Belgium, 1955), former pupil of animator-teacher Raoul Servais, founded his studio in 1983 and worked mainly in the field of advertising. Another studio of some size was Magic Touch, which specialized in computer animation. Riccardo Capecchi, Italian by birth, in 1989 directed *Walk Tall*, aimed at 'enhancing the pride of the miners', and some more

very short films such as *Cotton,
Ghost Pops II, Mondi Ro-
tarim, Yogi Sip*. We must also

mention Peter Templeton, who
in 1970 made *My Eye*.

Chapter 23

New realities in Asia

In many Oriental and Middle-Eastern countries, such as India, Hong Kong, Indonesia, the Philippines, Taiwan and Turkey, a frail animation industry contrasts with the prosperous production of live-action cinema. It has become common practice for Western producers to commission labour intensive tasks (like animation, 'inbetweening', and painting) to workers in the East. Because of the economic structure of the countries involved, this practice has been profitable for both parties. In other countries, production was nationalized in a way analogous to Eastern Europe.

Israel

In the 1950s, small animation teams made films on commission as well as some experimental works. Israeli artists included Josef Bau in Tel-Aviv, Tuvia Carmeli in Haifa and Yoram Gross, creator of the country's first animated feature film, *Joseph the Dreamer* (1961). Gross' later activity, which took place in Australia, is discussed more extensively in the next chapter.

Production grew in the following decades as well, albeit within the areas of education and advertising. One notable work was the Hebraic version of the popular children's programme *Sesame Street*. Other than the production groups owned by Educational Television (1965) and National Television (1967), two other major studios existed: Frame by Frame, led by Roni Oren, a creative filmmaker specializing in plasticine, and Eyn Gedi Productions[1], led by David 'Dudu' Shalita, director of the charming, 24-minute educational film, *Rhythm* (1985).

Yossi Aboulafia who worked for Israeli television and the National Film Board of Canada also had a dominant influence on the country's animation before returning to children's publishing. Arye Mambush, another singular talent, experimented with abstract cinema while working for educational children's films on commission. Ytzhak Yoresh, who began animating in 1964, produced a large number of educational and entertainment films such as *King in Jerusalem* (1969), on tourism; *The Widow and Her Lawsuit Against the Wind* (1971), based on a biblical story and *The Goal Is Production* (1976), on economic problems.

Independent artists included filmmaker and critic Tsvika Oren (Tel-Aviv, 1946); Avigdor Cohen (Vienna, Austria, 1920), director of *Samson's Love* (1979); Albert-Alain Kaminski (Brussels, Belgium, 1950), director of *Little Hirik* (1979) and *The Flower on Top of the World* (1980); and Agur Schiff (Tel-Aviv, 1955), best known for *Leon's Birthday* (1981) and *A Kid* (1983).

'Among Israel's schools of animation, one of the foremost was the Bezalel Academy for the Arts and Design in Jerusalem. Directed by Ytzhak Yoresh, the school trained a generation of young artists in the use of 'primitive' techniques instead of the traditional cel animation, and focused on artistic expression rather than the teaching of a trade. One of the most stimulating works created within this school is *Bitzbutz* (1984) by Gil Alkabetz (Beer Sheva, 1957).

Fig. 137. How the Boat of Belief Proceeded *by Tonguc Yasar (Turkey, 1972).*

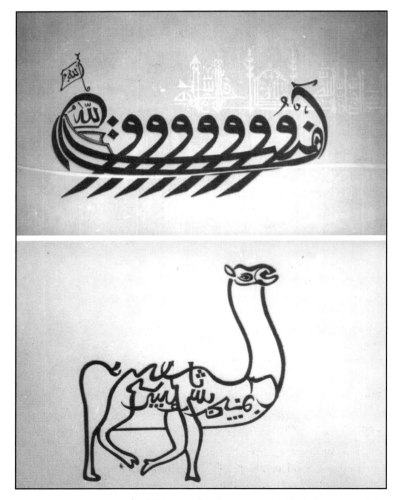

Turkey

In this Euro-Asiatic country animation began in the early 1960s, when advertising in the cinemas gained popularity and animated commercials were required. In these years agencies like Istanbul Reklam, Radar Reklam, Rare Reklam and Karikatur Reklam (later called Studio Cizgi, which produced the well-known *Evliya Celebi*) were established. Ferruh Dogan and Oguz Aral, who continued their careers in animation over the next 30 years, joined forces to establish a studio called Canli Karikatur and made some remarkable films, namely *Koca Yusuf* and *Direklerarasi*. This 'golden age' lasted only a few years, mainly because of the difficulty the caricaturists (who were the majority of the artists involved) experienced in adapting themselves to the assembly-line work of animated cartoons, and also because of their desire to go back to satirical vignettes as soon as possible.[2]

A second, but shorter, golden age of animated commercials started in March 1972, when Turkish television began broadcasting advertising. A new generation of animators made a debut: Dervis Pasin, Erim Gozen, Tunc Izberk, Emre Senan, Ruhi Goruney. But soon the animated cartoons, which took up to 30 per cent of the commercials, fell to 2 per cent and the studios had to close their doors. In 1972 Tonguc Yasar, who had cut his teeth at Studio Cizgi, made *How the Boat of Belief Proceeded*, a beautiful graphic exercise based on the shapes of the old – and today abandoned – Turkish alphabet. Screened at the Annecy Festival of 1973, this film enjoyed considerable success and influence, and was the one that opened the era of 'personal films' in Turkey. Tan Oral, who had made an interesting film called *Censure* in 1969, experimented later with a scratching technique in

---

1   This production company boasted the witty record of being the lowest in the world, being located below sea level, on the Dead Sea.

2   Turkish caricature, mainly in the form of costume and political satire, has a very brilliant history, which dates back to 1877, when the first humour magazine, *Diyojen*, was published.

The Line, and then used the magazine photographs of the early twentieth century for an animated collage film to be used by the Dostlar Theatre in its production of Berthold Brecht's *The Good Soldier Svejk*.

Among many difficulties, the production of auteur films continued. In 1974 Cemal Erez screened his *65-K*; in 1975 Emre Senan made *The Rhinoman*; in 1978 Meral Birden followed with *Cat*, while a contest, proposed by the Ministry of Culture for films about the traditional character Hogia Nasruddin, was attended by 10 filmmakers, with Tonguc Yasar sharing the first prize with Tunc Izberk (the two films had almost the same title: *Hodja and the Thief* and *Hodja and the Thieves*).

Ates Benice, who had been third in this competition with *Hodja One Day*, had his film *Stereo*, which describes a man wrestling with himself, screened at the Zagreb Festival of 1980. Two years later, Umit Solak (born in 1947 in Turkey but working in Paris) produced a fine essay with animated puppets, *A Story of Nasreddin Hodja: If It Worked!*, while in 1983 Erim Gozen received much praise for his film *Traffic*.

The most interesting personality of Turkish animation was Ali Murat Erkorkmaz (Istanbul, 1948), a dynamic director-producer who at various times opened studios not only in his own country, but also in the USA, Bahrain, Kuwait, England, Egypt, India and Sri Lanka. He created more than 3,800 shorts, including commercials and TV series; among these ones were *Non Commercial Commercials* (1976), *Aesop* (1980), *Rotto Botto Robotto* (1987), *Yok Yok TV* (1989) and *Babum Show* (1994). In 1989 he also began production of the feature *Woody and May*. Enis Tahsin Ozgur (Istanbul, 1956) had a catalyzing role: having studied and worked with the most brilliant animators in Canada, USA and Germany, he could give his colleagues and students a good example of high professionalism. Of the younger generation, Fethi Kaba (Es-

kisehir, 1967) made a good computer film in 1994, *The Stranger*, where a scarecrow is well designed and animated; Mahmut Tibet (1964) made, in 1993, *Error*, about a hand that is condemned to death for having murdered another hand; Bahadir Tosun (Ankara, 1973) with *Shadow Play* (1994) showed how a human being can exchange his role with his shadow.

Iran

The first to experiment with frame by frame cinema was Jafar Tejaratchi, an airforce colonel who made his earliest black-and-white animated films in 1958. He was later joined by Esphandiar Ahmadieh, whose activity in animation spanned more than thirty years and included works for other directors, such as Prague-educated Nosratolah Karimi. With the sponsorship of the Ministry of Culture and Art, the group (which was joined by camera operator Parviz Osanloo) obtained a small, modestly equipped studio and released films such as Ahmadieh's *The Satellite* (1959), and *The Jealous Duck* (1963); and Karimi's *Malek Jamshid* (1966) and *The Life* (1967).

When some of the most fertile suggestions of the post-Disney age were introduced at the first Teheran Festival in 1966, animation was rediscovered by audiences and young aspiring filmmakers. In 1969, the Institute for the Intellectual Development of Children and Young Adults opened a cinema department which favoured animation, giving rise to the second generation, or 'the Renaissance', of Iranian animation. Meanwhile, small private studios, mainly devoted to advertising, released highly professional work.

In 1974 an Iranian centre for experimental animation was founded; and in 1977, Farabi University opened a graduate programme in animation led by the centre's director, Nooreddin Zarrinkelk. Production came to a standstill during the turmoil which led to the Shah's fall in 1979 and to the establishment of the Islamic Republic. It started up again in the mid-1980s, still supported by the Institute for the Intellectual Development. The rich production was enhanced by animators such as Vahik Martirossian (*The Mouse and the Cat*, a Bulgarian co-production based on an old comic poem by Obeid Zakani) and Nooreddin Zarrinkelk, creator of feature films.

Long-time professionals include: Farshid Mesghali (Isfahan, 1940) who made his debut with *Mister Monster* (1970), a critique of the power of a technological society. His second film, *Misunderstanding* (1970) was graphically and conceptually an easier work. It featured a man who benignly shows his tongue to strangers passing by. Other films followed: *The Boy, the Bird and the Musical Instrument* (1971); *The Grey City* (1972); *A Very Good Worm* (1973) about an ill-fated worm who wishes to be universally praised; *Look Again* (1974), an invitation to find shapes in nature; *From Different Appearances* (1979); *How and Why* (1985) and *A Drop of Blood, A Drop of Oil* (1986). A draftsman with a Western style, Mesghali paid more attention to film graphics, than to their dramatic structure.

Similar limitations can be found in the works of Ali-Akbar Sadeghi (1937), who like Mesghali Sadeghi was a graduate of the University of Teheran. In 1971, he directed his first film, *Seven Cities*, followed one year later by *Floral Storm*. After *Boasting* (1973), which revolves around the proud declarations uttered by two opposing armies, he directed *The Tower* (1974) which features a chess tower, and *Malek Khorshid* (1975), about a prince who falls in love with a girl he sees in a portrait. In 1977, Sadeghi focussed on his most ambitious project – a 25-minute film based on *The Book of Kings* by the ancient Persian poet Firdusi. Entitled *The Albino and the Phoenix*, the film is a beautifully drawn tale about the albino son of the powerful Saam of Narimaan who was rejected by his father and saved by the phoenix.

Parviz Naderi, perhaps a more refined filmmaker, displayed curiously amoeboid drawings in films such as *Independence* (1973) and *The Man and the Cloud* (1975). After some unproductive years, he directed *The Apple* in 1982. Arapik Bagdasarian (1942–1985) directed *The Weightlifter* (1970, see Colour Plate 86), an internationally praised comic film about a muscle man whose primary aim is to win his audiences' approval. Morteza Momayez (1937) directed *The One Who Fantasized and the One Who Acted* (1971) and *The Bird in the Ruin* (1973), a fable about evil told with incisive drawings.

Fig. 138. The Man and the Cloud *by Parviz Naderi (Iran, 1975).*

Nafiseh Riahi (1943) was one of the few women directors in Iranian animation. After *How Much Do I Know?* (1972), she made *Rainbow* (1973), about the struggle to bring light and colour to everyday gloom, and *The Purple Pencil* (1975), about a child's fantasies. From 1977 to 1987 she made *From Teheran to Teheran*, in co-direction with woman director Soudabeh Agah author of *The Circle* (1977).

Other artists, worked only briefly in animation. They include painter Parviz Kalantari (*Freedom American Style*, 1980), live-action director Sohrab Shahid-Saless (*Black and White*, 1971, made with pixillation, a technique by which live people are animated) and Ahmad Asbaghi, whose *Careless* (1974, about a man who leaves the city to find peace in nature and ends up building a new house) made a contribution to the typically Iranian form of aphorism-films.

Among 'third generation' animators the following are to be commended: Vajiholah Fard Moghadam (*The Troublesome*, 1976, a brief satire on a malfunctioning alarm clock, *Imitation*, 1979 and *The Return*, 1987); Abdollah Alimorad (*Paper and Fold*, 1984, and *Seeing*, 1985); Berlin-educated Hamid Navim (director of a educational TV series about hygiene in the 1980s, and *The Birth*, 1987); Ahmad Arabani (*The Axe*, 1982, and *The Treasure*, 1987); and Nazenin Sarbandi (*The Carpet*, 1980, and *Solidarity*, 1987).

Nooreddin Zarrinkelk was responsible for some of the most interesting productions. Born in Mashhad (11 April 1937), he was taught calligraphy and painting by his father and began publishing his drawings and caricatures in newspapers while still a student. In 1964, he became a book illustrator. His encounter with cinema dates back to the late 1960s, when a fellowship from the Institute for the Intellectual Development of Children and Young Adults allowed him to spend some years at Raoul Ser-

vais' School in Belgium. It was here that he directed his first film, the one-minute *Duty First*.

Having returned to Iran he developed a programme for teaching and promoting animation. He also continued his activity as a book illustrator and an animator. Zarrinkelk's films include *Association of Ideas* (1973), *Atal Matal* (1974) and *Crazy, Crazy, Crazy World* (1975), which was internationally praised, and which gave Zarrinkelk a position of leadership among Iranian filmmakers. *Crazy, Crazy, Crazy World*, a satirical allegory of the quarrelsome planet, was based on the curious and unusual idea of bringing the world's map to life. Scandinavia becomes a hungry little animal and devours Denmark; Borneo and New Guinea fight over Celebes; Alaska and Siberia are two chickens pecking at each other.

Amir Hamzeh (1977) is a pleasantly ironic tale about a hunter freeing a princess who had been transformed into a zebra by a demon. *One, Two, Three, More* (1982), featuring the adventures of diamond-hunters, is a collection of five variations on the theme of greed and its consequences. Here Zarrinkelk displayed his strongest skill – to capture the core of a situation and represent it as

Fig. 139. Amir Hamzeh *by Nooreddin Zarrinkelk (Iran, 1977).*

a moral judgement with dry humour. In 1987 he released *Plus and Minus* and began work on the feature film *Sindbad and the Secret of the Snow Land*, an adventurous fairy tale made with Finnish financial contributions.

China

As mentioned previously, the Cultural Revolution interrupted the activity of the Shanghai studio for several years. Work resumed timidly in 1972, while production still bowed to the dictates of propaganda. *The Little Trumpeter* (1972), made by Yan Dingsian (27 September 1936) and Wang Shushen but released anonymously, is a good example of the producers' collectivist ideology. The film featured the story of Hsiao Yung, a little shepherd who became a trumpeter in the Red Army during the second civil war (1927–1937). In the film, Chiang Kai-shek's soldiers resemble demons, while the Red Army soldiers jump magically from mountain to mountain. The historical theme becomes a fight between the old and the new, with images echoing the magniloquence of Mao's Red Guards.

When the Gang of Four fell from power in October 1976, the Shanghai animation studio acquired new vitality. Under the leadership of veterans such as Te Wei and Jin Shi, it produced six films in 1978, ten in 1979, and seventeen in 1980.

The major Chinese animator of this time was Xu Jingda (Shanghai, 1934 – Beijing, 15 February 1987), known in artistic circles as 'A Da'. Educated at the Soochow Institute of Art and at the Beijing Academy of Cinema, he went to Shanghai in 1953 and worked as a set-designer, layout artist and director until he was purged by the Red Army and sent to a labour camp in the countryside. He returned to his creative pursuits with *A Night in an Art Gallery* (1978). Along with his colleagues Wang Shushen and Yan Dingsian, A Da directed the feature film *Nezha Triumphs over King Dragon* (or Nezha Shakes the Sea, 1979, see Colour Plate 87), based on the mythological novel *The Gods' Investiture*. Influenced by Chinese traditional art, but also by classical animated drawings, the film is about a boy, Nezha, who saves a girl from the King Dragon of the Eastern Seas. *The Three Buddhist Monks* (1980), perhaps A Da's best work, was a gently ironic tale about three quarrelsome monks who finally agree to rebuild their temple after a fire destroys it. Characterized by quiet rhythm and sober animation, the film is a fable dealing with the rediscovery of solidarity in times of danger. *The Spring of Butterflies* (1984), one of the few Chinese animated films for adults rather than children, tells a sweet love story. *San Mao's Wanderings* is a sort of mini-series taken from a popular 1930s comic strip.[1] Finally, *36 Chinese Characters* (1985, see Colour Plate 88) features the few characters of Chinese calligraphy which still resemble the objects they describe – an elephant, a bird, water, sun, and a deer. Despite its premise, the film is not educational but rather an amiable graphic comedy.

The Shanghai studio operated in three sectors – animated drawings on cels, puppets and cut-outs. Among the animators of drawings, Hu Jinqing (21 March 1936) made *The Snipe-Clam Grapple* (1984) using the 'lavis' (Chinese watercolours). Centered on the proverb 'In the fight between the snipe and the clam, the fisherman has the best of it', the Eastern version of 'while two dogs fight for a bone the third runs away with it', the film is well animated and conveys the expression and psychology of the two characters without transforming them into caricatures. Other artists include Tang Cheng (5 June 1919 – 18 February 1986), one of the few Asian

---

1   *San Mao* (literally, 'three strands of hair') was created as a comic strip by Zhang Leping in 1935; it was the character of a ten year old boy living in the streets of Shanghai.

women animators, who made *An Elephant of Little Resemblance* (1978) and *The Deer's Rattle* (1982); the director of the above-mentioned *Where is Mama?* Qian Jajun, who directed *The Spotted Deer* (1981) using the famous drawings of the Dunhuang caves; and Pu Jaziang (19 April 1932), who made *The Hairdresser Squirrel* (1982) with a modern style of drawings and vivid colours. Wang Shuchen (*The Curious Book Which Came From the Sky*, 1984), and Te Wei (*The King of the Monkeys Eliminates the Witch*, 1985), both makers of feature films, deserve mention.

Jin Shi, director of the successful *Effendi* (1980), a tale from Uigur folklore, was the leader among puppet animators. Specialists in animated cut-outs at the Shanghai studio also produced stimulating works. Zhou Keqin (28 March 1942) directed *The Monkeys Fish for the Moon* (1981), based on the proverb 'the monkeys fish for the moon but do not catch anything'. The film was characterized by a beautiful design (monkey cut-outs on velvet paper were drawn by A Da), and an expert use of lighting. Hu Xionghua again made a name for himself with *The Fox Cheats the Hunter* (1978), displaying an original use of

colours and a well matched sound-track. Qian Yunda animated a character from the classic *Chronicles of the Three Kingdoms*, in the film *Zhang Fei Judges the Theft of a Watermelon* (1979, made in collaboration with Ge Guiyun, born on 4 November 1933). The film contains 'sophisticated paper cut-outs, marvelous colours, and opera music in the tradition of shadow theatre.'[1] Finally, Qian Jaxin (23 February 1929) found inspiration from ancient bas-reliefs for *Mr. Nanguo* (1981). Centred on a musically ignorant man who is employed as a court musician, the film is an expression of shrewdness and argumentativeness.

In the past, the Shanghai studio was the only one that consistently released productions. More recently the Institute for Science and Education in Beijing has placed itself in the running, while the television broadcasting services in Beijing, Shanghai and other cities have similarly equipped their studios in order to fulfill their production needs.

Vietnam

While the country was still divided, animation continued to develop, particularly in the North. In

Fig. 140. The Snipe-Clam Grapple *by Hu Jinqing (China, 1984)*.

1   Marie-Claire Quiquemelle, *Les frères Wan et 60 ans de dessins animés chinois*/The Wan Brothers and 60 Years of Animated Films in China, Annecy Festival (Annecy, 1985).

1959, Le Minh Hien and Truong Qua, who studied at Soyuzmultfilm in Moscow, held training courses for young animators. Even before a state-sponsored studio opened in Hanoi in 1962, Le Minh Hien released *What the Fox Deserves* (1960). Filmed with makeshift equipment, it was an allegory on the necessity of working together to defeat the enemies. Animated puppets appeared in 1962 in a Vietnamese tale, *The Hare Goes to School* (1960) by Czechoslovakian-trained Ngueyen Tik.

Despite inexperience and a lack of means, work in animation continued. In 1966, Ngo Manh Lan's *The Kitty* was awarded the Silver Pelican at the Mamaia film festival – the country's first international recognition of animation. The film told the story of a kitty whose quiet life is interrupted by a huge rat and its rodent army; the kitty organizes a resistance and chases the invaders away. Here, as well as in other films, the propagandistic meaning of the story is clear. In fact, during the war against South Vietnam and the United States, approximately half of the animated works coming out of North Vietnam were explicitly propagandistic. (The other half consisted of traditional tales or satires.) For instance, in 1967, Ngo Manh Lan directed *The Talking Blackbird*, a film with distinctly stylized drawings about a South Vietnamese boy who, accompanied by a talking blackbird, defeats the Americans. In this, Vietnamese animation is similar to the animation of other communist countries, persisting as a smooth blend of subjects and images rooted in national folklore with particular attention given to children's audiences and political propaganda (which was intensified during the war).

Only after 1967 was the first colour film introduced – *Carved in the Rock*, by Truong Qua

created in collaboration with Nguyen Yen. The film is an epic poem on three generations of partisans in the jungle. Qua later directed *The Legend of the Region* (1970). Considered the studio's finest film, *The Legend of the Region* intertwines a story of national heroism with scenes of idyllic country fairs. After Vietnam's unification in 1975, a state-sponsored studio was opened in Ho Chi Minh City (formerly Saigon). Yearly production consisted of a dozen movies filmed in the North and approximately six in the South.

India

The first Indian animated film was *Agkadyanchi Mouj* (Matchsticks' Fun, 1915) by Dhundiraj Govind 'Dadasaheb' Phalke, who was also the founder of Indian live-action cinema. The materials used suggest that this short film was inspired by Emile Cohl's *Les allumettes animées*. As for sound cinema, the first Indian animated film with a soundtrack[1] was *On a Moonlit Night*, released in 1934 and attributed to R.C. Boral who was a composer and orchestra director with the production company New Theatres[2]. Also in 1930 the Prabhat Film Company distributed *Jambu the Fox* (the name of the director is unknown), together with the live-action feature film *Amrit Manthan*[3].

In 1935 Mohan Bhavnani, one of the country's first documentarists, produced *Lafanga Longoor*, featuring the adventures of a funny little monkey. This short work was filmed and animated by a German operator whose name was not released. In 1939 G.K. Gokhale (Born 1915) made his debut with *Superman Myth,* produced in Bombay by Indian Cartoon Pictures and followed by several commercials. In 1947 the Madras-based Gemini Studios produced *Cinema Kadamban,* an eight minute short, filmed under

1   The first Indian live-action sound film was *Beauty of the World* (1931) by Ardeshir Irani.

2   Firoze Rangoonwalla *Seventy-five years of Indian Cinema* (New Delhi: Indian Book Company) 1975, p. 89.

3   Directed by V. Shantaram, one of the best artists of Indian cinema, this film was meant as a protest against religious obscurantism. It was highly praised by audiences and critics alike.

the supervision of noted cartoonist N. Thanu.

Continuous production only started in 1956 with the opening of a Cartoon Film Unit within the Films Division – a large state-funded organization established in 1948 and engaged in producing newsreels and documentaries. The small, but well-equipped, team was able to enjoy the expertise of G.K. Gokhale and of the American Clair H. Weeks, a former animator at Disney Studios who was visiting India as part of a cultural exchange programme. The first release was *Banyan Tree* by Weeks and Gokhale, which was based on a Buddhist Jataka story. Afterward, the animation unit produced about two films per year until 1962 when this number doubled. The subjects chosen were mostly educational or social, but some art films were also made. The first film in this latter category was *Radha and Krishna* (1958) which was based on a traditional Hindu legend and Pahari painting. It won several awards. Directed by Shanti Varma and by Jehangir S Bhownagary (born in 1921), the film was strongly influenced by the personality of Bhownagary who was a writer, painter, actor and whose interests in the plastic arts deeply influenced the Films Division where he was a deputy chief producer.

The production of art films increased after the 1960s thanks to Pramod Pati, who studied in Czechoslovakia with Trnka, Brdecka and Hofman, and who worked in Zagreb and in the United States of America. Promoted to be a deputy chief producer in the Films Division, Pati focussed on the production of documentaries but proved also to be an excellent director of animated films. His best animated works include the comic *Wives and Wives* (1962), *Trip* (1970) – a film made using pixillation techniques and which depicted the transitoriness of life – and *Abid* (1972), a re-interpretation of the world of pop artist Abid Surti.

After *Banyan Tree*, G.K. Gokhale remained

with the Films Division until 1974 when he left the company to work as a free-lancer. In *Tandava* he retold the Hindu legend of the god Shiva who, angered by his wife Sati's suicide, threw himself into the dance of destruction called 'Tandava'. Other works by Gokhale include *Homo Saps* (1966) and *Chaos* (1969), both focus on environmental themes and both won several awards.

Ram Mohan (born in 1931) scripted, designed and animated many of the cartoons produced by Films Division from 1956 to 1967. In 1968 he joined Prasad Productions as chief of their animated division, and in 1972 established his own production company, Ram Mohan Biographics. His films include *Baap Re Baap*, *You Said It* (1972), *Harmony* and *Fire Games*. In 1974 Ram Mohan was commissioned to make an educational series called *Down to Earth* which met with enormous success all over the country. *The Tree* (1991) is a beautiful fable about the lifelong, joyful relationship between a man and a tree.

V.G. Samant joined the Cartoon Film Unit at the Films Division in 1959 where he produced and directed a large number of educational films including *Law of Nature*, *Precious Water*, *Race with Death*, *Tree of Unity* and *Mouji's Neigh-*

Fig. 141. The Tree by Ram Mogan (India, 1991).

bour (the last of these encouraged parents to set the ideal number of children at one or two per family). In 1981 he made a foray into the entertainment field with *The Lion and the Rabbit*, a story from the *Panchatranta,* the Indian treasury of tales.

Another Films Division stalwart was script-writer, designer, animator and director A.R. Sen who joined the Cartoon Film Unit in 1957. His films include *Skin in the Bin* (1974) and *The Thinker* (1981), which shows the evolution of man from the cave to the modern city and the environmental problems that have resulted. In 1974, in collaboration with B.R. Dohling, Sen made the much praised *Synthesis*, a six minute film scrolling through the entire history of India and relating the spirit of tolerance which brought about a colourful harmony in spite of the great diversity of the country.

Another much praised artist was B.R. Shendge (born in 1936) who won numerous awards. His films include *Umbrella* (1969), an educational film about family planning; *The Brahmin's Goat* (1976), based on a tale from the *Panchatranta,* whose moral is 'one should not be carried by the opinions of others'; *Precious Water* (1980),

about water pollution; *A Little Thought* (1981), about good manners and civic sense; and *The Balloon* (1985), which teaches that 'rumours can turn a molehill into a mountain'.

Other artists employed by the animation unit of the Films Division include producer, live-action director and animator G.H. Saraiya (*My Wise Daddy* 1965), R.A. Shaikh (*Happy Wedding* 1969), R.R. Swamy (born in 1941 and known for *Connoisseur*, 1988), and V.K. Wankhede (born in 1936) who directed *The Ungrateful Man* (1974) and *Warli Painting* (1985). Layout technician Kewaldas Bansod directed *Piety Prospers* (1985), a much praised film on the childhood of Prince Sidharth, who grew up to become Buddha. Among the younger generation artists at Films Division, Arun Gondade (born in 1950) won many national and international awards for *A B See* (1986, a film about child blindness), *End Game* (1988) and *Shanti* (1990, a film which appeals for peace).

Women artists also found an albeit limited place within Indian animation. Shaila Paralkar (born in 1940) animated *The Thinker* (which was directed by Sen) and turned to direction with films such as *Bottled Cannibals* (1978, an anti-alcoholism film), *Dosti* (1990) and *The Last Drop* (1991). Rani D. Burra directed *Louse Story* (1977), a musical fable based on traditional Kalamkari design and featuring a hard-working louse who defeats a wicked king. Outside the Films Division, Nina Sabnani (born in 1956) taught animation and graphic design at the National Institute of Design in Ahmedabad. Her films, produced by the Institute, include *Drawing Drawing* (1982), the beautiful *Shubh Vivah* (1984), *A Summer Story* (1987) and *All About Nothing* (1990).

The National Institute of Design also produced films by Binita Desai including *Cirrus Skies* and *Patang* (both 1984), and by R.L. Mistry including *Din Pratidin* and the award winning *National*

Fig. 142. Shanti by Arun Gongade (India, 1990).

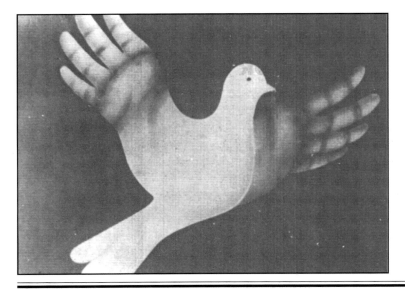

Highway (1985). Kantilal Rathod, a graduate from the Art Institute of Chicago, worked on a number of well-made documentaries, fiction films and animation films. The latter include *Peace Time Armada* (1967). *Tested Berries* (1973) tells a story from Ramayana about the values of equality even in a society divided into social castes. *Business is People* (1975) stresses the importance of co-operation between employees and employers.

Finally, Bhimsain (born in 1936), a musician, producer and director of live-action and documentary films, ran Climb Films, the first Indian production company to specialize in computer animation. Bhimsain's films include *The Climb,* winner of the Silver Hugo award at the Chicago International Film Festival in 1970, *The Fire* (1975) which uses beautifully spare drawings, *Munni* (1976) which is about water conservation and *Chalak Kauva* (1991), a story about enmity that turns to friendship.

Overall, in comparison with live-action productions, Indian animation is as a pygmy to a giant. The animated films produced in a year, consisting of television series or educational films by Films Division and totalling one hour, pale in front of the 800–900 live action feature films released each year – a world record unbeaten in the last decade. The style of Indian animation, moreover, betrays the ethnic heritage of local animators and almost always borrows from Western productions. The few films referring to the extremely rich figurative, pictorial and colourist tradition of the country can be counted on the fingers of one hand and – to quote a young Indian animator and journalist – 'Animation in India is still waiting for a prince'[1].

Sri Lanka

In 1976, Singhalese architect Tilak Samarawickrema directed a short film, *Andere of Sri Lanka,*

featuring the popular child-figure, Andere, in his little village. Filmed in Italy, *Andere* displays curvilinear, sensual drawings based on the alphabet of Sri Lanka. *King Dutugemunu* (1978), a feature film by Givantha Arthasad, was censored by the government. Other than these few isolated works, the only other Sri Lankan animated films were produced for educational purposes by the Institute for Television Training. ITT's Turkish-born Nelly Welzel (1955) was responsible for *Health through Hygiene* (1985), *Do Not Take Drugs* (1986) and *Environmental Protection* (1987).

Indonesia

Indonesian productions, usually released by the state-owned organization for cinema (PPFN), were for the most part either educational or for children's entertainment. Two very successful series starred Unyil (puppet animation) and Huma (animated drawings). Graphic artist and video expert Sasonohardjo (Kertosono, 28 April 1944) stood out with *Baru Klinting* (1985), a mid-length film based on a traditional dragon legend.

Thailand

Payut Ngaokrachang (the Prachuab Kirkhan province, 1 April 1929) is one of the major figures of Thai animation. A graduate of the Poa Chang art school in Bangkok, he was attracted to animation by his love for a local form of shadow theatre (nan talung), and by the Fleischers' and Disney's movies. However it was not until 1955 that he was able to make his first film with equipment and material collected in the difficult post-war era. Entitled *The Magnificent Cause* or *One Night a Miracle Happened*, it's a short comic film about a huge car wreck that occurs when a strikingly beautiful woman walks by. In the end, it turns out that the collision is merely a dream. In

---

1   Kireet Khurana *World of Animation Cinema* (Bombay: Bombay International Film Festival) 1992.

1957, Ngaokrachang filmed *Hanuman's New Adventure*, a political satire in which Hanuman, the big white monkey of the Indian Ramayana, organizes a riot against the government. In 1960, he created *Children and the Big Bear*, a promotional film for SEATO.[1]

In the 1960s the director founded a studio with a staff of fifty, which produced advertising for television and movie theatres. In 1976, he released *Soodsakorn* (see Colour Plate 89), one of his finest works and the first Thai feature film. The prodigious child Soodsakorn, son of a siren and the powerful Phra Aphai Manee, rides a dragon-horse, and has many adventures while searching for his father, helped by a magic cane. Based on *Phra Aphai Manee*, one of the most popular short stories by the classical poet Soonthornpoo (1784–1854), the film displays rich colours and gives a suggestive, modern interpretation of the country's graphic tradition. *Soodsakorn* is a good example of assimilation, rather than an imitation of the Disney lesson.

Monthol Amorapat (Bangkok, 2 May 1949) was a photographer and an expert in documentaries and educational films. In 1977, he directed *Unity Is Strength*, featuring a fight between two peoples, the 'Circles' and the 'Triangles'. *The Path to the Gods* (1978) tells of a poor honest woodcutter who remains faithful to his old axe despite the seductive offers by the God of the Woods. Finally, *Kraitong- Chalawan* (1986) is based on a popular tale. A crocodile-demon, Chalawan, kidnaps a girl to be his bride, but the hero Kraitong kills him, saving the girl.

Taiwan

The aggressive economic expansion that the island underwent during the 1970s, 1980s and early 1990s involved live action cinema and even animation cinema. In 1978 James Wang, a graduate of Indiana University, USA, founded Wang Films, whose animation branch, Cuckoo's Nest Studio, became, in ten years time, one out of the two or three most important production studios of Asia (874 employees in 1991).

Excellently equipped and very well organized (the various production teams worked like small independent studios within the frame of the overall structure), Cuckoo's Nest was esentially an executant on behalf of other companies, basically the American studio Hanna & Barbera. The only exception was the feature film *Uncle Niou's Great Adventure* (1982), produced for the head office, Wang Films. Among the other production centres of Taiwan, Green Paddy Animation Studio, advertising specialist, and Dragon Animation, devoted to educational and governmental films, deserve a mention.

Mongolia

The first animated film entitled *Three Brothers*, (puppet animation), which was an apologue of friendship among children, was made in Mongolia in 1964 by T. Zagiraa. Only 11 years later, in 1975, it was followed by the start of an animation movement: filmmakers from Mongolkino and from the State-owned television made some experimental productions. These were not very satisfying to begin with because of the lack of experience and technical equipment. It was in the 1980s that the Mongolian animation industry really flourished, with about sixty animators working full time in three studios: they were the Mongol Studio for animated films (15 people led by the most prestigious Mongolian animator, Sodnompilin Miagmar), Ulzi Film, and Mongolkino. The subject of *Burto Chino* (1992), by Sodnompilin Miagmar, was based on the traditional XIII century *Mongol Secret History*; the drawings were by R. Togoldor and B. Baterdene, the music by B. Sharav. It was screened at the

---

1   South East Asia Treaty Organization, an agreement signed by United States, Thailand, the Philippines, Pakistan, Great Britain, France, Australia and New Zealand. It dissolved in 1977.

Hiroshima Animation Festival in 1992.

Singapore

Singapore's most important animators were K. Subramaniam and Johnny Lau. At his company, Animata Productions (Singapore's first animation studio), Subramaniam (Singapore, 9 August 1955) made animated advertising and promotional films (his 1988 film, *Little Pink Elephant*, produced for the Community Chest of Singapore, is regarded as Singapore's first narrative animated cartoon), educational animated films for the Singaporean government (his 1993 film, *FIDRANT*, was made for the National Fire Prevention Council), and films for his own artistic expression. His best known work is *The Cage* (1990), a quiet, eleven minute exploration of the life of an elderly Chinese Singaporean who eventually releases his pet bird from its cage, allowing it the freedom that he himself feels he will never know in his secure, but highly structured and ultimately boring life. *The Cage* won a Special Jury Prize at the 1991 Singapore International Film Festival. 'Subra', as he is known professionally, is currently working on a feature-length animated film on the life of the Buddha, which he hopes to complete by the end of 1994.

Johnny Lau (born in London, UK, 25 July 1964, although he is a Singaporean citizen) was best known as the creator of 'Mr Kiasu' (*kiasu* is a Chinese term which means something like 'the fear of losing out'), a popular comic book in Singapore. Lau and his creation became well known throughout Singapore due, in large part, to a promotion by the local McDonald's fast food chain, which not only sold a 'kiasu burger' (a sandwich made of chicken and sweet chilli sauce, a popular combination in Singapore), but also sponsored a series of quite clever and colourful animated commercials featuring Mr Kiasu. In production is a feature length animated film, and 13 episodes of a television series (probably to be broadcast across Asia by Hong Kong's Star TV satellite sys-

tem), starring Mr Kiasu, who is a parody of the average Singaporean; he takes anything that is free (whether he really wants it or not), takes more than he can possibly eat at buffets, and thinks of little more than money. These animated works are being directed by Lau and co-produced with K. Subramaniam at Animata Productions.

Malaysia

Malaysia's greatest hopes for a spot on the animation map were Mohamad Nor Khalid and Ibrahim Mohd Noor. Mohamad Nor Khalid, better known by his pen name, 'Lat', was by far the best known and best loved cartoonist in Malaysia, and devoted most of his time to animation. His cartoons, which appear three times weekly in *The New Straits Times*, Malaysia's leading English-language newspaper, gently poke fun at Malaysians and their customs, whether Malay, Chinese or Indian, as do his cartoon books, which feature the autobiographical 'Kampung (village) Boy'. Currently, however, he is working, with other animators in Canada and the Phillippines, on a series of animated cartoons for television featuring the Kampung Boy.

The other important animator from Malaysia is Ibrahim Mohd Noor (born in 1966), known professionally as 'Ujang', a singer, cartoonist, and writer. While a cartoonist at *Glla-glla* (glla means 'mad' or 'crazy' in Malay), a Malaysian humour magazine, Ujang got the idea for an animated television series, which eventually became *Usop Sontorian*, currently in production. Ujang, who is responsible for the concept, stories, and scripts of the cartoons, as well as much of the drawing (the cartoons utilize, in part, computer animation), described the series as a Malaysian version of *The Simpsons*.

The Philippines

The country's first animation studio, which opened in 1982, was a branch of the Sydney-based

Burbank Films. In only two and a half years, the company doubled its staff, which originally consisted of 80 novice Philippine animators and five Australian trainers. Thus the studio existed as one of the numerous Far Eastern businesses which executed low-cost work for Western, mainly American, producers. Fil-Cartoons (a branch of Hanna & Barbera) achieved enormous success, as well as Los Angeles Animation and Island Animation, doing the same low-cost work.

In 1986, Gerardo A. Garcia (Manila, 29 June 1951) founded GAGAVEP, a local production company. That same year, he released *Ang Panday*, the country's first series, and a conventional adventure story that features a character resembling the popular actor Fernando Poe Jr. The success of the series spurred Garcia to continue with other enterprises. Other animation groups were Mega Scope Graphcs, an advertising-oriented company, and Alcazaren Bros., who specialize in plasticine animation.

Hong Kong

Beyond making inserts and special effects for live-action films (the industry of cinema in Hong Kong has long been a thriving one), local animators worked in the fields of advertising and series production. In 1974, one year after the death of actor Bruce Lee, the country that created kung-fu movies released *The History of the Chinese*. Produced by Chan Ying Motion Pictures and advertised with the slogan 'See Bruce Lee in action again', it featured kings, demons and battles from Chinese mythology. Most recently, the Single Frame studio has acquired a prominent place for its interesting, autonomous productions.

North Korea

The Pyongyang animation studio opened in 1948, the same year the region located north of the 38th parallel became a Communist Republic.

In over forty years of activity, the studio produced more than two hundred films. Its fortune extended well into the 1980s when it employed approximately six hundred people, twenty of whom were directors.

More than any other communist country, animation in North Korea functioned as an ideological educator for children. Its films (with animated drawings, puppets or cut-outs) had marked educational contents; many were based on tales 'narrated to the youth by the country's leader, Marshal Kim Il Sung'.

The pervasive style of Korean animated films strongly resembles that of the Soviet films of the 1950s, with delicate ways and fluid animation but decidedly conventional drawings. The characters' movements and mimes may be autochthonous, rather than drawn from the international repertoire, but are scarcely incisive. At times, these productions share similarities with Japanese series, especially in the deformed caricatures of monsters (for example, Kim Gwang Song's *The Boy Who Defeated the Thieves*, 1985); but this is probably due to common traits in figurative culture rather than stylistic imitation.

North Korea's finest film is *The Flying Horse* (1986) by Kim Chun Ok. A feature film, it tells of a man with three sons, the youngest of whom is able to ride a flying horse and defeat foreign invaders. Based on a short story by Kim Il Sung, the film won an award at the Varna film festival. Another award-winner was the more modest *An Ant Which Rolled a Cantaloupe* (1985), by Ryu Chung Ung. The film tells the story of an ant whose powerful intellect triumphs over his lack of physical strength. Other films, like Chang Young Hwan's *The Butterfly and the Rooster* and *Two Generals*, and Kim Chun Ok's *The Squirrel and the Hedgehog*, all share the principle that to defend one's country one needs strength of body and mind.[1]

1   Yun Wun Ik, Catalogue of Korean Film Export & Import Corporation, 1986.

South Korea

Because of its skillful, disciplined and low-cost labour force,[1] South Korea became a paradise for American, Japanese and Western-European 'runaway' productions. Out of the many companies which executed work for foreign studios, a branch of Japan's Toei and Dong-Seo Animation (whose revealing name means 'East-West Animation') prospered enormously. With over 400 full-time animators, Dong-Seo Animation was able to complete up to two-and-a-half hours of finished product each week. The giant of the 1980s was called Sun Woo Animation. Its president Kang Han Young could boast that their job was 'producing feature films, shorts, series, anything, for an army of clients all over the world'. Another big production company was Anitel. The pioneer of South Korean animation was Dong-Hun Shin (Seoul, 1 April 1927), known for his comic strips and the numerous short films he directed in the 1960s.

Japan's expansion

The industrial expansion of Japanese animation began in 1958 with the release of Taiji Yabushita's *The White Snake*, a successful feature film about a boy's unrequited love for a girl who had previously been incarnated as a reptile. Toei, the production company responsible for the film, flooded the market with feature films (at least one per year) that dealt with such topics as legends from the Far East and international tales or science-fiction. These were mainly entertainment films, professionally made by draftsmen and set designers and soon imitated by Toei's competitors, Otogi, Kyodo, Nihon Eiga and Toho to name a few. Despite some fine work, these efforts often suffered from hurried preparation. Unlike their American counterparts, they usually neglected painstaking drawings and musical intermezzos, favouring fast editing, breathtaking

action, illustrations of dream-like worlds, and quite often, violence.

The few exceptions to the rule include *Shaka no Shoga* (Life of Buddha, 1961), by Noburo Ofuji. A black-and-white film made with Ofuji's own technique of transparent figures, it seemed anachronistic when compared to the fast-paced, polychromatic works of the competition. This was the last film by Ofuji, who died on 18 June 1974.

In 1959 the production company Gakken, specializing in educational cinema, opened a puppet animation studio under the leadership of one of the few women directors in Japanese animation, Matsue Jinbo (Naka, April 1928). In 1975, Jinbo's *Match uri no Shojo* (The Little Match Girl, 1967) won the Golden Mermaid Award at the Copenhagen festival commemorating the one hundredth anniversary of Hans Christian Andersen's death.

The production company Otogi, founded by Ryuichi Yokoyama in 1955, released *Otogino Sekai Ryoko* (Journey in Fairyland, 1962), a well-crafted collection of stories by staff members. Osamu Tezuka (discussed later in this chapter) directed *Pictures at an Exhibition*. Eiichi Yamamoto[2] (Kyoto, 22 November 1936) directed several television series for the production company Mushi and collaborated on Tezuka's *Senya Ichiya Monogatari* (One Thousand and One Nights, 1969) and *Cleopatra* (1970). In 1973, he directed *Belladonna*, based on a novel by French author Jules Michelet. An ambitious film for adult audiences, it was praised by a small group of art film *aficionados*, but was a box-office failure. The soft, erotic themes of these films put them in line with the most advanced works by European and American animators of the time.

Another noteworthy artist in the 1960s and 1970s was Yugo Serikawa (Tokyo, 26 June

---

1   The weekly wage of South Korean animators averaged about US$300 in 1985 – less than half of an American animator's wage, but still high when compared to the cost of living in South Korea.
2   Not to be confused with Zenjiro 'Sanae' Yamamoto.

1931), who competed with Yabushita for leadership in the production of Japanese animated feature films. A connoisseur of action movies, he deserves mention for *Wanpaku Oji no Orochi Taiji* (The Little Prince and the Dragon with Seven Heads, 1963), *Chibikko Remi to Meikan Kapi* (Little Remi and Kapi the Dog, 1970), *Panda no Daiboken* (Panda's Adventures, 1973) and a variety of television productions.

Since the early 1960s, television was a determining factor for Japanese mass animation. Osamu Tezuka led the way with *Tetsuwan Atom* (Astro Boy, 1963). New companies were founded and, still in 1963, television broadcast six new animated series: two by Mushi (Tezuka's production company), three by TCJ and one by Toei.

Two years later, twelve series were produced by seven different studios. Tatsunoko Productions, founded by cartoonist Tatsuo Yoshida, released *Uchu Ace* (Ace, the Space Boy); TCJ produced *Tetsujin 28-go* (Steelman Number 28), created and drawn by cartoonist Mitsuteru Yokoyama; and Toei introduced *Ookami Shonen Ken* (Ken, the Wolf Boy), directed by Sadao Tsukioka. The esteemed Mushi continued to focus on innovation, releasing the first colour animated series, *Jungle Taitei* (The Emperor of the Jungle, 1965); and when the honoured Mochinaga retired in 1967, his staff reorganized the production company under a new name, Video Tokyo Productions.

In 1968, Tokyo Movie introduced a higher level of formal elegance with works such as *Kyojin no Hoshi* (The Giants' Star) and *Moomin*, based on the children's story by Finnish author Tove Jansson. *Sazae-San* (1969), featuring the daily adventures of a popular comic-strip housewife, stands out for its anti-conformist style amidst the huge production of conventional series and specials.

Television of the 1970s began with a sports-oriented production, *Attack No. 1* (1969–71);

with 104 episodes, the series features the deeds and misdeeds of a female volleyball team. Analogous series followed, dealing with boxers, baseball and football players. Other animated works produced in the 1970s became very successful on European television and gave way to a true Japanese invasion (less so in the United States of America, where the market is usually not as receptive to foreign films and television productions). *Mazinger Z* (based on a Goo Nagai comic strip and released by Toei) and *Grendizer* (Atlas Ufo Robot Goldrake or Goldorak), also based on Goo Nagai's drawings and released by Toei, are science-fiction war sagas; *Alps no Shoojo Heidi* (Heidi), based on a children's novel by Swiss author Johanna Spyri, directed by Isao Takahata and produced by Taurus Film/Toei) is a calm, gentle story. All three series started in 1972. *Candy Candy*, a Toei production based on comic strips by Mizuki and Igarashi, was released in 1976.

Among the innumerable series about monstrous robots defending the earth from galactic monsters, *Uchyu-Kansen Yamato* (Cosmic Warship Yamato), directed by comic strip artist Reiji Matsumoto, transforms World War II into a futuristic space war. Matsumoto also directed *Ghinga Tetsudo 999* (Galactic Express 999, 1978–81). Based on a comic strip, the film features a boy who travels on a space-train in search of a legendary planet where he can transplant his brain into the immortal body of a robot. Another science-fiction series is *Gundam* (1979–80), a Nippon Sunrise production based on a story by Yoshiyuki Tomino, with drawings by Yoshikazu Yasuhiko. These science-fiction war stories, featuring believable characters with realistic psychological reactions, represented a departure from the stereotypical productions of the past.

The series mentioned here are noted for their success or quality, but overall, this mass production requires little attention as far as creativity is concerned. Two hundred series were produced by 1976, and by 1983 the number doubled. In Tokyo alone there were more than ten thousand professional animators. In 1985, the production giant Toei employed over one thousand people in its Tokyo artistic department, and even more in its Seoul-based South Korean subsidiary; overall it was able to release twenty-six minutes of finished animation daily. The resulting series were broadcast daily during children's prime time from 5 to 7 pm by the country's eight major networks. Production usually followed this routine: the television broadcasters would sell their programming time to advertising agencies, which in turn would find sponsors among the manufacturers of toys, candies or other products for children. Finally, animated films would be set up on the basis of marketing needs and would then be commissioned to a production company.

Regularly employed personnel executed only a segment of the work; the rest was assigned to freelancers or to cost-effective subsidiaries and sub-contractors in other Far Eastern countries. In the 1980s, the practice of 'pen renting' became quite popular in Tokyo, where professional teams working for producers unfamiliar with animation, packaged films or series to be released with the producers' names. This led to an expansion in the field. A true boost, however, came with the opening of the videocassette market in 1985.[1] Many of these works for the home entertainment industry introduced heretofore unthinkable themes such as violence, brutality and pornography.

In 1987, more than 1600 hours of film were produced, including 24 feature films for movie-theatres and 72 mid-length or feature films exclusively for the home entertainment industry. Animation was surrounded by a whole constellation of movie-buffs and buyers. Merchandising developed in every direction, but particularly in the toy industry which favoured moveable, plastic figures. In major cities, specialty stores sold original cels for collectors as well as drawing and filming materials, posters, videodiscs and videocassettes. The publishing industry developed trade magazines with such titles as *Animec, Animage, Animedia, This Is Animation* and *Love Animation*.

Finally, the popularity of television series renewed an interest in feature films. Many series were reworked and offered to movie-theatre audiences. Some of these works even established box-office records. The aforementioned *Cosmic Warship Yamato* was released in 1977 as a feature film, while a feature film version of *Galactic Express 999* was released in 1979. *Akira* (1988) was directed by Katsuhiro Otamo (see Colour Plate 90), who is also the author of the comic strip from which it is derived. Set in 2030 AD among trash and technology, it is a monument to gore and adventure.

The new king of feature films was Hayao Miyazaki (Tokyo, 1941). A former trainee at Toei who made a name for himself as the art director of *Heidi*, he directed feature films which were praised as masterpieces by both viewers and colleagues alike. His finest works include *Kaliostro no Shiro* (Cagliostro's Castle, 1979), *Rupan Sansei* (Lupin III, 1980), *Kaze no Tani no Naushika* (Nausicaa, 1984) and especially *Tenku no Siro Rapyuta* (Laputa, the Castle in the Sky, 1986)[2].

Isao Takahata (Ise-shi, Mie-ken, 29 October 1935), director of the series *Heidi*, went from his hectic activity as a professional of mass production to the making of a meticulously sculpted feature film for children. Entitled *Celo Hiki no Goshu* (Goshu the Cellist, 1980), this OH Productions' release took six years to complete with little or no division of labour. Based on a 1920s

1   Frederick Patten, 'Full Circle,' *Witty World*, 1, No. 1 (Summer 1987).
2   Takuya Mori, 'Short History of Japanese Animation', *Hiroshima Festival, Daily Bulletin* (1987), n. 6.

short story by writer Kenji Miyazawa, the film is about the spiritual growth of a child who performs with his 'cello.

As for puppet animation, Kihachiro Kawamoto (who will be discussed shortly) and scriptwriter Tadasu Iizawa left Tadahito Mochinaga's studio and founded Shiba Productions. In a similar move, Tadanari Okamoto (Osaka, 1931–90) founded Echo Productions. As a director, Okamoto won praise at international festivals for films such as *Hana to Mogura* (The Flowers and the Mole, 1970), *Mochi-Mochi no Ki* (Mochi-Mochi Tree, 1972), *Namu ichibyo sokusai* (The Happy Weakling, 1973), *Niji ni Mukatte* (Toward the Rainbow, 1977) and *Okonjoruri* (1982).

Osamu Tezuka

Osamu Tezuka (Toyonaka, Osaka, 3 November 1926 – Tokyo, 9 February 1989) managed a curious balancing act between mass production and art. He was both a comic strip artist and an animator. Working first as a comic strip artist, this continued to be his primary commitment. In Japan, where comic strip artists enjoyed the same consideration as novelists and painters, he was considered a living legend. His portrait, with his characteristic black beret, appeared as an endorsement testimonial in advertisements. And while others were called 'masters' or 'great masters', he was referred to as the 'God of comicstrips'. His production was remarkable for its quality and quantity, including over 75,000 drawn poster boards and a record 250,000,000 copies sold by the mid-1980s.

As a teenager, Tezuka was attracted by Chaplin's, the Fleischers' and Disney's movies and began drawing at an early age. In 1947, he entered medical school at the University of Osaka, from which he graduated in 1952. His artistic activity, however, underwent such growth as to completely distract him from a medical career. In 1947, he published *Shin Takara Jima* (The New Treasure Island), which sold an unexpected half-

a-million copies and made him famous. With this work, Tezuka broke with the Japanese static, theatre-like drawings and began a stylistic revolution by introducing cinema-like dynamism and assembly. He soon became supervisor of his own team, producing all kinds of works, from science-fiction to fairy tales, to horror stories, to novellas, and to national legends. He broke into animation in 1959, when he was hired by Toei to co-direct and write the production *Saiyuki* (Western Diary), a film based on an old Chinese story about a journey West which Tezuka had re-written in 1953.

In 1961, the artist founded a production company, Mushi. A famous character from his comic strips (a superpowerful teenaged robot who is brave but also melancholy in his longing to be human) is the protagonist of the first Japanese animated television series. The black-and-white production, entitled *Tetsuwan Atom* (Atom With an Iron Core), was broadcast for the first time on 2 January 1963, and became popular in the West as *Astro Boy*. In 1965, Tezuka was the first to introduce colour, with *Jungle Taitei* (The Emperor of the Jungle, known in the West as Kimba the White Lion).

Throughout the 1960s and well into the 1970s, Mushi continued with the production of television series and feature films; Tezuka always maintained artistic control, usually as a supervisor. Inspired by Mussorgsky's music, he directed a feature film for Toei in 1966 entitled *Tenrankai no E* (Pictures at an Exhibition). The film was a collection of ten satirical vignettes, each illustrating an aspect of human folly and displaying characteristics similar to those of the Zagreb School.

When Mushi suffered several setbacks in 1973 Osamu Tezuka created Tezuka Productions, a more flexible organization catering to his interests as an individual creator. In 1980, he produced and directed *2772, Ai no Cosmozone* (2772, The Cosmic Zone of Love), a feature film based on the last episode of his long running comic strip saga about the Phoenix, Japan's sacred bird. This was the artist's own answer to *Hi no tori* (The Phoenix, 1980), a live-action feature film with animated inserts directed in 1980 by Kon Ichikawa. *Hi no tori*, which Tezuka found to be unsatisfactory, was also based on Tezuka's comic strip.

Despite the many years devoted to productions for larger audiences, Tezuka did not neglect his nature as an artist and the social responsibilities that this implied. His works centred on the values of peace, love for nature and social participation. Twice, in the 1960s and in the 1980s, he helped found and promote international animation festivals aimed at showing art animation to the public. From an artistic standpoint, he produced a limited but creative number of original shorts, including *Aru Machi Kado no Monogatari* (A Story of the Street Corner, 1962), a film without human characters or dialogue, exclusively narrated by visual means, and *Osu* (Male, 1962), a more experimental film displaying the distortion of image in CinemaScope.

In 1984, he made *Jumping*, a 'subjective' film which the viewer's eyes see from the same perspective as the protagonist's – an unknown creature that jumps higher and higher, flying over oceans and plunging into hell. Tezuka trusted this unconventional, creative film with an ethical message:

> 'Those who jump are you, the public, humanity. We humans have the tendency to go too far with what we do. Often this becomes a dilemma or a catastrophe.'[1]

Onboro Film (Broken Down Film, 1985), one of Tezuka's best, is a parodied salute to American silent movies. The film goes so far as to simulate the accidents that marred silent film screenings such as torn film stock and scratched images. The mid-length *Legend of the Forest* (1988) is a less satisfactory film. Poorly combining an ostenta-

tious salute to the classics of animation with ecological messages and bizarre stylistic research, the film is a tear-jerking medley that lacks self-irony.

Art productions

Similar to the majority of industrialized nations, Japan also saw the birth of spontaneous, chaotic productions outside the framework of the official market. These were self-financed animators who often worked in painting, graphics or advertising (since here as in many other countries, support by the state or by private foundations was non-existent). A true beacon for this movement was Tokyo Image Forum, a prestigious centre for avant-garde cinema and the arts.

Kihachiro Kawamoto (Sendagaya, 11 January 1925) gained a solid reputation with audiences as well as critics as one of the world's major experts of puppet animation. Gifted with a remarkable theatrical spirit, he was a master at modelling the faces and bodies of his wooden puppets and at directing their acting. A student of Mochinaga's, Kawamoto founded his own production company with Iizawa, but soon left for Prague, where

Fig. 143. Jumping by Osamu Tezuka (Japan, 1984).

1   Cited in: 'Osamu Tezuka,' *Banc-Titre*, No. 44 (October 1984), p. 28.

he specialized at Jiří Trnka's school. In 1965, he returned to Japan and divided his activity in three main directions: children's educational or entertainment works for television; puppet theatre shows for adult audiences, which he himself wrote and directed and which toured the country; and animation films. His first film, *Hanaori* (Do Not Break the Branches, 1968), based on a popular comedy from the Middle-Ages, won a silver medal at the Mamaia Animation Film Festival.

After *Kenju Giga* (An Anthropo-Cynical Farce, 1970), he made *Oni* (The She-Devil, 1972). The film which is based on a medieval subject shows Kawamoto's style at its best – personal, modern, and also linked to Trnka's school and Japan's own traditions. For his puppets, the filmmaker did not imitate human models, but instead selected the Japanese Noh masks and the Bunraku puppets as sources of inspiration. Since puppets don't have facial muscles to express emotions, he indicated a change of feelings with camera angles and lighting, in the best Japanese tradition.[1] *Tabi* (The Trip, 1973) and *Shijin no Shogai* (Life as a poet, 1974), two films with cut-outs, were followed by the distinguished film *Dojoji* (The Dojoji Temple, 1976). *Dojoji* is about a young monk who is desperately loved by a widow. When she chases him into the temple they encounter a tragic destiny.

In 1979, Kawamoto finished *Kataku* (The House in Flames, see Colour Plate 91), the story of a girl who is undecided about two gentlemen callers. Choosing death as her final suitor, her soul becomes embraced by a burning house. Kawamoto's first work to be released by an outside producer is *Rennyo to sono Haha* (Rennyo the Priest and His Mother, 1981), a feature film inspired by an event in Japanese history. It won the grand prize at the Varna festival.

Renzo Kinoshita (Abeno-ku, Osaka, 3 September 1936), in collaboration with his wife Sayoko,

CARTOONS
Bendazzi

416

directed *Made in Japan* (1972) and *Japanese* (1977). Both are bitingly amusing satires on Japanese stereotypes. *Pica Don* (1978) features 6 August 1945 – the fateful day of the bombing of Hiroshima. Despite an excessive lingering over decaying bodies, it was a powerful pacifist film.

A collaborator of Yoji Kuri's, Taku Furukawa (Uno-shi, 25 September 1941) was internationally renowned for *Headspoon* (1972). In 1975, he earned an award at Annecy for *Odoroki-ban* (Phenakistiscope), an original salute to the origins of animation by a modern animator. His talent as a visionary emerged in other films, such as *Utsukushiihoshi* (Beautiful Planet, 1976), *Coffee Break* (1978) and *Speed* (1981).

Harugutsu Fukushima (Fuji-shi, 16 October 1941) directed *Tobira* (The Door, 1971), the accomplished *The Great Tour* (1972) and *Cube* (1987).

Sadao Tsukioka (Niigata-ken, 15 May 1939), a former director of the 1963 Toei series *Ken, The Wolf-Boy*, switched to advertising and independent productions. His films include *Shin-tenchisozo* (New Creation of the World, 1970), the series *Science Non-Fiction* (original title in English, 1973) and *Yoake* (Dawn, 1985). Hideo Koide succesfully created avant-garde visual effects in *Stonegame* (1973), a mix of abstract and Pop Art. Andy Warhol's Pop Art was also explicitly mentioned by a more important filmmaker, Keiichi Tanaami (Tokyo, 1936). A genial painter and sculptor, gifted with a traditional style, he broke into avant-garde cinema several times with films such as *Goodbye Elvis* (1971), *USA* (1971), *Goodbye Marilyn* (1975) and *Crayon Angel* (1979).

Other avant-garde artists used video-techniques and computer aided animation. They include Koh Nakajima (Tokyo, 11 January 1941), director of *Kage* (The Shadow, 1969) and Masaki Fu-

1   Kihachiro Kawamoto. Letter to author, 17 November 1987.

jihata (Tokyo, 1956), internationally praised director of *Mandala 1983* (1983) and *Miroku* (1984).

Shinichi Suzuki (Nagasaki, December 1933) was a more traditional filmmaker. Inspired by Disney's work, he learned animation at Otogi during the 1950s. Later, he founded Studio Zero, where he produced a wide variety of animation work, including art films. Dead-pan humour and drawings based on thin lines characterize *Ten* (Points, 1971) and *Hyotan* (The Pumpkin, 1961). *The Bubble* (1980) features a child's mind as it transforms bubbles into fantastical shapes. *Gag Menso* (Gag-Kaleidoscope, 1981) is a comic anthology of unrelated stories. Nobuhiro Aihara (Naga-gun, Kanawagaken, 17 October 1944) was a surrealist and a lover of black and white. An active animator since the mid-1960s, he exhibited his best work in *Stone* (1975), by applying drawing to rocks and houses (with a technique similar to Carmen D'Avino's) amidst a filmed Swedish landscape. *Kumo no Ito* (Cloud Thread, 1976) was also a highly praised film by the same director.

Finally, Tatsuo Shimamura should be credited for *Kachofugetsu* (Japan's Four Seasons, 1985), in which animated drawings, computer graphics, plasticine animation and other effects create evocative, flowing images of Japanese culture and nature.

Yoji Kuri

Yoji Kuri was born on 9 April 1928 in Sabae-cho, in the Fukui prefecture. The second-born son of an officer of the Imperial Army, he attended military high-school. During World War II, he worked in an aeroplane factory which was frequently bombed. When the war ended, Kuri abandoned the military and pursued his inborn vocation, drawing. After a short stay at the Kyoto School

of Fine Arts, he transferred to Tokyo Bunga Gakuin, the country's most respected art academy. In the capital, he met caricaturist Yokohama who first introduced him to comic drawing. From 1950, Yoji Kuri became a successful artist, who was published in newspapers and magazines. In 1955, he had his first one-man art show, more proof of his versatility, in the related fields of caricature, painting, sculpture and, later, animation. One year later, Kuri published his first volume of *COO*, a collection of drawn stories without words, and won the national prize offered by *Bungei Shuniu* magazine. This award was the most prestigious of the many prizes he had already been awarded up to that time. In 1960, the artist opened Kuri Jikken Manga Kobo, a production company devoted to short films. Later, with his colleagues Manabe and Yanagihara, he founded the Three Designers, a polemical movement claiming that Japan's cartoonists and animators should follow the very rich iconographic tradition of Japan rather than foreign suggestions. Actually, Kuri himself often neglected this very rule. In *Human Zoo* (1962),[1] one of his first films, he found inspiration in the Western theatre of the absurd, while his style was influenced by surrealism and by artists such as McLaren, Hubley and Dunning. His graphics are more reminiscent of the American tradition than of Hokusai's style.

Kuri's film production is extremely rich and difficult to classify. Over the years, for instance, he made nearly one thousand films for television, each lasting one or two minutes. He claimed that he made three thousand films in the 1970s alone.[2] In the 1960s, beside the highly prized *Human Zoo*, his productions included *Locus* (1963), *Love* (1963) and *AOS* (1964). The latter, which features indescribable events that take place inside a crate, shocked its viewers with its

1   As the Japanese titles of Kuri's films were not always available, they have been indicated here with the titles used at their release during international festivals.

2   Yoji Kuri. Personal communication to author, 1983. Kuri has never denied his wish to surprise, even during private conversations. This last figure seems to be most unlikely.

violence and sensuality. An analogous film is *The Man Next Door* (1965), about the relationship between men and women, seen from a decidedly misogynous standpoint. Many works followed, all reiterating the same formula with different degrees of originality. Instead of looking for new inspiration, Kuri preferred to look for new techniques and switched from animated drawings to the animation of live-actors (he himself appeared as an actor in *The Bathroom*, 1971).

A turning point in his production was *Midnight Parasites* (1972) a salute to Hieronymus Bosch, stylistically inspired by Bosch as well as the nineteenth century European models of Borowczyk and Topor. Here he abandoned his typically provocative taste for a more rhythmic, thoughtful structure and substituted frescoes of horror for absurd games. *Manga* (1977) marked a return to his previous manner. In the years which followed, Kuri displayed a renewed interest in plastic arts (during this period he participated as a painter in

major expositions in Basle, Washington and New York). Putting aside his caustic humour and bloody taste for the absurd, he favoured formal combinations of caricature and geometric figures with light effects.

Kuri's filmmaking is anti-cinema par excellence. As he tries to offend his viewers with 'unpleasant' drawings, unattractive colours and a shrieking sound track, he also wants to entertain. He goes against the rules of timing and the rhythm of images in motion, with unbearably motionless characters, exasperatingly inconclusive repetitions or overly rapid events which escape comprehension. As for themes, Kuri (who usually likes to talk about himself) prefers not to speak, but lets the viewers see for themselves such topics as existential despair, anti-authoritarianism (politically, Kuri is a leftist), the Japanese cruelty of *hara-kiri* and so on. His strong misogynous attitude mixes with an openly declared taste for sadism and sexual deviance: Kuri never minds being too gruesome or exaggerated.

Fig. 144. Midnight Parasites *by Yoji Kuri (Japan, 1972).*

Chapter 24

Australasia

Australia

Australian cinema dates back to 1896, with the production of documentaries. The very first feature film within living memory, Charles Tait's *The Story of the Kelly Gang* (1906), was Australian. That florid age ended with the arrival of the sound track, and except for one or two unusual films, the Australian filmmaking industry did not regain prominence until the 1970s and 1980s when government agencies offered opportunities to talented actors and directors.

During World War I, Harry Julius animated political vignettes with cut-outs for the newsreel *Australian Gazette*. These one or two-minute films exhibited better than average drawing and technique, and presumably, Julius incorporated such skills into the lightning sketches he created for his later films. Other animators worked during the 1920s and 1930s, leaving no record except for some advertising spots and a few vignettes on daily events, such as a cricket match. Eric Porter, whose work will be discussed later in this chapter, and who is considered the founder of Australian animation, worked in the 1930s and 1940s. During World War II, the Owen brothers of Melbourne made two-minute propaganda films commissioned by the Department of Information.

Australia's animation reached its maturity with the diffusion of television in 1956; the initial production of advertising and commissioned films was joined by television specials and series, and only gradually, by feature films and art animation. Major and minor studios were founded in several cities. In 1983, Bob Hanlon counted thirteen in Sydney, four in Melbourne and three in Adelaide, adding that, in fact, there were many more.[1] There were also many independent and freelance professionals. A large number of animators moved to St Leonards, a Sydney suburb. 'Chandos Street in that suburb was also called Animation Row, home to animation companies representing every form and style[2].' Except for advertising, however, the country's internal market was weak, and did not offer opportunities to local animators, who turned to the much larger markets of other English speaking nations such as the United States of America and Great Britain. This, and the lack of a solid tradition, were probably the cause for the scarcity of original Australian animation, which was technically advanced but lacked a character of its own.

Fascinated by the first appearances of Mickey Mouse, Eric Porter (Sydney, 8 February 1911 – 21 December 1983) was the well-known father of Australian animation. He convinced producer Ken Hall, at Cinesound, to finance some experiments. Before he was twenty, Porter completed his first animated film – an advertising spot for an Adelaide butcher. Subsequently, he founded a studio which he supported with advertising while his attempts at entertainment cinema failed. In 1938, he began work on *Waste Not, Want Not*, featuring the character of Willie the Wombat; the film was distributed only after the war. In 1940, he contributed to war propaganda with *Adolf in Plunderland*, a short film mocking Adolf Hitler. Before the birth of television, however, Porter's attempts to build a solid, productive activity in Australia failed. He made two pilots for the US market, *Bimbo's Auto* and *Rabbit Stew* in the early 1950s, but neither series was produced. *Ten Little Cyclists* (1953), a work commissioned by the Department of Transportation was critically praised, but over all, Porter supported himself by making commercials.

In 1956, he joined the Artransa Studios, and for the next two years organized the animation department and trained its filmmakers. Finally, he devoted himself in grand style to Eric Porter Pro-

ductions. Together with series for the US market (*Superfriends, Cool McCool, Charlie Chan* and *Abbott & Costello*), the studio released series made for Australian audiences such as *The Yellow House*, which satisfied Porter artistically, but was otherwise a financial failure. Porter also produced a huge number of advertising spots for television, launching characters which soon became popular, such as Louis the Fly, Mr. Sheen and Friar Tuck.

During the 1972 Christmas season, Porter presented the first Australian animated feature film, *Marco Polo Jr. vs. the Red Dragon*.[3] A descendant of the ancient traveller, Marco Polo Junior takes a journey to Xanadu, carrying one half of the friendship medal. Meanwhile, Xanadu has fallen into the hands of the cruel Red Dragon, who has imprisoned the princess. After many adventures, Marco manages to unite the two halves of the medal. Audiences loved the film, and Porter was openly proud of his creation; as for the critics, they were divided into those who liked the

Fig. 145. *Advertising sketch for* Waste Not, Want Not *by Eric Porter (Australia, 1938).*

1   Bob Hanlon, 'Animation Down Undeer', *Animator's Newsletter*, No. 7 (St. Albans, Great Britain, Winter 1983–84). Production centres opened also in Queensland, Western Australia and Tasmania.

2   Tim Mendham & Keith Hepper, 'Animation in Australia', *Industrial & Commercial Photography Yearbook 1978* (Sydney, 1978).

3   The original title Porter had chosen was Marco Polo Junior. The production company changed it later, but both titles currently appear in the credits.

film for its pictorial qualities and sophisticated humour and those who saw it as a catalogue of cliches. In any case, Porter suffered a financial setback, for which he accused his American partner. Constant problems haunted the studio and eventually Porter was forced to close it.

In the panorama of Australian animation, Porter can be considered the founder of the first professional production company. As a trainer of young animators, he respected the individual skills and dispositions of his collaborators and allowed them to express their own unique style. As for his artistic credo, he remained faithful to Disney, stating that *Fantasia* was 'unquestionably every animator's ideal', and in 1978 he claimed, 'Animation reached its peak about 18 years ago, and has gradually declined since then, including Disney.'[1]

Among the largest Australian studios the most important was Hanna & Barbera Australia. Founded in 1972, this studio was responsible for 25 per cent of the series work produced globally by the multinational corporation in the 1970s. Its advertising department which opened in 1974, captured up to 35 per cent of the Australian market in its first years of operation. The studio also released some locally produced specials.

Another large organization was Air Programs International, founded in the early 1960s by Walter Hucker with his wife Wendy. In 1966, Air Programs released the first series entirely created and produced in Australia, *King Arthur & the Square Knights of the Round Table*, comprised of 39 half-hour episodes. In 1969, the studio's version of Charles Dickens' *A Christmas Carol*[2] was acquired by the American corporation CBS; this gave rise to an anthology of similar specials, titled *English Classics*.

Other works released by this production company

pany include *Gentlemen of Titipu*, a controversially updated version of Gilbert and Sullivan's 1885 operetta, *The Mikado* (the music was also modernized); and the 17 episodes of *Funky Phantom*, a co-production with Hanna & Barbera made in 1971, before the Californian corporation opened its local subsidiary.

In the tradition of Air Programs International, Burbank Films brought the classics to the screen. In the 1980s, the company produced eight feature film specials based on Charles Dickens' novels including *The Old Curiosity Shop* and *Oliver Twist*, mid-length versions of four Sherlock Holmes novels, and other mid-length adaptations. A prolific producer of live-action movies

Fig. 146. Marco Polo Jr. vs. the Red Dragon *by Eric Porter (Australia, 1972)*

---

1   'What! Me Make Another Animated Feature? No Way!', *Industrial & Commercial Photography Yearbook*, 1978, (Sydney, 1978).

2   This *Christmas Carol* should not be confused with the film directed by Richard Williams in 1971.

and documentaries as well, Burbank Films opened a studio in the Philippines to take advantage of low-cost labour in that nation.

Other companies include David Denneen's Film Graphics, producer of many award-winning advertising films and of *Leisure*, directed by Bruce Petty; ZAP production, of the Croatian Zoran Janjic (a former employee at Zagreb Film who moved to Sydney in 1960; his films include *Tale of One City*, a history of urban development); Graphic Animation; and Raymond Lea Animation, founded by Ray Leach, a veteran who broke into animation in 1951, at the age of sixteen, and worked for Eric Porter. Under Steve French's direction, Second Banana Films produced *There's Dragons* (1982) and *Dudu and the Line*, in which a character with a rooster-like head fights against a drawn line.

Among the companies not satisfied with advertising work or made-on-commission films, the small Jollification Cartoon, founded in 1980 by Anne Jolliffe, deserves mention. Born in Tasmania (1933) and schooled in Melbourne, Jolliffe worked in London from 1964 to 1978, where she animated works such as George Dunning's *Yellow Submarine* and Bob Godfrey's *Great.* While still in London, she directed her first film, *The Cranky Princess* (1972). After a short stay in Melbourne, she began her company in Sydney. In 1987, she released the children's series *The Bunyip* (made with Raoul Barré's old-fashioned technique of the slash system) and the environmental tale *Neptune's Ultimatum*, in which the sea-god threatens to take away the privilege of water from human polluters.

As for companies working primarily in television, Fable Film produced the mid-length *The Island of Nevawuz* (1979) and *The Black Planet* (1982), which was shown in movie theatres as well. Both works were directed by Paul Williams. Nicholson Cartoon Productions became well-

CARTOONS
Bendazzi

422

known for *Rubbery Figures* (1987), a television series of political satire featuring animated rubber figures. The ATAM Animation Studios filmed many episodes of *Kaboodle*, a series produced in the late 1980s by the Australian Children's Television Foundation.

An interesting representative of Australian animation was Alexander Stitt, a solid professional not without intellectual ambitions. Born in Melbourne (3 January 1937), from 1958 to 1962 he was art director at Fanfare Films; afterward, he founded the studio Al *et al.*,[1] which produced films and all kinds of graphic services. The director of mid-length films such as *One Designer, Two Designers* (1978), shown at the 1979 Annecy Film Festival, he became popular for *Grendel Grendel Grendel* (1981), the first Australian feature film which addressed adult audiences. Grendel, a green spotted monster, over nine-feet long who alternates his love for humans with a taste for terrorizing them, is challenged by the hero Beowulf whom the Scandinavian king Hrothgar has called in. The film is based on the Early Middle Ages poem, *Beowulf*, or rather, on the manipulated version *Grendel* by the American John Gardner (1972). Despite good animation and structuring, the film won tepid praise because of its slow pace. In 1984, Stitt released another feature film, *Abra Cadabra*, an anti-conformist version of the *The Pied Piper of Hamelin*, made with the help of technological novelties such as multiplane and Dolby Stereo (though not in 3D as advertised).

Yoram Gross

Yoram Gross' Australian activity is only one aspect of the overall production by this experienced filmmaker, which took place on over three continents. Born in Krakow, Poland (18 October 1926), initially he studied music with the intention of becoming a composer, but changed his mind and joined the newly opened Polish In-

1   A pun: 'Al (Stitt) *et al.*'.

stitute for Cinema. After some work as an assistant director with documentary specialist Joris Ivens among others, he moved to Israel in 1950, where he advanced quickly from a camera operator to director and producer, and learned the tricks of scriptwriting from Carl Foreman, author of *High Noon*. In 1958, Gross made his first animation films, which years later he still considered his best: *Chansons sans paroles* (Songs Without Words, 1958), a story of love and death, with animated matches and crumpled paper; and *We Shall Never Die* (1958), an experimental film with three candles, barbed wire and other simple objects. *We Shall Never Die* was dedicated to those who did not return from Nazi concentration camps. In 1961, Gross finished *Joseph the Dreamer*. With animated puppets, the film is based on a biblical subject. This was Gross' first feature film as well as Israel's. Despite being highly praised by critics, it attracted only small audiences. Three years later, the opposite happened to *One Pound Only*, a live-action slapstick comedy which was the box-office leader for that year.

Tired of the tension in the war-torn region, Gross emigrated again in 1968, this time to Sydney. For the next nine years, he produced and directed short films (*To Nefertiti*, 1971), documentaries (*The Politicians*, 1970) and a large number of commercials which, however, he disliked.

> 'I didn't see any reasons, apart from financial, for helping sell a product which I didn't use and didn't like. I felt it was time to be a filmmaker who made only what he wanted to make, not what Mr. Cigarette or Mr. Food wanted me to make,' he told an interviewer.[1]

In 1977, Gross returned to feature films with *Dot and the Kangaroo*. Based on E. Pedley's novel

by the same title, published in 1899, the book had become very popular in Australia (a stage version opened in 1924). *Dot and the Kangaroo* (see Colour Plate 92) tells the adventures of a little girl named Dot. Dot gets lost in the Australian bush, finds cover in the pouch of a large kangaroo, meets several animals and finally, finds her way home. For this film, Gross used a technique which later became his trademark. Combining drawn and animated figures with live-action backgrounds, he was able to present the Australian landscape and fauna in all their beauty.

After the success of this film, Gross continued expanding his production company to include a staff of forty. Over a period of nine years, he produced eleven other animated feature films, seven of which starred Dot. Gross' commercial success came with the development of cable television in the United States of America. The cable industry was interested in his family oriented productions and let him into the American market.

Technically impeccable and a delight to behold, his films were usually well received by reviewers, although Gross himself acknowledged that they were less interesting then his avant-garde works. His decision to make feature films was dictated by the market:

> 'Short films have no market today,' he said, adding that he wanted to show the films he made, 'not keep them at home.'[2]

One film which maintained links to Gross' first production, at least thematically, was *Sarah* (1980). Set in World War II, it featured an abandoned little girl, helped only by the animals of the forest, who determinedly fights a battle against militarism by destroying a railway bridge used for transporting arms. Actress Mia Farrow starred in the live-action part. 'I like films that have a lot of messages,' said Gross.[3] Actually, his films are

1   Antoinette Starkiewicz, 'Yoram Gross,' *Cinema Papers*, (Melbourne, October 1984).
2   Antoinette Starkiewicz, 'Yoram Gross.'
3   Antoinette Starkiewicz, 'Yoram Gross.'

ethical, educational manifestos, suggesting topics such as peace, the respect for traditions, the love of nature and the acceptance of one's own personality. His is the point of view of the classical filmmaker for children, who constantly risks becoming preachy, and whose greatest strength is verve and good spirits.

Independent filmmakers

The most distinguished among independent artists was Bruce Petty. Born to a family of small land holders in Doncaster, near Melbourne (1929), he began drawing at a young age. In 1952 he found employment with a small advertising company. One year later, he moved to London and found expression for his vocation as a satirical cartoonist, publishing in prestigious newspapers and magazines such as the English *Punch* and the American *New Yorker*. In 1959,

Petty returned to his home country where he reinforced his fame for social commentary in the pages of *The Mirror*, *The Australian* and later, *Age*. In his first film, *Hearts and Minds* (1967), he argued against the Australian interests in the Vietnam war. 'With *Australian History*,' a film of 1970, 'I was trying to put our kind of peripheral debates in the context of world debates which are going on simultaneously, but which we are excluded from,' said Petty.[1] A winner of international awards, and much loved in Australia for its clever anti-conformism, this film was Petty's favourite. After several other animated and live action films, Petty released *Leisure* (1976), a comic sequence of sketches on what people do in their free time, which earned him an Oscar in 1977. He was joined in this project by David Denneen's Film Graphics which contributed substantial ideas.

In *Karl Marx* (1977), a biography of the nineteenth century philosopher with animated drawings and live actors, Petty did not hesitate narrating the sexual life of his subject, whom he described as a male chauvinist. After other less stimulating films, in 1986 he released *The Movers*, a mix of animation and live actors (a technique called Ultimatte). *The Movers* once again explores historical moments. An artist with a dry, ungracious style of drawing and anti-conformist political and social positions, Petty brought his polemic spirit from newspapers to the screen and considered himself an artist involved in several media rather than solely an animator. A self-proclaimed leftist, he used cinema as a vehicle for social commentary, protest and the overturning of consolidated opinion. 'I think films only really work if they've got some ideological thread through them. I don't think any film works unless someone is making some sort of judgement about behaviour be it individually or collectively,' he told an interviewer.[2] All things

Fig. 147. Self portrait by Bruce Petty (Australia, 1979).

1 Antoinette Starkiewicz, 'Petty,' *Cinema Papers*, (Melbourne, July–August 1979).
2 Nick Herd, Susan Lambert, Barbara Alysen, 'Bruce Petty,' *Filmnews* (Sydney, May 1977).

considered, Petty was a moralist in the good sense of the word; however, at times he was limited by the frailty of his themes, and by a certain intellectualism.

Antoinette Starkiewicz (Bielsko Biala, Poland, 30 June 1950) began studying dance and voice at the age of four, at ten she moved to Australia, and at twenty she was working as a dancer. But she had also developed an interest in the visual arts while studying at the National Gallery of the Victoria School of Art. After a first, still quite raw film entitled *Secret of Madam X* (1971), she moved to Great Britain and attended the London Film School. In eight months of work she finished *Putting on the Ritz* (1974), which thrust her onto the international stage. This was the first of the many film-ballets in which she combined her dual inspiration as artist and choreographer. Based on a motif sung by Fred Astaire, *Putting on the Ritz* displayed vaguely floral drawings and imaginative, tender and mischievous dancing. The same can be said of *High Fidelity* (1976) and *Pussy Pumps Up* (1979), both filmed in Australia, although the former is copyrighted to the British Film Institute's Production Board. The latter contains the finer graphics, movement and suggestive quality (it features a seductive dance by a cat-woman).

The main characteristics of Starkiewicz's inspiration returned in later works such as the musical fantasies *Koko's History of Music* (1981) and *Piano Forte* (1984). In these films, however, elegance, sensuality and musical interpretation seem more academic and manneristic. Linear drawings against white backgrounds have been replaced by pictorialism and this figurative choice gives viewers a feeling of material weight which suffers in comparison to the ethereal traits of earlier works.

Denis Tupicoff (Ipswich, Queensland, 23 March 1951), graduated in fine art studies and cinema before releasing his first short films and advertising spots. His first work, *Please Don't Bury Me*

(1976) was followed by *My Big Chance* (1977), *Changes* (1977) and *Puffed Out* (1981). His most successful short, *Dance of Death* (1983), is about a television game-show in which some spectators lose their lives. *Dance of Death* is an uncommon example of black humour well-supported by good taste. Tupicoff then turned to scriptwriting and live-action cinema.

Max Bannah (Brisbane, 1947) made his debut with *Violet and Brutal* (1982), a sour comedy about a couple's relationship. *Bird Brain* (1983), about the association between a man and a bird, and *The Lone Sailor* (1984), a geopolitical allegory, ensued. John Skibinski (Geelong, Victoria, 1957) made *Freize* (1980), *Foxbat and the Mimi* (1980) and *Foxbat and the Demon* (1983). Bruce Currie (Adelaide, 1957), directed *Flank Breeder* (1982), *Anatomy of a Businessman* (1984), *One Potato Moor* (1986) and *Tar Baby* (1986), using elaborate drawings inspired by the comics. Philip Pepper put his name to *Ironbark Bill in the Champion Buckjumper* (1985), an entertaining cinematographic version of the tall tales by Australian writer Dal Stivens. David Johnson directed the animated puppet *Air Pirates of the Outback* (1987), a comedy set in the 1920s.

Among women, the most popular was Lee Whitmore (Sidney, Februry 22, 1947), director of *Ned Wethered* (1984). A former set designer, she made her directing and animation debut by putting together fragments of memories about a family friend, artist Ned Wethered, in a moving example of personal film. Other female filmmakers of distinction include Sonia Hofmann for *Letter to a Friend* (1978), a message of love expressed with interesting graphics; Julie Cunningham for *Double X* (1986), a feminist film which explains how biological differences between men and women have forged history; and Pamela Lofts for *Dunbi the Owl* (1986), an aboriginal legend narrated by animating children's paintings.

As for avant-garde animation, little information is available. Dusan Marek gave his contribution to a vast programme of experimental works entitled *Embryo*, which toured artistic and student circles in Melbourne and Sydney in 1963–1964. Other experimental filmmakers include Albie Thomas and David Perry, founders of the company Ubu Films. Thomas' productions include *Bluto* (a combination of video techniques and painted or engraved stock), *The Second Bardo*, *Tribute to America* and *Moon Virility*. Perry created *Puncture* (obtained by puncturing the stock), *Divertimento* and *Jimmy*.

Other Australian animators to remember are Browyn Steven-Jones filmed *Gone with the Wind the Second* and John Bell made *John Bell No. 1*, followed by sequels *2*, *3*, and *The Everything & the Nothing*. Abigail Day created *Inversible Invaders*. Finally, Arthur and Corinna Cantrill, a husband and wife team renowned for their research work, made some animated films. In *Harry Hooton* (1970), a feature film dedicated to the poet who died in Sydney in 1961, the finale was not filmed with a camera, but was impressed directly on stock with the help of coloured lights.

New Zealand

Animation in New Zealand began in the 1940s at the New Zealand National Film Unit.[1] Still in an embryonic form, it consisted of support work (head titles and inserts) created by Cecil Forsberg and Martin Townsend for the films produced by the organization. In 1948, Robert Morrow (Glasgow, 1918 – Wellington, 1980) arrived from Great Britain. A former collaborator of David Hand when the production company Rank was attempting Disney-style animation, Morrow worked at first for the National Film Unit and later founded a studio involved with advertising work, initiating independent professional animation in New Zealand.

Another filmmaker was Fred O'Neill (1920–85) a businessman from Dunedin who animated puppets, at first as an amateur and later with professional commitment. A true pioneer in the field, he used plasticine for his first film, *Plastimania* (1958), at a time when this material was quite unusual. Other works, many of which won international awards, include *Phantasm* (1960), *Fiddlesticks* (1961) and three films based on Maori legends: *Hotupatu and the Birdwoman* (1962, with rare recordings of native songs of the early twentieth century); *The Legend of Rotorua* (1967, on the volcanic origins of the land of Rotorua) and *The Great Fish of Maui* (1967, on how Maui fished the North Island from the deep of the ocean). Later, O'Neill created three children's series for national television. Although he did not have direct followers, his example motivated an unusually large group of local filmmakers to animation.

The age of television and small screen advertising expanded in the 1960s. Two prominent animators in this field were Sam Harvey (who later created the most famous animated work in the nation, the sign-off *Good Night*), and the American John Ewing. A former animator at Disney, for which he worked for eleven years, Texas born Ewing (1928) moved to Auckland in 1967 and began a profitable career in advertising and educational films. The growth of television also led to development in the area of television services, where animation was used for titles and graphics. A major initiator was Tom Rowell, an assiduous promoter of technical and stylistic improvements

---

1   The National Film Unit (founded in 1941), a state-owned organization with headquarters near the capital city of Wellington, specialized in the production of documentaries and fiction films which were to reflect the country's life and culture and establish common ground between the New Zealanders and people all over the world. In the 1980s, Martin Townsend (born in 1927) and producer Hugh MacDonald managed to spread their conviction that animated films should become independent products of the Design Department rather than being mere supplements for live action films. This philosophy provided opportunities for animators such as Robert Stenhouse, Larry Nelson and Nicki Dennis.

until his death in 1979.

The outbreak of a true animated production did not happen until the late 1970s. Murray Freeth (Nelson, 1954) produced and directed *The Boy Who Bounced* (1978) from his Christchurch studio. Presented in Ottawa, this was the first New Zealand fiction film to be shown at a major international festival of animation. In 1986, Freeth returned to the international stage, this time in Zagreb, with *Number One*, a playful ghost story.

In 1976 the English immigrant David Waters founded the Paint Pot Film Studios. Four years later, the company released the country's first animated series, *Rozzo the Goldminer*, featuring the threesome of goldminer Rozzo and his friends Washington (a donkey) and Santana (a vulture). Having fallen asleep in the 1870s, they wake up one hundred years later. The show's comicality derives from the trio's anachronistic reactions to modern life. In an attempt to penetrate the American market, Waters set the series in the West.

Animators again found inspiration in the culture of the Maori people, the country's first inhabitants. Auckland-based, Joe Wylie (1948) and Susan Wilson (1945) were mostly involved with advertising, until they made a name for themselves with *Te Rerenga Wairua* (1984). Beautifully illustrated, with a contemporary setting, the film is about the Maori philosophy of the spirit's (wairua) journey toward the place of eternal rest (te rerenga). Nicki Dennis (Ashburton, 1956) also drew upon her ancestry. A former camera operator, she directed seven colourful, well drawn *Maori Legends of New Zealand* (1986). Here, she favoured the technique of animated cut-outs. The films were produced for children by the National Film Unit.

Euan Frizzell (Darfield, 3 January 1954) directed his first film in 1975. Entitled *Peaceful Partisans of the World*, it dealt with the theme of solitude

in the big city. Based on the editing of photographs, *A Speck of Truth* (1976) was more avant-garde. In 1977, Frizzell directed *Good Night Old Man*, about ghosts who haunt an alcoholic old man. It was released by Gnome Productions, a company founded by Frizzell. This realistic film displayed a cinematograhic language in the style of live-action cinema. After some months of specialization in London with Halas & Batchelor, Frizzell released a constant flow of works that included children's feature films such as *The Wizard of Wallaby Wallow* (1984), *Greedy Cat* (1985), *A Bubbling Crocodile* (1985) and *Shopping with a Crocodile* (1985).

Independent animators include Murray Reece (England, 1941), an advertising artist who created *Rachel Dustbin's Dog and the Law* (1985), an educational film for children about the legislative process; advertising artist Alistair Byrt (1951); Robert Jahnke (1951), director of *Te Utu – Battle of the Gods* (1980), and Mark Winter, a cartoonist, animator and documentary film maker who ran a studio in the southernmost city in the world, Invercargill. His films include *The Letter X* (1989), *The Great Escape* (1991), *Headlines* (1991), and above all *Not My Type* (1991), a typographical ugly duckling story, with a Times Roman serif letter 'I' caught in a sans-serif Helvetica font.

The country's first animated feature film, *Footrot Flats – The Dog's Tale*, reached the screen in 1986. Based on Murray Ball's comic strip characters which were published daily in over 120 newspapers in New Zealand and Australia, the film was written and directed by Ball himself. It was highly prosperous (with record earninngs among New Zealand productions), and was also well received by the reviewers who appreciated its striking drawings, ironic humour, study of human nature and especially, its reproduction of the landscape and mentality of rural New Zealand. The actual production, however, took place in Australia, a country better equipped in personnel and animation instruments. Robbert Smit, an Australian of Dutch descent and a former advertising director at Hanna & Barbera Australia, was the director of animation.

Finally, Larry Nelson and Robert Stenhouse, both with the National Film Unit, have linked their names to art animation. Born in England (4 August 1943), Nelson moved to his new country at a very young age. In 1972, he found employment at the state-funded production company and while working there, he explored the opportunities offered by animation. In 1981, he made *Parallel Line* about New Zealand's evolution, from the formation of the archipelago to the arrival of the first humans, the Maori. An educational film displaying all the characteristics of an art film, *Parallel Line* describes the episodes of natural history, through a fluid metamorphosis of parallel lines which are simultaneously pleasant and incisive. In 1987, Nelson released *Spacescape*, an avant-garde story which discusses the problem of teenagers in love with videogames.

Robert Stenhouse (Dunedin, 3 November 1944) joined the National Film Unit in 1980, after twelve years at Television New Zealand. As with his previous employer, he was responsible for titles and inserts. He also found time to draw and direct *The Domino* (1981), a cutting satire about bureaucracy featuring a man who is happy with his work, but is gradually suffocated.

In 1986, Stenhouse's *The Frog, The Dog and The Devil* (see Colour Plate 93) won an award at the international festival of Hamilton (the first international award ever won by New Zealand). The film, which also received an Oscar nomination, was based on a popular ballad from the South Island about a shepherd who, one dark night after a long stay at a saloon, gets into trouble with a frog and a dog and is persecuted by images of the devil. Exuberantly rich in special effects, an unusual foreshortening of light, sharp drawings and original timing, *The Frog The Dog and The Devil* is an innovative stylistic work and a small jewel of grotesque cinema.

Chapter 25

The Globe Trotters of Animation

Jan Lenica

Jan Lenica (Poznan, Poland, 4 January 1928) received an eclectic education in fine arts (his father Alfred was a painter), architecture, and music. He began working on caricatures and journalistic satire because of the freedom these artistic expressions offered to his activism. Later, searching for more thoughtful, intellectual approaches to social and existential problems, he looked into other branches of graphics. The dialogue between his artwork and a cerebral awareness led to his well known posters which started a new current in Polish poster art that was soon to be appreciated world-wide.

Toward the late 1950s Lenica joined Walerian Borowczyk in making cryptic and stylistically innovative films made by quasi-amateurish means. In 1959, the year of his first stay in Paris, Lenica chose filmmaking as his primary activity, although he did not abandon painting, illustrating and graphic design. By then, Lenica preferred to work alone, and did so in France, Germany, and Poland. His only collaborative effort was *Monsieur Tête* (1959), co-directed with Henri Gruel. This disturbing, ironic film was praised by reviewers as the first example of animation in which 'atmosphere' and 'setting' prevailed over plot.

In Poland, Lenica made *Nowy Janko muzykant* (Janko the New Musician, 1960), a stylish graphic experiment along the lines of *Monsieur Tête*, and *Labyrinth* (1962), a slow-paced, mournful work and one of Lenica's most monumental. Set in a ghostly, nocturnal town, *Labyrinth* features a winged man who is chased by conformist monsters, and is eventually devoured by vultures.

In 1963, having moved to the German Federal Republic, Lenica made *Die Nashorner*, a film adaptation of Ionesco's *Rhinoceros*. *Monsieur Tête* was also based on a subject by Ionesco, one of Lenica's favourite writers. The following year he released *A*, a parable in which power prevails despite the individual's struggle for personal freedom.

From 1966 to 1969, Lenica worked on his first feature film, *Adam II*, a story about the long, sad journey of Adam – a modern-day, lonely man. In the 1969 press release for the film, Lenica wrote:

'I prefer the technique of animated drawing, because it allows me to actualize my intentions just as I like, without the need for an army of technicians and assistants. As far as I know, no other film has ever been made with a crew of three as we did for *Adam II*. My only collaborators were the cameraman and the composer. *Adam II* is the result of an effort lasting more than three years. If somebody asked me to summarize the subject of this film, I could answer: *Adam II* is a film about curiosity. Adam is curious. On his own, he discovers the world, willingly or by chance. Curiosity is, in my opinion, one of human nature's most interesting phenomena, an instinct which seems ridiculous to me because it does not have any practical results. I could also say *Adam II* is a film about solitude. My Adam is even more lonely than his namesake, the first man – he does not even have a companion. I did not wish to deal with a problem. I intended to make a biography, or rather, to sketch a portrait. One should not give the name "Adam" too much relevance. In my short films, his name was Monsieur Tête or Janko the Musician; in *Labyrinth*, he remained anonymous. I stopped, deprived of autobiographic traits. Every artist who paints a portrait gives it something of himself, without necessarily transforming it into a self-portrait.'

After *Fantorro, le dernier justicier* (Fantorro, the Last Arbiter, 1971), Lenica made *Enfer* (Hell, 1973) and in 1974 while lecturing at Harvard University he completed *Landscape*. These films were followed by a large project on Alfred Jarry, which included *Ubu roi* (1976, a 50-minute-long special produced by a West German broadcasting company), and the feature film *Ubu et la grande gidouille* (1979, a French production, based also on *Ubu cocu* and *Ubu enchaîné*, lesser-known works by Jarry). In the latter work, Lenica broke his artistic belief in silent films and used Jarry's text.

'Lenica's work is not without obsessive motifs, transposed into numerous contexts,' Marek Borowski wrote. 'The cruel conflicts between the individual and the surrounding world find expression in the power of the authorities, in the destruction of personality and of those who are non-conformist, and in reducing people to instruments.'[1]

Alf Brustellin wrote: 'Lenica has a time reference, he is an existentialist even when forgetting the attributes and emblems of reality and only shapes the visionary material of the imagination. However free Lenica's invention, however deformed or decorated his creations, his story remains concrete, comprehensible, having a habitation and a name.

'His art is no doubt literary and has literary ancestors. The film artist Lenica can hardly be conceived without Kafka and Ionesco, and far

Fig. 148. Labyrinth *by Jan Lenica (France, 1962).*

1   Marek Borowski, 'Jan Lenica's Film Quest / Les recherches cinématographiques de Jan Lenica,' *Animafilm*, No. 2 (Warsaw, April–June 1980), p. 10.

less understood.'[1]

In fact, the main characteristic of this exceptional animator can be found in his graphics. His films are terrific adventures by a man who fantasizes; and are like the uninterrupted creation of a pictorial and architectural universe. The thick, dark lines and depths of field (which Lenica obtains from ancient prints, old postcards or the contrast of milky whites to nuanceless blacks) create a sense of shadow and mystery appealing more to the eye and the subconscious than the intellect. The formal, subtle refinement pleases the movie expert as in *Fantorro*, where the protagonist offers the damsel-in-distress a rose which is hand-painted directly on film stock.

This colouration on frame within a live-action film marks a return to Méliès and the origins of cinema.

Peter Földes

An ingenious, vagrant artist, Földes (Budapest 22 August, 1924 – Paris, 29 March 1977), made his first two films *Animated Genesis* (1952) and *A Short Vision* (1956) while in Great Britain. He then worked exclusively on his painting without following the main pictorial currents of his times, but rather developing his own style in a neo-figurative direction. In 1956, he moved to Paris, using the city as a base for his frequent travels to exhibitions and, in later years, to pursue film projects.

Fig. 149. Ubu et la grande gidouille *by Jan Lenica (France, 1979).*

1   Alf Brustellin, '*Adam 2*, a New Cartoon Film by Jan Lenica,' *Graphics*, No. 145 (1969–70).

He spent some time in New York, the capital of major artistic movements of the period; then he returned to France where he made *Appétit d'oiseau* (Appetite of a Bird, 1964). From that time until his death, he constantly worked on movies of every genre – high and low quality films, advertising spots, computerized experiments (done mainly in Canada), and also a feature film, entitled *Je, tu, elles* (I, You, They, 1971), which uses actors and special effects. Employing the traditional technique of cel animation, he made two of his finest movies, *Un garçon plein d'avenir* (A Boy with a Great Future, 1965) and the stylish *Visages des femmes* (Women's Faces, metamorphoses of lines portraying female faces and bodies, 1968). After an initial unsatisfactory attempt at using a computer to assist him in the creation of an animated film (*Meta Data*, 1970), he made the limpid, well-built *La faim* (Hunger, 1974).

'I am not capable of staying still,' he wrote. 'I am in constant transformation, I always need something new. That's why I chose to use a computer, which is the animator's new frontier.'[1]

Transformation intended as research beyond the present is not only an artistic expression to Földes, but also the first landmark of inspiration. His films are not the development of ideas, but rather the constant growth of one drawing into another, with the unquenchable desire to bring every drawing to maturity. Földes' second requisite of inspiration is purity. An excellent draftsman, he played with the purity of lines as few artists could. In his last movies, made with the help of electronic techniques, he attained a movement so uniform as to be almost ecstatic. *Au delá du temps* (Beyond Time), part of a feature film which was left unfinished at the time of the artist's death, is an example where this purity goes too far into Arcadia, with delicate faces, lim-

Fig. 150. Visages des femmes *by Peter Földes (France, 1968).*

1   Peter Földes, personal communication (1973).

pid waters and black lines traced on candid spaces.

Földes' themes are less decipherable. Obsession and anguish, fears and impulses emerge in a universe which moves quickly from harmony to violence. Erotic visions or suggestions are constantly present. Overall, one has the impression that a dream has been transposed into a film, which maintains the analogical associations of the oneiric condition.

As an artist of his century, Földes supported and justified the creative uses of inhuman tools borrowed from science and mathematics.

'The art of the 20th century is cinema,' he said. 'The language of the 20th century is technology. In my films, I made metamorphosis. *Visages de femmes* was a perpetual metamorphosis, created by hand-made drawings. With a computer, I can still make metamorphoses, but with greater control over each line of the drawing, [a line] which I can move as I please. And I work faster, because the machine frees the artist from the fatigue of labour. A miniaturist can work for seven years on a single work; nobody says that Rembrandt's paintings are less beautiful only because he spent less time on them.

'In the Middle Ages, stones were dug out, cleaned, pulverized and mixed with glue for paint. Will anybody claim that the Impressionists have not been good painters? Yet they bought their colours in tubes; they bought brushes. Whenever they could, they finished their paintings in the time-span of a day. I did not make the computer. I did not write the programme. I just make movies. The machine does not create anything. It only does what I tell it to do. Nothing keeps me from creating.'[1]

Jimmy Teru Murakami

Another 'vagrant' artist was Jimmy Teru Mu-

rakami (San Jose, California, 5 June 1933). Murakami and his family were among the thousands of Japanese-Americans interned by the American government in prison camps during World War II. He graduated from the Chouinard Art Institute of Los Angeles, a school that forged many animators. In the mid-1950s, he found employment as a draftsman and animator at Bosustow's UPA. In 1958, he moved to New York, where he worked with Ernest Pintoff contributing to *The Violinist*, one of Pintoff's finest shorts. The following year Murakami left the United States for Japan, Great Britain, France, Italy and The Netherlands.

In 1965, Murakami returned to California and co-founded a Hollywood-based production company with Fred Wolf. He directed commissioned works as well as some interesting art shorts. *The Top* (1965) offers a criticism of the myth of success, illustrating how people use others to reach the top. *Breath* (1967), an award-winner at the Annecy Festival, is an apologue describing life and its cruelties in terms of breath (a creature 'breathes' another one and so on); the soundtrack as well is based on breath. This kind of black humour also appears in *Good Friends* (1969). Here, a man literally gives himself to another man – eyes, mouth, and so on – until the latter leaves with the donor's woman.

After dissolving his partnership with Wolf, in 1972, Murakami moved to Ireland. In 1979 he released a film that dealt with suicide, *Death of a Bullet*, another harsh, sarcastic film, although perhaps less inspired than previous works.

Murakami's major achievement, and the work which brought him fame, is *When the Wind Blows* (1986), see Colour Plate 94). A feature film with an anti-nuclear theme, *When the Wind Blows* is based on a popular illustrated book by British author Raymond Briggs and produced by London's TVC. The protagonists are an elderly couple called Jim and Hilda who lead a quiet life

1   Personal communication to the author, 1973.

in their country home. When the radio announces an imminent world conflict, Jim tries to protect their lives and property from an atomic explosion by obeying the ridiculous instructions given by the authorities. In the end, the explosion does take place and the couple quietly dies. The mundane activity and characters (the latter are rendered even more credible by the well-balanced voices of John Mills and Peggy Ashcroft) invites the audiences to identify with the protagonists and react emotionally against the atomic threat.

When the Wind Blows is clearly a polemical work, powerful in its calibrated pathos, with interesting figurative choices (such as the two-dimensional animated drawings against a three-dimensional background) and music by pol-

itically active rock'n'roll musicians such as Roger Waters and David Bowie. As in other works, here also Murakami reveals his nature as an iron-fisted filmmaker and a demanding, if not always original, professional.

He belongs to the generation of specialists who were trained or inspired by UPA, and is among the first of the American intellectuals who found their social awareness during the difficult 1950s – educated, sensitive artists devoted not so much to finding absolutes in art as to creating intelligently tasteful, ethical films for large audiences. In his art films, Murakami (whose professional productions and world-wide influence should not be undervalued) employs a somewhat surrealistic narrative and graphic style to describe the cruelty of people and ages.

V
Afterword

Chapter 26

The electronic age

In industrialized countries, the 1960s and 1970s were the years of television and its related communication functions, particularly advertising. As a result, the motion-picture industry suffered dramatically. Supermarkets or gas-stations replaced old movie theatres, more than a half of which went out of business. With the 1960s came a severe crisis, particularly in the United States where Hollywood workers petitioned the government for economic aid reserved for depressed areas. Affected by reduced markets and cost increases, the producers of traditional cartoons were forced to thin out or close their studios. Animated characters survived in boring television series which became the new fad. Made with little money, stifling self-censorship, rushed deadlines and limited animation, these series represented an artistic regression, but the insatiable demand for hours and hours of films (mainly for children) created opportunities with little demand for quality.

The animators who worked in advertising were slaves to efficiency and to the fact that effective advertising spots were usually bad films from an artistic standpoint. Still, advertising offered appreciable opportunities which went beyond the field of commercials. Many animators made their 16mm art films outside the workplace; others, usually in charge of small advertising agencies, used their down-time to produce brief works of no commercial purpose. In both cases, the training in television and advertising taught filmmakers that animated films did not necessarily have to be seven-minutes long like Californian one-reelers, or two hours long like feature films; rather, just like commercials, art films could convey their messages in a few seconds. The animators who worked in advertising adopted the same technical and stylistic novelties which were constantly being incorporated into commercials to attract inattentive audiences. From television, which constantly required films of varying length, they also developed an extraordinary sense of timing.

In the 1960s more than in any other age, the young animators who were often recruited from the Art Institutes did not forget their background, but transposed onto the screen the influences of plastic movements, research and pictorial and graphic styles. The art animation of the 1960s emphasized visualization over narration, painting over cinema, poetry over story-telling, and aimed at suggestion and synthesis while breaking its links with logic – in short, the colours used to indicate the occurrence of events counted more than the events themselves.

The relationship between animation and comic strips weakened, with the exception of television series. Extremely popular characters such as Mickey or Popeye – who had generated laughter as well as a sense of identification in millions of spectators – lost ground, as animation advanced toward the 'death of the character'. Artists gave expression to an age of uncertainty, in which one no longer had time, desire nor reason for laughter. Just like the comic genre as a whole, comic animation temporarily celebrated its own funeral rites.

Those filmmakers who made movies on their own encountered problems with distribution. It was precisely for this reason that, in the United States, animation and the experiences of the underground merged – when the commercial circuit of movie theatres was joined by a large organized non-theatrical distribution industry made up of university and college cinema clubs and cultural institutes. The new age was also characterized by a tendency to associate. Animators, including artists, producers, organizers of cultural events and critics, met officially for the first time in Cannes in 1956, on the occasion of a specialized section promoted by the film festival. After years spent working alone, they were feeling the need to share experiences.

A second meeting was organized in 1958, again in Cannes. Finally, the first specialized festival was organized in 1960, in Annecy, Haute Savoie. On that occasion, after several preparatory meetings, an international committee for animated film was founded, ASIFA (Association Internationale du Film d'Animation), and one year later a temporary board of directors was elected, with Norman McLaren as president. The first of-

ficial newsletter explained the purposes of the association. As animation was constantly advancing and becoming popular, ASIFA aimed at supporting its growth by helping the development of audiovisual communications, by fighting against the isolation of artists and by giving the public, the press and the authorities the information they often lacked.

The first general assembly of ASIFA was held on 29 June 1962. On that occasion, John Hubley was elected president of the board of directors, which included Paul Grimault, John Halas, Ivan Ivanov-Vano, Ion Popescu-Gopo, Norman McLaren and Bobe Cannon. Afterward, ASIFA helped organize specialized festivals worldwide.

The founding of ASIFA and of animation festivals simply ratified a *fait accompli*. The revolution initiated by UPA and the lessons of individuals such as McLaren or Alexeïeff had evolved into an international 'new' animation, characterized by research and quality, addressed to adults and to a somewhat cultural élite. From the late 1950s on, this new animation began detaching itself in an ever more marked way from traditional cartoons, and formed a new cultural 'movement' worldwide whose implicit manifesto was the development of innovative technical and stylistic research. Every country of the world, at different times and different ways, helped establish the stylistic and expressive possibilities of this formula-free animation which is the most important and interesting branch of animation.

Chapter 27

Computers and animation

The most exciting and potentially revolutionary event that has happened to the world of animation has been the invention of the computer, the development of computer graphics, simulation and computer animation. And yet, after 20 years, the computer has only recently begun to realize the wondes of a few visionary animators foresaw. A look at the relatively brief, constantly changing, history of computer animation will help but the industry's current status in perspective in relation to the animation industry as a whole.

The first graphics, images or drawings, that were produced with the aid of computers in the mid-1960s, were output on to graphics plotters. These devices drew the picture that had been generated with the aid of a computer on to sheets of paper as single-colour line drawings. It wasn't until someone at the Massachusetts Institute of Technology's Lincoln Lab had the bright idea of hooking-up the computer to a Cathode Ray Tube (CRT) – an instrument used for a television set – that the actual possibility of computer animation was unleashed. This enabled Ivan Sutherland, also working at MIT's Lincoln Lab, to write his 'Sketchpad' programme; the first interactive computer graphics programme which is often referred to as the true genesis of practical computer graphics. However, even though these pictures were still single colour, two-dimensional line drawings that generated relatively simple images ismilar tothose seen on early radar sets, it was not long before the powerof this new medium was recognized by scientists looking for a means to make visual representations of images and scenes that could not be easily photographed, and by artists an danimators looking for new methods of creative expression.

By the early 1970s considerable financing was made available through various United States Government sources to rapidly develop this new technology for space simulations, interactive flight simulators for pilot training, and communications. Much of the pioneering work in computer generated simulations was done at the Jet Propulsion Laboratory (JPL) at NASA, and funded by the US Department of Defense. Involved inthese early phases were several people who continue to be very active in the industry: James Blinn of JPL, David Evans, Ivan Sutherland and Nelson Max. But not all progress was the result of US government/NASA requirements. In 1969, Tom DeFanti joined Charles Csuri at Ohio State University where he was already earning a reputation as a major force in computer graphics development. Over the next three years,

DeFanti developed 'GRASS', a powerful computer graphics programming language, for Csuri.

During this same period, other institutions and people were also devoted to the foundling science of computer graphics. At the University of Utah, which also played a leading role in computer graphics development, Ed Catmull did his major work in surface representation, and Phong Bui-Tuong created the lighting and shading model that bears his name and is still widely used in the industry. At the New York Institute of Technology, Alvy Ray Smith created the programming for his PAINT system that has since become the standard. Richard Shoup of XEROX PARC computer science lab took the next step using the newly developed frame-buffer technology to create his 'Superpaint' system which led to the first commercially viable raster graphics productions.

It appears that the bulk of activity during the 1970s took place in the United States and Canada. Fueled to a large extent by the demands of North America's highly competitive television networks, computer animation and its effects became an excellent medium for the stations to display their call-letters in on-air promos and identification spots.

While the Japanese quickly became involved in the early development of computer animation in the 1960s, further work in Japan almost came to a halt during the following decade. The Japanese, strong on hardware but weak in software design, concentrated instead on developing computers to assist production in their growing manufacturing industries. When Japanese interest in computer animation was revived in the early 1980s, they quickly made their presence felt with the unique Links 1 system, designed by Koichi Omura of Osaka University. Operating quite differently from most other systems of that period, Links 1 is a 'parallel processing' system which ties together a large number of small, inex-

pensive computers and distributes the work load among them so each can simultaneously progress on a small portion of the image.

In Great Britain and Europe, lacking the budgets and impetus of competitive commercial television networks, interest and concurrent development was more directed to the artistic aspects of the medium. While they did not have the raw computer power available to the Americans, software and graphic designers, as well as filmmakers made excellent use of what technology they did have available. Accessible programs such as John Vince's PICASO, Britain's Digital Pictures, CAL Videographics and France's INA and Sogitec, inspired artists to concentrate on design, and the movement of objects, and to integrate their computer generated images with other media.

While great strides were made in 'digital' computer animation to serve the needs of the government, by NASA, the entertainment industry, and a small artistic circle led by the innovative John Whitney Sr, the first viable commercial productions came from Denver's Computer Image Corporation. There, Lee Harrison's analog 'Scanimate' animation computer, soon to be joined by his 'Caesar' animation computer, was turning out two-dimensional computer animation daily, including character animation, graphics, and visual effects for television commercials and film. Instead of building pictures digitally in the computer's memory by assembling groups of geometric shapes in which each pixel or point of light on the video screen is stored as a separate piece of information in the computer's memory, 'Scanimate' and 'Caesar' worked with black-and-white images, scanned into the computer from prepared artwork as analog video signals by specially modified video cameras. These images could then be manipulated, modified and coloured in 'real time', as you watched, either in whole or in their various parts, to create the desired animated images.

By the late 1970s, computer animation was beginning to be recognized as a serious visual communications and artistic medium, even though very few people knew how to handle it properly, or even understood its many ramifications. Perhaps because of this, there existed a great lack of artistic support from the bulk of the international animation community. However, several animators were looking closely at this new technology as a means of advancing their art. Walt Disney Studios did some early experimental work with the University of Utah, and Hanna & Barbera worked hard to develop a combination, or computer assisted, 'cel' animation system. By 1981, computer animation had become a well-established graphics medium, and the rapid growth the industry is currently experiencing began to gain momentum.

One of the first 'traditional' animators to embrace the computer was England's John Halas who in 1981 produced his fully computer generated short film *Dilemma* at Computer Creations in the United States. This was followed by Disney's *The Wild Things*, test produced with MAGI Synthavision, a computer animation and rendering system developed by Philip Mittleman. This short production used the best of two mediums: 'soft' cel animated characters combined with computer generated three-dimensional backgrounds that could be manipulated frame-by-frame. The young Disney animator who developed this project, his first experience with computer animation, was John Lasseter.

Despite major advancements between 1978 and 1982, computer animation's mathematical structure, based on rigid geometric shapes, still made it a poor means for character animation production. Traditional animators continued to view computer animation with great scepticism. It was not the personal type of expressive medium they were used to working with. Serious involvement required large mainframe computers that cost hundreds of thousands of dollars, considerable financial resources and necessitated collaboration with technicians. At the 1984 Canadian International Animation Festival, *The Wild Things* was given a special presentation. This film intrigued many animators and first opened their eyes to computer animation's coming uses. Two following films, Susan Van Baerle's *Snoot and Muttly* (see Colour Plate 95) and Lucasfilm's *The Adventures of Andre and Wally B*, clearly showed that computers would soon be quite adept at producing character animation, complete with 'stretch and squeeze' and 'motion blur'. Both these productions have since won numerous awards at animation festivals world-wide.

Refinement of the medium received additional impetus by traditionally trained animators who now work in computer animation, and continue to win awards for their creations. Chris Wedge, whose first job out of animation school was to work on MAGI Synthavision's film *TRON*, produced the delightful *Tuber's Two Step* which chronicles a family's joy at witnessing their infant's first steps. And John Lasseter of Pixar, who designed and animated *Andre and Wally B*, went on to design and animate the internationally acclaimed 1986 production *Luxo Jr*. A traditional piece of computer generated character animation about happy parent and child 'Luxo' lamps.

Though used more and more in film and television since the mid-1980s, computer animation still had not become the 'movie star' that some claimed would be its ultimate potential, be it creating complete scenes and simulations of natural events or producing computer animated replicas of actors and actresses. From *2001*, through *TRON, The Last Starfighter, Explorers, 2010* and many other movies, filmmakers slowly became aware of how to handle the new medium and integrate it into their other visual tools. In short, it was a question of learning how a computer handles images.

Computer generated images are not constrained by the laws of gravity. They can go anywhere the director wants them to go, at any speed, at any time during a sequence. Reality can be mixed with the unreal at the flip of a switch. Unlike models used in stop-motion or miniature photography where a shot's length is limited by the size and available travel of the motion control device used, computer generated scenes can be almost any length desired, allowing the director great latitude in planning sequences. However, like a child with a new toy, all too often when filmmakers used computer animation for the first time, they became carried away by the lack of constraints and over-used the medium. Yet, cinema is still perhaps one of the greatest vehicles for computer animation, and Hollywood is now using it in a great variety of ways for a multitude of productions. All this development reached a climax in April, 1989, when John Lasseter at Pixar created his film, *Tin Toy*, and won the first Oscar ever awarded for a computer animated film.

Television advertising is also a prominent user of computer animation which has tremendous attention-grabbing power and adds memorability to the advertiser's message. Once again, there was a problem of overuse by directors and creative people. Not understanding the strengths of the medium, they often used computer anima-

tion purely for a visual effect without considering the message they were attempting to communicate.

At its most successful, computer animation has been integrated with live-action and other visual media and effects. Recent television commercials by Pacific Data Images (PDI), one of the oldest computer animation production companies, using its 'morph' effect that changes video images as you watch, have been particularly powerful. Other, completely computer animated commercials, or combinations of computer animation and live action, by such companies as Rhythm & Hues, Rez-N8, and Metrolight in the United States, Topix Computer Animation in Canada, Electric Image and Moving Picture Company in England, and Ex-Machina, and Fantome in France, are setting new standards for the use of computer animation in television commercials, and are gaining new acceptance for the medium.

Because of their great time saving benefits, the 'behind the scenes' uses of computer animation has been catching on quickly in the film industry. By building scenes in quick 'wireframe' line form, or simple coloured and shaded images, and then using set computer programs to position light sources, camera angles and even actor placement, a director can preview a scene, and quickly determine whether the staging is accurate.

The history of computer animation is one of constant change. This has been particularly true since early 1990. With a series of very rapid advancements in computer technology, the cost of a PC has dropped to almost universally affordable prices. Concurrently, the power of a graphic workstation has also increased, while the cost is now similar to that of a high-end personal computer based animation system. Software and systems seem to be up-graded and improved daily. And as they do, the equipment becomes easier to use, and costs keep dropping.

Although still spearheaded by very few 'develop-

Fig. 151. Luxo Jr. by John Lasseter (USA, 1986).

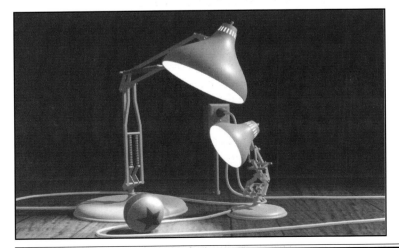

mental' producers who create software to run on their own graphics workstations and rendering computers, the computer animation production industry is now almost totally turn-key system based. Most of these are smaller companies.

The large companies that originally gave form to this industry are gone. Canada's Omnibus Computer Graphics grew to be by far the largest company in the industry. Omnibus Computer Graphics absorbed first Los Angeles based Digital Productions, and its US$12 million Cray X/MP super-computer, and then the early creative standard-bearers Robert Abel & Associates; Cranston/Csuri; MAGI Synthavision; Sogitec of France; and Japan Computer Graphics Lab. These companies were all victims of advancing technology. No longer able to carry the heavy debt they had accumulated buying large million dollar mainframe computers, and developing the software to run them, they were superseded by companies that bought the new turn-key systems – software and hardware – for under US$500,000. Today, even more powerful and competent systems cost well under US$100,000.

Computer animation continues to be the most exciting change in the industry. It is responsible for the explosive growth; that is, the rapid rise of the 'turn-key' market segment, represented by the ever increasing number of software packages and complete computer animation systems becoming available. Today's turn-key systems show an impressive range of capabilities, whether they are designed to run on the industry standard Silicon Graphics (SGI) IRIS line of graphics workstations, or personal computers such as the IBM-PC and its many 'compatibles', the Apple Macintosh, or even the Commodore Amiga. Computer animation software for these systems range from SGI IRIS based systems from Alias Research and Soft Image of Canada, Wavefront Technologies of the USA, and TDI Explore from France. For the PC, and Macintosh, there are systems avail-

able from Byte by Byte, Digital Arts, Time Arts, AT&T Graphics Software Labs, Symbolics, and Autodesk, among others. These are mainly USA based companies, whose complete PC based systems can cost in the US$15,000 to $25,000 range.

However, the most interesting development from the traditional animator's standpoint is the new two-dimensional computer animation systems, designed specifically to assist the animator in producing his work faster, and with better quality. QuickCel from AXA, and Animation Stand from Linker Systems, both in the USA, are leaders in this area, as are the Venice and Atalis systems from France's Getris Images. They all join Alan Kitching's venerable Antics as computer animation systems designed specifically for animators.

Major animation studios, such as Walt Disney Productions and Sullivan Bluth, also use both 2-D, and particularly 3-D, computer animation systems to aid in their film production. Hanna & Barbera worked for several years to develop its own system, but now also uses proprietary turn-key systems as well. The computer animation produced by these studios is skilfully blended with their traditional cel production techniques so that its use is transparent to the viewer. They aim for better images, better overall animated films and reduced production costs, replacing the increasingly expensive handwork with computer techniques. Going one step further, in DATE Walt Disney Productions signed an agreement with Pixar for the production of a feature length 3-D computer animated film, under the direction of John Lasseter.

With much more frequency, traditional filmmakers are incorporating animation into their productions. Recent films of which computer animated segments are major components of the story include *The Abyss*, *Total Recall*, and to the largest extent, *Terminator 2*. Some of the specialists to whom Hollywood turns include Lucasfilm's Industrial Light and Magic Division who use the Alias system, and companies such as Pacific Data Images, Rhythm & Hues, and Metrolight. It is interesting that these companies are now seeking traditionally trained animators, particularly those adept at character animation, to add to their creative teams. They are not looking for people with computer knowledge, or experience, but rather people who are pure animators. This is indicative of the state reached by current computer animation systems.

These new, affordable, easy to use, but still very capable and powerful systems have brought computer animation within reach of just about any animator, artist, designer or filmmaker. They are equally applicable to a large studio, or the individual animator. They allow the animator to work in a simple studio environment with the computer work-station as an adjunct to, or even replacing, the traditional animator's light table. The animator can even use a pen, drawing images into the computer with a digitizing tablet, and then manipulating them by selecting commands from the on-screen menus, or with simple key-strokes on the computer's keyboard. Output can be directly on to videotape or via the traditional frame-by-frame photographic film methods to which the animator is accustomed.

Computers animation systems can be used to create the complete image – characters and background – in either 2-D or 3-D; to plot layout and movement for traditional cel creation; to produce 'in-betweens'; to ink and paint hand drawn cels; to produce backgrounds that can change from frame to frame, into which traditional hand-drawn characters can be inserted; to record and preview hand drawn sequences; to add effects to cel animated, or live action images, or images produced by any other animation medium. The versatility of computer animation is only limited by the creativity of its user.

The result is a greatly increased creative output. The computer animation industry, particularly in North America, has suffered from too much technical input and not enough creative exposure. Now, with much easier access through these smaller, less expensive systems, it is up to the animators to push this technology to its creative limits. And all over the world animators, artists and designers are introducing a tremendous amount of creative input into this maturing medium. Animators are the key to its success. Animation computers will broaden the animator's scope like no tool ever before. The technology still has scope for improvement, but the animator's input will give it the direction needed.

The computer animation industry continues to grow at an average annual rate of 30 per cent. Computer animation devices are opening a whole new creative venue and production capability for filmmakers, television commercial producers and particularly animators. The acceptance of the computer animation medium by animators, and its new found accessibility for them, is an important step to the industry's continued growth and expansion. After several viewings even the most visually astounding, technically awesome, computer generated images can quickly pale if they have no more substance than mechanical wizardry. A good piece of animation lives forever, in any language.

Written by Robi Roncarelli
2 September 1991

VI
Reference

A bibliography

___

International animation cinema magazines

Animafilm, Warsaw (in English, French, Russian and Polish), from 1978 to 1981. New Series Turin (in English and French), from 1984 to 1988. New series under the name *Asifa News* Brussels (in English, French and Russian) from 1988 to 1992. New series under the same name Prague (in English, French and Russian) from 1993. Official magazine of the Asifa (International Association of Animators).

Animation Journal Tustin. Since 1992.

Animation Magazine Los Angeles, then Agoura Hills. Since 1987.

The Animation Report Canoga Park. Since 1992.

Animatographe Paris, 1987.

Animator St. Albans (UK). Since 1982.

Animator Los Angeles. Since 1984.

Animatrix Los Angeles. Since 1984.

Banc Titre Paris. From 1978 to 1985.

Cinémaction no. 51, April 1989, Paris. Special issue on animation edited by Pascal Vimenet and Michel Roudevitch.

Dossier de l'audiovisuel no. 10, Le dessin animé, Paris, Nov.–Dec. 1986.

Ecran 73 no. 11, Paris, Jan. 1973. Special issue on animation.

Film History vol. 5, no. 2, London, June 1993. Special issue on animation edited by Mark Langer.

Plateau Ghent (Belgium). Since 1980.

Positif no. 297, November 1985; no. 370, December 1991; no. 371, January 1992, Paris (France). Dossiers on world animation edited by Michel Ciment.

Sightlines vol. 19, no. 2, New York, Winter 1985–86. Special issue on animation edited by John Canemaker.

International animation cinema books

Anitei, Elvira (edtior): *Nous mêmes – Ourselves*, Asifa, Bucharest, 1973, 164 pp. In English and French. It contains autobiographical texts by Alexeïeff, Ivanov-Vano, Hubley, Halas, Brdecka, Ansorge, Böttge, Bozzetto, Reisenbuchler, Godfrey, Truica, Varasteanu, Antonescu, Balasa.

Asenin, Sergey: *Mir Multfilma*, Moscow, Iskusstvo, 1986, 288 pp. Panorama of animation in different Communist countries (In Russian).

Mudrost' Vimisla, Moscow, Iskusstvo, 1983, 207 pp. Collection of protraits of various masters of international animation.

Volsevniki Ekrana, Moscow, Iskusstvo, 1974, 288 pp. Short history of world animation.

Benayoun, Robert: *Le dessin animé après Walt Disney*, Paris, Pauvert, 1961, 174 pp.

Bendazzi, Giannalberto: *Topolino e poi*, Milan, Il formichiere, 1978, 250 pp. Short history of world animation.

Bendazzi, Giannalberto and Michelone, Guido (editors): *Il movimento creato*, Turin, Pluriverso,

1983, 222 pp. A collection of essays from 26 contributors on various topics of international animation.

Caldiron, Orio and Fedele, Turi: *Il film d'animazione in Europa*, Abano Terme (Italy), Archivio internazionale del film d'animazione, 1971, 130 pp. Proceedings of the Colloquium held in Abano Terme on European animation, 13–14 March 1970.

Chevalier, Denis: *J'aime le dessin animé*, Paris, Denoël, 1962.

Crafton, Donal: *Before Mickey – The Animated Film 1898–1982*, Cambridge–London, MIT Press, 1982, 413 pp.

Curtis, David and Francis, Richard: *Film as Film*, London, Hayward Gallery, 1979, 152 pp. Various essays on cinematographic avant-garde with references to abstract animation.

Edera, Bruno: *Full-length Animated Feature Films*, London–New York, Focal Press, 1977, 198 pp.

Gifford, Denis: *The Great Cartoon Stars – A Who's Who's*, London, Jupiter, 1979, 128 pp.

Halas, John: *Masters of Animation,* London, BBC Books, 1987, 136 pp.

Holman, L.B.: *Puppet Animation in the Cinema – History and Technique*, Cranbury (New Jersey)– London, Barnes/Tantivy, 1975, 120 pp.

Lichtenstein, Manfred (ed.): *Animationsfilm socialisticher Länder*, Berlin, Staatliches Filmarchiv der DDR, 1978, 246 pp. Essays on animation in various Communist countries.

Lenburg, Jeff. *The Encyclopaedia of Animated Cartoons*, Facts on file, New York–Oxford, 1991, 466 pp.

Lo Duca, Giuseppe Maria: *Le dessin animé*, Paris, 1948. First attempt at publishuing a world history of animation.

CARTOONS
Bendazzi

448

Pilling, Jayne (ed.): *Women and Animation – A compendium*, BFI, London, 1992, 144 pp.

Rondolino, Gianni: *Storia del cinema d'animazione*, Turin, Einaudi, 1974, 430 pp. First serious 'history' of world animation.

Solomon, Charles and Stark, Ron: *The Complete Kodak Animation Book*, Rochester, Eastman Kodak, 1983, 192 pp.

Stephenson, Ralph: *The Animated Film*, London–New York, Tantivy/Barnes, 1973, 206 pp. Updated version of *Animation in the Cinema*, London, Zwemmer/Barnes, 1967.

National publications

Brazil

Moreno, Antonio: *A experiencia brasileira no cinema de animação*, Rio de Janeiro, Artenova/Embrafilme, 1978, 127 pp.

Bulgaria

Micheli, Sergio: *Cinema di animazione in Bulgaria*, Bologna, Cappelli, 1975, 198 pp.

Canada

Asifa Canada, magazine of the Canadian chapter of Asifa; Montreal, since 1970.

Séquences, n. 91, Jan. 1978, Montreal. Special issue on Canadian animation edited by Léo Bonneville.

Beaudet, Louise, 'L'animation' in *Les cinémas canadiens*, edited by Pierre Véronneau, Paris (France) – Montreal, Lherminier/Cinémathéque Québécoise, 1978.

China

Quiquemelle, Marie-Claire: *The Wan Brothers*

and 60 Years of Animated Film in China, Annecy, Jica Diffusion, 1985, 38. pp

Biagini, Alessandra: *Lo stile nazionale nel cinema d'animazione cinese: proposta di analisi attraverso l'esame di Danao Tiangong di Wan Laiming*, University thesis ms., Venezia, 1993, 131 pp.

Czechoslovakia

Horejsi, Jan and Struska, Jirí, *Occhio magico – Il cinema d'animazione cecoslovacco 1944–1969*, Prague, Cinema Artists' Union and Ceskoslovensky Filmexport, 1069, 150 pp. (in Italian).

Kolman, Vladimir: *Vom Millionär, der Sonne Stahl – Geschichte des Tschekoslowakischen Animationsfilm*, Frankfurt, Deutsches Filmmuseum, 1981, 120 pp.

Estonia

Asenin, Sergey: *Etuude eesti multifilmidest – Ja nende loojatest*, Tallinn, Perioodika, 1986, 319 pp. In Estonian, Russian and English.

France

Image et Son n. 207, June/July 1967, Paris. Monograph on French animation.

L'avant-scène cinéma no. 149/150, July/September 1974, Paris. Monograph issue on French animation and particularly on Laloux-Topor's *La planète sauvage*.

Maillet, Raymond: *Le dessin animé français*, Lyon, Institute Lumière, 1983, 128 pp.

Le dessin animé français, Paris, Musée-galerie de la Seita, 1982, 34 pp.

Great Britain

Gifford, Denis: *British Animated Films 1895–1985 – A Filmography*, Jefferson (South Carolina), McFarland, 1987, 345 pp.

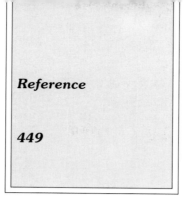

Reference

449

The Netherlands

Holland Animation, Haarlem-Den Haag. Since 1973. National magazine of Dutch animators, with regular editions in English.

Italy

Monographs published by Incontri internazionali sul cinema d'animazione, Genoa, 1983–85. Booklets on: Gianini and Luzzati (by Sara Cortellazzo), Guido Manuli (by Giannalberto Bendazzi), Osvaldo Cavadoli (by Giannalberto Bendazzi), Bruno Bozzetto (by Alfio Bastiancich), Manfredo Manfredi (by Oscar Cosulich).

Zanotto, Piero and Zangrando, Fiorello: *L'Italia di Cartone*, Padua, Liviana, 1973, 186 pp.

Spain

Manzanera, María: *Cine de animación en España – Largometrajes 1945–1985*, Murcia, Universidad de Murcia, 1992, 235 pp.

Switzerland

Cosandey, Roland: *Langages et imaginaire dans le cinéma suisse d'animation*, Etagnières, Groupement Suisse du film d'animation, 1988, 153 pp.

United States of America

Magazine AFI Report, vol. 5 no. 2, Washington DC, 1974. Monographic issue on American animation of the bulletin of the American Film Insitute.

Animania (originally *Mindrot*), Minneapolis. From 1975 to 1984.

Funnyworld, Little Rock (Arkansas) then New York, from 1966 to 1979.

Film Comment vol. 11, no. 1, New York, January 1975. Monograph issue devoted to American animation.

Books

Adams Sitney, P.: *Visionary Film – The American Avant-Garde*, New York, Oxford University Press, 1974, 452 pp. Chapter 8 (Absolute Animation) deals with Smith, Belson, Breer and others.

Blanc, Mel: *That's Not All, Folks! My Life in the Golden Age of Cartoons and Radio*, New York, Warner Books, 1988, 276 pp. Autobiography of the man who gave his voice to Bugs Bunny and many other American characters.

Brasch, Walter M.: *Cartoon Monickers – An Insight into the Animation Industry*, Bowling Green (Ohio), Bowling Green University Popular Press, 1983, 180 pp.

Culhane, Shamus: *Talking Animals and Other People*, New York, St. Martin's Press, 1986, 463 pp. Autobiography of a living legend of American animation.

Friedwald, Will and Beck, Jerry. *The Warner Brothers Cartoons*, Metuchen (New Jersey) – London (GB), The Scarecrow Press, 1981, 271 pp. Filmography from 1930 to 1969.

Furniss, Maureen Ruth: *The Current State of American Independent Animation and a Prediction for its Future*, University thesis, San Diego, 1987, 172 pp.

Griffin, George (ed.): *Frames – A Selection of Drawings and Statements by Independent American Animators*, New York, Griffin, 1978, 96 pp.

Korkis, Jim and Cawley, John: *Cartoon Confidential*, Malibu Graphics Malibu, 1992, 170 pp. Historical gossip and curiosities about American animation.

Lenburg, Jeff: *The Great Cartoon Directors*, Jefferson (North Carolina), McFarland, 1983, 147 pp.

Maltin, Leonard: *Of Mice and Magic – A History of American Animated Cartoon*, New

York, New American Library, 1980, 470 pp.

Peary, Danny and Peary, Gerald: *The American Animated Cartoon – A Critical Anthology*, New York, Dutton, 1980, 310 pp.

Pilling, Jayne: *That's Not All, Folks! A Primer in Cartoon Knowledge*, BFI Distribution, London, 1986, 38 pp.

Solomon, Charles: *Enchanted Drawings – The History of Animation*, New York, Knopf, 1989, 322 pp.

Woolery, George, W.: *Children's Television: The First Thirty-Five Years, 1946–1981. Part I: Animated Cartoon Series*, Metuchen (New Jersey)–London, The Scarecrow Press, 1983, 386 pp.

Animated TV Specials – The Complete Directory of the First Twenty-five Years, 1962–1987, Metuchen (New Jersey) – London, The Scarecrow Press, 1989, 542 pp.

Characters

Bugs Bunny

Adamson, Joe: *Bugs Bunny – Fifty Years and Only One Grey Hare*, London, Pyramid Books, 1990, 192 pp.

Sylvester and Tweety

Beck, Jerry, with Shalom Auslander: *I Tawt I Taw A Puddy Tat: Fifty Years of Sylvester and Tweety*, New York, Holt & Co., 1991, 160 pp.

Tom and Jerry

Adams, T.R.: *Tom and Jerry. Fifty Years of Cat and Mouse*, New York, Crescent Books, 1991, 159 pp.

Brion, Patrick: *Tom et Jerry*, Paris, Chène, 1987, 176 pp.

Felix the Cat

Canemaker, John: *Felix – The Twisted Tale of the World's Most Famous Cat*, New York, Pantheon, 1991, 178 pp.

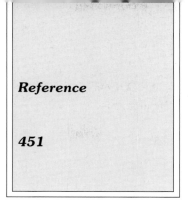

James Stuart Blackton

Blackton-Trible, Marian: *J. Stuart Blackton – A Personal Biography by His Daughter*, Metuchen (New Jersey)–London, The Scarecrow Press, 1985, 210 pp.

Filmmakers

Alexandre Alexeïeff and Claire Parker

Arnault, Hubert: 'Tableaux d'une exposition d'Alexandre Alexeïeff et Claire Parker'. *Cinéma Pratique*, XIX, No. 132, Paris, May/June 1973. Technical description of the pinscreen.

Bendazzi, Giannalberto (ed.): *Pages d'Alexeïeff*, Annecy (France), AAA, 1983, 68 pp. Anthology of the essays on film theory written by Alexeïeff.

Salomon, Nicole and Just, Jackie: *Entretien Avec Alexandre Alexeïeff et Claire Parker*. Annecy, Salomon, 1979, 84 pp.

Tex Avery

Tex Avery, La folie du cartoon, Montreuil, 1979, p. 112. Monograph issue of the magazine *Fantasmagorie*. Publishers uncredited.

Adamson, Joe: *Tex Avery, King of Cartoons*, New York, Popular Library, 1975, 238 pp.

Benayoun, Robert: *Le mystère Tex Avery*, Paris, Seuil, 1988, 110 pp.

Brion, Patrick: *Tex Avery*, Paris, Chène, 1984, 124 pp. Well documented, with good illustrations.

Brion, Patrick: *Tex Avery, les dessins*, Paris, Nathan, 1998, 110 pp.

Ford, Greg: *Avery Program Notes*, in Zagreb '78 Retrospectives, Zagreb International Animation Festival, (1978 Croatia, then Yugoslavia). This essay has been published many times in many editions.

Don Bluth

Cawley, John: *The Animated Films of Don Bluth*, New York, Image Publishing, 1991, 156 pp.

Bruno Bozzetto

Bendazzi, Giannalberto: *Bruno Bozzetto – Animazione primo amore*, Milan, Isca, 1972, 40 pp.

Candia, Renato: *Sul filo della matita – Il cinema di Bruno Bozzetto*, Venezia, Cinit, 1993, 191 pp.

Robert Breer

Mendelson, Lois: *Robert Breer – A Study of His Work in the Context of the Modernist Tradition*, Ann Arbor, Umi Research Press, 1981, 169 pp.

Emile Cohl

Crafton, Donald: *Emile Cohl, Caricature, and Film*, Princeton, Princeton University Press, 1990, 404 pp.

Quirino Cristiani

Bendazzi, Giannalberto: *Due volte l'oceano – Vita di Quirino Cristiani, pioniere del cinema d'animazione*, Florence, La Casa Usher, 1983, 138 pp.

Segundo de Chomón

Beaudet, Louise: *In Search of Segundo de Chomón*, Annecy, Jica Diffusion, 1985, 84 pp.

Fernandez Cuenca, Carlos: *Segundo de Chomón*, Zaragoza, Prensas Univesitarias de Zaragoza, 1988, 317 pp.

Viking Eggeling

O'Konor, Louise: *Viking Eggeling, 1880–1925, Artist and Film Maker, Life and Work*, Stockholm, Almqvist & Wiksell, 1971, 302 pp. (in English).

Oskar Fischinger

Moritz, William: 'The Films of Oskar Fischinger', *Film Culture* no. 58-59-60, New York, 1974.

Fleischer Brothers

Cabarga, Leslie: *The Fleischer Story*. Nostalgia Press, New York, 1974 and 1988.

Langer, Mark: *Max e Dave Fleischer: da Ko-Ko the Clown a Superman*. Venice: Arsenale, 1980, 116 pp.

Paul Grimault

Grimault, Paul: *Traits de Mémoire*. Paris: Seuil, 1991, 259 pp.

Grimault, Paul & Prévert, Jacques: *Le roi et l'oiseau*. Paris: Gallimard, 1980, 77 pp. Book version of the film by the same title.

Pagliano, Jean-Pierre: *Paul Grimault*, Paris: L'herminier, 1986, 151 pp.

John Halas

Manvell, Roger: *Art & Animation*. London: Halas and Batchelor, 1980, 128 pp. Analysis of 40 years of activity of the Halas and Batchelor Studio (1940–1980).

Ub Iwerks

Griffithiana, no. 3, September 1980, Genoa. Monograph issue of the magazine.

Chuck Jones

Jones, Chuck: *Chuck Amuck – The Life and Times of an Animated Cartoonist*. New York: Farrar–Straus–Giroux, 1989, 304 pp.

Jean-François Laguionie

Salachas, Gilbert: *Le chateau des singes – Le livre d'avant le film de Jean-François La-*

guionie, Paris, Atelier Akimbo, 1992, 95 pp.

Walter Lantz

Adamson, Joe: *The Walter Lantz Story – With Woody Woodpecker and Friends*. New York, G.B. Putnam's Sons, 1985, 254 pp.

Len Lye

Brownson, Ron (ed.): *Len Lye – A Personal Mythology*, Auckland: Auckland City Art Gallery, 1980, 91 pp.

Curnow, Wystan and Horrocks, Roger (editors): *Figures of Motion – Len Lye, Selected Writings*, Auckland: Auckland University Press/Oxford University Press, 1984, 152 pp.

The Films of Len Lye, *Film Library Quarterly*, vol. 14, n. 3–5. New York, 1981.

Winsor McCay

Canemaker, John: *Winsor McCay – His Life and Art*, New York: Abbeville Press, 1987, 223 pp.

Norman McLaren

Asifa Canada, vol. 15, vo. 1. April 1987, Montreal, 25 pp. Special monograph issue on McLaren.

Sequences, no. 82, October 1975, Montreal, 155 pp. Special monograph issue on McLaren.

Anonymous (Guy Glover): *McLaren*, Montreal, NFB of Canada, 1980, 32 pp.

Anonymous (Michael White): *The Drawings of/Les dessins de Norman McLaren*, Montreal, Tundra Books/Les livres Toundra, 1975, 192 pp. Non-cinematographic drawings by the master.

Bastiancich, Alfio: *L'opera di Norman McLaren*, Turin, Giappichelli, 1981, 209 pp. A fundamental book on the master.

Collins, Maynard: *Norman McLaren*, Ottawa,

Canadian Film Institute, 1976, 119 pp.

Martin, André: i x i = ... ou le cinéma de deux mains. *Cahiers du cinéma* bis, 79, 80, 81, 82, January, February, March, April, 1958, Paris.

Richard, Valliere T.: *Norman McLaren, Manipulator of Movement – The National Film Board Years, 1947–1967*, East Brunswick (Canada), Ontario Film Institute/Associated University Presses, 1982, 128 pp.

Lotte Reiniger

Bastiancich, Alfio (editor); *Lotte Reiniger*, Turin, Assemblea teatro/Compagnia del bagatto, 1982, 116 pp.

Reiniger, Lotte: *Die Abenteuer des Prinzen Achmed*, Tubingen, Wasmuth, 1972, 32 pp. Book version of the film by the same title.

Reiniger, Lotte: *Shadow Theatres and Shadow Films*, London–New York, Batsford/Watson & Guptill, 1970, 128 pp.

Emile Reynaud

Talon, Gérard: 'Emile Reynaud, coll.' *Anthologie du cinéma* no. 69. A supplement to *L'avant-scène du cinéma*, no. 129, October 1972, Paris, 55 pp.

Walther Ruttmann

Goergen, Jeanpaul: *Walther Ruttmann, eine Dokumentation*, Berlin: Freunde der Deutsche Kinemathek, 1989, 184 pp.

Paul Sharits

Film Culture, no. 65–66, New York, 1978. Monograph issue devoted to Sharits.

Ladislas Starewich

Béatrice, Léona and Martin, François: *Ladislas Starewitch, filmographie illustrée*, Annecy, Jica Diffusion, 1991, 80 pp.

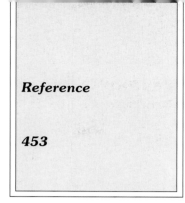

Reference

453

Jirí Trnka

Jirí Trnka, Montreuil, 1981, 144 pp. Monograph issue of *Fantasmagorie*. Publishers uncredited.

Benesova, Marie: *Jirí Trnka*, Prague, Ceskoslovensky Filmexport, 1970, 30 pp (English).

Bocek, Jaroslav: *Jirí Trnka*, Prague, Artia, 1964, 267 pp. (German).

Boilat, Jean-Marc: 'Trnka, coll.' *Anthologie du cinéma* no. 79, supplement to *L'avant-scène du cinéma*, no. 149–150, July–September 1974, Paris, 63 pp.

John Whitney

Whitney, John: *Digital Harmony – On the Complementarity of Music and Visual Art*, Peterborough, Byte Books/McGraw Hill, 1980, 235 pp.

Richard Williams

Canemaker, John: *The Animated Raggedy Ann & Andy – An Intimate Look at the Art of Animation: Its History, Techniques and Artists*, Indianapolis–New York: Bobbs–Merrill, 1977, 292 pp. Documentary book on the feature film directed by Williams and about Williams himself.

Karel Zeman

Asenin, Sergey: *Fantasticesky kinomir Karela Zemana*, Moscow, Iskusstvo, 1979, 129 pp.

Walt Disney

Anonymous: *Treasures of Disney Animation Art*, New York, Abbeville, 1982, 319 pp. Luxurious collection of preparatory and inspirational drawings, sketches and backgrounds.

Bruno, Edoardo and Ghezzi, Enrico (ed.): *Walt Disney*, Venice: La Biennale di Venezia, 1985, 263 pp.

Charlot, Jean: 'But Is It Art? A Disney Disquisition'. *American Scholar* vol. 8, no. 3, Summer 1939. The animated cartoon seen as specific artistic language.

Culhane, John: *Walt Disney's* Fantasia, New York, Abrams, 1983, 222 pp.

Feild, Robert: *The Art of Walt Disney*, New York, Macmillan, 1942, 290 pp. First book on Disney: it illustrates the studio, the artistic principles, the way of working.

Finch, Christopher: *The Art of Walt Disney – From Mickey Mouse to the Magic Kingdoms*, New York, Abrams, 1973, 458 pp. Very luxurious book made for the prestige of the studio. Very well documented.

Grant, John: *Encyclopaedia of Walt Disney's Animated Characters*, London, Hamlyn, 1987, 320 pp.

Kinney, Jack: *Walt Disney and Assorted Other Characters – An Unauthorized Account of the Early Days at Disney's*. New York, Harmony, 1988, 207 pp. The autobiography of one of the Disney stalwarts.

Leebron, Elizabeth and Gartley, Lynn: *Walt Disney – A Guide to References and Resources*. Boston, Hall, 1979, 226 pp. See particularly part 4, formed by 88 pages of bibliography.

Leyda, Jay: *Eisenstein on Disney*, Calcutta, Seagull, 1986, 114 pp.

Merritt, Russell and Kaufmann, J.B.: *Nel Paese delle meraviglie. I cartoni animati muti di Walt Disney/Walt in Wonderland – The Silent Films of Walt Disney*, Pordenone (Italy), Le giornate del cinema muto/Biblioteca dell'immagine, 1992, 235 pp.

Miller Disney, Diana: *The Story of Walt Disney*, New York, Holt, 1957, 247 pp. First biography

CARTOONS
Bendazzi

454

of Disney, written by his daughter in collaboration with journalist Pete Martin.

Schickel, Richard: *The Disney Version – The Life, Times, Art and Commerce of Walt Disney*, New York, Simon & Schuster, 1968, 330 pp. Unfriendly biography where Disney is depicted as a tycoon without artistic gifts. It is nevertheless interesting.

Shale, Richard: *Donald Duck Joins Up*, Ann Arbor (Michigan), Umi Research Press, 1982, 185 pp. Detailed account of the war propaganda element of Disney production.

Thomas, Bob: *Walt Disney, an American Original*, New York, Simon & Schuster, 1978, 380 pp. A biography rich in first-hand information.

Thomas, Bob: *Disney's Art of Animation: From Mickey Mouse to* Beauty and the Beast, New York, Hyperion, 1991, 208 pp.

Thomas, Frank & Johnston, Ollie: *Disney Animation: The Illusion of Life*, New York, Abbeville, 1983, 575 pp. Methods and philosophy of Walt Disney and his crew. The authors are two of the famous 'Nine Old Men'.

Thomas, Frank & Johnston, Ollie: *Walt Disney's* Bambi – *The Story and the Film*, New York, Stewart Tabori & Chang, 1990, 208 pp. It contains a flip-book with examples of animation of four characters of the film.

Tietyen, David: *The Musical World of Walt Disney*, Milwaukee, Leonard, 1990, 158 pp.

Aesthetics, education, repertories

Asifa News, 1974, p. 376, Proceedings of the colloquium on problems of theory in animation, Repino (Russia), 26 March – 2 April 1974 (English, French, Russian).

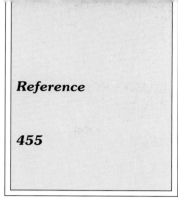

Amya, Pierre and Maillet, Raymond: *Bibliographie du film d'animation*, Ghent, Bilifa, 1976, 36 pp.

Cholodenko, Alan (ed.): *The Illusion of Life – Essays on Animation.* Sydney, Power/Australian Film Commission, 1991, 312 pp.

Halas, John and Manvell, Roger: *Art in Movement – New Directions in Animation*, London, Studio Vista, 1970, 192 pp.

Halas, John: *Graphics in motion – Vom Trickfilm bis zur Holografik/From Special Effects Film to Holographics*, Munchen, Bruckmann, 1981, 206 pp.

Hoffer, T.W.: *Animation – A Reference Guide*, Westport (Connecticut)–London, Greenwood, 1981, 386 pp.

Jouvanceau, Pierre: *Esthétique du film de silhouettes*, University thesis, Université de Paris 1, Pantéon, Sorbonne, 992, 431 pp.

Lermen, Birgit and Loewen, Matthias: *Der Trickfilm als didaktische Ausgabe. I: Zugänge, exemplarische Analysen und didaktisch-methodische Aspekte. II: Semiotische Einführung und exemplarische Analysen*, Hollfeld, Bange: 1983 and 1984, 232 pp. and 210 pp.

Munitic, Ranko: *Uvod u estetiku kinematografske animacije*, Belgrade–Zagreb, Univerzitet Umetnosti/Filmoteka 16, 1982, 317 pp (with summary in English).

Poncet, Marie-Thérèse: *L'esthétique du dessin animé*, Paris, Nizet, 1952, 279 pp. First attempt at building an aesthetic theory of animation.

Sifianos, Georges: *Langage et esthétique du film d'animation*, University thesis, Université de Paris 1, Panthéon Sorbonne, Paris, 1987, 333 pp.

Reference

455

Manuals

Blair, Preston: *Animation – Learn How to Draw Animated Cartoons*, Tustin (California), Foster, 1949, 40 pp. Completed by *How to Animate Film Cartoons*, same author, same publisher, 1980.

Engler, Robi: *Film Animation Workshop – Handbook for Film Animation Workshops and Low-Cost Animated Film Production*, Munich, Friedrich Ebert Stiftung, 1981, 687 pp. Same book in German and in French.

Halas, John & Privett, Bob: *How to Cartoon*, London–New York, Focal Press, 1951, 131 pp.

Halas, John & Manvell, Roger: *The Technique of Film Animation*, London–New York, Focal Press, 1980, 360 pp.

Hayward, Stan: *Scriptwriting for Animation*, London–New York, Focal Press–Hastings House, 1977, 160 pp.

Laybourne, Kit: *The Animation Book – A Complete Guide to Animation Filmmaking, from Flip-books to Sound Cartoons*, New York, Crown, 1979, 272 pp.

Lutz, E.G.: *Animated Cartoons – How They Are Made, Their Origin and Development*, New York: Charles Scribner's Sons, 1920, 261 pp. First manual and also first book on animation.

Noake, Roger: *Animation Techniques – Planning and Producing Animation with Today's Technologies*, Secaucus (New Jersey), Chartwell, 1988, 159 pp.

Perisic, Zoran: *Special Optical Effects*, London–New York, Focal Press, 1980, 185 pp.

Pevisic, Zoran: *The Focal Guide to Shooting Animation*, London–New York, Focal Press, 1981, 142 pp.

White, Tony, *The Animator's Workbook*, New York, Watson & Guptill, 1986, 160 pp.

Computer Animation

Pixel – The Computer Animation Newsletter, Toronto. Since 1984.

Halas, John (editor): *Computer Animation*, London–New York, Focal Press, 1974, 176 pp. First book on this subject.

CARTOONS
Bendazzi

456

Hayward, Stan: *Computers for Animation*, London–New York, Focal Press, 1984, 144 pp.

Lewell, J. *Computer Graphics*, London, Orbis, 1985, 160 pp.

Roncarelli, Robi: *The Computer Animation Dictionary*, New York, Springer, 1989, 124 pp.

VII

Indexes: Names and Titles

Name Index

Title Index

F

O

S